THE LAWBOOK EXCHANGE, LTD.

# Foundations of Spanish, Mexican and Civil Law Series

WARREN M. BILLINGS, Series Editor

*Distinguished Professor of History, Emeritus,*
*University of New Orleans and Visiting Professor of Law,*
*William and Mary School of Law*

**This series addresses the history of the civil law in the Americas, with an emphasis on Spanish and Mexican law**

---

# The Laws of Mexico

**A Compilation and Treatise Relating to Real Property, Mines, Water Rights, Personal Rights, Contracts and Inheritances**

## Books in the Series

**A Compilation of Spanish and Mexican Law, in Relation to Mines and Titles to Real Estate, in Force in California, Texas and New Mexico**
**And in the Territories Acquired under the Louisiana and Florida Treaties When Annexed to the United States. Volume I [All Published]**

JOHN A. ROCKWELL
With a New Introduction by **Peter L. Reich** *Whittier Law School*

**Laws and Decrees of the State of Coahuila and Texas**
**In Spanish and English**

J. P. KIMBALL, translator
With a New Introduction by **Joseph W. McKnight** *SMU Dedman School of Law*

**The Laws of Mexico**
**A Compilation and Treatise Relating to Real Property, Mines, Water Rights, Personal Rights, Contracts and Inheritances**

FREDERIC HALL
With a New Introduction by **Peter L. Reich** *Whittier Law School*

**A New Collection of Laws, Charters and Local Ordinances of the Governments of Great Britain, France and Spain Relating to the Concessions of Land in their Respective Colonies**
**Together with the Laws of Mexico and Texas on the Same Subject, to Which is Prefixed Judge Johnson's Translation of Azo and Manuel's Institutes of the Civil Law of Spain**

JOSEPH M. WHITE
With a New Introduction by **Agustín Parise** *LSU Law Center*

### Forthcoming

**Hamilton's Mexican Law**
**A Compilation of Mexican Legislation Affecting Foreigners, Commercial Law, Property Real and Personal...**

LEONIDAS HAMILTON
With a New Introduction by **Peter L. Reich** *Whittier Law School*

THE

# LAWS OF MEXICO:

## A COMPILATION AND TREATISE

RELATING TO

## REAL PROPERTY, MINES, WATER RIGHTS, PERSONAL RIGHTS, CONTRACTS,

AND

## INHERITANCES.

BY

FREDERIC HALL,

COUNSELOR AT LAW.

**With a New Introduction by**

**Peter L. Reich**

*Professor of Law and Sumner Scholar,*
*Whittier Law School*

THE LAWBOOK EXCHANGE, LTD.

Clark, New Jersey

ISBN 978-1-58477-995-7 (hardcover)
ISBN 978-1-61619-077-4 (paperback)



Lawbook Exchange edition 2016

*The quality of this reprint is equivalent to the quality of the original work.*

**The Lawbook Exchange, Ltd.**
33 Terminal Avenue
Clark, New Jersey 07066-1321

*Please see our website for a selection of our other publications and fine facsimile reprints of classic works of legal history:*
www.lawbookexchange.com

**Library of Congress Cataloging-in-Publication Data**

Names: Hall, Frederic, 1825-1898, author. | Reich, Peter L., 1955- writer of introduction.
Title: The laws of Mexico : a compilation and treatise relating to real property, mines, water rights, personal rights, contracts, and inheritances / by Frederic Hall ; with a new introduction by Peter L. Reich, Professor of Law, Whittier Law School.
Description: Lawbook exchange ed. | Clark, NJ : The Lawbook Exchange, Ltd., 2016. | Includes bibliographical references and index.
Identifiers: LCCN 2016003866| ISBN 9781584779957 (hardcover : alk. paper) | ISBN 9781616190774 (pbk. : alk. paper)
Subjects: LCSH: Law--Mexico.
Classification: LCC KGF327 .H35 2016 | DDC 349.72--dc23
LC record available at http://lccn.loc.gov/2016003866

*Printed in the United States of America on acid-free paper*

# INTRODUCTION[1]

Frederic Hall's preface to his 1885 treatise, *The Laws of Mexico*, announced its twin purpose: to address "questions arising under Mexican laws" in the territories Mexico ceded to the United States, and those presented by "the increase of trade, of progress, and of the transfer of property within the present domain of the republic of Mexico."[2] Hall well understood the relevance of Mexican law to these issues, for his legal career had taken him from post-Conquest California to Mexico in the 1860s and 1880s. These experiences let him compile one of the most widely-used English references on the subject—and one cited in judicial opinions as late as the 1960s. This essay discusses Hall's legal practice in California, his career in Mexico as an attorney and journalist, the context and production of his treatise, and its influence on subsequent jurisprudence.

Born in Rutland, Vermont, in 1825, Hall was the son of a local probate judge, and left home after high school to clerk in several New England businesses before securing employment in 1848 in a New Orleans import-export house.[3] There he learned Spanish in the course of

---

[1] The research for this project was initiated by Michael Widener, Rare Book Librarian at Yale Law School, and Emma Molina Widener of the Southern Connecticut State University Department of World Languages, who provided essential leads. The essay's sources are contained in various repositories, including the Bancroft Library at U.C. Berkeley, the Los Angeles County Law Library, and the U.C.L.A. Law Library. The author is grateful for the valuable assistance of the librarians at these institutions, and to Whittier Law Librarians Curtis Jones and Margot McLaren for obtaining rare periodicals through interlibrary loan. Thanks are also due to Whittier Law School for supporting the project with a Faculty Summer Research Stipend.

[2] FREDERIC HALL, THE LAWS OF MEXICO: A COMPILATION AND TREATISE RELATING TO REAL PROPERTY, MINES, WATER RIGHTS, PERSONAL RIGHTS, CONTRACTS, AND INHERITANCES iii (1885). The ceded territories included most of the contemporary U.S. Southwest, which was transferred at the end of the Mexico-U.S. War. Treaty of Peace, Friendship, Limits, and Settlement with the Republic of Mexico, Feb. 2, 1848, U.S.-Mex., ch. 27, 9 Stat. 922 (1848).

[3] Some of the basic facts of Hall's life can be found in obituaries. *See Frederick* [sic] *Hall, a Pioneer Attorney, Has Passed Away*, SAN FRANCISCO CALL, Dec. 27, 1898, at 10; *Attorney Frederick* [sic] *Hall Dies of Heart Disease*, SAN FRANCISCO EXAMINER, Dec. 28, 1898, at 10. The only biography is Kenneth M. Johnson, *Frederic Hall*, 38 CAL. HIST. SOC'Y Q. 47 (1959). Johnson had the unique opportunity to interview Hall's daughter, Mrs. Rollo R. Millar of San Francisco, on several occasions. *Id.* At 57 n.2.

Frederic Hall, from his obituary
(*San Francisco Call, Dec. 27, 1898, at 10*)

dealings with Mexico, where he traveled and worked briefly as a private tutor.[4] Hearing of the gold discovery in California while in Mexico City, Hall and several friends trekked north, arriving in Monterey in late 1849.[5] By the end of the year he had established himself in San José and began to study law.[6]

In San José Hall also took up journalism on legal and political subjects—an interest he would maintain throughout his life. For his hometown paper, *The Rutland Herald*, he covered California's 1851 gubernatorial election, in which Democrat John Bigler defeated Whig Pierson B. Reading.[7] After noting that the Whigs, among whom Hall

---

[4] Johnson, *supra* note 3, at 48.
[5] *Id.*
[6] *Id.* at 48–49.
[7] Frederic Hall, *For the Herald, San José, California, Sept. 12, 1851*, THE RUTLAND HERALD, Oct. 30, 1851, at 1. *See generally* WILLIAM HENRY ELLISON, A SELF-GOVERNING DOMINION: CALIFORNIA, 1849–1860 (1950) (discussing politics in 1850s California, including the different perspectives of the Democratic and Whig parties).

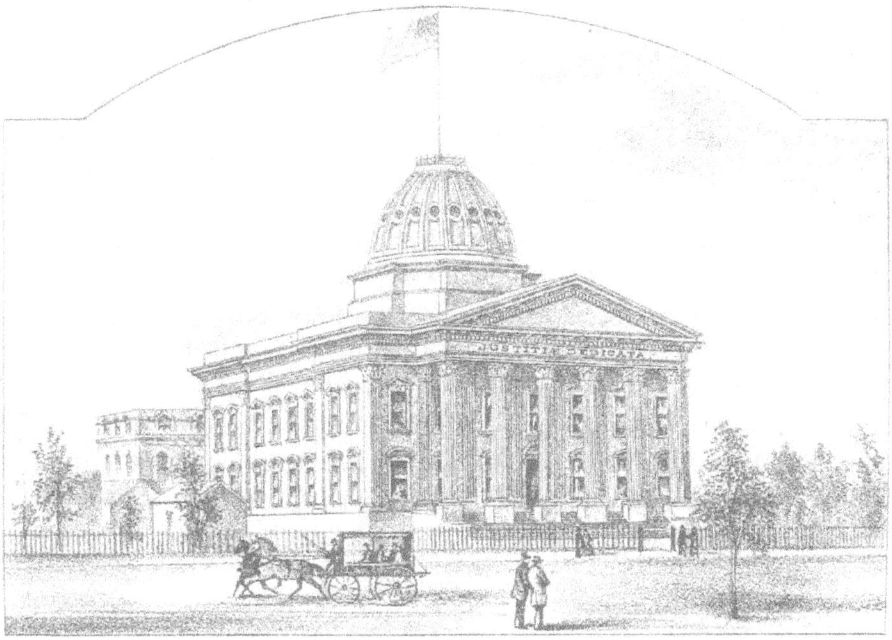

San Jose Court House
*(frontispiece of Frederic Hall,* The History of San Jose *(San Francisco: A.L. Bancroft & Company, 1871))*

counted himself, were disappointed at the results, he broached the larger issue then preoccupying the country: the North-South antagonism over slavery.[8] Like many Whigs of the period, Hall bemoaned the contemporary sectional divide and suggested that if only northerners and southerners would travel to each other's regions, "there would be a happier and more brotherly feeling existing between them."[9] In this attitude he resembled his fellow Whig and earlier Hispanic law expert, John A. Rockwell, who also hoped that war over slavery might be avoided.[10] At the same time Hall expressed faith in California's future, if a railroad could connect it with the East and contested land titles could be settled.[11]

---

[8] *Id.*
[9] *Id.*
[10] *See* Peter L. Reich, *Introduction, in* JOHN A. ROCKWELL, A COMPILATION OF SPANISH AND MEXICAN LAW IN RELATION TO MINES AND TITLES TO REAL ESTATE, IN FORCE IN CALIFORNIA, TEXAS, AND NEW MEXICO v, xv–xvi (Lawbook Exchange 2011) (1851) (discussing the 1854 disintegration of the Whigs due to conflicts over slavery, and Rockwell's faith in the party's ideology of reason and neutrality).
[11] Hall, *supra* note 7.

Admitted to the bar in 1852, Hall pursued his new profession, representing clients in property disputes, many of which hinged on balancing relevant Mexican with American law.[12] As he described two decades later in his history of San José, a major controversy arose in the 1850s and 1860s from the city's claim to, and later attempt to mortgage, its "pueblo" lands (communal municipal property), so the litigation required attorneys well versed in Hispanic law.[13] In *Branham v. Mayor and Common Council of San José* (1864), a case in which he participated, the California Supreme Court held that the city could not mortgage its pueblo tracts in order to pay its obligations.[14] Later Hall, a landowner himself, became a party in a suit to partition a former Mexican land grant.[15] The case turned on the recognition of a parol (oral) sale from which his title descended, so he cited the *Siete Partidas* (the medieval Spanish law code) and several Louisiana and California cases supporting the validity of such contracts in Hispanic law, convincing the court to rule is his favor.[16]

Perhaps seeking adventure, and armed with his language skills and legal knowledge, Hall journeyed to Mexico City in 1867. He moved in circles of ex-Confederates allied with the French-backed interventionist regime of Emperor Maximilian von Habsburg, some of whom signed a petition for Hall's appointment to the post of U.S. Minister to Mexico.[17]

---

[12] Johnson, *supra* note 3, at 49.

[13] *See* FREDERIC HALL, THE HISTORY OF SAN JOSÉ AND SURROUNDINGS, WITH BIOGRAPHICAL SKETCHES OF EARLY SETTLERS iv, 333–349 (1871) (describing Mexican legal sources in local archives and San José's pueblo land cases). *See also* Peter L. Reich, *Dismantling the Pueblo: Hispanic Municipal Land Rights in California Since 1850,* 45 AM. J. LEGAL HIST. 353 (2001) (discussing how U.S. successor cities to Spanish and Mexican municipalities tried to alienate public property despite traditional restrictions).

[14] 24 Cal. 585 (1864); HALL, *supra* note 13, at 345–347; Johnson, *supra* note 3, at 51.

[15] Hall v. Yoell, et al., 45 Cal. 584 (1873).

[16] Brief of Respondent Hall at 17, *Hall v. Yoell*; Points and Authorities of Frederic Hall at 3, *Hall v. Yoell* (originals in Bancroft Library, U.C. Berkeley). *See generally* Peter L. Reich, *Siete Partidas in My Saddlebags: The Transmission of Hispanic Law from Antebellum Louisiana to Texas and California*, 22 TUL. EUR. & CIV. L.F. 79 (2007) (discussing the influence of Louisiana jurisprudence on the interpretation of Hispanic law by southwestern courts).

[17] *See* Frank A. Knapp, Jr., *A New Source on the Confederate Exodus to Mexico: The Two Republics*, 19 J.S.HIST. 363, 369–370 (1953) (discussing the southern expatriate community in Mexico City and its support of Hall for U.S. Minister). *See also* ANDREW ROLLE, THE LOST CAUSE: THE CONFEDERATE EXODUS TO MEXICO (1965) (relating Confederate exiles' involvement with Maximilian and failed colonization attempts); TODD W. WAHLSTROM, THE SOUTHERN EXODUS TO

According to his account of the intervention, in May 1867 Hall visited the Emperor, imprisoned by opposition forces under Benito Juárez, and brought an international law treatise to assist in Maximilian's defense against treason charges.[18] An eyewitness to these events, German Princess Agnes Salm-Salm, saw Hall as "an able lawyer, well versed in Mexican law," and arranged for him to draft a brief for the Emperor's trial.[19] The brief challenged the jurisdiction of the military court trying Maximilian, argued that the sovereign head of a *de facto* government could not be tried by another government, and reasoned that in any event he could not be guilty of treason since he was not Mexican but Austrian.[20] Hall was expelled by the *Juaristas* before he could take part in the trial, which condemned the Emperor to be executed a month later, but the California lawyer always maintained that the sentence disregarded the weight of the evidence and thus violated international law.[21]

After resettling in California for over a decade to practice law and write his history of San José, in 1880 Hall returned to Mexico as liaison for a Massachusetts railway company, the Ferrocarril Central Mexicano.[22] The development of Mexican railroads was a project of U.S. financiers and industrialists, who supported dictator Porfirio Díaz's 1876 overthrow of elected President Sebastián Lerdo de Tejada.[23] American investors laid the bulk of Mexico's track between 1880 and 1900, helped

---

MEXICO: MIGRATION ACROSS THE BORDERLANDS AFTER THE AMERICAN CIVIL WAR (2015) (placing the multiracial southern migration in the context of transnational economic development).

[18] FREDERIC HALL, INVASION OF MEXICO BY THE FRENCH; AND THE REIGN OF MAXIMILIAN I, WITH A SKETCH OF THE EMPRESS CARLOTA 200–212 (1868). *See also* EL IMPERIO NAPOLEÓNICO Y LA MONARQUÍA EN MÉXICO (Patricia Galeana ed., 2012) (explaining various aspects of the French invasion, installation of Maximilian, and resistance by Juárez's Liberal movement in 1862–1867).

[19] PRINCESS FELIX SALM-SALM, TEN YEARS OF MY LIFE 204 (1877).

[20] HALL, *supra* note 18, at 224–230.

[21] *Id.* at 212, 236, 298–299.

[22] Johnson, *supra* note 3, at 55.

[23] JOHN MASON HART, EMPIRE AND REVOLUTION: THE AMERICANS IN MEXICO SINCE THE CIVIL WAR 68 (2002). *See also* DANIEL LEWIS, IRON HORSE IMPERIALISM: THE SOUTHERN PACIFIC IN MEXICO, 1880–1951 (2007) (a case study of a U.S. railway corporation's Mexican subsidiary).

General Porfirio Díaz, President of the Republic of Mexico
*(Henry C.R. Becher,* A Trip to Mexico *(Toronto: Willing & Williamson, 1880), p. 79)*

by subsidies from the Díaz regime.[24] Promotion of railways, mining, and other capital-intensive enterprises required attorneys expert in local law (like Hall) to purchase land, secure titles, and deal with a multitude of unfamiliar legalities.[25] American ventures were also facilitated by a close-knit expatriate community in Mexico City, often connected to Mexican political elites through marriage and retaining ties to particular U.S. regions, including California.[26] While many American observers viewed U.S.-backed development as beneficial to both countries, Díaz's Mexican critics feared that this massive capital

---

[24] HART, *supra* note 23, at 122–123; Friedrich Katz, *The Liberal Republic and the Porfiriato, 1867–1910, in* MEXICO SINCE INDEPENDENCE 49, 70 (Leslie Bethell ed., 1991). The 1876–1910 period of Díaz's political control, most of it spent as President, is referred to as the "Porfiriato."

[25] *See* RACHEL ST. JOHN, LINE IN THE SAND: A HISTORY OF THE WESTERN U.S.-MEXICO BORDER 82 (2011) (discussing the reliance of U.S. investors in Mexico on specialized professionals, including lawyers).

[26] *See* WILLIAM SCHELL, JR., INTEGRAL OUTSIDERS: THE AMERICAN COLONY IN MEXICO CITY, 1876–1911 (2001) (discussing the role of familial and geographic relationships in Mexico-U.S. business). *See also* Paul Bryan Gray, *Judge Ignacio Sepulveda: A Life in Los Angeles and Mexico City, 1842–1916*, 95 S. CAL. Q. 141 (2013) (a biography of a lawyer from a leading Hispanic California family who brokered American investment in Porfirian Mexico). Commerce between California and Mexico was increasing rapidly in the 1880s, with Mexico being the state's largest western hemisphere trading partner in 1882. *California and Mexico*, THE MEXICAN FINANCIER/FINANCIERO MEXICANO, May 26, 1883, at 120.

influx would threaten national sovereignty and increase the risk of another foreign intervention.[27]

Practicing law in addition to representing the railroad, Hall quickly became enmeshed in Mexico City's American colony and socialized with diplomatic personnel to help him obtain clients. U.S. Consul General David Hunter Strother noted in 1882 that Hall had secured the release of a U.S. citizen accused of murder.[28] Hall haunted the Consulate trolling for business, and on one occasion was accused by a former client of agreeing to an insufficient settlement.[29] By 1884 Strother had become exasperated with his hanging on, writing that "Judge Hall ... has turned out to be a regular sponge & dead beat & also a candidate for office."[30] But whatever his professional abilities or personal foibles, Hall's participation in one of the major legal-political controversies of the 1880s—the right of foreigners to own land—made him a public figure in Mexico.

For a month in 1883, he engaged in a newspaper debate with Ignacio L. Vallarta, the prominent Minister of Foreign Relations (1876–1878) and President (Chief Justice) of the Supreme Court (1878– 1882), over limitations on property ownership by foreigners.[31] Writing in *The Mexican Financier/Financiero Mexicano*, a bilingual weekly boosting international commerce, Hall took aim at the federal legislation restricting non-Mexicans from acquiring land within twenty leagues of the border and five leagues of the coast, as well as requiring them to sell

---

[27] *See* HUBERT HOWE BANCROFT, 6 HISTORY OF MEXICO 463 (1888) (viewing "the mutual commercial advantages to be derived by peace and reciprocal comity"); Katz, *supra* note 24, at 70 (discussing contemporary fears of instability and invasion).

[28] DAVID HUNTER STROTHER, PORTE CRAYON'S MEXICO: DAVID HUNTER STROTHER'S DIARIES IN THE EARLY PORFIRIAN ERA, 1879–1885 472 (John E. Stealey III ed., 2006).

[29] *Id.* at 611, 634.

[30] *Id.* at 833. In addition to his failed attempt to be appointed U.S. Minister to Mexico in 1875, Hall ran unsuccessfully for a San Francisco probate judgeship in 1875. Johnson, *supra* note 3, at 54. This candidacy may be the origin of Strother's various references to "Judge" Hall.

[31] *See* Sergio Ortega Noriega, *Prólogo*, *in* IGNACIO L. VALLARTA, LA PROPIEDAD INMUEBLE POR EXTRANJEROS 13–22 (Secretaría de Relaciones Exteriores, 1986) (1883) (detailing the constitutional and legislative background of the foreign ownership controversy). *See also* Matthew C. Mirow, *Case Law in Mexico 1861 to 1919: The Work of Ignacio Luis Vallarta*, *in* RATIO DECIDIENDI: GUIDING PRINCIPLES OF JUDICIAL DECISIONS 223 (W. Hamilton Bryson & Serge Dauchy eds., 2006) (on Mexico's innovative development of constitutional case law, unusual for a civil law country, beginning with Vallarta's Supreme Court term).

any holdings if they moved or resided abroad.[32] He argued that the limitations violated articles of the 1857 Constitution protecting property acquisition as a "right of man" (art. 1), which right was possessed by foreigners (art. 33), and the reservation of non-express powers to the states (art. 117).[33] Further, Hall considered that the provisions were a trap for investors: "The Government of Mexico cannot afford to play the roll [sic] of the spider, and assign that of the fly to the foreigner; and thus invite him within her borders by relating to him that gold and silver lie hidden within her hills ... and then ... under color of law, deprive him of his richly cultivated and well-earned estate."[34]

Responding two weeks later in *The Two Republics*, Vallarta acknowledged that the Mexican Constitution indeed gave citizens and foreigners the same basic rights, but maintained that the statutory restrictions merely counterbalanced the latter's access to diplomatic intervention against confiscation, since otherwise "the absurdity would follow that the legal position of the foreigner would be better than that of a native."[35] Hall retorted that Vallarta had not produced any authority for his position, and reiterated his critique of the anti-foreign legislation in a *Mexican Financier/Financiero Mexicano* editorial.[36] Mexico's Congress reentered the debate at the end of the year, passing a new statute compensating private (including foreign) companies for their expenses

---

[32] *See* MANUEL AZPIROZ, CÓDIGO DE EXTRANJERÍA DE LOS ESTADOS UNIDOS MEXICANOS: ENSAYO DE CODIFICACIÓN 27–28 (1876); LEONIDAS HAMILTON, HAMILTON'S MEXICAN LAW: A COMPILATION OF LEGISLATION 10–13 (1882) (presenting the 1842, 1854, and 1856 statutory provisions on foreign ownership).

[33] Frederic Hall, *Foreigner's Rights in Mexico*, THE MEXICAN FINANCIER/ FINANCIERO MEXICANO, Aug. 11, 1883, at 299, 301, 303. *See also* www.juridicas.unam.mx/infjur/leg/conhist/1857.pdf (text of the 1857 Constitution).

[34] *Id.* at 305.

[35] I.L. Vallarta, *Ex-Chief Justice Vallarta's Opinion*, THE TWO REPUBLICS, Aug. 25, 1883, at 4.

[36] Frederic Hall, *The Rights of Foreigners*, THE MEXICAN FINANCIER/FINANCIERO MEXICANO, Sept. 15, 1883, at 387. *See also* Luis Méndez, *Rights of Foreigners in Mexico*, THE MEXICAN FINANCIER/FINANCIERO MEXICANO, Aug. 25, 1883, at 335–341 (reinforcing Hall's position).

Plaza de Armas, City of Mexico, showing the Cathedral, Sagrario and National Palace
*(Henry C.R. Becher,* A Trip to Mexico *(Toronto: Willing & Williamson, 1880), p. 55)*

surveying land the companies themselves determined to be "public" with one-third of such land.[37] Vallarta had vainly objected to the legislation on the grounds that it undermined federal power over citizenship, colonization, and naturalization.[38] The conflict over foreign property rights and the transfer of public land to private businesses underscores the government's redistribution of wealth to moneyed elites, a process Hall endorsed.[39]

Based on his practice and forays into legal journalism, Hall felt that Mexican law was "sadly in need of organization & regulation," as he remarked to Consul General Strother early in 1883.[40] This problem was noted by other observers of Porfirian Mexico such as historian and publisher Hubert Howe Bancroft, who commented that inconsistencies in judicial administration and frequent regime changes made the country's law a "mass of odd, feudal, and medieval hasty and contradictory enactments."[41] Hall engaged Bancroft's San Francisco firm, which had issued his San José narrative and now had an active law department, to publish his compilation of Spanish and Mexican codes

---

[37] Ley de 15 de Diciembre de 1883 (1883), *reprinted in* LEGISLACIÓN Y JURISPRUDENCIA SOBRE TERRENOS BALDÍOS 806 (Wistano Luis Orozco ed., 1895).
[38] IGNACIO L. VALLARTA, LA PROPIEDAD INMUEBLE POR EXTRANJEROS 23–96 (Secretaría de Relaciones Exteriores, 1986) (1883). Vallarta's opinion on the law had been solicited in advance of its passage by the Ministry of Public Works.
[39] *See* Katz, *supra* note 24, at 72 (analyzing the survey law's facilitation of land concentration at the expense of small plot holders).
[40] STROTHER, *supra* note 28, at 528.
[41] BANCROFT, *supra* note 27, at 484.

for attorneys advising investors in Mexico and dealing with Hispanic legal questions in the U.S. Southwest.[42] In September, 1884, Strother wrote in his diary that "Judge Hall it seems has gone to Calafornia [sic] to publish his Law Book."[43]

Hall's decision to produce a new English compilation of Mexican law to supersede prior works contextualizes his writing within the nineteenth-century tradition of legal treatise literature. According to historian Morton Horwitz, the devotion of U.S. jurists between 1820 and 1920 "to the proposition that law was a science and that most of its basic problems could be solved through the intensive application of reason"[44] fueled the systematic attempt to collect and summarize legal sources, and explains the contemporary prominence of the treatise. Its growing importance derived also from another major mid-nineteenth-century debate, that over codifying the notoriously inconsistent common law (reducing it to statutory form). Treatises appeared to some as the stepping stones to a code, and to others as making codification unnecessary. But proponents of either perspective believed treatises would unify and simplify jurisprudence.[45] Given Hall's views on the disorganized state of Mexican law, and the authoritative role of treatises in the civil law tradition of which Mexico partook, it is not surprising that he would seek to secure his reputation by creating the most comprehensive lawbook on the subject.[46]

Hall stated his goals of illuminating issues arising under Mexican law still pertaining in territories ceded to the United States and those concerning trade and property within Mexico proper.[47] His sources—published works and primary material in the Mexican national archives—

---

[42] *See* JOHN WALTON CAUGHEY, HUBERT HOWE BANCROFT, HISTORIAN OF THE WEST 59 (1946) (describing Bancroft's law department and its production of case reports, codes, and treatises).

[43] STROTHER, *supra* note 28, at 778.

[44] Morton J. Horwitz, *Part III—Treatise Literature*, 69 LAW LIBR. J. 460, 460 (1976).

[45] Angela Fernandez & Markus D. Dubber, *Introduction: Putting the Legal Treatise in Its Place*, *in* LAW BOOKS IN ACTION: ESSAYS ON THE ANGLO-AMERICAN LEGAL TREATISE 1, 10 (Angela Fernandez & Markus D. Dubber eds., 2012). *See also* CHARLES M. COOK, THE AMERICAN CODIFICATION MOVEMENT: A STUDY OF ANTEBELLUM LEGAL REFORM (1881) (on the U.S. trend to codify the law and its critics).

[46] *See* JOHN HENRY MERRYMAN & ROGELIO PÉREZ-PERDOMO, THE CIVIL LAW TRADITION: AN INTRODUCTION TO THE LEGAL SYSTEM OF EUROPE AND LATIN AMERICA (3d ed. 2007) (highlighting the scholarly treatise's authority in civil law jurisdictions).

[47] HALL, *supra* note 2, at iii.

included the medieval law code, the *Siete Partidas* (1348), the colonial compilations *Recopilación de las Indias* (1774) and *Novísima Recopilación* (1805), the mining code *Reales Ordenanzas... de la Minería* (1783), Joaquín Escriche's treatise *Diccionario Razonado de Legislación y Jurisprudencia* (1847), and the 1870 *Código Civil* (Civil Code).[48] Hall acknowledged previous English-language compilers and translators of Hispanic law, specifically Charles Thomson, John A. Rockwell, and Henry Halleck, but considered his version more accurate.[49] He also recognized the assistance of his opponent in the property rights debate, Ex-Chief Justice Vallarta, as well as of prominent attorneys Luis Méndez (a drafter of the *Código Civil)* and Emilio Pardo.[50] In addition to these sources, though, readers received the benefit of his on-the-ground expertise in applying and explicating Mexico's civil law methodology.

Following a translation of the 1857 Mexican Constitution, Hall divided the contents into three parts: First, Spanish Crown lands, Mexican public lands, and mines; then, individual property rights prior to the 1870 Civil Code; and, finally, rights set out in that Code. One particularly thorough chapter in the second part, based on Escriche's *Diccionario Razonado*, covered water law, including irrigation canals, upper and lower riparian (riverbank) owners' rights, tidelands, and the consequences of watercourse changes.[51] Hall was aware that the law was not static and foresaw the passage of a new federal mining code, which occurred in 1884, too late to be included.[52] Throughout the work, he

---

[48] *Id.* at iv–v.

[49] *See* THE ORDINANCES OF THE MINES OF NEW SPAIN (Charles Thomson trans., 1825); JOHN A. ROCKWELL, A COMPILATION OF SPANISH AND MEXICAN LAW IN RELATION TO MINES AND TITLES TO REAL ESTATE, IN FORCE IN CALIFORNIA, TEXAS AND NEW MEXICO (Lawbook Exchange, 2011) (1851); H.W. HALLECK, A COLLECTION OF MINING LAWS OF SPAIN AND MEXICO (1859).

[50] HALL, *supra* note 2, at v. *See also* Peter L. Reich, *Regime Change and Legal Change—The Legacy of Mexico's Second Empire*, 2015 OXFORD U. COMP. L. F., ouclf.ius.org/articles/reich/shtml (discussing Méndez's code-drafting role).

[51] *Id.* at 399– 419. *See* 1 JOAQUÍN ESCRICHE, DICCIONARIO RAZONADO DE JURISPRUDENCIA Y LEGISLACIÓN 79–80, 130–135 (1847) (detailing *acequías* or irrigation canals, and riparian servitudes); 2 JOAQUÍN ESCRICHE, DICCIONARIO RAZONADO DE JURISPRUDENCIA Y LEGISLACIÓN 827–828 (1847) (detailing tidelands and watercourse changes).

[52] HALL, *supra* note 2, at 398. The *Código Minero* was designed to appeal to foreign investors by expressly granting surface proprietors ownership of most mineral deposits below their lands, which had previously been government property. *Código de Minería*

compared the past translations with his own interpretations of the sources' language, and consulted his Mexican advisers when in doubt.[53]

Released in 1885, *The Laws of Mexico* was well received by commercial and legal periodicals. Simeon Levy, publisher of *The Mexican Financier/Financiero Mexicano*, lauded the book for its historical comprehensiveness and praised Hall for having "spared no pains in his researches and … indefatigable industry and patience in this great amount of translation," despite a few minor errors.[54] Levy considered that "[t]he great value of the work consists in its presenting, not simply the present law on the subjects treated, but the whole series of legislation, royal, imperial, and republican, from which the laws of to-day have originated, thus giving that which to the student is most interesting but at the same time most difficult to obtain."[55] A shorter, unattributed review in the *American Law Review* of Philadelphia noted the utility of Hall's book in Mexican law disputes within the ceded territories, as well as in matters touching U.S. investment in Mexico, especially because its contents had "always been difficult of access to American lawyers, locked up in a little known foreign language, clothed in ancient form and doubtful phrase."[56] One commentator, reflecting U.S. paternalism toward Latin America in the era, marveled that the translated Mexican Constitution of 1857 contained "all those essential guarantees of civil liberty, which the English-speaking people have been accustomed to prize so highly."[57] Another remarked that, while the work would be "more highly appreciated" in the U.S. Southwest and Pacific slope, its interest was not confined to that region but was "well worthy of a place in every well-appointed Eastern law library."[58]

Beyond the immediate plaudits it garnered, *The Laws of Mexico* exerted a lasting influence on property jurisprudence in the U.S. Southwest—one of Hall's principal aims in writing it. In 1888 the New Mexico Territorial Supreme Court held that a federal land grant patent to a former Mexican citizen did not convey any mineral title, referencing Hall's explanation that Spanish and Mexican law had recognized

---

*de la República Mexicana* (1884). *See* MARVIN D. BERNSTEIN, THE MEXICAN - MINING INDUSTRY, 1890–1950 18–19 (1965) (discussing the history and substance of the 1884 Mining Code).

[53] HALL, *supra* note 2, at v.

[54] Simeon Levy, *The Laws of Mexico*, THE MEXICAN FINANCIER/FINANCIERO MEXICANO, Feb. 21, 1885, at 323–324.

[55] *Id.* at 324.

[56] *The Laws of Mexico*, 2 AM. L. J. 280 (1884–1885).

[57] *Hall's Mexican Law*, 20 CENT. L.J. 279 (1885).

[58] *The Laws of Mexico*, 6 CRIM. L. MAG. 409 (1885).

subsurface rights as belonging to the sovereign and thus as incapable of being "passed out of it by mere grant."[59] U.S. Supreme Court Justice Oliver Wendell Holmes, Jr., relied on Hall's translation of Mexico's 1824 and 1830 colonization laws to rule in 1921 that a reservation of tidelands for public use did not justify U.S. government expropriation without compensation of private property granted in that zone.[60] And the U.S. Fifth Circuit Court of Appeals resolved a dispute over oil and gas deposits under tidelands added to an ocean beach by using Hall's definition of the seashore, taken from the *Siete Partidas*, as land covered by the "highest swells of the sea."[61]

*The Laws of Mexico* played a similarly key role in the half-century conflict over whether there was an Hispanic law basis for the irrigation rights of riparian owners in Texas.[62] In 1926, the Texas Supreme Court held that riparian proprietors could prevent non-riparians from diverting water, citing Hall's water law chapter, which stated that non-navigable streams passing through properties could be used by the owners "for the utility of their farms or industries" and, if passing between tracts, could be used by each owner "for the utility of his estate or any other object."[63] But three decades later, a scholarly critique of the decision pointed out that it had omitted significant passages requiring that any irrigation be "[w]ithout prejudice to the common use" and consistent with "ordinances and customs."[64] After a thorough examination of Hispanic law, including a reference to *The Laws of Mexico*, the Texas Court of Civil Appeals

---

[59] United States v. San Pedro & Canon del Agua Co., 17 P. 337, 404 (N.M. 1888), *aff'd on other grounds* 146 U.S. 120 (1892) (citing HALL, *supra* note 2 §§ 1210–1213, 1235). *See generally* Peter L. Reich, *Western Courts and the Privatization of Hispanic Mineral Rights Since 1850: An Alchemy of Title*, 23 COLUM. J. ENVT'L L. 57 (1998) (discussing southwestern case law on the validity of Hispanic mineral titles).

[60] United States v. Coronado Beach Co., 255 U.S. 472, 485–486 (1921) (citing HALL, *supra* note 2 §§ 291, 492).

[61] Humble Oil & Refining Col, et al. v. Sun Oil Co., et al., 191 F.2d 705, 720 (5th Cir. 1951) (quoting HALL, *supra* note 2 § 1466).

[62] Riparian water rights are based on users owning land adjacent to a watercourse and typically exclude use by non-riparians. *See generally* Peter L. Reich, *Mission Revival Jurisprudence: State Courts and Hispanic Water Law Since 1850*, 69 WASH. L. REV. 869, 914–923 (1994) (analyzing the historical background of Texas judicial decisions initially accepting and ultimately rejecting riparian irrigation rights).

[63] Motl v. Boyd, 286 S.W. 458, 465 (Tex. 1926) (quoting HALL, *supra* note 2 §§ 1388, 1391).

[64] A.R. White & Will Wilson, *The Flow and Underflow of Motl v. Boyd—The Conclusion*, 9 SW.L.J. 377, 381–383 (1955) (quoting HALL, *supra* note 2 §§ 1388, 1389). All the passages cited and omitted by the court were direct translations of ESCRICHE, *supra* note 51, at 134.

THE MINING LAWS

— OF THE —

STATE OF CALIFORNIA

1849 to 1897

— BY —

FREDERIC HALL

— AUTHOR OF —

"HALL'S MEXICAN LAW."

*Including the Attorney General's Opinion on the New Location Law, also Opinion by J. F. Cowdrey on same, with United States and California Court Decisions on Important Points in Mining Law — and Statistics of Mineral Productions of California for 1896.*

FIRST EDITION.

Price, 25 Cents.

J. BELL, PUBLISHER,
LOS ANGELES, CAL.
1897.

Hall's California Mining Law Compilation
(*title page of Frederic Hall*, The Mining Laws of the State of California, 1849 to 1897 (*Los Angeles: J. Bell, 1897*))

found in 1961 that irrigation rights did not automatically accompany riparian land grants in the colonial and Mexican periods, and overruled the 1926 holding.[65]

The success of Hall's second purpose—to provide a legal guide for U.S. investors in Mexico—is harder to trace. Two subsequent English-language compilations and translations did not mention *The Laws of*

---

[65] State v. Valmont Plantations, 346 S.W. 2d 853, 859 (Tex. Ct. App. 1961), *opinion adopted* 355 S.W. 2d 502 (Tex. 1962) (citing HALL, *supra* note 2, at 2). The Texas Supreme Court lauded the appellate opinion as "exhaustive and well documented." Valmont Plantations v. State, 355 S.W. 2d 502, 503 (Tex. 1962).

*Mexico* in their prefatory acknowledgments.[66] Indeed, one referred to other similar works, pointedly ignoring Hall's.[67] Of course, the book's effect on myriad negotiations over property rights, and on unpublished judgments in a non-precedent-based legal system, would necessarily have left little if any documentation. In any event, Frederic Hall did not live to witness his book's influence. He returned from Mexico in 1884 and practiced law in Los Angeles, where he compiled a pamphlet of California mining legislation and case summaries.[68] After his appointment as an archivist of pre-statehood materials in the U.S. Surveyor General's Office in San Francisco, Hall died of a heart attack in that city on December 26, 1898.[69]

Drawn from a life filled with adventures in international litigation, journalism, and politics, *The Laws of Mexico* became Hall's most enduring legacy. His experiences researching Hispanic sources in Gold Rush-era California and Porfirian Mexico allowed him to produce a treatise useful to both courts and practitioners. As historian Christopher Tomlins wrote, the worth of a legal treatise "lies not only in its exposition of law as a particular form of knowledge, but also in its purposeful advocacy of structures … that animate the way that particular knowledge is expressed."[70] Indeed, at its publication *The Laws of Mexico* was the most up-to-date resource for Anglo-American attorneys not only on Mexican legal material, but on the civil law methodology for applying it—the author cautioning his readers that "precedents, neither in the courts of continental Europe nor in those of Spanish America, have the same force and authority as in the courts of the United States."[71] Hall's work has been superseded by more recent bibliographic reference guides and practice-oriented summaries, but its translations and comprehensive coverage of property, mining, and water law helped

---

[66] *See* ROBERT JOSEPH KERR, A HANDBOOK OF MEXICAN LAW iii–iv (1909); JOSEPH WHELESS, COMPENDIUM OF THE LAWS OF MEXICO ix–x (1910).
[67] WHELESS, *supra* note 66, at ix (citing HAMILTON, *supra* note 32, and KERR, *supra* note 66).
[68] JOHNSON, *supra* note 3, at 55–56; FREDERIC HALL, THE MINING LAWS OF THE STATE OF CALIFORNIA, 1849 to 1897 (1897).
[69] JOHNSON, *supra* note 3, at 56. *See* obituaries cited *supra* note 3.
[70] Christopher Tomlins, *Commentary: Effects of Scale: Toward a History of the Literature of Law*, *in* LAW BOOKS IN ACTION, *supra* note 45, at 220, 242).
[71] HALL, *supra* note 2, at 398.

shape the judicial approach to the Hispanic tradition still pervading U.S. law in the Southwest.[72]

Peter L. Reich<br>
Costa Mesa, California, and México, D.F.<br>
January, 2016

[72] *See* HELEN L. CLAGETT & DANIEL M. VALDERRAMA, A REVISED GUIDE TO THE LAW AND LEGAL LITERATURE OF MEXICO (1973) (detailing legislation and treatises on a range of topics); JORGE A. VARGAS, MEXICAN LAW FOR THE AMERICAN LAWYER (2009) (presenting substantive law combined with litigation and transaction strategies).

THE

# LAWS OF MEXICO:

A COMPILATION AND TREATISE

RELATING TO

## REAL PROPERTY, MINES, WATER RIGHTS, PERSONAL RIGHTS, CONTRACTS,

AND

## INHERITANCES.

BY

FREDERIC HALL,

COUNSELOR AT LAW.

SAN FRANCISCO:

A. L. BANCROFT AND COMPANY,

LAW BOOK PUBLISHERS, BOOKSELLERS, AND STATIONERS.

1885.

# PREFACE.

The author and compiler undertook this work for the purpose of furnishing the profession in the United States what seemed to him a deficiency or a necessity. The difficulties which have presented themselves in the territories ceded to the United States by Mexico relative to the rights pertaining to real estate have been exceedingly great. There are many questions arising under Mexican laws in said territories yet unsettled, and innumerable ones must necessarily arise by virtue of the increase of trade, of progress, and of the transfer of property within the present domain of the republic of Mexico. It can hardly be denied that the present work will be of value to the English-speaking race who are about to invest their wealth and make their abode within the confines of Mexican territory. The history of Spanish and Mexican jurisprudence has been difficult of access, in a great degree, to American lawyers, from the fact that much of it has been clothed in a foreign language, of an ancient form, and without sufficient precedents of judicial interpretation to show what was in force and what repealed; or to make it clearly known what has been the universal construction, if any, upon doubtful phrases or language. It is indeed yet an open question in Mexico how much of Spanish jurisprudence is binding upon the people of the republic.

The question has lately been raised in the supreme court whether all of the laws of the Novisima Recopilacion are in force here by virtue of their being within said code, or whether only such laws therein are in force as were communicated to the viceroy, by order of the king, through the council of the Indies, and promulgated there. The court held, in the case of Garza against Milmo, July 1, 1882, that such communication and promulgation were necessary.

The author has endeavored to present the laws of Mexico, and a brief commentary thereon, pertaining to real estate, from the time of the conquest by Cortés until the present. This undertaking has been attended with much labor and perplexity, in the search of books and their contents, and examination in the general archives of Mexico for royal decrees.

The laws referred to in this work as Las Siete Partidas are divided into *seven* parts; hence the name. The work was commenced in the year 1255 and finished in 1263. It was not sanctioned and published until 1348. It is difficult, and in fact impossible, to read these ancient laws without the aid of the glossary which is usually attached to the later editions, and published in the same ancient style and orthography as the first edition. This form has been followed, lest any change therein might produce a modification of the true spirit and intent of the laws as originally promulgated.

So much of this celebrated code as was deemed requisite for the clear understanding of Spanish jurisprudence applicable to the rights of property in Louisiana was translated by Messrs. Moreau and Carleton, under the sanction of said state and at the expense thereof. The translation was published in 1808. The author has availed himself of this translation, with a very few corrections of style rather than of substance.

The Recopilacion de Indias and the Ordenanzas de Intendentes have been referred to and explained in the body of this work. The Novisima Recopilacion was published in 1805, varying in method and order from the previous codes of Spanish laws. The mining code now in force, promulgated by Charles III. in 1783, has been stripped by the author of this work of those portions which are inapplicable to the republic and at variance with its constitution and laws. This mining code was translated by Charles Thompson, Esq., of Lincoln's Inn, barrister at law, and published at London in 1825. This translation was adopted by Rockwell in his work on "Spanish and Mexican Law," as he says, "with the few corrections which were deemed proper after a careful comparison of it with the original." With all due respect to the ability of both Mr. Thompson and Mr. Rockwell, the translation in article 22, title 6, relative to the substances which are subject to be denounced, is perfectly astounding. Many have been misled by it, and among them the author hereof, prior to his examination of the original. The foregoing translation makes *every production* of the earth subject to the ordinances. Halleck, in his work on the "Mining Laws of Spain and Mexico," did better. But he was too limited in his construction, while the other above-mentioned authors were without limits. By reference to the chapter on mines herein, the reader may see the construction placed upon the phraseology in question by the author.

The author has followed chiefly the translation of Thompson, but in some places he has adopted the language of Halleck, and in others his own, after a comparison with the original. Whenever any doubt has arisen in the mind of the author as to the correctness of his translation, he has not failed to bring to his aid the learning of scholarly Mexicans.

No treatise or compilation of Spanish and Mexican jurisprudence pertaining to real estate exactly like the present work has ever been published in any language. The bringing together in a compact form the legislation on that subject-matter must necessarily be of great convenience to those desirous of obtaining a knowledge thereof.

The task of the author and compiler might have fallen to the lot of an abler mind. How well the work has been executed is submitted to the indulgence of the reader. If he has "opened the windows of the law to let in more light to the student," though feeble be its rays, it will be a great satisfaction to him, and a recompense for his labor.

During the author's residence in the city of Mexico, he received much aid from the members of the profession with whom it was his good fortune to be acquainted, and he can not close without specially acknowledging his obligations, for valuable assistance and suggestions, to the Hon. Ignacio L. Vallarta, ex-chief justice of the supreme court of justice, and also to Señores Luis Mendez and Emilio Pardo, distinguished members of the Mexican bar. Nor is the author less indebted to Don Justino Rubio, keeper of the general archives of Mexico, for his valuable services rendered in search of royal decrees.

FREDERIC HALL.

SAN FRANCISCO, CALIFORNIA, January, 1885.

# CONTENTS.

## PART FIRST.

### CROWN LANDS OF SPAIN, PUBLIC LANDS OF MEXICO, AND MINES.

### CHAPTER I.

POSSESSION AND EARLY GOVERNMENT OF MÈXICO BY SPAIN.



### CHAPTER II.

GRANTS AND COMPOSITIONS OF LANDS, AND ROYAL CÉDULAS AND DECREES PERTAINING THERETO.

## CHAPTER III.

LAWS OF THE INDIES, BOOK 4, TITLE 12, AS TO THE SALES, COMPOSITIONS, AND DISTRIBUTION OF LANDS, HOUSE-LOTS, AND WATERS.



## CHAPTER IV.

COMMENTARY ON THE ROYAL CÉDULA OF OCTOBER 15, 1754.

## CHAPTER V.

CÉDULA OF THE KING, DATED OCTOBER 15, 1754, REPEALING THAT OF NOVEMBER 24, 1735—CONFIRMATION OF TITLES BY ROYAL AUDIENCIAS.



## CHAPTER VI.

ORDINANCE OF INTENDENTS OF DECEMBER 4, 1786—ORDER OF PEDRO NAVA, MILITARY COMMANDER, 1791—ROYAL CÉDULA, MARCH 23, 1798—DECREE OF JANUARY 4, 1813—CÉDULAS AND DECREES, 1814–1822.

## CHAPTER VII.

### PUEBLOS OR TOWNS.

## CHAPTER VIII.

### RIGHTS OF INDIANS.



## CHAPTER IX.

### MANNER OF OBTAINING GRANTS UNDER THE SPANISH GOVERNMENT.



## CHAPTER X.

### DEPOSITORY OR ARCHIVES OF GRANTS.

## CHAPTER XI.

### AGRARIAN MEASURES UNDER SPANISH AND MEXICAN GOVERNMENT.



## CHAPTER XII.

### LOWER CALIFORNIA.

## CHAPTER XIII.

### COLONIZATION.

## CHAPTER XIV.

### COLONIZATION.

## CHAPTER XV.

### GRANTS ANNULLED—LAWS REPEALED—PRE-EMPTION LAW—CIRCULARS.

## CHAPTER XVI.

### RIGHTS OF FOREIGNERS TO PURCHASE, HOLD, AND DISPOSE OF REAL PROPERTY.

## CHAPTER XVII.

### FORESTS AND TIMBER CUTTING.

## CHAPTER XVIII.

### THE DESAMORTIZACION AND NATIONALIZATION OF PROPERTY.

## CHAPTER XIX.

### CONFISCATION OF THE PROPERTY OF TRAITORS.

## CHAPTER XX.

### SUSPENSION OF CONSTITUTIONAL GUARANTIES.

# CHAPTER XXI.

## STATE AND CHURCH.



# CHAPTER XXII.

## MINES IN GENERAL.

# PART SECOND.

## OF INDIVIDUAL RIGHTS, UNDER SPAIN AND MEXICO, RELATIVE TO REAL PROPERTY, PRIOR TO THE CODE OF 1871.

---

## CHAPTER I.

### WATER AND RIPARIAN RIGHTS.

## CHAPTER II.

### OF THE SERVICES (SERVIDUMBRES) WHICH SOME THINGS HAVE UPON OTHERS, AND HOW THEY ARE CREATED.

PARTIDA 3, TITLE 31.

# CHAPTER III.

## OF NEW WORKS AND WATER RIGHTS.

### Partida 3, Title 32.



# CHAPTER IV.

## THINGS OF WHICH ONE MAY ACQUIRE THE PROPERTY, AND HOW IT IS ACQUIRED.

### Partida 3, Title 28.

## CHAPTER V.

### OF SALE AND PURCHASE.

### Partida 3, Title 5.

## CHAPTER VI.

### OF PRESCRIPTION OR LIMITATION.

PARTIDA 3, TITLE 29, AND THE LAWS OF TORO.

## CHAPTER VII.

### SALES AND INSTRUMENTS IN WRITING.



---

# PART THIRD.

## CIVIL CODE—PERSONAL RIGHTS, REAL PROPERTY, CONTRACTS, AND INHERITANCE.

---

## CHAPTER I.

### COMMENTARY—EFFECTS OF THE LAWS—PERSONS, DOMICILES, ASSOCIATIONS, AND CORPORATIONS.

## CHAPTER II.

### IMMOVABLE PROPERTIES.

## CHAPTER III.

### PROPERTY IN GENERAL.

## CHAPTER IV.

### POSSESSION.

## CHAPTER V.

### USUFRUCTS IN GENERAL—USE AND HABITATION.

## CHAPTER VI.

SERVICES (SERVIDUMBRES).

## CHAPTER VII.

### PRESCRIPTION.

## CHAPTER VIII.

PARTIES TO SALES, LEASES, ETC.

## CHAPTER IX.

### PURCHASE AND SALE.

## CHAPTER X.

### ANTICRESIS AND MORTGAGES.

## CHAPTER XI.

### LEASES AND RURAL PARTNERSHIP.

## CHAPTER XII.

### CONTRACTS IN GENERAL.

## CHAPTER XIII.

### CONTRACTS OF MARRIAGE RELATIVE TO THE PROPERTY OF THE CONSORTS.

# CHAPTER XIV.

## DOWER.

# CHAPTER XV.

## DONATIONS.

## CHAPTER XVI.

### CENSOS OR ANNUAL PENSIONS OR ANNUITIES.

## CHAPTER XVII.

### SUCCESSIONS.

## CHAPTER XVIII.

### EXECUTORS OF LAST WILLS.

## CHAPTER XIX.

### OF THE FORM OF WILLS AND SUCCESSION.

# CHAPTER XX.

## DISPOSITIONS COMMON TO THE TESTAMENTARY AND TO THE LEGITIMATE SUCCESSION.

## CHAPTER XXI.

### INVENTORY.

## CHAPTER XXII.

### COLLATIONS.

## CHAPTER XXIII.

### PARTITIONS.

# CHAPTER XXIV.

## PUBLIC REGISTER.

## APPENDIX I.



## APPENDIX II.

# THE CONSTITUTION OF MEXICO.

---

Ignacio Comonfort, substitute president of the Mexican republic, to the inhabitants thereof, know ye: That the extraordinary constituent congress has decreed the following: The representatives of the different states of the district, and of the territories which compose the republic of Mexico, called by the plan proclaimed in Ayutla, the first of March, 1854, reformed in Acapulco the eleventh day of the same month and year, and by the letter of convocation issued the seventeenth of October, 1855, in order to constitute the nation under the popular, representative, democratic, republican form, exercising the powers with which they are vested, fulfill their high charge by decreeing the following: The political constitution of the Mexican republic, on the indestructible basis of its legitimate independence, proclaimed the sixteenth of September, 1810, and consummated the twenty-seventh of September, 1821.

## TITLE I.

### SECTION I. OF THE RIGHTS OF MAN.

Art. 1. The Mexican people recognize that the rights of man are the basis and the object of social institutions. Consequently they declare that all the laws and all the authorities of the country must respect and sustain the guaranties which the present constitution grants.

Art. 2. In the republic all are born free. Slaves who tread the national territory recover, by that act alone, their liberty, and have a right to the protection of the laws.

Art. 3. Instruction is free. The law shall determine what professions require a diploma for their exercise, and with what requisites they must be issued.

Art. 4. All men are free to adopt the profession, industry, or labor which suits them, the same being useful and honest, and to avail themselves of their products. They can not be prevented from exercising either, except by judicial sentence when they attack the rights of a third party, or by a governmental resolution, dictated in the terms which the law marks out, when they offend the rights of society.

Art. 5. Nobody can be obliged to give his personal labor without a just recompense, and without his full consent. The law can not authorize any contract which has for its object the loss or the irrevocable sacrifice of the liberty of man, whether through the cause of labor, education, or religious vow. Neither can contracts be authorized in which a man agrees to his proscription or exile.

Art. 6. The manifestation of ideas can not be the object of any judicial or administrative inquisition, unless, in case it attacks morality, the rights of a third party, provokes some crime or misdemeanor, or disturbs public order.

Art. 7. The liberty of writing or publishing writings upon any matter is inviolable. No law nor authority can establish previous censure, nor require security from authors or printers, nor restrain the liberty of the press, which has no further limits than the respect of private life, morality, and the public peace. The crimes of the press shall be tried by a jury which shall decide the fact, and by another which applies the law and designates the punishment.

Art. 8. The right of petition in writing, in a peaceful and respectful manner, is inviolable; but in political matters the citizens of the republic only can exercise the right. Every petition must be followed by a written answer from the authority to which it may have been addressed, and the latter is under obligation to make the result known to the petitioner.

Art. 9. Nobody can be deprived of the right of peacefully associating or uniting with others for any lawful object; but only citizens of the republic can do so to take part in the political affairs of the country. No armed meeting has a right to deliberate.

Art. 10. Every man has a right to possess and carry arms for his security and legitimate defense. The law shall designate which are prohibited, and the punishment which those shall incur who carry them.

Art. 11. Every man has a right to enter and to go out of the republic, to travel through its territory and change his residence, without the necessity of any safeguard, passport, letter of safe conduct, or other like requisite.

Art. 12. There are no titles of nobility, nor prerogatives,

nor hereditary honors, nor are they recognized in the republic. The people alone legitimately represented can decree recompenses in honor of those who have given or shall give eminent services to the country or to humanity.

Art. 13. In the Mexican republic no one can be tried by special laws nor by special tribunals. No person or corporation can have laws, nor enjoy emoluments which may not be a compensation for a public service, and be fixed by law. The law of war only subsists for crimes and faults which have an exact connection with military discipline. The law shall fix with all clearness the cases of this description.

Art. 14. No retroactive law can be enacted. No one can be tried nor sentenced except by laws made prior to the act and exactly applicable to it, and by the tribunal which has been previously established by law.

Art. 15. Treaties shall never be made for the extradition of political prisoners, nor for the extradition of those offenders of the common order who may have held the condition of slaves in the country where they committed the crime; nor agreements or treaties in virtue of those which shall alter the guaranties and rights which this constitution grants to man and to the citizen.

Art. 16. No one can be molested in his person, family, domicile, papers, or possessions, except in virtue of a writ written by competent authority, which establishes and assigns a legal cause for the proceedings. In the case of *in flagrante delicto*, every person can apprehend the delinquent and his accomplices, placing them, without delay, at the disposition of the immediate authority.

Art. 17. No one can be arrested for debt of a purely civil character. No one can exercise violence to reclaim his right. The tribunals will always be expeditious to administer justice. This shall be gratuitous, judicial cost being consequently abolished.

Art. 18. Imprisonment shall only take place for crimes which deserve corporal punishment. In any state of the process in which it shall appear that such a punishment can not be imposed upon the accused, he shall be set at liberty under bail. In no case can the imprisonment or detention be prolonged for want of the payment of fees, or any other supply of money.

Art. 19. No detention can exceed the term of three days, unless justified by a writ showing cause of imprisonment and other requisites which the law establishes. The lapse of this term alone constitutes a responsibility with the authority which orders it or consents to it, and the agents, ministers, warden, or jailer who executes it. Every maltreatment in the apprehension or in the prisons, every molestation which shall be declared without a legal reason, every tax or contribution in the prisons, is an abuse which the laws must correct and the authorities severely punish.

Art. 20. In every criminal trial the accused shall have the following guaranties: 1. That the grounds of the proceedings and the name of the accuser, if there shall be one, shall be made known to him; 2. That his preparatory declaration shall be taken within forty-eight hours, counting from the time he may be at the disposition of the judge; 3. That he shall be confronted with the witnesses who depose against him; 4. That he shall be facilitated with the *data* which he requires and which appear in the process, in order to prepare for his defense; 5. That he shall be heard in his defense by himself or by a person of his confidence, or by both, according to his will. In case he should have no one to defend him, a list of the official defenders shall be presented to him, in order that he may elect the one or those who may suit him.

Art. 21. The application of the punishments properly as such is exclusively of the judicial authority. The political or administrative authority can only impose, as a correction, to the extent of five hundred dollars as a fine, or to the extent of one month's confinement, in the cases and in the manner which the law shall expressly determine.

Art. 22. Punishments by mutilation and infamy, by marks, lashes, sticks, torment of any kind, excessive fine, confiscation of property, and any other unusual or transcendental punishment, shall be forever prohibited.

Art. 23. For the abolition of the punishment of death, it shall be the care of the administrative power to establish, within the greatest brevity, a penitentiary regimen. In the mean time it shall be abolished for political crimes, and shall not extend to other cases except those of a traitor to the country in a foreign war, of a highway robber, of an incendiary, of a parricide, of a homicide by treachery, premeditation, or advantage; to cases of grave crimes of the military order, and to those of piracy which the law shall define.

Art. 24. No criminal trial can have more than three instances. No one can be tried twice for the same crime, whether it be a trial which absolves or condemns him. The practice of absolving from the instance is abolished.

Art. 25. The correspondence which under cover circulates through the post-office is free from all registry. The violation of this guaranty is an offense which the law will punish severely.

Art. 26. In time of peace no military man can require lodging nor supplies, nor other real or personal service, without the consent of the proprietor. In time of war they can only be required in the terms which the law establishes.

Art. 27. The property of persons can not be occupied without their consent, unless for a cause of public utility and a previous indemnification. The law shall determine the authority which must make expropriation and the requisites with which it must be done. No civil or ecclesiastical corporation, whatever may be its character, denomination, or object, shall have legal capacity to acquire in property (as owner) or administer by itself real estate, with the only exception of the edifices destined immmediately and directly to the service or object of the institution.

Art. 28. There shall be no monopolies, nor privileged places (estancos) of any kind, nor prohibitions with titles of protection to industry. Those only shall be excepted which relate to the coining of money, to the post-offices, and the privileges which, for a limited time, the law may concede to inventors or perfecters of some improvement.

Art. 29. In cases of invasion, grave disturbances of the public peace, or any other cases which may place society in great danger or conflict, by the president of the republic only, with the consent of the council of ministers, and with the approbation of the congress of the union, and in the recess of the latter, of the permanent deputation, can the guaranties granted in this constitution be suspended, with the exception of those which insure the life of man; but he must do so for a limited time, through the means of general provisions, and without the suspension being limited to a determined individual. If the suspension should take place while congress is in session, the latter will concede the authorizations which it may esteem necessary in order that the executive may meet the situation. If the supension should be made in time of recess, the permanent deputation will convoke congress without delay, in order that it may resolve the authorizations.

## Section II. Of Mexicans.

Art. 30. Mexicans are: 1. All those born within or without the territory of the republic of Mexican parents; 2. Foreigners who are naturalized in conformity with the laws of the federation; 3. Foreigners who acquire real estate in the republic, or who may have Mexican children, provided they do not manifest the resolution of preserving their nationality.

Art. 31. It is an obligation of every Mexican: 1. To defend the independence, the territory, the honor, the rights, and interests of his country; 2. To contribute for the public expenses, as well of the federation as of the state and municipality in which he resides, in the proportional and equitable manner which the laws may provide.

Art. 32. Mexicans shall be preferred to foreigners in equal circumstances for all employments, charges, or commissions of appointment by the authorities in which the condition of citizen may not be indispensable. Laws shall be issued to improve the condition of laboring Mexicans, rewarding those who shall distinguish themselves in any science or art, stimulating labor, and founding practical colleges and schools of art and trades.

### Section III. Of Foreigners.

Art. 33. Foreigners are those who possess the qualities determined in article 30. They have a right to the guaranties granted in section 1, title 1, of the present constitution, save in all cases the power which the government has to expel pernicious foreigners. They are under the obligation to contribute for the public expenses in the manner which the laws provide, and to obey and respect the institutions, laws, and authorities of the country, subjecting themselves to the judgments and decrees of the tribunals without being able to institute other recourses than those which the laws concede to Mexicans.

### Section IV. Of Mexican Citizens.

Art. 34. All those having the quality of Mexicans and the following conditions are citizens of the republic: 1. Having completed the age of eighteen years and being married, or twenty-one without being married; 2. Having an honest mode of living.

Art. 35. The prerogatives of a citizen are: 1. To vote at the popular elections; 2. To be voted for for all offices of popular election, and to be appointed for any other employment or commission, having the qualities which the law establishes; 3. To associate together in order to treat of the political affairs of the country; 4. To take up arms in the army or in the national guard, for the defense of the republic and its institutions; 5. To exercise in all classes of business the right of petition.

Art. 36. The obligations of the citizen of the republic are: 1. To be inscribed on the municipal roll, manifesting the property which he has, or the industry, profession, or labor by which he subsists; 2. To enlist in the national guard; 3. To vote at the popular elections in the district in which he belongs; 4. To perform the charges of the popular election of the federation, which in no case shall be gratuitous.

Art. 37. The quality of citizen is lost: 1. By naturalization in a foreign country; 2. By serving officially the government of another country, or receiving from it decorations, titles, or functions, without a previous license from the federal congress, excepting literary, scientific, and humanitarian titles, which may be accepted freely.

Art. 38. The law shall fix the cases and the form in which the rights of the citizen shall be lost or suspended, and the manner of reinstating them.

## TITLE II.

### Section I. Of the National Sovereignty, and of the Form of the Government.

Art. 39. The national sovereignty resides essentially and originally in the people. All public power emanates from the people, and is instituted for their benefit. The people have at all times the inalienable right of altering or modifying the form of their government.

Art. 40. It is the will of the Mexican people to constitute themselves into a representative, democratic, and federal republic, composed of free and sovereign states, in all that concerns their interior regimen; but united in a federation established according to the principles of this fundamental law.

Art. 41. The people exercise their sovereignty through the means of the powers of the union in the cases of their competency, and through those of the states touching their interior regimen, in the terms respectively established by this federal constitution, and the special ones of the states, which in no case can contravene the stipulations of the federal compact.

### Section II. Of the Integral Parts of the Federation and of the National Territory.

Art. 42. The national territory comprehends that of the integral parts of the federation, and besides, that of the adjacent islands in both oceans.

Art. 43. The integral parts of the federation are the states of

Aguascalientes, Colima, Chiapas, Chihuahua, Durango, Guanajuato, Guerrero, Jalisco, Mexico, Michoacan, Nuevo Leon and Coahuila, Oaxaca, Puebla, Querétaro, San Luis Potosí, Sinaloa, Sonora, Tabasco, Tamaulipas, Tlaxcala, Valle de Mexico, Vera Cruz, Yucatan, Zacatecas, and the territory of Lower California.

Art. 44. The states of Aguascalientes, Chiapas, Chihuahua, Durango, Guerrero, Mexico, Puebla, Querétaro, Sinaloa, Sonora, Tamaulipas, and the territory of Lower California will preserve the limits they now have.

Art. 45. The states of Colima and Tlaxcala will preserve, in their new character of states, the limits which they have had as territories of the federation.

Art. 46. The state of the Valle de Mexico will be formed of the territory which at present comprehends the federal district; but this erection will only have effect when the supreme federal powers are transferred to another place.

Art. 47. The state of Nuevo Leon and Coahuila will comprehend the territory which has belonged to the two distinct states which to-day form it, separating the part of the hacienda of Bonanza, which will be reincorporated into Zacatecas, on the same terms in which it was before its incorporation into Coahuila.

Art. 48. The states of Guanajuato, Jalisco, Michoacan, Oaxaca, San Luis Potosí, Tabasco, Vera Cruz, Yucatan, and Zacatecas will recover the extension and limits which they have on the thirty-first of December, 1852, with the alterations which the following article establishes.

Art. 49. The town of Contepec, which has belonged to Guanajuato, will be incorporated into Michoacan. The municipality of Ahualulco, which has belonged to Zacatecas, will be incorporated into San Luis Potosí. The municipalities of Ojo Caliente and San Francisco de los Adames, which have belonged to San Luis, as well as the towns of Nueva Tlaxcala and San Andres del Teul, which have belonged to Jalisco, will be incorporated into Zacatecas. The department of Tuxpan will continue to form a part of Vera Cruz. The canton of Huimanguillo, which has belonged to Vera Cruz, will be incorporated into Tabasco.

## TITLE III.

### OF THE DIVISION OF POWERS.

Art. 50. The supreme power of the federation is divided for its exercise into legislative, executive, and judicial. There can never be united in one person or corporation two or more of these powers, nor the legislative power deposited in one individual.

### Section I. Of the Legislative Power.

Art. 51. The exercise of the supreme legislative power is deposited in an assembly, which shall be denominated the congress of the union.

#### PARAGRAPH I. OF THE ELECTION AND INSTALLATION OF CONGRESS.

Art. 52. The congress of the union shall be composed of representatives, elected in their totality every two years by the Mexican citizens.

Art. 53. One deputy shall be appointed for each forty thousand inhabitants, or for a fraction which exceeds twenty thousand. The territory in which the population shall be less than that which is fixed in this article shall appoint, notwithstanding, one deputy.

Art. 54. For each proprietary deputy shall be appointed one substitute (suplente).

Art. 55. The election for deputies shall be indirect in the first grade, and en escrutinio secreto (by ballot) in the terms which the electoral law may provide.

Art. 56. In order to be a deputy, it is required to be a Mexican citizen in the exercise of his rights; to be of the age of twenty-five years complete on the day of the opening of the session; to be a citizen of the state or territory which makes the election; and not to belong to the ecclesiastical state. Citizenship of a place (vecindad) is not lost by absence or the performance of a public charge of popular election.

Art. 57. The charge of a deputy is incompatible with any other commission or destiny of the union in which a salary is enjoyed.

Art. 58. The proprietary deputies, from the day of their election to the day on which their charge is concluded, can not accept any employment or appointment from the executive of the union by which he enjoys a salary, without a previous license from congress. The same requisite is necessary for the substitute deputies when they are in the exercise of their functions.

Art. 59. The deputies are inviolable for their opinions manifested in the performance of their charge, and they never can be called to account therefor.

Art. 60. Congress qualifies the election of its members, and resolves the doubts relative thereto.

Art. 61. Congress can not open its sessions nor exercise its charge without the concurrence of more than half of the total number of its members; but those present must meet on the day designated by law, and compel those absent to appear, under the penalties which it shall designate.

Art. 62. Congress shall have each year two periods of ordinary sessions: the first shall commence the sixteenth of September and terminate the fifteenth of December; and the second (improrogable) shall commence the first of April and terminate the last of May.

Art. 63. At the opening of the sessions of congress the president of the union shall be present, and shall pronounce a discourse, in which he shall manifest the condition which the country is in. The president of congress shall answer in general terms.

Art. 64. Every resolution of congress shall have no other character than that of a law or economic resolution. The laws shall be communicated to the executive signed by the president and two secretaries, and the economic resolutions by two secretaries alone.

PARAGRAPH II. OF THE INITIATIVE AND FORMATION OF THE LAWS.

Art. 65. The right of initiating laws belongs: 1. To the president of the union; 2. To the deputies of the federal congress; 3. To the legislatures of the states.

Art. 66. The initiatives presented by the president of the republic, the legislatures of the states, or the deputations of the same shall pass immediately to a commission. Those which the deputies may present shall be subject to the procedure which the rules of debate shall designate.

Art. 67. Every bill which shall be rejected by congress shall not again be presented during the sessions of the year.

Art. 68. The second period of sessions shall be destined, with all preference, to the examination and voting of the appropriations of the following fiscal year; to the decreeing of the contributions to cover them, and to the revision of the account of the preceding year which the executive shall present.

Art. 69. The penultimate day of the first period of sessions the executive shall present to congress a bill of appropriations for the next year, and an account of the preceding year. Both shall pass to a committee composed of five representatives appointed on the same day, which will be under obligations to examine both documents, and present their opinion on them in the second session of the second period.

Art. 70. The initiatives or bills must be subject to the following procedure: 1. An opinion of a committee; 2. One or two discussions in the terms which the following fractions express; 3. The first discussion shall be had on the day which the president of congress shall designate, in conformity with the regulations; 4. The discussion being concluded, a copy of the bill shall be passed to the executive, in order that within the term of seven days he may manifest his opinion, or declare that he will not use that power; 5. If the opinion of the executive should be in accord therewith, they will proceed without further discussion to vote upon the bill; 6. If in said opinion there should be a discrepancy, in whole or in part thereof, the bill will be returned to the committee, in order that, with the presence of the observations of the government, the committee may again examine the matter; 7. The new report of the committee shall receive another discussion; and this being concluded, the voting will proceed; 8. An approbation of the absolute majority of the deputies present.

Art. 71. In the case of notorious agency, qualified by the vote of two thirds of the deputies present, congress can narrow or dispense with the procedure established in article 70.

#### PARAGRAPH III. OF THE POWERS OF CONGRESS.

Art. 72. Congress has the power: 1. To admit new states or territories into the federal union, incorporating them into the nation. 2. To erect territories into states when they shall have a population of eighty thousand inhabitants, and the necessary elements to provide for their political existence. 3. To form new states within the limits of those existing, provided that a population of eighty thousand prove that they have the necessary elements to provide for their political existence. Congress will hear in every case the legislatures of the territory which is treated of, and the resolution of congress will only have effect if it be ratified by the majority of the legislatures of the states. 4. To regulate definitely the limits of the states, terminating the differences which may arise between them relative to the demarkation of their respective territories, except when those differences have a contentious character. 5. To change the residence of the supreme powers of the federation. 6. To regulate the interior of the federal district and territories, having as a basis the regulation that the citizens shall elect popularly the political, municipal, and judicial authorities, designating for them a revenue to cover their local observance. 7. To approve the appropriations of the expenses of the federation which the executive must annually present to it, and to impose the necessary taxes to cover them. 8. To give the bases upon which the executive can make loans upon the credit of the nation, to approve of those said loans, and to recognize and order the national debt to be paid. 9. To issue a list of duties relative to foreign commerce, and to prevent, by the means of general bases, onerous restrictions from being established in the commerce from state to state. 10. To establish the general bases of mercantile legislation. 11. To create and suppress public employments of the federation; to designate, increase, or diminish their dotations. 12. To ratify the appointments which the executive may make of ministers, diplomatic agents, and consuls, of the superior employés of the treasury, of the colonels and other superior officers of the national army and navy. 13. To approve of the treaties, diplomatic agreements, or conventions which the executive may make. 14. To declare war in view of the *data* which the executive shall present to it. 15. To regulate the manner in which letters of marque shall be issued; to dictate laws, according to which must be declared good or bad the prizes on sea and land; and to issue those laws relative to maritime rights in peace and war. 16. To concede or deny the entrance of foreign troops into the territory of the republic, and to consent to the station of squadrons of another power for more than a month in the waters of the republic. 17. To permit the departure of national troops out of the limits of the republic. 18. To raise and sustain the army and navy of the union, and regulate their organization and service. 19. To give regulations with the object of organizing, arming, and disciplining the national guard, reserving to the citizens that form it the respective appointment of chiefs and officials, and to the states the power of instructing it in conformity with the discipline prescribed by said regulations. 20. To give its consent in order that the executive may dispose of the national guard, out of their respective states or territories, fixing the necessary force. 21. To dictate laws on naturalization, colonization, and citizenship. 22. To dictate laws on general ways of communication, and on post-stages and post-offices. 23. To establish mints, fix the conditions which the money ought to have, to determine the value of foreign money, and to adopt a general system of weights and measures. 24. To fix the rules to which the occupation and alienation of public lands ought to be subject, and the price of said lands.

25. To concede amnesties for crimes, the trials of which belong to the tribunals of the federation. 26. To concede premiums or compensations for eminent services given to the country or to humanity, and privileges for a limited time to inventors or perfecters of any improvement. 27. To prorogue for thirty working days the first period of its ordinary sessions. 28. To form its interior regulation, and to take the necessary measures to cause absent deputies to appear, and to correct the faults or omissions of those present. 29. To appoint and freely remove the employés of its secretaryship, and those of the chief auditorship, which shall be organized accordingly as the law provides. 30. To issue all laws which may be necessary and proper to make effective the foregoing faculties, and all others conceded by this constitution to the powers of the union.

#### PARAGRAPH IV. OF THE PERMANENT DEPUTATION.

Art. 73. During the recess of the congress of the union, there shall be a permanent deputation, composed of one deputy for each state and territory, which congress shall appoint the evening before the closing of its sessions.

Art. 74. The attributes of the permanent deputation are the following: 1. To give its consent for the use of the national guard, in the cases spoken of in fraction 20 of article 72; 2. To resolve by itself, or on petition of the executive, the convocation of congress to extraordinary sessions; 3. To approve the appointments made in the cases referred to in fraction 3, article 85; 4. To receive the oath from the president of the republic, and from the ministers of the supreme court of justice in the cases provided by this constitution; 5. To report on all the business which remains without resolution in the bills, in order that the legislature which follows may immediately commence upon said business.

### SECTION II. OF THE EXECUTIVE POWER.

Art. 75. The exercise of the supreme executive power of the union is deposited in one sole individual, who shall be denominated "President of the Mexican United States."

Art. 76. The election of president shall be indirect in the first grade and en escrutinio secreto (by ballot), in the terms which the electoral law shall provide.

Art. 77. To be president it is required to be a Mexican citizen by birth, in the exercise of his rights, of thirty-five years of age, complete at the time of the election; not to belong to the ecclesiastical state, and to reside in the country at the time the election is carried on.

Art. 78. The president shall enter upon the exercise of his functions the first of December, and shall remain in charge thereof four years.

Art. 79. In the temporary defaults of the president of the republic, and in the absolute, until the newly elected one shall be presented, the president of the supreme court of justice shall enter upon the exercise of the power.

Art. 80. If the default of the president should be absolute, a new election will be proceeded with according to the provision in article 76, and the newly elected one will exercise his functions until the last day of November of the fourth year following his election.

Art. 81. The office of president of the union is renounceable only for grave cause, qualified by congress, before which the renunciation shall be presented.

Art. 82. If for any reason the election of president should not be had and published for the first of December, on which the place ought to be refilled, or the person elected should not be ready to enter upon the exercise of his functions, the former president shall cease acting notwithstanding, and the supreme executive power shall be deposited in the interim in the president of the supreme court of justice.

Art. 83. The president, on taking possession of his office, shall swear before congress, and in its recess before the permanent deputation, under the following formula: "I swear to perform loyally and patriotically the charge of president of the Mexican United States in conformity with the constitution, watching everything for the good and prosperity of the union."

Art. 84. The president can not remove from the place of the residence of the federal powers, nor from that of the exercise of his functions, without grave reasons qualified by congress, and in the recesses thereof, by the permanent deputation.

Art. 85. The powers and obligations of the president are the following: 1. To promulgate and execute the laws which the congress of the union shall issue, proceeding in the administrative sphere with its exact observance; 2. To freely appoint and remove the secretaries of the cabinet, to remove diplomatic agents and superior employés of the treasury, and to freely appoint and remove all other employés of the union, whose appointment and removal shall not be determined in any other manner in the constitution or in the laws; 3. To appoint ministers, diplomatic agents, and consuls general, with the approbation of congress, and in its recess, with the approval of the permanent deputation; 4. To appoint, with the approbation of congress, the colonels and other superior officers of the national army and navy, and the superior employés of the treasury; 5. To appoint the other officers of the national army and navy, according to the laws; 6. To dispose of the permanent armed force on sea and land for the interior security and exterior defense of the federation; 7. To dispose of the national guard for the same objects, in the terms which fraction 20 of article 72 provides; 8. To declare war in the name of the Mexican United States, after a previous law therefor of the congress of the union; 9. To grant letters of marque, with subjection to the bases fixed by congress; 10. To direct diplomatic affairs and celebrate treaties with foreign powers, submitting them for the ratification of the federal congress; 11. To receive ministers and other envoys from foreign powers; 12. To convoke congress to extraordinary sessions, when the permanent deputation shall consent to it; 13. To facilitate the judicial power with the necessary auxiliaries for the speedy exercise of its functions; 14. To create all kinds of ports, to establish maritime and frontier custom-houses, and designate their location; 15. To grant, in conformity with the laws, pardons to criminals sentenced for crimes within the jurisdiction of the federal tribunals.

Art. 86. For the dispatch of the business in the administrative order of the federation, there shall be the number of secretaries which congress may establish by a law, which shall make the distribution of the business which must be in charge of each secretaryship.

Art. 87. To be a secretary of the cabinet it is required to be a Mexican citizen by birth, to be in the exercise of his rights, and to be twenty-five years of age in full.

Art. 88. All the regulations, decrees, and orders of the president must be signed by the secretary of the department charged with the branch to which the affair belongs. Without this requisite they shall not be obeyed.

Art. 89. The secretaries of the cabinet, as soon as shall be opened the sessions of the first period, shall report to congress the state of their respective branches.

### Section III. Of the Judicial Power.

Art. 90. The exercise of the judicial power of the federation shall be deposited in a supreme court of justice, and in district and circuit tribunals.

Art. 91. The supreme court of justice shall be composed of eleven proprietary ministers, four supernumeraries, one attorney (fiscal) and attorney general (procurador general).

Art. 92. Each one of the individuals of the supreme court of justice shall remain in his office six years, and his election shall be indirect in the first grade (primary), in the terms which the electoral law shall provide.

Art. 93. To be elected a member of the supreme court of justice, it is necessary to be learned in the science of law, in the judgment of the electors, to be thirty-five years of age and a Mexican citizen by birth, in the exercise of his rights.

Art. 94. The members of the supreme court of justice, on entering to exercise their charge, shall take an oath before congress, and in its recess before the permanent deputation, in the following form: "You swear to perform loyally and patriotically the charge of magistrate of the supreme court of justice, which the people have conferred upon you, in conformity with the constitution, and viewing everything for the good and the prosperity of the union."

Art. 95. The office of a member of the supreme court of justice is only renounceable for grave cause, qualified by congress, before which the renunciation shall be presented. In the recesses of congress the qualification shall be made by the permanent deputation.

Art. 96. The law shall establish and organize the circuit and district tribunals.

Art. 97. It belongs to the tribunals of the federation to try: 1. All controversies which relate to the fulfillment and application of the federal laws; 2. Those controversies which rest on maritime law; 3. Those in which the federation may be a party; 4. Those which arise between two or more states; 5. Those which arise between one state and one or more citizens of another; 6. Those of a civil or criminal order, which arise in consequence of the treaties made with foreign powers; 7. Those cases concerning diplomatic agents and consuls.

Art. 98. The trial of the controversies which arise of one state with another, and of those in which the union may be a party, belongs to the supreme court of justice, in the first instance.

Art. 99. It belongs also to the supreme court of justice to determine the questions of jurisdiction which arise between the tribunals of the federation, between these and those of the states, or between those of one state and those of another.

Art. 100. In the other cases comprehended in article 97, the supreme court of justice shall be an appellate tribunal, or rather of the last instance, in conformity with the graduation which the law shall make of the attributes of the circuit and and district tribunals.

Art. 101. The tribunals of the federation shall resolve all controversies which arise: 1. By laws or acts of any authority which violate individual guaranties; 2. By laws or acts of the federal authority which violate or restrain the sovereignty of the states; 3. By laws or acts of the authorities of the latter which invade the sphere of federal authority.

Art. 102. All the trials of which the preceding article speaks shall be prosecuted by a petition of the aggrieved party, by means of proceedings and forms of juridical order which the law shall determine. The judgment shall always be such that it shall only affect private individuals, and shall be limited to the protection and maintenance of those whose rights arise in the special case under consideration, without making any general declaration respecting the law or act which gave rise to the case.

## TITLE IV.

### OF THE RESPONSIBILITY OF PUBLIC FUNCTIONARIES.

Art. 103. The deputies to the congress of the union, the members of the supreme court of justice, and the secretaries of the cabinet are responsible for the common crimes which they may commit during the time of their office, and for crimes, defaults, or omissions which they incur in the exercise of that same office. The governors of the states are equally responsible for the infraction of the constitution and federal laws. The president of the republic is also responsible; but during the time of his office he can only be accused of the crimes of treason to the country, of express violation of the constitution, of attacking the electoral freedom, and of grave crimes of the common order.

Art. 104. If the crime should be a common one, congress, being erected into a grand jury, shall declare by an absolute majority of votes if there is or not cause to proceed against the accused. In a negative case, no further proceedings shall take place. In the affirmative, the accused shall remain by said act separated from his charge, and subject to an action of the common tribunals.

Art. 105. Congress as a jury of accusation, and the supreme court of justice as a jury of judgment, shall take cognizance of official crimes. The jury of accusation shall have for its object to declare by an absolute majority of votes if the accused is or not guilty. If the declaration should be absolutory, the functionary will continue in the exercise of his charge; if it should be condemnatory, he shall remain immediately separated from said charge, and shall be placed at the disposition of the supreme court of justice. This court, in full bench and formed into a jury of judgment, in the presence of the criminal, of the fiscal, and of the accuser, should there be one, shall proceed to apply, by an absolue majority of votes, the punishment which the law designates.

Art. 106. A judgment of responsibility for an official crime having been pronounced, no favor of pardon can be granted to the criminal.

Art. 107. The responsibility for official crimes and defaults can only be exacted during the period in which the functionary exercises his charge, and one year after.

Art. 108. In demands of a civil order there shall be no law, nor immunity for any public functionary.

## TITLE V.

### OF THE STATES OF THE FEDERATION.

Art. 109. The states shall adopt for their interior regimen the form of a popular representative republican government.

Art. 110. The states may regulate between themselves, by friendly agreements, their respective limits; but those regulations shall not be carried into effect without the approbation of the congress of the union.

Art. 111. The states can in no case: 1. Celebrate an alliance, treaty, or coalition with another state, nor with foreign powers—the coalition is excepted which the frontier states may make for an offensive or defensive war against the Indians: 2. Issue letters of marque or of reprisals; 3. Coin money, issue paper money or sealed paper.

Art. 112. Neither can the states, without the consent of the congress of the union: 1. Establish tonnage duties, nor any port duties, nor impose taxes or duties on importations or exportations; 2. Have at any time permanent troops, nor vessels of war; 3. Make war by itself with any foreign power. The cases of invasion, or dangers so imminent that they admit of no delay, are excepted. In these cases they will report immediately to the president of the republic.

Art. 113. Each state is under obligation to deliver without delay the criminals of other states to the authority that claims them.

Art. 114. The governors of the states are obliged to publish and to cause the federal laws to be complied with.

Art. 115. In each state of the federation there shall be given entire faith and credit to the public acts, records, and judicial proceedings of all the others. Congress may, by the means of general laws, prescribe the manner of proving said acts, records, and proceedings, and the effect thereof.

Art. 116. The powers of the union are bound to protect the states against all foreign invasion and violence. In case of insurrection or internal disturbance, they shall give them like protection, provided they shall be required by the legislature of the state, or by its executive if the legislature be not in session.

## TITLE VI.

### GENERAL PROVISIONS.

Art. 117. The powers that are not expressly granted by this constitution to the federal functionaries are understood as reserved to the states.

Art. 118. No individual can perform at the same time two offices of the union by popular election; but the person appointed may elect which of the two he wishes to perform.

Art. 119. No payment can be made which is not comprehended in the appropriation or determined by a posterior law.

Art. 120. The president of the republic, the members of the supreme court of justice, the deputies, and other public functionaries of the federation, by popular election, shall receive a compensation for their services, which shall be determined by law and paid by the federal treasury. This compensation is not renounceable, and the law which increases or diminishes it can not have effect during the period in which a functionary exercises his charge.

Art. 121. Every public functionary, without any exception, before taking possession of his office, shall take an oath to maintain this constitution and the laws which emanate therefrom.

Art. 122. In time of peace no military authority can exercise more functions than those which have an exact connection with military discipline. There shall only be fixed and permanent military commands in the forts, fortresses, and magazines which are immediately under the government of the union; or in the camps, quarters, or depositories which, out of towns, shall be established for the station of troops.

Art. 123. It belongs exclusively to the federal powers to exercise, in matters of religious worship and external discipline, the intervention which the laws designate.

Art. 124. On the first day of June, 1858, the taxes on sales of property (alcabalas) and internal custom-houses shall be abolished in all the republic.

Art. 125. The forts, military quarters, magazines of deposits, and other edifices necessary for the government of the union shall be under the immediate inspection of the federal powers.

Art. 126. This constitution, the laws of the congress of the union which emanate therefrom, and all the treaties made or which shall be made by the president of the republic, with the approbation of congress, shall be the supreme law of the whole union. The judges of each state shall be guided by said constitution, laws, and treaties, in spite of the provisions contrary thereto which there may be in the constitutions or laws of the states.

## TITLE VII.

### OF THE REFORM OF THE CONSTITUTION.

Art. 127. The present constitution can be enlarged or reformed. In order that additions or reforms shall become a part of the constitution, it shall require that the congress of the union, by a vote of two thirds of the members present, shall agree to the reforms or additions, and that these shall be approved by a majority of the legislatures of the states. The congress of the union shall make the computation of the votes of the legislatures and the declaration that the additions and reforms have been approved.

## TITLE VIII.

### OF THE INVIOLABILITY OF THE CONSTITUTION.

Art. 128. This constitution shall not lose its force and vigor, even when through any rebellion its observance shall be interrupted. In case that by any public disturbance a government contrary to the principles which it sanctions shall be established, as soon as the people recover their liberty its observance shall be re-established, and according to it and the laws which shall be issued in virtue of it shall be tried those who shall have figured in the government emanating from the rebellion, as well as those who shall have co-operated with this.

### TRANSITORY ARTICLE.

This constitution shall be published immediately, and it shall be sworn to with the greatest solemnity in the whole republic;

but with the exceptions of the provisions relative to elections of the supreme federal powers and of the states, it shall not commence to govern until the sixteenth day of September next, on which day the first constitutional congress must be installed. Thenceforth the president of the republic and the supreme court of justice, who must continue in office until the constitutionally elected individuals shall take possession of the same, shall be guided in the performance of their obligations and powers by the precepts of the constitution.

Given in the department of the sessions of congress, in Mexico, the fifth of February, 1857, and the thirty-seventh of the independence.

(Here follow the signatures of the members of the convention or congress.)

Wherefore I command that it be printed, published, circulated, and that due compliance be given to it, in the terms which it expresses. Palace of the national government, in Mexico, February 12, 1857. Ignacio Comonfort. To the citizen Ignacio de la Llave, secretary of state and of the department of government. And I communicate it to you for its publication and fulfillment. God and liberty. Mexico, February 12, 1857. Llave.

## AMENDMENTS TO THE CONSTITUTION.

Sebastian Lerdo de Tejada, constitutional president of the Mexican United States, to all the inhabitants thereof, know ye: That the congress of the union has decreed the following: The congress of the Mexican United States, in the exercise of the power which article 127 of the political constitution, promulgated the twelfth of February, 1857, concedes to it, and the previous approbation by the majority of the legislatures of the republic declares: The additions and amendments to the said constitution are:

Art. 1. The state and the church are independent between themselves. Congress can not dictate laws establishing or prohibiting any religion.

Art. 2. Marriage is a civil contract. This and the other acts of the civil state of persons are of the exclusive jurisdiction of the functionaries and authorities of the civil order, in the terms provided by the laws, and they shall have the force and the validity which the same shall attribute to them.

Art. 3. No religious institution can acquire real estate nor capitals imposed upon it, with the sole exception established in article 27 of the constitution.

Art. 4. The simple promise to say the truth and to comply with the obligations which are contracted shall be substituted for the religious oath, with its effects and penalties.

Art. 5. No person can be obligated to give personal service without just compensation and without his full consent. The state can not permit any contract, pact, or agreement to be carried into effect which shall have for its object the diminution, loss, or irrevocable sacrifice of the liberty of man, whether it be for a cause of labor, education, or religious worship. The law, consequently, does not recognize monastic orders, nor can their establishment be permitted, whatever may be the denomination or object with which they claim to be established. Neither can an agreement be admitted in which a man stipulates for his proscription or banishment.

TRANSITORY.

The foregoing additions and amendments to the constitution shall be published immediately, with the greatest solemnity, in all the republic. Palace of the congress of the union. Mexico, September 25, 1873. (Here follow the signatures of the members.) Given in the national palace of Mexico, the twenty-fifth of September, 1873.

The congress of the union, in exercise of the power which article 127 of the federal constitution concedes to it, declares the amendments hereinafter expressed to be approved by the majority of the legislatures of the states, and to be a part of the same constitution. These amendments shall commence to govern the sixteenth of September of the next year, 1875.

## TITLE III.

### SECTION I. OF THE LEGISLATIVE POWER.

Art. 51. The legislative power of the nation is deposited in a general congress, which shall be divided into two houses, one of deputies and the other of senators.

#### PARAGRAPH I. OF THE ELECTION AND INSTALLATION OF CONGRESS.

Art. 52. The house of deputies shall be composed of representatives of the nation, elected in their totality every two years by the Mexican citizens.

Art. 57. The offices of deputy and senator are incompatible with any other commission or employment of the union by which a salary is enjoyed.

Art. 58. The proprietary deputies and senators, from the day of their election to the day on which they conclude their charge, can not accept any commission or employment by appointment of the federal executive, by which he shall enjoy a salary, without a previous license from the respective house. The same requisite is necessary for the substitute deputies and senators in the exercise of their duties.

A. The senate shall be composed of two senators from each state, and two from the federal district. The election of senators shall be indirect in the first step. The legislature of each state shall declare elected him who shall have obtained the absolute majority of the votes cast, or shall elect among those who shall have obtained a relative majority, on the terms which the electoral law shall provide. For each proprietary senator shall be elected one substitute.

B. The senate shall be renewed by halves every two years. The senators elected in the second place shall cease at the end of the first two years, and thereafter the oldest.

C. In order to be a senator, the same qualities shall be required as to be a deputy, except that of age, which shall be that of thirty years, completed the day of the opening of the sessions.

Art. 59. The deputies and senators are inviolable for their opinions manifested in the performance of their duties, and can never be reprimanded therefor.

Art. 60. Each house shall judge of the elections of its members, and solve the doubts which there may be thereon.

Art. 61. The houses can not open their sessions nor exercise their charge without the concurrence in that of the senators of two thirds part, and in that of the deputies of more than the half of the whole number of its members; but those present in either must meet on the day designated by law, and compel the absent ones under the penalties which the law shall designate.

Art. 62. Congress shall have each year two periods of sessions: the first, prorogable for thirty working days, shall commence the sixteenth day of September and shall terminate the fifteenth day of December; and the second, prorogable for fifteen working days, shall commence the first of April and terminate the last day of the month of May.

Art. 64. Every resolution of congress shall have the character of a law or decree. The laws and decrees shall be communicated to the executive, signed by the presidents of both houses, and by a secretary of each one of them, and shall be promulgated in this form: "The Congress of the Mexican United States decrees." (Text of the law or decree.)

PARAGRAPH II. OF THE INITIATIVE AND FORMATION OF THE LAWS.

Art. 65. The right to initiate laws or decrees belongs: 1. To the president of the union; 2. To the deputies and senators of the general congress; 3. To the legislatures of the states.

Art. 66. The initiatives presented by the president of the republic, by the legislatures of the states, or by the deputations of the same shall pass immediately to a commission. Those which the deputies or senators shall present shall be subject to the rules which the regulation of debate shall designate.

Art. 67. Every bill which shall be rejected in the house of its origin before passing to the revisory one, can not be again presented in the sessions of that year.

Art. 69. The last day but one of the first period of sessions the executive shall present to the house of deputies the bill of appropriations for the next year following, and the accounts of the prior one. The latter and the former shall pass to a commission of five representatives, appointed on the same day, which shall be under obligation to examine said documents, and present a report thereon in the second session of the second period.

Art. 70. The formation of the laws and of the decrees may commence indiscriminately in any of the two houses, with the exception of bills which treat on loans, taxes, or imposts, and on the recruiting of troops, all which must be discussed first in the house of deputies.

Art. 71. Every bill, the resolution of which may not be exclusively of one of the houses, shall be discussed successively in both, observing the regulation of debate relative to the form, intervals, and manner of proceeding in the discussions and voting.

A. A bill having been approved in the house of its origin, it shall pass for discussion to the other house. If the latter should approve it, it will be remitted to the executive, who, if he shall have no observations to make, shall publish it immediately.

B. Every bill shall be reputed as approved by the executive power which is not returned with observations to the house of its origin within ten working days, unless during this term congress shall have closed or suspended its sessions, in which case the return must be made the first working day on which it shall meet.

C. A bill rejected in whole or in part by the executive must be returned with his observations to the house of its origin. It must be discussed again by the latter, and if it should be confirmed by an absolute majority of votes, it shall pass again to the revisory house. If it should be sanctioned by the latter with the same majority, the bill shall be a law or decree, and returned to the executive for its promulgation. The voting on the law or decree shall be nominal.

D. If any bill should be rejected in its totality by the house of revision, it shall be returned to that of its origin with the observations which the former shall have made upon it. If being examined again it should be approved by an absolute majority of the members present, it shall be returned to the house which rejected it, which shall again take it into consideration; and if it should approve it by the same majority, it shall pass to the executive for the effects of fraction A; but if it should reject it, it can not again be presented until the following sessions.

E. If a bill should be rejected only in part, or modified, or receive addition by the revisory house, the new discussion in the house of its origin shall be had only on the part rejected or on the amendments or additions, without altering in any manner the articles approved. If the additions or amendments made by the revisory house should be approved by the absolute majority of the votes present in the house of its origin, all the bills shall pass to the executive for the effects of fraction A. But if the additions or amendments made by the revisory house should be rejected by the majority of the votes in the house of its origin, they shall be returned to the former in order that the reasons of the latter may be taken into consideration; and if by the absolute majority of the votes present said additions or amendments shall be rejected on this second revision, the bill, as to what has been approved by both houses, shall pass to the executive for the effects of fraction A; but if the revisory house should insist, by an absolute majority of votes present, on said additions or amendments, the whole bill can not again be presented until the following sessions, or unless both houses agree, by an absolute majority of members present, that the law or decree shall be issued solely with the articles approved, and that the additions or amendments shall be reserved for their examination and voting in the following sessions.

F. In the interpretation, amendment, or repeal of the laws or decrees, the same rules established for their formation shall be observed.

G. Both houses shall reside in the same place, and they can not remove to another without first agreeing to the removal and on the time and manner of making it, designating the same point for the meeting of both. But if both agreeing to the removal should differ as to the time, manner, or place, the executive shall terminate the difference by electing one of the points in question. Neither house can suspend its sessions for more than three days without the consent of the other.

H. When the general congress shall meet in extraordinary sessions it shall occupy itself exclusively with the object or objects designated in the order of convocation; and if they should not be fulfilled the day on which the ordinary sessions ought to be opened, notwithstanding, the former shall be closed, leaving the points pending to be treated of in the latter. The executive of the union can not make observations on the resolutions of congress, when the latter prorogues its sessions or exercises functions as an electoral body or as a jury.

PARAGRAPH III. OF THE POWERS OF THE GENERAL CONGRESS.

Art. 72. Congress has power: 3. To form new states within the limits of those existing, being necessary for the purpose: 1. That the fraction or fractions which ask to be established into a state shall number a population of one hundred and twenty thousand inhabitants at least; 2. That it shall be proved before congress that they have sufficient elements to provide for their political existence; 3. That the legislatures of the states, the territories of which are in question, shall be heard on the expediency or inexpediency of the establishment of the new state, and they shall be obliged to make their report within six months, counted from the day on which the relative communication shall have been remitted to them; 4. That the executive of the federation shall likewise be heard, who shall send his report within seven days, counted from the date on which he shall be asked therefor; 5. That the establishment of the new estate shall be voted for by two thirds of the deputies and senators present in their respective houses; 6. That the resolution of congress shall be ratified by the majority of the legislatures of the states, after examining a copy of the proceedings (expediente); provided, that the legislatures of the states, the territory of which is in question, shall have given their consent; 7. If the legislatures of the states, the territory of which is in question, shall not have given their consent, the ratification of which the preceding fraction speaks must be made by two thirds of the legislatures of the other states.

A. The exclusive powers of the house of deputies are: 1. To form itself into an electoral college in order to exercise the powers which the law may assign it, in respect to the election of the constitutional president of the republic, magistrates of the supreme court, and senators for the federal district; 2. To judge and decide upon the resignations which the president of the republic or the magistrates of the supreme court of justice shall make—the same attribute belongs to it in treating of licenses solicited by the first; 3. To watch over, by means of an inspecting commission from its own body, the exact performance of the functions of the chief auditor; 4. To appoint the chiefs and other employés of the same; 5. To form itself into a jury of accusation for the high functionaries of which article 103 of the constitution treats; 6. To examine the account which the executive must present to it annually; to approve of the annual appropriation of expenses, and to initiate the taxes which in its judgment ought to be decreed to cover the former.

B. The exclusive powers of the senate are: 1. To approve the treaties and diplomatic conventions which the executive may make with foreign powers. 2. To ratify the appointments which the president of the republic may make of ministers, diplomatic agents, consuls-general, superior employés of the treasury, colonels, and other superior officers of the national army and navy, on the terms which the law shall provide. 3. To authorize the executive in order that he may permit the going of national troops out of the limits of the republic, the passage of foreign troops through the national territory, and the station of squadrons of other nations for more than a month in the waters of the republic. 4. To give its consent in order that the executive may dispose of the national guard out of their respective states or territories, fixing the necessary force. 5. To declare when the constitutional, legislative, and executive powers of a state shall have disappeared, that the case has arrived to appoint a provisional governor, who shall convoke elections in conformity with the constitutional laws of the said state. The appointment of governor shall be made by the federal executive with the approbation of the senate, and in its recess with that of the permanent commission. Said functionary can not be elected constitutional governor at the elections which are had in virtue of the convocation which he shall issue. 6. To resolve the political questions which shall arise between the powers of a state, when any of them shall appear with that object in the senate, or when on account of said questions constitutional order shall have been interrupted during a conflict of arms. In this case the senate shall dictate its resolution, being subject to the general constitution of the republic and to that of the state. The law shall regulate the exercise of that power and that of the preceding. 7. To form itself into a jury of judgment in conformity with article 105 of the constitution.

C. Each one of the houses can, without the intervention of the other: 1. Dictate economic resolutions relative to its internal regimen; 2. Communicate within itself, and with the executive of the union, through the means of commissions of its own body; 3. Appoint the employés of its secretaryship, and make internal regulations for the same; 4. Issue convocations for extraordinary elections, with the object of filling the vacancies of its respective members.

PARAGRAPH IV. OF THE PERMANENT DEPUTATION.

Art. 73. During the recess of congress there shall be a permanent commission composed of twenty-nine members, of whom fifteen shall be deputies and fourteen senators, appointed by their respective houses the evening before the close of the sessions.

Art. 74. The attributes of the permanent commission are: To resolve by itself or with the proposal of the executive, after hearing him in the first place, the convocation of congress, or of one house alone, for extraordinary sessions, the vote of two thirds part of the individuals present being necessary in both cases. The convocation shall designate the object or objects of the extraordinary sessions.

Article 103 of the constitution shall be in these terms: The senators, the deputies, the individuals of the supreme court of justice, and the secretaries of the cabinet are responsible for the common crimes which they may commit during the time of their office, and for the crimes, faults, or omissions which they shall incur in the exercise of that same office. The governors of the states are likewise so responsible for the infraction of the constitution and federal laws. The president of the republic is also so responsible; but during the time of his office he can only be accused of the crimes of treason to the country, express violation of the constitution, attack on the electoral liberty, and grave crimes of the common order.

To the preceding article 103 of the constitution shall be added the following: The high functionaries of the federation shall not enjoy any constitutional privilege for the official crimes, faults, or omissions into which they may fall in the performance of any employment, charge, or public commission which they shall have accepted during the period in which in conformity with the law they shall have been elected. The same shall happen with respect to those crimes which they may commit during the performance of said employment, charge, or commission. In order that the cause may be initiated when the high functionary shall have returned to exercise his proper functions, he must be proceeded with according to the provision in article 104 of the constitution.

Articles 104 and 105 of the constitution shall be in these terms: If the crime should be a common one, the house of representatives, formed into a grand jury, shall declare, by an absolute majority of votes, if there has been or not ground to proceed against the accused. In the negative case, there shall be no ground for further proceeding. In the affirmative, the accused shall be, by the said act, separated from his office and subject to the action of the common tribunals.

Art. 105. The house of deputies shall have jurisdiction of official crimes as a jury of accusation, and that of the senate as a jury of judgment. The jury of accusation shall have for its object to declare, by an absolute majority of votes, if the accused is or is not culpable. If the declaration should be absolvatory, the functionary shall continue in the exercise of his office; if it should be condemnatory, he shall be immediately separated from said office, and shall be placed at the disposition of the house of senators. The latter shall be formed into a jury of judgment, and, with the presence of the criminal, and of the accuser, if there should be one, it shall proceed to apply, by an absolute majority of votes, the punishment which the law designates.

TRANSITORY.

This declaration shall be promulgated by a national proclamation. Palace of the legislative power, Mexico, November 6, 1874. (Signed by all the members.) Wherefore I order it to be printed, published, circulated, and that due fulfillment be given it. Given in the national palace of Mexico the thirteenth of November, 1874. Sebastian Lerdo de Tejada. To the citizen Lic. Cayetano Gómez y Perez, charged with the department of government. And I communicate it to you for your knowledge and consequent effects. Independence and liberty. Mexico, November 13, 1874. Cayetano Gómez y Perez.

Department of state and that of government. Section 1. The citizen president of the republic has been pleased to direct to me the decree as follows: Porfirio Diaz, constitutional president of the Mexican United States, to the inhabitants thereof, know ye: That the congress of the union has decreed the following: The congress of the Mexican United States, in the exercise of the power which article 127 of the federal constitution concedes to it, and the previous approbation of the majority of the legislatures of the states, declares amended articles 78 and 109 of the constitution, in the following terms:

Art. 78. The president shall enter into the exercise of his office the first of December, and shall remain in it four years; and he can not be re-elected for the next period, nor occupy the presidency for any reason, except until four years shall have passed after the exercise of his functions.

Art. 109. The states shall adopt for their internal regimen the form of a popular, representative, republican government, and they shall determine in their respective constitutions the terms on which the re-election of their governors shall be prohibited. The character of governor of a state, whatever may be the titles with which he shall exercise the power, is incompatible in every case with his election for the following period. The local constitutions shall compel this precept in the terms which the legislatures may esteem proper.

TRANSITORY.

The declaration shall be promulgated by national proclamation on the fifth of May next. (Signed by all the members.) Wherefore I order it to be printed, published, circulated, and that due compliance be given it. Given in the national palace in Mexico on the fifth of May, 1878. Porfirio Diaz. To the citizen Trinidad García, secretary of state and of that of government. And I communicate it to you for your knowledge and consequent ends. Liberty and constitution. Mexico, May 5, 1878. García.

Department of state and that of government. Section 1. The citizen president of the republic has been pleased to direct me the following decree: Manuel Gonzales, constitutional president of the Mexican United States, to the inhabitants thereof, know ye: That the congress of the union has thought proper to direct me the following decree: The congress of the Mexican United States, in the exercise of the power which article 127 of the federal union concedes to it, and the previous approbation of the majority of the legislatures of the states, declares article

124 of the said constitution to be amended in the following terms:

Art. 124. By the first day of December, 1884, at the latest, the alcabalas and interior custom-houses in the district and territory of the federation, and in the states which shall not have suppressed them, shall be abolished.

(Signed by all the members.)

Wherefore I order it to be printed, published, and circulated for its due fulfillment. Given in the national palace of Mexico, the seventeenth of May, 1882. Manuel Gonzales. To the citizen Manuel Mercado, first assistant, charged with the department of state and that of government. And I communicate it to you for your knowledge and consequent effects. Liberty in the constitution. Mexico, May 17, 1882. M. A. Mercado.

Department of state and that of government. Section 1. The president of the republic has thought proper to direct me the following decree: Manuel Gonzales, constitutional president of the Mexican United States, to the inhabitants thereof, know ye: That the congress of the union has been pleased to issue the decree which follows: The congress of the Mexican United States, in use of the power which article 127 of the federal constitution concedes to it, and the previous approbation of the majority of the legislatures of the states, declares fraction 26 of article 72 to be amended, and an addition to article 85 of the constitution, in the following terms:

Art. 1. Fraction 26 of article 72 of the constitution is amended, which shall be in the following terms: 26. To concede premiums or recompenses for eminent services given to the country or to humanity.

Art. 2. Article 85 of the constitution is amended by adding the following fraction: 16. To concede exclusive privileges for a limited time, and according to the respective law, to discoverers, inventors, or perfectioners of any branch of industry.

(Signed by all the members.)

Wherefore, I order the same to be printed, published, and circulated for its fulfillment. Given in the national palace of Mexico, on the second of June, 1882. Manuel Gonzales. To the citizen Lic. Manuel A. Mercado, first assistant, charged with the department of state and that of government. I communicate to you for its effects. Liberty in the constitution. Mexico, June 2, 1882. M. A. Mercado, assistant.

Department of state and of that of government. Section 1. The president of the republic has been pleased to direct to me the following decree: Manuel Gonzales, constitutional president of the Mexican United States, to the inhabitants thereof, know ye: That the congress of the union has thought proper to decree what follows: The congress of the Mexican United States, in the exercise of the power which article 127 of the federal constitution concedes to it, and the previous approbation of the majority of the legislatures of the states, declares articles 79, 80, and 82 of the constitution to be amended in the following terms:

Art. 79. In the temporary default of the president of the republic, and in the absolute, until the newly elected shall present himself, the citizen who shall have performed the charge of president or vice-president of the senate, or of the permanent commission in the periods of recess, during the month prior to that in which said defaults shall occur, shall enter into the exercise of the executive power of the union.

A. The president and the vice-president of the senate and of the permanent commission can not be re-elected for those charges until a year after having performed them.

B. If the period of sessions of the senate, or of the permanent commission, shall commence within the second fifteen days of a month, the defaults of the president of the republic shall be covered by the president or vice-president who shall have performed his functions in the senate or in the permanent commission during the first fifteen days of said month.

C. The senate and the permanent commission shall renew their president and vice-president the last day of each month. For these charges the permanent commission shall elect alternately in a month two deputies, and in the following two senators.

D. When the default of the president of the republic shall be absolute, the functionary who shall enter constitutionally as his substitute must issue, within the precise term of fifteen days, a convocation in order to proceed with a new election, which shall be made within the term of three months, and according to the provision in article 76 of this constitution. The provisional president can not be elected as proprietary president at the elections which are made in order to put an end to his provisional term.

E. If, on account of death or any other reason, the functionaries to whom it shall belong according to these amendments should not be able, in an absolute manner, to substitute themselves for the president of the republic, the citizen who shall have been president or vice-president in the exercise of his duty of the senate or of the permanent commission, in the month prior to that in which they performed those offices, shall be substituted in the terms provided.

F. When the absolute default of the president of the republic shall occur within the last six months of the constitutional period, this shall terminate the functionary who shall be substituted for the president.

G. In order to be president or vice-president of the senate or permanent commission it shall be necessary to be a Mexican citizen by birth.

H. If the default of the president of the republic should occur when the permanent commission and the senate shall be performing their functions at the same time in extraordinary sessions, the president of the commission shall supply the default in the terms designated in this article.

I. The vice-president of the senate or of the permanent commission shall enter to perform the functions which this article confers upon them, in the absolute default of the president of the senate or of the permanent commission, and in the seasons solely while the impediment shall last.

J. The president newly elected shall enter into the exercise of his functions at the latest sixty days after that of the election. In case the house of deputies shall not be in session, extraordinary sessions shall be convoked in order to make the computation of votes within the term mentioned.

Art. 80. In the absolute default of the president, the period of the newly elected shall be computed from the first of December of the year prior to that of his election, provided that he shall not have taken possession of his office on the date which article 78 determines.

Art. 82. If for any reason the election of president should not be had and published for the first of December, on which the fulfillment of office ought to be made, or the elect should not be ready to enter into the exercise of his functions, the old one will cease notwithstanding, and the supreme executive power shall be deposited provisionally in the functionary to whom it belongs, according to the provision in the amended article 79 of this constitution.

### Article Transitory.

The foregoing amendments shall be published by a national proclamation in all the republic. (Signed by all the members.)

Wherefore I order it to be printed, published, and circulated for its fulfillment. Given in the national palace of Mexico, on the third of October, 1882. Manuel Gonzales. To the citizen general, Cárlos Diez Gutierrez, department of state and that of government. Liberty in the constitution. Mexico. And I communicate it to you for its effects. October 3, 1882. Diez Gutierrez.

# HALL'S LAWS OF MEXICO.

# COMPILATION AND TREATISE

ON THE

# LAWS OF MEXICO.

---

## PART FIRST.

## CROWN LANDS OF SPAIN, PUBLIC LANDS OF MEXICO, AND MINES.

---

### CHAPTER I.

#### POSSESSION AND EARLY GOVERNMENT OF MEXICO BY SPAIN.

§ 1. *Grant by the Pope.*—For the purposes of overthrowing heathenism, and advancing the Roman Catholic religion, Alexander the sixth issued a bull in 1493, granting to the crown of Castile the whole of the vast domain then discovered, or to be discovered, between the north and south poles, or so much thereof as was not considered in the possession of any Christian power. "Ut fides Catholica et Christiana religio nostres præsertim temporibus exaltetur, etc., ac barbaræ nationes deprimentur, et ad fidem ipsam reducantur," was the language of the bull: 1 Haz. Coll. 3.

§ 2. *Right by Discovery.*—But Spain did not rest her title alone on the grant of the pope. She with other European nations also claimed and exercised the right of discovery—a right which they deemed sufficient to maintain a title to any part of the globe. Under such views, the rights of the native Mexicans to their own soil became subordinate to the dominion of the discoverer and conqueror.

§ 3. *Mexico Reconquered.*—The republic of Mexico, now composed of twenty-seven states, one district, and one territory, was for three centuries, by virtue of discovery and conquest, the crown jewel of Spain. The embattled chivalry of Spanish power once spread its banner and its laws over nearly all of the American domain. The vast numerical strength of the half-civilized Aztecs was insufficient to resist the advancing searchers for new lands, armored in steel, and skilled in the use of powder and ball. But the coursing of Spanish blood for three centuries in the veins of the native dwellers of Anáhuac, and the advanced ideas of the latter, produced a race of such improved intellectual force, that Spanish pride and Spanish arms were compelled to release the once conquered soil of Mexico to its birthright owners.

§ 4. *Progress.*—To-day, the adventurous Americans, with hopes as brilliant as any cherished by Castilian knight who won laurels under Ferdinand, are turning their backs to the north and looking towards the lands of milder climes—lands inlaid with silver and gold, where nature invites their capital. Railroads are opening the way; and with them progress and the arts and sciences of civilization are advancing into Mexican domain. While metallic wealth is enchanting, it must be admitted that perfect agriculture is the true foundation of the riches of the state. Those who desire to build their fortunes on this foundation will not be unmindful of the care requisite in ascertaining the tenure by which landed estates are held. I purpose to trace the chain of Mexican land titles from the time of the conquest by Cortés to the present day.

§ 5. *Cortés as Governor.*—Hernan Cortés entered the city of Mexico on the thirteenth day of August, 1521. Soon after this the country received the appellation of New Spain. Cortés received the appointment of governor and captain-general thereof on the fifteenth day of October, 1522. He acted as chief justice, and had powers to appoint lieutenants and other high officers; also, among other powers, to grant lands.

§ 6. *Supreme Council of the Indies.*—The consejo supremo de Indias, or the supreme council of the Indies, sometimes termed the consejo de Indias, or India council, was formed on the first of August, 1524. It held its sessions at Madrid, Spain. Different dates have been assigned by different authors as to the time of the creation of this council. It is said that the error was occasioned by the fact that certain officers had acted informally as advisers of the king, prior to said date, in like manner as members of the council. This council had a very extensive jurisdiction. Its powers were both judicial and executive. Civil, military, ecclesiastical, and commercial cases came within the sphere of its action. Its powers were exclusive of all others as regards the governmental affairs of New Spain. The resolutions or ordinances emanating from that body received a two-thirds vote. Otherwise they would not have been approved by the king. This council continued the exercise of its powers until the year 1834.

§ 7. *Audiencias of the Indies and Viceroy.*—The emperor Charles V. adopted the system of audiencias for the government of the Indies. The first audiencia arrived in the city of Mexico in December, 1528. The first viceroy was not appointed until April 17, 1535, when Señor Don Antonio Mendoza was selected to fill that high position. On the same day he was made president of the royal audiencia, according to law 3, title 15, book 2, of the Recopilacion de las Indias. The body known as the royal audiencia and chancery was composed of the viceroy, as governor and captain-general of the viceroyalty, and lieutenant; he was also president, as before stated; eight oidores, who were magistrates or judges; four alcaldes of criminal jurisdiction, and two fiscales or counselors at law, one for civil and the other for criminal proceedings; one alguacil mayor, or high constable; one lieutenant of chancery; and other necessary ministers and officials. The number of oidores was subsequently increased to twelve, and afterwards reduced to ten. This body possessed executive and judicial functions, and was divided into departments. The oidores had jurisdiction of contentions or judicial matters, principally with appellate powers. In certain cases called casos de corte, being cases of importance, it exercised original jurisdiction. The executive and governmental functions were exercised by the viceroy or president, or by the senior oidor, who acted as president in case of the death, absence, or inability of the viceroy.

§ 8. *Powers of Audiencia and Viceroy.*—The viceroy was not to interfere in judicial matters, which the oidores alone were to decide; nor were the latter to take cognizance of governmental affairs, as appears by laws 32 and 33, title 15, book 2, of said recopilacion. But by law 35 of said title and book, the oidores had power to hear on appeal cases pertaining to governmental questions decided by the viceroy as president, or by the acting president of the audiencia, where the latter were to do justice according to the law and the ordinances. The viceroys and presidents were commanded not to impede the process of said appeals, and not to be present at the appellate trial. By a subsequent cédula of May 19, 1768, it was provided that said appeals should be taken through the formality of first asking permission of the viceroy, according to the former custom. To the same effect was the cédula of February 14, 1797. By another cédula of August 29, 1806, the governmental affairs belonged to the viceroys and presidents of the audiencias. The archives of the audiencias were under the care of the chancellor (canciller). Regents were attached to the audiencias by a cédula of April, 6, 1776. They performed duties similar to those of a chief justice, empowered to designate the functions of the oidores, to a certain degree; to form special courts; to sit as judges in any court, and to preside in the absence of the viceroy or president.

§ 9. *Audiencia at Compostela.*—By a royal cédula it was decreed that an audiencia should be established in Compostela, in the kingdom of New Galicia, now state of Jalisco, with four oidores and alcaldes mayores. The latter were not generally jueces de letras, or judges learned in the law. The members appointed for this audience arrived at Compostela on the nineteenth of January, 1549, and on the twenty-first of said month took possession of their office and commenced to govern.

§ 10. *Audiencia Moved to Guadalajara.*—Señor Don Pedro de Azala, bishop, who took possession of his bishopric in said place, informed his majesty the emperor, in 1559, that the episcopal see as well as the audiencia would be better situated if placed in Guadalajara. In consequence of the suggestion his majesty, by a royal cédula dated May 10, 1560, ordered the members of the audiencia to remove to said city. They reached there on the tenth of December of that year. On the seventh of the following month they commenced their official duties.

§ 11. *Provinces and Kingdoms.*—Before proceeding further, it will be essential to speak of the territorial divisions of the country; of the various offices, and of the occupants who exercised the respective functions thereof. The country was divided into provinces and kingdoms in the earlier periods. Although the country received the appellation of New Spain as a whole, when spoken of in general terms, yet that name was specially given to a part of the now Mexican territory embracing less than half of its original domain. This was denominated the kingdom of New Spain. Another portion was termed the kingdom of Nueva Vizcaya; another that of Nueva Galicia. Nueva Vizcaya included the state of Chihuahua south of about thirty degrees north latitude, and that part of Durango north of twenty-four degrees of said latitude; embracing also that part of Coahuila south of said thirty degrees and west of Nuevo Leon. Nueva Galicia included the states of Aguas Calientes, Zacatecas, and the state of Jalisco, except the provinces of Avalos that lie south of Autlan and Gazala. The whole of the Mexican territory was divided and termed kingdoms and provinces, as follows:

1. The kingdom of Mexico, now the state of Mexico and the federal district.
2. The kingdom of Nueva Galicia, now state of Jalisco.
3. The kingdom of Leon, now state of Nuevo Leon.
4. The colony of Nuevo Santander, now state of Tamaulipas.
5. The province of Texas, now state of Texas.
6. The province of Coahuila, now state of Coahuila.
7. The province of Nueva Vizcaya, now Durango and Chihuahua, as above described.
8. The province of Sonora and Sinaloa, now two states.
9. The province of Nuevo Mexico, now territory of New Mexico.
10. The province of Upper and Lower California.

§ 12. *Jurisdiction of Audiencias.*—As I have already shown, there were audiencias; and as they exercised certain jurisdiction over land titles, it is essential to know their respective territorial limits. The kingdoms of Nueva Vizcaya and Nueva Galicia, together with the province of Sonora and Sinaloa, belonged to the jurisdition of the audience of Guadalajara. As a dividing line between the two audiencias, we may take the west boundary of the state of Nuevo Leon; thence running southward near Matehuala, including a part of the state of San Luis Potosí, to and southward along the west line of the state of Guanajuato; thence southward to the parallel of twenty degrees of north latitude; thence west to the Pacific ocean. All east and south of the line thus described was within the jurisdiction of the audiencia of New Spain, sitting in the city of Mexico. The city of San Luis Potosí was within the limits of the latter audiencia. Texas and Nuevo Leon were within the bishopric of Guadalajara, but not within the jurisdiction of the audiencia of that city. Neither were New Mexico nor the Californias within the jurisdiction of the audiencia of Guadalupe, at least, during the sixteenth and seventeenth centuries. According to the royal cédula of October 15, 1778, the audiencia of Guadalajara had its jurisdiction extended over six provinces, to a certain degree, namely: Nueva Galicia, Zacatecas, Nueva Vizcaya, Sonora and Sinaloa, New Mexico, and the Californias: Bancroft's Hist. of Mex., vol. 3, p. 299, note. The state of Tamaulipas was formerly known as the province of Santander. Texas was first designated as the province of Nueva Felipinas, having been discovered in the reign of Philip V.

§ 13. *Various Officers and their Powers.*—The Indies were principally governed by viceroys, audiencias, royal chancellors, royal officials, adelantados, corregidores, alcaldes mayores, alcaldes ordinarios, ayuntamientos, and tenientes de justicia. The royal officials were revenue officers, residing in their respective districts. Adelantado was an early term for governor. Each kingdom or province was under the charge of a governor; and in the capitals of each was a corregidor. Each kingdom or province was divided into partidos, or districts, under the jurisdiction of an alcalde mayor (according to law 1, book 5, title 1, Recop. Indias); and the pueblos of each partido had a teniente de justicia, a lieutenant of justice. According to law 1, title 3, book 5, of the Recopilacion de las Indias, in cities and pueblos where there was no governor or lieutenant, two alcaldes ordinarios were to be elected, who tried all suits, causes, and matters which the governor or his lieutenant could try, in all civil and criminal matters; and the appeals which were interposed from their decrees and sentences were to go to the audiencias, governors, or ayuntamientos (town councils), in conformity as they were ordered by the laws of Spain or of the kingdoms of Mexico.

Alcaldes mayores and corregidores had prior to the date of the ordinance of intendencias, December 4, 1786, and for nearly three centuries, exercised the functions of magistrates of their respective partidos, with political powers also. They sometimes acted as governors. In the matter of the sale and composition of land and water, they were usually made subdelegates, as will be hereafter explained.

§ 14. *Municipalities.*—Municipalities were generally governed by regidores, or councilmen, and alcaldes. Large cities and towns had twelve councilmen, and small ones six. Law 2, title 7, book 4, of the Recopilacion de las Indias, which was ordinance No. 43 of Philip II., provides as follows: "The land, province, and place having been elected in which a new settlement is to be made, and the convenience and availability which there may be having been examined, the governor in whose district it may be or confined shall declare whether the pueblo which is to be settled must be a city, villa, or place, and in conformity with what he shall declare shall be formed the council, government, and officials thereof; so that if it should be a metropolitan city, it shall have a judge, with the title of adelantado, or alcalde mayor, or corregidor, or alcalde ordinario, who shall exercise jurisdiction *in solidum;* and jointly with the town council (regimiento), shall have the administration of the city; two or three officials of the royal treasury; twelve councilmen (regidores); two faithful executors; two jurados of each parish; one attorney-general (procurador general); one mayordomo; one notary of the council; two notaries public; one of mines and registers; one public crier; one exchange broker; two porters; and if a diocese or suffragan, eight councilmen, and the other perpetual officials; for the villas and places, an alcalde ordinario; four councilmen; one alguacil (constable); one notary of the council, and a notary public; and one mayordomo." The above law 1, title 3, book 5, was issued by the Emperor Charles V. in 1537. The words "cabildo," "ayuntamiento," and "regimiento," each and every one signify a city or town council. If a governor died without leaving a lieutenant, an alcalde ordinario governed: Law 12, title 3, book 5, of said recopilacion. If there should be no alcalde in such a case, the oldest councilman governed: Law 13. Where there was a governor or corregidor the alcalde ordinario could not appear in the council: Law 14.

§ 15. *Intendencias.*—By article 1 of the royal ordinance of intendents, bearing date December 4, 1786, Mexico, without including the Californias and New Mexico, was divided into twelve intendencias, each one bearing the name of its respective capital except Sonora. There was one intendencia general for the province of Mexico; and the others were designated as follows: Intendencias of Guadalajara, Zacatecas, Durango, Sonora including Sinaloa, Puebla, Vera Cruz, Merida, Oajaca, Valladolid (now state of Michoacan), Guanajuato, and San Luis Potosí. These divisions embraced two hundred and forty-two alcaldias mayores, or partidos. The capital of Sonora was Arispe. March 17, 1787, Sinaloa was made a separate intendencia.

§ 16. *Intendent of Guadalajara.*—An audiencia, an episcopal see, and a university having been established at Guadalajara, a high military officer was appointed as intendent for that city, who was styled commander-general, president, governor, intendent of the provinces embraced within the kingdom of Nueva Galicia. He was president of the audiencia of that city. The arrival of the several intendents appointed by the king for Mexico did not take place until 1787. The head towns and residents of the intendents were made the seats of corregimientos. The said ordinance of intendents discontinued the offices of alcaldes mayores, and asesores, subdelegates, and alcaldes ordinarios were created. The asesor was an attorney at law, who acted as legal adviser of the chief officers. This government by intendents continued until the independence of Mexico.

§ 17. *Comandancia General and Comandante.*—Visitador general Señor Galvez, jointly with the Marqués de Croix, viceroy in 1768, suggested to the king that a plan should be provided for the formation of a government under a comandancia general, and superintendencia de hacienda, entirely independent. On the twenty-second of August, 1776, a royal cédula was issued, appointing Don Teodoro de Croix, comandante general of the provinces of Sinaloa, Sonora, Californias, Nueva Vizcaya, Coahuila, Texas, and New Mexico. His residence was fixed at Arispe, in Sonora. This cédula embraced what was termed instructions, setting forth the powers of the comandante over these provincias internas. He was entirely independent of the viceroy at the city of Mexico. There seems to be no direct language in the cédula in regard to selling lands, but nearly all powers in general. The power exercised by the comandante Don Pedro Nava, in authorizing captains of presidios to form pueblos under the protection of the presidios, and make grants of house-lots and other lands within the same, by his order of March 22, 1791, dated at Chihuahua, may have been exercised under his unlimited military power, as the presidios, being military garrisons, were considered under his exclusive jurisdiction. He seems to have had a doubt as to his power to sell land. The comandante had also the patronato real, or royal patrónage.

§ 18. *Provincias Internas.*—By a cédula of November 23, 1792, the comandancia general de provincias internas included Sonora and Sinaloa, Nueva Vizcaya, New Mexico, Texas, and Coahuila, independent of the viceroy. The two Californias, Nuevo Leon, and the colony of Nuevo Santander were attached to the viceroyalty of New Spain. This cédula attached to the comandancia general the subdelegated superintendence of the royal treasury, which gave the power to sell and compromise lands and waters, evidently the same which was vested in the intendents by the ordinance of 1786. Under this latter cédula the comandante was ordered to fix his residence at Chihuahua. He went wherever he thought it necessary to go within his comandancia, on tours of inspection, and issued orders whenever and wherever he deemed it expedient.

# CHAPTER II.

## GRANTS AND COMPOSITIONS OF LANDS, AND ROYAL CÉDULAS AND DECREES PERTAINING THERETO.

§ 19. The Crown Enriched by Private Enterprise.
§ 20. First Grant to Cortés; Grants by Him.
§ 21. Cédulas of 1591 as to Lands Possessed without Title; Viceroy Commissioned to Sell and Compromise.
§ 22. Compromise and Compositions, how Made.
§ 23. Royal Cédula of November 1, 1591.
§ 24. Sales and Compromises of Crown Lands.
§ 25. Commissioners Sent to Make Sales and Compromises.
§ 26. Confirmation of Grants by the King, and afterwards Dispensed with.
§ 27. Cédula of 1735 again Requiring Confirmation by the King.
§ 28. Cédula of 1754, dispensing with Said Confirmation.
§ 29. General Laws as to Crown Lands.
§ 30. Ordinances of Intendents of 1786.
§ 31. Power of the Treasury of the Indies.

§ 19. *The Crown Enriched by Private Enterprise.*—Having thus referred to the origin of Spanish authority over American soil, and having delineated the territorial divisions of Mexico under that authority, and also having enumerated the respective rulers who governed the same in their several capacities, I shall now consider the method of transferring to private individuals, as early settlers and their descendants, the title to the various tracts of that vast domain—a measure which gave great vigor to private enterprise and enriched the crown.

§ 20. *Grants to and by Cortés.*—The first grants were made by the king to Cortés, Marqués de Valle, and other grand personages, without any pecuniary consideration. Cortés, while governor, was also in like manner generous. Then the viceroys with a prodigal hand made many the owners of vast possessions, with a view of promoting settlements by Spaniards. No formalities of great importance were required in thus obtaining grants of mercedes graciosas (grants without remuneration), except in the surveys. The country had but few if any skilled in the use of the compass and chain; the surveys were very inaccurate, and the tracts granted usually contained much more than the language of the titles would warrant, even more than double the quantity in many instances. The commissioned justices to whom was assigned the authority to make the surveys, in most cases, assumed as correct the various statements made by the claimants, as to the amount of land within the demarkations petitioned for; and thus they reported the surveys, and in accordance therewith the grants were issued. Many large tracts were occupied without any titles or warrants of any kind whatever, from the fact that in such vast domains there were none to dispossess them.

§ 21. *Cédulas of* 1591 *as to Possession and Sale of Lands* —In the latter part of the sixteenth century the king, having been for some time informed of the large estates possessed by persons who had in no manner remunerated the public exchequer therefor, and being desirous of creating a great armada to protect his immense possessions and his commerce, issued on the first of November, 1591, two royal cédulas. In the first he ordered the viceroy to cause all lands occupied without just and legal titles to be restored to the crown. In the second, with the concurrence of the royal council of the Indies, he commissioned the viceroy to sell and compromise the lands so possessed, as should appear to him just and reasonable, according to the quantity and quality. The viceroy was authorized thereby to grant and confirm said titles; so that by his grants the titles became perfect.

§ 22. The compromise or composition was only made with those who had been in the possession of their respective tracts for some time; and in consideration of their having settled and made some improvements, some equitable arrangement was to be made by which they could hold their lands by paying a moderate price therefor. And those who possessed lands by just titles, but having within their boundaries more land than their grants called for, were admitted, as to such excess, to a composition. To this effect was the royal decree of Philip IV., May 17, 1631; and which decree is law 15, title 12, book 4, of the Recopilacion of the Laws of the Indies. By a subsequent decree of June 30, 1646, which is law 19 of said title and book, it was provided that none should be admitted to a composition who had not been in possession of their respective tracts for the term of ten years.

§ 23. *Cédula of November* 1, 1591.—The foregoing royal cédula of November 1, 1591, is as follows:

The first royal disposition made pertaining to the sales and compositions of lands in New Spain or Mexico by cédula dated November 1, 1591, ordering the viceroy to have restored all lands occupied without just titles, and authorizing the viceroy to make sales and compositions.

The king. My D. Luis de Velasco, my viceroy, governor, and captain-general of New Spain. By another cédula of mine of this date, I order you that you cause to be restored to me all the lands that any persons have and possess in those provinces without just and legitimate titles; that you will cause said titles to be examined therefor, because said lands are mine and belong to me. And as I could justly execute what is contained in said cédula for some just causes and considerations, and principally to make grants to my vassals, I have thought proper and do think proper that said lands may be admitted to some convenient composition, in order that I may have what may be just to establish and put on the sea a great navy to secure these and those kingdoms, and the fleets which go and come therefrom, and that they may not receive damages from the enemies as they try to inflict them before being punished. The lands which they possess shall be confirmed to them, and by these presents, with the advice and judgment of my royal council of the Indies, I give you commission, power, and faculty, in order that reserving before all things what shall appear to you necessary for squares (ejidos), common lands of the towns (propios), lands for revenue, pastures and sheep lands of the places and municipal lands (consejos), which are populated, as well what belongs to the present condition as for the future, and to the increase and growth which may take place in each one, and to the Indians what may be necessary for them to sow, cultivate, and to raise stock; all the rest you can compromise, the possessors paying me for said lands, Indian farms (chacaras), small grazing farms (estancias), farms (cortijos), and cavallerias, for what shall appear to you just and reasonable, according to the quantity and quality of the lands which they have and possess without just and legal titles; for which lands you will give and confirm to them new titles. And in order that the same possessors and any others who, although they may possess some of said lands, Indian farms (charcaras), and farms with new titles, may wish new confirmation of them, you can concede such to them with the clauses and security (firmeza) which may be proper for them; they paying me therefor what may be just and for what you can agree with them therefor. And besides, after reserving out of the lands which have not been occupied and distributed those which may be necessary for the small towns and municipalities (consejos) populated, which it shall be proper to people anew, and what shall be necessary for the Indians, and which they shall lack for their fields and stock raising; all the rest you can give and concede anew for farms, chacaras, and lands for grist mills (ejidos de molinos), to whomsoever shall ask and wish for them by the means of said composition—regulating the composition in conformity with what shall be given them; and in case that any persons should refuse and should not wish said composition, you shall proceed with such persons in conformity with the law; by virtue of my said cédula. You will restore to me before all things all that you may find which has been occupied and possessed without valid and legal titles; and this even which may be restored to me, you may concede anew to whomsoever that shall ask you for it and wish it, by the means of said composition in the form declared in use; and all that you may thus compromise and confirm and concede anew I, by these presents, approve, confirm, and concede, being in conformity with what is in this our cédula decreed; which, it is my will, shall be incorporated in the titles, confirmations, and dispatches which you may give of said lands; in order that by means of said securities (recaudos) they may have as true owners and legitimate possessors of what they are not as such now. Dated in Pardo, the first of November, one thousand five hundred and ninety-one. I the king. By order of the king our lord, Juan de Ibarra.

By a decree of the twelfth of March, 1593, it was ordered that the foregoing royal cédula should be obeyed and published in the accustomed places in the city.

§ 24. *Sales and Compromises of Vacant Lands.*—Afterwards, and in pursuance of the foregoing cédula in the beginning of the following century, the viceroy commenced to sell the vacant lands and to make compositions with those persons in possession of lands occupied without just titles. These sales and compositions were made by orders from the viceroy through judges commissioned for that purpose. Near the close of the seventeenth century, the members of the council of the Indies (to whom his majesty had delegated the powers thus to act, and to give jurisdiction and government of this branch of the royal treasury) appointed ministers of the audiencias to make the sales and compositions, and to cause surveys and the valuations of the lands to be thus disposed of. Subsequently this power of appointment over this branch of the treasury was taken from the council of the Indies and given to the secretaries of state and of the universal department of the Indies.

§ 25. *Commissioners Sent to Make Sales and Compromises.*—As soon as the subdelegated ministers commenced to perform their duties they sent commissioners to all the principal places within their respective districts. That is to say, the ministers of the audiencia of New Spain, at the city of Mexico, sent their commissioners to the places within the jurisdiction of their audiencia; and the ministers of the audiencia established at Guadalajara dispatched their subdelegates or commissioners to the chief places within their district. The major part of these commissioners thus sent were generally true to their trust, and acted with energy; but there were not wanting those who made such personal arrangements with the occupants and tillers of the soil as resulted injuriously to the treasury department. They favored some by permitting their boundaries to lap on the claims possessed by others, and gave to many more land than was designated in their petitions and grants. Thus litigation was produced between the claimants, and between the claimants and the fiscal department of the crown. The commissioners often gave titles to the claimants which never received the approval of any higher authority.

§ 26. *Confirmation of Grants by the King.*—Law 16, title 12, book 4, of the Recopilacion de las Indias required the confirmation of the king to the titles issued. The latter part of that law contains the order for royal approbation. The last marginal date given thereto is June 17, 1617. Probably that was the date of the order requiring such confirmation. It is evident that such royal confirmation was, at some subsequent period, dispensed with, as will appear by the cédula of 1735.

§ 27. *Cédula of* 1735 *as to Confirmations.*—His majesty, having long been dissatisfied with the manner of issuing grants, and with the illegal occupancy of lands in this distant domain, decided to make himself better acquainted with the facts and circumstances pertaining to the subject-matter. With that view, he issued, on the twenty-fourth of November, 1735, a royal cédula, whereby he reserved the right to personally examine all solicitations for lands, and the right of confirmation or the rejection thereof. But a few years of experience under this rule made it manifest to the king that the distance and the expense were too great for his vassals to lay their respective applications before his royal person for confirmation. The result of the foregoing cédula was to lessen the sales of land, and to diminish the treasury; to increase the extent of lands occupied with imperfect titles, and those occupied with no titles at all;

and to cause the occupants to make but trifling improvements, lest they should be deprived of them by the denouncements made by others.

§ 28. *Cédula of* 1754 *Dispensing with Confirmation by the King.*—On the fifteenth of October, 1754, another royal cédula was issued relieving the solicitants for titles from transmitting them to the king for confirmation. The power of confirmation became thereby vested in the two audiencias respectively; that is, each audiencia had power to confirm titles to the lands within their respective territorial jurisdiction. As the questions usually to be considered in these cases of confirmation were not of law or contentious questions, the oidores had no voice in the matter. It was for the consideration of the president of the audiencia alone, whether it were the viceroy or the senior oidor acting as the president. In cases where legal questions had arisen before the local judge, as to the rights of the solicitant, then the case went upon an appeal to the audiencia having jurisdiction. Then the appeal was heard and decided by the oidores, as the judges or magistrates of that tribunal, and the viceroy had no voice in the decision of the legal questions. The judgments were, however, signed by the president, whoever he might have been, whether viceroy or senior oidor.

§ 29. *General Laws.*—The general laws governing the dispositions of the crown lands until 1786 consisted of numerous decrees and ordinances, commencing in the year 1513, and created at various epochs thereafter; all of which were collated and published in the Recopilacion de las Indias, except the foregoing cedulas of 1591, 1735, and 1754. Said laws are to be found in title 12, book 4, of said recopilacion. The decrees and ordinances of which said laws are composed are not chronologically arranged; and the several dates which are assigned as marginal notes thereto make it difficult and even impossible to distinguish what parts of said laws were created at the time of the respective dates; or whether the later dates merely refer to decrees or ordinances which were but confirmatory of what had been decreed under the prior date or dates. This recopilacion was declared by a royal decree of the eighteenth of May, 1680, to contain the laws in force up to that date; and any laws conflicting therewith were declared to be null. In the following year the king ordered the book to be printed under the superintendence of the council of the Indies, which was done. The laws of said title 12 will be found herein.

§ 30. *Ordinances of Intendents of* 1786.—Under the foregoing laws and cédulas, the titles to lands were held, until the ordinances of intendents, which was signed on the fourth of December, 1786; except the instruction of José de Galvez, dated August 12, 1768, which was applicable only to Lower California, and which will be found herein.

§ 31. *Power of the Treasury of the Indies.*—By the record of royal cédulas in the archives at the city of Mexico, it appears that a resolution was made by the council of the Indies, before a full board at Madrid, on the twenty-third of December, 1818, and approved by the king, declaring that all business pertaining to the alienation of land in New Spain should belong to the department of the office of the treasury of the Indies.

# CHAPTER III.

## LAWS OF THE INDIES, BOOK 4, TITLE 12, AS TO THE SALES, COMPOSITIONS, AND DISTRIBUTION OF LANDS, HOUSE-LOTS, AND WATERS.[1]

§ 32. Distribution of Pueblo or Town Lands.
§ 33. Manner of Making Distributions.
§ 34. Houses to be Built; Pastures Stocked.
§ 35. Viceroys may Grant Lands to Settlers.
§ 36. Advice of City Council to be Taken.
§ 37. Assistance of the Procurador.
§ 38. No Acceptation of Persons Permitted.
§ 39. Before Whom Lands and Water to be Asked.
§ 40. Indians not to be Prejudiced.
§ 41. Discoverers and Settlers to have Lands, but not Ecclesiastics.
§ 42. Improvements to be Made within Three Months.
§ 43. A Distance to be Made between Lands of Spaniards and Indians.
§ 44. Cattle to be Withdrawn and Wheat Sown.
§ 45. Lands Possessed without Title Restored to the King.
§ 46. What Lands Admitted to Composition.
§ 47. Titles to be Confirmed by the King.
§ 48. Certain Lands not Admitted to Composition.
§ 49. Lands Left to the Indians.
§ 50. Ten Years' Possession Required for Composition.
§ 51. Grants by City Council not Confirmed by the King shall be Revoked.
§ 52. Sales and Compositions, unless Necessary, not to be Made.

§ 32. *Distribution of Pueblo Lands.*—Law First: In order that our vassals may be encouraged to make discoveries and settlements in the Indies, and that they may live with comfort and convenience, which we desire, it is our will that house-lots, lands, cavallerias, and peonias be partitioned and distributed to all those who shall go to settle new lands in towns and places (pueblos y lugares), which shall be assigned them by the governor of the new settlement, a distinction being made between esquires (escuderos) and laboring men (peones) and those who may be of less grade and merit; and these grants may be extended and improved in a measure corresponding to the services that each grantee shall render, so as to stimulate them in

[1] Ferdinand V., Valladolid, June 18 and August 9, 1513; Emperor Charles V., June 26, 1523; and at Toledo May 19, 1525; Philip II., chap. of instructions, at Toledo, May 25, 1596.

the tilling of the land and rearing of cattle; and having on said lands their residences, and having planted them and having resided in those towns four years, we concede to them power thenceforth to sell them, and to do with them according to their will freely, as a thing of their own. And likewise, in conformity with the quality of the settlers, the governor, or whoever shall have our power, shall assign Indians to them in the distribution he may make, in order that they may enjoy the profits and labors (demoras) in conformity with the taxes and what is ordered. And because it might happen that on apportioning the lands there might be a doubt as to the measures, we declare that a peonia is a house-lot of fifty feet in width and one hundred in length, one hundred fanegas[1] of cultivatable land, of wheat or barley, ten of corn, two huebras[2] of land for an orchard, and eight of dry land for planting other trees; pasture land for ten breeding sows, twenty cows, and five mares, one hundred sheep, and twenty goats. A cavalleria is a house-lot of one hundred feet in width and two hundred in length; and all the rest, as five peonias, which will be five hundred fanegas of cultivatable land for wheat bread or barley, fifty of corn, ten huebras of land for orchards, forty of dry land for the planting of other trees; pasture land for fifty breeding hogs, one hundred cows, twenty mares, five hundred sheep, and one hundred goats. And we order that the distribution be made in such a manner that all will participate in the good and in the mediocre, and of that which should not be such, in the part which ought to be assigned to each one.

§ 33. Law Second: *That gives the manner of making the apportionments in new settlement.*—To those who in the new settlement of any province may have lands and house-lots in a town, other lands and house-lots can not be given in another town, unless they should leave the first residence, and go to live in that which should be more recently settled; save if in the first they should have lived the four years required to obtain the title, or should leave said lands, and should not avail themselves of them by not having completed the four years' residence; and we declare the apportionment which shall be made contrary to the decision of this law to be null, and we condemn those who shall have made it to the penalty of our mercy and ten thousand maravedis for our house.[3]

[1] Fanega is as much land as is necessary to sow a fanega of wheat or corn, which is about four hundred fathoms square. A fanega of grain weighs about one hundred pounds.

[2] Huebra of land is about what a pair of oxen will plow in a day.

[3] Emperor Charles V., Toledo, May 19, 1525.

§ 34. Law Third: *That within a certain time houses shall be built, and the pastures stocked, under penalty of this law.*—Those who shall accept a tract of cavallerias and peonias shall be obligėd to have the house-lots built upon, their houses inhabited, to have made and partitioned the plats of cultivatable lands, to have them cultivated and planted, and the pastures stocked, within a limited time divided into terms; and declaring what is to be done in each term, under the penalty of losing the apportionment of house-lots and lands, and besides, a certain quantity of maravedis for the municipality (republic) with an obligation in public form, and a complete and responsible security.[1]

§ 35. Law Fourth: *That the viceroys may give lands and house-lots to those who go to settle.*—If in that which is already discovered in the Indias, there should be any places (sitias) and districts so good that it may be proper to found settlements, and any persons should make application to settle and reside in them, in order that with a greater will and profit they may do so, the viceroys and presidents may give them in our name lands, house-lots, and waters, in conformity with the disposition of the land; provided it be not in prejudice to third parties, and that it be for the time which may be our will.[2]

§ 36. Law Fifth: *That the apportionment of lands shall be made with the advice of the city or town council, and that the councilmen shall be preferred.*—Having to apportion the lands, waters, and watering places and pastures among those who may go to settle, the viceroys or governors, who may have the power from us, will make the apportionment with the advice of the councils of the cities or villas (small towns), taking in consideration that the councilmen (regidores) may be preferred, if they should have no equivalent lands and house-lots; and that to the Indians should be left their lands, cultivated lands, and pastures, in such a manner that they may not lack what is necessary, and that they may have all the comfort and repose possible for the sustenance of their houses and families.[3]

§ 37. Law Sixth: *That the apportionment of the lands shall be made with the assistance of the attorney (procurador) of the place.*—On the apportionment of the vicinages, cavallerias, and peonias of lands, that shall be given to the settlers, we order that the procurador of the city or villa where it has to be done shall be present.[4]

---

[1] Philip II., Ordinance 107.
[2] 1568; May 18, 1572; Feb. 15, 1586.
[3] Emp. Charles V., April 4, 1532; Philip II., 1563; May 25, 1596.
[4] Emp. Charles V., June 26, 1523; May 24, 1534.

§ 38. Law Seventh: *That the lands shall be apportioned without any acceptation of persons or damage to the Indians.*—We order that the apportionment of lands in the new settlements, as well as in those which may be already settled, be made with all justification, without admitting any singularity, acceptation of persons, or any damage to the Indians.[1]

§ 39. Law Eighth: *That declares before whom must be asked house-lots, lands, and waters.*—We order that if there should be presented a petition asking for house-lots or lands in a city or villa where our audiencia resides, the presentation must be made before the council; and they having conferred thereon, they shall appoint two deputy councilmen, who shall make known to the viceroy or president how it appears to the council; and it being examined by the viceroy, or president and deputies, the title (despacho) shall be given, signed by all in the presence of the notary of the council (escribano de cabildo), in order that he may record it in the book of the council; and if the petition should be for the distribution of waters, and lands for sugar plantations, it will be presented before the viceroy or president, and he will remit it to the council, who likewise having conferred thereon, will send its opinion by a councilman, in order that after the same has been examined by the viceroy or president he may decree what he may think proper.[2]

§ 40. Law Ninth: *That lands shall not be given to the prejudice of the Indians; and those thus given shall be returned to the owners.*—We command that the farms (estancias) and lands which shall be given to the Spaniards shall be without prejudice to the Indians; and that those which have been given to their prejudice and damage shall be returned to whom by law they may belong.[3]

§ 41. Law Tenth: *That the lands shall be apportioned to the discoverers and settlers, and can not be sold to the ecclesiastics.*—The lands shall be apportioned without excess among the discoverers and old settlers, and their descendants, who must remain on the land, and the most qualified shall be preferred; and they can not sell the lands to a church nor monastery, nor to any ecclesiasticial person, under the penalty that they shall lose them, and that said lands may be apportioned to others.[4]

§ 42. Law Eleventh: *Possession shall be taken of the lands apportioned, within three months, and they shall make planta-*

[1] Philip II., April 6, 1588.
[2] Philip II., Ordinance of 1563.
[3] Philip II., June 11, 1594.
[4] Emperor Charles V., October 27, 1535.

*tions (plantios), under penalty of losing said lands.*—All the residents and dwellers to whom apportionment of lands shall be made shall be obliged, within three months from the time they shall have been assigned to them, to take possession of said lands, and to plant all the landmarks and confines which are contiguous to other lands with willow trees (and other trees suitable for the season), so that besides putting the land in a good and pleasant condition, there shall be a part to be availed of for firewood, which may be necessary; under a penalty that if the term shall have passed and the said trees shall not have been planted, they will lose the land, in order that they may be decreed and given to any other settler; which not only shall take place on the lands, but in the towns and within the ditches which they may have, and which may be within the limits of each city or villa.[1]

§ 43. Law Twelfth: *The stock farms shall be given (at a distance) from the towns, and from the sown fields of the Indians.*—Because the stock farms of cattle, mares, hogs, and other large and small cattle do great damage to the cornfields of the Indians, and especially those which are at a distance from the settlements and without a keeper, we command that no farms shall be given in parts or places where damage can result, and that if this can not be avoided, they shall at least be far from the towns of the Indians and from their sown fields; since for the cattle there are separate lands, and grasses where they can pasture and graze without damage; and the justices will cause the owners of cattle, and persons interested in the public good, to put shepherds and keepers, which may be sufficient to avoid damage; and in case any should happen, the owners shall make satisfaction therefor.[2]

§ 44. Law Thirteenth: *The viceroy shall cause the cattle to be withdrawn from the irrigable lands, and that said lands be sown with wheat.*—We order the viceroys to inform themselves as to the lands which there may be that are irrigable; and that they order the cattle to be taken therefrom, and that said lands be sown in wheat, unless the owners have titles for this quality of farms.[3]

§ 45. Law Fourteenth: *The possessors of lands, farms, chacras (Indian farms), and cavallerias, with legitimate titles, shall be*

[1] November 20, 1536.

[2] Emp. Charles V., March 24 and May 2, 1550. See Law 20, title 3, and law 19, title 9, book 6.

[3] Philip III., June 11, 1612, chap. 3 of instructions to Viceroys; Philip IV., June 18, 1624.

*protected in their possessions, and the others shall be restored to the king.*—We having succeeded to the seigniory of the Indies, and the vacant lands, soils, and lands which have not been conceded by the lord kings our predecessors, or by us, or in our name, belonging to our patrimony and royal crown, it is proper that all the lands which are possessed without just and true titles should be restored to us, accordingly as they belong to us; and that there shall be reserved before all things what to us, or the viceroys, audiencias, and governors shall appear necessary for squares, exidos, propias, pastures, and vacant lands of the towns and municipalities (lugares y concejos) which are populated, as well as for what belongs to the present condition in which they are as for the future, and the increase which they may have; and there shall be apportioned to the Indians what may be conveniently necessary for them to cultivate and to sow and to raise cattle; and the lands which they now have shall be confirmed to them, and others which may be necessary shall be given them. The rest of the land shall remain free and disencumbered, to be granted and disposed of according to our will. For all which we order and command the viceroys and presidents of the pretorial audiencias, that whenever it shall appear proper to them, they shall designate a competent term for the possessors to exhibit before them and the ministers of the audiencias, whom they shall appoint, the titles of lands, farms (estancias), Indian farms (chacras), and cavallerias. Those who may possess with good titles and evidences of titles (recaudos), or just prescription shall be protected, and the other lands shall be returned and restored to us, to be disposed of according to our will.[1]

§ 46. Law Fifteenth: *What lands shall be admitted to a composition.*—Considering the great benefit of our vassals, we order and command the viceroys and president governors to make no innovation in the lands compromised by their predecessors; but they shall leave the owners in the peaceable possession thereof. Those who have usurped and gone into possession of more land than belongs to them in conformity with the measurement may be admitted as to the excess to a moderate composition, and new titles shall be issued to them. And all those lands which are about to be compromised,[2] the viceroy and president governor shall absolutely cause to be sold at public auction, and struck off to the highest bidder, giving them á

[1] Philip II., Nov. 20, 1578, March 8, 1589, Nov. 1, 1591.

[2] This evidently means lands where the possessor has no title to any part thereof.

razon de censo al quitar,[1] in conformity with the laws and pragmatics of these kingdoms of Castile. And we remit to the viceroys and presidents the mode and form of the execution of all the foregoing, in order that they may be disposed of with the least cost possible; and to avoid what may follow from the collection, the viceroys and presidents will order our royal officers of each district to make the collection with their own hands, without sending executors, availing themselves of our royal audiencias; and where there are none, of the corregidores. And because some titles of lands have been given by ministers who had no power to apportion them, and which have been confirmed by us in our council, we command that those who may have cédulas of confirmation shall be preserved in them, and shall be protected in the possession thereof within the limits contained in said cédula; and as to the excess, they may be admitted to the benefit of this law.[2]

§ 47. Law Sixteenth: *The lands shall be given and sold with the conditions of this law, and the titles given to the interested parties must bear confirmation of the king.*—In order to avoid the inconvenience and damages which may follow from giving or selling cavallerias, peonias, and other measures of land to the Spaniards, in prejudice of the Indians, from preceding suspicious informations of witnesses, we order and command that when they are given or sold, it shall be with citation of the fiscales (attorneys) of our royal audiencias of the district, who will be obliged to see and examine with diligence the quality and depositions of the witnesses; and the presidents and audiencias, if they govern, shall give or sell the lands with the advice of the board of the treasury (junta de hacienda), where it must appear that they belong to us; and they shall be offered and sold at public auction as our other landed property, keeping always in view the welfare of the Indians; and in case they have been given or sold by the viceroys, it is our will that none of the said ministers shall intervene; and the titles which shall be given to the interested parties must bear our confirmation within the ordinary term which is observed in the grants of assignments of Indians.[3]

§ 48. Law Seventeenth: *Lands which shall have been of the Indians shall not be admitted to composition, or those with vicious titles, and the fiscales and protectors shall prosecute their rights.*—

---

[1] An annuity or quit rent, which may be redeemed at any time.

[2] Philip IV., May 17, 1631.

[3] Feb. 27, 1531, Dec. 14, 1615, June 17, 1617.

In order to favor and protect the Indians, and that they shall not receive damages, we command that the compositions of lands shall not be of those which the Spaniards shall have acquired of the Indians, contrary to our royal cédulas and ordinances, or which they may possess by vicious titles, because in this it is our will that the fiscales-protectors, or the fiscales of the audiencias, if there should not be any fiscales-protectors, prosecute their rights, and the rights which belong to them by the cédulas and ordinances, and to ask that such contracts be nullified. And we charge the viceroys, presidents, and audiencias, that they shall give them all assistance for their entire compliance.[1]

§ 49. Law Eighteenth: *Lands shall be left to the Indians.*—We order that the sale, benefit, and composition of lands be made with such consideration that the Indians be left with, above all, what lands shall belong to them, as well to the individual Indian as to the communities, and the waters and places of irrigations; and the lands in which they have made ditches (acequias) for irrigation or any other benefit, with which by their personal industry they have fertilized, shall be reserved in the first place, and in no case can they be sold or alienated. And the judges who shall be sent for this purpose shall specify the Indians which they shall find on the lands, and the lands which they leave to each one of the old renters (tributarias viejos), retired ones (reservados), caciques, governors, absent ones, and communities.[2]

§ 50. Law Nineteenth: *Those who have not been in possession ten years shall not be admitted to a composition; and the Indians shall be preferred.*—He who has not been in possession of lands for ten years will not be admitted to make a composition of them; although he may allege that he is in possession of them; because this pretext is not sufficient, and the communities of Indians shall be admitted to compositions in preference to other individual persons, and every convenience shall be made for them.[3]

§ 51. Law Twentieth: *The viceroys and presidents shall revoke the grants made by the city councils not confirmed by the king, but shall admit them to composition.*—It is our will that viceroys and president governors shall revoke and annul grants which the city councils have made or shall make

---

[1] Philip IV., June 30, 1646.
[2] Philip IV., March 16, 1642, June 30, 1646.
[3] Philip IV., June 30, 1646.

of lands in their districts unless they be confirmed by us; and if they should be of the lands of the Indians, said viceroys and president governors will order said lands to be returned to the Indians; and the vacant lands will remain as such, and be admitted to composition by those who may have them, and they shall pay us therefor what may be just.[1]

§ 52. Law Twenty-first: *The viceroys and presidents shall not issue commissions of compositions and sales of lands without evident necessity and notifying the king thereof.*—If any private individuals shall have occupied lands of public places, small towns, and concegiles, lands of the cities, they must restore them, in conformity with the law of Toledo, and the viceroys and presidents shall provide that restoration shall be made, and regulate the law of prescription with which private individuals may defend themselves. And we command that the viceroys and presidents shall not give commissions for the composition of lands unless there be evident necessity therefor, and by first notifying us of the causes which move them to make them, and in what places said lands are, to whom they belong, since when were they possessed, and the quality of those without trees (calmas), and those planted with them (plantias). And we order that when they shall have to give these commissions, they shall appoint persons whose age, experience, and good parts will correspond with the best execution.[2]

Law Twenty-second: This law relates to the lands of Tolu, Carthegena.

Law Twenty-third: This law relates to Cuba.

Title 12 is composed of the foregoing twenty-three laws only.

---

[1] Philip II., Madrid, January 10, 1589.

[2] Philip III., San Lorenzo, April 26, 1618.

# CHAPTER IV.

## COMMENTARY ON THE ROYAL CÉDULA OF OCTOBER 15, 1754.



§ 53. *Grants to be made by Viceroys and Presidents of the Audiences.*—Article 1 vested the power of appointing subdelegates to sell and compromise the lands of the Spanish crown in the Indies in the viceroys and presidents of the audiencias; thereby removing from Spain to Mexico all power and jurisdiction over Mexican domain, save, of course, the right of the sovereign to modify the same at pleasure.

§ 54. *Duty of Subdelegates.*—By article 2, the subdelegates were to proceed mildly with the Indians, and with verbal process, and not judicially. And if their possessions had been usurped by Spaniards, they were to have been restored, and also other lands were to have been given them according to their requirements. Laws 14, 15, 17, and 19, of title 12, book 4, of the Recopilacion de las Indias, were to have been especially observed.

§ 55. *Notices to be Given by Sudelegates.*—By article 3, the subdelegates, immediately after receiving their appointment, were to publish the same by proclamation in their respective districts; and the people were also to be notified in said proclamation that those who possessed lands, whether the same were settled upon, cultivated, and worked, or not, since the year 1700, up to the publication of said proclamation, should appear, by themselves or attorney, before the subdelegates and exhibit their titles and dispatches by virtue of which they claimed possession. For this exhibition they were to have time allotted to them according to the distance they had to travel. They were likewise notified that if they did not so appear and make the said exhibition, they would be ejected from said lands, and grants thereof would be made to others, unless they should present some good excuse for not so appearing.

§ 56. *Possession Prior to* 1700 *to be Held as a Title.*—Article 4 declares that if it appeared by the titles or instruments which were thus presented, or by any other legal means, that the parties were in possession of said land by virtue of any sale or composition made by the subdelegates before the year 1700, although the titles had not been confirmed by the king, or by the viceroy, or president of the audiences, the parties were to be left in the peaceful possession thereof, and not to be molested; nor were they to pay any fees for these proceedings, in conformity with law 18, title 12, book 4, of said Recopilacion de las Indias. These facts were to be noted in the title, in order that in the future they should not be molested. If they had no titles, proof of their ancient possession was sufficient to hold by prescription or limitation; with the understanding, if they had not cultivated or worked the said lands, they were to have assigned them the term of three months, which law 11 of said title and book provides, with a notice, if they did not so cultivate the said lands, the same would be granted to whomsoever might denounce them; with the same obligation attached. This article is an important one. It is held in Mexico that prescription does not run against the sovereign, under the Roman or Spanish law, where no title is shown. The law of prescription is based on a title and possession in good faith at the time possession was first taken. It is further held that a title with fixed boundaries, although containing more than the grant calls for, may be sustained by prescription for the whole thereof, against the sovereign.

But if the grantee of the sovereign or his vendee has been in possession of a larger tract than designated in the grant, without fixed and determinate boundaries, then the said grantee or his vendee can not hold the overplus against the sovereign by prescription. There are many ancient titles in the republic, and especially in the northern states thereof, the limits of which are not well defined. This question of unfixed boundaries has already become a vexed one in Mexico. The federal government seems inclined to claim the overplus in grants without defined boundaries, and the possessors are equally inclined to resist the claims of the government, upon the ground that such ancient peaceable possession justly entitles them to all within the limits so long occupied by them and their ancestors.

The doctrine of the United States supreme court is, that thirty years' possession is sufficient to hold lands on the ground of the presumption of a grant. The language of the court is a follows: "If it were necessary, an unmolested possession of thirty years would authorize the presumption of a grant:" Barclay v. Howell's Lessee, 6 Pet. 498. That part of the decision will be found on page 513. No such doctrine has been laid down by the courts of Mexico. It is evident that by virtue of the foregoing cédula of 1754 all possessions with or without titles, or with fixed or undetermined boundaries in the grants, or the possession of more land than is designated in the grant, since any time prior to the year 1700, can be held as against the sovereign.

§ 57. *Titles Subsequent to* 1700.—By article 5 it is declared that those who had titles to the lands they possessed, which had been sold to them or compromised by the subdelegates since the year 1700, could not be molested in their possessions, if their titles had been confirmed by the king, or by the viceroy or presidents of the audiencias of the respective districts, within the respective periods in which said personages had power to confirm them. Such a declaration would seem unnecessary, as it is but declaratory of what the law already was. But it proceeds to provide that if their titles had not been so confirmed, they were bound to present themselves immediately, and solicit confirmations from the audiencia of the respective district, and other ministers to whom was committed such power by this new instruction. It would seem from the whole cédula (and especially from article 9), that no other persons but the presidents of the audiencias, whether viceroy or senior oidor acting as president, could confirm titles. The value and measure were to be examined, to see that no fraud had been committed; and the advice of the fiscales or attorneys was to be had thereon prior to a confirmation.

§ 57 *a*. *Valuation and Measurement.*—Article 6 provides that valuation and measurement were absolutely essential before a confirmation.

§ 58. *Possession of Land in Excess of That Granted.*—By article

7 it appears that the subdelegates were to state in their general orders to the judges of the capitals or partidos of their districts the clause that the persons who had included in their limits more land than they had purchased, or more than they had compromised for, whether they had been confirmed or not, should appear before the subdelegates for a composition as to the excess, according to the measure and value thereof, with a notice if they did not so appear their lands, that is, the excess, would be adjudged as crown lands, and that they would be sold to third parties, although they might have been cultivated and improved. This, it was declared, should be done without acceptation of persons or communities. There seems to have been a determination on the part of the Spanish sovereigns to confine land-holders to the quantity granted to them.

§ 59. *Informers Compensated.*—Article 8 provides that those who gave information or denounced persons who were thus possessing lands without just titles should be given a corresponding recompense therefor; and also that they should be admitted to a composition of said lands for a moderate sum. The subdelegates were commanded to include a notice to this effect in the proclamations they were ordered to publish in their respective districts.

§ 60. *Audiencias to Issue Titles.*—By article 9 the respective audiencias were to issue for the provinces in the king's name the confirmations, after the fiscales had given an opinion favorable thereto.

§ 61. *Proceedings Transmitted by Subdelegates.*—Article 10 prudently provided that in order to avoid costs and unnecessary proceedings in the issuing of titles, which might have happened if the audiencias should have ordered new surveys and new valuations, the subdelegates should transmit the proceedings to the audiencia for consultation before issuing the titles; so that body might order what it deemed proper to be done before the issuing of the final title, and thus save a duplication of titles.

§ 62. *Audiencias to Hear Appeals.*—Article 11 declares that the audiencias were to hear on appeal all cases tried before the subdelegates, which were litigious or judicial in their nature, pertaining to the rights of the petitioners. In this manner they were saved the costs of appealing to the council of the Indies at Madrid. In these cases the oidores were to decide the questions without the voice of the viceroy; but the latter, if presiding, signed the judgments.

§ 63. *Confirmation in Distant Provinces.*—By article 12 it is provided that in the provinces distant from the audiencias or beyond the seas, the confirmations might have been issued by the governors, with the consent of the royal officers (oficiales reales), and of the lieutenant-general learned in the law, where there was one.

§ 64. *Separate Account of Moneys.*—By article 13 the amount received for sales and compositions was to be kept in separate books, and the governors, the audiencias, presidents, and royal officials were to report each year to the secretary of the department of the Indies what this branch of the royal treasury had produced.

§ 65. *No Fees to Subdelegates.*—Article 14 provides that the subdelegates were not to exact any fees from the parties for their services; but two per cent of the sales were assigned to them, as the council had resolved in 1696; and the notaries were to receive as fees only what had been prescribed by the regular tariff.

# CHAPTER V.

## CÉDULA OF THE KING, DATED OCTOBER 15, 1754, REPEALING THAT OF NOVEMBER 24, 1735—CONFIRMATION OF TITLES BY ROYAL AUDIENCIAS.



§ 66. *Reasons for the Cédula.*—The king. Experience having shown the injuries which the decree that was given by a royal cédula of the twenty-fourth of November of 1735 causes my vassals in the kingdom of the Indias, requiring those who should enter into the crown lands (realengos) of those dominions absolutely to have recourse to my royal person to solicit their confirmation in the term which was assigned them, under the penalty of losing said land if they should not do so—whereby many persons fail to avail themselves of this benefit, on account of not being able to pay the cost of soliciting this court for the confirmation—being of little value or of small sitios (sites or places), or of only a few cavallerias, the lands which they have compromised or purchased; and those who have such recourse on account of their purchases being of greater consideration, are at a great expense, for the certified copies which they have to present, the remission of funds, appointment of agents, and other indispensable expenses which exceed, generally, in a great measure, the principal costs which they have made for the purchase or composition of the said crown lands before the subdelegates; whereby consequently are to be found many sitios and lands without cultivation, which would supply with their cultivation and the raising of cattle the immediate provinces; and because other persons may maintain themselves on usurped lands through defect of title, without giving them all the work which corresponds to a high state of cultivation, through fear of being denounced and prosecuted in regard to them; from which equally results injuries to my royal treasury, as well for the want of product from the sales of said lands as from what consequently flows to the public and the state of husbandry and the rearing of stock, I have resolved that in the grants, sales, and compositions of crown lands, sitios, and vacant lands (baldios) made at present, and which may be made in the future, shall be observed and practiced precisely what is contained in this instruction.

§ 67. *Subdelegates, how Appointed.*—1. That from the date of this my royal resolution, henceforth shall be solely in charge of the viceroys and presidents of my royal audiencias of those dominions the power to appoint the subdelegated ministers who are to make and execute the sale and composition of the lands and vacant lands (baldios) which belong to me in those dominions. The appointment or respective title must be issued to them with an authentic copy of this instruction, of the exact character of which the said viceroys and presidents must give punctual notice to my secretary of state and of the universal department of the Indias; of the ministers whom they may respectively delegate in their districts and the places which have been in the custom to have them, or in which it should appear necessary to establish anew by their approbation; and those ministers who are at present in the exercise of said commission must continue therein; it being understood that these, and those whom said viceroys and presidents may appoint in the future, may subdelegate their commissions to others for the parts and provinces distant from their residences, as it was done before. My council of the Indias and their ministers are, in virtue of this decree, prohibited from the direction and management of this branch of the royal treasury.

§ 68. *Duty of Subdelegates.*—2. That the judges and ministers in whom is subdelegated the jurisdiction for the sale and composition of the crown-lands shall proceed with suavity, temperance, and moderation, with verbal process, and not judicial, with those lands which the Indians may possess, and with the rest which may be particularly necessary for their working, cultivation, and the rearing of cattle. And as regarding those of a community, and those which are conceded to their pueblos for pastures and common lands (exidos), they are not to be changed; but the Indians are to be maintained in the possession of them, and are to be reinstated in those which may have been taken from them; and greater extensions of lands are to be conceded to them according to the exigency of the population. Neither is severity to be used in regard to those lands which the Spaniards and other castes may now possess; but must be borne in mind toward both the provisions of the laws 14 and 15, 17 and 19, title 12, book 4, of the Recopilacion de las Indias.

§ 69. *Orders and Notices to be Given by Subdelegates.*—3. As soon as shall have been received by each one of the principal delegates which are now and in the future may be appointed in each province, this instruction and the appointment which, in the form stated in chapter 1, must be issued to them, they will issue on their part general orders to the justices of the capitals of the provinces and principal places of their respective districts, commanding said orders to be published in said places, in the form which is practiced, with other general orders which the viceroys, presidents, and audiencias in the business of my service may require them; in order that all and every person who may possess crown lands, being or not populated, cultivated, and worked, since the year 1700 up to the day of the notoriety and publication of said order, may appear and show before the said subdelegate, by themselves or by their corresponding attorney, the titles and dispatches by virtue of which they possess said lands. For this exhibition will be assigned them a competent and proportionate term, according to the distances, with a warning that they will be dispossessed and ejected from said lands, and that a grant of them will be made to another, if within the term assigned they should fail to appear, without a just and legitimate cause, with an exhibition of their titles.

§ 70. *Titles Prior to* 1700.—4. That if it should appear by the titles or instruments which should be thus presented, or by any other legal means, that they are in possession of said crown lands in virtue of a sale or composition made by the subdelegates who have been of this commission before the said year 1700, although they may not have been confirmed by my royal person, neither by the viceroys and presidents, the possessors will be left in the free and quiet possession of said lands, without being caused the least molestation; nor will any fees be exacted from them for these proceedings, in conformity with law 18, title 4, of the Recopilacion de las Indias. A note will be made on the titles which may be exhibited that this obligation has been complied with, in order that in the future the possessors may not be disturbed, summoned, nor denounced, nor their successors in said crown lands; and not having titles, the proof which they shall make of their ancient possession will be sufficient for them, as a title of just prescription; with the understanding that if such crown lands should not have been cultivated or worked, the term of three months must be assigned them, which law 11 of said title and book prescribes, or that which may appear sufficient in order that they may so cultivate them; with a warning that otherwise grants will be made of said lands to those who may denounce them, with the same obligation to cultivate them.

§ 71. *Titles Subsequent to* 1700.—5. That the possessors of lands sold or compromised by the respective subdelegates, from the said year 1700 to the present, can not either be molested, disquieted, nor denounced, now nor in the future, if it appear that said lands have been confirmed by my royal person, or by the viceroys and presidents of the audiencias of their district and other ministers to whom is committed this power by this new instruction; who, in view of the suits which may have been formed by the subdelegates, with regard to the measure and value of said lands, and of the titles which may have been issued to them, will examine if the sale and composition are made without fraud or collusion, and for proportionate and equitable prices; with an examination and hearing by the attorneys (fiscales), in order that, in consideration that there appearing to have been paid into the royal treasury the price of the sale or composition, and the respective half-year's tax (derecho de media anata), and their making again that pecuniary service which may appear to correspond, the audiencias will issue to said possessors in my name the confirmation of their titles; with which they will be legalized in the possession and ownership of said lands, waters, or vacant lands (baldios); and said possessors can not ever be disquieted in the possession thereof, neither their universal nor particular successors.

§ 72. *Valuation and Measurement.*—6. That if, by the suits which ought to have been formed for the sales and composition not confirmed since the year 1700, it should appear that such crown lands have not been measured nor valued, as it is understood has happened in some province, the issuing of the confirmation will be suspended until such acts be executed; and according to the greatest value which may result from the measurement and valuation, the pecuniary service will be regulated, which must precede the confirmation.

§ 73. *Lands Held in Excess of the Grants.*—7. In the general orders, which, as has been said, must be issued by the subdelegates to the justices of the capitals (cabeceras) of the provinces or partidos, there must be equally contained the clause that the persons who may have exceeded the limits of the purchase or composition, adding thereto or entering into more land than was conceded, whether the principal possession be confirmed or not, must absolutely appear before said subdelegates with their composition, in order that of the excess, the measurement and valuation having first been made, the title and confirmation may be issued to them, with a warning that the lands so occupied will be adjudicated for a moderate sum to those who may denounce them; and that likewise they will be adjudicated to the royal patrimony in order to sell them to other third parties, although the crown lands occupied without titles be worked, planted, or have sugar mills, if the term which shall have been assigned is passed and the intrusive possessors have not appeared to show their titles, and to treat for their composition and confirmation, which must be complied with and executed without acceptation of persons or communities of whatever condition or quality they may be.

§ 74. *Denouncers Compensated.*—8. That to those who may denounce lands, grounds, sitios, water, vacant, and desert lands, will be given a corresponding recompense, and will be admitted to a moderate composition of those lands which are occupied without a just title, and that this will also be included in the proclamation which the subdelegates who may be appointed must cause to be published in their respective districts.

§ 75. *Confirmations by the Audiencias.*—9. That by the respective audiencias shall be issued for the provinces and in my royal name the confirmations, with a preceding fiscal review thereof, as is heretofore expressed, without further judicial cost from the parties than that of the fees of such provision, according to the tariff; to which end the audiencias will collect from the subdelegates of their districts the proceedings (autos) which they shall have made about the sale or composition of which confirmation may be asked; with which and according to the value for which the lands have been regulated (and considering the benefit which I have thought proper to dispense to them my vassals by relieving them from the costs of having recourse to my royal person for the compositions), they can judge of the pecuniary service which they must make for this new grant.

§ 76. *Costs Avoided.*—10. That in order to avoid costs and proceedings in the expedition of these cases, as would happen if after the titles have been issued by the subdelegates, the audiencias should order new proceedings of measurements and valuations, or others, the subdelegates must remit for consultation to the respective audiencias the proceedings (autos) which may have been made in each case, and which they considered as concluded and in a condition to have the titles issued, in order that after being examined by the said audiencias with the hearing of my fiscales, the titles may be returned by them, or either in order that they may issue the titles, there being no objections offered, or in order to complete the proceedings which said subdelegates may be ordered to carry out, and to facilitate in this manner the speedy expedition of the royal confirmations without the duplication of new titles.

§ 77. *Appeals by the Audiencias.*—11. That the said audiencias may try by way of appeal from the determination and judgments which the subdelegates may give in any suit which may arise about the sale or composition of crown lands, their denunciations, measure, and taxation; by which decree will be avoided the costly recourse of those vassals to the council, which expense some are unable to make and will abandon their rights.

§ 78. *Confirmation in Distant Provinces.*—12. That in the provinces distant from the audiencias, or in those which are beyond the sea, as Caracas, Havana, Carthaginia, Buenos Aires, Panama, Yucatan, Cumani, Magarita, Puerto Rico, and others in equal circumstances, the confirmation may be issued by their governors, with the advice of the royal officers and of the lieutenant-general learned in the law, where there may be one; and said ministers may determine equally the appeals which may be interposed from the subdelegates which may have been appointed or may be appointed in each one of said provinces and islands, without having recourse to the audiencia or chancery of the district, except in case the two judgments do not agree (and this officially) and by way of consultation to avoid the costs of the recourse by appeal; and where there may be two royal officers, the most recent one will perform the office of defender of the royal treasury in these causes, and the oldest one (in commission) that of associate judge with the governor; and any lawyer in or out of the district may act as asesor (legal adviser) when there is a doubtful question of law; and where there may be only one royal officer, any intelligent person in the vicinity may be appointed as defender of the royal treasury; being equally the duty of the governors with their associate judges to examine in regard to the compositions of the subdelegates the same as is expressed towards the audiencias.

§ 79. *Separate Account of Moneys Received.*—13. That whatever the sales and compositions of each audiencia and partido may amount to, and the pecuniary service which may be paid for confirmations, they shall be kept in a separate account and in a separate book in the corresponding royal cash accounts; and the audiencias and presidents thereof, the governors and royal officers of the partidos, shall give me an account through my secretary of the department of the Indias, what this branch of the royal treasury may have produced in each year, in order that upon notice thereof, I may give this fund the destiny which may be most convenient for my service.

§ 80. *No Fees to Subdelegates.*—14. Considering that, for what services may be done by the subdelegates who may be appointed for the administration of this branch, they must not require of the parties any fee, I have thought proper to assign to each one, by way of paying cost, two per cent of the amount of the sales and compositions which they may make, as the council resolved in their instruction of the year 1696; and the notaries before whom the proceedings are made must only receive the fees according to the tariff, to which they must certify at the end of the proceedings; and the respective audiencias and governors must proceed against them in case they contravene this law.

§ 81. *This Instruction to be Obeyed and Registered.*—15. It is my will that all that which is provided in this instruction be executed exactly and punctually by my vassals, viceroys, audiencias, presidents, and governors of all my dominions of the Indias; and by the subdelegates and other persons to whom the fulfillment thereof belongs or may belong, without going against the tenor thereof, for any cause or motive, it being what is proper for my royal service and the good of those vassals. And I command that this instruction be registered in the general auditor's office of the council of the Indias (contaduria), and in the offices of the audiencias, of chancery, governments, and cities; the same to be entered in the respective books and in the tribunals and auditor's office of the royal treasury, and other parts which may be proper, in order that all and every one may understand, observe, and keep it precisely and indispensable in the part which may belong to him. Given in San Lorenzo palace, the fifteenth day of October, 1754. I, the king. D. Julian Arriga.

§ 82. *Compliance Given by the Council.*—16. By decree of the royal council of the twenty-first of April, 1755, compliance with the royal instruction was given.

# CHAPTER VI.

ORDINANCE OF INTENDENTS OF DECEMBER 4, 1786—ORDER OF PEDRO NAVA, MILITARY COMMANDER, 1791—ROYAL CÉDULA, MARCH 23, 1798—DECREE OF JANUARY 4, 1813—CÉDULAS AND DECREES, 1814–1822.



§ 83. *Board of the Royal Treasury*.—It is provided in article 4 of said ordinance that a superior board of the royal treasury (junta superior de la real hacienda) should be established at the city of Mexico, the president of which should be the viceroy; composed also, in conformity with law 8, title 3, Recopilacion de las Indias, of the regent of the pretorial audiencia; of the fiscal of the royal treasury, with a vote in all affairs to which he was not a party;

of the senior minister of the tribunal of the auditory of accounts (del ministro mas antiguo del tribunal de la contaduria de cuentas); and of the senior auditor or treasurer general of the army and royal treasury.

§ 84. *Grants and Confirmation.*—Article 81 thereof states the manner of obtaining titles and the confirmation of the same by the said superior board of the treasury. The cédula of 1754 was to govern when not in conflict with the said ordinance. Said article 81 was modified by a royal cédula dated March 23, 1798, so that it became unnecessary to transmit the titles to the junta superior de hacienda for confirmation, provided the petitioners for land would pay two per cent on the value of the land, as a pecuniary service to the king. And when the value of the land did not exceed the sum of two hundred dollars, no fees were to be paid for the proceedings before the intendents or junta superior.

The foregoing article reads as follows: "Article 81. The intendents shall be special judges of the incidental questions, matters, and causes which may occur in the districts of their provinces over sales, compositions, and distributions of crown lands and those of the seignories; and it shall be the duty of the possessors, and those who claim new grants of those lands, to present their rights and make their petitions before the said intendents, in order that these proceedings being legally drawn up, with the sanction of the agent (promoter) of my royal treasury, whom they, the intendents, shall appoint, they, the intendents, shall decide the matter in question according to law, with the opinion of their lawyers (asesores ordinarios) who advise the ordinary judges; and they, the intendents, shall admit appeals to the superior board of the treasury (junta superior de hacienda); or they shall give an account of the matter to the junta, in case the interested parties do not interpose an appeal with the original proceedings whenever they shall consider these in a condition to issue the title; in order that, being examined by the junta, the said documents may be returned to the intendents, so that they, the intendents, may either issue the title, if no objection is offered by the junta, or in order that, before issuing the title, the intendents may carry out the proceedings which the junta may find wanting, and which it may order them to carry out; by means of which, without further embarrassment, the junta will be able to dictate in due time the corresponding confirmation of the title. The junta will proceed in the affair, as well as the intendents, their subdelegates, and others, according to the provisions of the royal instructions of October 15, 1754, so far as they are not opposed to the resolution of this ordinance, without losing sight of the salutary provisions of the laws which are cited in it, and those of law 9, title 12, book 4."[1]

§ 85. *Laws in Force up to* 1792.—On the twentieth of November, 1792, Señores Carlos de Urrutia and Fabian de Fonseca reported to the viceroy, Count de Revillagigedo, all the laws then in force pertaining to the sales and compositions of land and waters in Mexico. This report is embraced in the fourth volume of the General History of the Royal Treasury ("Historia General de Real Hacienda"), commencing on page 398. This work was written by order of the viceroy. According to said report, the foregoing laws, cédulas, and ordinances were the only ones in force generally up to the date thereof.

There were some others of certain special matters, having application to certain locations only.

1. There was the instruction of Don José de Galvez, of the council of the Indies, intendent of the army, and visitor-general. This bears date August 12, 1768, and relates entirely to the peninsula of Lower California, and which will be found in this work.

2. There was a cédula relating to the town of Pitic, now Hermosillo, Sonora, declaring that the pueblo should contain four square leagues.

3. The decree of the military commander, Pedro de Nava, dated March 22, 1791, addressed to the govornor of the province of California, which related alone to presidios or military posts, and which is set forth herein.

4. On the fourteenth of February, 1805, a royal cédula was issued approving of the resolution of the superior board of the treasury, dated May 10, 1802, which declared that said board would not adjudicate any more than three or four leagues of land to any one person in the province of Nuevo Santander (now Tamaulipas), Nuevo Leon, and Coahuila. This resolution was passed on account of the large tracts containing forty and fifty leagues which some possessed. The cédula refers to law 11, title 12, book 4 of the said recopilacion, and also to the royal cédula of 1754, showing that said laws and cédula were then in force. There seems to have been no law or cédula issued

[1] Said law is of the Recopilacion de las Indias, and refers to the rights of the Indians, and declares they shall not be disturbed in their rights. Said law will be found in chapter 3 of part 1 of this work.

by the sovereigns of Spain, repealing said laws of the Indies, nor the cédula of 1754, nor the ordinance of intendents. They must, therefore, be considered as having been in force up to the independence of Mexico; except so far as the one subsequent in date repealed that which was prior in date and in conflict therewith.

§ 86. *Order of Pedro de Nava.*—"In conformity with the opinion of the asesor of the comandaucia general, I have determined in a decree of this date that, notwithstanding the provisions made in the eighty-first article of the ordinance of intendentes, the captains of presidios are authorized to grant and distribute house-lots and lands to the soldiers and citizens who may solicit them to fix their residences on.

"And considering the extent of four common leagues measured from the center of the presidio square, viz., two leagues in every direction, to be sufficient for the new pueblos to be found under the protection of said presidios, I have likewise determined, in order to avoid doubts and disputes in future, that said captains restrict themselves henceforward to the quantity of house-lots and lands within the four leagues already mentioned, without exceeding in any manner said limits, leaving free and open the exclusive jurisdiction belonging to the intendentes of the royal (hacienda) treasury, respecting the sale, composition, and distribution of the remainder of the land in the respective districts.

"And that this may be punctually observed and carried into effect, you will circulate it to the captains and commandants of the presidios of your province, informing me of having done so.

"God preserve you many years. PEDRO DE NAVA.

"Chihuahua, March 22, 1791.

"SEÑOR DON JOSEPH ANTONIO ROMEN."

The royal cédula of March 23, 1798, mentioned herein, is as follows:

§ 87. *Royal Cédula of March 23, 1798—Confirmation by Board of Treasury, when not Required.*—The king. Whereas, in a letter of the twentieth of April, 1792, the viceroy who was in New Spain, Count de Revillagigedo, represents with testimony that the judge of lands of the audiencia of Guadalajara showed by reason of having sold at public sale to Don Cristobal Feliz, a resident of the village of Fuerte, in the province of Sinaloa, two sitios de ganado mayor and five cavallerias of land, that the observance of article 81 of the ordinance of intendents was onerous and prejudicial to the parties, as to the remission of the proceedings to the superior board (junta superior), for the approbation and confirmation of the title of public and crown lands of small quantities in the interior and remote provinces, on account of having to suffer for the costs of the courier and other fees more than the value of said lands; in proof of which he had transmitted certificates in fourteen cases of this kind, in which the highest did not reach thirty-six dollars, besides others which were found pending in different tribunals; from which one would infer that by not paying such great costs many would retain viciously and clandestinely the crown lands, and others, in consideration of not being informed against, will abandon their plantations and fields. The advantages thus failing, which might result to the state from the industry and application of said vassals—on account of which, and the same being founded on the example of the royal cédula of the fifteenth of October, 1754, which for the benefit of my vassals revoked that of the twenty-fourth of November, 1735, in order that those who had to repair to my royal person for the confirmation of the crown lands should apply in the future to the audiencias, the judge asked the viceroy that they should take in the affair the determination most convenient, the urgency of which the present president and commandant-general and intendent of those provinces, Don Jacobo Ugarte de Loyola, reiterated to him, on account of D. Luis Jimenez, resident of the jurisdiction of the pueblo of Atematica, having solicited that he should be excused from remitting to the junta superior the expedient of the dominion of land in the site called "La Agua Zarca;" adding that although the said junta superior had ordered lately that the parties should be free from petitioning said junta for the confirmation of titles by the pecuniary service which had to be made of the two per cent on the value of the lands, there remained, notwithstanding, in force the first part of said article, as to the remission and return of the original proceedings. Wherefore, it was considered opportune that the small cases should be excepted from the ordinary solemnities and proceedings, and that the amount or value of those crown lands should be designated, in which the provisions of the ordinance should be practiced; in virtue of which, and to solve the point with due consideration, the said viceroy commanded that the expediente should be carried to the junta superior, with a previous audience of the fiscal; and in a resolution made the twenty-fourth of February of the said year of 1792, it was declared that in consideration of being obviated, the injuries (represented in the decrees which the said junta had dictated on the twenty-third of July, 1790), of those who should solicit compositions of lands or should make denouncements of the public lands, that they should be excused from appearing for the confirmation of their titles, after having paid the two per cent of their value in the respective auditor's office, there was no reason now which would obligate a change to be made; wherefore (adding a copy of said decree), he would report to me, as he did, my said viceroy, to the effect that he would condescend to make the resolution, which would be of my royal pleasure. And the foregoing having been examined in my royal council of the Indies before a full bench of two departments, with what the general auditor's office gave as its understanding, and what my fiscales expressed, I have resolved in consultation on the fifth of December of the year last past, to approve, as by these presents I do approve, the resolution of the superior board of Mexico of the twenty-third of July, 1790, and ratified on the twenty-fourth of February, 1792, by which those who solicited compositions or made denouncement of public lands should be excused from repairing to said board for the confirmation of their titles, after having paid the two per cent of the value in the respective auditor's office; it being well understood that when the amount of the lands denounced or compromised do not reach the sum of two hundred dollars, they shall proceed officially (that is, without pay) in the courts of intendents and in that of the superior board, with the end that these crown lands may be denounced and compromised by the residents of little means; the promotores fiscales of the royal treasury of said audiences, taking care that the foregoing be complied with, and that not the least contravention nor omission be made in returning the proceedings of sale or composition of crown lands remitted for the judgment of the superior board. That in the rest shall be observed the provisions of article 81 of the said ordinance, with the modification of the resolution cited of the superior board of Mexico, so far as it suppressed for the benefit of the purchasers the second remission of proceedings to it, for the confirmation of the title and assignment of the pecuniary service for the dispensation of repairing for the confirmation to my royal person, as was practiced formerly, and afterwards to the audiencias by royal cédula of the fifteenth of October, 1754. Wherefore, I command my viceroys, audiencias, intendents, and superior boards of my kingdoms of the Indies and the adjacent places, that they comply and keep, and that they cause to be kept, complied with, and executed punctually and duly this my royal deliberation, on account of such being my will, and that from the present my royal cédula be recorded in the general auditor's office mentioned.

§ 88. *Decree of the Fourth of January*, 1813, *on Reducing Vacant and Crown Lands and Other Common Lands to Private Dominion—Suertes Ceded to the Defenders of the Country and to the Citizens not Proprietors.*—The general and extraordinary córtes considering that the reduction of the common lands to private dominion is one of the provisions which the welfare of the pueblos and improvement of agriculture and industry most imperiously claim, and wishing at the same time to give with this class of lands an aid to the public necessities, by a premium to the well-merited defenders of the country and a help to the citizens not proprietors, they decree:

§ 89. *Land Reduced to Private Ownership.*—1. All the vacant or crown lands and municipal property (propios and arbitrios), with wooded lands and lands not wooded, as well on the peninsula and adjacent islands as in the provinces beyond the seas, except the exidos necessary for the pueblos, shall be reduced to private property, taking care that in those of propios and arbitrios their annual incomes be supplied by the most opportune means, which by the proposal of the respective provincial deputations the córtes shall approve.

§ 90. *Titles to be in Fee.*—2. In whatever manner the lands shall be distributed, it shall be in fee and with the right of inclosure, in order that their owners may inclose them (without prejudice to the sheep-walks (cañadas), cross-ways, watering-places, and services), and enjoy them freely and exclusively, and to destine them to the use or cultivation which may best suit them; but they can not ever entail them, or pass them at any time into mortmain.

§ 91. *Residents Preferred.*—3. In the alienation of said lands, the residents of the pueblos within the limits in which the lands exist, and the common people (comuneros) in the enjoyment of said lands, shall be preferred.

§ 92. *Manner of Carrying the Law into Effect.*—4. The provincial deputations shall propose to the córtes by means of the regency the time and the terms on which it will be most proper to carry into effect this provision, in their respective provisions, according to the circumstances of the country, and the lands which may be indispensable to preserve for the pueblos, in order that the córtes may resolve what may be most proper to each territory.

§ 93. *Regencies and Secretaries.*—5. This business is recommended to the zeal of the regency of the kingdom, and to the secretaries of the government, in order that they may promote it and illustrate it to the córtes whenever they direct to them the proposals of the provincial deputations.

§ 94. *One Half of the Lands to be Reserved.*—6. Without prejudice to what is provided, the half of the vacant and crown lands of the monarchy, excepting the exidos, shall be reserved, in order that all or the part which may be deemed necessary shall be subject as a mortgage for the payment of the national debt, and with preference to that of the credits which the residents of the pueblos to which the lands belong have against the nation; and the first place must be given among these credits to those which proceed from the furnishing of the national armies or loans for the war, which the said residents may have made since the first of May, 1808.

§ 95. *Residents to Have Preference in the Purchases.*—7. On alienating this half of the vacant and crown lands, or the part which is esteemed necessary to mortgage on account of the public debt, the residents of the respective pueblos shall be preferred in the purchase, and the comuneros in the enjoyment, of the said lands; and to both shall be admitted in payment for all their value the competent liquidated credits which they may have on account of said supplies and loans, and in default thereof any other legitimate national credit with which they may be found.

§ 96. *Lands Already Sold.*—8. In the said half of vacant and crown lands must be comprehended and computed the part which has already been justly and legally sold in any provinces for the expenses of the present war.

§ 97. *How Distributed.*—9. In the remaining vacant and crown lands, or of the arable lands of the propios and arbitrios, shall be given gratuitously one suerte of the land most suited to cultivation to each captain, lieutenant, or sublieutenant, who by his advanced age, or on account of having been in the military service, has been retired with a proper furlough, without remarks, and with legitimate documents which prove his good conduct; and the same to each sergeant, corporal, soldier, trumpeter and drummer, who for the same cause, or by having completed his time, shall obtain a final discharge, without any black marks, whether they be natives or foreigners, provided that in the districts in which they fix their residences there shall be this class of lands.

§ 98. *Suertes of Land.*—10. The suertes which in each pueblo are conceded to officers or to soldiers shall be equal in value in proportion to the capacity and quality of the same, and greater or less in some countries than in others, according to the circumstances of these, and the small or great extension of the lands; and if it is possible, each suerte shall be such as, if regularly cultivated, shall be sufficient for the maintenance of one individual.

§ 99. *Designation of Suertes.*—11. The designation of these suertes shall be made by the constitutional ayuntamientos of the pueblos to which the lands belong, as soon as the interested parties shall present their documents which prove their good service and retirement, hearing above all briefly and governmentally the attorneys of the pueblos (procuradores síndicos), and without their requiring costs or fees. Next the expediente shall be remitted to the provincial deputations, in order that the latter may approve it and rectify any error.

§ 100. *To Whom Concessions Given.*—12. The concessions of these suertes, which shall be called patriotic premiums (premio patriótico), shall not be extended now to other individuals than those who may serve or have served in the present war, or in the pacification of the present turbulences, in any provinces beyond the sea. But the premium comprehends the captains, lieutenants, sublieutenants, and troops who, having served in both, have been retired without black marks, and with a legitimate discharge on account of having been maimed or made helpless in the action of war, and not otherwise.

§ 101. *Persons not Military.*—13. Also it comprehends individuals not military, who having served in parties, or contributed in any manner to the national defense in this war, or in the turbulences of America, and who remained or remain maimed and unable to work from the result of the action of war.

§ 102. *Other Premises not a Bar.*—14. The favors shall be conceded to said subjects, although for their services and actions designated they may enjoy other premises.

§ 103. *How Lands to be Assigned.*—15. Of the remaining said vacant and crown lands shall be assigned the most suitable for cultivation ; and to every resident of the respective pueblos who may ask it, and who has no other land of his own, shall be given him gratuitously, by drawing lots (por sorteo), and once only, a suerte proportioned to the extent of lands, provided that the total of those which are so divided in any case do not exceed the fourth part of said vacant and crown lands; and if these should not be sufficient, the suerte shall be given in the arable lands of the propios and arbitrios, imposing on it in such case a redeemable tax (canon) equivalent to the rents of the same for the term of five years (quinquenio), until the end of 1817, in order that the municipal funds may not fall off.

§ 104. *Failure to Pay Taxes.*—16. If any of the favored parties by the preceding article should fail in two consecutive years to pay the tax (canon), the suerte being his own, or having it as common land of the pueblo, it shall be conceded to another resident more industrious, who lacks land of his own.

§ 105. *Concessions without Cost.*—17. The proceedings for these concessions shall be made also without any costs by the ayuntamientos, and the provincial deputation shall approve them.

§ 106. *Suertes Unalienable until Four Years.*—18. All the suertes which are conceded in conformity with articles 9, 10, 12, 13, and 15 shall be also in fee for the favored ones and their successors on the terms and with the faculties which article 2 expresses; but the owners of these suertes can not alienate them before four years from the time they shall have been conceded, nor subject them even to entailment, nor pass them at any time by any title in mortmain.

§ 107. *Exemption from Taxes Eight Years.*—19. Any of the favored persons referred to and their successors who establish their permanent dwelling on the said suerte shall be exempt for eight years from all tax or imposts on that land or its products.

§ 108. *Publication of Decree.*—20. This decree shall be circulated not only among all the pueblos of the monarchy, but also among all the national armies, and it shall be published in every manner, that it may reach all the individuals who compose them.

§ 109. *Abrogation of the Decree—Various Decrees.*—The foregoing decree was abrogated by a royal cédula of the eighth of July, 1814. In 1818 the sale of the vacant and crown lands was again ordered, to pay the interest and the funding of the public debt; and afterwards, in 1819, rules were determined upon for the execution thereof. But in 1820 the constitutional régime inaugurated in 1812, being re-established, the distribution of the vacant crown lands was again ordered by the córtes on the eighth of November of that year; and others were issued on the twenty-ninth of June, 1821, and on the same date of the year 1822. These decrees subsequent to that of January 4, 1813, are not considered as essential to be given herein at length.

# CHAPTER VII.

## PUEBLOS OR TOWNS.

§ 110. Methods of Establishing Pueblos.
§ 111. Powers of the Contractor.
§ 112. Division of the Land.
§ 113. Form of Pueblos.
§ 114. Towns Established by Government.
§ 115. Division of Land in Such Towns.
§ 116. Exidos, how Measured.
§ 117. Limits of Pueblos.
§ 118. United States Decisions.
§ 119. Special Laws.
§ 120. Limits Fixed by the Discretion of the Viceroy and Governor.
§ 121. Opinion of Pedro Nava.
§ 122. Fee in the Sovereign.
§ 123. Petitions for Land.
§ 124. Revocation of Grants.
§ 125. Record of Proceedings of Ayuntamientos.
§ 126. Titles under Law of 1813.
§ 127. Ayuntamientos or Town Councils.
§ 128. Number of Inhabitants for an Ayuntamiento.
§ 129. Members of Ayuntamiento.
§ 130. Provincial Deputation.
§ 131. Municipal Ordinances.
§ 132. Government of Provinces.
§ 133. Pueblos of Less than One Thousand Inhabitants.
§ 134. Government by Ayuntamientos.
§ 135. American Courts.
§ 136. Under Mexican Authority.
§ 137. Lower California.
§ 138. Alcaldes.
§ 139. Petition to Ayuntamiento Necessary to Obtain Land—Alcaldes had no Power to Grant without Consent of the Ayuntamiento.
§ 140. House-lots Only Sold Prior to 1856.
§ 141. All Community Lands to be Sold by Law of 1856.
§ 142. Agreements for Settlements.
§ 143. Settlements with not Less than Ten Families.
§ 144. Possession by and Register of Colonists.
§ 145. Book for the Registry of All Proceedings.
§ 146. Cédulas to be Opened before the Council.
§ 147. Cédulas to be Kept in the Coffers.
§ 148. Letters Addressed to the Councils.
§ 149. Original Papers not to be Withdrawn.

§ 110. *Methods of Establishing Pueblos.*—There were two methods of establishing towns: 1. By virtue of a capitulation or agreement entered into between a given person and the government, whereby the contractor was to establish a town upon the conditions established by law. According to the ordinances 88 and 89 of Philip II., which are embodied in law 6, book 4, title 5, of the Recopilacion de las Indias, the contractor was to furnish at least thirty inhabitants (vecinas), and each of them to build a house, and to furnish a certain number of stock; and if he complied with all the conditions, he was to have assigned him four square leagues of land in a square or oblong form according to the condition of the land. The limits of the town were not to be within five leagues of any other town of Spaniards; nor to do any damage to any Indian town or to any private person. Ordinance 100 of Philip II., which is law 7 of said book and title, modifies the foregoing by permitting the contractor to furnish not less than ten inhabitants.

§ 111. *Powers of the Contractor.*—According to ordinance 95, which is law 11 of said book, the contractor had civil and criminal jurisdiction in the first instance, during his life, and also one son or heir had the same. He could appoint councilmen (alcaldes ordinarios) and other officers of the council. Appeals could be taken to the alcalde mayor or to the audiencia in the district wherein the town was situated.

§ 112. *Division of the Land.*—Ordinance 90, or law 7, book 4, title 7, of said recopilacion, designates the manner in which the contractor shall divide the land, which is as follows: first there shall be measured off what shall be necessary for house-lots (solares) and commons (exidos); then beyond and adjoining the exidos was to be designated the dehesa or community lands for the pasture of the stock belonging to the inhabitants of the town. The exidos were the common or place of recreation for the inhabitants. Next was to be measured the proprios, which were lands to be rented out by the ayuntamiento or town council; the proceeds of which were used to defray the municipal expenses. The remainder of the land was to be divided into four parts: one part was given to the contractor or founder of the town, and the other three parts were to be divided into suerte lots equally among the other settlers. By ordinance 103, which is law 9, book 4, title 5, peonias and cavallerias of land were to be given to the settlers.

§ 113. *Form of Pueblos.*—The form of the plaza or square was to be an oblong square, which should be as two to three as regards its width and length. The size should be in proportion to the inhabitants and according to the probabilities of the growth of the town. No plaza was to be less than two hundred feet wide and three hundred long; nor greater than five hundred and thirty-two feet wide and eight hundred long: Law 9, said book and title.

§ 114. *Towns Established by Government.*—2. Towns were established by the government. The governor of the province examined the locations as to the conveniences and advantages which would arise from the establishment of towns in certain places; and he determined whether the town to be established should be a city, villa, or place; and in conformity with what he declared, the municipal government was formed: Law 2, book 4, title 7.

§ 115. *Division of Land in Towns Established by Government.* In the towns established by the government, after the house-lots, exidos, dehesas, and propios were measured off, the rest was divided into suertes, or lands for cultivation. The suertes were in number equal to the house-lots or more, so that each poblador or founder received a suerte; and if there were irrigable lands, they were also divided into suertes and given to the pobladors. The remainder of the suertes remained for the king to grant to other persons who might think proper to settle in said towns.

§ 116. *Exidos.*—Law 13, book 4, title 7, required the exidos to be measured at such a distance from the ground for house-lots, that the growth of the town may leave sufficient space in the exidos for recreation. When all the ground for house-lots was occupied, house-lots were sold out of the exidos, as in no other way could the town extend.

§ 117. *Limits of Pueblos.*—There never existed any general law fixing four square leagues as the extent of pueblos or towns. That extent of land was assigned to pueblos founded by contractors for Spaniards, by law 6, title 5, book 4, of the laws of the Indies. Those formed by the government, independent of contractors, were only limited by the discretion of the governors of the provinces, and viceroys, subject to approval or disapproval of the king. There are numerous pueblos in Mexico which have less and many that have more than four square leagues.

§ 118. *United States Decisions.*—The United States supreme court, in *Townsend* v. *Greely*, 5 Wall. 337, and *Grisar* v. *McDowell*, 6 Id. 363, and the supreme court of California in *Welch*

v. *Sullivan*, 8 Cal. 187, were in error in holding that a general law existed declaring four square leagues as the seperfice of of pueblos. The jurists of Mexico are unacquainted with any such provision of Spanish jurisprudence.

§ 119. *Special Laws.*—There were some special laws and cédulas issued in relation to certain locations which designated that amount of land. The royal cédula as to the town of Pitic, now Hermosillo, in Sonora, provided four square leagues for that settlement.

But this decree or cédula states that it is issued in accordance with law 6, title 5, book 4, of the laws of the Indies, for the formation of pueblos by Spaniards (not Indians), and which law is for the government of pueblos founded by virtue of a capitulacion, an agreement with some founder. And it is but a reiteration of said law, namely, that in the future all pueblos to be formed by founders in that commandancy shall be of the same extent of four square leagues. This decree has been misconstrued by the United States courts, in regard to pueblos to be subsequently made. The order of Don Pedro de Nava, military commandant of Chihuahua, issued March 22, 1791, to the governor of Upper California, was a special order which restricted the captains of presidios to the extent of four square leagues, in the formation of pueblos.

§ 120. *Limits Fixed by Discretion of Viceroy and Governors.*—Law 1, book 4, title 13, Recopilacion de las Indias, is as follows: "The viceroys and governors who may have the power shall designate to each villa and place which is to be founded and populated anew the lands and house-lots (solares) which shall be necessary, and they shall give them without prejudice to third parties (propios); and they shall send us a statement of what they have designated and given to each one, in order that we may command the same to be confirmed."

Here, then, is a discretionary power vested in the viceroys and governors as to the quantity of land to be assigned to each town, And further: it must be apparent that had a general law existed requiring all pueblos to contain four square leagues, there would have been no necessity of mentioning the quantity when it was intended that the extent of four leagues should be the exact limit. But there being no such general law, it became essential to specify the extent when the sovereign desired to grant only four leagues by his royal cédula to any particular pueblo.

§ 121. *Opinion of Nava.*—Don Pedro Nava, commandant at

Chihuahua, must have taken the same view of the law, when he fixed the extent of four leagues in his order "to avoid doubts and disputes in the future," and because he "considered it to be sufficient." Had a general law been in force as to the limits of all pueblos to be founded, there would have been no room for "doubts and disputes in the future," as to the quantity of land each and every pueblo was entitled to, and he would not have had "to consider what amount was sufficient." It would seem that the above law 1, book 4, title 13, and the said order, placed the question beyond discussion.

§ 122. *Fee in the Sovereign.*—The fee of the land embraced within the limits of pueblos continued to remain in the sovereign, and never in the pueblo as a corporate body. Under the jurisprudence of Spain, no lands within a pueblo were ever sold to a private individual, except the house-lots (solares), the suertes, peonias, and cavallerias, which were given to the settlers or pobladors for cultivation. These were to be possessed and worked continuously for four years before the grantee could dispose of them as his own, as provided in law 1, book 4, title 12, of the laws of the Indies. All the other pueblo lands were held by the sovereign for the benefit of the inhabitants thereof. The proprios were lands that were rented out in order to produce a revenue to assist in the support of the municipal government. The leases of these lands were sold by the town council (ayuntamiento) at public auction to the highest bidder, as provided in law 3, book 4, title 13, of said laws. The exidos were the commons or grounds for recreation. The dehesas were the pastures and woodlands for the benefit of all the community, According to law 5, book 4, title 12, the distribution of these lands among the settlers was to be made by the viceroy or governors, with the consent of the ayuntamiento, or cabildo, which is the same as town council.

§ 123. *Petitions for Lands.*—By law 8, said book and title, petitions were to be made before the council for lands. Law 6, of said book and title, required the city attorney or procurador to be present when distributions of peonias and cavallerias of land were to be made.

§ 124. *Revocation of Grants.*—Law 20 of said book and title provided that the viceroys, presidents of the audiencias, and governors of the provinces could revoke and annul all grants of lands made by the town councils which had not been approved by the king. It seems to have been a discretionary power. It would seem to be evidence that the ayuntamientos did make the grants.

§ 125. *Records.*—Law 16, book 4, title 9, required every act of the ayuntamiento to be recorded in a book kept for that purpose, and all of the proceedings of that body were transmitted annually to the king for his approval. All titles issued by the ayuntamiento were thus in a position to be confirmed or rejected by his majesty. It would seem that all lots held by the grantees for more than a year would be presumed to have been approved by the king.

§ 126. *Titles under Law of* 1813.—The law of the córtes of January, 1813 (see chapter 6), granting to soldiers the right to claim suertes of land in pueblos, vested the power in the council to designate the lands to be given them, and also to execute all the proceedings relative thereto; that is, to make the titles for said lands.

§ 127. *Ayuntamientos.*—Spain formed a constitution by the córtes, March 18, 1812. Article 309 thereof, for the government of pueblos, provided that there should be an ayuntamiento composed of the alcalde or alcaldes, councilmen, and city attorney (procurador síndico). When the political chief was present he was entitled to preside over the council. When not present, the alcalde has to preside. If there were two alcaldes, the first was to take the position.

§ 128. *Number of Inhabitants.*—By article 310 it was requisite that a pueblo should have a thousand inhabitants to be entitled to an ayuntamiento, unless in consideration of agricultural or other important interest, it was essential to have one where a less number of inhabitants resided.

§ 129. *Members of Ayuntamientos.*—Article 311 declared that the laws should determine the number of individuals which should compose the ayuntamientos.

§ 130. *Provincial Deputation.*—Articles 325 and 326 provided that there should be a provincial deputation, to be presided over by the political chief, and that it should be composed of the president, the intendent, and seven individuals to be elected in the manner which shall be established.

§ 131. *Municipal Ordinances.*—Article 321 empowered the ayuntamientos to form municipal ordinances for their respective pueblos, and to present to the córtes for approbation, through the provincial deputation; which body was also to express its views thereon.

§ 132. *Government of Provinces.*—The general and extraordinary córtes enacted a law on May 23, 1812, for the government of the provinces. Article 1 thereof provided that pueblos without ayuntamientos, and not having a thousand inhabitants, and which from certain circumstances ought to have one, could apply to the provincial deputation for one.

§ 133. *Having Less than One Thousand Inhabitants.*—By article 2, pueblos not having a thousand inhabitants nor an ayuntamiento will be attached to the ayuntamientos to which they had been annexed until then; and those pueblos which should be newly established should be under the control of the ayuntamiento of the nearest pueblo having one.

§ 134. *Government by Ayuntamientos.*—By article 10 of the law of córtes of June 23, 1813, the general measures of good government which ought to be taken to assure and protect the persons and property of the inhabitants shall be resolved by the ayuntamiento, and executed by the alcalde or alcaldes.

§ 135. *American Courts.*—In the American courts, the question as to where the power to sell pueblo lands was vested was not an easy one for solution. This was not altogether without reason. The constitution of Spain of 1812, the laws under it, and the federal laws of Mexico seem to be silent upon the question. The fact is, the laws of the Indies herein referred to have never been repealed. The power seemed to be a joint one, requiring the action of the ayuntamiento, and that of the highest political power of the province, or that of the viceroy, president of the audiencia, or king, under Spanish rule. The practice was for the person wishing a grant of a lot to present a petition to the ayuntamiento, soliciting a given lot, accurately described. Notices of the same were posted at the court-house (juzgado), churches, and other public places for a certain period, in order that if any person was aware of any objections to the granting of said lot, they could present the same to the ayuntamiento. There being no objection, the grant was made in accordance with the ordinances established by the ayuntamiento, and approved by the governor of the province; or according to the instructions issued by the governor to that body. Sometimes they were signed by the president of the ayuntamiento. The records of each ayuntamiento will show the authority for their method of issuing the titles. Those issued in the capital of Mexico were issued by the ayuntamiento and approved by the viceroy, or president of the audiencia. Of late years, under Mexican regulations, the titles in the capital were executed by a commission of the treasury. There existed no general law or decree of the sovereign designating the manner of issuing such titles.

§ 136. *Under Mexican Authority.*—After the independence of Mexico, the states became to a certain extent sovereign powers; and the rights and jurisdiction of the crown of Spain over pueblos became vested in the states respectively. Each state enacted its own laws pertaining to its pueblo. The power was given to the ayuntamientos, and to alcaldes where no ayuntamiento existed.

§ 137. *Lower California.*—By article 4 of instructions issued from the department of the interior, Mexico, February 12, 1827, for the government of Lower California, the ayuntamientos were authorized to issue titles for town lots, to be signed by the president thereof, the city attorney (procurador síndico), and the secretary.

§ 138. *The Alcaldes.*—There never was any law enacted by Spain or Mexico that permitted an alcalde or any other officer to execute deeds to pueblo lands, where an ayuntamiento existed without the consent of that body. Even in small pueblos where no ayuntamiento governed, the lands thereof were subject to the control of the ayuntamiento of the nearest pueblo. Article 2 of the law of the córtes of May 23, 1812, expressly declares that to be the law, and that it had been the rule.

§ 139. *Petition to Ayuntamiento Necessary.*—In every case a petition had to be presented to the ayuntamiento for action, before the alcalde or other person could execute a deed of pueblo land. There being really but three pueblos ever established in California—San José, Los Angeles, and Branciforte—and those scarcely having inhabitants for many years to require ayuntamientos; and there being smaller settlements at a great distance from the pueblos, it became necessary to authorize alcaldes to execute deeds of town lots in such settlements; and likewise in the pueblos when no ayuntamiento was in being.

§ 140. *House-lots Only Sold Prior to* 1856.—Since the independence of Mexico, as well as prior thereto, the proprios, exidos, and dehesas were never sold until the enactment of the law of June 25, 1856. This law, with its regulation of the thirtieth of July following, those of the twelfth and thirteenth of July, 1859, and that of the fifth of February, 1861, form the special legislation for the desamortizacion and nationalization of the community lands of civil and ecclesiastical corporations.

§ 141. *All Community Lands Sold.*—The said law of June 25, 1856, compelled the pueblos throughout the republic to sell all their community lands, except what was necessary for the use and the public service of the pueblos. These sales were to be made under state legislation, subject, however, to the said federal law, which will be found herein. Article 27 of the federal constitution is a confirmation of said law, and prohibits any civil or ecclesiastical corporation from acquiring or administering real estate except edifices and the lands requisite therefor, according to the real objects of their institutions.

§ 142. *Book 4, Title 5, Recopilacion of the Indias.*—Law Sixth: *That the Capitulation (Agreement for Settlement) for Villas of Alcaldes Ordinarios and Councilmen shall be Made in Conformity with This Law.*—If the disposition of the land shall give a place to settle any villa of Spaniards, with a council of alcaldes ordinarios and councilmen, and there shall be a person who will take the site to settle it, the agreement (capitulacion) shall be made with these conditions: that within the term which shall be designated to him, he shall have at least thirty settlers, and each one of them a house, ten breeding cows, four oxen, or two oxen and two steers, one breeding mare, one breeding sow, twenty Castilian breeding ewes, and six hens and one rooster; he shall also appoint a clergyman, who shall administer the holy sacrament, which appointment the first time shall be made at his election, and at other times in conformity with our royal patronage; and he shall provide the church with ornaments and things necessary for divine worship; and he shall give securities that he will comply with the conditions within said time; and if he does not comply therewith, he shall lose what he shall have constructed, worked, and cultivated, which we will apply to our royal patrimony; and he shall further incur a penalty of one thousand dollars in gold for our house; and if he shall comply with his obligation, shall be given him an extent of four leagues of territory in a square or oblong, according to the condition of the land, in a manner that when delineated there shall be four square leagues (cuatro leguas en cuadro), with the condition that the limits of said territory shall be distant at least five leagues from any city, villa, or place of Spaniards which shall have been settled before; and he shall do no injury to any Indian pueblo, nor to any private person.[1]

§ 143. Law Seventh: *That having a Capitulation of More or Less Settlers, It shall be Made Respectively with the Same Terms and Territory, and with the Same Conditions.*—There being a person who wishes to obligate himself to make a new settlement in the

[1] Ordinances of Philip II., Nos. 88, 89.

manner ordered, with more or less than thirty settlers, provided there shall not be less than ten, the same terms and territory shall be respectively conceded to him and with the same conditions.[1]

§ 144. Law Ninth: *That the Principal Poblador shall Take Possession with Each Settler or Colonist Who shall be Registered to Settle.*—In the possession of new settlements which the government shall make, or he who shall have power in the Indies by virtue of a contract with a city, governor (adelantado), alcalde mayor, or corregidor, he shall take possession and also cause each settler to register himself to settle; and he shall obligate himself to give in the pueblo designated house-lots (solares) on which to build houses, pasture lands, and cultivatable lands (labores), in as many peonias and cavallerias as each one of the settlers (pobladores) will obligate himself to build upon, provided he does not exceed nor give to each one more than five peonias, nor more than three cavallerias, according to the distinction, difference, and measure expressed in the laws of the title of the distribution of lands, house-lots, and waters: Ordinance No. 103.

§ 145. *Book* 4, *Title* 9.—Law Sixteenth: *That in the Council there shall be Kept a Book in Which shall be Entered All that shall be Resolved.*—In the council of each city there shall be a book in which shall be entered all that shall be resolved, as well to give us an account thereof as for any other effect which may be offered; let it be kept in secret, to be used when proper.[2]

§ 146. Law Seventeenth: *That the Royal Cédulas for the Councils shall be Opened in Them.*—Our cédulas and provisions for cities shall only be opened in the council, and shall be there entered in the book by the notary of the council, and the originals shall be placed in the coffer or chest of the council, as it is ordered.[3]

§ 147. Law Eighteenth: *That the Cédulas for the Government of the Provinces shall be in the Coffers of the Councils.*—We command that all the cédulas, provisions, ordinances, and private instructions which shall be sent to the Indies, and the particular and general ones for the good government of the Indies, the treatment and preservation of the natives, and the good collection of our royal treasury, all shall be collected and placed in the coffers of the councils of the cities, villas, and places, in order that they may be kept with the decency which

---

[1] Ordinance of Philip II., No. 100.
[2] May 26, 1573.
[3] February 27, 1575.

is proper, each city leaving a copy of all of them in a book, to be used how and where it may be proper.[1]

§ 148. Law Nineteenth: *That the Letters of the Viceroys, Ministers, and Officials Addressed to the Councils shall be Entered in their Books.*—We order that the letters of the viceroys, ministers, and officials for the councils of the cities, villas, and places shall be entered in the books of the council by the notary thereof.[2]

§ 149. Law Twentieth: *That the Judge Who may Wish Any Paper from the Archives shall Ask for It, and in No Case shall He Withdraw from the Council the Box Containing the Writings.*—If any ordinary judge or delegate shall have a necessity for papers or writings of the archives, he shall ask for them, declaring that he must see, recognize, and copy them; and in no case shall the original paper be withdrawn from the council, nor the council, nor the box with its writings; and as to the visitors, shall be kept what is ordered by law 16, title 34, book 2.[3]

---

[1] 1565, and June 15, 1628.
[2] February 27, 1575.
[3] May 1, 1586.

# CHAPTER VIII.

## RIGHTS OF INDIANS.



§ 150. *Perplexities.*—It has not always been easy to comprehend the exact relative condition of the white and red man of America pertaining to their rights to the soil. The demands of civilization have caused the former to enter upon the lands long held by the latter as their hunting-ground. Public policy, progress, civilization, and Christianity form the substructure which supports the right and title of the white man to the vast domain of America. Nor has there been altogether a want of respect for the fair and just right of the red man to a sufficiency of his native soil for his support.

§ 151. *Protection.*—The broad field of Spanish jurisprudence bristled all over with fortifications for the protection of the Indians. The government of Spain, while careful of their proprietary rights, expended much for their conversion to Christianity.

§ 152. *Encomiendas.*—The motive and origin of the assignment of Indians to the colonists (encomiendas) were for the spiritual and temporal good of that race. The persons to whom the Indians were assigned (encomenderos) were charged to protect their person and property, and to furnish them with ministers who should teach them the doctrine of the Christian faith, and administer to them the sacrament.

§ 153. *Peaceful Indians.*—As soon as the Indians became sufficiently pacified, the governors (adelantados) were to distribute them among the colonists, who were to take charge of them and watch over their welfare, as provided in book 6 of the Recopilacion de las Indias.

§ 154. *Indian Pueblos.*—Laws were provided for the founding of Indian pueblos or towns, designating the qualities they were to have, their limits and privileges. The first law in the codes is that of the Emperor Charles V., given in Cigales on the twenty-first of March, 1551, and reproduced by King Philip II., as appears in law 1, title 2, book 6, of the Recopilacion de las Indias. It provides that the Indians shall be reduced to pueblos, and that they should not live separated in the mountains, depriving themselves of all spiritual and temporal benefits.

§ 155. *Plan of Pueblos.*—Law 8, title 3, book 6, of said recopilacion, is as follows: "The sites on which pueblos and reductions must be formed shall have convenience of water, land, and wood, entrance and departure, and lands for cultivation (labranzas), and an exido of a league in length, where the Indians can have their cattle without their mixing with those of the Spaniards."

§ 156. *Limits not Clear.*—This description of the amount of the land is not very clear. It is probably intended, in speaking of the exido being a league in length, to be understood to be a league in each direction.

§ 157. *Unlimited Power of Viceroy as to Boundaries.*—There seems to have been no other law defining the extent of an Indian pueblo. But the royal cédula of June 4, 1687, is of a date subsequent to that of said law 8, title 3, book 6,[1] and that gives unlimited power to the viceroy and president of the royal audiencia in fixing the amount of land either within or without pueblos to be given to the Indians. This cédula does not appear to have been repealed by any subsequent law or decree.

[1] The first part of said law 8, title 3, book 6, is noted as being of December 1, 1573; and the latter part thereof of date of October 10, 1618.

The royal cédula of July 12, 1695, addressed to the alcaldes mayores of the jurisdiction of Tezcoco, and for the government of that district or jurisdiction is a regulation for the distances between Indian pueblos and settlements or farms of the Spaniards. It in no manner curtails the power of the viceroy or the president of the audiencia in the exercise of their discretion in granting lands to the Indians.

§ 158. *Four Leagues Never the Limit.*—There never was any general law fixing the amount of four square leagues for an Indian pueblo. Law 6, title 5, book 4, of the Recopilacion de las Indias, which embraced ordinances Nos. 88 and 89 of Philip II., and which will be found in chapter 7 of this work, refers expressly to towns of the Spaniards, and has no application to those occupied by Indians.

§ 159. *Indians Entitled to All They Possessed.*—It is clear from the whole tenor of the Spanish and Mexican laws, whether in the form of pueblos or ranchos, that the Indians are entitled, in equity and good conscience, and even according to the strict rigor of the laws, to all the lands they have or have had in actual possession for cultivation, pasture, or habitation, when such domain can be ascertained to have had any tolerably well defined boundaries. Both Spain and Mexico have acknowledged this principle to be a just one. President Juarez acted in accordance therewith when on the thirtieth day of September, 1867, he issued his circular to the governor of Chihuahua, and also extended the same to all the republic, in which he declared that the Indians were entitled to the lands of which they had the actual, real, and true possession. The said governor was ordered to notify them of their rights, and also that they should appear and obtain titles for their respective possessions within six months from the date of said circular. This time has also been extended.

§ 160. *Sales by Indians.*—By virtue of law 27, title 1, book 6 of said recopilacion, the Indians could sell their real and personal property; but the same were to be sold at public auction in presence of the judge, after a notice of thirty days if real estate, and if personal after a notice of nine days. The judge could shorten the time of selling personal property if good reason was shown therefor. Inasmuch as on small sales there might be too much cost, the law provides that these proceedings need not be strictly observed as to giving notice; and that when the property was of less value than thirty dollars in gold, the seller could appear before the ordinary judge and obtain a license to sell, provided it appeared that the property belonged to the seller, and that the sale thereof would be no damage to him. This license was attached to the bill of sale. Sales otherwise made were null and void.

§ 161. On the twenty-third of February, 1781, the viceroy, D. Martin Mayorga, published a decree of the audiencia (auto acordado), prohibiting the Indians from selling their real estate without a license from the proper authority. This remained in force until the independence of Mexico, which made all the inhabitants of the Mexican nation equal before the law. The plan of Iguala, adopted the twenty-fourth of February, 1821, declared that "all the inhabitants of New Spain, Africans or Indians, are citizens of this monarchy, with a right to be employed in any post according to their merit and virtues;" and that "the person and property of every citizen shall be respected and protected by the government." The treaty of Córdova, August 24, 1821, between the Spanish viceroy and the revolutionary party, and the declaration of independence issued on the twenty-eighth of September, 1821, reaffirm the principles of said plan. The decree of the Mexican congress, adopted on the twenty-fourth of February, 1822, says: "The sovereign congress declares the equality of civil rights to all free inhabitants of the empire, whatever may be their origin in the four quarters of the earth." The decree of April 9, 1823, reaffirms also the plan of Iguala. The United States supreme court, in the case of United States *v.* Ritchie, 17 How. 525, held that an Indian could purchase, hold, and sell real estate under the Mexican law. The following laws, and those in book 4, title 12 of said Recopilacion de las Indias, which will be found in chapter 3 of this work, and the cédula of 1754, all show the care and protection given to the Indians as regards both their person and property:

§ 162. *Royal Cédula of June 4, 1687, upon the Fundo Legal*[1] *of the So-called Indians—The Ancient Mode of Measuring It, and the Increase of a Hundred Varas above the Five Hundred of the Primitive Ordinance.*—The king: Whereas in my royal council of the Indies there is information that the Marqués de Falces, Count de Santisteván, being viceroy of the provinces of New Spain, made an ordinance on the twenty-sixth of May, in the year of 1567, by which he ordered that the Indian pueblos which should need lands for the Indians to live upon and to sow, five hundred varas should be given them, and whatever more they should

[1] Limits for the building of houses.

need; and that from that time henceforth grants should not be given to any person of any farm (estancia) nor land, unless it could be placed a thousand varas of cloth and silk measure distant and out of the way of the settlement (poblacion) and houses of the Indians. And whereas it appears from the copy (testimonio) of said ordinance which has reached the council that against all custom, order, and practice the owners of farms and lands who have obtained grants that should be five hundred varas distant from the settlements of the Indians, are encroaching upon the lands of the latter, taking the same away from them, either by fraud or violence, by reason of the poor Indians abandoning their houses and settlements, this being what the Spaniards long for and aim at, and therefore these one thousand varas of five hundred varas, which must be separated from the pueblo, are measured from the church or hermitage (ermita) or chapel, which is ordinarily in the center of the place; and as these five hundred varas are taken in by the pueblo, it results that no free space is left between the outskirts of the pueblo and the farms of the Spaniards, while it must be understood that the last five hundred varas must be measured on all sides of the town as is ordered and commanded in laws 12 and 18 of title 12, book 4, of the new Recopilacion de las Indias; and on account of the many inconveniences, damages, and losses which thereby result to those poor natives, it has been considered that it will be proper to order that those Indian pueblos which shall need lands for the Indians to live upon and to sow, not only five hundred varas shall be given them, which the said ordinance provides, but all that they may require, measuring these five hundred varas from the last boundaries and houses of the place, outward all around the town, to the east, west, north, and south; which space must remain vacant. These five hundred varas are to be given, not only to the pueblos which may be the capital towns, but to all those others which shall ask for and need lands, as well in those newly populated as in those to be populated and founded in the future; as by this means they will all have lands to sow and on which their cattle can eat and pasture; it being just, and very much according to my royal piety, to look again after the Indians, who suffer so many injustices and molestations of which I have notice; and in view of the fact that they pay the most revenue, benefit and fortify my royal crown, and all my vassals. In consideration of which, and having heard what the fiscal of my said council has expressed, after due examination of the points in question, and of the already cited copy of the ordinance and laws 12 and 18 of the new Recopilacion de las Indias, I have thought proper to resolve and order, as by these presents I do, that in conformity with the ordinance which the viceroy, Count de Santisteván, made and ordered on the twenty-sixth of May, in the year 1567, and of the laws compiled which are cited, that you shall give generally to the Indian pueblos of all the provinces of New Spain, for their sowing lands, not only the five hundred varas of land around the settlement, which shall not be measured from the church, but from the last house in the place, as well on the eastern and western part as on the north and south; and that not only they shall have five hundred varas, but one hundred varas more, making the complement of six hundred varas; and that if the place or town should have more than an ordinary population, and it should not appear entirely sufficient, my viceroy of New Spain and my royal audiencia of Mexico shall have care, as I charge and command them, to distribute to them a much greater quantity; and that to said places and settlements they shall distribute and assign as many more varas of land as shall appear to them necessary, without limitation. And as to the farms (estancias) for cattle, it is my will and I command that not only shall they be separated from the settlements and places of the Indians by the one thousand varas assigned by said ordinance of the twenty-sixth of May, 1567, but by one hundred varas more, and that these one thousand one hundred varas shall be measured from the last house of the settlement or place, and not from the church; and if to my viceroys of New Spain it shall appear that the estancias ought to be at a greater distance than that of said one thousand one hundred varas, they shall order it as soon as they receive this dispatch or that it is manifest to them. For all the aforesaid, I give to my royal audiencia of Mexico the power and faculty to order to be done and executed what may be necessary without any limitation, charging them, as I do, that they look all possible ways for the relief, good treatment, and preservation of the Indians; not only in that which maintains and preserves them in what is ordered and provided by the ordinance of the twenty-sixth of May, 1567, and laws 12 and 18 of the new Recopilacion de las Indias, which are cited, but that this may be with the increase of varas which in this dispatch are granted, as much in what refers to the lands which must be given, and which the Indians are to have in all New Spain to live on and to sow, as in the distance at which the estancias must be; and not only this quantity of varas, but that which my said viceroy and royal audiencia of Mexico may perceive that they need, and which they shall distribute and designate to them. For such is my will, and as it is proper for my service; and of what shall be executed in this matter, a general account and record shall be given me on all occasions; because I desire to be informed of all that shall be done for the benefit of the Indians. Dated in Madrid, June 4, 1687. I, the king. By order of the king our lord, D. Antonio Hortiz de Ottalora. [Stamped with four rubrics.]

§ 163. *Royal Cédula of July* 12, 1695, *Explanatory of That of June* 4, 1867, *Pertaining to Tezcoco.*—Don Ferdinand VI., by the grace of God, king of Castille, etc. To you my alcaldes mayores of the jurisdiction of Tezcoco. Know ye: That to the president and oidores of my royal audiencia of Mexico. On the part of the farmers of New Spain, it has been represented to me that the vexations and molestations which they receive and suffer are many on account of the suits which the Indians are continually moving against them, from which flows a loss not only to their treasuries, but to mine also; and for a remedy they beg that I may be pleased to order that the privileges which are conceded to them by the lord kings, my predecessors, may be preserved to them; that they shall be observed literally, without interpretation; and that may be conceded to them a protector for their causes, and that he may be one of the ministers of the audiencia. They further represent that the Indians, in order to dispossess the farmers of their haciendas, have recourse to the construction of huts of palm, wood, mud, and stone; and then apply to the audiencia for the purpose of having the five hundred varas measured, which according to the ordinance of the Marqués de Falces, Count de Santi-Esteban, of the twenty-sixth of May, 1567, ought to intervene between their haciendas and those of the farmers; succeeding by this means in encroaching upon the haciendas of the latter. And although this injury is of so much gravity, yet that which results from the cédula issued on the fourth of June, 1687, is greater, since another hundred varas over and above the five hundred is conceded to the Indians; and it being ordered that these be measured to them according to the four cardinal points, from the last house, leaving free the limits of the occupied part of the pueblo (el casco del pueblo); and this being so detrimental to the farmers, they ask it not to be put in practice, and that the decision of the ordinance be understood in those pueblos which were settled before the grants and founding of their haciendas, and that the measures be understood not from the last house of the pueblo, but from the center of the church, which is in the center, and that this be only with those pueblos which are capital towns where the holy sacrament, governors, and alcaldes mayores were; since that, to be understood generically in any town, and district or congregation, would be the gravest injury on account of having many of these subjects at the capitals where necessarily they congregate at the administration of the holy sacrament. And as for measuring the said varas to the Indians from the church as the farmers ask, it is a sufficient reason therefor that the Indians do not build their houses in a regular form; because some are distant from the others thirty and forty varas, and some almost a quarter of a league, by which their haciendas are damaged; and the farmers ask that the Indians be not permitted to made huts nor chapels on the lands of their labores, as by this reason they form false information, and make said lands appear to be a pueblo, and grants of lands are there given them, and they (the farmers) are despoiled of their haciendas; and other points of complaint about the sales of which the Indians make of those lands and other properties, and the amounts which the farmers can advance to the Indian laborers; the felling of trees; the fires which they make in the woods; and the visits which the governors and alcaldes mayores make on their haciendas and farms for those private ends and interests, receiving large salaries. My council in the Indies having duly examined the matter, as also what you thereupon informed me in your letter of the seventeenth of January, and taking into consideration what the fiscal said, I have resolved that the aforecited cédula issued on the fourth of June of the past year 1687, the reception of which you advised me, shall be kept, complied with, and precisely executed, and it being understood that the distance which there must be between the lands and fields of the Indians of that jurisdiction and those of the farmers shall be reckoned from the center of the pueblos, that is, from the church thereof and not from the last house; and that the same shall be practiced as to the distance of the one thousand one hundred varas which there must be from the pueblo to the farmers; and if in this manner should be experienced an injury, as well to the lands distributed to the Indians as to those of the farmers, both shall be compensated by lengthening their distances, through the place which shall be recognized as the most fit and the least prejudicial to either party; and should there not be lands as well for the distribution to the Indians as for compositions with the farmers, to compensate for the loss, the compensation shall be made out of lands belonging to me; and you will have much care that it be done with such equality that no grounds of complaint will be given to the Indians nor to the farmers, nor that suits will arise among them; rather that all be used with so much equity, that each one will be encouraged to remain in the limits which belong to him, and you will attend to the well-being and success of the Indians as I have commanded it, so that as far as capable they will be benefited, as such is my will. And of the receipt of this dispatch and the fulfillment of what is herein ordered, you will advise me at the first opportunity. Dated in Madrid, the twelfth of July, in the year 1695. I, the king. By command of the king our lord, D. Bernadino Antonio de Pardiñas Villar de Franco. [Sealed with three rubrics.]

§ 164. *Decree* 20, *January* 5, 1811, *Protecting Indians.*—The scandalous abuses which are observed and innumerable vexations which are practiced with the primitive native Indians of America and Asia having called very particularly the attention of the general and extraordinary córtes; and those worthy subjects meriting a special consideration of the córtes by all the circumstances, they order that the viceroys, presidents of the audiencias, governors, intendents, and other magistrates to whom it respectively belongs, dedicate themselves with particular care and attention to cutting the root of so many abuses condemned by religion, sound reason, and justice; they shall prohibit with all rigor that under no pretext, however rational it may appear, shall any person constituted in ecclesiastical, civil, or military authority, or any other, of any class or condition whatever, afflict on the Indian in his person or occasion him an injury however slight in his property; of which all the magistrates and chiefs must take care with the most scrupulous vigilance. The córtes likewise declare that any infraction which may be made of this solemn declaration of the national will shall deserve their displeasure and a most severe punishment, and that any one who shall contravene this its sovereign will shall be punished with all the rigor of the laws. They likewise order that the protectors of the Indians shall take care to duly comply with the sacred charge of defending their personal liberty, their privileges, and other exemptions; in the mean while the córtes, after being informed of all that may appear further necessary and proper in this matter, will proceed with the successive dispositions and regulations which may be deemed opportune. Finally, the córtes orders that this decree shall be circulated with all parish curates in every point of America, in order that, after being read for three consecutive days at the parish mass, copies of it shall be sent to each one of the town councils (cabildos) of the Indians, and it may appear by this means to those worthy subjects the watch and paternal solicitude with which the entire nation, represented by their general and extraordinary córtes, occupies itself for the happiness of all and each one of them. The council of the regencia will inform itself of this decree in order to command the most exact fulfillment thereof in all its parts, and to cause it to be printed, published, and circulated. Given at the royal island of Leon, the fifth of January, 1811. Alonzo Cañedo, president. Josef Martinez, deputy secretary. Josef Aznares, deputy secretary. To the council of regency. Reg., fol. 28.

§ 165. *Indian Rights—Decree* 31 *of the Ninth of February*, 1811. The general and extraordinary córtes, always constant in their principles sanctioned in their decree of the fifteenth of October of the year last past, and desiring to secure forever to the Americans, Spaniards as well as the original natives of those vast dominions of the Spanish monarchy, the rights which as an integrant part of the same they must enjoy in the future, decree:

§ 166. *Equal Rights as Spaniards.*—Art. 1. That one of the principal rights of the Spanish people being that of their competent representation in the national córtes, the representation of the American part of the Spanish monarchy, in all the córtes which shall be celebrated in the future, shall be entirely equal in manner and form to that which is established in the peninsula; the regulation of this representation must be fixed in the constitution upon the basis of perfect equality in conformity with said decree of the fifteenth of last October.

§ 167. *Natives may Cultivate.*—Art. 2. That the natives and inhabitants of America can sow and cultivate as much as nature and art shall make competent for them in those climates, and in the same manner promote the manufacturing industry and the arts in all their extension.

§ 168. *Equality of Rights in Every Place.*—Art. 3. That the Americans, Spaniards as well as Indians, and the children of both classes, shall have equal option as the European Spaniards for all classes of employment or destiny, as well in the córtes as in any other place of the monarchy, whether they be of an ecclesiastical, political, or military career. The council of regency must bear this in mind, and shall order what may be necessary for its fulfillment, and shall command it to be printed, published, and circulated. Given on the royal island of Leon, the ninth of February, 1811. Antonio Joaquin Perez, president. Josef Aznarez, deputy secretary. Vincente Tomás Traver, deputy secretary. To the council of regency. Reg., fol. 48.

§ 169. *Exemption from Tribute.—Decree* 42 *of the Thirteenth of March*, 1811. The general and extraordinary córtes having examined attentively the decree issued by the foregoing council of regency, on the royal island of Leon, the twenty-sixth of March of the year last past, of 1810, and the proclamation which for its execution the viceroy of New Spain, D. Francisco Xavier Venegas, ordered published in Mexico, bearing date October 5th of the same year, at the same time that they have thought proper to approve the exemption from tribute conceded to the Indians in that decree, with the extension declared by said viceroy in the said proclamation in favor of the casts of mulattoes, negroes, and others who have maintained themselves faithful to the sacred cause of the country in the district of that viceroyalty, they decree:

1. That the mentioned grace of the exemption from tribute shall extend to the Indians and the casts of the other provinces of America.

§ 170. *Distribution of Lands.*—2. That the grace of the distribution of lands of the pueblos of the Indians shall not extend to the casts.

§ 171. *Justices not to Traffic in their Jurisdiction.*—3. That the royal orders and dispositions which prohibit the abuse of the justices in trafficking in the district of their respective jurisdictions, under the specious title of distributions, shall be fulfilled with the greatest rigor. The council of regency must bear this in mind, and shall cause it to be printed, published, and circulated. Given in Cadiz, the thirteenth of March, 1811. Baron de Antella, president. Vicente Tomás Traver, deputy secretary. Juan Polo y Catalina, deputy secretary. To the council of regency. Reg., fol. 61.

# CHAPTER IX.

## MANNER OF OBTAINING GRANTS UNDER THE SPANISH GOVERNMENT.



§ 172. *The Manner of Obtaining Grants under the Spanish Government.*—The mercedes or grants of land and water which the viceroys of New Spain conceded to pueblos as well as to private individuals were made in the following manner: The party desiring land presented his petition to the viceroy declaring said land described to be public and vacant, and asking that it be granted to him. The petition was made by the party wishing the land, or by his attorney or representative. In virtue of this declaration or denouncement (denuncio), the viceroy issued an order directed to the alcalde mayor, the lieutenant of the alcalde mayor, or the corregidor of the partido or district, in which the solicited land was situated, in order to ascertain by the necessary proceedings whether the land was vacant or claimed by some third party. These proceedings consisted in publishing in the town or place nearest to the said solicited land the said order of the viceroy. This notice was posted at the church and other places on feast-days, in Spanish, and in the idiom of the Indians in that neighborhood, so that the latter might declare whether the land solicited belonged to them or not. Some person who understood the idiom read it aloud in the presence of the Indians, and they informed others of the contents of the notices. A report was made stating whether or not the Indians claimed any of the land petitioned for, which was signed officially by five witnesses, each one respectively declaring whether he was a Spaniard or Indian. Then the surrounding neighbors were cited to appear, and the commissioned judge went and examined the land personally; and made a map of it, stating the location, with an explanation as to the distance it was from any pueblo or hacienda. Then the judge sent this information sealed to the viceroy, who ordered the same to be examined by the fiscal of the royal treasury, who conceded or denied the same according to his judgment. If conceded, a title of concession was made expressing the limits of the land by the judge. This document, signed by the viceroy and countersigned by the escribano de gobernacion, was given to the interested party, by virtue of which he was placed in possession by the local authorities. A note of this document or title was made in the book of gobernacion.

§ 173. *Modification of the Manner.*—But subsequently the manner was somewhat modified. Petitions were also addressed to the president of the audiencia having jurisdiction over the territory in which the solicited land was situated. As has been observed in this work, there were two audiencias—one at the city of Mexico, the other at Guadalajara. Petitions were also addressed to the ministers or subdelegates of the audiencias commissioned and sent out to make grants; also to the commissioners who were sent out through the country for the purpose of attending to the distribution of the lands, as has been herein stated, at distant places. Under the ordinance of intendents of December 4, 1786, petitions were addressed to the intendent general of his respective intendency. He ordered the examination of the land to be made, the same to be surveyed, and the surrounding neighbors were notified that they might protest if they had good reasons therefor. A report of the condition of the land, a survey thereof, and all important circumstances pertaining thereto was made by the juez subdelegado, and transmitted to the intendent. He transmitted the same to the city of Mexico for the consideration of the fiscal and the superior board of the treasury (junta superior de la hacienda) for confirmation; and if confirmed, it was returned to the local authorities to be delivered to the interested party, with the possession of the land. In the preliminary proceedings under the intendents, the lands were measured and appraised and offered for sale publicly every day for thirty days, and sold to the highest bidder. It is hardly necessary to mention every step in the proceedings to obtain grants.

# CHAPTER X.

## DEPOSITORY OR ARCHIVES OF GRANTS.



§ 174. *First Titles in Mexico and Madrid.*—The titles first issued by the king, and those afterwards by the viceroy, ought to be found in the archives in the city of Mexico. The records of those by the king will also be found at Madrid.

§ 175. *First Titles by the Viceroy in Mexico.*—Under the cédula of 1591, the viceroy was first empowered to sell and compromise lands, and to approve the titles therefor. Such titles must be sought for likewise in the archives of said city.

§ 176. *In Mexico and Madrid.*—Law 16, title 12, book 4, of the Recopilacion de las Indias, which was probably decreed June 17, 1617, required the king's approval. They also are to be found in said archives and at Madrid.

§ 177. *In Mexico and Madrid.*—The royal cédula of 1735 required the king's approval. It is evident upon its face that at some time prior thereto, and subsequent to said law of June 17, 1617, the viceroy's approval of titles was sufficient. The titles issued while the cédula of 1735 was in force, and until the cédula of 1754 went into effect, will be also found in said archives and at Madrid.

§ 178. *In Mexico and Guadalajara.*—Titles issued by virtue of the cédula of 1754 were to be approved by the presidents of the respective audiencias. Those given for lands lying within the jurisdiction of the audiencia of Guadalajara will be found in the archives of that city. As to the boundary line between the two audiencias, see chapter 1.

§ 179. *Titles Approved at Guadalajara.*—The grants made within the territorial jurisdiction of the audiencia of Guadalajara, which required under the earliest laws the approval of the viceroy or the king, will probably be found in both archives; that is to say, the approvals in the archives of the city of Mexico, and official copies in the archives of Guadalajara. It is difficult to determine whether the approvals and communications of the king pertaining to lands lying within said jurisdiction were sent directly to the president of that audiencia, or whether they went through the hands of the viceroy. I am of opinion that they were addressed to the viceroy, as he was legally president of both audiencias, but did not preside over the one at Guadalajara. And yet the cédula of 1789, pertaining to Pitic, now Hermosillo, and Sonora, does nor appear in the volume of the royal cédulas of that year, and is probably in the archives of Guadalajara, and an official copy at Hermosillo.[1] If this be so in fact, it would indicate that the king communicated directly through his secretary with the president of the audiencia at Guadalajara.

§ 180. *Grants by Intendents.*—The grants issued under the ordinance of intendents of December 4, 1786, required the approval of the superior board of the treasury (junta superior de hacienda). As that board was established at the city of Mexico, the approvals of all grants by it must be found in the archives thereof. In the archives of the capital of each province, where the respective intendents resided, will be found the records of all grants executed by them by virtue of said ordinance. The intendents did not arrive from Spain until the year 1787.

§ 181. *San Luis Potosí.*—Texas, Coahuila, Nuevo Leon, and Tamaulipas were within the jurisdiction of the intendency of San Luis Potosí. The various records of grants made of lands in those states ought to appear in the archives of said city.

§ 182. *Durango Archives.*—Chihuahua was part of the jurisdiction of the intendency of Durango.

[1] An authentic copy is also to be found in the archives of the surveyor-general's office in San Francisco.

§ 183. *California and New Mexico.*—The record of grants made of lands in the Californias and New Mexico ought to be at the city of Mexico.

§ 184. *Intendency of Sinaloa.*—Sonora and Sinaloa at first belonged to one and the same intendency; but on the seventeenth day of March, 1787, Sinaloa was made a separate one. See chapter 1.

§ 185. *Provincias Internas.*—As has been said in chapter 1, by a royal cédula of August 22, 1776, Don Teodoro de Croix was appointed commandant general of the provinces of Sinaloa, Sonora, the Californias, Nueva Vizcaya, Coahuila, Texas, and New Mexico. His residence was fixed at Arispe, Sonora. This cédula embraced what was termed instructions, setting forth the powers of the commandant over the provincias internas. The express power, in clear language, to sell lands does not appear in the cédula; but a general power for nearly all purposes, independent of the viceroys. The power exercised by the commandant Don Pedro Nava, authorizing captains of presidios to form pueblos under the protection of said presidios, and make grants of lots and other lands within the same, by his order of March 22, 1791, dated at Chihuahua, may have been exercised under his unlimited military power; as the presidios were military garrison, they were under his exclusive jurisdiction. He seems to have had a doubt as to his powers to grant lands. He says he "leaves free and open the exclusive jurisdiction belonging to the intendentes of the royal hacienda, respecting the sale, composition, and distribution of the remainder of the land in the respective district." He certainly confined his power to the formation of pueblos at the presidios, for the colonization of soldiers and citizens who desired to fix their residences in them. Whatever orders the commandant issued pertaining to lands must be found at the place of his residence.

§ 186. *Jurisdiction Modified.*—By a cédula of November 23, 1792, the comandancia general de provincias internas included Sonora and Sinaloa, Nueva Vizcaya, New Mexico, Texas, and Coahuila, independant of the viceroy. This cédula changed the residence of the commandant to Chihuahua. It also attached to the comandancia general the subdelegated superintendence of the royal treasury, which evidently gave the same power to sell and compromise lands as was vested in the intendentes, by the ordinance of December 4, 1786. The records of the commandants must be found respectively at Arispe and Chihuahua, and the approvals thereof at the city of Mexico.

§ 187. *Board of the Treasury not Required to Approve.*—By virtue of the royal cédula of March 23, 1798, it became unnecessary to transmit titles to the junta superior of the treasury, provided the grantee would pay two per cent extra on the appraised value of the land, as a pecuniary service to the king. Grants thus made and paid for will be found in the archives of the respective capitals where the intendents resided.

§ 188. *Treasury of the Indies.*—By a resolution of the council of the Indies before a full board at Madrid, on the twenty-third of December, 1818, and approved by the king, it was declared that all business pertaining to the alienation of land in New Spain should belong to the department of the office of the treasury of the Indies, at Madrid. This was probably issued on account of the revolutionary condition of Mexico at that epoch; as this was but three years prior to the independence of the Mexican nation.[1]

§ 189. *Grants after* 1818.—Probably not many grants were made between the years 1818 and 1821. If so, their approvals would be found at Madrid, and communications thereof to the viceroy in the archives at the city of Mexico.

§ 190. *Records, how Kept.*—The records of land grants are placed within covers in the form of volumes, in folio size, and numbered; but the documents are not arranged in chronological order, and it is with some difficulty they are found. The royal cédulas are arranged with more method, and will usually be found in the volumes marked with the year of their respective dates.

§ 191. *Mexican Archives under the Republic.*—After the independence of Mexico, the records of land grants were under the direction of the department of foreign relations. Within that department was a board called the mercantile board (junta mercantil), which had supervision of these records. On the twenty-second of April, 1853, the department of fomento, or of public works, was established. In the following May it assumed the functions assigned it. The records of grants made subsequent thereto were kept in said department. Also many of the grants made prior thereto were transferred to this department. Revolutions and foreign wars have been destructive to some extent of said records. The records of grants made subsequent to the independence and prior to May, 1853, may be sought for, either in the department of foreign relations or that of fomento.

[1] And yet it does not appear that the cédula of 1754 or ordinance of December 4, 1786, was ever repealed.

# CHAPTER XI.

## AGRARIAN MEASURES UNDER SPANISH AND MEXICAN GOVERNMENT.



§ 192. *Ancient Land Measures.*—It appears that the most ancient measure in Spain is the foot, root of all the measures of intervals or of length; and it is divided into sixteen fingers, and the finger into a half, quarter, eighth, and a sixteenth; as also into twelve inches, and the inch into twelve lines.

§ 193. *The League and Other Measures.*—The league, which is the regular travel of an hour, is twenty thousand feet, and three feet make a vara of the pattern of Burgess. The estadal for measuring lands contains four varas, or twelve feet. The aranzada is a square of twenty estadales on each side, making four hundred square estadales. The fanega of land is a square of twenty-four estadales on each side, or having a superfice of five hundred and seventy-six square estadales; and it is divided into twelve celemines; the latter is divided into two halves and four quarters.

§ 194. *The Agrarian Measure of New Spain.*—The first measure known in New Spain as legal is that which appears in the following fragment of the original of the agrarian measures, according to the ordinance of D. Antonio de Mendoza, first viceroy of New Spain, which was made in the year 1536. It says: It appears it was made and provided in this said council on the ninth of March, 1536, and it is declared that each foot of said measure must be one third, and each step of five feet; and also it appears to be confirmed with the intervention of the lawyer, Loayza, by the viceroy D. Antonio de Mendoza, and proclaimed in the great square (plaza mayor) of Mexico, the same fourth of July, 1536, by the voice of Juan de Bausilla, public crier. Besides, whereas in this city there is no measure with which lands are measured, his excellency the señor viceroy ordered a measure made, as well for the city as for all of New Spain, so that all the measures may be equal, and with it the lands are measured which are to be measured, as well in the city as out of it, and that this city shall have it as a pattern, and that the number for the land shall be and shall give for the cabezadas ninety-six varas of said measure, and for the double lengths the varas, which are one hundred and ninety-two of the proper measure, and because it is understood what an entire cavalleria of land is, it must be a measure of one hundred and ninety-two varas of said measure for the head (cabezada), and double for the length, which are three hundred and eighty-four varas of said measure, and so respectively. (Cabezada is the land which forms the side of the parallelogram.)

§ 195. *Confirmation of the Measure.*—Don Gaston de Peralta, Marqués de Falces, third viceroy of New Spain, caused due fulfillment to be given these ordinances; and for that purpose he caused them to be revised, confirmed them, and added some which appeared to him necessary, and ordered them to be published again in Mexico on the nineteenth of September, 1567. These ordinances deserved to be confirmed and reproduced in divers other epochs by the viceroys and royal orders and provisions coming from Madrid.

§ 196. *Mexican Vara.*—The unity of measure has been the Mexican vara, which was the unity of all the measures of length, the pattern or size of which is taken from the Castilian vara from the mark of Burgess, and has been the legal measure until the adoption of the metrical-decimal system. The Mexican vara is divided into two halves, three thirds or feet, four fourths, six sixths, and thirty-six inches. Another legal division is also made, corresponding with the ancient vara of Toledo; by which of the vara is made two halves, three thirds or feet, four quarters or palms, six sixths, eight eighths, and forty-eight fingers. A finger is divided into three straws or into four grains. Fifty Mexican varas make a measure called cordel, which instrument has served for the measuring of lands.

§ 197. *The League.*—The league has one hundred cordeles of fifty varas each, which make five thousand varas. The league is divided in two halves and four quarters. Anciently the Mexican league was divided into three miles, a mile into a thousand steps or paces of Solomon, and each step had five thirds or feet of the Mexican vara; consequently the league is three thousand steps or paces of Solomon. This division is recognized as legal, but it has not been used for a long time, the same as the pace of Solomon, which in that epoch was called a vara, and served for the measure of lands.

§ 198. *Reduction of Solomon's Steps to Varas.*—In order to reduce the Solomon steps or paces to varas, a cipher will be written at the end of the number which expresses them, and the result will be divided by six, and the quotient will be the number of varas.

§ 199. *The Mark.*—The mark was a measure which was equivalent to two varas and seven eighths, that is, eight marks had twenty-three varas, and served for the measure of lands.

§ 200. *The Cordel.*—The cordel of sixty-nine varas was used also to measure a cavalleria.

§ 201. *Sitios.*—The ancient ordinances provided that the sides or heads of a tract of a square league (sitio de ganado mayor) must be marked in the direction of east and west, and of north and south, so that starting from the center the four cardinal points would be followed, each line making a distance of two thousand five hundred varas; and the line which measures from the center to any of the corners must have three thousand five hundred and thirty-five and one half varas; and from one corner to the other, seven thousand and seventy-one. The surperfice which results from this measure is twenty-five million square varas, because each side of the square has five thousand varas, or one hundred cordels of fifty varas each.

§ 202. *Reasons for Giving These Measures.*—This comparative table of ancient agrarian measures has been given because these measures appear in many titles and grants of property in past years, where the first grants were made by the council and municipality of Mexico, which resided in Coyoacan before Governor Hernan Cortés came to Mexico.

§ 203. *Classes of Land.*—Three classes of land were distinguished by the law in order to mark different values: 1. The land which had no irrigation was called de pan sembrar; 2. That which had water of the season, that is, rain enough, was called de pan cojer; and 3. That land which had water to irrigate at will, and by which the crops were made secure, was called de pan llevar. The agrarian measures have been changed, but nothing has been said of that classification. The last law published on this subject is the following: Department of justice, public works, and public instruction. Section of public works. The citizen president of the republic has been pleased to address me the decree which follows: Benito Juarez, constitutional president of the Mexican United States, to its inhabitants, know ye: That in the use of the faculties with which I find myself vested, I have thought proper to decree the following:

§ 204. *Metrical System.*—Art. 1. The measures of land and those of water, whether for irrigation or power, shall be estimated by the engineers and surveyors, according to the metrical-decimal system; at the same time, and during ten years, their reduction shall be given to the units of measure which have been in use up to to-day.

§ 205. *Values Reduced to the New Unit.*—Art. 2. The values of the lands and those of waters shall be derived from the present ones, and they shall be reduced to the new units of measure. The prices of these shall be those which are expressed in all the statements (partidas) of value.

§ 206. *Contentions as to Water Measure.*—Art. 3. When there shall be a contention over the waters because a right to a quantity is alleged, the titles and documents of which, anterior to the sanction of the law, give the measure in surcos, the terms heretofore fixed to determine the controverted quantity shall not be employed, unless when there is no other material proof as to what that quantity has been; but if this can be proved by any other means which imports full proof, it shall be decided in conformity therewith.

§ 207. *Metrico-decimal System of* 1857 *Sanctioned.*—Art. 4. The longitudinal and itinerary measures and those of superfice will be henceforth those fixed by the table sanctioned by the minister of justice, public works, and public instruction, on the tenth of November, 1862, relative to the metrico-decimal system established by the law of the fifteenth of March, 1857.

§ 208. *Forming Value of Land.*—Art. 5. On forming a value, the engineers or surveyors must comply with the following provisions: 1. Indicate the agricultural quality of the lands. 2.

Present a plan, if it is so agreed; or if there is no such agreement, the sketch of the lands which have been sold, in which will appear the longitude of the lines and the amplitude of the angles, the value of which can be reported, besides the fees of the valuation. 3. In every plan or sketch will be marked the astronomic orientation, and besides the magnetic, the declination which shall have been observed shall be noted, and the date on which the observation is made. 4. The plans or sketches shall be formed according to the horizontal projection of the lands, in conformity with the principles of topography. 5. In the surveys of the distances and in the measures which may be necessary to make in the possessory acts of boundary, or any other judicial ones, the engineers or surveyors shall indicate the reduction which the material measures must have, when by not being horizontal they have to be corrected, according to the inclination which they present.

§ 209. *The Measure of Water.*—Art. 6. The liter, that is, the capacity of a cubic decimeter, shall be henceforth the only measure for waters in the country and in cities. In the computation of the first, the second shall be taken as a unit of time, and in that of the cities, the minute.

Art. 7. One surco shall be considered equal to six liters and a half a second, in the country measures, and in the cities, the paja will be considered equal to forty-five hundredths of a liter a minute.

Art. 8. The engineers, surveyors, and the hydromeasurers shall regulate in each case the rustic (country) and urban (town or city) *data*, which shall correspond with the elements of inclination, distance of the taking or pressure, which must be taken into account, and in each case they must present the formulas which they shall employ, and the reasons of their proceedings.

Art. 9. The measure for the mechanical powers shall be the kilogrameter, that is, one kilogram per second with the height of a meter, forming seventy-five kilogrameters, one horse power of steam.

Wherefore, I order that it be printed, published, circulated, and that due fulfillment be given it. At the palace of the federal government, in San Luis Potosí, the second of August, 1863. Benito Juarez, A. C. Jesus Terán, minister of justice, public works, and public instruction. And I communicate it to you for your understanding and fulfillment. God and liberty. San Luis Potosí, August 2, 1863. Terán.

## § 210. *Table of Agrarian Measures.*

| NAMES OF THE MEASURES. | ANCIENT, IN VARAS. Length of the figure in varas.* | ANCIENT, IN VARAS. Breadth in varas. | Superficial Areas—Square varas. | Area in Caballerias and Fractions. | ANCIENT MEASURE. Solomon's Steps, or Pasos. Pasos or Steps. | ANCIENT MEASURE. Pasos or Steps. | ANCIENT MEASURE. Square Pasos or Steps. | MODERN MEASURE. Metrical-Decimal. Hec. | MODERN MEASURE. Aras | MODERN MEASURE. Hun. | MODERN MEASURE. Fractions. | ACRES. |
|---|---|---|---|---|---|---|---|---|---|---|---|---|
| 1 Hacienda | 25,000 | 5,000 | 125,000,000 | 205.215 | 13,000 | 3,000 | 45,000,000 | 8,778 | 05 | 0 | 0 | |
| 1 Sitio de ganado mayor | 5,000 | 5,000 | 25,000,000 | 41.230 | 3,000 | 3,000 | 9,000,000 | 1,775 | 61 | 0 | 0 | 4,338.464† |
| 1 Sitio de ganado menor | 3,333⅓ | 3,333⅓ | 11,111,111⅑ | 18.332 | 2,000 | 2,000 | 4,000,000 | 780 | 27 | 11 | 111 | 1,928.464 |
| 1 Criadero de ganado mayor. | 2,500 | 2,500 | 6,250,000 | 10.265 | .... | .... | ........ | 438 | 90 | 25 | 0 | |
| 1 Criadero de ganado menor | 1,666⅔ | 1,666⅔ | 2,777,777⅑ | 4.558 | .... | .... | ........ | 195 | 7 | 77 | | |
| 1 Fundo legal for pueblo or town | 1,200 | 1,200 | 1,440,000 | 2.360 | .... | .... | ........ | 101 | 12 | 31 | ... | |
| 1 Labor | 1,000 | 1,000 | 1,000,000 | 1.641 | .... | .... | ........ | 70 | 22 | 44 | ... | 105.756 |
| 1 Caballeria de tierra | 1,104 | 552 | 609,408 | 1.000 | .... | .... | ........ | 42 | 79 | 33 | 111 | |
| ½ Caballeria de tierra | 552 | 552 | 304,704 | .500 | .... | .... | ........ | 21 | 39 | 76 | 555 | |
| ¼ Caballeria de tierra | 552 | 276 | 152,352 | .250 | .... | .... | ........ | 10 | 69 | 88 | 277 | |
| Fauega de sembradura maiz. | 276 | 184 | 50,784 | .125 | .... | .... | ........ | 3 | 56 | 62 | 752 | |
| Solar (lot) for a house, millor | 50 | 50 | 2,500 | .004 | .... | .... | ........ | 0 | 17 | 55 | 61 | |
| Caballeria de tierra Mendoza | 640 | 320 | 204,800 | 3.219 | 384 | 192 | 73,728 | 16 | 76 | 0 | 0 | |
| ¼ Caballeria of March 9, 1536 | 320 | 160 | 51,200 | .805 | 192 | 96 | 18,432 | 4 | 19 | 0 | 0 | |

* The vara is considered 837 milimeters, and the yard, 914.

† According to what was declared in the twentieth order, by the provision in article 7 of the law of the first of June, 1839.

§ 211. *Recapitulation of the Metrical-decimal System.*

| | Lineal. | | Superficial or Square. | |
|---|---|---|---|---|
| | Meters. | Thousandths | Meters. | Thousandths. |
| Mirimeter—ten thousand.......... | 10,000 | .... | 100,000,000 | |
| Kilómeter—a thousand............ | 1,000 | .... | 1,000,000 | |
| Hectometer—a hundred........... | 100 | .... | 10,000 | |
| Decameter—ten.... .............. | 10 | .... | 100 | |
| The meter—a unit............... | 1 | .... | 1 | |
| Decimeter—a tenth .............. | .... | 100 | ........ | 000010 |
| Centimeter—a hundredth.......... | .... | 010 | ........ | 000001 |
| Milimeter—a thousandth .......... | .... | 001 | ........ | 0000001 |

The meter, or the ten thousandth part of a quarter of the terrestrial meridian, shall be the unit of lineal or longitudinal measure. The ara is equivalent to a square of ten meters on each side; and it shall be the unit for superficial or agrarian measures. Decree of the fifteenth of March, 1857. Ignacio Comonfort, Manuel Siliceo.

# CHAPTER XII.

## LOWER CALIFORNIA.

§ 212. Archives of Grants.
§ 213. Colonization.
§ 214. Instructions of Count de Galvez, August 12, 1768.
§ 215. Grant of House-lots.
§ 216. Grant of Suertes.
§ 217. Grant to be Hereditary in Sons.
§ 218. Grant not to be Encumbered.
§ 219. Water and Pasture Privileges.
§ 220. Exemption from Tithes or Other Taxes.
§ 221. Tithes Paid after Three Years.
§ 222. Payment in Produce for the Fee in the Land.
§ 223. Raising of Hogs Indispensable.
§ 224. Stock and Implements of Agriculture.
§ 225. Compensation for Digging Wells.
§ 225 *a*. Honors to the Colonists Granted.
§ 226. Grants Recorded and Placed in the Archives.
§ 227. Resolution of the Ayuntamiento of San Antonio on Titles, September 28, 1828.
§ 228. Ratification of Titles by Said Resolution.
§ 229. New Petitions to be Presented in Certain Cases.
§ 230. Memorials for Sitios.
§ 231. Titles not Given by the Ayuntamiento Invalid.
§ 232. Mission Lands may be Granted.
§ 233. Title of Address to the Ayuntamiento.
§ 234. Order Relative to Law of 1824 and Regulations of 1828.
§ 235. Grants Annulled by Law of March 10, 1857.
§ 236. Confirmation of Federal Government Essential.
§ 237. Grantees to Present their Titles to Department of Public Works.
§ 238. Foreigners' Titles Null unless Approved.
§ 239. Statement by the Governor of All Grants.
§ 240. Titles to be Presented within Six Months.
§ 241. Decree of March 14, 1861, Annulling Certain Grants.
§ 242. Consent of Federal Government Necessary.
§ 243. Grants Annulled Enumerated.
§ 244. Ratification of 1859 Invalid.
§ 245. Said Rights may be Reobtained.
§ 246. Lands to be Peopled and Cultivated.
§ 247. Amount of Land and Price Limited.
§ 248. Lands Given to the Poor.
§ 249. Provisions of June 9, 1856, to Govern.
§ 250. Twenty Leagues Set Apart for Colonization.
§ 251. Articles Free from Duty.

§ 212. *Archives of Grants.*—The territory of Lower California has had for the government of its land titles some special enactments. Its archives are deposited in various places. From 1697 to 1830 Loreto was its capital, and there may be found many of its records. The same fate befell them which has been the misfortune of those of other places of vastly more importance to receive. In 1822 the town was sacked by the crew of the Chilean cruiser brig Araucario. In 1846 it is said that cartridges were made of some of its records. San Antonio also possessed some of the territorial documents. In 1830 the capital was changed to La Paz, where also will be found a portion of its archives.

§ 213. *Colonization.*—The colonization of the territory will be found subject to four laws, in the main: 1. The instruction of the visitor, Count de José de Galvez, of the twelfth of August, 1768; 2. The general law of colonization of August 18, 1824; 3. The regulations of said law bearing date November 21, 1828; 4. The general law of colonization of July 20, 1863. The said law of 1824 and the regulations of 1828 did not go into effect in the territory of Lower California until the year 1830, when on the twenty-fifth of February of that year they were circulated in the peninsula by D. José Maria de Echeandia. But that year had nearly ended before all the ayuntamientos received them. The proclamation by said Echeandia in reference thereto is herein annexed. The instruction of Count de Galvez of 1768 remained in full force until 1830; and indeed, in some parts has continued to be operative, when not in conflict with the subsequent laws, up to the date of the colonization law of July 20, 1863. Prior to the date of the said law of 1863, the patents issued by the federal government for lands in Lower California contained a reference to the said three laws in these words: " That in conformity with the instruction which for the new colonists of Lower California, was issued by the royal commissioner, Count de D. José de Galvez, in the town of Santa Anna, of that peninsula, the twelfth of August, 1768; the law of colonization decreed by the general sovereign congress on the eighteenth of August, 1824; and its supreme regulations for the territories of the republic, issued on the twenty-first of November, 1828, I have thought proper, by virtue of the faculties with which I find myself vested, to confirm and approve the allineation made on the day of ," etc. The special laws relating to Lower California will be found in this chapter: those of the general colonization laws, in chapter 13. The departmental deputation and the ayuntamientos of the peninsula made laws and regulations beyond their jurisdiction, which the federal government of Mexico considers of no binding effect.

§ 214. *Instruction of Count de Galvez of the Twelfth of August, 1768.*—Don José de Galvez of the council and chamber of his catholic majesty in the royal and supreme council of the Indies, intendent of the army, visitor-general of all the tribunals of justice, coffers, and other branches of the royal treasury of these kingdoms, and commissioner with all the ample faculties of his excellency the Marques de Croix, viceroy, governor, and captain-general of New Spain, etc. For the benefit of the new colonist of California, and using his attributes as visitor and royal commissioner, he formed, in order that it should be kept, the following instruction, which contains the prerogatives and indispensable conditions with which, in the name of the king our lord, he concedes grants of house-lots and suertes of land in the new pueblos and districts of the three missions of this department of the south of California, and in other places which they are colonizing in it.

§ 215. *Grant of House-lots.*—1. The house-lots granted to the new colonists must be designated by the royal commissaries whom I shall appoint on the sites, and with the extension corresponding to that which the land may have where the new pueblos may be established, so that their squares and streets shall be formed by right lines; and the latter shall have, if possible, from fourteen to sixteen varas in width, so that before each house and near it the owner can put two trees at equal distance from the door and two varas from the front wall, and which will serve as a comfort and defense from the burning of the sun, and will beautify and fertilize the pueblos.

§ 216. *Grant of Suertes.*—2. Each suerte of land, whether capable of irrigation where there is such, or dependent on the season, or dry (de temporal i secano), must be two hundred varas in length and one hundred in width, on account of this being the area of land generally occupied in the sowing of one fanega of corn; and as I propose to grant the suertes to the new colonists in greater or less number, according to the quality and merit of each one, they shall also be marked out by the royal commissaries with the approval of the reverend father missionaries, if the distribution be made in the district of the missions where they are charged with the economical administration of their temporalities; and these distributions of land must be made without prejudice to the native Indians, to disbanded soldiers and other Spaniards of good habits.

§ 217. *Grants to be Hereditary.*—3. The houses built on the house-lots (solares) granted and designated to the new pobladores, and the suertes of land comprehended within their respective grants, shall be perpetually hereditary in their sons and descendents, or their daughters who shall marry useful colonists, and who have received no grants of suertes for themselves; provided all of them comply with the conditions which are expressed in this instruction; and in order that the sons of the possessors of these grants observe the obedience and respect which they owe to their fathers, the latter shall be freely authorized, if they should have one or more sons, to elect which one of them they may wish, he being a layman, as heir to their house and suertes of the colony; and they can likewise, if they should possess more than one, dispose of them among their children; but no one suerte shall be divided, because they must all and each one be indivisible and perpetually unalienable.

§ 218. *Grants not to be Encumbered.*—4. Neither can the colonists nor their heirs impose on the house or suertes granted to them any tax, entail, reversion, mortgage, or any other burden, although it be for pious purposes; and should any one do so in violation of this just prohibition, he shall irremediably be deprived of his property, and his grant shall *ipso facto* be given to another colonist who may be useful and obedient.

§ 219. *Water and Pasture Privileges.*—5. The new colonists and their descendents shall enjoy, for the purpose of maintaining their cattle, the common privilege of the water and pasturage to be designated in the new pueblos or missions; and besides, each one shall conclusively enjoy the pasture of his own land; but with the condition that if they are able to possess and breed all kinds of large and small cattle, they shall keep them under herdsmen's charge (so that they shall not become wild and stray away), and no colonist is to possess more than fifty head of each kind, in order that in this manner the profit produced by the cattle shall be distributed among all, and that the true riches of the pueblos be not monopolized by a few inhabitants.

§ 220. *Exemption from Tithes or Other Taxes.*—6. The new colonists shall be free and exempt for the term of three years from paying tithes or any other tax on the fruits and produce of the lands given to them, provided that within a year from the day on which the house-lots and suertes shall have been designated to them they shall have constructed their houses in the best way they can, and shall inhabit them, and that they inclose them or make trenches to separate and protect, each one, the lands designated to him, placing on the boundary lines or margins instead of landmarks, fruit trees or wild ones of some utility, at the rate of ten to each suerte.

§ 221. *Tithes Paid after Three Years.*—7. After the expiration of the three years they shall pay the tithes to his majesty, for him to dispose of according to his royal pleasure, as belonging solely to him, not only on account of the absolute royal patronage which he possesses in these dominions, but also because they are the produce of uncultivated and abandoned lands which are about to become fruitful at the cost of the large outlays and expenses which the great expeditions caused.

§ 222. *Payment in Produce for the Fee in the Land.*—8. At the expiration of the said term of three years, the new pobladores and their descendents shall pay, in acknowledgment of the direct and supreme dominion (fee in the land) which belongs to the sovereign, annually, one almud of wheat or corn for each suerte of temporal land, and a quarter (una cuartilla) for each irrigable suerte, and for their own benefit they shall be collectively under the indispensable obligation of attending to the repair of the trenches of water, and the other public works of their pueblos, including those of the church, whether they be parochial or of the mission where they may have their parish.

§ 223. *Raising of Hogs Indispensable.*—9. Under the supposition that the hog is the most useful animal everywhere, and that in this part of the south of the peninsula, where it is entirely lacking, it is made indispensable on account of its destroying the vipers and locusts, in proportion as they multiply, it will be a necessary obligation on the part of the new colonists, to increase each year, for the first ten years, two breeding sows and maintain these cattle in the pastures, as all the other kinds, so that the leopards and coyotes will not destroy them, as has happened heretofore.

§ 224. *Stock and Implements of Agriculture.*—10. Besides the breeding sows, the new colonists shall be obliged to have within the two first years, a yoke of oxen or cows, a plow, two plow-points to work the land, two pick-axes, one ax, one hammer, one hunter's cutlass, five sheep or goats, and two mares with their brands in pasture; and they shall have entirely finished their houses in the pueblo, and each one shall have within the same time five hens and one cock.

§ 225. *Compensation for Digging Wells.*—11. As a recompense of the greater application in the culture and working of the lands, shall be granted to the colonist who shall make a well to irrigate them two suertes more of dry or temporal ones than now is to be granted and designated to them; and if by two should be made a well for the common benefit of both, each one shall have his increase of a suerte, by only making it so appear to him who may govern in this department.

§ 225 *a*. *Honors to the Colonists Granted.*—12. As a greater and distinctive honor to the new Spanish colonists, I grant to them in the name of his majesty, the military law (fuero mílitar), and the privileges and exemptions, which by the royal ordinances the provisional military enjoy, on condition that each colonist, the head of a family, shall have his horse, a gun or escopet, a broad sword, and his spear and shield to meet for the defense of the country, whenever any inimical invasion offers itself; and to assist the government or the ministers of the missions, if a case should occur of any commotion or internal rising of the Indians; for which purpose the colonists will be enlisted and distributed in one or two companies which I shall order to be formed in this department of the south.

§ 226. *Grants Recorded and Placed in the Archives.*—13. And the corresponding titles of grants having been made by me, of house-lots, lands, and waters, which I shall concede to the new pobladores, they must be presented to the royal commissary and lieutenant of the governor of this department, Don Manuel Espinosa de las Monteras, so that they may be entered in the general book of the pueblo which I have ordered to be made, and which must be kept in the archives of the government, with the memorials and decrees of concessions; and if these grants be made within the limits of any of the missions, they will also be exhibited to the father minister of the mission, in order that a registry may be made in the private book of the pueblo and of the apportionment of the mission.

Given in the mining town (real) of Santa Ana, the twelfth

of August, 1768. Don Joseph de Galvez. By order of his illustrious lordship, Miguel Joseph de Azanza.

§ 227. *Resolutions of the Ayuntamiento of San Antonio, on Titles, September* 28, 1828.—The illustrious ayuntamiento (town council) of the mining town (real) of San Antonio, to the citizens of its district (partido). It having been declared by the provisional political chief of the province that the distribution of the public territory or vacant lands, in favor of the citizens who need it, as well as to execute the instruments and writings appertaining to their possessions, is the peculiar province of the ayuntamientos, it has declared by resolution (de comun acuerdo) to decree the following:

§ 228. *Ratification of Titles.*—1. That it ratifies and makes valid all the sitios and possessions which have been given, up to the day of the date on which this proclamation is published, as if granted by superior and legitimate authority, even when the instruments and writings of these lack some requisite of the law, which now, by their antiquity or by some defect of the public archives, can not be found; their own prescription being sufficient for them to enjoy their properties without any contradiction.

§ 229. *New Petitions to be Made in Certain Cases.*—2. That all those sitios the memorials of which have been presented and decreed prior to the date of the publication of this law, and the possessions of which have not been taken by the interested parties— these must present themselves before the ayuntamiento by means of a memorial, in order that by its authority and knowledge titles may be given to said parties.

§ 230. *Memorials for Sitios.*—3. That in the future every citizen of this partido must absolutely, when they need one or more sitios for the breeding of cattle, present themselves by means of a memorial to this ayuntamiento in order to obtain this favor, which will be granted to them as justice and the public right may require it.

§ 231. *Titles not Given by the Ayuntamiento Invalid.*—4. That all the possessions and writings which shall be given by any other authority than that of the ayuntamiento, posterior to the date of the publication of this, are declared null and of no value, and consequently without any right which can benefit the interested party that obtains them.

§ 232. *Mission Lands may be Granted.*— 5. That as the scarcity of grain and cotton in all these parts is notorious, and that the missions have vacant lands, the inhabitants who wish to dedicate themselves to cultivation can solicit the reverend fathers of the same to grant them the use of said lands (franquear en calidad de prestado), as well for the common good as for the individual good which will result; provided it be for the products above mentioned.

§ 233. *Title of Address to the Ayuntamiento.*—6. That in every memorial or petition which is presented for the purpose to this ayuntamiento must be given it by law the title of Illustrious, and in the body of it that of V. S., because those not presented in these terms will be refused. And for its due fulfillment it is ordered published by proclamation in this capital (cabecera), and in the other places belonging to the jurisdiction of the partido.

Given in the town hall (sala consistorial) of the mining town of San Antonio the twenty-eighth of September, 1828. Raznundo Carrillo, Juan Bautista Talamantes. Antonio Navarro, sindic attorney. Julian Perez, secretary.

§ 234. *Order of José Maria Echeandia, to the Principal Commander and Subaltern Political Chief of Lower California, Relative to the Law of August* 18, 1824, *and its Regulation of the Twenty-first of November*, 1828.—Superior political government of both Californias. With this date I circulated with the alcaldes what I copy: I transmit you a copy of the law of the eighteenth of August, 1824, and another of the general provisions given on the twenty-first of November, 1828, by the supreme government for the fulfillment of said law in the territories of our republic. Both copies you will publish in the demarkation of your command, giving notice that all individuals who occupy sitios, with whatever motive, shall make their presentations to this government for the corresponding confirmation of their titles in legal form, through the channel of the principal commander of that territory, if he should be pleased to charge himself with the subaltern political (jefatura) office, minutely as article 2 of said general provisions of the supreme government provides; adding by documents all merits believed to be in their favor. Those who up to date have made petitions to obtain sitios, in order to have their petitions taken into consideration hereafter, can renew them by complying with the provision in the cited article 2, and calling attention to their former petitions. I transcribe it to you, and accompany it with said number of copies for your understanding and government, in case that you have been pleased to take charge of the subaltern political government of that territory. God and liberty. Santa Barbara, February 25, 1830. José Maria Echeandia. To the principal commander and subaltern political chief of Lower California. Loreto.

§ 235. *Grants Annulled—Law of March* 10, 1857, *Annulling Grants in Lower California Made Since* 1821, *and not Approved by the Supreme Government.*—Department of public works, colonization, industry, and commerce of the Mexican republic. Section 4. His excellency the president of the republic has been pleased to direct to me the decree which follows. The citizen Ignacio Comonfort, president of the Mexican republic.

§ 236. *Confirmation of Federal Government Essential.*—Art. 1. The sales or alienation of the islands or public lands of Lower California, which have been made since the year 1821 up to the present time, by political chiefs, governors, and any other civil or military authority of the territory or department of both Californias, are null and of no value, whilst they have not obtained the ratification of the supreme government.

§ 237. *Grantees to Present their Titles.*—Art. 2. To this end the holders of said titles shall present them to the department of public works, either directly or through the agent in Lower California, in order to examine if they were issued in conformity with the law of August 18, 1824, and whether the previous license and approbation of the supreme government were obtained. In case they lack these requisites, the islands and lands contracted for therein shall be returned to the national domain.

§ 238. *Foreigners.*—Art. 3. The sales, transfers, or leases of the islands or lands which shall have been made to foreigners, by the possessors of any kind of titles, are null, provided they have been made without the knowledge and approbation of the said supreme government, according as it is provided in the laws of March 11, 1842, and February 1, 1856. Consequently the authorities of said territory and the others of the republic shall prevent by all possible means the possession, use, and dominion of the islands or lands to be taken by foreign individuals or companies whose rights are founded on the sales, transfers, or leases which shall have been made to them.

§ 239. *Statement by the Governor.*—Art. 4. The political chief of the territory of Lower California, placing himself in accord with the agent of the department of public works, shall remit within three months, counted from the date of the present law, a detailed statement of all the alienations of islands and public lands which have been made by the authorities of said territory from the year 1821 up to the present time.

§ 240. *Titles to be Presented within Six Months.*—Art. 5. The islands and public lands alienated by said authorities, the titles of which shall not be presented for the review of the said department within six months, counted from the day on which this law shall have been published in the capital of Lower California, shall return by this sole fact to the national domain.

Wherefore I command that it be printed, published, circulated, and that due compliance be given it. Given in the national palace of Mexico the tenth of March, 1857. Ignacio Comonfort. To the citizen Manuel Siliceo. And I communicate it to you for your understanding and consequent ends. God and liberty. Mexico, March 10, 1857. Siliceo.

§ 241. *March* 14, 1861—*A Decree of the Government Declaring Null Various Alienations of Vacant Lands in Lower California.*—Excellent Señor. His excellency the president has been pleased to address me the decree which follows: The C. Benito Juarez, provisional constitutional president of the Mexican United States, to all the inhabitants thereof, know ye: That in use of the ample faculties with which I find myself vested, I have thought proper to decree the following:

§ 242. *Consent of Federal Government Necessary.*—Art. 1. No political or military authority of the territory of Lower California could alienate, without the consent of the general government, the vacant lands existing in that part of the republic; consequently are null and of no value the alienations which lack that requisite, in conformity with the disposition in the decree of March 10, 1857.

§ 243. *Annulled Grants Enumerated.*—Art. 2. Are also null the following grants, because the grantees have not complied with the condition imposed upon them: That of Don Custodio Sousa, of fourteen leagues in the missions of San Miguel and Guadalupe; that of Matias Moreno in the plains (llanos) of San Quintin and San Vicente; that of Ricardo Palacio, in the mission of Santa Catarina; that of Julio Morner, of one league, and that of Jesus Delgado, of a half-league, which they were to mark and measure at their expense; that of Miguel Arriga, in the lands called San Felipe; that of forty-five leagues made to Francisco Gochicoa, for the establishment of a colony; those of José Maria Esteva, of three leagues in the island of San Juan, and of four leagues in the place called Llano del Diablo.

§ 244. *Ratification of* 1859 *Invalid.*—Art. 3. The ratification accorded on the eighth of August, 1859, to various alienations made by the political chiefs and military authorities of the northern frontier of Lower California, is also without value or effect, because the original titles were not remitted, as was provided, in order that they could be reviewed by the department of public works.

§ 245. *Said Rights may be Reobtained.*—Art. 4. Those comprehended within the preceding article, if they wish to acquire the right to the lands which have been conceded to them, must remit to the said department the original titles or copies certified to by the agent of the said department, and besides, a voucher which will prove that they have taken possession of their respective land, after having marked and measured it, and that they have peopled and cultivated it.

§ 246. *Lands must be Peopled and Cultivated.*—Art. 5. The possessors of the lands not comprehended in article 3, the alienation of which has been ratified by the general government, will lose the right to them if, within two years from this date, they do not comply with the obligations imposed upon them to people and cultivate them. This time having passed without these requisites having been fulfilled, the lands will be returned to the national domain, and they will be given by preference to him who may denounce them and obligate himself to comply with said requisites.

§ 247. *Amount of Land and Price Limited.*—Art. 6. In the future a sale can not be conceded of vacant lands in Lower California, for a greater extension than that of three leagues (sitios de ganado mayor), nor for a less value than that of from two hundred to three hundred dollars for each one, according to its class. If, notwithstanding this probibition, there should be fraudulently united in one single person a greater extent of land, he that may have it will lose the excess, which shall be given to whoever may denounce it.

§ 248. *Lands Given to the Poor.*—Art. 7. To the poor inhabitants of Lower California, and to the rest who may wish to reside therein, shall be given *gratis* for each person up to two cavallerias of vacant land, in the place which they may select, but with the condition of peopling and cultivating them. For this object they will address their petition to the agent of the department of public works, with a certificate from the respective political authority, in which it may appear that the land which they claim is vacant, and that employé will appoint an expert who shall make the measurement and marking of the limits, which proceedings he shall remit to said department, in order that the corresponding title of property may be issued.

§ 249. *Provisions of June* 9, 1856, *to Govern.*—Art. 8. In all the alienations which shall be claimed of said vacant lands, the solicitors and public functionaries shall be governed by the provisions in the circular number 102 of the ninth of June, 1856.

§ 250. *Twenty Leagues Set Apart for Colonization.*—Art. 9. Of the vacant lands which are residues in virtue of the nullity declared in article 2, there shall be destined in two places immediate to the frontier which may be thought convenient twenty sitios de ganado mayor (twenty leagues) for the formation of two colonies, which shall be composed absolutely of the Mexicans, who shall have remained in the territory of the United States, and who may wish to return to the republic. To this end the agent of the department of public works (fomento), with the concurrence of the political chief of the territory of Lower California, shall immediately designate said places, and remit to the proper office a minute description of their situation, climate, and productions, in order with the presence of those *data* shall be regulated the distribution of the lands destined to each colony, and auxiliaries which the government has to give for the establishment of the colonists. The transport of these will be on their account.

§ 251. *Articles Free from Duty.*—Art. 10. The provisions, instruments, machines, and other tools which those who establish themselves in said colonies may carry with them shall be free of all duty at their introduction in said colonies.

§ 252. *Products Free from All Duty or Taxes.*—Art. 11. The products of the said colonies and the estates (fincas) and lands of the settlers shall also be free of all duty and all tax, whatever may be its denomination, during five years; and the settlers shall be for the same time free from all forced military service, except in the case of foreign invasion.

§ 253. *Removal of Families from Upper California.*—Art. 12. The department of public works, with the presence of the proposals which have been made to it on the translation of Mexican families from Upper California, will dictate the proper orders in order that the present decree may have effect.

Palace of the federal government in Mexico, the fourteenth of March, 1861. Benito Juarez. To the C. Ignacio Ramirez, minister of public works, colonization, industry, and commerce. And I communicate to Y. E. for your knowledge and consequent ends. God and liberty. Mexico, etc. Ramirez.

*Law of December* 14, 1874, *Granting to Certain Parties Lands in Lower California, Gratis.*—Department of public works, colonization, industry, and commerce of the Mexican republic. Section 1. The citizen president of the republic has been pleased to direct to me the decree which follows: Sebastian Lerdo de Tejada, constitutional president of the Mexican United States, to the inhabitants thereof, know ye: That the congress of the Union has thought proper to decree the following. The congress of the Union decrees:

§ 253 *a*. *Titles to be Issued by the Executive—To Whom without Compensation.*—Art. 1. The executive is authorized to issue through the department of public works the corresponding titles of property to the public lands in Lower California, a previous measurement and demarkation being made, and without requiring any price from the interested parties who shall be found comprehended in any of the following clauses:

1. Those who shall prove that on the day of the sanctioning of this law by the executive they were in the quiet and peaceable possession in their own name, or by their legitimate representatives, in the terms of article 921 of the civil code;[1] which they have not acquired clandestinely, not being foreigners, in contravention of the laws of the eleventh of March, 1842, and first of February, 1856, and that they have the lands peopled, cultivated, bounded, or being worked.

2. Those who having before possessed any lands without opposition, and for want of ratification of their titles have been ejected by denouncements made in conformity with the law of the twentieth of July, 1863, to whom shall be adjudicated lands which as far as possible shall be equivalent in extension and quality to those which they lost, provided that they shall designate the location of the lands which they desire within the said territory of Lower California. They shall solicit said land within the term of six months, counted from the day on which the commission treated of in article 2 shall commence to exercise their functions; without the grantees of the alienations declared nominally null by the law of the fourteenth of March, 1861, considering themselves comprehended within this favor.

3. The former Mexican inhabitants of the territory ceded to the United States, who with whatever title and in whatever time they shall have established themselves, or shall establish

[1] Art. 921. Those who are capable of acquiring are capable of possessing. Those incapacitated in conformity with the law may possess by means of their legitimate representatives.

themselves within the term of five years, counted from the publication of this law, in Lower California, who shall have a right to the adjudication provided in article 7 of the said law of the fourteenth of March, 1861; they being, as well as those comprehended in the preceding clauses, under the obligation which the laws impose, of peopling, cultivating, or working the lands which shall be adjudicated to them.

§ 253 *b*. *Commission.*—Art. 2. The executive shall exercise these authorizations through the means of a commission which also shall be charged with fulfilling the provision of said articles 7 and 9 of said law, and its plant shall be as follows:

| | |
|---|---|
| 1 commissioner | $4,000 |
| 1 secretary | 1,800 |
| 1 clerk | 600 |
| 1 first engineer | 3,500 |
| 1 second engineer | 2,300 |
| Traveling expenses of the commission | 3,000 |
| Expenses of the operations of measurement and unforeseen expenses | 2,400 |
| | $17,600 |

§ 253 *c*. *Commission Suspended by Litigation.*—Art. 3. If there should be a litigation anterior to the publication of this law, relative to any of the lands occupied, or if there should be raised any litigation in the course of the operations of the commission referred to in the preceding article, the latter will suspend all proceedings until the question be resolved by competent judicial authority.

§ 253 *d*. *Certain Persons Exempt from Duties.*—Art. 4. From the individuals spoken of in the third clause of article 1, who in the future may come to establish themselves in the territory of Lower California, no duties shall be collected on their live-stock, utensils, and effects which for use they may introduce.

Palace of the legislative power, Mexico, December 14, 1874, Nicolás Lémus, deputy president. Luis G. Alvirez, deputy secretary. Antonio Gómez, deputy secretary. Wherefore I command that it be printed, published, circulated, and that due compliance be given it. Given in the national palace of Mexico, the fourteenth of December, 1874. S. Lerdo de Tejada. To citizen Blas Balcárcel, minister of public works, colonization, industry, and commerce. And I communicate it to you for the consequent ends. Independence and liberty. Mexico, December 14, 1874. Balcárcel.

# CHAPTER XIII.

## COLONIZATION.

§ 254. Division of the Laws.
§ 255. Enumeration of the Laws of this Chapter.
§ 256. Law of January 4, 1823—Catholics Receive Protection.
§ 257. Lands on Conditions.
§ 258. Empresarios.
§ 259. Families of Immigrants.
§ 260. Measurement of Lands.
§ 261. Distribution of Lands.
§ 262. Labor of Land.
§ 263. Farmers.
§ 264. Amount of Land may be Increased.
§ 265. Establishments not Completed.
§ 266. Division of Large Tracts.
§ 267. Towns and Cities.
§ 268. Plan of Towns.
§ 269. Provinces Formed.
§ 270. Government of Towns.
§ 271. Spiritual Pastors.
§ 272. The Most Important Places to be Settled.
§ 273. Natives Have Preference.
§ 274. Rights of Empresarios.
§ 275. Proprietors must Alienate Two Thirds.
§ 276. Explanation of the Two Prior Articles.
§ 277. The Date of a Concession Important.
§ 278. Lands to be Cultivated within Two Years.
§ 279. No Tithes or Taxes for Six Years.
§ 280. Half Tithes and Taxes after Six Years.
§ 281. Certain Articles Free of Duty.
§ 282. Foreigners Considered as Naturalized.
§ 283. Letters of Citizenship.
§ 284. Every Person may Sell and Leave the Country.
§ 285. Modification of Slavery.
§ 286. Foreigners with Prior Rights.
§ 287. Executive may Sell or Lease.
§ 288. Decree of April 6, 1830—Importation of Cotton Goods.
§ 289. Application of Duties.
§ 290. Commissioners to Visit Colonies.
§ 291. Right of Eminent Domain.
§ 292. Convicts may be Sent to Colonies.
§ 293. Employment of Convicts.
§ 294. Mexican Families, Conveyance of, Free.
§ 295. Federal and State Laws to be Obeyed.

§ 343. Decree of December 4, 1846—Reasons for the Decree of Regulations.
§ 344. Substitutes in Case of Absence of Officers..
§ 345. Disability of the President.
§ 346. Decision of a Majority Necessary.
§ 347. Term of Office.
§ 348. Duty of the President.
§ 349. Clerks, how Appointed.
§ 350. Plats of Lands to be Made.
§ 351. Surveys of the Lands.
§ 352. Oath of Surveyors.
§ 353. Surveyors to Obey Orders.
§ 354. Surveys, how Made.
§ 355. Division of Land.
§ 356. Service of Surveyors in Person.
§ 357. Lines, how Drawn—Water, Minerals, etc., Noted.
§ 358. Divisions of Sitios Numbered.
§ 359. Squares of a Mile—Lots No. 16 to Remain Unsold.
§ 360. Responsibility of Surveyors.
§ 361. Salaries of Surveyors.
§ 362. Payment of Salaries may be Advanced.
§ 363. Plats to be Filed.
§ 364. Mines Reserved.
§ 365. Sixth of the Land Reserved.
§ 366. Price of Land.
§ 367. Adjacent Owners to be Summoned.
§ 368. Landmarks.
§ 369. Plats Open to Inspection.
§ 370. Sales at the Office of Direction.
§ 371. Sales Made at Public Auction.
§ 372. Notice of Sale.
§ 373. Method of Sale.
§ 374. Payments.
§ 375. Contracts of Sale.
§ 376. Bidder to Receive Title.
§ 377. Bill of Sale.
§ 378. No Fees to be Paid.
§ 379. Sales Suspended when No Bidders Appear.
§ 380. Monthly Notice of Unsold Lands.
§ 381. Contracts for New Colonies.
§ 382. Who may not be Colonists.
§ 383. Slaves not Permitted.
§ 384. Default of Surveyors.
§ 385. Prices, how Paid.
§ 386. Families Introduced in a Certain Period.
§ 387. Default of Conditions.
§ 388. Contracts of Settlement.
§ 389. Banks—Highways.
§ 390. What Lands to be Granted.
§ 391. Distribution of Land by Contractors.
§ 392. Enforcement of Contracts.

§ 254. *Division of the Laws.*—It seems proper, for the sake of the convenience of the reader and the proper connection of matter, to divide the laws of colonization into two chapters, without following a chronological order in the division. This chapter will contain the following:

§ 255. *Enumeration of the Laws.*—1. Colonization law of January 4, 1823, which remained in force but a short time. 2. The decree of April 6, 1830, relating to importations of goods, the frontier lands, convicts, slaves, and other matters touch the main subject. 3. The decree of November 25, 1833, repealing the eleventh article of the law of 1830; and authorizing the government to expend money for the colonization of the territories, and to do certain other acts. 4. The circular of February 4, 1834, in the relation to the colonization of the lands of the state of Coahuila and Texas (both being then one state). 5. The law of April 24, 1835, in relation to the decree of the legislature of Coahuila and Texas, and the unoccupied land of those states, passed March 14th of said year. 6. The law of April 4, 1837, for the redemption of the national debt, by means of sale and mortgage. 7. The decree of April 12, 1837, in virtue of the authority conferred by the law of the fourth of said month, for the creation of a national consolidated stock for the express purposes of converting the entire foreign debt and redeeming the same on the terms expressed. 8. The decree of November 27, 1846, establishing a board of colonization. 9. The decree of December 4, 1846, establishing regulations for the direction of colonization. 10. The colonization law of the state of Coahuila and Texas, dated March 24, 1825. 11. The instructions of the commissioners appointed by the legislature of said state, dated September 4, 1827. This division of the laws into two chapters has been made, because the matters in this chapter, except the first law of 1823, relate more to special subjects pertaining to colonization than to general laws thereon.

§ 256. *National Colonization Law of January 4, 1823—Catholics will Receive Protection.*—Art. 1. The government of the Mexican nation will protect the liberty, property, and civil rights, of all foreigners who profess the Roman Catholic apostolic religion, the established religion of the empire.

§ 257. *Lands on Conditions.*—Art. 2. To facilitate their establishment, the executive will distribute lands to them, under the conditions and terms herein expressed.

§ 258. *Empresarios.*—Art. 3. The empresarios, by whom is understood those who introduce at least two hundred families, shall previously contract with the executive, and inform it what branch of industry they propose to follow, the property or resources they intend to introduce for that purpose, and any other particulars they may deem necessary; in order that with this necessary information, the executive may designate the province to which they must direct themselves, the lands which they can occupy with the right of property, and the other circumstances which may be considered necessary.

§ 259. *Families of Immigrants.*—Art. 4. Families who immigrate, not included in a contract, shall immediately present themselves to the ayuntamiento of the place where they wish to settle, in order that this body, in conformity with the instructions of the executive, may designate the lands corresponding to them, agreeably to the industry which they may establish.

§ 260. *Measurement of Lands.*—Art. 5. The measurement of land shall be the following: Establishing the vara at three geometrical feet, a straight line of five thousand varas shall be a league; a square, each of the sides of which shall be one league, shall be called a sitio; and this shall be the unity of counting one, two, or more sitios; five sitios shall compose one hacienda.

§ 261. *Distribution of Lands.*—Art. 6. In the distribution made by government of lands to the colonists for the formation of villages, towns, cities, and provinces, a distinction shall be made between grazing lands destined for the raising of stock, and lands suitable for farming or planting, on account of the facility of irrigating.

§ 262. *Labor of Land.*—Art. 7. One labor shall be composed of one million square varas, that is to say one thousand varas on each side, which measurement shall be the unity for counting one, two, or more labores. These labores can be divided into halves and quarters, but not into lesser portions.

§ 263. *Farmers.*—Art. 8. To the colonists whose occupation is farming, there can not be given less than one labor, and to those whose occupation is stock-raising, there can not be given less than one sitio.

§ 264. *Amount of Land may be Increased.*—Art. 9. The government itself, or by means of the authorities authorized for that purpose, can augment said portions of land as may be deemed proper, agreeably to the conditions and circumstances of the colonists.

§ 265. *Establishments not Completed.*—Art. 10. Establishments made under the former government, which are now pending, shall be regulated by this law in all matters that may occur; but those that are finished shall remain in that state.

§ 266. *Division of Large Tracts.*—Art. 11. As one of the

principal objects of laws in free governments ought to be to approximate, so far as is possible, to an equal distribution of property; the government, taking into consideration the provisions of this law, will adopt measures for dividing out the lands which may have accumulated in large portions on the hands of individuals or corporations, and which are not cultivated, indemnifying the proprietors for the just price of such lands, to be fixed by appraisers.

§ 267. *Towns and Cities.*—Art. 12. The union of many families at one place shall be called a village, town, or city, agreeably to the number of its inhabitants, its extension, locality, and other circumstances which may characterize it, in conformity with the law on that subject. The same regulations for its internal improvement and police shall be observed as in the others of the same class in the empire.

§ 268. *Plan of Towns.*—Art. 13. Care shall be taken in the formation of said new towns that, so far as the situation of the ground will permit, the streets shall be laid off straight, running north and south, east and west.

§ 269. *Provinces.*—Art. 14. Provinces shall be formed, the superficies of which shall be six hundred square leagues.

§ 270. *Government of Towns.*—Art. 15. As soon as a sufficient number of families may be united to form one or more towns, their local government shall be regulated, and the constitutional ayuntamientos and other legal establishments formed, in conformity with the laws.

§ 271. *Spiritual Pastors.*—Art. 16. The government shall take care, in accord with the respective ecclesiastical authority, that these new towns are provided with a sufficient number of spiritual pastors, and in like manner it will propose to congress a plan for their decent support.

§ 272. *The Most Important Places to be Settled.*—Art. 17. In the distribution of lands for settlement among the different provinces, the government shall take care that the colonists shall be located in those which it may consider the most important to settle. As a general rule, the colonists who arrive first shall have the preference in the selection of land.

§ 273. *Natives Have Preference.*—Art. 18. Natives of the country shall have a preference in the distribution of land; and particularly the military of the army, of the three guaranties, in conformity with the decree of the twenty-seventh of March, 1821; and also those who served in the first epoch of the insurrection.

§ 274. *Rights of Empresarios.*—Art. 19. To each empresario

who introduces and establishes families in any of the provinces designated for colonization, there shall be granted at the rate of three haciendas and two labores for each two hundred families so introduced by him; but he will lose the right of property over said lands should he not have populated and cultivated them in twelve years from the date of the concession. The premium can not exceed nine haciendas and six labores, whatever may be the number of families he introduces.

§ 275. *Proprietors must Alienate Two Thirds after Twenty Years.*—Art. 20. At the end of twenty years the proprietors of the lands acquired in virtue of the foregoing article must alienate two thirds part of said lands, either by sale, donation, or in any other manner he pleases. The law authorizes him to hold in full property and dominion one third part.

§ 276. *Explanation of the Two Prior Articles.*—Art. 21. The two foregoing articles are to be understood as governing the contracts made within six months, as after that time, counting from the day of the promulgation of this law, the executive can diminish the premium as it may deem proper, giving an account thereof to congress, with such information as may be deemed necessary.

§ 277. *The Date of a Concession Important.*—Art. 22. The date of the concession for lands constitutes an inviolable law, for the right of property and legal ownership; should any one, through error or by subsequent concession, occupy land belonging to another, he shall have no right to it, further than a preference in case of sale, at the current price.

§ 278. *Lands to be Cultivated within Two Years.*—Art. 23. If, after two years from the date of the concession, the colonist should not have cultivated his land, the right of property shall be considered as renounced; in which case the respective ayuntamiento can grant it to another.

§ 279. *No Tithes or Taxes for Six Years.*—Art. 24. During the first six years from the date of the concession the colonists shall not pay tithes, duties on their produce, nor any contribution under whatever name it may be called.

§ 280. *Half Tithes and Taxes after Six Years.*—Art. 25. The next six years from the same date they shall pay half tithes and the half of the contributions, whether direct or indirect, that are paid by the other citizens of the empire. After this time they shall in all things relating to taxes and contributions be placed on the same footing with the other citizens.

§ 281. *Certain Articles Free of Duty.*—Art. 26. All the instruments of husbandry, machinery, and other utensils that are introduced by the colonists for their use, at the time of their coming to the empire, shall be free, as also the merchandise introduced by each family, to the amount of two thousand dollars.

§ 282. *Foreigners Considered as Naturalized.*—Art. 27. All foreigners who come to establish themselves in the empire shall be considered as naturalized, should they exercise any useful profession or industry by which, at the end of three years, they have a capital to support themselves with decency, and are married. Those who, with the foregoing qualifications, marry Mexicans will acquire particular merit for the obtaining letters of citizenship.

§ 283. *Letters of Citizenship.*—Art. 28. Congress will grant letters of citizenship to those who solicit them in conformity with the constitution of the empire.

§ 284. *Every Person may Sell and Leave the Country.*—Art. 29. Every person shall be free to leave the empire, and can alienate the lands over which he may have acquired the right of property, agreeably to the tenor of this law, and he can likewise take away from the country all his property, by paying the duties established by law.

§ 285. *Modification of Slavery.*—Art. 30. After the publication of this law there can be no sale or purchase of slaves which may be introduced into the empire. The children of slaves born in the empire shall be free at fourteen years of age.

§ 286. *Foreigners with Prior Rights.*—Art. 31. All foreigners who may have established themselves in any of the provinces of the empire, under a permission of the former government, will remain on the lands which they may have occupied, being governed by the tenor of this law in the distribution of said lands.

§ 287. *Executive may Sell or Lease.*—Art. 32. The executive, as it may deem necessary, will sell or lease the lands which, on account of their situation, may be the most important, being governed with respect to all others by the provisions of this law.

This law shall be presented to his imperial majesty for his sanction, publication, and fulfillment. Mexico, January 3, 1823, third of the independence of the empire. Juan Francisco, bishop of Durango, president. Antonio de Mier, member and secretary. Juan Bautista de Arispe, member and secretary. Therefore we order all tribunals, judges, chiefs, governors, and all other authorities, as well civil as military and ecclesiastical, of whatever class or dignity they may be, to comply with this decree, and cause it to be complied with in all its parts; and you will cause it to be printed, published, and circulated. Given in Mexico, January 4, 1823. Signed by the emperor. To Don José Manuel de Herrera, minister of interior and exterior relations.

*Decree of April* 6, 1830.—The vice-president of the Mexican United States to the inhabitants of the republic, know ye: that the general congress has decreed as follows:

§ 288. *Importation of Cotton Goods.*—Art. 1. The entry of those descriptions of cotton goods prohibited by the law of the twenty-second of May last shall be permitted in the ports of the republic generally, until the last of June, 1831.

§ 289. *Application of Duties.*—Art. 2. The duties arising from the importation of such goods shall be appropriated to maintaining the indivisibility of the Mexican territory, to the formation of a fund of reserve, to be used in case of a Spanish invasion, and to the encouragement of national industry.

§ 290. *Commissioners to Visit Colonies.*—Art. 3. The government shall appoint one or more commissioners whose duty it shall be to visit the colonies of the frontier states; to contract with the legislatures of said states for the purchase by the nation of lands suitable for the establishment of new colonies of Mexicans and foreigners; to enter into such arrangements as they may deem proper for the security of the republic, with the colonies already established; to watch over the exact compliance of the contracts on the entrance of new co'onists; and to investigate how far the contracts already made have been complied with.

§ 291. *Right of Eminent Domain.*—Art. 4. The executive is empowered to take possession of such lands as may be suitable for fortifications and arsenals, and for the new colonies, indemnifying the state in which such lands are situated, by a deduction from the debt due by such state to the federation.

§ 292. *Convicts may be Sent to Colonies.*—Art. 5. The government may cause such number of the convicts destined for Vera Cruz and other places, as it may deem proper, to be conducted to the colonies it may establish, paying at the same time the expense of removal of such families as may desire to accompany them.

§ 293. *Employment of Convicts.*—Art. 6. The said convicts shall be employed in the construction of the fortifications, public buildings, and roads, which the respective commissioner may judge necessary; and every convict who, at the expiration of his term of service, shall desire to become a colonist shall receive a grant of land, and shall be furnished with implements of husbandry and a subsistence during one year.

§ 294. *Mexican Families.*—Art. 7. Mexican families who may voluntarily desire to become colonists shall be conveyed free of expense, subsisted during the first year, and receive a grant of land and the necessary implements of husbandry.

§ 295. *Federal and State Laws to be Obeyed.*—Art. 8. The individuals spoken of in the anterior articles shall conform to the laws of colonization of the federation, and the state in which they are settled.

§ 296. *Entry of Foreigners on Northern Frontier Prohibited.* Art. 9. The entrance of foreigners by the frontier of the north, under any pretense whatsoever, is prohibited, unless furnished with a passport, signed by an agent of the republic in the country from which the individual may come.

§ 297. *No Change in Colonies Established.*—Art. 10. No change will be made with respect to the colonies already established, nor with respect to the slaves which they now contain; but the general government, and that of each particular state, shall exact, under the strictest responsibilities, the observance of the colonization laws, and the prevention of the further introduction of slaves.

§ 298. *Foreigners from Adjacent Countries.*—Art. 11. In exercise of the right reserved to the general congress, by the seventh article of the law of the eighteenth of August, 1824, the citizens of foreign countries lying adjacent to the Mexican territory are prohibited from settling as colonists in the states or territories of the republic adjoining such countries. These contracts of colonization, the terms of which are opposed to the present article, and which are not yet complied with, shall consequently be suspended.

§ 299. *Foreign Coasting Vessels.*—Art. 12. For and during the term of four years, the coasting trade shall be free to foreign vessels for transportation of produce of the colonies to the ports of Matamoras, Tampico, and Vera Cruz.

§ 300. *Houses and Provisions Free of Duty at Matagorda and Galveston.*—Art. 13. For and during the term of two years, the introduction of frame houses and of every kind of foreign provisions shall be admitted into the ports of Galveston and Matagorda free of duty.

§ 301. *Expenditures for Building and Transportation.*—Art. 14. The government is authorized to expend in the construction of fortifications and public buildings on the frontier, in the transportation of convicts and Mexican families to the new colonies, in the subsistence of such during one year, in implements of husbandry, transportation of troops, and premiums to agriculturists who may distinguish themselves among the colonists, and for the general purposes contemplated by the foregoing articles, the sum of five hundred thousand dollars.

§ 302. *Loan for the Government.*—Art. 15. For the purpose of raising promptly one half of the said sum, the government is authorized to negotiate a loan, payable from the duties received on coarse cotton goods, at the rate of three per cent per month, to be paid at the term fixed by the arancel.

§ 303. *Cotton Factories.*—Art. 16. The twentieth part of the above-mentioned duties shall be employed to encourage cotton manufactories by purchasing machines and looms, by furnishing small sums to aid in their establishment, and by such other means as the government may deem most advisable; apportioning the aid among the states where this branch of industry exists. This appropriation shall be placed at the disposition of the minister of relations, to be applied to the above-stated interesting objects.

§ 304. *Reservation of Funds.*—Art. 17. Out of the produce of said duties shall also be reserved three hundred thousand dollars for the formation of a fund, to be deposited in the treasury, under the most strict responsibility of the government that it shall not be touched except in case of a Spanish invasion.

§ 305. *Regulations for New Colonies.*—Art. 18. The government shall form a system for the regulation of the new colonies, and shall, within one year, lay before congress an account of the colonies established under this law, and a statement of the increase of the new settlement on the frontiers. José Dominguez, president of the chamber of deputies. Miguel Duque de Estrada, president of the senate. Juan Vicente Campos, deputy secretary. Rafael Delgado, secretary of the senate. Wherefore I command it to be printed, published, and circulated, and fulfilled. Palace of the federal government, Mexico, April 6, 1830. Anstacio Bustamente. To D. Lucas Alaman.

§ 306. *Decree of November 25, 1833—Article 11 of Prior Law Repealed.*—Art. 1. The eleventh article of the law of the sixth of April, 1830, is repealed in all its parts.

§ 307. *Expenditure of Funds.*—Art. 2. The government is authorized to expend the sums necessary in the colonization of the territories of the confederation, and other vacant places which it has the right to colonize.

§ 308. *Discretion of Government.*—Art. 3. The government is also authorized, with respect to lands subject to colonization, to adopt such measures as they may consider conducive to the security, advancement, and stability of the colonies which shall be established.

§ 309. *Repeal in Article* 1 *Takes Effect in Six Months.*—Art. 4. The repeal spoken of in the first article of this decree shall not take effect until the expiration of six months after its publication.

§ 310. *Fortresses.*—Art. 5. In the authority conceded by the second article is comprehended that of raising fortresses at those points on the frontiers where the executive may think them useful and expedient.

§ 311. *Circular of February* 4, 1834, *of the Secretary of Relations, in Relation to the Colonization of Coahuila and Texas—Reasons for the Circular.*—The vice-president of the Mexican United States, in the exercise of the supreme executive power, availing himself of the authority conferred upon him by the law of the sixth of April, 1830, and impressed with the necessity of relieving a multitude of persons whose condition has been and now is most unfortunate by reason of political errors, the paralyzation of trade, the destruction of fortunes, and all those evils which attend a state in a condition of constant revolution, as has been the state of this republic for many years, it has resulted in the opening of the coffers of the public in order to repair as far as possible a state of things so deplorable. The territories situated adjoining the dividing line of our republic, all crossed by navigable rivers, situated immediately on the Atlantic Ocean, open to commerce, unexhausted by cultivation and fruitful in the extreme, and inviting the robust arms of the Mexican to all kinds of employment which can nowhere else be so well rewarded and the same facilities afforded as within their limits. No other measures are necessary to effect the colonization of those beautiful and fruitful territories but the incipient advances for the enterprise, and the supreme government have the disposition and power to make them. The public funds should not be wasted; but neither should the necessary means be niggardly applied, nor those affected be withheld, anticipating on proper occasions the means of bringing into action the industry of the nation, until their accumulated means shall place the colonists in a position not only of supplying for themselves the bare necessaries of life, but to form for themselves a capital by which to extend their operations and to reproduce continually the product of agricultural industry, the true source of wealth, and that upon which alone new communities can rely. The republic finds itself infested by families which, in one mode or another, from this or that cause, have lost their fortune and their peace; all such the supreme government invites to better their condition in the peaceful pursuits of agriculture; this will restore their estates, improve their fortunes, cause them to forget their errors and wanderings, and convert into useful citizens a multitude of persons whom the pressure of circumstances has widely separated from the existing communities, and the imperious necessity of living which could not be satisfied by lawful means has ranked with the class of criminals. The vice-president is sincerely desirous of attaining this happy result, but he can not omit adopting the precautions to secure it by avoiding the result that the transport of the colonists shall possess no other character than that of a costly journey. If they are to abandon their land shortly after their arrival, and if they are to do nothing to render it productive by their labor, and confine themselves to consuming the appropriations made for the sacred purpose of supplying their want of capital, the object is entirely frustrated, and the republic, instead of recovering its erring citizens, only loses its funds, and increases its wants by an enterprise which instead of securing exposes to greater risks the integrity of its territory. At no period has it been so important to provide for the security of the frontiers, and to give employment to the innumerable hands which by the most sad fatality are found unemployed. To objects so beneficent and salutary has the attention of the government been directed, and he believes that the following provisions are not unlikely to secure them:

§ 312. *Who may Colonize.*—1. Every person who is free and not under local engagements in other parts of the republic shall be admitted to colonize the lands which are or may be at the disposition of the supreme government in the state of Coahuila and Texas.

§ 313. *Officers and Soldiers.*—2. This invitation is most particularly given to the officers and soldiers who have been thrown out of employment from having taken part in the present revolution, to those who are under obligation for debts due to the government, to those expelled from the states, and to those who already remain with arms in their hands.

§ 314. *A Tenth Sitio to a Family.*—3. To each family which shall engage to colonize in said state there shall be given a tenth part of a sitio de ganado mayor.

§ 315. *Transportation.*—4. To every person more than fifteen years of age, the expense of cattle or carts necessary for transportation shall be borne by the government, and they shall become the property of such persons at the moment of arriving at the sitio where they intend colonizing.

§ 316. *Persons over Fifteen.*—5. Each of the persons aforesaid past the age of fifteen years shall be assisted from the day of his departure from the place of his residence to the end of a year, by receiving four reales daily, and to those less than fifteen years of age two reales.

§ 317. *Persons must Remain Two Years.*—6. No person shall separate from the colony before the expiration of two years without the permission of the government, and those who do so shall lose the land which had been given to them, and continue bound to pay whatever may have been received from the government.

§ 318. *Supply of Stock and Tools.*—7. To each of the families comprising the colonies shall be given a yoke of cattle and a cow, or their value, two plows, and such carpentering and farming tools as the government shall consider necessary.

§ 319. *Building Lots.*—8. From the land which is appropriated for a village there shall be given to each family a building lot on which to erect a house as his own dwelling.

§ 320. *Transportation.*—9. Transportation shall be conducted under the direction of the person or persons whom the government shall select.

§ 321. *Political Government.*—10. The colonies shall be subject to such political regulations as the government shall direct, and when they shall have distributed their house-lots, they shall establish a municipal government. Published by a decree, on the sixth instant. In the declaration circulated by the secretary of the treasury of the eleventh of April of this year, and published by decree of the thirteenth, the tenth article is published in the following terms: "The colonies shall be subject to such political ruler or rulers as the government shall designate; and when they shall have distributed their house-lots, they shall establish a municipal government in conformity with the laws of the same."

§ 322. *Law of April* 24, 1835, *in Relation to the Decree of the Legislature of Coahuila and Texas, and the Unoccupied Lands of Those States—Sales under Texas Law Void.*—1. The decree of the legislature of Coahuila and Texas, of the fourth of March of the present year, is contrary in its first and second articles to the law of the eighteenth of August, 1824; consequently the alienations of property made in pursuance of said decree are void, and of no effect.

§ 323. *States Prohibited from Selling.*—2. In the exercise of the power which is reserved to the general congress in the seventh article of said law of the eighteenth of August, 1824, the states on the frontiers and on the coast are prohibited from alienating their vacant lands for colonization until the regulations proper to be observed therein shall be established.

§ 324. *States must Obtain Federal Consent to Sell.*—3. If any one of those states desire to alienate any portion of their vacant lands, they can not do so without the previous approbation of the general government; said government in every case shall be preferred, if they see fit to take it, and shall give to the state the corresponding indemnification.

§ 325. *General Government may Purchase from Coahuila and Texas.*—4. The general government may, in accordance with the third and fourth articles of the law of the sixth of April, 1830, purchase of the state of Coahuila and Texas the amount of four hundred sitios which it says it is under the necessity of selling. Circulated by the secretary of relations on said twenty-fifth of April, and published by edict on the second of the following May.

§ 326. *Law of Coahuila and Texas.*—The decree cited in article 1 of the foregoing law is as follows: "Supreme government of the free state of Coahuila and Texas. The provisional governor of the state of Coahuila and Texas, in the exercise of supreme executive power, to all the inhabitants thereof. Know ye: That the congress of said state have decreed as follows: The constitutional congress of the free, sovereign, and independent state of Coahuila and Texas have thought proper to decree: 1. The government may dispose to the extent of four hundred sitios of land, of the vacant lands of the state, in order to meet the urgent wants of the public, which are actually existing. 2. The colonization of said lands shall be regulated on the bases and conditions which may be considered expedient, without being subject to the provisions of the law of the twenty-sixth of March of last year. 3. The government will direct the measures necessary for the collection of the amounts due the state, whatever their sources and origin. The provisional constitutional governor will cause the same to be complied with, and to be printed, published, and circulated. José Antonio Tejerina, president. Andres de la Viesca y Montes, deputy secretary. Diego, grand deputy secretary. Monclava, March 14, 1835."

*Law of the Fourth of April*, 1837, *Providing for Rendering Effective the Colonization of the Lands Which are or should be the Property of the Republic.*—All directions heretofore issued in relation to colonization, so far as they are contrary to this law, are repealed. (See decree of the supreme government of the twelfth of the present month.)

§ 327. *Colonization to be Made Effective.*—The government, with the consent of the council, will proceed to give effect to the colonization of the lands which are or should be the property of the republic, by means of sale, enfiteusis, or mortgage, applying the amount (which for the best lands should not be less than ten reales per acre) to the redemption of the national debt, contracted or to be contracted, reserving always a sufficient amount in order to fulfill the promise to the troops who aided in achieving the independence, and for the rewards and grants decreed by congress in favor of the native tribes or nations, and of those aiding in the restoration of Texas; not being hindered by the laws heretofore passed in relation to colonization, the provisions of which, so far as they are contrary to this law, are repealed—the prohibition of the eleventh article of the law of the sixth of April, 1830, being renewed.

*Decree of April* 12, 1837.—Decree of the supreme government, in virtue of the authority conferred by the law of the fourth instant. Creation of a national consolidated stock, at an interest of five per cent per annum, for the express purpose of converting the entire foreign debt, and redeeming the same on the terms expressed.

§ 328. *Funding of the National Debt.*—1. A consolidated national stock, with interest at five per cent per annum, is hereby created for the sole and determinate object of converting the entire foreign debt, if the existing creditors consent, and for the redemption of the same in the manner expressed in the following articles. For this purpose Messrs. F. de Lizardy & Co. are appointed as agents for the republic in said transaction, and are authorized in the name of the Mexican nation to issue accordingly the bonds of said consolidated national stock in pounds sterling, payable in London on the first of October, 1866, with coupons for interest in the margin, payable every six months, and running to the aforesaid date. These bonds shall also be viséed by the minister plenipotentiary of the republic at London, or by the person acting in his stead.

§ 329. *Holders of Bonds.*—2. The holders of the bonds of the foreign debt in circulation (the proceeds of the two loans negotiated in London at five and six per cent interest) may convert the same, together with the interest coupons overdue, into bonds of the new consolidated stock on the following conditions: 1. That the bonds of five per cent interest shall be received in exchange cent per cent; 2. That those of six per cent interest shall be at the rate of a hundred and twelve and a half for a hundred; 3. That the over-due coupons of interest of both loans shall be exchanged cent per cent; 4. That they shall receive in payment of the sums which they desire to convert one half of the amount in bonds of the consolidated stock at five per cent interest, and the other half in public land scrip in the departments of Texas, Chihuahua, New Mexico, Sonora, and the Californias, at the rate of four acres per pound sterling; and this scrip shall also bear interest at five per cent to the day on which the owners are placed in possession of the lands, increasing thereby proportionally the amount of property acquired, and security shall be given by those interested that they will be present to take possession within the period designated in article 5.

§ 330. *Payment of Interest.*—3. The interest on the bonds of the national consolidated stock shall be payable in London, at intervals of six months on the first days of April and October of each year, commencing on the first of October of the present year, 1837. In the mean time and until arrangements are made for remitting periodically the funds destined to this object, the holders of the interest coupons which become due shall have the right to present them. to the agents of the republic in London on the day of their maturity, and to require of them in exchange for such coupons a certificate of their value, viséed in like manner by the minister of the republic at said court; and these shall be received on presentation as ready money in payment of a sixth part of the duties collected at the maritime custom-houses of Vera Cruz and Santa Anna de Tamaulipas. The agents of the republic in London shall not consequently be at liberty to refuse to give such certificates when thereto requested by the holders of the unpaid coupons. In such case the value of each pound sterling shall be computed at the rate of five dollars, and the amount of each certificate shall be increased six per cent, in full compensation for difference of exchange and all expenses, including in such six per cent one per cent, which the persons interested shall pay on receiving the certificates to the agents, one fourth part of which they shall relinquish in favor of the minister plenipotentary of the republic.

§ 331.—4. The public land scrip shall in like manner be issued in the name of the Mexican nation by the agents aforesaid, and shall be viséed by the diplomatic agent accredited at London, the tenor of which shall be as follows: "To all whom these present shall come—Know ye, that the Mexican nation acknowledges that [the name], or his representative, is the proprietor of [the number] acres of land in the department [the place], of which he shall be placed in immediate and full possession by competent authority, with the aid of the public surveyor, and on the delivery of this scrip. Dated at London [the day of the year]." No scrip shall be issued for less than four hundred acres nor for more than ten thousand. Those interested shall pay to the agents, on receiving their scrip, at the rate of twelve reales for every hundred acres, and of these three reales shall belong to the minister that visées them.

§ 332. *Land Passes by Indorsement of Scrip.*—5. The property of the land scrip may pass from person to person by indorsement; but after taking possession of the land of which the scrip gives the right, and receiving a new title, the same can not be transferred to another person except in virtue of a public instrument of sale.

§ 333. *Presentation of Scrip.*—6. It is necessary that the scrip should be presented when the same is to be redeemed by the delivery of lands at the office of the secretary of the several departmental goverments, in order that he may make a list of them as presented (obtaining a book for that purpose), with the view of giving to those interested a preference in the selection of land according to the order of presentation. For the same purpose, shall be delivered to them a certificate, in which shall appear the number and place entered in the scrip, in order that it may be presented to the local authorities, and thus, with the aid of the surveyor of the department, will give to them possession of the land which they select, taking care, without fail, to observe the eleventh article of the law of the sixth of April, 1830, which declares: "In the exercise of the authority reserved to the general congress in the seventh article of the law of the eighteenth of August, 1824, the colonization of foreigners of adjacent countries is prohibited in those states and territories which adjoin such foreign nations; consequently, contracts which are opposed to this law shall be suspended."

§ 334. *Land Pledged.*—7. For the greater security of the payment of the principal and interest of this consolidated stock, the Mexican goverment, in the name of the nation, specially pledges one hundred millions of acres of public land in the departments of the Californias, Chihuahua, New Mexico, Sornora, and Texas, as a special guaranty of said stock until the total extinction of said debts; but if any sale shall be made of said lands so pledged, it shall be at least at the rate of four acres to the pound, and the proceeds shall be paid by the purchaser to the government agents in London, from whom alone can he receive the corresponding scrip, and they shall use the product of the sale in the redemption of the bonds of the new consolidated stock, which also may be received in payment for said lands at the price said bonds bear in market.

§ 335. *Change of Securities.*—8. The proper period for making the application for the change of securities treated of in article 2 of this decree will be from the day on which the appropriate notice is published in London by the agents of the republic till the corresponding day of the following year; when this period shall have passed, no further opportunity shall be afforded for such change.

§ 336. *Land Scrip may be Taken in Exchange for Bonds.*—9. During said period, and until the thirty-first day of December, 1839, the holders of the bonds of the consolidated stock shall have the right, either on receiving them from the agents or at any other time, for the purpose of extinguishing the same, to take in exchange public land scrip for the amount, with ten per cent premium added to the same, at the rate as aforesaid, of four acres to the pound sterling; but if this be not done before the first of January, 1840, although the right will be at all times recognized of extinguishing these bonds by receiving scrip in like manner with ten per cent premium, there shall not be granted to them more than three acres to the pound sterling.

§ 337. *Rights of Foreigners Who Sold Scrip.*—10. Finally, those foreigners who, in virtue of the scrip which they hold, come to the republic and establish themselves in their new estates shall acquire from that moment the title of colonists, and they and their families shall enjoy all the rights and advantages which are or may be granted by law to all naturalized foreigners, and on the same conditions; but it shall not be allowed that there be held by a single person or the owner more than a league square of five thousand varas of regadio, four of superficie temporal, and six leagues of surperficie de abrevadero;

and the usufruct of the mines which are found in said lands shall be subject to the provisions of the general mining ordinances. (Circulated on the same day by the department of the treasury, and published by edict on the seventeenth of May following.)

§ 338. *Decree of November* 27, 1846, *Relative to the Board of Colonization—Reasons for This Decree.*—Department of the interior and foreign relations. His excellency the general charged with the supreme power has been pleased to send me the following decree: José Mariano de Salas, general charged with the executive power of the Mexican United States, to the inhabitants of the republic, know ye: That being authorized by the plan proclaimed in the citadel on the fourth of August last to dictate all the measures which the security of the republic may demand, and considering that one of the most necessary and urgent is that of promoting foreign immigration in order to people our immense lands which are at this time the object of foreign cupidity; that for this purpose it is indispensable to establish the board of colonization heretofore decreed, so that it may labor with zeal and industry in the rapid increase of the population, upon which great benefits will depend; that the economy of the treasury is now more than ever necessary, and requires that the aforesaid board be established in the office of industry, which junction does not in any other view present any inconvenience—I have thought proper to decree as follows:

§ 339. *Establishment of the Board according to Law of June* 1, 1839.—1. In conformity with the provision in the sixteenth article of the regulations issued for the execution of the law of the first of June, 1839, the board of colonization is established under the immediate consent of the department of relations.

§ 340. *Board of Three Persons.*—2. This board shall be composed, as provided in the foregoing regulations, of three persons, appointed by the supreme government.

§ 341. *Location and Duty of the Board.*—3. In order to save expense, the board of colonization shall be established in the office of industry, and shall exercise the functions and attributes thereof. In regard to colonization, it shall promote the same effectually by all means possible, consulting the government with respect to those involving expenses which its funds may not meet, and endeavoring to combine the rapid increase of population with the revenue coming to the treasury from the sales it shall make of the public lands. It shall also exercise the faculties given to it by the aforesaid regulation of the first of June, 1839, and those which shall be specified in the one it shall draw up and present for the approval of the government.

§ 342. *Funds Assigned the Board.*—4. The board of colonization and industry shall have the funds assigned to the board of this name in the decree of the second of October, 1843, the five per cent from the sales of lands belonging to the confederation, and the proceeds of the prohibited goods confiscated, which shall be sold, but which can not be passed through the country by permits, but consumed in the precise place of sale; or the twenty per cent of the duties which these goods shall give rise to, on their importation, should it be hereafter permitted.

Wherefore I order the same to be printed, published, circulated, and carried into full effect. Palace of the general government. José Mariano de Salas. To Don José Maria Lafragua. And I inclose it to you for your information. God and liberty. Mexico, November 27, 1846. Lafragua.

*Decree of December 4, 1846—Regulations Governing Colonization.*—His excellency the general charged with the supreme executive power has been pleased to transmit to me the following decree: José Mariano de Salas, general of brigade, charged with supreme executive power of the Mexican United States, to the inhabitants of the republic. Know ye:

§ 343. *Reasons for This Decree.*—That being constantly desirous of rendering available the benefits which the system of colonization ought to produce in the republic, and considering that the decree issued on the twenty-seventh of last month, which established the direction of the branch, will not produce all the effects which ought to be anticipated if its powers are not at once detailed; keeping in view the project in which these are proposed, presented by the same direction which has been so diligently and efficaciously engaged in drawing up the same from the moment of entering upon its duties, in compliance with the provisions in article 3 of the aforesaid decree of the twenty-seventh of last month, and whilst the congress, taking into consideration the initiative which the government has consented to make, is digesting the principal bases on which will depend the advancement of colonization—I have thought proper to decree the following regulations:

§ 344. *Substitutes.*—1. In order that the direction of colonization may not suspend its labors from accidental impediments to its members, three substitutes shall be appointed who shall be called upon in the order of their appointment whenever any disability or absence of any of the members shall occur.

§ 345. *Disability of the President.*—2. In case of the absence or disability of the president, who shall always be the first named, the second shall discharge his duties; and in case of his absence or disability, the third shall do so.

§ 346. *Decision of a Majority Necessary.*—3. In order to have concord in the direction, the concurrence of a majority of the members and the joint vote of two shall be sufficient.

§ 347. *Term of Office.*—4. The proprietary members and substitutes of the direction shall remain four years in the exercise of their functions.

§ 348. *Duty of the President.*—5. The president shall have in his charge the correspondence and the whole management of the office.

§ 349. *Clerks.*—6. The appointment of clerks in the office appertains to the board, with the approbation of the government; the provisions of the eleventh article of the decree organizing the direction of industry, of the second of December, 1842, governing in regard to the perpetuity of these employments.

§ 350. *Plats of Lands.*—7. The direction of colonization shall use particular diligence in having plats drawn of the lands of the republic which may be colonized, and in collecting the *data* which are filed in the archives, in order to know whatever may be of importance for the better direction of the business relating to colonization; procuring information and reports of the kind of land, of their waters, mountains, mineral and salt regions, and also of the climate and production of the said lands.

§ 351. *Surveys of the Lands.*—8. The same direction shall appoint competent persons, who shall without any delay make surveys of the public lands which either now or hereafter may belong to the confederation, it being understood by such public lands those lands which are not the property of individuals, societies, or corporations; and if hereafter it be thought proper, it may appoint a surveyor general, by commission, to reside in that capital, who may revise the plats and surveys. In these duties and others it may employ, by commission, the retiring and withdrawing clerks, and those who are in actual service.

§ 352. *Oath of Surveyors.*—9. These surveyors shall take an oath before the direction or the authority whom it may intrust therewith, to faithfully execute the surveys. Those employed in carrying the chains in the said surveys shall take an oath before the surveyors. The direction shall have power to remove these to save expense, from failure to perform their duties, and to appoint others in their stead when their positions become vacant from illness, death, or resignation.

§ 353. *Surveyors to Obey Orders.*—10. The surveyors shall work and proceed in their surveys in entire conformity with the orders they may receive from the direction.

§ 354. *Surveys, how Made* —11. The surveys shall be made by sitios, which shall be squares of six miles of one thousand six hundred and sixty-six and two-thirds Mexican varas per side, or eighteen thousand nine hundred and forty-eight and six one hundredths acres. The lines to form the squares shall be drawn due north and south, one to each mile. Upon these lines shall be drawn others from east to west, at the same distance of one mile from each other, forming perfect squares by right angles; so that each square shall be one mile square.

§ 355. *Division of Land.*—12. This division must not fail to be made in the surveys, save when physical and legal obstacles prevent it; that is to say, when natural obstructions or the ownership of lands in contact do not permit; but then the surveyors shall always endeavor, so far as possible, to make the surveys in squares.

§ 356. *Service of Surveyors in Person.*—13. The surveyors shall assist in person in drawing the first and last lines from north to south and from west to east, and all those lines which on account of the surface of the land are necessarily irregular.

§ 357. *Lines, how Drawn—Water, Mineral, etc., to be Noted.*—14. The lines must be drawn with a straight iron rope or chain, and exactly copied or drawn in the plat which must be made. By notes on the same plat, the streams of water which may be in the land will be indicated, their courses to be drawn in the places through which they pass, and their capacity estimated. Mention shall also be made of the lakes, pools, mountains, mineral regions, salt regions, and others, the climate of the locality, and the apparent character of the soil, and everything else which may give an idea of the improvements of which they may be susceptible.

§ 358. *Division of Sitios Numbered.*—15. The squares into which a sitio is divided will be numbered on the plat, beginning with No. 1.

§ 359. *Squares of a Mile—Lot No. 16 to Remain Unsold.*—16. Each square of one mile square will make a lot of five hundred and twenty-six and thirty-three and one-half hundredths acres. The lot No. 16 shall always remain unsold for the public uses to which the government may think proper to appropriate it.

§ 360. *Responsibility of Surveyors.*—17. The surveyors, being responsible for the correctness of the surveys, will take the greatest care to execute them well, and in the variations of the compass will state and note the true meridian.

§ 361. *Salaries of Surveyors.*—18. The surveyors shall have the salary which they shall agree for with the direction.

§ 362. *Payment of Salaries may be Advanced.*—19. The same direction may advance to the surveyors under bond the amounts which in its discretion they may require, and at the end of each year it shall settle them and pay what they have earned, or they shall return what they may not have earned of the previous advances, if they should not continue.

§ 363. *Plats to be Filed.*—20. With this intent, and in order that the drawn plats may be on file in the office of the direction, the surveyors shall transmit them thereto, retaining copies.

§ 364. *Mines Reserved.*—21. The confederation reserves to itself the mines discovered and to be discovered in the public lands, which were not known at the time the lands may have been alienated.

§ 365. *Sixth of the Land Reserved.*—22. It will also reserve the sixth part of the lands which may be surveyed at the disposal of the war department for military rewards, and the portion necessary in the judgment of the direction to make a capital for the salaries of the persons employed who may desire to retire from the service; this capital being made by giving them in value a quantity of land which invested at five per cent will produce the amount of the annual salary they receive.

§ 366. *Price of Lands.*—23. The price of each acre of land for the present, and so long as the direction of colonization does not propose any modification, and the government does not decree in conformity therewith, shall be at least four reales, except in Lower California, where it shall not exceed two reales per acre. The price of the public lands shall be hereafter increased by the government on the proposition of the direction, where their situation, the improvements which may be given them, and other circumstances render them peculiarly valuable.

§ 367. *Adjacent Owners to be Summoned.*—24. The surveyors when they survey lands lying alongside of private property, or surrounded thereby, shall summon the parties interested in said property to concur therein, and exhibit their titles. In case of any dispute, the survey shall be made, considering as public land what the surveyor may judge to be such, and the business shall be referred to the respective district court for its judicial decision. Connivance or corruption between the proprietors and the surveyors shall be reputed as a fraud on the public treasury, and the latter shall be tried as such defrauders, for the sole fact of not reporting to the direction of colonization, without delay, the public lands which they may discover occupied without a right thereto at the time of making the surveys. Those who report those lands which may be possessed without right by individuals, companies, or corporations, shall be rewarded with twenty-five per cent of their value, on the sale of the land by the direction, in the funds in which the price of the sale may be paid, or in the land itself if it can be conveniently divided, in the opinion of the said direction, with the obligation of cultivating and settling it.

§ 368. *Landmarks.*—25. All surveyed lands shall remain with the landmarks used by the surveyors, or marked by permanent bounds, of which mention shall be made in the plats.

§ 369. *Plats Open to Inspection.*—26. The plats of the surveyed lands shall be open for inspection in the office of the direction of colonization, and in those of its agents in the states and territories where sales of the land are to take place.

§ 370. *Sales.*—27. These sales shall take place in the office of the direction of colonization, and by the agents and commissioners thereof in the states and territories; they shall be conformable with the regulations of this decree, and with those which may be received from the said direction of the branch.

§ 371. *Sales Made at Public Auction.*—28. The said sales shall be made at public auction, to the highest bidder, under the following rules:

§ 372. *Notice of Sale.*—1. As soon as the direction receives the plat of a portion of land, it shall publish in the newspapers the announcement of its sale three months beforehand, specifying the place where it will take place; and if it is to be effected by its agents, the latter will also advertise the same at least one month beforehand.

§ 373. *Method of Sale.*—2. On the specified day, the land will be put up at auction at the price and on the conditions established by this decree. That situation will be held as the best in which the introduction of the greatest number of families may be secured in a given period. The shortest period for this introduction will be considered the best; and in default of bidding upon this basis, the best bid offered, with proposals for ready money and those with cash, will be accepted.

§ 374. *Payments.*—3. Payment will be made with twenty per cent in money, which will be payable in four installments, one at once, and the three others in the twelve months ensuing, one installment every four months. The remainder shall be paid within two years counted from the day of sale or auction, in money or in credits against the treasury, of the internal or external debt, which may be in the course of payment, and which may cause revenue.

§ 375. *Contracts of Sale.*—29. As a general rule, in all contracts of sale the purchaser shall bind himself to settle the land he purchases with at least two families, of five individuals each, per square mile, within the space of two years counted from the date of the sale or purchase.

§ 376. *Bidder to Receive Title.*—30. To the person with whom the bidding shall close, which being once accomplished can not be reopened, shall be issued the corresponding evidence of title by the direction of the branch.

§ 377. *Bill of Sale.*—31. Each bill of sale shall be signed by the board, and shall be recorded in the general treasury of the confederation.

§ 378. *No Fees to be Paid.*—32. Neither for the auction nor for the issue of the title of ownership shall any fees be incurred. The purchasers shall pay no more than the cost of the stamped paper upon which the title is written out, which shall in all cases be of the third seal, and two dollars to the office in which the auction may take place.

§ 379. *Sales Suspended.*—33. When on the day specified for the auction of a portion of land no bidders appear, the sale shall be suspended until a purchaser shall present himself, to whom the sale shall be made.

§ 380. *Monthly Notice of Unsold Land.*—34. The direction of colonization shall announce every month in the newspapers of this capital the sale of the lands which have remained over unsold, from there not having been any bidder on the day specified for the auction.

§ 381. *Contracts for New Colonies.*—35. The same direction shall have power to make contracts with individuals or companies for the formation of new colonies upon the following bases:

§ 382. *Who may not be Colonists.*—1. That none of the colonists who may be introduced therein shall be a subject or native of or come from a nation whose territory lies contiguous to the lands which are to be granted, nor of a power with which the republic may be at war, save in the cases in which the government may make exceptions for special reasons and motives.

§ 383. *Slaves not Permitted.*—2. That in the colonies at no time shall slavery be permitted.

§ 384. *Default of Surveyors.*—3. That the plats of the surveys of the lands made by a competent person in its confidence shall be produced to the direction, which person in case of default herein shall be liable to the penalties laid down in article 23, within a period specified thereby, which shall not exceed two years, and that if the survey should have been already made, the cost thereof shall be paid.

§ 385. *Prices how Paid.*—4. That the price of the public lands shall be realized in annunities, or secured by credits in course of payment, which may cause revenue, on paying twenty per cent in money. The said price shall be fixed by the government on the proposition of the direction, according to the localities, and shall not be less than the half of that fixed in article 23.

§ 386. *Families Introduced in a Certain Period.*—5. That the number of families agreed upon with the direction shall be introduced within a determined period.

§ 387. *Default of Conditions.*—6. That the grants of land and payments made shall be forfeited in default of any of the foregoing conditions.

§ 388. *Contracts of Settlement.*—36. These contracts for new settlements shall be made at public auction, the right being granted for the same price to those who may have made the first proposals, unless from the nature of these and the circumstances of the case, this requisite in the opinion of the direction can not be proceeded with.

§ 389. *Banks—Highways.*—37. The direction shall also have power, with the approbation of the government, to contract for the establishment of banks for the colonization of large territories, and for the opening and constructing of highways for the colonies, with the pledge of the value of the public lands. In this case the government shall fix the price of the lands, and this shall be paid with the bills which the bank may issue. Its creation shall be fixed upon the bases contained in the decree of the twenty-fifth of October, 1842, the government signifying in each case the effective capital with which it is to be provided, the amount of bills it may issue, the time of their duration, and that of the redemption of the bills.

§ 390. *What Lands to be Granted.*—38. The lands which may be granted for new settlements shall be: 1. The public lands belonging to the confederation; 2. Those which the owners may cede for the purpose by agreements with the direction of the branch; 3. Those of ownership acquired by grants from the government, or by any other title, which remain uncultivated and unsettled, and which the direction may qualify as being open to colonization. With regard to these lands, the same direction shall require from their owners to cultivate and settle them, specifying to them a limited period, which shall not exceed five years; and if within that time they be not cultivated or settled at the rate of ten persons per square mile, it shall propose to them to put them up for sale to be colonized. If they do not consent thereto, the direction shall apply to the government, laying before it the case and the reasons for its opinion that the sale should take place, and if the government consider them well founded, it shall decree the occupation of the lands in the manner prescribed in the third paragraph of article 112 of the federal constitution.

§ 391. *Distributation of Land by Contractors.*—39. The contractors (empresarios) for colonization shall distribute the lands among the colonists, conformably with the contracts they may have made with them, saving the obligation of the recognition of the annuity upon the part upon which the price is not paid in ready money, which annuity the colonists will pay in proportion to the lands they may occupy.

§ 392. *Enforcement of Contracts.*—40. The judges and authorities of the republic shall enforce the fulfillment of said contracts on petition from the party interested.

§ 393. *Foreigners Become Citizens.*—41. The new foreign settlers shall be considered as citizens of the republic from their arrival in the colony, conformably with the decree of the tenth of September last.

§ 394. *Privileges of Contractors.*—42. The contractors (empresarios) for new settlements shall have, according to the decree of the third of October, 1843, a direct intervention in everything relating to the management of the colony and its primary organization in regard to the administrative and judicial branches, the laws of the republic will be observed, with the exceptions and privileges in favor of new settlements.

§ 395. *Spanish Language Used in Writings.*—43. All the public acts and documents of the colonies shall be written in the Spanish language.

§ 396. *Exemptions of Settlers.*—44. In conformity with the decrees of the twenty-fifth of October, 1842, and the fifth of November of the present year, the new settlements shall enjoy the following exemptions: 1. Exemption from active military service for twenty years, except in case of foreign aggression. 2. Exemption from all tax except municipal for the same term of twenty years. 3. Exemption from all duty for ten years after the colonies may be established, upon all articles of subsistence, clothing, furniture, and other articles useful in the construction and furnishing of houses, which may be imported into the colonies. These effects shall be conveyed to the colonies with proper precautions, in order to prevent their being carried to other places, and they can not be shipped from the colonies in the way of commerce without falling under the penalty of confiscation. 4. That of free importation, without payment of duties, of implements of art and agriculture, of books and printed matter, for twenty years, and for the same period no exaction will be imposed upon the country or town estates. 5. That of tonnage duty upon the vessels which may convey at least ten families of new settlers, or which may come fully laden with articles destined for the colonies.

§ 397. *Establishment of Military Colonies.*—45. Military colonies shall also be established, composed of Mexicans and of foreigners, or of both, on the coasts and frontiers where the government may indicate, especially for preventing the inroads of the savages; and in them shall be granted to the colonists, *gratis*, the lands which the direction of colonization may, with the approval of the government, designate for that purpose.

§ 398. *Classes of Persons in Military Colonies.*—46. The following classes shall appertain to the military colonies: 1. Retired and invalid soldiers of the republic, who may apply therefor. 2. Those who may be permitted by legal grant, and those who may desire to invest their savings in lands and settlements in order to cultivate them. 3. Mexican and foreign peasantry to whom the direction of colonization may grant the same. 4. Those who in future may be forcibly transported thither through the provisions of the laws. For the individuals of the military colonies the expense of their conveyance thither will be borne, and they will be furnished with a place of residence, implements and tools for labor or for the trades they may follow, and the means upon which to subsist during the first year.

§ 399. *Privileges of Military Colonies* —47. The military colonies shall have the same privileges as the other colonies, and shall be governed like those which are not military; but all the individuals who can bear arms shall be organized into companies and corps, it being the duty of the government to provide them with arms, ammunition, and everything requisite for the service. The government, upon a report from the direction of colonization, shall draw up the regulations for the instruction of and service which these militia are to perform, the pay they are to receive when in active service, and whatever else may concern these settlements in carrying out this object without withdrawing them from their domestic occupations.

§ 400. *Military Colony of Foreigners.*—48. A military colony composed wholly of foreigners can not be established unless contiguous to another composed of Mexicans or of other foreigners of various countries.

§ 401. *Schools and Doctors.*—49. The direction of colonization will make application for parishes to be erected in the military colonies, and shall establish in each of them a primary school and a medical practitioner.

§ 402. *Establishment of Missions.*—50. The same direction shall take the necessary steps for the founding of missions in the colonies nearest to the savage tribes, and shall propose to the government the means of sustaining and increasing them, and of encouraging those already existing.

§ 403. *Agents and Commissioners.*—51. The direction of colonization shall appoint agents, commissioners, or auxiliary boards in the states and territories, whose labors in the business of colonization shall be executed under the instruction of the same direction.

§ 404. *Agents in Foreign Countries.*—52. It shall also have power to appoint agents in foreign countries who may promote colonization, and enter into communication with the ministers and consuls of the republic, for the trust it may think proper to confide to them.

§ 405. *Frontiers—Navigation of Rivers.*—53. With the *data* which it shall collect together, the direction of colonization shall submit to the government the means of marking the boundaries of the lands on the frontiers of the republic, and whatever may concern the internal navigation of the rivers. Colonization of the frontiers shall not take place without the express approbation of the government, at less than twenty leagues from the boundaries of the republic, nor less than ten from the coasts, conformably with article 4 of the law of the thirteenth of August, 1844.

§ 406. *Registers of Lands—Record of Revenue of Lands, Measures.*—54. The office of the direction shall keep clear and methodical registers of all the public lands, of the titles of transfers which it may issue in consequence of sales at auction or by contracts, and of the documents of grants of lands where the issues of the title remain pending upon the surveys. It shall also keep the judicial record of the revenue which may arise from the amount of the price of the lands, and shall draw up a table showing the report of the measures which up to this time have been issued by the surveyors, with the measures of the acre and of the mile.

§ 407. *Reports of the Direction.*—55. The direction shall submit to the government everything which may have relation to the better administration and government of the new settlements; it shall report against the abuses which may be committed therein; and in order that they may be effective, shall report the guaranties and exemptions conceded to the colonists.

§ 408. *Powers of the Direction.*—56. The direction, as far as concerns the branches of the agricultural and manufacturing industry of the colonies, the district and the territory of the confederation, and as far as may be within the province of the general government in the states, shall exercise the following powers: 1. It shall be the organ of communication between the assemblages of manufacturing or agricultural industry of the colonies, and of the district and territories of the confederation and the supreme government, and through its channel all petitions or memorials which may be made to the government relative to matters appertaining to agriculture and the arts shall be conveyed to it, the direction expressing its opinion upon the same. 2. It shall enter into correspondence with the boards (juntas) of agriculture or industry of the states, in relation to the designs. 3. It shall make to the government such reports as may be desired in relation to matters of the same industry. 4. It shall have in its charge the formation of industrial statistics. 5. It shall promote the advancement of agriculture and the arts, by all proper means, and especially by premiums for industrial inventions, and improvements in cultivation, in vegetables, and breeding of animals, and by the establishment of schools of arts and agriculture, and the publication of instructive works. 6. It shall take cognizance of all the records of applications for patents for the invention, perfection, or introduction of new processes in industry, and in its archives shall be deposited the models and specifications presented by those who obtain patents, and it shall publish both, when the inventions become public property. 7. It shall take care that public exhibitions at stated periods shall be made in the capital of the republic of the national agricultural and manufacturing products. 8. It shall put into operation as early as possible the establishment of the schools of arts and of agriculture, which are placed under the inspection and care of the direction of industry, taking care immediately of the funds destined for said establishment.

§ 409. *Books—Rules to be Observed.*—57. In the treasury of the direction shall be kept a set of books, with the formalities which shall be decreed, on the recommendation of the board, and the following rules shall henceforth be observed: 1. No payment shall be made which shall not be decreed by law, without an order from the president, and without the assent of the board, and the further approval of the government, in the cases where the law expressly demands the same. 2. Every month there shall be a settlement of accounts, and a general settlement at the close of the fiscal year. 3. The treasury account shall be settled on the thirtieth of June of each year, and shall be presented before the month of November, together with a statement which shall comprehend the condition of the branch in charge of the direction, in which shall be exhibited the present state of colonization, and that of industry, their progress, or the causes of their backwardness, if such be the case, with an indication of what ought to be done to remedy the same, in order that the government, taking the whole into consideration, may on its part dictate such measures as may be within its functions, and may call the attention of congress at its next following session to what may be requisite from the legislative power.

Wherefore I order that the same be printed, published, circulated, and carried into full effect. Palace of the federal government of Mexico. José Mariano de Salas. To Don José Maria Lafragua. And I communicate it to you for its fulfillment. God and liberty. Mexico, December 4, 1846. Lafragua.

§ 410. *Colonization Law of the State of Coahuila and Texas, March* 24, 1825.—The governor provisionally appointed by the sovereign congress of this state. To all whom these presents may come, know ye: That the said congress have decreed: Decree No. 16. The constituent congress of the free, independent, and sovereign state of Coahuila and Texas, desiring by every possible means to augment the population of its territory, promote the cultivation of its fertile lands, the raising and multiplication of stock, and the progress of the arts and commerce; and being governed by the constitutional act, the federal constitution, and the basis established by the national decree of the general congress, No. 72, have thought proper to decree the following law of colonization:

§ 411. *Privileges of Foreigners.*—Art. 1. All foreigners who in virtue of the general law of the eighteenth of August, 1824, which guarantees the security of their persons and property in the territory of the Mexican nation, wish to remove to any of the settlements of the state of Coahuila and Texas are at liberty to do so; and the said state invites and calls them.

§ 412. *Further Privileges of Foreigners.*—Art. 2. Those who do so, instead of being incommoded, shall be admitted by the local authorities of said settlements, who shall freely permit them to pursue any branch of industry that they may think proper, provided they respect the general laws of the nation and those of the state.

§ 413. *Declaration to be Made by Foreigners.*—Art. 3. Any foreigner already in the limits of the state of Coahuila and Texas who wishes to settle himself in it shall make a declaration to that effect, before the ayuntamiento of the place which he selects as his residence. The ayuntamiento in such case shall administer to him the oath, which he must take, to obey the federal and state constitutions, and observe the religion which the former prescribes. The name of the person and his family, if he has any, shall then be registered in a book kept for that purpose, with a statement of where he was born, and whence from, his age, whether married, occupation, and that he has taken the oath prescribed, and considering him from that time, and not before, as domiciliated.

§ 414. *Foreigners may Solicit Land.*—Art. 4. From the day on which any foreigner has been enrolled as an inhabitant, in conformity with the foregoing article, he is at liberty to designate any vacant land, and the respective political authority will grant it to him in the same manner as to a native of the country, in conformity with the existing laws of the nation, under the condition that the proceedings shall be passed to the government for its approbation.

§ 415. *Foreigners may Form New Towns.*—Art. 5. Foreigners of any nation, or a native of any of the Mexican states, can project the formation of new towns on any lands entirely vacant, or even on those of an individual, in the case mentioned in article 35; but the new settlers who present themselves for admission must prove their Christianity, morality, and good habits by a certificate from the authorities where they formerly resided.

§ 416. *Regulations for Certain Foreigners.*—Art. 6. Foreigners who immigrate at the time in which the general sovereign congress may have prohibited their entrance for the purpose of colonizing, as they have the power to do after the year 1840, or previous to that time as respects those of any particular nation, shall not then be admitted; and those who apply in proper time shall always subject themselves to such precautionary measures of national security which the supreme government, without prejudicing the object of this law, may think proper to adopt relative to them.

§ 417. *Settlements within Twenty Leagues of North Frontier and Ten from the Coast Prohibited.*—Art. 7. The government shall take care that within the twenty leagues bordering on the limits of the United States of the north, and ten leagues in a straight line from the coast of the Gulf of Mexico, within the limits of this state, there shall be no other settlements except such as merit the approbation of the supreme government of the Union, for which object all petitions on the subject, whether made by Mexicans or foreigners, shall be passed to the superior government, accompanied by a corresponding report.

§ 418. *Projects for New Settlements.*—Art. 8. The projects for new settlements, in which one or more persons offer to bring at their expense one hundred or more families, shall be presented to the government, and if found conformable with this law they will be admitted; and the government will immediately designate to the contractors the land where they are to establish themselves, and the term of six years, within which they must present the number of families they contracted for, under the penalty of losing the rights and privileges offered in their favor in proportion to the number of families which they fail to introduce, and the contract totally annulled if they do not bring at least one hundred families.

§ 419. *Contractors Guaranteed.*—Art. 9. Contracts made by the contractors or undertakers (empresarios), with the families brought at their expense, are guaranteed by this law so far as they are conformable with its provisions.

§ 420. *Distribution of Lands.*—Art. 10. In the distribution of lands, a preference shall be given to the military entitled to them, by the diplomas issued by the supreme executive power, and to Mexican citizens who are not military, among whom there shall be no other distinction than that founded on their individual merit, or services performed for the country, or in equal circumstances, a residence in the place where the land may be situated; the quantity of land which may be granted is designated in the following articles.

§ 421. *Sitio.*—Art. 11. A square of land, which on each side has one league or five thousand varas, or what is the same thing, a superfice of twenty-five million varas, shall be called a sitio, and this shall be the unity for counting one, two, or more sitios; and also the unity for counting one, two, or more labores shall be one million square varas, or one thousand on each side, which shall compose a labor. The vara for this measurement shall be three geometrical feet.

§ 422. *Distinction of Lands—Premiums.*—Art. 12. Taking the above unity as a basis, and observing the distinction which must be made between grazing land, or that which is proper for raising of stock, and farming land, without the facility of irrigation; but they can only receive this premium for eight hundred families, although a greater number should be introduced, and no fraction whatever less than one hundred shall entitle them to any premium, not even proportionally.

§ 423. *Excess over Eleven Leagues.*—Art. 13. Should any contractor or contractors, in virtue of the number of families which he may have introduced, acquire, in conformity with the last article, more than eleven square leagues of land, it shall nevertheless be granted, but subject to the condition of alienating the excess within twelve years, and if it is not done, the respective political authority shall do it, by selling it at public auction, and delivering the proceeds to the owners, after deducting the costs of sale.

§ 424. *Amount of Land to One Family.*—Art. 14. To each family comprehended in a contract, whose sole occupation is cultivation of land, one labor shall be given; should he also be a stock raiser, grazing land shall be added to complete a sitio, and should his only occupation be raising of stock, he shall only receive a superfice of grazing land equal to twenty-four million square varas.

§ 425. *Effect of Marriage.*—Art. 15. Unmarried men shall receive the same quantity when they enter the matrimonial state, and foreigners who marry native Mexicans shall receive one fourth more; those who are entirely single, or who do not form a part of some family, whether foreigners or natives, shall content themselves with the fourth part of the above-mentioned quantity, which is all that can be given them until they marry.

§ 426. *Removing to New Towns.*—Art. 16. Families or unmarried men, who, entirely of their own accord, have immigrated, and may wish to unite themselves to any new towns, can at all times do so, and the same quantity of land shall be assigned them which is mentioned in the two last articles; but if they do so within the first six years from the establishment of the settlement, one labor more shall be given to families; and single men, in place of the quarter designated in the fifteenth article, shall have the third part.

§ 427. *Government may Increase the Amount of Land Given.* Art. 17. It appertains to the government to augment the quantity indicated in articles 14, 15, and 16, in proportion to the family industry and activity of the colonists, agreeably to the information given on these subjects by the ayuntamientos and commissioners; the said government always observing the provisions of article 12 of the decree of the general congress on the subject.

§ 428. *Immigrants to Present Themselves to the Authorities.* Art. 18. The families who immigrate in conformity with article 6 shall immediately present themselves to the political authority of the place which they may have chosen for their residence, who, finding in them the requisites prescribed by this law for new settlers, shall admit them and put them in possession of the corresponding lands, and shall immediately give an account thereof to the government, who of themselves, or by means of a person commissioned to that effect, will issue them a title.

§ 429. *Indians Traffic Free of Duty.*—Art. 19. The Indians of all nations bordering on the state, as well as wandering tribes that may be within its limits, shall be received in the markets, without paying any duty for commerce, in the products of the country; and if attracted by the moderation and confidence with which they shall be treated, any of them, after having first declared themselves in favor of our religion and institutions, wish to establish themselves in any settlements that are forming, they shall be admitted, and the same quantity of land given them as to the settlers spoken of in articles 14 and 15, preferring native Indians to strangers.

§ 430. *Lands—How Laid Off.*—Art. 20. In order that there may be no vacancies between tracts, of which great care shall be taken in the distribution of lands, it shall be laid off in squares, or other forms, although irregular, if the local situation requires it; and in said distribution as well as in the assignation of lands for new towns, previous notice shall be given to the adjoining proprietors, if any, in order to prevent dissensions and law-suits.

§ 431. *Errors in Concessions Rectified.*—Art. 21. If by error in the concession any land shall be granted belonging to another, on proof being made of that fact, an equal quantity shall be granted elsewhere to the person who may have thus obtained it for any improvements he may have made; the just value of which improvements shall be ascertained by appraisers.

§ 432. *Price of Lands.*—Art. 22. The new settlers, as an acknowledgment, shall pay to the state for each sitio of pasture land thirty dollars; two dollars and one half for each labor without the facility of irrigation, and three dollars and a half for each one that can be irrigated, and so on proportionally, according to the quantity and quality of the land distributed; but the said payments need not be made until six years after the settlement, and by thirds; the first within four years, the second within five years, and the last within six years, under the penalty of losing the land for a failure in any of said payments; are excepted from this payment, the contractors and the military spoken of in the tenth article; the former with respect to lands given them as a premium, and the latter for those which they obtained in conformity with their diplomas.

§ 433. *Collection of Funds by Ayuntamientos.*—Art. 23. The ayuntamiento of each municipality (comarca) shall collect the above mentioned funds, *gratis*, by means of a committee appointed either within or without the body, and shall remit them as they are collected to the treasurer of their funds, who will give the corresponding receipt, and without any other compensation than two and one half per cent, all that shall be allowed him, he shall hold them at the disposition of the government, rendering an account every month of the ingress and egress and of any remissness or fraud which he may observe in their collection; for the correct management of all which the person employed and the committee, and the individuals of the ayuntamientos who appoint them, shall be individually responsible; and that this responsibility may be at all times effectual, the said appointments shall be made *viva voce*, and information shall be given thereof immediately to the government.

§ 434. *Eleven Leagues Only to be Granted.*—Art. 24. The government will sell to Mexicans, and to them only, such lands as they may wish to purchase, taking care that there shall not be accumulated in the same hands more than eleven sitios; and under the condition that the purchaser must cultivate what he acquires of this title, within six years from its acquisition, under the penalty of losing them; the price of each sitio, subject to the foregoing condition, shall be one hundred dollars if it be pasture land; one hundred and fifty dollars if it can be irrigated.

§ 435. *This Law not to be Changed for Six Years.*—Art. 25. Until six years after the publication of this law, the legislature of this state can not alter it as regards the acknowledgment and price to be paid for land, or as regards the quantity and quality to be distributed to the new settlers or sold to Mexicans.

§ 436. *Rights of Settlers Lost.*—Art. 26. The new settlers who, within six years from the date of the possession, have not cultivated or occupied the lands granted to them, according to its quality, shall be considered to have renounced them, and the respective political authority shall immediately proceed to take possession of them, and recall the titles.

§ 437. *When Alienation of Lands can be Made.*—Art. 27. The contractors and the military heretofore spoken of, and those who by purchase have acquired lands, can alienate them at any time, but the successor is obliged to cultivate them in the same time that the original proprietor was bound to do; the other settlers can alienate theirs when they have totally cultivated them, and not before.

§ 438. *Disposition by Will.*—Art. 28. By testamentary will made in conformity with the existing laws, or those which may govern in future, any new colonist, from the day of his settlement, may dispose of his land, although he may not have cultivated it, and if he dies intestate, his property shall be inherited by the person or persons entitled by the laws to it; the heirs being subject to the same obligation and condition imposed on the original grantee.

§ 439. *Not to be Held in Mortmain.*—Art. 29. Lands acquired by virtue of this law shall not by any title whatever pass into mortmain.

§ 440. *Settlers may Leave the State on Conditions.*—Art. 30. The new settler who, wishing to establish himself in a foreign country, resolves to leave the territory of the state, can do so freely with all his property; but after leaving the state he shall not any longer hold the land, and if he had not previously sold it, or the sale should not be in conformity with the twenty-seventh article, it shall become entirely vacant.

§ 441. *Naturalization, how Made.*—Art. 31. Foreigners who in conformity with this law have obtained land and established themselves in any new settlement shall be considered from that moment naturalized in the country; and by marrying a Mexican, they acquire a particular merit to obtain letters of citizenship of the state, subject, however, to the provisions which may be made relative to both particulars in the constitution of the state.

§ 442. *Free from Taxes Ten Years.*—Art. 32. During the first ten years, counting from the day on which the new settlements may have been established, they shall be free from all contributions, of whatever denomination, with the exception of those which in case of invasion by an enemy, or to prevent it, are generally imposed, and all the produce of agriculture or industry of the new settlers shall be free from excise duty (alcabala), or other duties, throughout every part of the state, with the exception of the duties referred to in the next article; after the termination of that time the new settlements shall be on the same footing, as to taxes, with the old ones, and the colonists shall also in this particular be on the same footing with the other inhabitants of the state.

§ 443. *Settlers may Follow Any Industry, and Work Mines.*—Art. 33. From the day of their settlement the new colonists shall be at liberty to follow any branch of industry, and can also work mines of every description, communicating with the supreme government of the confederation relative to the general revenue appertaining to it, and subjecting themselves in all other particulars to the ordinances or taxes established or which may be established on this branch.

§ 444. *Most Suitable Sites to be Founded.*—Art. 34. Towns shall be founded on the sites deemed most suitable by the government or the person commissioned for this purpose, and for each one there shall be designated four square leagues, the area of which may be in a regular or irregular form, agreeable to the situation.

§ 445. *Private Lands may be Appropriated.*—Art. 35. If any of the said sites should be the property of an individual, and the establishment of new towns on them should notoriously be of general utility, they can notwithstanding be appropriated to this object, previously indemnifying the owner for its just value, to be determined by appraisers.

§ 446. *Building Lots Free.*—Art. 36. Building lots in the new towns shall be given *gratis* to the contractors of them, and also to artists of every class, as many as are necessary for the establishment of their trade; and to the other settlers they shall be sold at public auction, after having been previously valued, under the obligation to pay the purchase money by installments of one third each; the first in six months, the second in twelve months, and the third in eighteen months; but all owners of lots, including contractors and artists, shall annually pay one dollar for each lot, which, together with the produce of the sales, shall be collected by the ayuntamientos, and applied to the building of churches in said towns.

§ 447. *Natives and Foreigners to Settle Together.*—Art. 37. So far as is practicable, the towns shall be composed of natives and foreigners, and in their delineations great care shall be taken to lay off the streets straight, giving them a direction from north to south and from east to west, when the site will permit it.

§ 448. *Survey of Towns.*—Art. 38. For the better location of the said new towns, their regular formation and exact partition of their lands and lots, the government, on account of having admitted any project, and agreeing with the contractor or contractors who may have presented it, shall commission a person of intelligence and confidence, giving him such particular instructions as may be deemed necessary and expedient; and authorizing him, under his own responsibility, to appoint one or more surveyors to lay off the town scientifically, and to do whatever else may be required.

§ 449. *Fees, how Fixed.*—Art. 39. The governor, in conformity with the last fee bill (arancel) of notaries public of the ancient audiencia of Mexico, shall designate the fees of the commissioner, who, in conjunction with the colonists, shall fix the surveyor's fees; but both shall be paid by the colonists and in the manner which all parties among themselves may agree upon.

§ 450. *Forty Families Sufficient for a Settlement.*—Art. 40. As soon as at least forty families are united in one place they shall proceed to the formal establishment of the new town, and all of them shall take an oath to support the general and state constitutions; which oath will be administered by the commissioner. They shall then in his presence proceed for the first time to the election of their municipal authorities.

§ 451. *Ayuntamientos to be Elected.*—Art. 41. A new town,

whose inhabitants shall not be less than two hundred, shall elect an ayuntamiento, provided there is not another one established within eight leagues, in which case it shall be added to it. The number of individuals which are to compose the ayuntamiento shall be regulated by the existing laws.

§ 452. *Elective Franchise of Foreigners.*—Art. 42. Foreigners are eligible, subject to the provisions which the constitution of the state may prescribe, to elect the members of their municipal authorities, and to be elected to the same.

§ 453. *Provisions for Expenses.*—Art. 43. The municipal expenses and all others which may be necessary or of common utility to the new towns shall be proposed to the governor by the ayuntamientos through the political chief, accompanied with a plan of the taxes (arbitrios) which in their opinion may be just and best calculated to raise them, and should the proposed plan be approved by the governor, he shall order it to be executed, subject, however, to the resolution of the legislature, to which it shall be immediately passed with his report and that of the political chief, who will say whatever occurs to him on the subject.

§ 454. *Public Works and Highways.*—Art. 44. For the opening and improving of roads and other public works in Texas, the government will transmit to the chief of that department the individuals who in other parts of the state may have been sentenced to public works as vagrants or for other crimes; these same persons may be employed by individuals for competent wages, and as soon as the time of their condemnation is expired, they can unite themselves as colonists to any new settlement, and obtain the corresponding lands, if their reformation shall have made them worthy of such favor in the opinion of the chief of the department, without whose certificate they shall not be admitted.

§ 455. *Church Pastors.*—Art. 45. The government, in accord with the respective ordinary ecclesiastics, will take care to provide the new settlements with the competent number of pastors; and in accord with the same authority, shall propose to the legislature for its approbation the salary which the said pastors are to receive, which shall be paid by the new settlers.

§ 456. *Slaves.*—Art. 46. The new settlers, as regards the introduction of slaves, shall subject themselves to the existing laws, and those which may hereafter be established on the subject.

§ 457. *Petitions Now Pending.*—Art. 47. The petitions now

pending relative to the subject of this law shall be dispatched in conformity with it, and for this purpose they shall be passed to the governor; and the families who may be established within the limits of the state without having any land assigned them shall subject themselves to this law, and to the orders of the supreme government of the Union, with respect to those who are within twenty leagues of the limits of the United States of America, and ten leagues in a straight line of the coast of the Gulf of Mexico.

§ 458. *Publication of this Law.*—Art. 48. This law shall be published in all the villages of the state, and that it may reach the notice of all others throughout the Mexican confederation, it shall be communicated to their respective legislatures by the secretary of this state; and the governor will take particular care to send a certified copy of it, in compliance with the one hundred and sixty-first article of the federal constitution, to the two houses of congress and the supreme executive power of the nation, with a request to the latter to give it a general circulation through foreign states by means of our ambassadors.

The governor *pro tem.* of the state will cause it to be published and circulated. Saltillo, March 24, 1825. (Signed) Rafael Ramos y Valdez, president. Juan Vicente Campos, member and secretary. José Joaquin Arce Rosales, member and secretary. Therefore I command all authorities, as well civil as military and ecclesiastical, to obey and cause to be obeyed the present decree in all its parts. Rafael Gonzales, governor.

*Instructions to the Commissioners Appointed by the Legislature of the State.*—Executive department of the state of Coahuila and Texas. Instructions by which the commissioner shall be governed, in the partition of lands to the new colonists who may establish themselves in the state, in conformity with the colonization law of the twenty-fourth of March, 1825.

§ 459. *Duty of Commissioners.*—Art. 1. It shall be the duty of the commissioner, keeping in view the contract which an empresario may have entered into with the government, and also the certificates or recommendations which foreign immigrants must produce from the local authorities of the place where they removed from, accrediting their Christianity, morality, and steady habits, in conformity with the fifth article of said law; without which requisite they shall not be admitted to the colony.

§ 460. *Opinion of Empresario, when Required.*—Art. 2. In order to prevent being imposed upon by false recommendations, the commissioners shall not consider any as sufficient, without a previous opinion in writing as to their legitimacy from the empresario, for which purpose they shall be passed to him by the commissioner.

§ 461. *Oath of Colonists.*—Art. 3. The commissioner shall administer to each of the new colonists the oath in form, to observe the federal constitution of the United Mexican States, the constitution of the state, the general laws of the nation, and those of the state which they have adopted for their country.

§ 462. *Titles.*—Art. 4. He shall issue in the name of the state the titles for land, in conformity with the law, and put the new colonists in possession of their lands with all legal formalities, and the previous citation of adjoining proprietors, should there be any.

§ 463. *When Possession not Given.*—Art. 5. He shall not give possession to colonists who may have established, or who may wish to establish themselves within twenty leagues of the United States of the north, or within ten leagues of the coast, unless it should appear that the supreme government of the nation had approved thereof.

§ 464. *Vacant Spaces not Allowed.*—Art. 6. He shall take care that no vacant lands be left between possessions, and in order that the lines of each one may be clearly designated, he shall compel the colonists, within the term of one year, to mark their lines, and to establish fixed and permanent corners.

§ 465. *Scientific Surveys.*—Art. 7. He shall appoint, under his own responsibility, the surveyor, who must survey the land scientifically, requiring him previously to take an oath truly and faithfully to discharge the duties of his office.

§ 466. *Record of Titles.*—Art. 8. He shall form a manuscript book of paper of the third stamp, in which shall be written the titles of the lands distributed to the colonists, specifying the names, the boundaries, and other requisites and legal circumstances; and a certified copy of each title shall be taken from said book on paper of the second stamp, which shall be delivered to the interested party as his title.

§ 467. *Stamp Paper.*—Art. 9. Each settler shall pay the value of the stamp paper used in issuing his title, both for the original and copy.

§ 468. *Book of Records, where Kept.*—Art. 10. This book shall be preserved in the archives of the new colony, and an exact form of it shall be transmitted to the government, specifying the number of colonists, with their names, and the quantity of land granted to each one, distinguishing that which is farming land, with or without the facilities of irrigation, and that which is granted as grazing land.

§ 469. *Selection of Town Sites.*—Art. 11. He shall select the site which may be the most suitable for the establishment of the town or towns, which are to be founded agreeably to the number of families composing the colony, and keeping in view the provisions of the law of colonizations on this subject.

§ 470. *Base Lines, and Plan.*—Art. 12. After selecting the site destined for the new town, he shall take care that the base lines run north and south, east and west, and he will designate a public square, one hundred and twenty varas on each side, exclusive of the streets, which shall be called the principal or constitutional square; and this shall be the central point from which the streets shall run, for the formation of squares and blocks in conformity with the model hereto annexed.

§ 471. *Ecclesiastical and Public Buildings, etc.*—Art. 13. The block situated on the east side of the principal square shall be destined for the church, curate's house, and other ecclesiastical buildings. The block on the west side shall be designated for public buildings of the municipality. In some other suitable situation a block shall be designated for a market square, another for a jail and house of correction, another for a school and other edifices for public instruction, and another beyond the limits of the town for a burial-ground.

§ 472. *Streets.*—Art. 14. He shall, on his responsibility, cause the streets to be laid off straight, and that they are twenty varas wide, to promote the health of the town.

§ 473. *Mechanics' Privileges.*—Art. 15. Mechanics, who at the time of founding a new town, present themselves to settle it, shall have the right of receiving one lot apiece, without any other cost than the necessary stamp paper for issuing the title and the light tax of one dollar annually for the construction of the church.

§ 474. *Lots, how Distributed.*—Art. 16. The lots spoken of in the preceding article shall be distributed by lot, with the exception of the empresario, who shall be entitled to any two lots he may select.

§ 475. *Lots, how Appraised.*—Art. 17. The other lots shall be valued by appraisers according to their situation, and sold to the other colonists at their appraised value. In case there should be a number of applicants for the same lot, owing to its situation or other circumstances which may excite competition, it shall be decided by lot as prescribed in the preceding article;

the product of said lots shall be appropriated to the building of a church in said town.

§ 476. *Improvement of Towns.*—Art. 18. He shall, in union with the empresario, promote the settlement of each town by the inhabitants belonging to its jurisdiction, who take lots in it, and cause them to construct houses on said lots within a limited time, under the penalty of forfeiting them.

§ 477. *Record of Titles.*—Art. 19. He shall form a manuscript book of each new town, in which shall be written the titles of the lots which are given as a donation, or sold, specifying the boundaries and other necessary circumstances, a certified copy of each one of which on the corresponding stamp shall be delivered to the interested party as his title.

§ 478. *Topographical Plan.*—Art. 20. He shall form a topographical plan of each town that may be founded, and transmit to the government, keeping a copy of it in the said register book of the colony.

§ 479. *Ferries.*—Art. 21. He shall see that at the crossing of each of the rivers on the public roads where a town is founded a ferry is established at the cost of the inhabitants of said town; a moderate rate of ferriage shall be established to pay the salary of the ferrymen and the cost of the necessary boats, and the balance shall be applied to the public funds of the towns.

§ 480. *Ferries not in Towns.*—Art. 22. In places where there are no towns, and where ferries are necessary, the colonists who may be settled there shall be charged with the establishment of the ferry, collecting a moderate ferriage until such ferries are rented out for the use of the state. Any colonist who wishes to establish a ferry on the terms above indicated shall form an exact and certified account of the costs which he may be at for the building of boats, and also an account of the produce of the ferry, in order that when said ferry is rented out for the use of the state he shall have a right to receive the amount of said expenses which had not already been covered by the produce of the ferry, which for the present he will collect.

§ 481. *Elections.*—Art. 23. He shall preside at the popular elections mentioned in the fortieth article of the colonization law, for the election of the ayuntamiento, and shall put the elected parties in possession of their offices.

§ 482. *Surveys must be Accurate*—Art. 24. He shall take special care that the portions of land granted to the colonists by articles 14, 15, and 16 shall be measured by the surveyors with accuracy, and not permit any one to include more land than is designated by law, under the penalty of being personally responsible.

§ 483. *Increase of Land, how Obtained.*—Art. 25. Should any colonist solicit, in conformity with article 17 of the law, an increase of land beyond that designated in the preceding articles, on account of the size of his family, industry, or capital, he shall present his petition in writing to the commissioner, stating all the reasons on which he founds his petition, who shall transmit it to the governor of the state, together with his opinion, for which opinion he shall be responsible in the most rigid manner, in order that the governor may decide on the subject.

§ 484. *Spanish Language.*—Art. 26. All the public instruments, titles, or other documents issued by the commissioner shall be written in Spanish; the memorials, decrees, and reports of the colonists or empresarios on any subject whatever shall be written in the same language, whether they are to be transmitted to government or preserved in the archives of the colony.

§ 485. *Two Witnesses.*—Art. 27. All public instruments or titles of possession, and the copies signed by the commissioner, shall be attested by two assistant witnesses.

§ 486. *Reponsibility of Commissioners.*—Art. 28. The commissioner shall be personally responsible for all acts or measures performed by him, contrary to the colonization law or these instructions.

A copy. Saltillo, September 4, 1827. Tijerina, Arciniega, secretaries of the legislature. A copy. Juan Antonio Padilla, secretary of state.

# CHAPTER XIV.

## COLONIZATION.

§ 487. Enumeration of Laws.
§ 488. Decree of August 18, 1824—Security to Persons and Property.
§ 489. National Lands.
§ 490. State Laws.
§ 491. Lands Exempt.
§ 492. Lands for Public Use.
§ 493. Foreigners Exempt from Taxes.
§ 494. Foreigners, Entrance of.
§ 495. Foreigners, Security of Government against.
§ 496. Military Persons.
§ 497. Military Persons, Lands to.
§ 498. Extent of Land Granted.
§ 499. Mortmain.
§ 500. Guaranty of Contracts.
§ 501. Residence Necessary.
§ 502. Proceedings Governed by This Law.
§ 503. Regulations of November 21, 1828—Reasons therefor.
§ 504. Governors to Grant.
§ 505. Petition for Lands.
§ 506. Information by Governors.
§ 507. Grants according to Law.
§ 508. Approval of Departmental Assembly.
§ 509. Report to Supreme Government.
§ 510. Approval by Supreme Government.
§ 511. Title.
§ 512. Records of Petitions and Grants.
§ 513. Twelve Families Requisite.
§ 514. Conditions to be Performed.
§ 515. Proof of Performance.
§ 516. Government of Towns.
§ 517. Minimum of Land to be Given.
§ 518. House-lots.
§ 519. Vacant Spaces, how Distributed.
§ 520. Mission Lands not to be Colonized.
§ 521. Law of March 13, 1861—Foreigners Exempt from Taxes.
§ 522. Foreigners and Foreign Companies Exempt.
§ 523. Other Privileges of Foreigners.
§ 524. Taxes for Two Years not to be Paid.
§ 525. Municipal Funds.
§ 526. Quality of a Foreigner when Exercised.
§ 527. All Persons Subject to the Laws of the Country.
§ 528. Law of May 31, 1875—Executive's Powers.

§ 529. Bases of Contracts to be Made.
§ 530. Guaranties Required.
§ 531. Supplies.
§ 532. Fulfillment of Contracts.
§ 533. Exploring Commissions.
§ 534. Furnishing Public Land.
§ 535. Jurisdiction of Executive.
§ 536. Lands of Private Parties.
§ 537. Colony Lands Adopted for Private Persons.
§ 538. Privileges Cease in Ten Years.
§ 539. Two Hundred and Fifty Thousand Dollars for Expenses.
§ 540. Said Law Repealed December 15, 1883.
§ 541. Order of September 24, 1877—Monumental Ruins.
§ 542. Adjudication of Ruins Null.
§ 543. Authorities Notified.
§ 544. Law of December 15, 1883—Survey of Lands.
§ 545. Two Thousand Five Hundred Hectares to One Person.
§ 546. Foreigners and Natives may Hold Lands—Conditions.
§ 547. Duty of Executive as to Sales.
§ 548. Requisites of Foreign Colonists.
§ 549. Requisites of Resident Colonists.
§ 550. Proof of Character.
§ 551. Exemptions for Ten Years.
§ 552. Free Articles to be Designated.
§ 553. Planting of Trees.
§ 554. Subject to the Laws.
§ 555. Contracts to be Fulfilled.
§ 556. Declaration as to Reservation of Nationality.
§ 557. Laws and Tribunals of the Country.
§ 558. Abandonment.
§ 559. Rights of Founders.
§ 560. Mexican Colonists on Frontiers.
§ 561. Assistance to Colonists.
§ 562. Companies may Settle.
§ 563. Companies must Designate Land They Desire to Settle.
§ 564. District Judges Authorize Surveys.
§ 565. Third of Land Granted to Companies, with Conditions.
§ 566. Balance Ceded to Colonists.
§ 567. Operations to Commence in Three Months.
§ 568. Executive may Make Contracts with Conditions.
§ 569. Franchises and Exemptions.
§ 570. Foreign Companies Considered as Mexicans.
§ 571. Disputes Subject to Mexican Laws and Tribunals.
§ 572. Privileges of Private Persons Who Give Land for Colonization.
§ 573. Colonization of Islands.
§ 574. Executive may Buy Private Lands for Colonization.
§ 575. Prior Laws Repealed.

§ 487. *Enumeration of Laws.*—The general law of colonization which continued in force until the law of May 31, 1875, was that of August 18, 1824, together with regulations of November 21, 1828. In this chapter will be found the following laws, regulations, and order: 1. The law of August 18, 1824, and its regulations of November 21, 1828; 2. The law of March 13, 1861, in relation to foreigners or companies of foreigners who colonize, and their privileges; 3. The law of May 31, 1875, authorizing the executive to enact laws regulating all matters relating to colonization, and to make contracts with private enterprises therefor; 4. The order of September 24, 1877, ordering that lands possessing monumental ruins be preserved; 5. The general colonization law of December 15, 1883, repealing all others on the subject.

*Decree of August* 18, 1824.—The sovereign general constituent congress of the United Mexican States has been pleased to decree:

§ 488. *Security to Persons and Property.*—1. The Mexican nation promises to those foreigners who may come to establish themselves in its territory security in their persons and property, provided they subject themselves to the laws of the country.

§ 489. *National Lands.*—2. The objects of this law are those national lands which are neither private property nor belong to any corporation or town (pueblo), and can therefore be colonized.

§ 490. *State Laws.*—3. To this end the congress of the states will form, as soon as possible, the laws and regulations of colonization of their respective demarkation, with entire conformity to the constitutive act, the general constitution, and the rules established in this law.

§ 491. *Lands Exempt.*—4. Those territories comprised within twenty leagues of the boundaries of any foreign nation, or within ten leagues of the sea coast, can not be colonized without the previous approval of the supreme general executive power.

§ 492. *Land for Public Use.*—5. If for the defense or security of the nation the federal government should find it expedient to make use of any portion of these lands for the purpose of constructing warehouses, arsenals, or other public edifices, it may do so, with the approbation of the general congress, or during its recess with that of the government council.

§ 493. *Foreigners Exempt from Taxes.*—6. Before the expiration of four years after the publication of this law, no tax or duty (derecho) shall be imposed on the entry of the persons of foreigners who come to establish themselves for the first time in the nation.

§ 494. *Entrance of Foreigners.*—7. Previous to the year 1840, the general congress can not prohibit the entry of foreigners to colonize, except compelled to do so with respect to the individuals of some nation, by powerful reasons.

§ 495. *Security of Government respecting Foreigners.*—8. The government, without prejudicing the object of this law, will take the precautionary measures which it may consider necessary for the security of the federation, with respect to the foreigners who may come to colonize. In the distribution of lands, Mexican citizens are to be attended to in preference; and no distinction shall be made amongst these, except such only as is due to private merit and services rendered to the country, or inequality of circumstances, residence in the place to which the lands distributed belong.

§ 496. *Military Persons.*—9. Military persons who are entitled to lands by the promise made on the twenty-seventh of March, 1821, shall be attended to in the states, on producing the diplomas granted to them to that effect by the supreme executive power.

§ 497. *Lands to the Military.*—10. If by the decrees of capitulation, according to the probabilities of life, the supreme executive should see fit to alienate any portion of land in favor of any military or civil officers of the federation, it may so dispose of the vacant lands of the territories.

§ 498. *Extent of Land Granted.*—11. No one person shall be allowed to obtain the ownership of more than one square league of five thousand varas of irrigable land (de regadio); four superficial ones of land dependent on the seasons (de temporal); and six superficial ones for the purpose of rearing cattle (de abrevadero).

§ 499. *Mortmain.*—12. The new colonists can not transfer their possessions in mortmain (manos muertas).

§ 500. *Guaranty of Contracts.*—13. This law guarantees the contracts which the grantees (empresarios) may make with the families which they may bring out at their expense; provided they are not contrary to the laws.

§ 501. *Residence Necessary.*—14. No one who by virtue of this law shall acquire the ownership of lands shall retain them if he shall reside out of the territory of the republic.

§ 502. *Proceedings Governed by This Law.*—15. The government, in conformity with the principles established in this law, will proceed to the colonization of the territories of the republic.

§ 503. *General Rules and Regulations for the Colonization of*

*Territories of the Republic, Mexico, November* 21, 1828—*Reasons for Regulations.*—It being stipulated in the fifteenth article of the general law of colonization of the eighteenth of August, 1824, that the government, in conformity with the principles established in said law, shall proceed to the colonization of the territories of the republic; and it being very desirable, in order to give to said article the most punctual and exact fulfillment, to dictate some general rules for facilitating its execution in such cases as may occur, his excellency has seen fit to determine on the following articles:

§ 504. *Governors to Grant.*—1. The governors (gefes políticos) of the territories are authorized (in compliance with the law of the general congress of the eighteenth of August, 1824, and under the conditions hereafter specified) to grant vacant lands in their respective territories to such contractors (empresarios), families, or private persons, whether Mexicans or foreigners, who may ask for them for the pursose of cultivating and inhabiting them.

§ 505. *Petition.*—2. Every person soliciting lands, whether he be an empresario, head of a family, or private person, shall address to the governor of the respective territory a petition, expressing his name, country, profession, the number, description, religion, and other circumstances of the families or persons with whom he wishes to colonize, describing as distinctly as possible, by means of a map, the land asked for.

§ 506. *Information to be Obtained.*—3. The governor shall proceed immediately to obtain the necessary information whether the petition embraces the requisite conditions required by said law of the eighteenth of August, both as regards the land and the candidate, in order that the petitioner may at once be attended to; or if it be preferred, the respective municipal authority may be consulted, whether there be any objection to making the grant or not.

§ 507. *Grants Made according to Law.*—4. This being done, the governor will accede or not to such petition, in exact conformity with the laws on the subject, and especially to the before-mentioned one of the eighteenth of August, 1824.

§ 508. *Approval of Departmental Assembly.*—5. The grants made to families or private persons shall not be held to be definitely valid without the previous consent of the territorial deputation, to which end the respective documents (expedientes) shall be fowarded to it.

§ 509. *Report to Supreme Government.*—6. When the governor shall not obtain the approbation of the territorial deputation, he shall report to the supreme government, fowarding the necessary documents for its decision.

§ 510. *Approval by Supreme Government.*—7. The grants made to empresarios for them to colonize with many families shall not be held to be definitely valid until the approval of the supreme government be obtained; to which the necessary documents must be forwarded, along with the report of the territorial deputation.

§ 511. *Title.*—8. The definitive grant asked for being made, a document signed by the governor shall be given, to serve as a title to the interested party, wherein it must be stated that said grant is made in exact conformity with the provisions of the laws in virtue whereof possession shall be given.

§ 512. *Records of Petitions and Grants.*—9. The necessary record shall be kept in a book destined for the purpose, of all the petitions presented and grants made, with the maps of the lands granted, and the circumstantial report shall be forwarded quarterly to the supreme government.

§ 513. *Twelve Families Requisite.*—10. No capitulation shall be admitted for a new town, except the capitulator bind himself to present, as colonists, twelve familes at least.

§ 514. *Conditions to be Performed*—11. The governor shall designate to the new colonists a proportionate time within which he shall be bound to cultivate or occupy the land on the terms and with the number of persons or families which he may have capitulated for, it being understood that if he does not comply, the grant of the land shall remain void; nevertheless, the governor may revalidate it in proportion to the part which the party may have fulfilled.

§ 515. *Proof of Performance to be Made.*—12. Every new colonist, after having cultivated or occupied the land agreeably to his capitulation, will take care to prove the same before the municipal authority, in order that, the necessary record being made, he may consolidate and secure his right of ownership, so that he may dispose freely thereof.

§ 516. *Government of Towns.*—13. The reunion of many families into one town shall follow in its formation, interior government, and policy the rules established by the existing laws for the towns of the republic, special care being taken that the new ones are built with all possible regularity.

§ 517. *Minimum of Land to be Given.*—14. The minimum of irrigable land to be given to one person for colonization shall be two hundred varas square; the minimum of land called de temporal shall be eight hundred varas square; and the minimum for breeding cattle (de abrevadero) shall be one thousand two hundred varas square.

§ 518. *House-lots.*—15. The land given for a house-lot shall be one hundred varas.

§ 519. *Vacant Spaces, how Distributed.*—16. The spaces which may remain between the colonized lands may be distributed among the adjoining proprietors who shall have cultivated theirs with the most application, and have not received the whole extent of land allowed by the law, or to the children of said proprietor, who may ask them to combine the possessions of their families; but on this subject particular attention must be paid to the morality and industry of the parties.

§ 520. *Mission Lands not to be Colonized.*—In those territories where there are missions, the lands occupied by them can not be colonized at present, nor until it be determined whether they are to be considered as the property of the establishments of the neophytes, catechumens, and Mexican colonists.

*Law of March* 13, 1861.—Department of state and of public works, colonization, industry, and commerce. Section 4. The citizen Benito Juarez, constitutional president *ad interim* of the Mexican United States, to all the inhabitants thereof, know ye: That in the use of the ample faculties with which I find myself vested, I have thought proper to decree the following:

§ 521. *Foreigners Exempt from Taxes.*—Art. 1. Every foreigner, who for himself or in company with other foreigners buys land for agricultural labor or to establish a rustic estate, shall be excepted for five years, counted from the day on which they signed the deed (escretura publica) of purchase, from all classes of taxes, being obliged only to present the plan and survey of their possession to the minister of public works, without which requisite they can not enjoy the designated favor.

§ 522. *Foreigners and Companies of Foreigners Exempt from Taxes.*—Art. 2. Every foreigner or company of foreigners that purchases land for a colony, they and their colonists, are excepted for ten years, counted from the day on which they signed the deed of purchase, from all classes of taxes, unless they are municipal, which themselves impose; but they must present within a year the plan and survey of their possession to the minister of public works, under penalty of losing the favor conceded in this article.

§ 523. *Other Privileges of Foreigners.*—Art. 3. The foreigners comprehended within the preceding articles shall enjoy for five years more the favors which are conceded to them, provided that on the termination of said term they shall prove that they have on their lands or in their colonies employed a number of Mexicans which is not less than one third of all the workmen or colonists.

§ 524. *Taxes for Two Years not to be Paid.*—Art. 4. They shall not pay during two years any duties of importation nor of internation for the effects which shall be directly consigned for the consumption of the colonies or working of the lands. The effects which are sent out of the colonies or from the lands to circulate in commerce, and which come entirely from Europe, shall fall under the penalty of confiscation.

§ 525. *Municipal Funds.*—Art. 5. The colonies which are formed on the preceding bases, the principal one being that of planning with foreign capital, shall dispose with entire liberty of the municipal funds which they themselves furnish; and the authority will not intervene in the administration, except of those revenues which it designates to them.

§ 526. *Quality of a Foreigner Exercised, when.*—Art. 6. The lands being worked and the colonies thus formed, in what belongs to the fulfillment of the guaranties which are conceded to them by this law, and that of the guaranties which are found assigned in the constitution of the republic, they will enjoy for two years the rights of the quality of a foreigner (extranjeria), according to the nation to which the owner of the rustic estate or the majority of the colonists belong.

§ 527. *All Persons Subject to the Laws of the Country.*—Art. 7. On all points which are not expressly determined in this law, the owners of the estates and the colonists are entirely subject to the laws of the country, the same as on the termination of all and each one of the terms expressed in the preceding articles.

*The Law May* 31, 1875.—Department of public works, colonization, industry, and commerce of the Mexican republic. Section 1. The president of the republic has been pleased to direct to me the decree which follows: Sebastian Lerdo Tejada, constitutional president of the Mexican United States, to the inhabitants thereof, know ye: That the congress of the Union has decreed the following:

§ 528. *Executive Authorized to Regulate Colonization.*—Art. 1. The executive is hereby authorized in the interim to enact a law which shall definitely determine and regulate all that which relates to colonization; he may make it effective by his direct action, and by the means of contracts with private enterprises, upon the following bases:

§ 529. *Bases of Contracts to be Made.*—1. That of granting to the enterprise a subvention for a family established, or another smaller for a family landed in any port; an advancement with equitable interest, up to fifty per cent of said subvention; a sale on long time and at a low price, payable in annual bonds, of colonizable lands, with a previous survey, marking, and valuation; a premium for an immigrant family; exemption from port duties for every embarkation which brings to the republic ten or more families of such a character; a premium for a family of the indigenous race established in the colonies of the immigrants; a premium for a Mexican family established in the colonies of the frontier.

§ 530. *Guaranties Required.*—2. That of requiring from the enterprise sufficient guaranties for the fulfillment of the contracts, without omitting in them the forfeiture and respective fine; security that the colonists shall enjoy, in what on the contractors depend, the privileges which this law concedes.

§ 531. *Supplies.*—3. That of granting to the colonists; Mexican naturalization and citizenship in the case of being naturalized; a supply of the expenses of transportation and of subsistence until two years after being established, of implements of cultivation and of materials of construction for their habitations; an acquisition by sale at a low price, payable on long time by annual bonds, commencing to do it after the termination of the second year of their establishment, of a determined extension of land for cultivation and for a house; exemption from military service and all kinds of taxes except municipal ones; from every kind of importation duties, and interior duties on provisions, instruments for cultivation, tools, machinery, furniture, materials of construction for habitations, house-ware, and working-animals, breeding-animals, or blooded animals destined for the colonies, and also personal exemption and intransmissible of the duties of exportation on the products which they harvest; free transportation of their mail matter with their native country or their former residence, through the channel of the department of relations, or by the means of special seals; premiums and special protection for the introduction of a new cultivation or industry.

§ 532. *Fulfillment of Contracts.*—4. That of requiring from the colonists the fulfillment of their contracts in conformity with the common laws.

§ 533. *Exploring Commissions.*—5. That of appointing and putting into action the exploring commissions authorized by section 26 of the appropriation in force in order to obtain colonizable lands, with the requisites which they must have of measure, demarkation, value, and description.

§ 534. *Furnishing Public Land.*—6. That of furnishing a tract of public land, with the requisites which the preceding fraction requires, and that he who fulfills these requisites shall obtain the third part of said land or of its value, provided that he shall do it with due authorization.

§ 535. *Jurisdiction of Executive.*—7. That of this, it shall be of the exclusive jurisdiction of the said executive, who can not deny it to a state which claims it, in respect to a tract of land situated in its territory, remaining without effect and without the right of prorogation, the authorizations which are granted to the states and to private individuals, when after being obtained three months, the corresponding operations have not been undertaken.

§ 536. *Lands of Private Parties.*—8. That of acquiring in a proper case colonizable lands from private persons, by purchase, by cession, or by any other contract in conformity with the rules established for public lands in fraction 6.

§ 537. *Colony Land Adapted to Private Persons.*—9. That of adapting for lands of private persons, when they solicit them, the colonies of which he may dispose, by virtue of the contracts of immigration which shall have been made.

§ 538. *Privileges Cease in Ten Years.*—10. That of considering the colonies with this character, and with all their prerogatives, during ten years, on the termination of which, every privilege will cease.

§ 539. *Two Hundred and Fifty Thousand Dollars for Expenses.*—Art. 2. The executive is equally authorized in the next fiscal year to so regulate the amount that he may dispose of two hundred and fifty thousand dollars for the expenses which this law requires, inclusive of that for the exploring commission.

Palace of the legislative power of the Union, Mexico, May 31, 1875. Julio Zárate, deputy president. Antonio Gómez, deputy secretary. J. V. Villada, deputy secretary. Wherefore I command it to be printed, published, circulated, and that due compliance be given it. Palace of the executive power, Mexico, May 31, 1875. Sebastian Lerdo de Tejada. To citizen Blas

Balcárcel, minister of public works, colonization, industry, and commerce. And I communicate to you for your understanding and consequent ends. Independence and liberty. Mexico, May 31, 1875. Balcárcel.

§ 540. *Repeal.*—The above law was repealed by that of December 15, 1883.

*Order of September* 24, 1877.—Department of public works, colonization, industry, and commerce. Section 1.

§ 541. *Monumental Ruins Preserved.*—The citizen president of the republic, being convinced that the monumental ruins which our ancient founders left on our soil ought to be preserved with all care, has been pleased to order that the alienation of sites where they exist shall not be permitted, when these are on public lands; as they ought to remain as national property, they can not become private domain.

§ 542. *Adjudication of Ruins Null.*—This supreme order you will please remember in giving your report, which must be asked of you according to article 18 of the law of July 20, 1863, if by chance those lands should be denounced, because the adjudication thereof will be null, and of no value or effect.

§ 543. *Authorities Notified.*—At the same time I recommend to you to order the corresponding authorities that every monument which belongs to the nation, and all that which marks its ancient history, be preserved and respected as it is due. Liberty and the constitution. Mexico, September 24, 1877. Riva Palacio.

*Colonization Law of December* 15, 1883.—Department of state and of the office of public works, colonization, industry, and commerce of the Mexican republic. Section 1. The president of the republic has been pleased to direct to me the decree which follows: Manuel Gonzalez, constitutional president of the Mexican United States, to the inhabitants thereof, know ye: That the congress of the Union has thought proper to decree the following: The congress of the Mexican United States decrees:

### CHAPTER I.—OF THE DEMARKATION OF LANDS.

§ 544. *Survey of Lands.*—Art. 1. With the end of obtaining the necessary lands for the establishment of colonists, the executive will order the vacant lands or those of the national property which there may be in the republic to be marked out, measured, divided, and valued. For that purpose he will appoint commissions of engineers which he shall consider necessary, and he shall determine the system of operations which must be followed.

§ 545. *Two Thousand Five Hundred Hectares to One Person.*—Art. 2. The divisions shall not exceed in any case two thousand five hundred hectares, this being the greatest extension which can be adjudicated to one sole individual of age, and with legal capacity to contract.

§ 546. *Foreigners may Hold Lands.*—Art. 3. The lands marked out, measured, divided, and valued shall be ceded to foreign immigrants and to the inhabitants of the republic who may desire to establish themselves on them as colonists, with the following conditions: 1. By sale, at the price of the valuation made by the engineers, and approved by the department of public works, payable in bonds in ten years, commencing from the second year of the establishment of the colonist; 2. By sale, making the payment of the price with cash down, or in terms less than those of the preceding fraction; 3. By a gratuitous title, when the colonist may solicit it; but in this case the extent can not exceed one hundred hectares, nor will he obtain the title of property (in fee) except when he proves that he has preserved the land in his possession, and has cultivated it all, or an extension of it which is not less than the tenth part, during five consecutive years.

§ 547. *Duty of Executive as to Sales.*—Art. 4. As soon as there shall be proper lands for colonization, with the conditions which article 1 establishes, the executive shall determine which ought to be colonized immediately; and he shall publish the plan of them and the prices at which they ought to be sold; and he shall try in all cases to have the sale or cession of which the preceding article speaks made in alternate lots. The rest of the lands shall be reserved to be sold with the conditions which the law establishes, when they may be solicited; or when the executive shall so determine, he can mortgage them with the end of obtaining funds, which, united to the product of the sale of the lands, must be destined exclusively to carry out colonization.

## Chapter II.—Of the Colonists.

§ 548. *Requisites of a Foreign Colonist.*—Art. 5. In order to be considered as a colonist, and to have a right to the franchises which the present law grants, it shall be necessary, being a foreign immigrant, to come to the republic with a certificate of the consular agent or agent of immigration, issued on the petition of the said immigrant, or of the company or enterprise authorized by the executive to bring colonists to the republic.

§ 549. *Resident Colonists.*—If the petitioner resides in the republic, he must appear before the department of public works, or before the agents which the said department shall have authorized to admit colonists, in the colonies which shall be founded in the republic.

§ 550. *Proof of Character.*—Art. 6. In every case the solicitors must present certificates from the respective authorities, which shall prove their good habits, and the occupation which they have had before making the petition to be admitted as colonists.

§ 551. *Certain Exemptions for Ten Years.*—Art. 7. The colonists who shall establish themselves in the republic shall enjoy for ten years, counted from the date of their establishment, the following exemptions: 1. Exemption from military service; 2. Exemption from all classes of taxation, except municipal; 3. Exemption from duties of importation and interior duties on provisions of life, where there are none; on agricultural implements, tools, machinery, furniture, materials of construction for habitations, household ware, and breeding or blooded animals, destined for the colonies; 4. Personal exemption and untransferable from the duties of exportation on the fruits which they harvest; 5. Premiums for notable works, and prizes and special protection for the introduction of a new cultivation or industry; 6. Exemption from the fees of the legalization of signatures and the issuing of passports which consular agents grant to individuals who may come to the republic with destination for colonization, in virtue of contracts made by the government with any enterprise or enterprises.

§ 552. *Free Articles to be Designated.*—Art. 8. The department of public works shall determine the quantity and the class of objects which in each case must be introduced free from duties; and the treasury shall regulate the relative part with the manner of making the introductions, in order to avoid fraud and contraband, but without impeding the prompt dispatch of the objects.

§ 553. *Plantation of Trees.*—Art. 9. The colonists who shall establish themselves on lands unprovided with trees, and who shall prove that on a part of their lot, which shall not be less than the tenth part, they have made a plantation of trees in quantity proportionate to the extension, and two years before the term of the exemptions, shall enjoy for one year more freedom from taxation on all the land, and in general they shall have one year more of exemption for each tenth part which they shall destine to the cultivation of forests.

§ 554. *Subject to the Laws.*—Art. 10. The colonies shall be established under the municipal regimen, being subject, for the election of its authorities and for the establishment of imposts, to the general laws of the republic and to the laws of the state where they are found. The department of public works can, notwithstanding, constitute agents in the colonies, with the end of giving better direction to the works and of requiring reimbursement of the sums which they may owe to the federation for any title.

§ 555. *Contracts to be Fulfilled.*—Art. 11. The colonists are obliged to fulfill the contracts which they may make with the federal government, or with private persons or companies which shall transport and establish them in the republic.

§ 556. *Declaration as to Reservation of Nationality.*—Art. 12. Every foreign immigrant who shall establish himself in a colony shall manifest in the act of establishing himself, before the federal agent of colonization or before the respective notary or judge, if he has resolved to preserve his nationality, or whether he desires to obtain the Mexican nationality which the third part of article 30 of the constitution of the republic concedes to him.

§ 557. *Laws and Tribunals of the Country.*—Art. 13. The colonists will be considered with all the rights and obligations which the federal constitution concedes and imposes on Mexicans and foreigners in their case, and shall enjoy the temporary exemptions which the present law grants to them; but in all questions which shall arise, of whatever class they may be, they shall be subject to the decisions of the tribunals of the republic with the absolute exclusion of all foreign intervention.

§ 558. *Abandonment.*—Art. 14. The colonists who shall abandon, without a duly justifiable cause, for more than a year, and before having paid for the lands which shall have been ceded to them by sale, shall lose the right to said lands and to the part of the price which they shall have paid for them. In the case of fraction 3 of article 3, the right to the gratuitous title shall be lost by abandoning said land or failing to cultivate it for more than six months, without a duly justifiable cause.

§ 559. *Rights of Founders.*—Art. 15. In the places destined by the federal government for new towns, a lot shall be conceded *gratis* to the Mexican or foreign colonists who may wish to establish themselves in them, as founders; but they shall not acquire the property in said lot, except when they prove that before being established two years they have built in the town a dwelling; and in a contrary case, they shall lose their right to the acquisition. They shall endeavor to have the adjudication made by alternate lots.

§ 560. *Mexican Colonists on Frontiers.*—Art. 16. Mexicans who reside in foreign countries, and who may desire to establish themselves in deserted places on the frontiers of the republic, shall have a right to a gratuitous cession of land, with the conditions of fraction 3 of article 3, and of an extension of two hundred hectares, and the enjoyment for fifteen years of the exemptions which the present law grants.

§ 561. *Assistance to Colonists.*—Art. 17. The executive is authorized to assist the colonists or immigrants in the cases which he may think proper, and with subjection to the sums which are assigned in the law's appropriations, with the expenses of the transportation of themselves and their baggage by sea and into the interior, once, and to where the railroads reach; with the expenses of gratuitous maintenance for fifteen days in the places which he shall determine, and with tools, seeds, materials for habitations, and animals for working and breeding, these last supplies being reimbursable on the same terms as the value of the lands.

## Chapter III.—Of Companies.

§ 562. *Companies may Settle.*—Art. 18. The executive can authorize companies for the settlement of public lands, with the conditions of measurement, marking out, of dividing into lots, of valuation and description, and for the transportation of colonists and their establishment on said lands.

§ 563. *Companies must Designate Land They Desire to Settle.*—Art. 19. In order to obtain the authorization, the companies must designate the public land which they desire to settle, its approximate extension, and the number of colonists which they have to establish on them within a given time.

§ 564. *District Judge will Authorize Surveys.*—Art. 20. The proceedings of survey and demarkation shall be authorized by the district judge in whose demarkation the land is situated, and being once concluded, and there being no opponent, they shall be delivered to the company in order that it may present them to the department of public works, with the other conditions of which article 18 speaks. But should there be an opponent, the corresponding trial shall be proceeded with, and in which the representative of the federal treasury shall be considered as a party.

§ 565. *Third of Land Granted to Companies, with Conditions.*—Art. 21. In compensation for the expenses which the companies may make in the settlement of public lands, the executive can concede to them the third part of the lands which they may settle, or the value thereof; but with the exact conditions that they must not alienate the lands which are conceded to them to foreigners not authorized to acquire them, nor in greater extensions than two thousand five hundred hectares, under a penalty of losing in the two cases the divisions which shall have been alienated, if these conditions shall have been contravened; and which divisions shall immediately become the property of the nation.

§ 566. *Balance Ceded to Colonists.*—Art. 22. The lands marked out by the companies, and with the exception of those which may be ceded to these companies in compensation for expenses of settlement, shall be ceded to the colonists, or shall be reserved on the terms and conditions which articles 3 and 4 of this law establish.

§ 567. *Operations to Commence in Three Months.*—Art. 23. The authorizations which the executive shall grant for the settlement of public lands, shall remain without effect and without a right to prorogation, when the respective operations shall not have been commenced, within the improrogable time of three months.

§ 568. *Executive may Make Contracts with Conditions.*—Art. 24. The executive can make contracts with enterprises (empresas), or companies for the introduction into the republic and the establishment therein of colonists and foreign immigrants, with the following conditions: 1. The companies must fix the precise time within which they have to introduce a determined number of colonists. 2. The colonists or immigrants must fulfill the conditions established in articles 5 and 6 of this law. 3. The bases of the contracts which the companies must make with the colonists must be adjusted according to the prescriptions of this law, and must be submitted for the approbation of the department of public works. 4. The companies must guarantee to the satisfaction of the executive the fulfillment of the obligations which they shall make in their contracts, in which must be assigned the cases of forfeiture and respective fine.

§ 569. *Franchises and Exemptions.*—Art. 25. The companies which contract with the executive for the transportation to the republic and the establishment therein of foreign colonists shall enjoy for a term which must not exceed twenty years the following franchises and exemptions: 1. A sale on a long term and a moderate price of vacant lands or national property, with the exclusive object of colonizing them. 2. Exemption from taxation, except that of stamps, on the capitals destined for the enterprise. 3. Exemption from port dues, except those established for the improvement of said ports, on the ships which on account of the companies bring at least ten families of colonists to the republic. 4. Exemption from importation duties on tools, machinery, materials of construction, and working and breeding animals, all exclusively destined for an agricultural, mineral, or industrial colony, the formation of which the executive shall have authorized. 5. A prize for a family established, and a lesser one for a family disembarked (or landed in the country); a prize for a Mexican family established in a colony of foreigners. 6. Transportation of the colonists on account of the government on steamship lines and railroads subventionized.

§ 570. *Foreign Companies Considered as Mexicans.*—Art. 26. The foreign companies of colonization shall be always considered as Mexicans, and they must have their domicile in some of the cities of the republic, without prejudice to those which they may establish in foreign countries; and they shall be obliged to constitute in the country a part of their board of directors, and to have one or more attorneys in fact in the said republic, fully empowered to treat with the executive.

§ 571. *Disputes Subject to the Laws and Tribunals of Mexico.*—Art. 27. All the questions which may arise between the government and the companies shall be adjusted by the tribunals of the republic, and according to the laws thereof, without foreign diplomatic agents having any interference therewith.

## Chapter IV.

§ 572. *Privileges of Private Persons Who Give Lands for Colonization.*—Art. 28. Private persons who shall destine a part or the whole of their lands to colonize with ten families at least of foreign immigrants, the colonies which they may establish thereon shall have a right to enjoy the same franchises and exemption as the colonies which the federal government may establish, provided that they subject themselves to the conditions which the executive shall fix to insure the success of the colony, and provided that among those conditions shall be assigned that of this, that the colonists must acquire, by purchase or concession, one lot of land for cultivation. The executive can give foreign colonists to private individuals, stipulating with them the conditions with which they must establish them, and he can also assist them with the expenses of the transportation of the colonists.

§ 573. *Colonization of Islands.*—Art. 29. The colonization of the islands of both oceans shall be made by the federal executive, with subjection to the precepts of this law; the government necessarily reserving on each island an extension of fifty hectares for public uses. In case that the island should not have a superfice sufficient to make the separation provided in this article, no sale of land shall be made on it, and it can only be leased for a short term. In the colonies which may be established on the islands, there shall always be a number of Mexican families, which shall not be less than half of the total number of colonizing families.

§ 574. *Executive may Purchase Private Lands for Colonization.*—Art. 30. The executive is authorized to acquire, by purchase or cession, lands of private persons, whenever he shall think it proper, to establish thereon colonies, and with subjection to the estimate of expenses, which with such end are assigned in the laws of appropriations of expenditures.

§ 575. *Prior Laws Repealed.*—Art. 31. All laws prior to the present one on colonization are hereby repealed.

Ariste Mercado, deputy vice-president. Guillermo Palomino, senator-president. Saturnino Ayon, deputy secretary. Enrique Maria Rubio, senator-secretary. Wherefore I order it printed, published, circulated, and that due compliance be given it. Given in the palace of the executive power of the Union, in Mexico, on the fifteenth day of December, 1883. Manuel Gonzalez. To the citizen-general Carlos Pacheco, secretary of state and of the office of public works, colonization, industry, and commerce. And I communicate it to you for your knowledge and corresponding effects. Liberty and the constitution. Mexico, December 15, 1883. Pacheco.

# CHAPTER XV.

## GRANTS ANNULLED—LAWS REPEALED—PRE-EMPTION LAW—CIRCULARS.

§ 576. Law of November 25, 1853—Public Lands Belong to the Nation.
§ 577. Grants Annulled.
§ 578. Possession to be Surrendered to Government.
§ 579. Illegal Possessors No Redress.
§ 580. Law of July 7, 1854—Titles Made Since 1821.
§ 581. Titles to be Presented in Six Months.
§ 582. Receipts Given for Documents.
§ 583. Expedientes to be Made.
§ 584. Certain Grants Annulled.
§ 585. Certain Grants, if not for Colonization, Null.
§ 586. Grants with Conditions not Complied with, Null.
§ 587. Supreme Government may Validate Grants.
§ 588. All Grants may be Validated.
§ 589. Extension of Time.
§ 590. Foreigners can not Hold within Twenty Leagues of Boundary Line.
§ 591. Statistical Report.
§ 592. Public Lands under Care of Public Works Department.
§ 593. Law of November 25th in Force.
§ 594. Law of October 16, 1856—Decrees Annulled.
§ 595. Responsibility of Law-makers.
§ 596. Responsibility of Governors.
§ 597. Circular of February 13, 1861—Proceeding of Adjudication of Land.
§ 598. Commentary on the Law of 1863—Petition for Denouncement.
§ 599. Action of the Judge on the Petition.
§ 600. Notice Published—Adjudication when not Final.
§ 601. Questions of Construction of Statute.
§ 602. Minors can not Denounce.
§ 603. Women may Denounce.
§ 604. Companies, Adjudications by.
§ 605. Archæological Monuments Reserved.
§ 606. Payment of Price.
§ 607. Power of Attorney.
§ 608. Necessity of Fulfillment of Conditions.
§ 609. Title Only a Quitclaim.
§ 610. Cost Paid by Claimants.
§ 611. Schedule of Prices.
§ 612. Prescription.
§ 613. Law of July 22, 1863—What are Public Lands.
§ 614. Who may Denounce.
§ 615. List of Prices.

*Law of November* 25, 1853.—Department of government. His excellency the president of the republic has been pleased to direct to me the decree which follows: Antonio López de Santa Anna, know ye: That in use of the faculties which the nation has been pleased to confer on me, I have thought proper to decree the following:

§ 576. *Public Lands Belong to the Nation.*—Art. 1. It is declared that the public lands, as the exclusive property of the nation, never could have been alienated under any title, in virtue of decrees, orders, and provisions of the legislatures, governments, or private authorities of the states and territories of the republic.

§ 577. *Grants Annulled.*—Art. 2. Consequently, are also declared null, and of no value or effect, the sales, concessions, or any other kind of alienations of said public lands which have been made without the express mandate and sanction of the general powers in the form prescribed by law.

§ 578. *Possession to be Surrendered to the Government.*—Art. 3. The functionaries, authorities, and employés to whom shall belong the fulfillment of this decree shall proceed as soon as they receive it to claim and receive in the name of the nation the lands comprehended in what is provided by article 1, and which are found in possession of corporations or private individuals, whatever may be their prerogatives and category.

§ 579. *Illegal Possessors No Redress.*—Art. 4. The judicial, political, or administrative authorities shall not admit claims of any kind nor petitions which have for an object to receive indemnification from the public treasury for the injuries which the illegal possessors or proprietors may allege, in virtue of what is provided in the foregoing article; remaining only to them their right without diminution against those persons from whom they had the lands which now they are obliged to return.

Wherefore I command it to be printed, published, circulated, and that due compliance be given to it. Palace of the national government in Mexico, the twenty-fifth day of November, 1853. Antonio López de Santa Anna. To the minister of government. And I communicate it to you for your understanding and consequent ends. God and liberty. Mexico,

November 25, 1853. The minister of government. Ignacio Águilar.

*Law of July* 7, 1854.—Department of state and of the office of government. S. A. S., the president general, has been pleased to direct to me the decree which follows: Antonio López de Santa Anna, know ye: That in use of the faculties which the nation has been pleased to confer on me, I have thought proper to decree the following:

§ 580. *Titles Made Since* 1821.—Art. 1. The titles of all the alienations of public lands made in the territory of the republic since September of the year 1821 until the present time, whether by the general authorities, whether by that of the extinguished states and departments, shall be submitted to the review of the supreme government; and without it they shall have no value, nor shall they constitute any right of property.

§ 581. *Titles to be Presented in Six Months.*—Art. 2. To this end, the minister of public works shall appoint commissioners, who may be the agents which it now has in all the departments and territories, before whom the proprietors of public lands, or those who represent them, shall be obliged to present the titles of their acquisitions within the term of six months, counted from the date on which this law is published in the capital. For the effects of the present decree shall be admitted not only the original documents, but also in their default the authorized copies of them, in conformity with the laws being confronted with the commission that receives them. Proprietors who do not comply with the obligations which are imposed upon them in this and the preceding article shall be considered detainers without any title.

§ 582. *Receipts Given for Documents.*—Art. 3. It shall be the duty of the commissioners to issue to each proprietor a receipt for his documents, in which shall be specified their contents, under an exact enumeration. A copy of these receipts shall be copied into the book of registry, which must be kept with the due distinction of numbers and dates.

§ 583. *Expedientes to be Made.*—Art. 4. Immediately after the commissioners shall have received the documents belonging to a proprietor, they shall form with them a folio expediente, which they shall complete with all the information which they may judge necessary to obtain, and which the functionaries and authorities are obliged to furnish them, of whatever class they may be. The expedientes thus made up, the commission shall remit them, with its opinion and report, to the department of public works, in order that relative to them shall be made the supreme resolution which corresponds.

§ 584. *Certain Grants Null.*—Art. 5. The alienations of public lands, of whatever class they may be, are null, which shall not have been made by the authorities and functionaries of the departments (now states) without the knowledge and approbation of the general government, in the epochs in which the central system ruled in the republic.

§ 585. *Certain Grants, if not for Colonization, Null.*—Art. 6. Those made by the same authorities in the epochs of the extinguished federation are equally null, provided that they have not been made with the object of extending and improving colonization, which was that proposed by the law of the eighteenth of August, 1824.

§ 586. *Grants with Conditions not Complied with, Null.*—Art. 7. The concessions or sales of lands made in favor of private persons, companies, or corporations, under express conditions of colonizing them, and the possessors of which have not complied with the conditions in the terms expressed, are declared to be without any value.

§ 587. *Supreme Government may Validate Grants.*—Art. 8. The alienations made by the states or departments, and which are declared null by the three preceding articles, can notwithstanding subsist, if the possessors of the lands obtain the consent of the supreme government by the means of the indemnification to the public treasury, which the latter may judge proper to require for the value of the land, provided that they solicit the ratification within the term which article 1 designates; in which case only shall no innovation be made which shall molest or injure them.

§ 588. *All Invalid Grants may be Validated.*—Art. 9. According to the same regulation, the possessor of any public lands may seek for his title, who by any reason whatever lacks a legal one.

§ 589. *Extension of Time.*—Art. 10. Those who do not appear within the term designated to enjoy this benefit can only reach it within another equal term, by means of a composition with the supreme government by which the exchequer will be indemnified, not only with the price of the lands illegally possessed, but of the value of the profits and other advantages of them for all the time of the detention, according to the judgment of experts.

§ 590. *Foreigners can not Hold within Twenty Leagues of*

*Boundary Line.*—Art. 11. Foreigners not naturalized up to this date, are prohibited from acquiring country property, whether they are or are not public lands, situated within a zone of twenty leagues of the boundary line which is the dividing line between the republic and the neighboring nations. For the legitimate acquisition of said property a special permit from the supreme government shall be necessary, which shall be inserted in the corresponding writing.

§ 591. *Statistical Report.*—Art. 12. The department of public works, through the means of the commissioners of which this law speaks and of the others which it may be thought proper to appoint, shall collect within six months, counted from their publication in this capital, the statistical *data* relative to the public lands of the republic, in order to present with them to the supreme government a report, which comprehends them classified.

§ 592. *Public Lands under Care of Public Works Department.* Art. 13. All the cases which relate to public lands are of the exclusive province of the department of public works.

§ 593. *Law of November 25th in Force.*—Art. 14. The law of November 25th, of the year last past, shall remain in force, in all that is not opposed to the present decree.

Wherefore I command it to be printed, published, circulated, and that due compliance be given it. Given in the palace of the national government in Mexico, the seventh of July, 1854. Antonio López de Santa Anna. To the minister of government. And I communicate it to you for your understanding and consequent ends. God and liberty. Mexico, July 7, 1854. The minister of government. Ignacio Aguilar.

*Law of October* 16, 1856, *Declaring the Decrees of Santa Anna, Dated November* 25, 1853, *and July* 7, 1854, *Void.*—Department of state and office of government. His excellency the substitute president has been pleased to direct to me the decree which follows: Ignacio Comonfort, substitute president of the Mexican republic, to the inhabitants thereof, know ye: That the constituent congress, in use of the faculties which it has to review the acts of the executive, decrees what follows:

§ 594. *Decrees Annulled.*—1. The decree of November 25, 1853, and of July 7, 1854, are null.

§ 595. *Responsibility of Law-makers.*—2. D. Antonio López de Santa Anna, and the ministers who have intervened in their approbation and publication, are responsible with their property for the damage and losses which they have occasioned.

§ 596. *Responsibility of Governors.*—3. The governors of the departments are equally responsible with their property for the damages and losses which they have caused in executing the provisions relative to public lands, by going out of the limits marked in the respective rights. J. Maria Mata, president. Leon Guzman, deputy secretary. José Maria Cortés y Esparza, deputy secretary.

Wherefore I command it to be printed, published, circulated, and that due compliance be given it. Palace of the national government in Mexico, the sixteenth of October, 1856. Ignacio Comonfort. To the citizen José Maria Lafragua, minister of government. And I communicate it to you for your understanding. God and liberty. Mexico, October 16, 1856. Lafragua.

*February* 13, 1861—*Circular of the Minister of Public Works.*—The circular of the ninth of June, 1856, is repeated, on denouncements and alienation of vacant lands. With date of the ninth of June, 1856, was addressed to the agents of this department the following communication:

§ 597. *Proceedings on the Adjudication of Public Land.*—Circular No. 102. His excellency the substituted president of the republic has been pleased to order that whilst the law is being issued which regulates the proceedings in the denouncement and alienation of the vacant lands, the petitions and other affairs which in this branch may be pending shall be delivered by the authorities of the states to the agents of this department; and those which in the future shall be made shall be presented to the same agents, who will pass them to their excellencies the governors, in order that they may give information whether they consider the adjudication which they claim as advantageous or prejudicial to the respective state. That in case the said functionaries should agree thereto, the agents shall proceed to appoint an expert to mark and measure, at the expense of the petitioner, said land, regulating the same as far as possible according to the provisions dictated by the authorities of said states, remitting afterwards those proceedings to this department, in order that it may decide upon the price and terms of adjudication. And finally, that if the opinion of the respective governor should be contrary thereto, the agents shall remit said opinion immediately with the corresponding petition and the report which they may think opportune, in order that, with an examination of the reasons alleged, pro and con, the supreme government may resolve what it may esteem just.

Which by supreme order I say to you, for the corresponding effects. God and liberty. Mexico, the ninth of June, 1856. Silicio.

§ 598. *The Pre-emption Law of July* 22, 1863, *and Circulars Relative thereto—Petition for Denouncement.*—The pre-emption law of July 22, 1863, is still in force. To denounce land under this law is to claim it before the district judge having jurisdiction thereof. This claim is made in writing by setting forth the facts requisite to show that the land is vacant, and that the petitioner is one of the persons within the purview of the statute which declares who is entitled to make denouncement of public land. The judge, after the filing of the petition, appoints an expert or surveyor (perito), who is to survey the land, mark the boundaries, form a plan thereof, and present the same to the judge. Notice must be given prior to the survey to the parties claiming lands contiguous to the tract in question.

§ 599. *Action of the Judge on the Petition.*—The judge inquires of the treasury department (hacienda) if the said department is in possession of the land solicited. The object of this is to ascertain whether the land is really vacant or in possession of some third party. If it clearly appear that no one is in possession, the judge decides that the land can be adjudicated to the applicant, and does thus adjudicate it to him subject to the conditions provided in the law. The applicant, or person to whom it is adjudicated, is called the adjudicatario, a word for which there is no equivalent in English.

§ 600. *Notice to be Published—Adjudication, when not Final.* Should it appear that the government is not in possession, or in other words, the land is not vacant, a notice must be published for thirty days in the newspapers, and be also posted in public places. Should no one appear to oppose the claimant's right to the land, the possession will be adjudicated to him; but not the title in fee. (See article 17.) But this decree of adjudication is not final, as the approval of the department of public works (ministerio de fomento) is essential to vest the right of possession or the fee in the claimant.

§ 601. *Questions of Construction of Statute.*—While the proceedings are apparently simple, nevertheless questions of importance as to the construction of the statute often arise. As the words, "every inhabitant of the republic has a right to denounce," etc., some judges have admitted minors to receive the lands solicited by them under the foregoing law; not seeming to consider that they could not carry into effect the conditions prescribed by the law. As a minor can not make a valid contract, it must follow that lands can not be adjudicated to him fraught with conditions that the law can not make binding upon him or his property. Article 10 declares that the person to whom is thus adjudicated land is obliged to maintain on the land for the term of ten years one inhabitant at least for each two hundred hectares of land. How can a minor assume such a position, clothed with such an obligation?

§ 602. *Minors can not Denounce.*—The department of fomento has very justly held that a minor can not denounce land under said law, except when he has become of legal age by a special law, and authorized to make contracts; or in case where the father or mother of a minor had denounced land and had died subsequent thereto; for then the right passes to the minor as heir, and the adjudication may be made to the minor.

§ 603. *Women may Denounce.*—A woman, if not under paternal power (patria potestad), may denounce; and a married woman with the consent of her husband.

§ 604. *Companies, Adjudications by.*—As the amount of two thousand five hundred hectares, which is equal to six thousand one hundred and seventy-seven and a half acres, is allowed to each inhabitant who is entitled to denounce public land, it has therefore been contended by some that a company or copartnership of two or more persons could denounce in a body the sum of the amounts allowed to said number of persons. The decision of the department is to the contrary. Such a company or copartnership can only denounce two thousand five hundred hectares in a body. But each individual thereof, if there be no personal prohibition, may denounce two thousand five hundred hectares in such a manner that all of said tracts may be united in one body, and worked upon joint account of the company or copartnership. In such cases the adjudications are made separately, and the titles are issued separately to each claimant; and each one is responsible for the carrying out of the conditions prescribed by the law, as to his respective tract.

§ 605. *Archæological Monuments Reserved.*—By the circular of September 24, 1877, lands having upon them historical and archæological monuments are reserved from denouncement.

§ 606. *Payment of Price.*—After the adjudication by the judge, and the approval by the minister of fomento, the claimant must pay the price of the land into the treasury, before the title or possession of the land will be delivered to him. (See article 19.)

§ 607. *Powers of Attorney.*—Parties appearing for others must show a power of attorney legally authorized.

§ 608. *Necessity of the Fulfillment of Conditions.*—As the several officers of the government are required to watch with care all lands adjudicated, to see particularly if the condition in article 10 has been complied with, namely, that each two hundred hectares have at least thereon one inhabitant, it behooves the claimants to have care that said condition be strictly complied with; and thereby prevent the denouncement of said land by a third party.

§ 609. *Title Only a Quitclaim.*—A title by adjudication under this law is only a quitclaim deed of all the right of the government thereto. It is declared by article 20 that the adjudication of the possession gives a title as against the government and against third persons who appeared and were defeated; but as to other third parties, who have legal titles, such adjudications can not prevail against them.

§ 610. *Cost Paid by Claimants.*—All costs of surveys, and all other costs requisite to carry into effect the proceedings of adjudication are to be paid by the claimant. (See article 22.)

§ 611. *Schedule of Prices.*—Every two years the government issues a schedule or list of the prices of the public lands in each state and in the territory of Lower California; which prices continue to exist for the term of the two years thus designated.

§ 612. *Prescription.*—An important point or right is conceded by the government in this law which did not exist before; and that is, the right of holding against the government by prescription, or what is known in the United States and England as limitation. A party entitled to denounce under this law may hold by prescription two thousand five hundred hectares by a possession thereof for ten years. (See article 10.) Prior to this law, prescription did not run against the sovereign in Mexico.

*Pre-emption Law of July* 22, 1863.—Department of justice, public works, and public instruction. Section of public works, No. 1. The citizens constitutional president of the republic has been pleased to direct to me the decree which follows: Benito Juarez, constitutional president of the Mexican United States, to the inhabitants thereof, know ye: That in use of the ample faculties with which I find myself vested, and which fraction 24 of article 72 of the constitution concedes to the general congress, I have thought proper to decree the following law on the occupation and alienation of the public lands:

§ 613. *Public Land, What.*—Art. 1. All those lands of the republic which have not been destined to public use, by the authority empowered therefor by law, nor granted by the same, with an onerous or lucrative title, to any individual or corporation authorized to acquire them, are public lands for the effects of this law.

§ 614. *Who may Denounce.*—Art. 2. Every inhabitant of the republic has a right to denounce two thousand and five hundred hectares, and no more, of public land, with the exception of the natives of the nations bounding on the republic and those naturalized in said nations, who by no title can acquire public land in the states bordering on said nations.

§ 615. *List of Prices.*—Art. 3. The supreme general government will publish every two years the tariff of prices of the public lands in each state, the district, and the territory.

§ 616. *Price, how Paid.*—Art. 4. Two thirds of the price of the public lands shall be paid in money and the other in bonds of the national or foreign public debt. One half of the amount paid in money shall be applied to the federal treasury, and the other to that of the state in which the land is situated.

§ 617. *Rights of Parties Now in Actual Possession.*—Art. 5. The possessor of a tract of public land, of whatever extension it may be, which at this date is cultivated or bounded with a ditch, fence, or artificial landmarks, placed at least in all the angles of the periphery, has a right to have one half of the tariff price rebated, if he has had possession for ten years, or a title translative of dominion, although it be granted by him who had no right to grant it. Not having a title nor possession for ten years, the abatement will only be one quarter part; but in both cases the payment can be made by delivering the bonds at the time and the money by thirds, one in a year, another in two years, and the other in three years; the land in the mean while being especially mortgaged for the payment.

§ 618. *Abatement in Price, when Made.*—Art. 6. The sole possession of ten years, without the title of which the foregoing article speaks, or the latter without the former, does not give a right to any abatement; but if both concur, there shall be an abatement of one quarter part of the price, although the public land be not cultivated, nor limited, provided the possession shall have been preserved up to the day of denouncement. In this case, in order to determine the extent possessed, it shall be within the limits mentioned in the title, even when they are not in conformity with the amount of land, and it shall only be according to the amount of land, when the title does not fix the limits, or when it is impossible to ascertain the precise limits. In the case of this article the payment can be made in the terms prescribed in the preceding article.

§ 619. *Tracts Containing Public and Private Lands.*—Art. 7. In the two preceding articles is comprehended the public land confounded in its totality with the fields which are not so, or comprehended entirely within them, if the possessor of the public land has them in his possession, and the said public land has the condition of being cultivated, inclosed, or if he has a title or possession of ten years, accordingly as said articles require.

§ 620. *When Denouncement to be Made to Entitle to Abatement.*—Art. 8. The abatement of price granted by the preceding articles will only take place if he who has a right to it presents his denouncement within three months from the publication of this law, or afterwards if there should be no prior denouncer to oppose it; but should there be one, he will concede the land to the denouncer, or pay him its value according to the tariff price in cash down, and he will indemnify him in the same manner for the necessary expenses which he shall have made. All this without prejudice to the payment which he must make to the public treasury, according to the preceding provisions. During the three months of which this article speaks, the possessors only can denounce the public lands which are referred to; and in case of their not making a denouncement thereof, he who does so can only denounce two thousand five hundred hectares.

§ 621. *Actions of the Authorities not to be Interfered with.*—Art. 9. No one can oppose the measuring, marking, or the execution of any other acts by order of competent authority, necessary to ascertain the truth or legality of a denoucement on lands that are not public; but whenever the sentence declares the land denounced not to be public in whole or in part, there shall be a right to an indemnification for the damages and losses which by the denouncement have been spent, reserving a criminal action in case there should be cause for it.

§ 622. *Number of Persons to be Kept on the Land.*—Art. 10. The owners of public lands which may be adjudicated after this date are obliged to maintain on some place of their property, and during ten years counted from the adjudication, one inhabitant at least for each two hundred hectares adjudicated, without counting the fraction which shall not reach this number.

He who shall fail to have the inhabitants which correspond to him, four months in a year, shall lose the right to the land and to the price which shall have been paid by him.

§ 623. *Uses and Emphyteuses.*—Art. 11. Those who now have public lands in usufruct, emphyteuses, or by virtue of any other contract which has transferred to them the use without the fee in the land, shall enjoy an abatement of one half of the tariff price, if they are constituted denouncers in the terms and conditions of article 8; in the contrary case they are subject to the prescription of the same article.

§ 624. *Parties Holding Land by Contracts—Abatement to Them.* Art. 12. The present tenants and farming partners (aparceros) on public lands, and all those who have received them by virtue of a contract which has not transferred to them the use (dominio útil) nor the fee, are comprehended in the preceding article; but the abatement which shall be made to them shall be only one quarter of the tariff price. In case that they do not appropriate the land to themselves under this law, that is, adjudicate them, those who do (los adjudicatarios) shall fulfill the contract of partnership (aparceria), of lease, etc., for the whole time of their duration, if the time should be fixed, and if no term is fixed, to the end of the year in which the adjudication shall be decreed.

§ 625. *Contracts to be Made Only with Government.*—Art. 13. The president of the republic only, through the channel of the department of public works, can make contracts relative to public lands of which the two prior articles speak; but such contracts will not prevent alienation according to this law, whether they be or not for a fixed term, as they will only last until the end of the year in which the adjudication shall be decreed.

§ 626. *Denouncements to be Made before Judge of First Instance.*—Art. 14. The denouncement of public lands shall be made before the judge of first instance who has jurisdiction of federal affairs in the judicial district in which the land is situated.

§ 627. *Survey and Maps.*—Art. 15. A denouncement being presented, the survey and the drawing of the map will be proceeded with by an engineer, or practical expert in his default, whom the judge shall appoint.

§ 628. *Possession of Land by the Treasury.*—Art. 16. The survey and map having been made, inquiry shall be made in the office that has charge of the public lands, if the public treasury is in possession of the denounced land. If it should be, and there should be no opponent, the adjudication in property will be decreed without further steps to the denouncer; but if there should be an opponent, there shall be a previous trial between the opponent and the denouncer, a representative of the federal treasury being also a party thereto.

§ 629. *When the Treasury is not in Possession.*—Art. 17. If the public treasury should not be possession of the public land, the denouncement will be published three times, once every ten days, by the periodicals and by notices fixed up in public places. No opponent having presented himself, the adjudication will be decreed, not in property, but in possession; but if there should be an opponent, there shall be the respective previous trial between the opponent and the denouncer, the representative of the federal treasury being likewise a party thereto.

§ 630. *Approval of Department of Public Works.*—Art. 18. The judicial decree upon the adjudication of a tract of public land, whether in property or in possession, can not be complied with without being approved by the department of public works, where for that purpose shall be transmitted a copy of the proceedings (expediente) and a copy of the map through the channel of the governor of the state, who shall accompany the same with such report as he may think proper.

§ 631. *Delivery of Land and Title.*—Art. 19. The approval having been obtained of which the preceding article speaks, and proof of the value of the land having been paid into the respective office, in conformity with the tariff of the two years in which the denouncement was made, or the bonds when the payment is in installments, the judge will make the delivery of the land and of the title of property or of possession.

§ 632. *Third Parties not Affected by Title.*—Art. 20. The adjudication in possession gives also the property against the public treasury and against the opponents to the denouncement who have litigated and been defeated; but in respect to third parties, the property in this class of adjudications will only be gained by perscription, or other legal title.

§ 633. *Denouncers must not Make Default in the Proceedings.*—Art. 21. Every suspension in the proceedings of the denouncement which arises from the fault of the denouncer, whether it consists in not furnishing the necessary expenses, in absenting himself without leaving an attorney authorized to act and furnished with expense money, or simply in not promoting the proceedings which belong to the denouncement, or in any other thing, gives a right to the opponent to ask that a term be fixed, which shall not exceed six days, in order to continue said proceedings; and the denouncer not making preparations to go on with the proceedings within that time, it will be decreed that the denouncement shall be held as not made, and that the denouncer is too late (moroso), and he can not again denounce the same land. For want of the demand on the part of the opponent, the judge will officially fix that term.

§ 634. *Expenses Paid by Denouncer.*—Art. 22. The expenses of the survey, demarkation, possession, and any other expenses which are caused, shall be on account of the denouncer, without prejudice to his being indemnified when there has been an opponent who shall be condemned in costs.

§ 635. *Alcabala, when Paid.*—Art. 23. The adjudication of public land is free from tax (alcabala) if the person to whom the land is adjudicated (adjudicatario) should not be an adjacent owner, but being so, he will pay in money an alcabala of twenty-five per cent on the price, unless that he be comprehended in articles 5, 6, 7, 11, and 12, in which case, and provided that he is not an adjacent owner, he will only pay the ordinary alcabala which may be established.

§ 636. *Alcabala Paid for Ten Years.*—Art. 24. The alcabala of twenty-five per cent also shall be created for the term of ten years, counted from the adjudication, by the translation of dominion posterior to said adjudication, which shall be made in favor of the adjacent owners of the public land which shall be adjudicated from this date.

§ 637. *Form of the Land.*—Art. 25. If the public lands denounced should be bounded in all its circumference by lands not public, it can preserve the figure which it may have, whatever it may be. If it should be bounded only in part by lands of this class, the sides which are traced anew shall be rectilinear, and the angles the least sharp and obtuse possible; if it should be surrounded in its totality by public lands, the figure shall be necessarily a square.

§ 638. *Boundaries.*—Art. 26. When the public land denounced is near lands not public, the boundary of these shall be taken as the boundary of the land denounced, or shall be left between both, as the adjudicatario may prefer, a distance that shall not be less than one kilometer.

§ 639. *Repeal of Imprescriptibility.*—Art. 27. The provisions of the ancient laws which declare public lands imprescriptible are repealed from this date. Consequently, any individual can in the future, not excepted in article 2 of this law, prescribe by the possession of ten years two thousand and five hundred hectares, and no more, of public land, if the other requisites which the laws require for prescription should concur; and should there also be complied with during ten years what is required in article 10.

§ 640. *Proceedings Void, when.*—Art. 28. Every contract or provision relative to public lands that shall not be dictated in conformity with the prescriptions of this law and by the functionaries to whom is committed the power, is null in law, and does not constitute the public treasury responsible in anything.

Wherefore I command that it be printed, published, circulated, and that due compliance be given it. Given in the palace of the federal government, in San Luis Potosi, on the twentieth of July, 1863. Benito Juarez. To the citizen Jesus Terán, minister of justice, public works, and public instruction. And I communicate it to you for your intelligence and fulfillment. God and liberty. San Luis Potosi, July 22, 1863. Terán.

§ 641. *Modification of Article* 4.—This law has been in some matters modified as follows: Article 4 was modified by the law of May 30, 1868, in respect to the manner of making payments. This law, in article 1, says: "Are revenues and property of the federation: Fraction 5—the half of the product of the sale, rent, or working of the public lands in all of the republic; the other half remaining for the benefit of the states within the territory of which the lands are found."

§ 642. *Modification of Article* 8.—By the law of September 19, 1863, article 8 was made to read as follows: "The abatement of price granted by the preceding articles will only take place if he who has a right to it presents his denouncement within three months from the publication of this law, or afterwards if there should be no denouncer who should oppose it; but should there be one, he will concede the land to the denouncer, or he will pay him its value according to the tariff price in cash down, with a deduction of the part which must be paid to the public treasury, indemnifying him, besides, for the necessary expenses which he shall have made."

§ 643. *Modification of Articles* 23 *and* 24.—Articles 23 and 24 were modified by the law of May 30, 1868, which, in article 2 thereof, says: "The following imposts are suppressed for the federal exchequer" (among others): "That of the transfer of property (dominio) in all the republic." This is a repeal of the alcabala, which is nothing more nor less than a tax on the transfer of property.

§ 644. *Ratification of Sales in Chihuahua.*—November 23, 1864. Ratification of sales of vacant lands made by the state of Chihuahua. Department of state and that of the treasury and public credit. Section 2. In answer to the inquiry made by you on the twenty-seventh of last October, the citizen president has thought proper to decide that I shall say to you, that in conformity with the promise which was made to the government of that state, in the note which was addressed to you by this department on the eleventh of September, 1863, the concessions of vacant lands made up to the said date are ratified, without prejudice to third parties; but that this favor must be applied in each particular case, in order that it can be examined whether there is or not a prejudice to a third party, and likewise in order that the titles of property may be issued by this department, revalidating the prior ones which the decree of the fourteenth of April, 1862, declared null, under the idea that, in order that the interested parties shall not be prejudiced, the issuing of the titles will be free from fees and without any more cost than that of the sealed paper on which they must be drawn. Independence, liberty, and reform. Chihuahua, November 23, 1864. Iglesia, citizen chief of the treasury of this state, present.

§ 645. *Circular of the Thirtieth of September, 1867, Referring to and Embracing that of September 14, 1866, Pertaining to Lands in the Possession of Indians—Indians Protected in their Possessions* —On the fourteenth of September, 1866, the department of justice and public works addressed the governor and military commander of Chihuahua the following: In all the titles of property which are issued by the adjudication of public lands, care must be taken to express that they are given without injury to third parties; and although such injury does not exist, strictly speaking, in respect to the lands which are in possession of the Indians, when they lack their respective title, given by competent authority; notwithstanding the rule has been carried out, by reason of equity and public interest, of avoiding despoiling them of the possession which they may have of said lands. In this sense various resolution have been dictated in respect to divers cases which have offered themselves; but as their number is becoming considerable, it is made requisite to give a general disposition which may avoid unnecessary complications. The citizen president, therefore, orders that you will be pleased to issue a circular to the political chiefs of the cantons of that state, placing the rule mentioned within their knowledge, in order that they shall take care that said rule be complied with whenever an occasion to apply it is presented to them.

§ 646. *Whether the Indians Have Actual Possession must be Ascertained.*—In order to do so, they must take care to ascertain previously that the Indians in whose favor it is established are really and truly in the actual possession of the lands which they claim, for these are the only points to be considered, without amplifying in any case this favor to lands which are not actually possessed. Neither will it be permitted that other persons take the name of the said Indians, or induce them to make undue reclamations, as has already happened sometimes, soliciting the possession of lands which they do not possess, but their instigators. With the application of the rules contained in this note will follow, among other advantages, that of the Indians interested in the preservation of the lands which they possess, not having to come to this capital to carry on the dispatch of the business, since it will be sufficient for them to appear before the office of the respective political chiefs to act according to the present provision.

§ 647. *Notice to the Indians.*—It will be proper also that said offices of the chiefs notify the Indians, in order to avoid suits and future questions, who may appear immediately to solicit the respective title of the lands which they are in possession of, even when no one disputes them, under the conception that said title shall be issued to them *gratis*, the property being thus legitimized which otherwise might be claimed.

§ 648. *Same Resolution Extended to All the Republic.*—And the citizen president of the republic, considering that the reasons which were taken into consideration in dictating that resolution in the state of Chihuahua are common to the others of the federation, has thought proper to resolve that said resolution be extended to all the republic, fixing the term of six months counted from this date, in order that within that term may be put in practice the effects to which it refers; with the understanding that the time having once expired, they can not further enjoy the benefits which this resolution concedes.

Which I communicate to you, impressing upon you its most exact fulfillment. Independence and liberty. Mexico, September 30, 1867.

*Circular No.* 81, *of the Twentieth of May*, 1869, *Calling for a Statement of the Lands Adjudicated to Indians, in Virtue of the*

*Circular of September* 30, 1867.—Department of public works, colonization, industry, and commerce of the Mexican republic. Section 1. Circular No. 81.

§ 649. *Report of Lands to Indians Called for.*—The citizen president of the republic has thought proper to order that you be asked for a statement of the public lands adjudicated in that state to the Indians, in virtue of the circular of department of September 30, 1867, assigning in said statement the number of individuals to whom titles of property have been issued, the location of the lands and the extension thereof, even when it may not be more than approximation, expressing also if any adjudications are pending on account of their proceedings being prosecuted Independence and liberty. Mexico, May 20, 1869. Balcárcel.

§ 650. *Circular No.* 57, *of the Twenty-fourth of July,* 1868, *as to the Copies of the Expedientes in the Denouncement of Public Lands, to be Transmitted to the Department, What to Contain.*—With this date the following was stated to the judge of the district of the state of Tabasco: Your communication, dated the fifteenth ultimo, having been reported to the president of the republic, in which you manifest that when there are trials of opposition in the denouncements of public lands, the proceedings of that nature increase considerably the expedientes, causing the copies to be very expensive for the denouncers, causing delay in their dispatch and a useless charge for the consideration of the department on reviewing them for its approval; for which reason you had determined to proceed separately with the questions of opposition, and that the copies which must be remitted to the department shall comprehend only the trials of the denouncements, the plans and decrees of adjudication, which you immediately put in practice, subject to a supreme resolution; and the first magistrate being informed thereof, and taking into consideration that your conclusion tends to diminish the expenses which the denouncers of public lands spend, which must facilitate their sale, he has been pleased to approve of your determination, prescribing only that when there are trials of opposition shall be added to the expediente the pleadings of the opponents and the final judgment of the court. And the president, desiring that the denouncers of public lands in all the republic, may enjoy the benefit which this provision gives, has thought proper to resolve that it be circulated to the district courts; and with this object I communicate it to you, for your understanding and other ends. Independence and liberty. Mexico, July 24, 1868.

*A Correlative Circular, No.* 58, *of July* 27, 1868.—Department of public works, colonization, industry, and commerce. Section 1. Circular No. 58. With this date it is stated to the citizen district attorney (promotor fiscal) of the district court of Tabasco, the following:

§ 651. *Preamble of Circular.*—Your communication of the date of the sixteenth of last May was received in this department, in which you manifest that denouncements of public lands occur daily in that district court, forming a considerable number monthly; that the expedientes run with regularity until the moment in which the survey is concluded, and that thenceforth the denouncers suspend their actions until some extraneous reason, such as an opposition, another denouncement, or a question of boundaries, causes them to start again, to remove the difficulty which is presented to them. That you have thus found in the court expedientes concluded which date from 1862, and some from 1857; from which it results that private individuals enjoy in fact the lands from the moment in which the survey is concluded, without taking care to pay into the exchequer their value; and when they do it, by repeated compulsions, it is without any profit for the rent which, strictly speaking, they ought to satisfy. You add that the law in force authorizes that evil because it concedes abatements to the possessors of the lands, and the denouncers try to reach by all possible means the time when they shall fail to obtain them. That besides, as the value of the land is paid after the expedientes have been revised by this department to which they are remitted by copies made at the cost of the interested parties, the latter take but little care in complying with that requisite. That with the object of avoiding the certain and positive damage which the revenues in the branch of public lands suffer, you propose that the two following resolutions be dictated: 1. That it be declared that the dominion of the lands shall not be acquired until the respective title of property has been issued, obliging the denouncers to satisfy an annual rent of six per cent for all the time which without title they enjoy the use of the public land. 2. That the price of the lands denounced ought to be satisfied after the decree of adjudication shall have been pronounced, in which the fiscal and the interested parties are agreed; waiting in a contrary case for the decision of the supreme government.

§ 652. *Article 21 to be Enforced.*—And having reported to the citizen president of the republic said communication, and he taking into consideration the divers points which you embrace in it, he has been pleased to dictate the following resolutions: That in respect to the tardy denouncers, what is provided in article 21 of the general law in force ought to be carried into effect in all cases; that is to say, that even when there is no opponent to a denouncement, the attorney (promotor) ought to ask that a term be fixed for the denouncer in which to continue the proceedings, or the judge ought to fix it officially; and if the denouncer should not appear within the term which is assigned him, the judge will make the corresponding declaration, and will publish it in order that another may denounce the land.

§ 653. *Abatements.*—That as to the abatements, it ought to be understood that the law concedes them to the possessor of the lands which on the date of their publication had the conditions of being cultivated, inclosed, held by a title, or possessed for ten years; but that in no manner must the years of possession be counted which the denouncer may have of the land after the denouncement and after the publication of the law.

§ 654. *Tardy Denouncers.*—The president has also been pleased to declare that the denouncers who do not appear opportunely to furnish the necessary expenses for the copies of the expedientes and of the plans must be considered as tardy denouncers, and subject, therefore, to the provisions of article 21 of the law; but that in order to facilitate them in the manner of obtaining said copies, he recommends them to recollect the circular relative thereto, of this department, dated the twenty-fourth inst., as well as that they are not to be received without those expenses which are in every point indispensable.

§ 655. *Dominion of Land when Acquired.*—In respect to the measures which you propose to correct, the abuses which you mention, the citizen president has thought proper to resolve that you be told in answer that the law leaves in no doubt the moment in which the dominion of the land is acquired, since it provides in article 19 that the denouncer will not be put in possession of the said land, except when the decree of adjudication has been approved by the department of public works, and that the interested party has presented the proof of having made the payment, in which case the judge will also make delivery to him of the title issued by the president of the republic. As to the second part of said proposition, he has been pleased to order that the denouncers of public lands, whose expedientes have been approved by the department, and the value of those lands have not been paid, that they ought to pay the interest on that value, at the rate of six per cent per annum, except in the cases in which the law permits the payment to be made on time.

§ 656. *Practice as to Payment to be Continued.*—As to the payment being made before the approbation of the department, the citizen president has resolved that no variation shall be made in the practice followed up to to-day, considering that it is provided in the law, and also that on many occasions it is necessary to modify the value of the land, by the verification which the department makes of the surperfice, in which case there would be the necessity of returning to or requiring from the interested party some new amount.

And it being a duty to recollect in all denouncements of public lands the preceding provisions, through the resolution of the citizen president, I communicate them to you for your understanding and corresponding ends. Independence and liberty. Mexico, July 27, 1868. Balcárcel. To the citizen judge of the district of the state of ........

§ 657. *The Price Paid for Public Lands to be Divided between the Federal and State Governments, August* 7, 1868.—General treasury of the nation. Section 1. Circular No. 75. With this date I state to the citizen chief of the treasury of the state of Yucatan what I copy: The citizen minister of treasury and public credit, with date of the second of the present month, states to this treasury the following: The communication of that department, dated the twenty-fifth of the present month, in which was transcribed that of the citizen treasurer-general of the nation, and having inserted the opinion of the citizen chief of the treasury of the state of Yucatan, relative to the manner in which the payment of the public lands ought to be made, having been reported to the citizen president of the republic, he has thought proper to resolve the following: That in conformity with what the law of the classification of sales of the thirtieth of last May provides, the half of the price of the public lands must be applied to the federal exchequer and the other half to that of the state in which the land is situated. In like manner must be divided the part which has to be paid in bonds; one half in the credits of the state, and the other half in the credits of the general government. Which I transcribe to you, in answer to your official letter relative thereto, etc. Which I insert to you for your understanding and consequent ends. Independence and liberty. Mexico, August 7, 1868. M. P. Izaguire. To the citizen chief of the treasury of. . . . . . . . . . .

§ 658. *A Supreme Provision of the Tenth of December*, 1870, *in Reference to the State of Yucatan.*—Departments of public works, colonization, industry, and commerce. Section 1. You manifest to this department in your note of the thirteenth of July last the reasons which there are for subjecting the designation of the dimensions of the exidos of the towns of that state, to what is provided on this point by the special law of that state of the eighth of October, 1844, which orders that said exidos shall be extended five thousand Castilian veras in each cardinal direction, measured from the porch of the principal church of each pueblo, respecting the lands of private property which are found in them. With this object you state that said law has issued by the legislative assembly of that state when it had the necessary powers to legislate on public lands, at a time even when the constitution of 1857 was not in force; which law declared that this business was outside of federal powers; that besides all this, the government of the Union has recognized the permanence of said law, as on distinct occasions, finding itself vested with extraordinary powers, it has dictated resolutions commanding that the designation of exidos in the towns of that state should be made according to the provisions contained in said law; and lastly, in various towns they have already proceeded in the terms of said law, giving to the exidos the dimensions which this law indicates, having previously made the corresponding survey and demarkations. In view of these reasons, the citizen president of the republic has thought proper to resolve that you be informed that in that state will continue to be in force the special law of that state of October 8, 1844; but that by article 27 of the federal constitution denying the legal power to every civil corporation to acquire and administer real estate, the towns of that state can not possess nor work in common the four square leagues which the law which has been mentioned designates for the exidos.

§ 659. *Fundo Legal, Extent of.*—In order to conciliate, then, the provisions of this law with those of the general constitution of the Union, the citizen president has thought proper to order that within the four square leagues corresponding to the exidos of each town, the fundo legal shall be designated in a square of one thousand two hundred varas on each side, the center of which shall be the center of the town; the fundo being separated from the lands which, not being cultivatable, shall be destined to the establishment of pantheons, hospitals, slaughter-houses (rastros), and any other object of public use in each town; and the rest of the four leagues treated of shall be divided into lots, and adjudicated in property to the fathers or heads of families; and there shall be remitted to this department a sketch of the lands divided, and a list of the names of the persons among whom they shall have been distributed, with the object that this department may issue the corresponding titles of property. Independence and liberty. Mexico, December 10, 1870.

§ 660. *Supreme Provision of the Tenth of December*, 1873, *Referring to the State of Tabasco.*—Department of public works, colonization, industry, and commerce of the Mexican republic. Section 1. Having examined in this department the expediente formed in the district court of Tabasco on account of the denouncement made by C. Policarpo Valenzuela and his sons, of a tract of public land situated on the banks of the river Tonalá, in the jurisdiction of San Antonio de Cárdenes, it has been noted that even when the denouncers are not found to be in the case of article 5 of the law, an extension greater than that which article 2 permits to be denounced was adjudicated to them in common; there being also the fact that C. Policarpo Valenzuela, father, denounced and was adjudicated to him an extension of one thousand seven hundred and twenty-two hectares in the district (partido) of Comalcalco.

§ 661. *Companies Considered as Individuals.*—In view of this, the citizen president of the republic, to whom was reported the expediente, has thought proper to resolve that it be said to you that as the law establishes nothing in respect to companies, these must be considered with the same rights as an individual, and they are not permitted to denounce more than the maximum extension which article 2 of the said law fixes, except in the cases of article 5 and the following articles, in which may be denounced all the extension possessed. But that, as in the present case, when various persons have associated themselves together to denounce a tract of land, and do not wish to renounce the extension which the law permits a single individual to acquire, the land must be measured and divided so that an extension greater than two thousand five hundred hectares does not belong to any one denouncer, and making the adjudication individual, in order that also the title shall be issued separately to each person to whom the land was adjudicated (adjudicatario).

§ 662. *Divisions of Two Thousand Five Hundred Hectares.*—In conformity with this resolution, that court must cause the division of the public land to be made (warning the expert who shall designate the lines of division on the land and on the plan), so that no division shall have more than two thousand five hundred hectares; and as one thousand seven hundred and twenty-two hectares, fifty-one aras, and nine centiaras have been adjudicated to C. Policarpo Valenzuela, father (in the partido of Comalcalco), this circumstance must be borne in mind in order not to assign him in the land of Tonalá more than seven hundred and seventy-seven hectares, forty-eight aras, and ninety-one centiaras, which united to those of Comalcalco form the two thousand five hundred hectares which the law permits him to denounce. Independence and liberty. Mexico, December 10, 1873. Balcárcal. Citizen district judge of the state of Tabusco. San Juan Bautista.

§ 663. *Supreme Provision of March 26, 1878, in Reference to the State of Chiapas.*—Department of public works, colonization, industry, and commerce. Section of public lands. Report being made to the president of the republic with that of the official charged with the section of public lands of this department, relative to seven expedientes of the state of Chiapas, which existed, the greater part, in the archives of said section, since prior to the taking charge thereof by the new personnel that now performs that task, which expedientes, although relative to to divers affairs, all contain substantially the same question for the government and authorities of said state, relative to the grave difficulties which in said expedientes at each step are offered in reference to the public lands, or possessed in good faith by poor individnals of the Indian race, or by those called ladinos, whose lands may be denounced contrary to justice and public convenience, in conformity with the general law in force of July 22, 1863, on account of not having titles therefor, and of the difficulty of obtaining them; as well as the inconveniences and losses of another kind, which bring to the towns the question not defined and referring to lands designated or to be designated, with the character of exidos of the said towns, in conformity with the special laws in force in that state prior to the general law of July 22, 1863, which suspended the effect of those laws, and left undecided their rights to such lands, which also may be, against public interests, denounced by private persons without any right. And uniting these questions with the five points under consideration which embace the solution of all the difficult propositions, and which were addressed to this department by the government of Chiapas, as appear from the aforesaid expedientes, the president of the republic, in virtue of all this, has been pleased to resolve that:

§ 664. *Exidos to be Divided into Lots.*—1. By a supreme provision it is resolved that in the state of Chiapas all the lands assigned to the towns by the special laws of said state, previous to the general law of July 22, 1863, with the character of exidos, or at least which with such a character have been surveyed to them, must be divided into lots equal or equivalent to the distinct suertes of land which have been worked and cultivated (according to the circumstances of each particular case) among the indigenous and poor ladinos, fathers or heads of families of the respective towns, in conformity with the prescriptions and bases which hereinafter shall be prefixed.

§ 665. *Exidos to be Assigned where None have been.*—2. In the rest of the towns which, in conformity with the aforesaid laws of the state itself, shall not have their respective exidos even designated, or at least surveyed, can have them measured and designated in conformity with said laws, dividing them immediately according to the aforesaid provision.

§ 666. *Lots Adjudicated to Heads of Families not to be Sold for Eight Years.*—3. Every tract of land which, in conformity with the preceding divisions, shall be adjudicated in a lot to a father or head of a family, can not be alienated by said party within the term of eight years, to be counted from the date on which shall be issued to him by this department his title of adjudication.

§ 667. *Division by Whom and how Made.*—4. The divisions of which fractions 1 and 2 of this supreme provision speak shall be made by a surveyor or expert, appointed for that purpose by the governor of the state, and with the assistance of the síndico or commissioner appointed by the town council (ayuntamiento) belonging to the town the exidos of which shall be divided; the expert or surveyor of which shall draw a map of the division in lots, designating thereon the number of each lot, the name of the individual to whom it is adjudicated, and the general boundary of all the exido adjudicated, as well as the number of the general hectares and of the superfice of each lot; citing for the operation the adjacent owners and parties interested therein, and sending a copy of said map through the channel of the government of the state to this department; in order that, meeting with its approbation, the title of each lot shall be issued. Another copy of said plan shall remain in the archives of the government of the state; and a copy can also be given to the respective ayuntamiento and to the interested parties, if they should ask for it and pay for it.

§ 668. *Price how Paid.*—But as the stamp law of the twenty-eighth of March, 1876, provides that no title shall be issued without the respective stamps being canceled; and in order that this department can put them on and cancel them on the titles which shall be issued for lots of the division, the governor of the state shall take care that each father of a family interested shall pay the amount of the title which has to be issued to him, accordingly as the tariff of said law declares by the words "title of lands" or "public writing," and where it is provided that, considering the value of the land, by each hundred dollars and for the fraction less than a hundred dollars, a stamp of ten cents shall be put, besides that of the fifty cents which the page of the title must bear. It must be observed that, in order to value or appreciate the value of each lot, the price of the tariff in force at the time of making the division shall be considered. At the present time it is the tariff of the first of January 1872, which assigns to each hectare of public land of that state the value of twenty-five cents.

§ 669. *Tariff Extended.*—5. It is declared again to be in force, in the state of Chiapas alone, for the term of one year, to be counted from the date on which this department shall receive an answer of the reception of this supreme provision, the circular of the thirtieth of September, 1867, taking into account the provision of the circular of the twentieth of May, 1869, in order that each three months shall be remitted from that state to the section of public lands of this department the notice to which said circular refers.

All which, by supreme order, I say to you, for the corresponding effects, as a result of the considerations which the government of its worthy charge has directed in the matter to this department of public works. Liberty and the constitution. Mexico, March 26, 1878. Riva Palacio. To the governor of the state of Chiapas. San Cristóbal Las Casas.

# CHAPTER XVI.

## RIGHTS OF FOREIGNERS TO PURCHASE, HOLD, AND DISPOSE OF REAL PROPERTY.

§ 670. Commentary—Provisional Government.
§ 671. Foreigners Who are Residents may Purchase where.
§ 672. Powers under Article 7—Plan of Tacubaya.
§ 673. Santa Anna's Power to Organize.
§ 674. Plan of Ayutla.
§ 675. Comonfort.
§ 676. Law of 1863.
§ 677. Federal Constitution.
§ 678. Object of Article 1.
§ 679. Article 33 of the Constitution.
§ 680. The word "citizen" not mentioned.
§ 681. Rights of Implication.
§ 682. Interpretation of Language.
§ 683. Opinion of Velasco.
§ 684. Execution of Laws of 1842 and 1856 Prohibited.
§ 685. State Rights.
§ 686. United States *v.* Fox.
§ 687. Irvine *v.* Marshall.
§ 688. Laws of 1842 and 1856 Void.
§ 689. Purchase without Reservation of Nationality.
§ 690. European Doctrine.
§ 691. Consent for Expatriation Necessary.
§ 692. Division of Opinion in Mexico.
§ 693. Conclusions.
§ 694. Law of 1842—Reasons for the Law.
§ 695. Foreigners may Hold Property.
§ 696. Foreigners may Hold Mines.
§ 697. Foreigners can Only Hold Two Estates in Same Department.
§ 698. Right of Tanto, Preference.
§ 699. Foreigners Subject to the Laws.
§ 700. Non-intervention by Foreign Laws.
§ 701. Miners, Privileges of.
§ 702. Absence for Two Years, What Effect.
§ 703. Frontier not Included.
§ 704. Coasts.
§ 705. Citizenship.
§ 706. Public Lands.
§ 707. Law of 1856—Foreigners may Acquire Land and Mines.
§ 708. Frontier.
§ 709. Petition for Land must be Addressed to Department of Public Works.

§ 670. *Provisional Government.*—A provisional government was organized by the chiefs of the army, who assembled at Tacubaya on the twenty-eighth of September, 1841. The basis of that government was called the plan of Tacubaya. By virtue of that plan, the executive was authorized to establish a government. That authority rested on the seventh article of that plan, which reads as follows: "The powers of the provisional executive are all those which are necessary for the reorganization of all branches of public administration." Under that power Santa Anna issued the decree known as the law of March 11, 1842, herein contained.

§ 671. *Foreigners Who are Residents may Purchase where.*—Article 1 thereof provides that foreigners who are domiciled and residents in the republic may acquire and possess country or city property by purchase, adjudication, denouncement, or by any other title established by the laws. Article 3 provides that no one foreigner can acquire more than two estates within the same department, without the license of the supreme government. At that time the states were termed "departments." Article 8 prohibits a foreigner from holding lands after an absence of two years; that is, such an absence subjects the land to sale by the government; one tenth of the amount of the sale shall go to the informer and the remainder shall be deposited for the disposal of the owner. Article 10 prohibits foreigners from acquiring land within five leagues of the coast.

§ 672. *Powers under Article 7 of the Plan of Tacubaya.*—The power granted in article 7 of said plan of Tacubaya was limited to "the reorganization of all branches of public administration." Such a power was essential to bring into being an established form of government. When the government became reorganized the power ceased. The plan of Tacubaya was in the nature of a constitution. It was not intended to vest the law-making power in the executive beyond that of reorganization. Hence, any law after the formation of the government, made by Santa Anna, was *ultra vires*—beyond his power, therefore null and void.

§ 673. *Santa Anna's Power to Reorganize.*—On the seventeenth of March, 1853, Santa Anna was again declared to be elected president. Under the basis for the administration of the republic, issued by him April 22, 1853, he seems only to claim power in article 1, section 3, to "reorganize all the branches of public administration." But on the thirtieth of January, 1854, he issued a law which declared that of March 11, 1842, to be in force. He likewise herein exceeded his powers, as he did on decreeing the said law of March 11th.

§ 674. *Plan of Ayutla.*—On the first of March, 1854, the chiefs of the army assembled at Ayutla and proclaimed the plan of Ayutla. On the seventeenth of the said month certain officers met in the fort of San Diego, Acapulco, and modified the said plan. The third article of said reformed plan was as follows: "The provisional president, without any other restriction than that of respecting inviolably individual guaranties, shall be henceforth invested with ample faculties to reform all branches of the public administration, to attend to the security and independence of the nation, and to promote all that may lead to its prosperity, aggrandizement, and progress."

§ 675. *Comonfort.*—On the eighth day of December, 1855, Comonfort came into power as provisional president; and on the first day of February, 1856, relative to foreigners, which is cited in this chapter. Article 2 thereof prohibits foreigners from acquiring land on the frontiers within twenty leagues of the boundary, without the previous permission of the supreme government. By article 3, foreigners who desire to obtain land within said limit must present a petition to the department of public works (fomento), accompanied with a report of the governor of the state or territory where the land is located.

§ 676. *Law of* 1863.—The law of July 22, 1863, relative to what may be termed the pre-emption law, declared the foregoing law, of February 1, 1856, to be in force. This law, in the opinion of the author, gives no additional force to the former one.

§ 677. *Federal Constitution.*—The present constitution of Mexico was adopted February 5, 1857, and it would seem from its language that it has abrogated said laws of 1842 and 1856. Article 1, section 1, title 1 of the constitution reads as follows: "The Mexican people recognize that the rights of man are the basis and the object of social institutions. Consequently it declares that all the laws and all the authorities of the country must respect and sustain the guaranties which the present constitution grants." The interpretation of the rights of man by Blackstone is as follows: "The rights of man consist in the free use, disposal, and enjoyment of all his acquisitions, without any control or dimunition save only by the laws of the land:" 1 Bla. Com. 138.

§ 678. *Object of Said Article* 1.—Said article 1 was adopted for the very purpose of preventing any restraint being placed upon man in the free use, disposal, and enjoyment of his acquisitions, saving what may be essential for the welfare of the nation, such as taxes, the right of eminent domain, etc. These exceptions are applicable to mankind—to citizens as well as foreigners. This view is supported by article 33 of the constitution, which is as follows:

§ 679. *Article* 33 *of the Constitution.*—Foreigners are those who do not possess the qualities determined in article 30. They have the right to the guaranty granted in section 1, title 1, of the present constitution, save that in all cases the power which the government has in expelling pernicious foreigners. They are obliged to contribute to the public expenses in the manner which the law requires, and to obey and respect the institutions, laws, authorities of the country, being subject to the judgments and decrees of the tribunals, without being able to have any other resources than those which the law concedes to Mexicans.

§ 680. *The Word "Citizen" not Mentioned.*—It will be observed that the first section of the constitution, composed of twenty-nine articles, does not contain the word "citizen," but speaks of "man" and "persons." All the rights given to man in said section 1, title 1, are expressly guaranteed to foreigners in said article 33. It likewise impliedly guarantees to them all the recourses as regards property which Mexican citizens possess.

§ 681. *Rights by Implication.*—Chief Justice Marshall observed that when the constitution of the United States said that private property should not be taken for public use without a just compensation being paid therefor, it impliedly said that it could be taken by paying for it. When the Mexican constitution says that foreigners shall have no other recourses than those which the law concedes to Mexicans, it impliedly says that foreigners shall have all the recourses which Mexicans have. This is but a fair, unrestrained, and reasonable construction of the language of the constitution.

§ 682. *Interpretation of Language.*—A very just and salutary doctrine was laid down by the third United States circuit court in Pennsylvania upon the interpretation of language as follows: "Laws are construed strictly to save a right or avoid a penalty;

and liberally, to give a remedy or effect an object declared in the law."

§ 683. *Opinion of Velasco.*—Señor Maria del Castillo, a member of the constitutional convention in 1856, was a justice of the supreme court of Mexico when he published the work entitled "Observations for the Study of Mexican Constitutional Law" (1871), in which he uses the following language in speaking of article 33: "Foreigners have the right to the guaranties granted by the constitution, because they are in favor of the rights of man; with one limitation, and that is, the power which the government has to expel pernicious foreigners. The republic gives a free hospitality to all foreigners, and it invites them with the riches of the country." It would seem from the foregoing reasons, the said laws of 1842 and 1856 were clearly made nugatory by the constitution.

§ 684. *Execution of the Laws of* 1842 *and* 1856 *Prohibited.*—If the views herein expressed are not well supported by the reasoning advanced, other reasons may be given in the proposition that articles 22 and 27 of the constitution absolutely prohibit the execution of said laws of 1842 and 1856. By article 22, confiscation is forever prohibited. Article 27 reads as follows: "The property of persons can not be occupied without their consent, unless for the cause of public utility and previous indemnification." It may be observed that the word "person" is used, not "citizen." If a foreigner owning land in Mexico should absent himself for more than two years, and the property should be sold, that would be confiscation. If possession were taken without his consent, that would be in violation of article 27, as property can only be taken for public utility by paying for it. That is merely the right of eminent domain which belongs to every sovereign power, and is applicable to all persons within its jurisdiction, whether citizen or foreigner.

§ 685. *State Rights.*—If the opinion of the author be not correct as already expressed as to the interpretation of the constitution, then he submits that the federal government has no control of the subject-matter; and that it comes within the jurisdiction of state power. Article 117 of the Mexican federal constitution is as follows: "The powers which are not expressly conceded by this constitution to the federal functionaries are understood as reserved to the states." No power is given to the federal government over the subject-matter, unless as contended for herein, *supra*. Either the power is taken away by the federal constitution from all the authorities, to prohibit foreigners from holding real estate, as assumed herein, or it is vested in the states.

§ 686. *United States* v. *Fox.*—In the case of the United States *v.* Fox, 94 U. S. 315, the court held: "The several states of the Union possess the power to regulate the tenure of real property within their respective limits, the modes of acquisition and transfer, the rule of its descent, and the extent to which a testamentary disposition of it may be exercised by its owners. * * * The titles and modes of disposition of real property within the state, whether *inter vivos* or testamentary, are not matters placed under the control of federal authority. Such control would be foreign to the purpose for which the federal government was created, and would seriously embarrass the landed interests of the state."

§ 687. *Irvine* v. *Marshall.*—In the case of Irvine *v.* Marshall, 20 How. 558, the same court said: "The United States, being the owners of the public lands within the states and territories, have the right to say to whom, in what mode, and by what title they shall be conveyed. We hold the true principle to be this: that whenever the question in any court, state or federal, is whether a title to land which was once the property of the United States has passed, that question must be resolved by the laws of the United States; but wherever according to those laws the title shall have passed, then the property, like all other property in the state, is subject to the state legislation, so far as that legislation is consistent with the admission that the title passed and vested according to the laws of the United States."

§ 688. *Laws of* 1842 *and* 1856 *Void.*—Whether the federal constitution takes away the power from both federal and state legislatures over the subject-matter, or whether it is vested in the states, in either case the said laws of 1842 and 1856 are void.

§ 689. *As to the Effect of a Purchase of Land by a Foreigner without a Reservation of his Nationality.*—Article 30, section 2, designates who are Mexicans. Among that class are included foreign purchasers in the following language: "Foreigners who acquire real estate in the republic or have Mexican children, provided they do not manifest their resolution to preserve their nationality." If such a provision can be sustained, then a foreigner who purchases land and fails to make the reservation in the deed, either by accident, mistake, or otherwise, is deprived of the allegiance to his country without any affirmative act of his own.

§ 690. *European Doctrine.*—The general European doctrine is, that no person can by an act of his own, without the consent of the government, put off his allegiance and become alien. This doctrine of perpetual allegiance grew out of the feudel system. Expatriation is considered in the United States a fundamental right, and when manifested by a person's oath of allegiance to a foreign government, it is sufficient to establish the expatriation of such person, so as to render him no longer subject to the government of his country.

§ 691. *Consent for Expatriation Necessary.*—It never has been asserted that one government can compel a citizen or subject of another government to yield up his allegiance which he owes to his native country, against his own voluntary consent. It may be said that it is a presumption of law that every person is acquainted with the law of the country in which he resides; and therefore, a person buying land without a knowledge in fact of the constitution is nevertheless bound by its provisions. But such a doctrine can not be applied to the high privilege of allegiance to one's native land. Nothing less than a positive declaration in some form, with a *bona fide* intent to divest himself of his allegiance, can deprive a man thereof. And even this is further than European powers have gone, except by treaty stipulation.

§ 692. *Division of Opinion in Mexico.*—The Mexican jurists are divided in opinion on this question of the right of foreigners to purchase, hold, and dispose of real property in contravention of said laws of 1842 and 1856. The author is of opinion that the weight of authority among Mexicans is in favor of the affirmative—that foreigners have such right equally with Mexicans. They are also divided in opinion as to the interpretation of article 30, relative to the necessity of reservation of nationality when lands are purchased by foreigners.

§ 693. *Conclusions.*—Assuming that said laws of 1842 and 1856 are in force, it may be said in conclusion: 1. That foreigners may purchase and hold within the belt of twenty leagues from the frontier, by obtaining a permission from the executive of the federal government, upon petition therefor, accompanied by a favorable report from the governor of the state or territory where the land desired may be situated. 2. That they may purchase within the belt of five leagues from the coast, by obtaining a permission from congress. 3. That where they purchase outside of either of said belts, and if they wish to be absent, they may return to the country any time before the expiration of the two years, and remaining a short time, may again depart, thereby technically keeping within the provision of the law.

*The Laws of March* 11, 1842, *Relative to the Rights of Foreigners.*—Citizen Luis Gonzaga Vieyra, brevet brigadier-general, and governor of this department. By the department of foreign affairs and government the following has with this date been communicated to me: Most excellent sir: His excellency, the provisional president of the republic, has been pleased to transmit to me the following decree: Antonio Lopez de Santa Anna, general of division, well deserving (benemérito) of the country, and provisional president of the Mexican republic, to all the inhabitants thereof, know ye:

§ 694. *Reasons for the Law.*—That after a mature and the most cautious examination into the benefits which will result to the republic from permitting foreigners to acquire property, having heard the opinion of the council of representatives, who with the greatest exactitude examined this subject; the reports of several bodies of the departments, many well-informed persons, and the *pro* and *contra* supported in print; being also convinced that a frank policy and a well-understood interest demand that there should no longer be delayed a concession which may tend to the advancement of the republic, by the increase of population, the extension and division of property; which consequently makes the national wealth the greater; having also in consideration that by these means the safety of the nation may be more and more secured, since foreign proprietors will be so many more defenders of the national rights, at the same time that they are interested in the common property; considering also the impulse which will be given to agriculture, industry, and commerce, which are the sources of public wealth; and finally, that the opinion generally expressed is in favor of the said concession—I have thought proper, exercising the powers conceded to me by the seventh of the bases accorded in Tacubaya, and attested by the representatives of the departments, to decree as follows:

§ 695. *Foreigners may Hold Property.*—Art. 1. Foreigners not citizens residing in the republic may acquire and hold town and country property, by purchase, adjudication, denouncement, or any other title established by the laws.

§ 696. *Foreigners may Hold Mines.*—Art. 2. They may also acquire ownership in mines of gold, silver, copper, quicksilver, iron, and coal, of which they may be discoverers in conformity with the mining ordinance.

§ 697. *They can Only Hold Two Estates in Same Department.* Art 3. No individual foreigner can acquire more than two country estates in the same department, without a license from the supreme government, and only within the boundaries which they now have, each independent of the other.

§ 698. *Right of Preference.*—Art. 4. In the acquisition of town property in the cities, towns, and villages, as also in the lands contiguous thereto, in which they may wish to construct new estates, they shall enjoy the right del tanteo,[1] under similar circumstances and conditions.

§ 699. *Foreigners Subject to the Laws.*—Art. 5. Foreigners who in virtue of this law may acquire property are absolutely liable in regard to it to the existing laws, or those which may prevail in the republic as to transfer, use, preservation, and payment of imposts, without being able to allege in respect to these points the right of foreign protection (extranjeria).

§ 700. *Non-intervention by Foreign Laws.*—Art. 6. Consequently, all the questions of this nature which may arise shall be decided in the ordinary and usual manner of the national laws, with the exclusion of all other intervention whatsoever.

§ 701. *Miners, Privileges of.*—Art. 7. Foreigners who may acquire country property, city property, or property in mines, and foreigners who may labor in them as servants, laborers, or journeymen, are not obliged to take part in the service of arms, unless in the way of police; but they are to pay the imposts which have for their object to keep up the militia.

§ 702. *Absence, What Effect.*—Art. 8. If the foreign proprietor absent himself for more than two years with his family from the republic, without obtaining permission from the government, or if the property pass by inheritance or by any other title into the possession of persons non-resident in the republic, he shall be obliged to sell it within two years, counted from the day when his absence took place, or the change of ownership. If this be not done, the sale shall be officially proceeded with, with all the legal formalities, and of the proceeds the tenth part shall go to the informer; the nine tenths remaining shall be safely deposited at the disposal of the owner. This shall always be done when it is proved that the owner of the estate resides

[1] El tanteo in law signifies a right of preference; that is, a right to buy at the highest price offered by anybody else.

out of the republic, and he who is the nominal proprietor is only so in place of the absentee.

§ 703. *Frontier not Included.*—Art. 9. These arrangements do not include the departments on the frontier and bordering upon other nations, in regard to which special laws of colonization will be enacted, without the power in foreigners to ever acquire property in them, without the express license of the supreme government of the republic.

§ 704. *Coast.*—Art. 10. In the departments which are not on the frontier, and which may have coasts, only at five leagues distance from the coasts can foreigners acquire country property.

§ 705. *Citizenship.*—Art. 11. In order that foreigners who may have acquired property in the republic may be citizens thereof, it is sufficient that they are proprietors, that they have resided two years in the republic, and that they have conducted themselves well. The expediente drawn up in this manner will be sent to the proper department, by which the certificate of citizenship will be issued.

§ 706. *Public Lands.*—Art. 12. Foreigners can not acquire public lands in all the departments of the republic, without contracting for them with the government which possesses this right as representing the domain of the Mexican nation.

Wherefore, I order that it be printed, published, circulated, and carried into full effect. Palace of the national government, Mexico, March 11, 1842. Antonio López de Santa Anna. José Maria de Bocanegra, minister of foreign affairs and government. And I communicate to your excellency for your information and consequent action. God and liberty. Mexico, March 14, 1842. Bocanegra.

And in order that it may come to the knowledge of every one, I order that it be published by edict in this capital and the other cities, towns, and places within the limits of this department, exposed in the usual places, and circulated among those who are concerned in taking care to see it observed. Given in Mexico on the fourteenth of March, 1842. Luis G. Vieyra. Miguel Zerez, secretary.

*The Law of February* 1, 1856, *Pertaining to the Rights of Foreigners to Hold Land.*—Department of public works, colonization, industry, and commerce of the Mexican republic. Section 1. His excellency the substitute president of the republic has been pleased to direct to me the decree which follows: The citizen Ignacio Comonfort, substitute president of the republic, to the inhabitants thereof, know ye: That in use of the faculties which the plan proclaimed in Ayutla and reformed in Acapulco concede to me, I have thought proper to decree the following:

§ 707. *Foreigners may Acquire Lands and Mines.*—Art. 1. Foreigners who are denizens and residents in the republic may acquire possession of country and city property, including mines and all classes of metals and coal, whether by purchase, adjudication, denouncement, or any other title of domain established by the laws or by the mining ordinance.

§ 708. *Frontier.*—Art. 2. No foreigner can, without previous permission of the supreme government, acquire real estate in the frontier states or territories, except twenty leagues from the line of the frontier.

§ 709. *Petition for Lands must be Addressed to Department of Public Works.*—Art. 3. Foreigners who desire to obtain the permission of which the preceding article speaks must address their petition to the department of public works (fomento), in order that with a review of it, and the report of the government of the respective state or territory, what is proper may be resolved.

§ 710. *Lands for Building.*—Art. 4. In the acquisitions, in consequence of this law, which foreigners may wish to make of city estates or lands on which to construct improvements near the towns, the present tenants or lessees shall enjoy the right of tanteo [1] in equal circumstances and conditions.

§ 711. *Subject to the Laws.*—Art. 5. Foreigners who in virtue of this law acquire real estate, are subject, in all that relates to it, to the provisions which have been dictated or may be dictated in the future upon the transfer, use, and preservation of said property in the republic, as well as to the payment of every class of impost, without being able to allege at any time in respect to these points the right of foreign protection (extranjeria).

§ 712. *No Foreign Laws to Intervene.*—Art. 6. Consequently all the questions which relative to said property may arise shall be ventilated in the tribunals of the republic and in conformity with its laws, with the exclusion of all foreign intervention, whatever it may be.

§ 713. *Armed Service.*—Art. 7. Foreigners who acquire country, city, or mining property, in conformity with this law, shall be obliged to render armed services when the question is of the security of property or the preservation of order in the same

[1] A right to buy at the same price which has been offered to others.

town in which they are settled. Outside of these cases, such service can not be required of them.

§ 714. *Citizenship.*—Art. 8. In order that foreigners who may have acquired property in the republic may be citizens of it, it will be sufficient that they cause that circumstance to appear before the political authority of the place of their residence. This proof having been presented to the department of relaciones, with the respective petition, his letter of citizenship shall be issued to him.

Wherefore I command that it be printed, published, circulated, and that due fulfillment must be given it. Given in the national palace of Mexico, on the first of February, 1856. Ignacio Comonfort. To the citizen Manuel Siliceo. And I communicate it to you for your understanding and consequent ends. God and liberty. Mexico, first of February, 1856. Siliceo.

# CHAPTER XVII.

## FORESTS AND TIMBER CUTTING.

§ 715. Old Ordinance.
§ 716. Preservation and Increase.
§ 717. Employees.
§ 718. Forest-keepers.
§ 719. Duties of Agents.
§ 720. Distant Places.
§ 721. Duties of Subinspectors.
§ 722. Forest-keepers under Orders of Subinspectors.
§ 723. Authorities must Give Aid.
§ 724. Residence of Subinspectors and Keepers.
§ 725. Third Parties.
§ 726. Application of Fines.
§ 727. Permits Necessary to Cut.
§ 728. Cutting Only in Places Solicited
§ 729. Places to be Marked.
§ 730. Instructions to be Observed.
§ 731. Responsibility of Inspectors and Keepers.
§ 732. Permits not Transferable.
§ 733. Permits to Cut Give No Other Right.
§ 734. Rights in Permit can not be Exceeded.
§ 735. Renewal of Permits.
§ 736. Trespassers.
§ 737. Offensive Cutters.
§ 738. Keeper's Limits.
§ 739. Expenses of Examination.
§ 740. Officer's Faults.
§ 741. Settlement of Difficulties.
§ 742. Dye-wood.
§ 743. Commencement of This Regulation.
§ 744. Price of Wood.
§ 745. Character of Trees to be Cut.
§ 746. Reproduction of Trees.
§ 747. Reproduction of Sprouts or Plants.
§ 748. Artificial Reproduction.

§ 715. *Old Ordinance.*—Under the old ordinance pertaining to forests and the cutting of timber, the rights thereto were classified into five divisions: 1. National; 2. Municipal; 3. That of public establishments, such as hospitals and houses of charity; 4. Private; and 5. That of an undivided right belonging to two or more of the former classes. Since the enactment of the law of June 25, 1856, which compelled all civil and ecclesiastical corporations to dispose of all their common lands, and to reserve none but which were requisite for their buildings and the grounds specially needed for their respective institutions, the old ordinance has become necessarily modified, and it may be said, repealed. The pueblos or towns had their woodlands, to which all residents thereof resorted for the necessary fire-wood and timber of construction. By the said law of 1856, the pueblos disposed of all lands save the exidos, or commons for recreation, and lands for house-lots. The church and hospitals, and all other corporations, were likewise deprived of owning any lands save as before stated. Hence the only division of forest lands now remaining is that of national and private ownership. The owner of land is the owner of the forest thereon; therefore no law can effect such a vested right, except the will of the owner. The national forests and the cutting of timber thereon is now wholly governed by the following regulation: Department of state, and that of public works, colonization, industry, and commerce, of the Mexican republic. Section 1. The president of the republic, in use of the constitutional faculty and in compliance with the provision in the third paragraph of fraction 6 of article 2 of the law of income, of the thirty-first of May of the present year, has been pleased to resolve the following regulation, to which the cutting of timber in forests and on national lands must be subject:

## Chapter I.—Of the Agents Charged with Watching the Cutting of Timber.

§ 716. *Preservation and Increase.*—Art. 1. The preservation and increase of the forests and national lands of trees of building timber, of cabinet-woods and dye-woods, is commended immediately to the chiefs of the treasury, as agents of the department of public works in conformity with the resolution of the tenth of January, 1862, and to the subinspectors and forest-keepers, the number and pay of whom the said department shall designate.

§ 717. *Employés.*—Art. 2. These employés shall belong to the chief offices (jefaturas) of the treasury, to which demarkation the forests and lands belong. Consequently they shall perform all the orders and commissions relative to this branch which the chiefs of the treasury shall give them, although they may not be specified in this regulation.

§ 718. *Forest-keepers.*—Art. 3. The chiefs of the treasury, with the character of agents of the department of public works, shall appoint subinspectors and forest-keepers, preferring, as far as it may be possible, the natives of the country who shall have honesty, knowledge of land, and other necessary qualities for the performance of their employments.

§ 719. *Duties of Agents.*—Art. 4. The attributes corresponding to the agents for the performance of this regulation are the following: 1. To issue the permits which may be solicited for the cutting of the trees, expressing with clearness and exactness the number of them and the situation of the place where the cutting must be done. 2. To receive at the time of issuing the permit the total value corresponding to the number of trees which have to be cut. 3. To examine what are the woods and lands of national property which there may be in the state in which they exercise their functions, and to communicate them to the department of public works, in order that the necessary provisions may be dictated so that the public treasury may enter into possession of them. 4. To make the corresponding explanations to prove the offense of which article 21 speaks, and to pass the proofs which result to the respective judge, in order that he may impose the penalty which corresponds to the offender for the damages and losses which he may have caused the legitimate possessor. 5. To deny to the adjacent parties who cause offense to the vicinity of other cutters the legalization of their permits in the places where their presence prejudices. 6. To take care that the subinspectors make the examinations which the eighth part of article 6 of this regulation provides, reporting them to the department of public works. 7. To try to have the questions which arise among the cutters terminated peaceably by conciliation, and in case he can not do so, to transmit the *data* which he shall have collected to the judicial authority, if the litigant should carry their questions there. 8. To designate to the subinspectors and forest-keepers the demarkation which each one has to watch without prejudice to the moving of them, according as the best service may esteem it proper. 9. To impose and make effective a fine of six dollars for each tree which shall be cut without their authorization and consent, requiring besides the value of the tree, and reporting to the department of public works with the expediente which shall be formed, in order that it may examine if their proceedings have been regulated according to justice. If other damages and losses shall be caused, or should the offender not pay the fine, he will be assigned to the respective district judge in order that he may impose upon him the corresponding penalty. 10. To impose on the subinspectors and forest-keepers a fine even to the third part of the salaries which they enjoy, when they do not fulfill the obligations which in this regulation are imposed upon them, and they may also remove them. And in case the offense should be by dissimulation or connivance with the parties interested in the cutting of the trees which may be designated in the permit, they shall be assigned to the respective district judge, in order that he may apply to them the penalty which they shall merit. 11. To propose to the department of public works what the cutters ought to pay in the state in which they exercise their attributes for each tree that they cut, establishing the reasons which they may have for proposing the price which shall govern for the two years, commencing with the next year, 1882. In case the cutting be of dye-woods, or if the question is of using the trees which produce india-rubber or other gums or resins, the chief of the treasury, taking the necessary *data*, will propose the price which ought to be paid in that case.

§ 720. *Distant Places.*—Art. 5. When by the distance at which are found the places in which the cutting of timber is solicited, it shall be difficult to appear at the chief office (jefatura) of the treasury to solicit the permits of which faction 1 of article 4 aforesaid speaks, and for the same reason the chiefs of the treasury can not exercise due vigilance over said cutting, the department of public works shall designate the employés or federal agents which ought to be substituted for those in the exercise of the functions which the present regulation commits to them.

§ 721. *Duties of Subinspectors.*—Art. 6. The attributes of the subinspectors shall be the following: 1. To perform all the commissions of the service which the agent may think proper to order them to perform, and to inform themselves of the limits of the demarkation which are designated for them, which they must know for themselves in all its extension. 2. To give possession to the cutters of timber of the place in which they have to practice the cutting, according to the permit which the respective agent shall have issued to them. 3. To watch for themselves that timber is not cut without the consent of the agency; for that purpose they can require in the places (monterias) where the wood is cut, from the owners or persons charged with them, the permit by which they are doing the cutting, and they must stop it if it is done without permission; and they must take care to give notice immediately to the said agency, whenever they shall note any offense relative to this matter. 4. To collect carefully the *data* relative to the branches of wealth which the national forests contain, reporting what they may observe to the agent in or that he may place it within the knowledge of the department of public works. 5. To explain the true name of the places, when they are disputed by the cutters, with two or more different names. 6. To give a name to the national forests which have none, whenever wood-cutters are established, and to explain the true topographical position of the places, and to compare the notice which they must have of the permits issued with those which the cutters present to them, and to examine if said cutters do the cutting according to the corresponding permit. 7. To take care that the provisions in article 15 be complied with relative to the planting of seeds of mahogany or cedar, or other tree, or the cutting of trunks properly, in order that their production may be renewed. 8. To inform themselves on the sites where the cutting is done, of the questions which arise among the cutters, in order to place them within the knowledge of the agent, so that the latter may try to terminate them pacifically; and if this can not be effected, to remit the *data* which they may collect to the respective courts in case the interested parties appear there. 9. To prohibit them from cutting india-rubber and fruit trees for the sole purpose of availing themselves of the fruit of the latter, which fruit they may take without prejudice in any manner to the tree which produces it. 10. To take care also that tender trees are not cut, and that they are not destroyed at the time of cutting mature trees, governing themselves further as far as may be possible by the instructions which are found at the end of this regulation. 11. To watch that all the cutters comply with the provisions which belong to them to fulfill by this regulation. 12. To prevent fires from being made in the forests, which may cause the burning of them, and in case that any fire should occur, whether by this or any other cause, to try at all cost to extinguish it with the aid of the local authorities, and to try to procure the apprehension of those who shall have caused it, and to assign them then to the respective local judge, in order that the latter may practice the preliminary proceedings relative to the act, and in the mean time the subinspector will report to the agent of public works, in order that he may assign the guilty parties to the corresponding district judge. 13. To prohibit the cattle from crossing over the places of woods in which they can cause injury to the tender trees..

§ 722. *Forest-keepers Subject to the Orders of Subinspectors.*—Art. 7. The forest keepers shall be immediately dependent upon the subinspectors, without prejudice to the performance of the commissions or orders which the agent may give them, and they shall perform in default of the subinspectors the attributes which are assigned to them in the preceding article. Both are obliged to arm themselves at their own expense with a rifle or escopet and a hunter's cutlass.

§ 723. *Authorities must Give Aid.*—Art. 8. The subinspectors and forest-keepers shall always carry their titles or appointments, and as employés of the federal government they shall claim from all the authorities the aid which may be necessary for the performance of their employment; to which end the agent shall take care to report to the political authorities of the state the names of those employés and of the places where they exercise their vigilance.

§ 724. *Residence.*—Art. 9. They shall reside within the place of the demarkation which is assigned to them to watch, and they can not absent themselves from it nor change their residence without a previous permission from the agent. The latter can designate to them a tract of land which they can cultivate and form thereon their dwelling.

§ 725. *Third Parties.*—Art. 10. The subinspectors can not dictate any provision which may affect the interests of a third party without the knowledge of the agent in order that the latter may act with just information, and duly proved.

§ 726. *Application of Fines.*—Art. 11. The total amount of the fines which shall be imposed and collected in conformity with fraction 9 of article 4 will be divided by the respective agent of public works into two equal parts, one to be applied between the denouncer and apprehender or all of it if one person performed both services, and the other part shall be divided also into two portions, one to be destined for the repairing of the evil caused, by sowing the necessary seed for the purpose, and the other shall be for the employé who exercises the functions of agent of public works in that locality.

### Chapter II.—Of the Cutting of Timber.

§ 727. *Permits Necessary to Cut.*—Art. 12. Every person or company that wishes to dedicate itself to the cutting of timber in the national forests must first obtain of the agency of public works the corresponding permit, expressing in the petition which he makes with this object the name of the forest, and the immediate streams and trenches, and the direction of the way (salidero) out of the timber which he proposes to cut, as well as the adjacent owners nearest to the place where the cutting of the trees is to be effected.

§ 728. *Cutting must be Done in the Place Solicited.*—Art. 13. The permit by the agency having been conceded, the latter will order that the subinspector, accompanied by one of the forest-keepers, shall pass to the place designated by the cutter, in order to recognize that the cutting shall be done in the place asked for by the interested party; and if the forest-keeper should not agree to it, he shall report to the agency in order that it may dictate its orders to remedy the evil which might result by the change of names of the places in prejudice of the exchequer or of the said cutters.

§ 729. *Place to be Marked.*—Art. 14. The place having been recognized by the subinspector, and it having been ascertained that it is the same as designated by the petitioner, in the permit which he shall have asked to do the cutting, the subinspector shall cause the trees to be limited which shall belong to the place, by a clearing or path around them of a meter in width, and within which limit can not be comprehended more than the number of trees mentioned in its denouncement and designated in the permit from the agency. If on the land there should be any trench, stream, or low swamp, heavy timbers shall be placed at short distances, with a smaller one across them, which shall mark the distance to the timber which is legally being cut on the place, and with which requisite the right thereto is protected.

§ 730. *Instructions to be Observed.*—Art. 15. Every timber cutter shall direct his operations in conformity with the instructions which are inserted in the final part of this regulation, and in conformity with said instructions they shall be obliged to plant for each tree that they cut down at least ten seeds of mahogany, cedar, or other tree which the respective subinspector shall designate, who shall require from the cutter the plants produced from said seeds, or sprouts or renewals, as said instructions indicate.

§ 731. *Responsibility of Inspectors and Keepers.*—Art. 16. The subinspectors and forest-keepers shall be responsible in case that the provision in the preceding article is not complied with, relative to the delivery of the plants produced by the seeds, and the sprouts or renewals spoken of in said article, who shall take care to place them in proper places, in order that their growth may succeed, and shall preserve them with the necessary shelter to protect them from any cause that may destroy them.

§ 732. *Permits not Transferable.*—Art. 17. No individual who shall obtain a permit from the agency to cut trees on national lands can sell it, concede it, or transfer it to any other person.

§ 733. *Permits to Cut Give No Other Right.*—Art. 18. No person who shall have obtained a permit from the agency to cut trees on national lands can allege at any time any right of property, of possession, of retention, or of any other kind to said lands, they being only permitted to extract from them the timber on the precise terms which the permit fixes and proved to be corresponding to the permit by which it was cut, and the fees for which they have paid to the agency.

§ 734. *Rights in Permits can not be Exceeded.*—Art. 19. The permits conceded by the agency will only be useful to cut the number of trees which they designate in the course of the natural year to which the date corresponds on which they have been issued; and this time having passed, they will be null and of no value.

§ 735. *Renewal of Permits.*—Art. 20. The wood-cutters in the national forests can renew before the agency their permits annually, to cut in the forests adjacent to those on which they have established their wood-yards, but without this giving them any right to the possession or retention of the land, or to the trees which they have contiguous thereto, as they will have only such right to the trees for which they shall have satisfied the impost and which shall have been designated for each year, in which case they shall be subjected to the provision in article 14 of this regulation.

§ 736. *Trespassers Have No Rights—Their Liability.*—Art. 21. Every person who invades the forests marked in conformity with the provision in article 14 of this regulation shall lose the timber which he shall have cut, which shall remain on the place for the benefit of him who may have a right to it, who shall report it immediately to the agency, in order that it may make the corresponding explanations, and the offense being proved, he shall pass the expediente which he shall form to the corresponding judge, in order that he may impose the penalty on the offender for the damages and losses which he may have caused the legitimate possessor.

§ 737. *Offensive Cutters—Penalty.*—Art. 22. Every adjacent wood-cutter who shall cause offense to the vicinity of other cutters shall lose the right of having his permit legalized by the agency in the places where his presence is prejudicial, his offense having been proved in this sense.

§ 738. *Keeper's Limits.*—Art. 23. To each keeper shall be designated by the subinspector, and with the approbation of the agent, the extension of the woods which shall be considered proper for him to watch, according as the greater or less number of wood-yards established in it may require.

§ 739. *Expenses of Examination.*—Art. 24. Where cutters find it difficult to make their permits effective, and claim an ocular examination by the agent or by the subinspector, the expenses which may be caused thereby shall be on account of the parties who raise the question and consent to the examination.

§ 740. *Officers' Faults.*—Art. 25. Every person who shall note in the subinspectors and forest-keepers any fault in the compliance with this regulation shall notify the agent, in order that he may impose the fine which corresponds to the case from which the fault really results, and he shall receive a third part of the fine should there be occasion to require it.

§ 741. *Settlement of Difficulties.*—Art. 26. All the wood-cutters who do not agree with the deliberation of the agent of public works to terminate their difficulties pacifically, can carry them before the judicial authority which has jurisdiction to enforce their rights; but they can not allege any right against the interests of the exchequer for the cutting of timber on national lands, excepting that of the trees designated in the permits which they enjoy.

§ 742. *Dye-woods.*—Art. 27. In respect to the cutting of dye-wood, the cutters will be governed by the instructions which are found at the end of this regulation; and as to the impost which must be paid, the department of public works will solve it, in view of the proposal which, in conformity with fraction 11 of article 4, the agent has to make.

§ 743. *Commencement of This Regulation.*—Art. 28. This regulation shall commence to govern from the first of October of the present year, and all the wood-cutters shall be subject to its provisions, and the conditions which are expressed in the permits which the respective agents shall execute for them.

§ 744. *Transitory—Price of Wood.*—Until the value is fixed

which ought to be paid in each state or demarkation for a tree of building timber or of cabinet-wood, the cutters will continue to pay seventy-five cents, which the regulation of April 18, 1861, designated. Mexico, September 19, 1881. Carlos Pacheco.

*Instructions to Which the Preceding Regulation Refers in Order to Effectuate the Cutting of Timber and Reproduction of Trees.*

§ 745. *Of the Cutting of Trees.—Character of Trees to be Cut.* 1. They will endeavor to cut trees which shall have reached a proper age in order not to destroy the tender plants which can not produce seeds nor sprouts. If the trees are large which are found among others of less age, those which ought to be cut shall first be stripped of their branches and these thrown on the side which may be convenient in order to avoid destroying the plants and sprouts; if the forest has to be reproduced by new plants, the trees shall be cut close to the ground, with sharp instruments, in order not to bruise nor break off the bark. The cutting will be done obliquely, cutting from below upwards. The clearing (or cutting of trees) may be done by lots, by zones, or by picking out the trees, according to the facts, but with consideration of the rules which are here laid down to reproduce the forest.

§ 746. *Reproduction of Trees.*—2. This may be done by seeds, by sprouts and new plants, or by reproduction by seeds. It is done naturally or artificially. For the first case, certain trees must be left properly situated, and of good age, in order that they may produce prolific seeds; and they will endeavor to have the seeds fall on good, worked land, so that they can easily germinate. The quantity of seeds which these trees can shed and the area which they can cover are to be calculated in considering the situation in which they are to be left. If the plants grown under this care, or those which shall exist spontaneously, can not grow freely under the shade of other trees, care will be had that the cutting of trees will be made in preference at this point to facilitate the growth of the former.

§ 747. *Reproduction by Sprouts or Plants.*—3. The buds proceed from the roots or from the trunks; for these cases the trees may be cut even with the surface of the ground, or at a certain height; the latter is proper, above all, in case that they only avail themselves of the branches as combustibles, or when the cattle destroy the new plants if they are very low. In this system of reproduction care must be had that the trees which are cut be not very old, in order that they may give vigorous sprouts.

In certain cases some branches or young trees are left to be substituted for the tree which is cut; and as well in this case as in the preceding analogous ones, they shall try to do the cutting with much care in order to facilitate the sprouts. When the cutting is done with the object of protecting the plants care shall be taken to take out the timber to the roads before the buds commence, in order not to destroy them with the carrying of the former. This system of reproduction is not proper with resinous trees and some others, and the inspectors, guided by practice, will elect the proper kinds.

§ 748. *Artificial Reproduction.*—4. There are cases in which the replanting of the forests can not be done by the methods indicated, and the aspect of the fields will indicate to the inspectors if the spontaneous growth of the seeds will be sufficient for the reproduction of the plants. In case that it does not so appear, artificial sowings shall be made with new seeds well selected. For this purpose the ground shall be worked anew, either with a plow or with a spade, in order to sow broad-cast or in furrows, or holes shall be made of a half meter on a side, in which shall be placed a seed; and on inclined lands the furrows shall be made horizontally across the declivity, that the waters may not wash away the seeds. If these should be hard and heavy, they will be covered with a layer of earth of five or six centimeters, and if they are light or resinous, they shall be placed at a little depth. If it should be feared that the plantings might be maltreated by the wind, by animals, etc., they shall be covered with the remaining branches of the wood cutting. The seeds ought to be gathered at perfect maturity and before they fall from the trees, kept in dry places and well ventilated, and the sowing shall be made in the spring or at the beginning of the rainy season, according to the facts. Sometimes it is proper to transplant, in which case nurseries will be formed in opportune time, and the kinds will be transplanted, taking care to pull them up with sufficient roots, and that there shall not be lacking the necessary humidity in the place in which they are planted.

Mexico, September 19, 1881.

# CHAPTER XVIII.

## THE DESAMORTIZACION AND NATIONALIZATION OF PROPERTY.

§ 789. Back Rents to be Paid before Adjudication.
§ 790. Subrogation of a Denouncer.
§ 791. Interest, when to be Paid.
§ 792. Security.
§ 793. Collection of Interest.
§ 794. Leases to be Respected.
§ 795. Leases for an Indefinite Time.
§ 796. Property Acquired may be Alienated.
§ 797. Lands may be Divided for the Purpose of Sale.
§ 798. Preference of Burdens.
§ 799. Property Mortgaged can not be again Held by Corporations.
§ 800. Corporations can not Hold Real Estate—Exceptions to the Law.
§ 801. Capital may be Imposed on Private Property.
§ 802. Alienations must be Made by Public Writing.
§ 803. Report of Sales by Notaries.
§ 804. Titles, Executed by Whom.
§ 805. Trials to be before Judges of First Instance.
§ 806. Execution of Receipts.
§ 807. Alcabala.
§ 808. Purchaser Pays Alcabala.
§ 809. Application of Funds.
§ 810. Application of Interest.
§ 811. Ratification of Decree of June 25, 1856.
§ 812. Services when Due for Rent to be Valued.
§ 813. Services how Estimated.
§ 814. Usufructuaries.
§ 815. Corporations can not Acquire Usufructs.
§ 816. Estates á Censo Enfiteutico.
§ 817. Right of Preference.
§ 818. Mortgage Creditors.
§ 819. Attachments by Creditors.
§ 820. Right of Adjudication is Personal.
§ 821. Right of Lessee to Make Contracts.
§ 822. Conventional Sales.
§ 823. Conventional Sales of Rented Estates.
§ 824. No Prohibitions can have Effect.
§ 825. Corporations may Collect Interest, how and when.
§ 826. Corporations must Deliver Titles and Certificates of Mortgage.
§ 827. Political Authorities shall Execute Titles, when.
§ 828. The Term of Three Months how Counted.
§ 829. Registry of Denouncements.
§ 830. First Denouncer.
§ 831. Valuation.
§ 832. Notices of Sales.
§ 833. Duty of Political Authority, and of the Judge.
§ 834. Public Sales, where to be Made.
§ 835. Judgments of the Judges.
§ 836. Double Fees not to be Collected.
§ 837. Payment of Alcabala.
§ 838. Alcabala, where Paid.
§ 839. Separate Accounts of Alcabala.

§ 890. Expenses Paid by Purchasers.
§ 891. When Interest not to be Paid.
§ 892. Cash Down may be Paid.
§ 893. Certain Redemptions not to be Made for a Year.
§ 894. Tenants Protected.
§ 895. Estates Returned to the Clergy.
§ 896. Term for Redemption having Passed, Right of Other Denouncers.
§ 897. Denouncers of Property not Desamortizados.
§ 898. Favors to Denouncers, when Terminated.
§ 899. Denouncements to be Presented in Writing.
§ 900. Property within the Jurisdiction of the Usurper.
§ 901. Sums to be Preserved, how Fixed.
§ 902. Funds from Sales, how Disposed of.
§ 903. Five per Cent, how Distributed.
§ 904. Funding of the National Debt.
§ 905. Reports by Officers of the Impositions of Capitals.
§ 906. Statement of the Estates of Corporations, Order for.
§ 907. Money to be Sent to the Department by Draft.
§ 908. Adjudication of Property Leased.
§ 909. Explanation of the Law.
§ 910. In Pueblos, Adjudication to the Lessees.
§ 911. Waters for Public Use not Subject to Desamortizacion.
§ 912. Protocols of Adjudications Closed, September 26, 1856.
§ 913. Rooms Annexed to Edifices.
§ 914. Convent of Franciscans Suppressed.
§ 915. Security and Alienation of Property.
§ 916. Division of the Products.
§ 917. In Public Sales No Lesion Enorme.
§ 918. Governors may Delegate their Functions.
§ 919. Usual Proceedings in Lands not Valued over Two Hundred Dollars, not Followed.
§ 920. Protests and Reserves Prohibited.
§ 920*a*. Property how Renounced.
§ 921. Who may Revoke Reservations.
§ 922. Reserves being Known, Estates shall be Sold.
§ 923. Alcabala not to be Returned.
§ 924. Notice to Prior Proprietors.
§ 925. Possession of Estates.
§ 926. Proofs of Reserves.
§ 927. Fine of Notaries.
§ 928. Adjudicators, Who are.
§ 929. Void Sales.
§ 930. Favors Conceded on Conditions.
§ 931. Parties Included in Prior Articles.
§ 932. Purchases from the Clergy Void.
§ 933. Rights of Property Acquired are Free.
§ 934. Improvements on Property.
§ 935. Reoccupation of Property by the Clergy.
§ 936. Denouncements how Made.
§ 937. Validity of Denouncements.
§ 938. Legal Subrogation.

§ 1090. Concealed Estates.
§ 1091. Denouncer's Part.
§ 1092. Denouncements, where Made.
§ 1093. Book of Denouncements.
§ 1094. Denouncements to be Remitted to the Department.
§ 1095. Formalization of Values.
§ 1096. Redemption how Made.
§ 1097. New Valuation.
§ 1098. Redemption in Part with Credits.
§ 1099. Nominal Value of Bonds not Admitted.
§ 1100. Petitions for Adjudications, where Made.
§ 1101. Registry of Petitions.
§ 1102. Redemptions, where Made.
§ 1103. Convents not to be Adjudicated, Which.
§ 1104. Redemptions, when not Admissible.
§ 1105. Terms of Redemption.
§ 1106. Petitions, where Presented.
§ 1107. Registry of Petitions.
§ 1107 *a*. Redemptions, how Made.
§ 1108. Irredeemable Capitals, What.
§ 1109. Bases of Adjudication.
§ 1110. Division of Capital.
§ 1111. Bidding.
§ 1112. Two or More Bidders.
§ 1113. Delivery of Bonds and Certificates.
§ 1114. Application of Money.
§ 1115. Privileges of Censatarios.
§ 1116. Rights of Denouncers.
§ 1117. Nuns not Endowed.
§ 1118. Legacies, Representation of.
§ 1119. Payment in Notes.
§ 1119 *a*. Capitals, how Applied.
§ 1120. Concealed Properties, What.
§ 1121. Laws in Force.
§ 1122. Parties subrogated in place of Exchequer.
§ 1123. Contents of Promissory Notes.
§ 1124. Denouncements to be Remitted to the Treasury.
§ 1125. Annotations on Bonds.
§ 1126. Publication of Notices.
§ 1127. Nullified Promissory Notes.
§ 1128. Delivery of Satisfied Notes.
§ 1129. Copies of Liquidations to be Remitted to the Treasury.

§ 749. *Definitions of Desamortizacion, Nationalization, and Civil Corporation.*—The desamortizacion of property is to take it out of mortmain (dead hands); that is, to unloose it from the grasp, as it were, of ecclesiastical or civil corporations. The term "desamortizacion" has no equivalent in English; I shall therefore use the word, considering the foregoing signification sufficient for the understanding of the reader. The term "civil corporation," as used in the constitution and laws of Mexico, does not embrace what is known as a business corporation. The latter is known where the civil law is the basis of jurisprudence, as an anonymous society, in Spanish, sociedad anonima. By the corporate name, the shareholders' names are unknown to the world; and so far as their connection with the corporation is concerned, their own names may be said to be anonymous; that is, nameless. Hence the derivation of the term "anonymous," as applied to a body of persons associated together in the form of a company to transact any given business under a company name, which does not disclose any of their own. The nationalization of property is an act which denotes that it has become that of the nation by some process of law, whereby private individuals or corporations have been for specified reasons deprived thereof. The term "nationalization" is of a late coinage. It will not be found in the old English dictionaries, nor even in the first edition of Webster's unabridged. The word is derived from the French verb *nationaliser*, meaning to nationalize, or to bring a thing into the nomenclature of those which belong to a nation. Its equivalent in Spanish, nationalizacion, is not new, but of long usage.

§ 750. *List of Laws.*—The desamortizacion and nationalization of property in Mexico have been done under the following laws, regulations, decrees, and circulars: The law of the twenty-fifth of June, 1856, and its regulation of the thirtieth of the following July; the law of July 12, 1859, and its regulation of the thirteenth of said month and year; the regulation of February 5, 1861; the circulars and decrees explanatory thereof; and the law of December 10, 1869, and its regulation of the eleventh of said month and year. This latter law of December 10, 1869, and its regulation of the same day are still in force.

### I. Civil and Ecclesiastical Corporations.

§ 751. *The Amount of Corporate Property Detrimental.*—The law of June 25, 1856, was issued by President Comonfort; and on the twenty-eighth of said month it was ratified by congress. The vast amount of real estate held by ecclesiastical and civil corporations was considered a great detriment to the country. With a view of advancing the prosperity and aggrandizement of the nation, the government thought it wise and prudent to provide some means for the distribution of these landed estates among private individuals. Such were the reasons advanced for the enactment of the foregoing law.

§ 752. *Products of Sale.*—As will be observed by an examination of the law, the government did not provide for taking away from said corporations the products of the sales of said real estate, but only a means of distributing the same for a just compensation therefor among private individuals.

§ 753. *Conventional Sales.*—The corporations were permitted to make conventional sales of the estates, in accordance with the provisions of said law and its regulation. But the archbishop, bishops, and priests considered that they had no power to recognize the right of the civil government to enact such laws, or to enter into any agreement or give any assent thereto, until first authorized so to do by the pope. And as the term of three months awarded them in the law was too short to have communication with the pope, they remained quiet, and the sales were made according to the provisions of the law and regulation, without the assent of the church.

§ 754. *Federal Constitution.*—This prohibition against civil and ecclesiastical corporations having a right to hold or manage real estate became elevated to the dignity of being a part of the organic law of the nation, by the extraordinary constituent congress that formed the federal constitution, February 5, 1857. Article 27 thereof declares: "No civil or ecclesiastical corporation, whatever may be its character, denomination, or object, shall have legal capacity to acquire property (in fee), or manage for itself real estate, with the only exception of the edifices destined immediately and directly to the service or object of the institution."

§ 755. *Tenants.*—Those persons who occupied lands of the corporations, as tenants or lessees, were entitled to have said lands adjudicated to them upon paying the price; which was estimated according to the amount of the rent paid. If the rent was sixty dollars per annum, the value of the property was estimated at one thousand dollars; that is, in accordance with the law, the rent was equal to six per cent of the value of the property rented. Persons who received the lands under the adjudications were called adjudicatarios.

§ 756. *Á Censo Enfiteutico.*—Although an estate might have been held by parties as a copyhold estate, or á censo enfiteutico, the canon or rent paid was to be capitalized at six per cent, in order to determine the value of the estate. A censo is called enfiteutico when there is a right to require of another a certain canon or pension annually, on account of having transferred to that person forever certain real estate, but reserving the fee in the land. The owner who thus transfers the land is called the censualisto; and the person who pays the annuity is called the censatario.

§ 757. *Estates not Rented.*—Estates belonging to corporations which were not rented at the time of the publication of the law were to be sold at public auction to the best bidder by the first political authority of the partido in which the property was situated.

§ 758. *Adjudication to be Solicited in Three Months.*—After the publication of the law in the chief town or capital of each partido, three months were allowed for the lessees to solicit the adjudication of the respective lands held by them. If they failed to present their petition within that period, their sub-lessees or any other person might denounce the same.

§ 759. *Presentation of Petition for Adjudication.*—A party desirous of denouncing certain property presented his petition to the first political authority of the partido, stating that the property belongs to a certain corporation; that for certain reasons, as specified in the law, he as a denouncer was entitled to have the property adjudicated to him, upon his paying the price in accordance with the provisions of the law. The property was to be accurately described in the petition. Upon an examination of the facts, if it appeared that his petition was true, he was declared to be entitled to receive the property as his own upon payment of the estimated value. If he did not wish to pay the value in cash down, he could pay annually an installment, or interest equal to six per cent per annum on the estimated value; and the principal sum would be held as a lien on the property until the same should be paid. But the purchaser could redeem it by paying the principal sum at any time. In the district of Mexico the governor was the first political authority.

§ 760. *Back Rent.*—The lessees who were owing for back rent were not entitled to have the property adjudicated to them until they had paid up said rent, or consented that it should be added to the value of the property, which became a part of the principal. and was a lien upon the property.

§ 761. *Suits for Rents.*—For back rents the corporations were entitled to bring suit for the collection thereof. That is, rents due prior to the publication of the law.

§ 762. *Adjudicated Property Salable.*—The purchasers under the law, or the persons to whom the property was adjudicated, could sell the same freely, but with the conditions attached to it under the adjudication.

§ 763. *Deeds of Sale.*—If the representatives of the corporations refused to make the deeds of sale under the adjudications, after receiving a judicial notice to do so, then the first political authority, or the judge of first instance of the partido, executed the deed in the name of the corporation.

§ 764. *Legal Questions.*—If any legal questions arose as to the proceedings, it was to be decided in a summary manner by the judge of the first instance, without any right of appeal therefrom; except when it had reference to the question of the preference which one might have over the other to the adjudication, or as to the price at which it ought to be made; then if the amount was such that according to the common law an appeal could be taken, it was allowed in these cases.

§ 765. *Value of Services, how Ascertained.*—Where lands had been rented out by the corporations, or given á censo enfiteutico, or divided out into small tracts to the Indians or others, in consideration of certain services which had not been valued in money, the value of said services was to be ascertained by arbitration. That is, the censatario or lessee was to select one person, and the representative of the corporation another; and both were to appoint a third person in case of a disagreement of the two. The decision determined the value of the property at which it was to be adjudicated, for the purpose of sale under the law.

§ 766. *Delegation of Authority.*—The first political authority of the partido where the property was situated could delegate his powers to the judge of the first instance to intervene in the sales, whenever any business prevented him from attending to the same.

§ 767. *Reference to the Laws.*—For a more complete knowledge of all the proceedings, reference will be had to the law of 1856, its regulation, and the explanatory circulars issued by the treasury department, and also the decree of February 5, 1861.

## II. Of the Nationalization of Property.

§ 768. *Struggle between the Liberals and Church.*—The struggle between the church and liberal party in Mexico was of no mean import. It had existed for years. The liberal party, sometimes of late termed the Juarez party, and likewise the party of reform, determined to crush the popish power, and to sever church government from that of the state. It was patent to the party of reform that, whatever might be the effect of the teachings of the Roman church on the conscience of its disciples, it did not have any effect in rejecting human strife. The influence of church wealth against governmental reform was too apparent to be lost sight of. In fact, the riches of the church were but the handmaid of ecclesiastical sway.

§ 769. *Government of Reform.*—The government of reform viewed the ownership of ecclesiastical property in the same light as did some of the sovereigns of Spain. Charles III. and Charles IV. were of opinion that it was the property of the sovereign and always had been. The liberal party saw in this view of the premises an effectual way of cutting off the enemy's supplies and in some degree of replenishing their own coffers. As the constitution had deprived ecclesiastical and civil corporations from holding or managing real estate, except such as was requisite for the edifices necessary for the objects of their respective institutions, the taking away from these corporations their landed estates was but the exercise of a power in harmony with the organic law of the land.

§ 770. *Government Views as to Church Property.*—The government considered this constitutional provision as binding on its conscience in the regulation of public affairs. It likewise held that the disarming of their avowed enemy was a duty which devolved upon its rulers, as religiously as did the protection of its citizens. With these convictions, the right to deprive the church party of all property which it did not require for the advancement of Christianity did not admit of question.

§ 771. *Laws of Reform, when Issued.*—To hasten peace, and to establish civil authority, Benito Juarez, president of the republic, on the twelfth of July, 1859, with a fearless pen, signed the notable law known as the "Law of the nationalization of ecclesiastical properties." On the following day was issued the regulation for the fulfillment of said law. Also on the fifth of February, 1861, was issued the important decree explaining fully the laws of desamortizacion and nationalization. These laws and regulations, like the money of the republic, bear the impress and reform of Juarez; and it may be said that they have made the air too pure for the slaves of church rule to breathe. The sandy margin of the sounding sea is not the place where his name is written to be effaced by sea foam. It is embossed on the table of politic reform, that will be as lasting as the rock of ages.

§ 772. *Constitutionality of the Laws Settled.*—Here the question occurs, Are these laws constitutional? Two opinions existed as to the power of the government to thus decree. But the question now seems to be settled by both bench and bar. And titles are considered valid deraigned from these laws and regulations. Some whose religious conscience and church inclination have caused them to look with injustice upon the proceedings of the reform party, and who also with a view of placing their title to lands emanating from this source beyond a question, have procured a title from the church.

§ 773. *Bishoprics.*—Mexico is divided into three archbishoprics; an archbishop resides in the city of Mexico, another at Guadalajara, and the other at Morelia, Michoacan. Each state is likewise a bishopric, and in each resides a bishop.

§ 774. *Doubts about Titles, how Settled.*—Those who possess lands the titles of which are based upon the foregoing laws, if they deem it requisite, may apply to those heads of the church, and will doubtless obtain all of the right of the church thereto, for a moderate compensation.

§ 775. *Supreme Court Decisions.*—In the case of Cipriano Castillo Mercado in representation of the Indians of Chicontepec, state of Vera Cruz, against the political chief of the said place, on appeal from the federal district court of that state, to the supreme court of justice, the latter held that the foregoing laws, regulations, and circulars extinguished the juridical personality of said communities or Indian towns; that the law of desamortizacion was not in conflict with the constitution; and that towns or communities could not hold real estate nor manage the same, except as provided in said law and regulation. January 9, 1892, was the date of the decision. Also the same was held in the case of the pueblo of Tepetitlan, appealed from the state of Hidalgo November 9, 1882. Also in the case of the pueblo of Santiago Mitlatongo, state of Oaxaca, decided October 25, 1882.

### III. On the Desamortizacion of Property.

*Decree of June 25, 1856, on the Desamortizacion of Country and City Estates, which, as Proprietors, the Civil and Ecclesiastical Corporations of the Republic Administer.*—Department of state and that of the treasury and public credit. His excellency the substitute president of the republic has been pleased to direct to me the decree which follows: Ignacio Comonfort, substitute president of the Mexican republic, to the inhabitants thereof, know ye: That considering that one of the greatest obstacles in the way of the prosperity and aggrandizement of the nation is the want of movement or free circulation of a great part of the real estate, the fundamental basis of public wealth, and in use of the faculties which the plan proclaimed in Ayutla and reformed in Acapulco concedes to me, I have thought proper to decree the following:

§ 776. *Property of Corporations to be Sold.*—1. All the country or urban estates which to-day as proprietors the civil and ecclesiastical corporations of the republic have or administer shall be adjudicated in fee to those who have them rented, for the value corresponding to the rent which they now pay, calculated as an annual interest of six per cent.

§ 777. *Property Held á Censo Enfiteutico.*—2. The same adjudication shall be made to those who to-day hold á censo enfiteutico[1] county or urban estates of corporation, capitalizing at six per cent the tax (canon) which they pay, in order to determine the value of said estates.

§ 778. *Corporations, What are.*—3. Under the name of corporations are comprehended all religious communities of both sexes, confraternities, congregations, brotherhoods, parishes, town councils (ayuntamientos), colleges, and in general every establishment or foundation which may have the character of perpetual or indefinite duration.

§ 779. *Estates Rented Directly by Corporations.*—4. The urban estates rented directly by the corporations to various tenants shall be adjudicated, capitalizing the sum of the rents with that of the present tenant who pays the greatest rent, and in case of equality, to the oldest tenant. Respecting county estates which are found in the same case, to each lessee shall be adjudicated the part which he has rented.

§ 780. *Estates not Rented.*—5. The urban as well as country estates which shall not be rented at the date of the publication of this law shall be adjudicated to the best bidder at public auction, which shall be had before the first political authority of the district (partido).

§ 781. *Estates in Litigation.*—6. There being final judgments alreading obtained on the same date for the surrender of the possession (desocupacion) of any estates, they shall be considered as not rented, although the lessees in fact still occupy them; but these shall preserve the rights which the present law gives them if the trial should be pending for the possession (desocu-

[1] The right which we have to require of another a certain tax (canon) or annual pension, on account of having transferred to him forever certain real estate, but reserving the fee.

pacion). All those who have formally contracted for the lease of any country or urban estate shall also be considered as tenants or lessees, even when they are not yet in fact in possession of it.

§ 782. *Price of Estates.*—7. In all the adjudications of which this law treats, the price of them shall be imposed at six per cent annually, and á censo redimible,[1] on the same estates; and the new owners can when they wish redeem the whole or a part which shall not be less than a thousand dollars, respecting estates the value of which shall exceed two thousand two hundred and fifty dollars on those which go below said price.

§ 783. *Property Excepted from the Law.*—8. The edifices immediately and directly destined to the service or object of the institute of the corporations are only excepted from the alienation which is provided, even when a part not separated from them is rented, as convents, episcopals, or municipal palaces, colleges, hospitals, houses of charity, markets, houses of correction and of benevolence. A house which may be united to them and which those inhabit officially who serve the object of the institution, as the houses of the rectors and of the religious chaplains, may be comprehended in this exception, as a part of each one of said edifice. Of the properties belonging to ayuntamientos are excepted also the edifices, the exidos, and lands destined exclusively to the public service of the towns to which they belong.

§ 784. *Sales, when Made.*—9. The adjudications and public sales must be made within the term of three months, counted from the publication of this law in each head (capital) of a district (partido).

§ 785. *Elapse of Time for Adjudication.*—10. The three months having passed without the leasing tenant having formalized the adjudication, he will lose his right to do so; and the subtenant shall have an equal right to be subrogated in his place, or any other person who, in his default, shall present the denouncement before the first political authority of the partido, provided he causes the adjudication to be formalized in his favor within fifteen days following the date of the denouncement. In a contrary case, or the latter failing in this, the said authority shall cause the estate to be adjudicated at public auction to the best bidder.

§ 786. *Failure of Corporations to Proceed in Time.*—11. Any corporation not moving before the said authority within the

[1] A tax, canon, or pension which is redeemable.

term of three months for the public sale of the estates not rented, if there should be a denouncer of them, the eighth part of the price shall be applied to him, which for this purpose must be paid cash down by him to whom the sale is made, and the rest shall be recognized in favor of the corporation.

§ 787. *Adjudications in Favor of Lessees, and Parties Subrogated.*—12. When the adjudication shall be made in favor of the lessee, he can not discount from the price any sum for the reputation, transfer of the lease, or improvements; and when it shall be made in favor of one who shall be subrogated in his place, the latter shall pay in cash to the lessee only the amount of the good-will or improvements which the corporation shall have precisely recognized in writing before the publication of this law, all the price remaining in both cases in favor of the corporation, and the present rent being capitalized at six per cent. In case of a sale to the best bidder, there shall be discounted from the price that must be imposed upon the estate what ought to be paid to the lessee on account of his being recognized in the form expressed.

§ 788. *Suits for Back Rent.*—13. For the debts for rents prior to the adjudication, the corporation can have their actions in conformity with the common law.

§ 789. *Back Rents to be Paid before Adjudication.*—14. Besides, the tenant or lessee, being a debtor for rents, can not cause the adjudication to be formalized in his favor, without having first liquidated the debt by showing the last receipt, or he shall pay it in cash down, or he shall consent that it be noted in writing or in the adjudication, in order that on the price of the adjudication the estate shall be mortgaged for the amount of the debt, unless it be satisfied. This mortgage shall not draw interest, saving that the corporation laying aside its actions to require immediately the payment, as it may do, even asking in conformity with law the public sale of the estate adjudicated, it shall agree that for the amount of the debt an imposition shall be formalized on the said estate.

§ 790. *Subrogation of a Denouncer.*—15. When a denouncer is subrogated in the place of the lessee, the latter must, if the corporation ask it, present the last receipt, in order that, there being a debt for rents, it shall be noted in writing for all the effects of the prior article. Then the new owner can use the actions of the corporation to require the payment of that debt. But in the case of a sale to the best bidder the estate shall not remain obligated for that claim.

§ 791. *Interest, when Paid.*—16. Whenever other terms are not agreed upon, the interests caused by virtue of the sale or adjudication shall be paid at the end of three months on urban estates, and at the end of every six months on country estates.

§ 792. *Security.*—17. In every case of sale at public auction security shall be given for the interests, and also when the adjudication shall be made in favor of the lessee or whoever is subrogated in his place, if the former has given surety for his lease, but not otherwise.

§ 793. *Collection of Interest.*—18. The corporations not only can, in conformity with the law, collect the interests due, but should the new owners be indebted for six months (dos semestres) on urban estates, and a year on the country estates, if judicial citation should be made upon them for the collection and they should not have surety for interests, they will be obliged to give it immediately, even when they shall make the payment at any time after the citation.

§ 794. *Leases to be Respected.*—19. In cases of public sales, as well as in those of adjudication to the lessees, or to those who are subrogated in their place, and in the alienations which both make, the new owners must respect and fulfill the contracts of leases for definite time made before the publication of this law; and they will have no right to cause to cease or to modify those of indefinite time except after three years, counted from the same date. When the adjudication shall be made to the lessees they can not modify within said term the present subleases which shall have been made. The provisions in this article shall be understood without prejudice to the right of asking for the possession for other causes, in conformity with the laws in force.

§ 795. *Leases for an Indefinite Time.*—20. In general, all the present leases of country and urban estates of the republic, made for an indefinite time, can be renewed at the will of the owners after three years, counted from the publication of this law; henceforth for the future it shall always be understood that all the leases for an indefinite time have the said term of three years, in order that at that term the proprietors can freely renew the leases.

§ 796. *Property Acquired may be Alienated.*—21. Those who by public sale or by adjudication acquire country or urban estates by virtue of this law can at all times alienate them freely, and dispose of them as of a property legally acquired, remaining only to the corporations to which they belong the rights which in conformity with the laws correspond to the annuitant censualistas for the capital and interests.

§ 797. *Lands may be Divided for the Purpose of Sale.*—22. All those who by virtue of this law acquire the property of country estates may divide the lands thereof for the purpose of alienating them to various persons, without the corporations as annuitants being able to oppose the division, except only to use their rights in order that the recognition of capital be so distributed on the fractions of land in proportion to their value as that the said sum be secured as before recognized on all the estate.

§ 798. *Preference of Burdens.*—23. The capitals which as the price of the country or urban estates are imposed on them in favor of the corporations shall have the place and preference which in conformity with the law belongs to them, between the prior burdens of the estate and those which shall be imposed upon it in the future.

§ 799. *Property Mortgaged can not be again Held by the Corporations.*—24. Notwithstanding the mortgage by which the estates sold or adjudicated by this law are effected, they never can return to be the property of the corporations which in having their actions upon them they can only ask for the sale at public auction to the best bidder without prejudice to their personal rights against the debtor.

§ 800. *Corporations can not Hold Real Estate—Exceptions to the Law.*—25. From now henceforth no civil or ecclesiastical corporation, whatever may be its character, denomination, or object, shall have legal capacity to acquire in fee or to administer for itself real estate, with the only exception which article 8 expresses in respect to the edifices destined immediately and directly to the service or object of the institution.

§ 801. *Capital may be Imposed on Private Property.*—26. Consequently, all the sums of money which in the future shall come into the coffers of the corporations by the redemption of capitals, new donations, or by other titles, they may impose on private property, or invest them as shareholders in agricultural, industrial, or mercantile enterprises, without being able for this reason to acquire for themselves or manage any real estate.

§ 802. *Alienations must be Made by Public Writing.*—27. All the alienations which by adjudication or by auction shall be made by virtue of this law must appear by title (escritura publica); and there shall not be admitted as against said titles, and with the object of invalidating them in fraud of the law, at any time, any counter-document, whether in the form of private or public instruments; and those who shall pretend to make valid such counter-documents, as well as those who shall have subscribed them, shall be prosecuted criminally as forgers.

§ 803. *Report of Sales by Notaries.*—28. At the end of each week from the publication of this law the notaries (escribanos) of the district shall send directly to the department of the treasury a notice of all the titles of adjudication or sales executed before them, expressing the corporation which alienates, the price, and the name of the purchaser. The notaries of the states and territories shall send the same notice to the superior chief of the respective treasury, in order that the latter may direct it to the department. If the notaries do not comply with this obligation by the notice alone of their failure, which the department or the superior chief of the treasury shall give to the first political authority of the partido, the latter shall impose upon said notaries administratively, for the first time, a fine which shall not be less than one hundred dollars, nor exceed two hundred, or in default of payment, one month's imprisonment; for the second time, a double fine or imprisonment; and for the third time, a suspension from office for a year.

§ 804. *Titles Executed by Whom.*—29. The titles of adjudication or auction shall be executed to the purchasers by the representatives of the corporations which alienate; but if the latter should refuse, after judicial notice shall have been given them to appear for the execution, this will be done in the name of the corporation by the first authority or by the judge of first instance of the partido, who shall take into consideration the amount of the rent designated in the leases or in the last receipts which the lessees shall present.

§ 805. *Trials to be before Judges of First Instance.*—30. All the trials which may occur on points relative to the execution of this law, so far as it involves the necessity of any previous declaration, in order that they may immediately proceed to adjudicate or sell the estates, shall be substantiated verbally before the judges of first instance, whose judgments shall be executed without admitting any other recourse upon them than that of responsibility.

§ 806. *Execution of Receipts.*—31. Whenever, after a previous judicial notice, any corporation shall refuse to fully execute, without reserves or protests relative to the effects of this law, receipts of the payments of interests or redemptions of capitals which the new owners shall make, the latter shall remain free of all future responsibility as to those payments, but they shall be made in the respective offices of the general government, which shall receive them on deposit on account of the corporation.

§ 807. *Alcabala.*—32. All the transfers of dominion of country and urban estates, by virtue of this law, shall produce a tax (alcabala) of five per cent, which shall be paid into the corresponding offices of the general government; the law of the thirteenth of February of this year being repealed, in relation to this impost on the alienations of estates in mortmain. This alcabala shall be paid in the following form: one half in money and the other in consolidated bonds of interior debt for the adjudications which shall be made within the first month; two thirds part in money and one third in bonds for those which shall be made in the second month; and only one fourth part in bonds and three fourths in money for those which shall be done within the third month. After the completion of the three months, all alcabala shall be paid in money.

§ 808. *Purchaser Pays Alcabala.*—33. In the cases of adjudication, as well as in those of sale, the purchaser shall pay this alcabala, and he shall likewise pay the expenses of the sale or adjudication.

§ 809. *Application of Funds.*—34. From the product of these alcabalas shall be separated one million dollars, which, united to the other funds which a law which shall be dictated for this object shall designate, shall be applied to the funded capital for the benefit of retired employés, pawn offices (montepios), and civil and military pensions, as well as to the funding (amortizacion) of the savings of the civil and military employees in actual service.

§ 810. *Application of Interest.*—35. The interests of the capitals which the country and urban estates recognize, which shall be adjudicated or sold in conformity with this law, shall continue to be applied to the same objects to which the rents of said estates were destined.

Wherefore I command that it be printed, published, circulated, and that due fulfillment be given it. Given in the national palace of Mexico, on the twenty-fifth of June, 1856. Ignacio Comonfort. To citizen Miguel Lerdo de Tejada. And I communicate it to your excellency for your understanding and exact fulfillment. God and liberty. Mexico, June 25, 1856. Lerdo de Tejada.

*June* 28, 1856—*A Decree of the Constituent Congress* —The decree of the twenty-fifth day, on desamortizacion of the property of corporations, is ratified. Department of state and that of the treasury and public credit. Section 5. His excellency the substitute president of the republic has been pleased to direct to me the decree which follows: The citizen Ignacio Comonfort, substitute president of the Mexican republic, to the inhabitants thereof. Know ye: That the constituent congress, in use of the faculty which it has to revise the acts of the executive, decrees what follows:

§ 811. *Ratification of Decree of June* 25, 1856.—The decree of the twenty-fifth of the present month, issued by the government, on the desamortizacion of the country and urban estates of the civil and religious corporations of the republic, is ratified. Given in Mexico the twenty-eighth of June, 1856. Antonio Aguado, president. José Maria Cortés y Esparza, deputy secretary. Juan de D. Arias, deputy secretary. Wherefore I command it to be printed, published, circulated, and that due compliance be given it. Palace of the national government in Mexico, the twenty-eighth of June, 1856. Ignacio Comonfort. To the citizen Miguel Lerdo Tejada. And I communicate it to you for your understanding and consequent ends. God and liberty. Mexico, June 28, 1856. Lerdo de Tejada.

*July* 30, 1856—*Regulation Issued by the Department of the Treasury for the Execution of the Law of the Twenty-fifth of June Last, on the Desamortizacion of Properties of Corporations.*—Department of state and of the treasury. His excellency the substitute president of the republic has been pleased to approve the following regulation of the law of the twenty-fifth of June, 1856, on the desamortizacion of the properties of the civil and ecclesiastical corporations:

§ 812. *Services when Due for Rent, to be Valued.*—1. The country and urban estates of corporations, given in rent, á censo entiteutico,[1] or as lands of apportionment (repartimiento), in which the payment of all the rent in money has not been stipulated, but of which all or part shall be satisfied with the service of some thing or some personal service, which is not yet previously estimated, shall be adjudicated by previously valuing the services (prestacion), in order to fix the capital, and to de-

[1] The right which we have of requiring from another a certain annual canon or pension, on account of having transfered to that person forever some real estate, reserving the fee.

termine for the future the alternative obligation on the new owner of doing the service (prestacion), or to pay its value. In the cases of sale of the said estates, the bids shall be made with the condition of paying in money the interests, which the corporations shall take care to apply to their objects.

§ 813. *Services how Estimated.*—2. In order to estimate the services, the payer (censatario) of an annuity, or the lessee, and the representative of the corporation, shall appoint each one an expert, and a third person in case of disagreement; but if the representative of the corporation should refuse, after previous judicial notice, the judge of the first instance shall act in his place and make the appointment of an expert, and the first political authority of the partido shall make the appointment of the third person for the disagreement.

§ 814. *Usufructuaries.*—3. The estates in which the corporations, at the publication of the law, only had the property in fee, the usufruct being constituted in favor of another, shall be adjudicated to the usufructuary (usufructuario) according to the amount of the rent, if at that date they were rented; in the contrary case, or in the case of the former occupying them for himself, they will be adjudicated to him immediately, appraising, in the manner provided in the preceding article, the rent which must be paid at the end of the usufruct. In conformity with article 10 of the law, after the three months the subrogation of the denouncer or the sale will take place, transferring immediately in all cases the property without prejudice to the subsistence of the rights of the usufruct to its termination, in which it shall be consolidated with the property of the new owner, who shall then pay the interests to the corporation.

§ 815. *Corporation can not Acquire the Usufruct.*—4. According to the provisions in articles 25 and 26 of the law, which prohibits corporations from managing for themselves real estate, they can not retain nor acquire the usufruct of them. The usufruct which they may now have shall be consolidated with the property, adjudicating it to the proprietor for the sum of the rent, if the estate was rented, or appraising if it was not, the fixed rent at what in the place of the usufruct ought to be paid for the time of its duration. For want of adjudication the subrogation of the denouncer, or the sale of the rent to the best bidder, shall take place, in order that he may enjoy the usufruct by virtue of the payment of the rent.

§ 816. *Estates á Censo Enfiteutico.*—5. The provision of article 2 of the law, relative to the adjudication in favor of those who have á censo enfiteutico country or urban estates, comprehends as well the censos of the whole as well as those of a part of the value of them; and in the second case, the tax (canon) must also be capitalized at six per cent, in order to determine the sum which remains a redeemable tax (á censo redimible).

§ 817. *Right of Preference.*—6. The right of preference (del tanteo), which any one might have had at the publication of the law, by a written agreement or other title, for the case of a voluntary sale of an estate of corporation, is admissible in the sales, but not in the adjudications to the lessees, nor to them who may be subrogated in their place.

§ 818. *Mortgage Creditors.*—7. If any mortgage creditor of the estate of a corporation should have made an agreement with the corporation by the means of title (escritura publica) before the law, the expiration of the term of its credit, in case of sale, will be understood as completed by the sale or adjudication, which, in general, will not alter the terms and conditions of the burdens imposed previously on those estates.

§ 819. *Attachments by Creditors.*—8. There being any attachment by the creditors of the corporation, the sale or adjudication will be made; but the new owners will be obligated for the result of the judgment as to the sum and term of payment; but that obligation can not in any case exceed the sum which they may have acquired. In the future, for the sums which shall remain imposed á censo redimible, or redeemable tax, in favor of corporation, only their creditors can prosecute the rights thereof as censualitas.[1]

§ 820. *Right of Adjudication is Personal.*—9. The right is personal, which for the adjudication the law has conceded to the lessees, who in no manner can sell it or cede it in favor of other persons, except only they may transmit it legally with the lease in case of death. By this in nothing is the free faculty assigned in article 21 of the law prejudiced in disposing of the estates, and selling them at any time after the adjudication has been consummated.

§ 821. *Rights of Lessee to Make Contracts.*—10. If the lessee should renounce his right to the adjudication in order to make a conventional purchase of the estate, the corporation can sell it to him for the price and upon the conditions which they may stipulate, provided the writing shall be formalized within the three months designated in the law. For these conventional sales to the lessees, the corporations shall proceed with the

[1] Persons in whose favor an annuity has been imposed; a copyholder.

authorization and customary requisites according to their by-laws, without the ecclesiastical authority being required to acquire a special permission from the civil authority. The tax (alcabala) on these sales shall be paid by the purchaser, according to the price he stipulates; but if this price should be less, it will be paid as if the adjudication had been made on the basis of the amount of the rents in conformity with the law.

§ 822. *Conventional Sales.*—11. Within the three months designated in article 11 of the law to promote the sale, in place of this, the religious communities of both sexes, confraternities (cofradias), archconfraternities (archicofradias), congregations, brotherhoods, parishes, communities, and parties (parcialidades) of the indigenous, or natives, hospitals, houses of charity (hospicios), town councils (ayuntamientos), colleges, and in general all the civil and ecclesiastical corporations, can make conventional sales of the estates not rented, provided each and all of them obtain for each case the previous approbation of the general government, which when it has not been asked for before said government, the governors and political chiefs of the states and territories may grant in the name of the general government.

§ 823. *Conventional Sales of Rented Estates.*—12. With the renouncement which the lessees shall make of their right to the adjudication, the civil and ecclesiastical corporations can also make in favor of other persons conventional sales of estates rented, if they obtain for each case the previous approbation, in conformity with the preceding article.

§ 824. *No Prohibitions can have Effect.*—13. In none of the cases of adjudications or conventional or public sales made by virtue of the law will the effects of any prohibition take place, put on any foundation for the purpose of causing the corporation to make a voluntary sale, or to change the form or application of the property of those foundations (fundaciones), the clauses of which can in no manner contradict or limit the faculties of the supreme authority.

§ 825. *Corporations may Collect Interest, how and when.*—14. The corporations can not use their rights to collect interests and receive redemptions of the estates adjudicated or publicly sold, until they deliver the titles thereof, and the certificates of the offices of mortgages in which shall appear their freedom from claims or their encumbrances. In default of this proof, in order that the mortgage creditors shall preserve the right of not having their interests and capitals comprehended among the interests and redemptions of the corporation, they must appear within the three months designated in the law, and the first twenty days following, to make judicially known their credits to the new owners, or present a manifestation before the first political authority of the partido, respecting the estates not sold, in order that the encumbrances shall be borne in mind at the public sales.

§ 826. *Corporations must Deliver Titles and Certificates of Mortgage.*—15. If the corporations do not deliver the titles and certificates of mortgages, after a judicial notice, and the mortgage creditors do not present the manifestations provided in the preceding article, the new owners shall remain free of all future responsibility as to the payments of the interests and redemptions which they shall make in the corresponding offices of the general government, which shall receive them on deposit on the account respectively of the mortgage creditors and of the corporation.

§ 827. *Political Authorities shall Execute Titles, when.*—16. The first political authority, or the judge of the first instance, shall execute the titles of adjudication or public sale in the name of the corporations, when the latter do not take care to put in the partido any representative or administrator who can execute them, or on whom could be made the judicial notice provided for in case of refusing to do it. It being unknown whether or not there is in the partido the representative of the corporation, he shall be cited by the means of a notice published in the customary form, within the peremptory term of three days, and if he should not present himself they will proceed in the form which this article provides.

§ 828. *The Term of Three Months how Counted.*—17. The three months which for the desamortizacion the law designates shall be counted from date to date, completing itself on the working day (útil) immediately prior to the date of the month on which, three months before, the law was published. According to the provisions in its articles 9, 10, and 11, which concede that term to the lessees to adjudicate the estates, and to the corporations to move for the public sale of those not rented, the denouncements for want of having formalized the adjudication or moved for the public sale shall be admissible, from the first working day (útil) which follows the term of three months; and those which shall have been previously made shall not produce any right.

§ 829. *Registry of Denouncements.*—18. On that day a book

of registry of denouncements shall be opened in the department of the first political authority, in order that their presentation and preference may appear. The date and hour in which they are presented shall be noted in the book, if they are made for want of adjudication, or public sale of the estate, designating it, the name of the corporation, that of the denouncer, and those of the two witnesses which he shall have for that purpose. The secretary, the denouncer, and his two witnesses shall sign the note.

§ 830. *First Denouncer.*—19. He who makes the first denouncement shall have a preferred right; but if various persons appear at the same time, all will have equal rights. In this case, if the denouncement has been made for the public sale of an estate not rented, the eighth part of the price will be divided among them, conceded in article 11 of the law; and if it has been done for want of the adjudication of an estate rented, the first political authority shall cite the denouncers, with the object of making a public sale among them, in order that he who makes the best bid on the amount of the rent shall have preference in subrogating himself for the lessee. If he who becomes the best bidder does not formalize the adjudication in the peremptory term which, within the fifteen days of article 10 of the law, the said authority shall fix, the latter shall successively call those who follow in order of the bids, and he shall also fix for them a peremptory term for the adjudication.

§ 831. *Valuation.*—20. The value which may be declared for the payment of the contributions shall serve as a basis at the public sales of the estates; and in default thereof, whether through having been excepted, divided, found in construction, or other cause, they shall order to be valued, the corporation shall appoint one expert, the political authority the other, with the third one in case of discord; and the three shall be appointed by the said authority if the corporation should refuse to appoint. The bids which shall reach two third parts of the value shall be admissible, but between those of equal amounts the offering to make the greater redemptions in stated periods, or to pay a greater part of the price in cash down, shall be a reason of preference.

§ 832. *Notices of Sales.*—21. For the public sales the bidders shall be convoked for the term of nine days, designating the estates and the sum for which they shall be valued, by means of public notices in the official periodical, if there should be one, or in the place and form in which it is customary to publish the orders of the authority. In the notices shall be expressed also the hour and dates of the three auctions, designating for the first the first working day after the expiration of the nine of the term, and each third day the other two, with the observation that after the first the sale will end with the highest bidder, if it were admissible by reaching the two third parts of the value. If at the three auctions no admissible bid be made, the political authority shall order the estate to be again valued, and notices shall be published in the same manner for the new auctions.

§ 833. *Duty of Political Authority, and of the Judges.*—22. The first political authority of the partido in which the estates are situated, before whom the denouncements and the sales to be made must be presented, in conformity with articles 5, 10, and 11 of the law, shall submit to the judge of the first instance which require a previous judicial decision, and he can delegate to him his powers to intervene at the sales, provided any just reason prevents him from appearing thereat.

§ 834. *Public Sales, where to be Made.*—23. When the supreme government in the district, or the governors and political chiefs in the states and territories where the estates are situated, shall specially determine it for any cases, the public sales can be made in the respective capitals, ordering that then the notices shall be published, as well in the capital as in the head town of the partido.

§ 835. *Judgments of the Judges.*—24. Of the judgments which the judges of first instance shall pronounce when the points submitted for a verbal trial shall be relative to the preferred right of him who asks the adjudication, or relative to the price for which it ought to be made—if the interest of the trial permits it in conformity with common law—the appeal interposed in the act of the notification of the judgment, or within the third day, will be admissible without being conceded in any case a restitution of this term, and without prejudice to the execution immediately of those judgments fully, in the same manner and without any more requisites than the others of a declaration previous to the adjudication or public sale, relative to those which in conformity with article 30 of the law shall not be admitted further recourse than that of responsibility.

§ 836. *Double Fees not to be Collected.*—25. In no case shall double fees be collected for judicial acts, making of deeds, or any proceedings relative to the public sales or adjudication; and when the interests of these or the price of the estates do not exceed a thousand dollars, only one half of the fees designated in the respective tariff (arancel) can be collected, the titles to be drawn on paper of the fifth seal.

§ 837. *Payment of Alcabala.*—26. In order that the payment of tax (alcabala) may be regulated in the divers proportions of money and bonds, which in the three months article 32 of the law distinguishes, besides the execution of the title, the alcabala must have been paid within the respective term. In conformity with the same article, after the completion of the three months, all the alcabala shall be paid in money; and that of the transfer of the dominion which shall be made after the estates shall have been adjudicated or publicly sold, shall in the future be paid according to the common laws.

§ 838. *Alcabala, where Paid.*—27. For the adjudications or sales which shall be made in the district, the alcabala shall be paid in the principal administration of revenues of this city; for those which shall be made in the capitals of the states and territories, in the chief office (superior jefaturas) of the treasury; and for those which are made at the other points, in the administration of the post-offices of the chief towns of the partidos.

§ 839. *Separate Accounts of Alcabala.*—28. The principal administration of revenue of this city shall keep a separate account of what it collects of these alcabalas; also such separate account shall be kept by the superior chiefs of the treasury of what they collect, and the administrators of the post-offices in their demarkation.

§ 840. *The Estates Producing Alcabala to be Noted.*—29. In each one of the items of charge of said account shall be noted the estate by which the alcabala is produced, the name of the corporation to which it belonged, and that of the person to whom it was adjudicated or sold. Likewise shall be put a dated note on each one of the consolidated bonds of the interior debt, at the time of receiving them in payment, with an expression that by it they remain untransferable; and the chief of the office and the causante[1] shall sign these notes.

§ 841. *Money Collected to be Sent to the Treasury.*—30. The superior chiefs of the treasury shall take care to collect the bonds and amounts received by the administrators of the post-offices in their demarkation; they shall send to the department of the treasury by the first mail of each week a detailed notice of what they shall have collected directly or through the administrators in effective money or in bonds, expressing the

[1] The person from whom one desires any right which he has.

amount of money which they have in their possession; and they shall remit the bonds, noted on a sheet of paper certified by the said post-office, to the general treasury.

§ 842. *Fees.*—31. Two per cent, as fees on the amounts which they shall have collected in effective money, shall be passed as fees each month to the administrators of the post-offices.

§ 843. *Alcabala, Disposition of.*—32. The superior chiefs of the treasury can not, nor any other authority, without an express order from the department, dispose of, for any object, the sums proceeding from these alcabalas; and for any contravention thereof, said chiefs will be personally responsible.

And I communicate it to you for your understanding and consequent ends. God and liberty. Mexico, July 30, 1856. Lerdo de Tejada.

### IV. Nationalization of Ecclesiastic Properties.

*July* 12, 1859—*The Law of the Nationalization of Ecclesiastic Properties.*—Department of justice, ecclesiastic affairs, and public instruction. His excellency the constitutional provisional president of the republic has been pleased to direct to me the decree which follows: The citizen Benito Juarez, constitutional provisional president of the Mexican United States, to all the inhabitants thereof, know ye: That with the unanimous consent of the council of ministers, and—

§ 844. *Reasons for the Law.*—Considering that the principal reason of the present war moved and sustained by the clergy is to succeed in withdrawing itself from the dependence of the civil authority that when the latter, favoring the said .clergy, has wished to increase its revenues, the clergy by only not recognizing the authority which the sovereign had in it, has refused even its own benefice; that when the sovereign wished, putting in vigor the mandates even of the clergy relative to parochial obventions, to take from the latter the odiousness which the manner of collecting a part of their emoluments occasioned them, the clergy preferred to affect that they would let themselves perish before they would subject themselves to any law; that as the resolution showed upon this by the metropolitan (archbishop) proves that the clergy can maintain themselves in Mexico as in other countries, without the civil law regulating their collections and agreements with the faithful; that if in other times it could be doubted by any one that the clergy has been one of the constant hinderances in establishing the public peace to-day, all recognize that they are in open rebellion against the sovereign; that the clergy wasting the wealth which the faithful have confided to them for pious objects, they invest said wealth in the general destruction, sustaining, and imbruing with blood each day more the fratricidal struggle which moved in rebellion of the legitimate authority, and denying that the republic can be constituted; that having been useless until now efforts of every kind to terminate a war which is ruining the republic, the leaving longer in the hands of its sworn enemies the resources which they so gravely abuse would be to become their accomplice; and that it is an indispensable duty to put in execution all the means which may save the situation and society—I have thought proper to decree the following:

§ 845. *All Property Nationalized.*—1. All the properties which the secular and regular clergy have been managing with divers titles, whatever may be the class of estates, rights, and actions in which they consist, the name and application which they may have had enter into the dominion of the nation.

§ 846. *Special Law.*—2. A special law shall determine the manner and form of making all the properties of which the preceding article treats enter the treasure of the nation.

§ 847. *Independence between Church and State.*—3. There shall be a perfect independence between the affairs of the state and the affairs purely ecclesiastical. The government will confine itself to protecting with its authority the public worship of the catholic religion, as well as that of any other.

§ 848. *No Real Estate to be Received by the Church.*—4. The ministers of worship, through the administration of the sacraments and other functions of their ministry, can receive offerings which shall be furnished them, and they can settle freely with the persons who occupy them the indemnification which they ought to give them for the services which are asked of them. Neither the offerings nor the indemnifications can be made in real estate.

§ 849. *Order of Monks Suppressed.*—5. The orders of the regular monks which exist are suppressed in all the republic, whatever may be the denomination or advocation with which they have been erected, as well as also all the archbrotherhoods (archicofradias), confraternities (cofradias), congregations, or brotherhoods, annexed to the religious communities, to the cathedrals, parishes, or any other churches.

§ 850. *Convents Prohibited.*—6. The founding or erection

is prohibited of new convents of regulares; of archconfraternities, confraternities, congregations, or religious sisterhoods, whatever may be the form or denomination which they may wish to give them. Likewise is prohibited the use of habits or dresses of the suppressed orders.

§ 851. *Regular Ecclesiastics.*—7. The regular ecclesiastics of the suppressed orders, being by this law reduced to the secular clergy, shall be subject as the latter to the respective ecclesiastic ordinary in what concerns the exercise of its ministry.

§ 852. *Remuneration to Regular Ecclesiastics.*—8. To each one of the regular ecclesiastics of the suppressed orders who shall not be opposed to the provisions in this law, shall be furnished by the government the sum of five hundred dollars once. To the said regular ecclesiastics who by sickness or advanced age may be physically impeded from the exercise of their ministry, besides the five hundred dollars they shall receive a capital which has been secured on real estate, of three thousand dollars, to which they may look for their competent sustenance. They can dispose of both sums freely as of a thing of their property.

§ 853. *Furniture of Monks.*—9. The monks of the suppressed orders may carry to their houses the furniture and articles which for their personal use th y had in the convent.

§ 854. *Sacred Things of the Church.*—10. The images, ornaments, and sacred vases of the churches of the regulars suppressed shall be delivered by a formal inventory to the diocesan bishops.

§ 855. *Temples Reserved for Divine Service.*—11. The governor of the district and the governors of the states, on petition of the most reverend archbishop and of the right reverend diocesan bishops, shall designate the temples of the regulars suppressed which ought to remain intact for the divine offices, considering previously and scrupulously the necessity and utility of the case.

§ 856. *Books, Pictures, etc.*—12. The books, printed matter, manuscripts, pictures, antiquities, and other objects belonging to the religious communities suppressed, shall be applied to the museums, lyceums, libraries, and other public establishments.

§ 857. *Clerical Dresses not to be Used.*—13. The regular ecclesiastics of the suppressed orders who, after fifteen days from the publication of this law in each place, shall continue using the dress or living in community, shall not have a right to receive the quota which is assigned to them in article 8; and if after the term of fifteen days shall have passed, which this article fixes, they shall meet in any place to affect to follow the common life, they shall be expelled from the republic.

§ 858. *Convents of Nuns.*—14. The convents of nuns which now exist shall continue to exist and to observe the economic regulation of their cloisters. The convents of these nuns which were subject to the spiritual jurisdiction of any of the regulars suppressed shall remain under that of the diocesan bishops.

§ 859. *Rights of Nuns Expelled.*—15. Every nun who shall be expelled from the cloister shall receive at the time of her departure the sum which she may have brought to the convent in the quality of dower (dote), whether it proceeds from parapheral properties, whether it has been acquired by private donations, or finally, whether it has been obtained from any pious foundation. The nuns of mendicant orders who have brought nothing to their monasteries shall receive, notwithstanding, the sum of five hundred dollars at the time of their expulsion from the cloister. They can freely dispose of the dower and pension as of a thing of their own.

§ 860. *Dower and Payments Made Effective.*—16. The political and judicial authorities of the place shall impart, by way of caution, all kinds of help to the nuns expelled from the cloister, in order to make effective the restoration of the dower or the payment of the sum which was assigned them in the preceding article.

§ 861. *Capital Invested by Nuns Preserved.*—17. Each nun will preserve the capital which in the quality of dower she may have turned into the convent. This capital shall be secured to her in country or urban estates by the means of proper writings, which shall be executed individually in her favor.

§ 862. *Capital and Interest for Festivities and Expenses.*—18. To each one of the convents of nuns shall be left a capital sufficient, so that with its interests may be attended to the repairs of buildings and expenses of the festivities of their respective patrons, the nativity of Jesus Christ our Lord, holy week, the body, resurrection, and all-saints, and other expenses of community. The superiors and chaplains of the respective convents shall form the appropriations of these expenses, which shall be presented within fifteen days after the publication of this law to the governor of the district or to the governors of the respectice states for their revision and approbation.

§ 863. *The Balance to Belong to the Nation.*—19. All the remaining properties of said convents shall be turned into general treasury of the nation, in conformity with what is provided in article 1 of this law.

§ 863 *a*. *Nuns can Dispose of their Respective Dower.*—20. The nuns who are kept in the convents can dispose of their respective dower, freely bequeathing it in the form which the laws prescribe for every person. In case that they do not make any will, and have no relatives capable of receiving by inheritance *ab intestato*, the dower shall be turned into the public treasury.

§ 864. *Convents to be Closed.*—21. All apartments in the convents of nuns shall remain perpetually closed. The present novices can not profess, and on separating from the apartments, what they have turned into the convents shall be returned to them.

§ 865. *Sales with Consent of Government.*—22. All alienations which shall be made of the properties mentioned in this law, whether they be made by an individual of the clergy, or by any person who may not have received express authority from the constitutional government, are null and of no value. The purchaser, whether he be a Mexican or foreigner, shall be obliged to restore the thing purchased or its value, and shall besides pay a fine of five per cent, regulated according to the value of the thing. The notary who authorizes the contract shall be displaced and perpetually disqualified in his public office, and the witnesses of assistance, as well as the instrumental ones, shall suffer the punishment of from one to four years of imprisonment.

§ 866. *Violators of This Law Punished.*—23. All those who directly or indirectly are opposed or in any manner enervate the fulfillment of what is commanded in this law shall be, as the government may qualify the gravity of his culpability, expelled from the republic or assigned to the judicial authority. In this case they shall be tried and punished as conspirators. From the sentence which the competent tribunals shall pronounce against these criminals there shall be no recourse for pardon.

§ 867. *Punishment to be Made Effective.*—24. All the punishments which this law imposes shall be made effective by the judicial authorities of the nation, or by the political ones of the states; and they shall immediately make a report thereof to the general government.

§ 868. *Advice of the Government to be Requested.*—25. The governor of the district and the governors of the states, in their turn, shall consult the government about the provisions which they may esteem proper for the punctual fulfillment of this law.

Wherefore, I command it to be printed, published, and circulated to whom it corresponds. Given at the palace of the general government in Vera Cruz, the twelfth of July, 1859. Benito Juarez, Melchor Ocampo, president of cabinet, minister of government, charged with the department of relations and of that of war and of the navy. Lic. Manuel Ruiz, minister of justice, ecclesiastical affairs, and public instruction. Miguel Lerdo de Tejada, minister of the treasury, and charged with the branch of public works. And I communicate it to your excellency for your understanding and fulfillment. Palace of the general government in Vera Cruz, the twelfth of July, 1859. Ruiz.

*July* 13, 1859—*Regulation for the Fulfillment of the Law of Nationalization.*—Department of the treasury and public credit. Your excellency: His excellency the constitutional provisional president of the republic has been pleased to direct to me the decree which follows: The citizen Benito Juarez, constitutional provisional president of the republic, to the inhabitants thereof, know ye:

§ 869. *Object of the Law.*—That with the object that the alienation of the properties of which the law of the twelfth instant speaks, may efficaciously contribute to the subdivision of the territorial property and give a general benefit to the nation, which is the great end of the reform which it involves, I have thought proper to decree, with the unanimous consent of the cabinet, the following:

§ 870. *Occupation of Properties.*—1. The occupation of the properties which by the law cited enter into the dominion of the nation shall be made in the federal district through a special office, which for that purpose the government will establish, and in the states through the superior chief offices of the treasury (jefaturas superiores de hacienda), assisted by the principal administrations and collectorships of revenue in their respective districts.

§ 871. *Collection of Writings, Books, and Documents.*—2. The day following the publication of this law, in each place where any such properties exist, the first political authority shall appoint the commission or commissioners that may be necessary, in order that with a notary or two witnesses they may proceed immediately to collect from the respective procurador, sindico, administrator, or mayordomo, the writings, account books, and the other documents relative to the interests which they have had in their charge, in the state in which they are found, as well as the money existing, making the respective inventory and cash-balance sheet (cortes de caja), which the commissioner, the procurador or sindico, mayordomo or administrator, and the notary or witnesses, shall sign.

§ 872. *Disobedience, by Non-delivery and Making of Accounts.*—3. If the procuradores, sindicos, mayordomos, or administrators should not wish to sign the inventories and cortes de caja, of which the preceding article speaks, or in any other manner should refuse to make the delivery which is therein provided, the first political authority will order them to be apprehended and placed at the disposition of the judge of the treasury, in order that he may try them for their disobedience to the law and unjust detention of the public properties. In the cases which this article expresses, or in those in which resistance is opposed. the commissioner will proceed by himself alone with the notary or witnesses, asking the help of the police or armed force whenever it may be necessary.

§ 873. *Notice and Delivery by Commissioners.*—4. The commissioners shall proceed without interruption, giving daily to the authority which appointed them notice of what they may do in the performance of their charge; and as soon as they shall terminate it, they shall make delivery of all, with the inventory and cash-balance sheets, to the respective office of which article 1 speaks, which will take charge then of what it receives on account of the nation, in order to act in conformity with what this law provides.

§ 874. *Experts.*—5. Likewise the first political authority shall appoint one or more experts, in order that within the precise term of eight days they shall form plans of divisions in the edifices which the suppressed communities occupied, and shall submit them to the approbation of said authority. In these plans shall only be excluded those temples which shall be destined by the government to continue to be employed in divine service, in conformity with article 14 of the said law of the twelfth instant; and these plans being once approved, each one of the fractions thereof shall be valued separately.

§ 875. *Sales Made at Auction.*—6. This valuation being made, said fractions shall be sold at public auction, the sales being made in the federal district by the chief of the office which the government may establish, or by other persons which the latter may appoint for the purpose, and in the states by the superior chiefs of the treasury, administrators, or receivers of revenues.

§ 876. *Notices of Sales, and how Made.*—7. For these public sales shall be published notices, with terms of nine days, designating after that term three days which follow with an interval of one in each one of them, in order that the three auctions may be made. These notices shall be published in the chief town of the partido in which the edifices are situated, with a clear and express designation of what has to be sold, their value, and the place, days, and hours on which the three auctions have to be made, making the publications in the customary places and in the official periodical, if there should be one.

§ 877. *Bids how Made.*—8. At said auctions the bids shall be considered good when one third part of the value is offered in effective money, and another third part in the recognized national debt, whatever may be its origin or denomination. The basis of delivering the third part in money shall be unalterable, and the overbidding (pujas) must be made only on the part which has to be given on credit, being admitted as best the bid which offers the greatest amount on credit.

§ 878. *How Sold if No Bidders.*—9. From the first auction the sale will be made, if at it there should be an admissible bid, and if no such one should be presented in the three auctions, the chief of the office of the federal district and the chiefs of the treasury or the administrators of revenue in the states, shall afterwards privately accept the first admissible bid which shall be presented to them.

§ 879. *Payment.*—10. The payment of the values of the sales made according to the four preceding articles, as well in the money part as in the credit part, must be made at the time the respective deeds are signed; but the government can also, in all the cases in which it may judge proper, admit that the part in money shall remain as a lien on the said edifice or fraction thereof sold, for the term of five or nine years, and with annual interest at six per cent. Notwithstanding the provision in this article, preference will be given at the auctions to the bids in which it is offered to pay cash down, when they are equal in price, including the part of the credits with those that they propose shall remain as a lien on the property. The part in credits must in all cases be paid when the deed is executed.

§ 880. *Redemption of Capitals.*—11. All the capitals which are recognized in favor of the secular and regular clergy, whether they proceed from the impositions made before the law of June 25, 1856, or from the adjudications, conventional sales, or public sales, which in virtue thereof have been made up to the date of the publication of this law, can be redeemed by the present censatarios[1] in this form: three fifths parts in evidences or credits of the national debt, whatever may be their origin and denomination, and two fifth parts in effective money, payable in monthly credits, and in equal parts during forty months, counted from the date on which the contract of redemption is made.

§ 881. *Manner of Redeeming*—12. In order that said censatarios may enjoy the favor which is conceded to them in the prior article, they must appear at the office of the respective treasury cited in this law, and before thirty days counted from that of its publication, to manifest their will to redeem the amount which they recognize, delivering the corresponding part of the credits, and an obligation to pay the part in money on the terms which the preceding mentioned article expresses.

§ 882. *Obligations how Made.*—13. These obligations shall be made to the bearer, and shall preserve the said mortgage of the capital which must be redeemed, this circumstance being made to appear in the document, and being noted in the respective writing, which shall only be canceled when it is made to appear that that obligation has been complied with in all its parts before the chief of the office of the respective treasury, who shall then draw the corresponding order for the cancellation.

§ 883. *Obligations in the Interior.*—14. In interior places where there may be no credit of the national debt, the chiefs of the offices of the treasury to whom it corresponds can admit an obligation, which shall be delivered within a prudent term, according to the distance, whether in the capital of the state to which they may belong, or whether in the capital of the republic, when that returns to legal order. These obligations shall be remitted to the chief of the respective treasury, or to the office of the federal district, in order that the credits may be collected and utilized in the form which the law provides.

§ 884. *Renouncement of the Right of Redemption.*—15. If the thirty days spoken of in article 12 shall have passed without the present censatarios having appeared to make the redemption of the capitals which they recognize, they shall be considered as having renounced their right, and the redemption shall be ad-

[1] One who pays an annuity out of his estate.

mitted to the first who shall solicit it within the next ten days, the latter being subrogated in place of the exchequer. For the effects of this article, the special office of the district and the superior chief offices (jefaturas) and other offices of the treasury charged with the execution of this law, shall publish in the periodicals, if there are any, or in the customary places, a statement of all the impositions which must be redeemed in their respective demarkation, and each week shall publish also in the same manner a notice of those which during the week are redeemed. Of this and of the former, copies shall be sent through their respective channels to the department of the treasury.

§ 885. *Parties Subrogated.*—16. Those who, by virtue of the provision in the preceding article, shall be subrogated in place of the exchequer, shall pay the capital which they redeem on the same terms provided for the present censatarios, with the sole difference that their obligation, in order to cover the part in money, must be secured to the satisfaction of the chief of the office of the respective treasury.

§ 886. *Lapse of Term.*—17. The term of ten days once having passed, the chief of the special office of the district, and the chiefs of the treasury, administrators, or receivers of revenues in their respective demarkations, shall proceed to sell at public auction the capitals imposed, observing for the public sales the same provisions which article 7 of this law contains.

§ 887. *Bids Held Good, What.*—18. At these auctions shall be held as a good bid that which offers to deliver in money, in the times designated in article 11, the two fifth parts of the capital which is put up at auction, and the other three fifths in credits, the overbidding (pujas) being made on the latter, and not on the part in effective money.

§ 888. *Security for Obligations Given.*—19. The obligations which on the payment of money those make who sell at auction imposed capitals, in conformity with the preceding article, must be secured to the satisfaction of the chief of the office of the respective treasury, and the part of credits must be paid at the time of the execution of the title.

§ 889. *Manner of Sale of All Estates.*—20. In the same form and terms which the preceding articles express, with the sole difference that the values or declarations previously made shall serve as a basis for the public sale, they shall proceed to sell at public auction all the estates which, with divers titles, the regular and secular clergy have administered, and which at the date of the publication of this law have not been desamortizadas,[1] because the adjudication of them has not been formalized nor asked for in conformity with the law of June 25, 1856.

§ 890. *Expenses Paid by Purchasers.*—21. In these alienations, the same as in those which articles 6, 7, 8, and 9 of this law treat of, all the expenses shall be paid by the purchaser. But in none of the cases of redemption, subrogation, public sale, or other official act, can the chiefs of the offices of the treasury, of which this law speaks, collect fees from the interested parties. All these operations shall be free from the payment of tax (alcabala) on sales.

§ 891. *When Interest not to be Paid.*—22. The present payers of annuities (censatarios) who within the thirty days which article 12 concedes shall make redemption of capitals that are recognized shall remain exempt from paying the interests which at the date may be due. In case they do not do so, the government shall have its action directly against them for the sums due, or shall cede them, by virtue of an agreement, to those who may acquire said capitals.

§ 892. *Cash down may be Paid.*—23. Whenever any of those who may acquire properties of those of whom this law speaks, whether by direct redemption, or whether by subrogation and public sale, may not wish to enjoy the terms which article 11 concedes for the part in effective money, the government will admit the payment cash down, making them the corresponding discount for such advancement.

§ 893. *Certain Redemptions not to be Made for a Year.*—24. Those who, by subrogation or public sale, shall acquire imposed capitals for a time completed, or which must be completed before a year, counted from the date of this law, can not require their redemption of the present censatarios before said year. In respect to the impositions, where there has been stipulated for the redemption of the capital a term which exceeds the year, those who shall have acquired them by virtue of this law must respect the contracts, not requiring the redemption only at the date agreed upon in them.

§ 894. *Tenants Protected.*—25. Those who in conformity with article 20 acquire estates which ought to have been taken out of mortmain (desamortizarse), according to the law of June 25, 1856, shall be under the obligation of respecting towards their present tenants the rights which the said law conceded to them.

§ 895. *Estates Returned to the Clergy.*—26. The country estates

[1] Taken out of mortmain.

which, in virtue of having been returned to the clergy by the lessees who affected to adjudicate them in conformity with said law of June 25th, must be put up for sale again, shall be divided into lots of an extension which the governor of the respective state may judge proper. In the alienation of these lots, the present sublessees and residents of the said estate shall be preferred, and only in case that these do not make the acquisition in the term which for it the government of the state shall fix for them, they shall be sold to the best bidder, according to the provisions of this law.

§ 896. *Term for Redemption having Passed, Right of Other Denouncers.*—27. The thirty days having passed which by article 11 are granted to the present censatarios to redeem for themselves the capitals which they recognized, and the ten days which by article 17 are conceded to those who wish to be subrogated in place of the exchequer, every one who denounces an imposition not redeemed, and of which the office of the respective treasury has no knowledge, will have a right to be subrogated in the place of the exchequer, delivering sixty per cent of their value, in evidences of the public debt, and the rest in money, at the times which the said article 11 establishes.

§ 897. *Denouncers of Property not Desamortizadas.* — 28. Those who denounce estates which have not been taken out of mortmain (desamortizadas) in conformity with the law of June 25, 1856, and of which the office of he respective treasury has not notice, will have the right to have them adjudicated for the value declared for the payment of taxes, or in default thereof for that which corresponds to the rent which they at present bring, delivering the seventy per cent of its amount in credits, and the thirty in money, at the times which the said article 11 of this law fixes.

§ 898. *Favors to Denouncers, when Terminated.* — 29. The favor which by the preceding articles is conceded to the denouncers will only take place in case that within the twenty days following that of the denouncement they formalize for themselves or for the person whom they represent the subrogation or adjudication in the form which they provide. This term having passed without their so doing, they will lose their rights, and the respective office will proceed without delay to sell at public auction the annuities (censos) or estates in question, under the rules prescribed in this law.

§ 899. *Denouncements Presented in Writing.*—30. Said denouncements shall be presented in writing, in the federal district to the office which the government may establish therein, and in the states, to the chiefs of the treasury, administrators, or receivers of revenues in their respective demarkation.

§ 900. *Property within the Jurisdiction of the Usurper.*—31. In respect to the properties that, in conformity with this law, ought to be alienated in the part of the republic which to-day is found under the dominion of the government usurper of Mexico, the present payers of annuities (censatarios), or those who wish to substitute the latter, each one in his case, shall address himself to the supreme constitutional government to make the redemption, in conformity with what this same law provides; and the contracts of these operations shall be made before a notary public, taking care to note or cancel the respective writings, in order that when the towns return to the order in which are found the protocols in which the impositions so redeemed appear. The times having passed which for the redemptions articles 12 and 15 of this law concede, the government can order the sale of the properties at public auction whenever it thinks proper, on the terms provided in article 17.

§ 901. *Sums to be Preserved, how Fixed.*—32. In order to fix the sums of the imposed capitals which the religious communities have to preserve, in conformity with articles 8, 17, and 18 of the said law of the twelfth instant, if the mayordomos or chaplains of said communities shall not present, within fifteen days, a notice of the number of nuns who have introduced their dower, and the amount of said dowers, as well as the appropriation of the annual expenses of which said article 18 speaks, the office of the treasury to which it corresponds, together with the first political authority of the place, and with a review of the necessary *data*, shall fix the sum which ought to remain to each community for both objects, and shall designate the impositions which have to be applied to them, placing them at the disposition of the mayordomo or administrator of the community, with their respective inventory.

§ 902. *Funds from Sales, how Disposed of.*—33. Of the amount of money which the sales and redemptions of the properties, all of which this law speaks, shall produce in cash paid down on time, twenty-five per cent of what is sold and redeemed in their respective territories shall belong to the states, remaining to their charge to invest this product in the best roads and ways of communication, as well as in other objects of notorious public utility. In order to make this disposition effective, the chief offices (jefaturas) of the treasury in each state shall take care to deliver to the treasurer of the same the portion of the money and obligations which belong to it as they are collected.

§ 903. *Five per Cent, how Distributed.*—34. The special office which shall be established in the district, and the jefaturas of the treasury, administrations, and receiving offices of revenues, shall enjoy the five per cent of the money which each one of them collects in cash down or in installments, by virtue of what this law provides. The federal government in the district, and the governors of the states in each one of them, shall order the distribution which has to be made of the five per cent among the employés of said offices.

§ 904. *Funding of the National Debt.*—35. For the admission and funding that has to be made of the national debt, by the provisions of this law, all the rules established in the laws in force on the subject shall be observed, the supreme government being authorized to dictate all the measures it may think proper, with the object of assuring the interests of the nation, in all the operations which in conformity with this law must be executed. In none of the operations which emanate from this law shall be admitted as credits against the exchequer, the documents issued by the general treasury of Mexico, after the sixteenth of December, 1857, nor by any of the offices which have been or may be submitted to the so-called government of the capital.

§ 905. *Reports by Officers of the Impositions of Capitals.*—36. In order to avoid the concealments which in fraud of the provisions of this law might be made, all the notaries public and the registers of mortgages must present to the corresponding office of the treasury, within twenty days counted from the publication of this law, a nominal notice of the impositions of capitals which appear in their protocols, corresponding to the properties which it mentions. The want of the fulfillment of this provision will be a motive of a suspension of office for one or two years, according to the gravity of the case.

Wherefore, I command it to be printed, published, circulated, and that due fulfillment be given it. Given in the place of the national government, in Vera Cruz, on the thirteenth of July, 1859. Benito Juarez. To C. Miguel Lerdo de Tejàda, minister of the treasury and public credit. And I communicate it to you for your understanding and fulfillment. Palace of the national government of Vera Cruz, on the thirteenth of July, 1859. Lerdo de Tejada.

V. CIRCULARS OF THE DEPARTMENT OF THE TREASURY.

§ 906. *Order for the Formation of a Statement of the Estates of Corporations Existing at the Date of the Publication of the Law of June 25th.*—Department of state and that of the treasury and public credit. Circular. In order to facilitate the fulfillment of all the provisions of the law of the twenty-fifth of June last, and its regulation of July 30th, as well as to avoid secretions and frauds which might be committed in respect to the alienations which must be made in conformity with said law, his excellency the substitute president has thought proper to order that by all the governments of the states and territories of the republic shall be commanded to be formed immediately a detailed notice of the estates of corporations which at the date of the publication of the said law existed in the state or territory of their command, expressing the corporation or institution to which they belonged, the street and number of each urban estate, and the partido in which were found situated the country estates, as well as the value which each estate had fixed for the payment of the tax, according to *data* which existed in the respective office, and that said notice shall be published with the greatest possible brevity in the official periodical, or in the manner which may be most convenient to make the knowledge thereof general; and that a copy thereof be ordered to this department. Which by supreme order I have the honor to communicate to your excellency for its fulfillment, reiterating to you on this account the confidence of my consideration and particular appreciation. God and liberty. Mexico, August 9, 1856. Lerdo de Tejada.

*August* 13, 1856—*Circular Department of the Treasury—Explanation of the law of Desamortizacion.*—Department of state and that of the treasury and public credit. Section 2. In article 27 of the regulation of the law of the twenty-fifth of June last, issued on the thirtieth of July last passed, and which has already been communicated to your honor, it is provided that the payment of the alcabalas caused by the adjudications or public sales which shall be made in the capitals of the states and territories, shall be made in the superior offices (jefaturas) of the treasury; and those of the other points in the administration of the post-offices of the chief town of the partido. In article 30 of said regulation it is provided that the superior chiefs of the treasury shall take care to collect the bonds and sums received by the administrators of the post-offices in their demarkation; that they shall send to this department by the first mail of each week a detailed notice of what they may have collected directly or through the administrators, in effective money or in bonds, expressing the amount in money which they may have in their possession, and that they shall remit the bonds funded on a certified sheet, through the said post-office to the general treasury. Notwithstanding that the attributes and duties of the chief offices (jefaturas) of the treasury are marked with so much clearness, in respect to the desamortizacion of the properties of the civil and ecclesiastical corporations, his excellency the president ordered that the exact and faithful fulfillment of the provisions cited be especially recommended to your honor, in the conception that their non-observance or infraction will be perhaps the most strict responsibility for the employés culpable of either fault.

§ 907. *Money Sent to Department by Drafts.*—Likewise his excellency orders that whenever it may be possible to remit in drafts to the general treasury all or a part of what is collected, it shall be so done, and in case it can not, the money will be kept to the order of this department, without touching for any account that fund. I communicate it to your honor, by supreme order, for your knowledge and consequent effects. God and liberty. Mexico, August 13, 1856. Lerdo de Tejada.

§ 908. *August* 18, 1856—*Resolution of the Department of the Treasury—Explanation of the Law of Desamortizacion—Conventional Sales—Adjudication of Property Leased.*—Department of state and that of the treasury and public credit. Section 2. A report having been made to the president with your communication, of the date of the thirteenth of the present month, relative to the adjudication of the hacienda of Calpulalpan to the lessee D. Guadalupe Huitron of the appurtenance of the confraternity (cofradia) of the Santisimo, and that the mayordomo of the latter was at the adjudication of the forest of said hacienda, on account of Huitron being prohibited from cutting said wood to sell, and that he was only permitted to cut what was necessary for the service of the hacienda, and that further cutting was comprehended in the lease—his excellency has been pleased to determine that in virtue of the fact that said Huitron had rented the hacienda in question with the inclusion of the land on which is found the forest, with the only reservation of not cutting the wood for sale, said Huitron has a right to have all of said estate adjudicated to him, without any reservation of the rights of the ancient proprietor; that right which was reserved being appraised in conformity with the regulation of the thirtieth of the month last past, in order to unite its value to the sum of the lease, which recites the basis of the price of adjudication. At the same time his excellency orders that this rule shall be observed in all like cases. Which by supreme order I say to you for its fulfillment, and in answer to your cited communication. God and liberty. Mexico, August 18, 1856. Lerdo de Tejada. Señor judge of letters of the partido de Jilotepec.

§ 909. *August* 20, 1856—*Circular of the Department of the Treasury—Explanation of the Law of Desamortizacion—Explanation of the Law.*—Department of state and of that of the treasury and public credit. Section 2. In view of the inquiry of that subprefecture, dated the eleventh instant, relative to the fact that all the authorities of that partido, desirous of not being mistaken in the application of the law of the twenty-fifth of June last, on desamortizacion, solicit explanations to be made on the points which are expressed in said inquiry; his excellency the substitute president, to whom I reported, has been pleased to declare that the points 2, 3, 4, and 5 of said inquiry are resolved by articles 1, 2, and 25 of the regulations of July 30th; and that in respect to the first point, there is no doubt that are comprehended in the exception of article 8 of the law mentioned the woods of the municipalities of that subprefecture, in which the greater part of their uses is made directly for the residents of each municipality, although some of the advantages of those woods, such as the cutting heavy timber, is conceded by a lease. God and liberty. Mexico, August 20, 1856. Lerdo de Tejada. To the subprefect of the partido of Chalco.

§ 910. *August* 26, 1856—*Resolution of the Department of the Treasury—The Law of Desamortizacion is Explained—In Pueblo Lands, Adjudications to the Lessees.*—Department of state and that of the treasury and public credit. Section 2. A report having been made to his excellency the president, of your excellency's communication, No. 66, dated the thirtieth of the last month of July, relative to your excellency's being empowered, in order that with due consideration of the circumstances the common property (bienes comunales) may be sold on the terms which the law of desamortizacion provides, to the residents of the pueblos which possess them, and not be adjudicated to the lessees, for the reasons which your excellency expresses—his excellency the president, in view thereof, has been pleased to resolve that your excellency be answered, as I have the honor to do, that it would destroy completely the basis of the law, to take from the lessees the right of adjudication which has been granted to them, and that consequently only in case that they renounce the right can sales be made in favor of the residents of the pueblos which possess said bienes comunales. Which I say to your excellency in answer, reiterating the considerations of my particular appreciation. God and liberty. Mexico, August 26, 1856. Lerdo de Tejada. To his excellency the governor of the state of Oaxaca.

*August* 27, 1856—*Resolution of the Department of the Treasury—Waters.*—The waters comprehended in the lands of corporations are subject to desamortizacion.

§ 911. *Waters for Public Use not Subject to Desamortizacion.* Department of state and of that of the treasury and public credit. Section 2. Most excellent sir: In view of your communication, No. 100, dated the twenty-eighth of July last passed, in which is inserted that of the prefect of the district of Texcoco, as to whether the waters belonging to the municipality of said district ought or not to be considered with the character of country estates, his excellency the president has been pleased to resolve that I answer your excellency, as I have the honor to do, that if the waters are of public or common use, they are not comprehended in the law of desamortizacion; but they are comprehended in it, in case that they are stagnant waters and belong to lands of the corporations. I say this to your excellency in answer to your cited communication. God and liberty. August 27, 1856. Lerdo de Tejada. His excellency the governor of the state of Mexico.

§ 912. *Protocols of Adjudications Closed, September* 26, 1856. Department of state and that of the treasury and public credit. Section 2. His excellency the president desiring that the provisions of the law of the twenty-fifth of June, and the regulation of the thirtieth of July should be duly fulfilled, he has been pleased to order that by circular your government notify the notaries (escribanos) of this capital that precisely on the twenty-sixth of this month they close their protocols of adjudications of the estates of civil and ecclesiastical corporations, and that they shall give your excellency directly a detailed notice of all those which have been made before each one of them, in order that with the presence of those *data* it may be immediately known whether or not the denouncements are admissible, which are presented on account of the adjudication not having been formalized, or the public sale made. On designating the twenty-sixth day for the remission of said notices, it has been taken into consideration that the twenty-seventh is a festal day on which the third and last term of the law is completed. I communicate it to your excellency by supreme order for your understanding and consequent effects. God and liberty. Mexico, September 5, 1856. Lerdo de Tejada. His excellency the governor of the district.

§ 913. *Rooms Annexed to Edifices Occupied by Corporations are not Desamortized, even when They are Rented.*—Department of state and that of the treasury and public credit. Section 2. Your excellency: A report having been made to his excellency the president with your excellency's communication of the date of the first instant, in which you manifest that the adjudications which, in conformity with the law of the twenty-fifth of June last, have been made of the properties of the college of San Juan de Letran, of which your excellency is the worthy rector, it has been verified that are included in the adjudications a part of the said edifice of the college, the high rooms of which are occupied by the college, or on the contrary, the lower rooms or the higher parts are destined and are now used for the offices which are necessary for the college, and perhaps because having various entrances from the principal part of the edifice, these parts have been considered as separated therefrom, and not comprehended in article 8 of said law, and you solicit that it be declared in conformity with said article that shall be excepted from adjudication those parts of the edifices occupied by the corporations, which although they are rented and have various entrances from the principal part of the edifice, they form respectively the upper and lower rooms of others occupied by the corporations. His excellency, in view thereof, has been pleased to resolve that in the exception of article 8 of said law, in respect to the edifices immediately and directly destined to the service and object of the institute of the corporations, even when any part not separated from them is rented, although the distinct edifices from the principal one occupied by the corporations are not comprehended, and although in some manner they may be united or contiguous to the same, it is clear that the parts or rooms which constitute it are comprehended in the exception; and that consequently the rooms rented of the higher or lower stories which correspond to the lower or higher stories occupied by the respective corporation, as parts of the edifice directly destined for the service or object of the institution, even when they have distinct entrances from the principal one of the same edifice, are excepted from the alienation provided by the law. Which I have the honor to say to your excellency by supreme order in answer to your said communication. God and liberty. Mexico, September 5, 1856. Lerdo de Tejada. His excellency Don José Maria Lacunza, rector of the national college of San Juan de Letran.

September 17, 1856. Department of justice, ecclesiastical affairs, and public instruction. His excellency the president has been pleased to direct to me the decree which follows: Ignacio Comonfort, substitute president of the Mexican republic, to the inhabitants thereof, know ye: That in use of the faculties which article 3 of the plan of Ayutla, reformed in Acapulco, concedes to me, and in consideration that on the morning of the fifteenth of the present month a sedition broke out in the convent of San Francisco of this city, and many conspirators being surprised *flagrante delicto* in the cloisters and cells, and among them various monks, I have decreed, with the unanimous consent of the council of ministers, the following:

§ 914. *Convent of Franciscans Suppressed.*—1. The convent of Franciscans of the city of Mexico is suppressed, and the properties which have belonged to it up to this date are declared national properties, excepting the principal church and the chapels, which with their sacred vases, sacerdotal ornaments, relics, and images will be placed at the disposition of the illustrious archbishop, that they may be destined to divine worship.

§ 915. *Security and Alienation of Property.*—2. The department of public works shall dictate the measures conducive to the security and alienation of the properties declared national in this decree.

§ 916. *Division of the Products.*—3. The product of said properties shall be divided immediately among the orphanage, house of lunatics, house of charity (hospicio), college of secondary education for girls, and school of arts, etc.

§ 917. *In the Public Sales of the Estates Desamortizadas there is No Restitution nor Lesion Enorme.*[1]—Department of state and that of the treasury and public credit. Section 2. His excellency the president, to whom I reported your petition, in which you manifest that the hacienda of beneficiating ores called pardo, situated on the edge of that city, and the property of the town council (ayuntamiento) of that capital, was put at auction, and the sale struck off in your favor, and that the representative of the ayuntamiento has presented himself saying the sale

[1] Great damage, for which a sale may be rescinded.

was null, and besides that two persons, by a subsequent act, appeared and advanced the bid, alleging that the municipal corporation enjoyed the benefit of restitution *in integrum;*[1] that the overbid was admissible, and that the first sale ought to be rescinded; which question has been submitted to judicial authority—his excellency has been pleased to resolve that in the public sales made according to the law of the twenty-fifth of June, relative to desamortizacion, restitution *in integrum* nor rescission for lesion enorme does not take place, notwithstanding these recourses are valid in ordinary cases. I say this to you by supreme order as the result of your petition relative thereto. God and liberty. Mexico, September 17, 1856. To Señor D. Ignacio Arizmendi. Lerdo de Tejada.

§ 918. *It is Ordered that the Governor of the District may Delegate his Functions to the Judges of First Instance and to their Substitutes (Suplentes), to Preside over the Auctions of Estates Desamortizadas.*—Department of state and that of the treasury and public credit. Section 2. In order that the provisions of the law of the 25th of June and the regulation of July 30th may have due effect, his excellency the president has thought proper to resolve that for the auctions at which must be sold the estates of civil and ecclesiastical-corporations which have not been adjudicated, nor publicly sold in the legal term of three months, your excellency may not only delegate your powers to the judges of first instance, in conformity with the provisions of said regulation, but may do so also to their substitutes, and to other persons in whom your excellency may deem it opportune to deposit your confidence for the execution of said act, in which it is of the greatest interests that there should be no delay for want of authority to preside over them. Likewise his excellency has resolved that the notice which the notaries of this capital must give to that government, of the adjudications made before each one of them up to the twenty-sixth day, they shall remit precisely on the twenty-seventh day, in spite of its being a festive day. God and liberty. Mexico, September 17, 1856. Lerdo de Tejada.

§ 919. *October* 9, 1856.—*Communication from the Department of the Treasury, on the Objects of the Law of Desamortizacion—Lands that do not Pass Two Hundred Dollars in Value Need not Follow the Usual Proceedings.*—Department of state and that of the treasury and public credit. His excellency the president has had the necessity of taking into consideration that

[1] Restitution of property where fraud may be proved.

the ignorance of the poor laborer is being abused, and specially that of the indigenous (Indians), in order to make them view in opposition to their interests the law of desamortizacion, the principal object of which was, on the contrary, that of favoring the classes most destitute; to which is added that a great part of the lessees of land have not been able to have them adjudicated, either through a want of resources for the necessary expenses, or either by the impediments which the avarice of speculators has placed in their way, with the well-known view of depriving them of the right which the law conceded to them, subrogating themselves in their place as soon as the time designated in the same may pass for the adjudications, and which they have not been left to enjoy freely. The law would be nullified in one of its principal ends, which is that of the subdivision of country property, if the consummation of acts so reproved should not be prevented; with such end, as well as with that of facilitating the needy in the acquisition of the fee in the land, his excellency the president orders that all land the value of which does not pass that of two hundred dollars, in conformity with the law of the twenty-fifth of June, shall be adjudicated to the respective lessees, whether they have them by apportionment, whether they belong to the ayuntamientos, or be in any other manner subject to the desamortizacion, without any alcabala being collected from them, or their being obliged to pay any fee, and without any necessity either of the execution of any deed (escritura) of adjudication, as to constitute them owners and proprietors in every form of what shall be sold them, the title which the political authority shall give them on paper marked with their official seal will be sufficient, protocolizing in the archives of the said office the documents which are issued. This disposition would be inefficacious, in case the term of three months fixed for the adjudications should be held as passed; a term which has not passed for the indigenous and other needy laborers, whom the government proposes to protect, since that for the reasons already expressed they have found themselves under a positive impossibility to comply with the law. It is therefore as just as it is proper to resolve, and as his excellency does so, that no adjudication nor public sale shall be made in respect to lands the value of which has already been fixed, except in the case that the lessees expressly renounce their right, taking care, in order to avoid all fraud, that that renunciation be made to appear precisely in the deed which shall be executed in favor of another person, and that it comprehends the point that he who makes the renunciation has been previously informed of the law, of the regulation, and of the other provisions given for their benefit. In the fulfillment of these supreme dispositions, the public peace, the well-being of the most needy classes, and the realization and the carrying out of the rules dictated to move property are simultaneously interested. The attainment of ends so important requires that this circular be scattered in profusion, and that care be scrupulously taken that it be not infringed upon by any private person or authority, who will be warned that the responsibility which they contract will be made effective; and on both points his excellency the president hopes to find in your excellency the co-operation which he has never missed in the affairs concerning the public service. God and liberty. Mexico, October 9, 1856. Lerdo de Tejada.

§ 920. *December* 18, 1856. *Circular from the Department of the Treasury—All Protests or Reserves in the Adjudications of Desamortizadas Estates are Prohibited.*—Department of state and that of the treasury and public credit. Section 2. Circular. Your excellency: His excellency the substitute president has taken into consideration that as the acquisitions of estates of corporations have been declared null, when any protest or reservation contrary to the law of the twenty-fifth of June of this year is put in the writings, likewise must be rescinded those in which, after the adjudication has been formalized or the public sale, any like protest or reserve shall have been executed in writing; and therefore his excellency has been pleased to resolve that the following provisions shall be observed:

§ 920 *a*. *Property how Renounced.*—1. Every one who having acquired by adjudication or public sale an estate of a corporation shall execute in writing, whether by a public or private instrument, which is entitled to credit in court, any reserve or protest to return at any time the estate of the corporation, although it may be with the pretext or for the case that the law in force may be derogated, it shall be understood that from that moment he has renounced the property of that corporation, for the purpose that it may be again denounced or resold.

§ 921. *Who may Revoke Reservations.*—2. Those who before these provisions shall have made such reserves or protests can revoke them, appearing with that object before the first political authority of the partido, within fifteen days after the publication of this circular. This term having passed without its being done, they will remain with the case of the preceding article.

§ 922. *Reserves being Known, Estates shall be Sold.*—3. The reserve or protest being known, the first political authority shall officially order the estate to be sold, unless some denouncement thereof shall have been presented before; in which case the said authority shall declare to the first denouncer the right of subrogation in the place of the prior proprietor, for the same price and conditions which he had acquired by the adjudication or public sale.

§ 923. *Alcabala not to be Returned.*—4. He who by the reserve or protest shall lose the property in an estate shall lose no right to have the alcabala returned to him; and he who by subrogation or public sale may acquire the property again shall pay one half of the alcabala in money and the other half in bonds, as in the common transfers of the dominion.

§ 924. *Notice to Prior Proprietor.*—5. In order to proceed with the subrogation of the denouncer, or with the public sale officially, the prior proprietor shall be notified with the document of the reserve or protest, and if he should deny it, the point shall be submitted to the decision of the judge of the first instance. The latter shall proceed by a verbal trial, immediately rendering his judgment, without prejudice to an appeal being granted, if the interest in the case permits it in conformity with the common law.

§ 925. *Possession of Estate.*—6. Those who acquire the property of an estate, by subrogation or by public sale, in virtue of the renunciation consequent upon the reserve or protest of the prior proprietor, can ask that the latter quit the possession thereof immediately. In order to obligate him to quit, if he should refuse, they shall proceed by a verbal trial, the judgment of which must be immediately executed, and an appeal can be taken therefrom as in the prior article.

§ 926. *Proofs of Reserve.*—7. For the effects of this circular, after the adjudication has been formalized, or the public sale taken place, the receipts which a proprietor has admitted shall be admissible as proofs of reserve or protest contrary to the law, when in them the corporation shall manifest that it receives the incomes as a rent, and not as an interest on the censo or lien which the proprietor recognizes. Besides, those receipts shall not be evidence to prove the payment, the proprietor who admits them being obligated for a second payment, as well in respect to the corporation as in respect to any person who may represent their right.

§ 927. *Fine of Notaries.*—8. The first political authority of the partido, or the judge of the first instance, shall impose economically on the notary who authorizes any document of reserve or protest a fine of one hundred or two hundred dollars, and a suspension from office for a term of two or four months.

Which I communicate to your excellency for your knowledge, and that you may please to order it published for the corresponding ends. God and liberty. Mexico, December 18, 1856. M. Lerdo de Tejada.

*February* 5, 1861—*A Decree of the Government Explaining the Laws of Desamortizacion and Nationalization.*— His excellency the president has been pleased to address me the decree which follows: The citizen Benito Juarez, constitutional provisional president of the Mexican United States, to the inhabitants thereof, know ye: That in use of the faculties with which I find myself vested, I have thought proper to decree the following:

TITLE I. OF THE ADJUDICATARIOS.

§ 928. *Adjudicatarios, Who Are.*—1. Those comprehended in the following classifications are actually and permanently legitimate adjudicatarios.

2. Those who did not return their title of adjudication, nor retract the certificate of the return of the tax-sales (alcabala).

3. Those who returned their title without any note and did not retract their certificate.

4. Those who did return it at the point of death (en artículo de muerte), whatever may be the note with which the return was made; and in case of their death, their heirs.

5. The maids, widows, or female orphans who, although they have returned the title with a note in conformity, and have drawn the certificate of the return of the alcabala, may have exceeded more than five years of living in the house, the title of the adjudication of which they returned, provided that it is a question of one sole estate (finca).

6. The minors whose tutors or curators made the return in the name of said minors, whatever may be the note which they may have given, and even when they may have drawn the certificate of the return of the alcabala.

7. Those who returned the title with a note in which may appear a simple subjection to the so-called law of the twenty-

eighth of February, 1858, without there being any word which may denote conformity or consent.

8. Those who were subrogated in the place of the adjudicatarios by purchase, concession, donation, or any other title translative of dominion, provided that neither they nor those of whom they acquired the right shall have lost it in conformity with this law. Those who shall have made denouncements in conformity with the laws are included in this number.

9. Those who are not comprehended in any of the foregoing articles, and those who have defaulted in the conditions of the law of the twenty-fifth of June, 1856, and its regulation, have failed to be adjudicatarios.

### Title II. Of the Purchasers.

§ 929. *Void Sales.*—10. Every sale, whether of estates (fincas), or of any other thing, made by the clergy without express authorization from the constitutional authorities, is null and of no value or effect.

§ 930. *Favors Conceded on Conditions.*—11. Those who, possessing titles of adjudication, conventional bid, or sale, prior to the seventeenth of December, 1857, or given subsequently by constitutional authorities, made purchases with the clergy of the same properties (fincas) on which they had titles, lost their right of adjudicatarios, conventional bidders, or purchasers, as they acquired none of the contract made with the clergy, nor preserve the right to any return, nor indemnifiation, whatever may be the amounts which they have given to the clergy, or to any other person or authority which is not constitutional. If they should wish now to recover the primitive rights of adjudicatarios, bidders, or purchasers, the government will concede this favor, without prejudice to third parties, with the condition that the capital shall be increased twenty per cent, which was recognized by the adjudication, conventional bid or sale, which twenty per cent will follow, for the redemptions or recognition, the same fate as the primitive capital. Those who may wish to enjoy this favor will so manifest it within thirty days from the publication of this law.

§ 931. *Parties Included in Prior Article.*—12. Those who purchased from the clergy, making themselves owners at the same time of the rights of the adjudicatarios, are comprehended in the resolutions of the foregoing article.

§ 932. *Purchases from the Clergy Void.*—13. Those who purchased from the clergy without having made themselves owners of the rights of the adjudicatarios have not acquired a right of any kind; in consequence, the adjudicatarios can enter immediately, through the medium of judicial authority, into the possession of the estates (fincas) which were adjudicated to them.

§ 933. *Rights of Property Acquired are Free.*—14. Those who, by adjudication, conventional or public sale, acquired rights of property are entirely free to exercise them, provided they may not have lost them in conformity with this law.

§ 934. *Improvements on Property.*—15. Those who, in virtue of the declarations made by the law, continue in the dominion and possession of the houses purchased from the clergy will be obliged to indemnify the illegitimate purchasers of the same for the improvements made on the properties from the date of the purchase, with a valuation by experts, and in case of disagreement, by a third party, according to the laws. In respect to the improvements anterior to the law of July 25, 1850, said law shall govern.

§ 935. *Reoccupation of Property by the Cleryg.*—16. When the property adjudicated was reoccupied by the clergy, and not sold afterwards by it to another person, the adjudicatario who enters again into the possession will not be obliged to pay for any of the improvements which may have been made on the property after the reoccupation, of whatsoever class they may be.

17. Those who can not do in the act of payment what article 15 speaks of will acknowledge the amount as a mortgage on the said houses for nine years, with annual interest at the rate of six per cent.

### Title III. Of the Denouncers.

§ 936. *Denouncements how Made.*—18. The denouncements will not be valid unless made before the corresponding authorities, with entire conformity to the law of the twenty-fifth of June, 1856, and relative posterior circulars, or those made before the general government or revalidated by it.

§ 937. *Validity of Denouncements.*—19. For the validity of the denouncement before the constitutional authorities, two epochs must be borne in mind: 1. That of the twenty-fifth of June, 1856, to thirteenth of July, 1859; 2. That of the thirteenth of July, 1859, to the date of this law. For the validity of those of the first epoch, the certificate of the denouncement and of the payment of the tax (alcabala) is necessary, in conformity with the provisions in the law of the twenty-fifth of June, 1856. For the validity of those of the second, the certificate of the denouncement and proof of the payment having been made is required in the terms which the law of the thirteenth of July, 1859, and the circular of the twenty-seventh of the same month, provide. The denouncements which may have been made before the government and the constitutional authorities of the properties which were in the places occupied by the reaction, do not prejudice the rights acquired in virtue of the anterior laws, and which may not have been lost by the express declaration of the law.

§ 938. *Legal Subrogation.*—20. The existence being supposed of the requisites mentioned in the two anterior articles, the denouncers of properties voluntarily returned by them were legally subrogated in the place of the primitive adjudicatarios, bidders, or conventional purchasers; it being understood by voluntary return all those which are comprehended in articles 3, 4, 5, 6, and 7 of this law.

§ 939. *Withdrawal of Certificates.*—21. The denouncers of properties, the owners of which withdrew the certificate of the return of the alcabala, were also legally subrogated in the place of the primitive adjudicatarios, bidders, or conventional purchasers.

§ 940. *Denouncers Free for Subrogation.*—22. The denouncers of properties or capitals, the adjudicatarios or censatario (one who pays an annuity to another) of which have let or should let the term pass designated by the law of the thirteenth of June, 1859, for the manifestation marked in article 12 thereof, are free for the subrogation.

§ 941. *Disputes Settled by the Tribunals.*—23. Whenever there may be a dispute between two or more denouncers, or between one denouncer and an adjudicatario, bidder, or conventional purchaser, on the right of preference, and in general, in every case of doubt on the right of property of nationalized properties, the question shall be decided by the tribunals according to the laws.

§ 942. *Alcabala Returned.*—24. The sums which the government may receive for redemptions or payment of tax (alcabala), which may not belong to the government because the titles in virtue of which they may have been paid have not been declared valid, will be returned with all preference in the same terms in which they shall have been received.

§ 943. *Rights Lost how Regained.*—25. The adjudicatarios who may have lost their rights as such for any cause, and whose properties have not been denounced by other persons, can denounce the same properties, and they shall be adjudicated to them again for the price of the old adjudication; being in the class of denouncers for the payment and redemption of capital, who can only act with the security required by article 16 of the law of the thirteenth of July, 1859.

§ 944. *Denouncements now Non-admissible.*—26. Outside of the denouncements comprehended in the preceding article, none are now legally admissible, except those authorized by the law of the twenty-fifth of June, 1856, and relative posterior circulars, and by the law of the thirteenth of July, 1859.

### Title IV. Of the Legal Terms.

§ 945. *Publications.*—27. For the course of terms designated in the laws and decrees concerning the nationalization of ecclesiastical properties, the official publication of said dispositions will be required in each locality.

§ 946. *Occupation by Reactionists.*—28. The time of occupation by the reactionists shall be discounted from the terms mentioned in the towns in which the official publication should have already had effect.

§ 947. *Terms how Counted.*—29. All the terms shall be counted from moment to moment, with the exclusion of holidays, without giving place to an interpretation taken from the spirit of the laws for the increase or diminution of said terms, but it shall be according to the letter thereof.

§ 948. *Terms Relate to Location of Property.*—30. The terms relate to the place where the properties are situated, and not to the domicile of the owners thereof.

§ 949. *Terms to be Extended.*—31. In the future no prorogation shall be conceded of the terms designated for the delivery of the money and credits with which the redemption of capitals must be made, except to persons who may have some of the following qualities: To ask the prorogation for one single property, country or city, which has been adjudicated to the adjudicatario because he had lived in it; especial and eminent service in the constitutional cause, or of the national independence in a foreign war; having lost in defense of one or the other father, son, or brother, the only sustainer of the family.

### Title V. Of the Redemptions.

§ 950. *Separation of Fifteen per Cent.*—32. In conformity with what is ordered in the decree of the seventeenth of December, 1860, the chief offices of the treasury, and the section of desamortizacion and redemptions of the department of the same branch, shall separate the fifteen per cent designated in union with other funds for the payment of the respective reclamations; and the infraction of this disposition will be a case of responsibility and destitution of employment.

§ 951. *Compensation No Longer Admitted.*—33. From the date of this law compensation of no class will be admitted in the money part, however privileged the credit may be of the one in whose favor it is solicited.

§ 952. *Punctual Collections.*—34. Exact and punctual collection will be made with the greatest efficacy of the monthly notes signed by the censatarias for the redemption of the capitals which they recognize.

§ 953. *Negotiation of Notes Prohibited.*—35. The negotiation of said notes is expressly prohibited, under the penalty of deprivation of office, without the express order of the general government.

§ 954. *Prompt Payment or Extra Charge.*—36. He who has signed a note is obliged to deliver the amount within the first eight days of each completed month, and if he should not do it, he will incur the penalty of an extra charge of one half per cent for each day that passes up to thirty; if the delay should pass this term and reach two months, he shall pay twenty-five per cent more; and if it reaches three months, he shall lose the right of enjoying the terms for the redemption of the part which may be pending.

§ 955. *Coercive Power may be Used.*—And he can be compelled by coercive power to make immediately the redemption in full; and for that purpose the property must be sold, unless the real payment be made; and there shall be collected from the product, with preference to all other credit, the complete amount of the capital, with twenty-five per cent extra.

§ 956. *Non-delivery of Bonds, Consequence thereof.*—37. Those who within the term designated shall not deliver the bonds or credits for the payment of which they are obligated shall pay fifty per cent extra on said bonds or credits; and if they do not do it, public sale of the property will be proceeded with, and coercive power used; from which sale the seller will immediately make, in bonds or credits, the payment of what is due, with the extra mentioned.

§ 957.—*Discount on Cash Payments.*—38. To those who shall redeem at once the whole of what they are to pay in money, a conventional discount will be made to them in the district, and that of twenty-five per cent in the states. To those who in the future may wish to redeem altogether, a discount will be made equivalent to one per cent monthly.

TITLE VI. OF THE OFFICES OF REDEMPTION.

§ 958. *Treasury Officers Responsible to That Department Only.* 39. The offices of the chiefs of the treasury and the special section of the district are dependent, only and exclusively, on the department of that branch.

§ 959. *Fifteen per Cent, Separation of.*—40. It is an obligation of the chiefs of the said mentioned offices to separate daily the fifteen per cent spoken of in article 32.

§ 960. *Three per Cent, Separation and Distribution.*—41. It is equally the obligation of the said chiefs to separate daily the three per cent, to which is reduced the five per cent destined by the law for the proper offices, and the distribution of which will be made as follows: In the special section of the district will belong; the one per cent. to the assistant of the department and section of public credit; one quarter of one per cent to the general treasurer; one half of one per cent to the attorney (asesor) of the section of redemptions; three quarters of one per cent to the chief of the same; and one half of one per cent to the employees thereof. In the office of the chiefs (jefaturas), the one half per cent to the chief; the same (idem) to the asesor which shall be appointed by the department of the treasury; the same (idem) to the employees of the office of the chief: and one and a half per cent to the administrators, receivers of rents, in conformity with the distribution which the governors of the states may make.

§ 961. *Separation and Application of Funds.*—42. The special section of the district will make the separations already expressed of the three and fifteen per cent, the first of which it will reserve in its possession, and the second it will remit to the board created by the decree of the seventeenth of December, 1860. The eighty-two per cent remaining will be entered into the same general treasury for the common considerations of the exchequer.

43. The chief offices of the treasury will make the same sepations of the three and fifteen per cent, and also that of the twenty per cent for the states; and the penalties imposed for the infractions of the provisions of this law shall be extended to the chiefs. The sixty-two per cent remaining will be employed in conformity with the special orders of the department of the treasury.

§ 962. *Bonds and Credits Received Canceled.*—44. The bonds and credits of every class which shall be entered in the offices of redemption shall be rendered useless at the time by taking out a small piece from the center of them, and in this particular all that is established in the provisions in force on the matter shall be observed.

§ 963. *Balance Sheet.*—45. Besides the obligations expressed, the offices of redemption are obliged to remit monthly to the department of the treasury the balance sheet of the ingress and egress corresponding to the said branch of redemptions, and shall give this document to the press.

§ 964. *Publication of Operations.*—46. They shall likewise remit and publish a statement of all the operations in their own branch which they shall have made from the publication of the law of the thirteenth of July, 1859, with an expression of the names of the redeemers, the situation of the properties, the prices thereof, and the corporations to which they belonged.

§ 965. *Disputes Settled by Treasury Department.*—47. All the grave doubts which they may have on points relative to this law they shall submit to the department of the treasury, the resolution of which they shall await before proceeding any further in the matter. In doubtful cases the opinion of the attorney (asesor) will be given in writing.

§ 966. *Report Sent to the Department.*—48. In order that the resolution shall be dictated with full knowledge, an exact and detailed report of the antecedents of the matter shall be sent to the department, accompanied by a certified copy of the documents which may be indispensable to entirely understand the matter.

§ 967. *Separation of Accounts.*—49. The offices of the chiefs shall keep, with due separation, the accounts of the twenty per cent corresponding to the states, and that of the eighty per cent of the general government, in which shall be opportunely made the credits due.

## Title VII. Of the Bonds and Creidts.

§ 968. *Bonds and Credits, how Admitted.*—50. In the offices of redemptions shall not be admitted bonds nor other classes of credits proceeding from offices or authorities that are not constitutional. In the district, the general treasury will examine every credit, without which requisite they will not be admitted. In the states, the admission will be made under the responsibility of the chiefs of the treasury, being undisputed those of the credits examined by the general treasury.

§ 969. *Close Examination of Bonds.*—51. The offices shall scrupulously take care, under the responsibility of their chiefs, of the examination of the bonds which shall be presented to them, as well not to admit those of a date anterior to that of the seventeenth of December, 1857, as to exclude also those which may be proved to be forged, of which it is public a considerable number exists. If there should appear culpability in him who may present them, they will assign him immediately to the judge of the district.

52. The admission of money in payment, in place of bonds or credits, is expressly prohibited.

## Title VIII. Of Public Sales.

§ 970. *Property not Adjudicated Sold at Auction.*—53. Every property to which no adjudicatario, bidder, conventional purchaser, or denouncer may have a right, shall be put up at public auction, which shall take place in the department of the treasury in respect to the district.

§ 971. *Provisions of Law to be Observed.*—54. Being included in these sales the convents and other edifices comprehended in the law of June 13, 1859, the provisions in articles 5, 6, 7, 8, 9, and 10 thereof will be observed literally.

§ 972. *Product from the Sales of Convents.*—55. The product of the sale of the convents not sold up to the said twenty-fourth of October, and which must be alienated in conformity with the law of the thirteenth of July, 1859, being especially assigned by the decree of the twenty-fourth of October, 1860, to the payment of the transportation train occupied by the constitutional forces in September of the same year, and to the indemnification of damages caused by this occupation, the provisions of said decree will be observed literally; and of the products of said sale shall be formed a separate fund, and deposited with such character into the safes of the general treasury; and the penalty of destitution of the treasurer should be imposed if it be destined to other uses.

## Title IX. Of the Chaplaincies.

§ 973. *Chaplaincies of Blood.*—56. The chaplaincies of blood will be disentailed by the present chaplain paying the ten per cent on the value of the capital, if he should make the payment at the time, or the fifteen per cent if he should wait to collect from the censatario. If the capital should become due before two years, he will wait until the expiration of that term; and if it should become due afterwards, it will be required at the date of its maturity. It is declared that by chaplaincy of blood is only understood that in which the founder has called for the chaplains of his relatives or other person expressly appointed, and in that the present chaplain may be one of the relatives called. Without the union of those two circumstances the chaplaincy is not of blood.

§ 974. *Term of Two Months Conceded for the Enjoyment of Benefits.*—57. In order to enjoy the benefit which the prior article concedes, the last and unprorogable term of two months from the publication of this law is conceded. This term having passed without the chaplain having appeared to avail himself of the benefit which is granted to him, he will lose his right, the censatario being subrogated in his place, to whom will be admitted the redemption, the same as for any other capital which he may acknowledge.

§ 975. *Redemption of Chaplaincies of Blood.*—58. The chaplaincies which may not be of blood shall be redeemed, the chaplains paying two fifth parts in money of the amount of the capital, and three fifths in bonds or credits. In order to require the capital, what is ordered in respect to the chaplaincies of blood shall be observed.

§ 976. *Term of Redemption.*—59. The chaplains of whom the prior article speaks will have the same term of two months to solicit the redemption. If the term should pass without their doing it, the censatario will be subrogated in his place, or in default of the latter, he who may solicit it.

§ 977. *Chaplains not Ordained.*—60. Those who enjoy chaplaincies, whether of blood or not, without being ordained, being less than of thirty years, shall obtain, in order to pay the ten or the forty per cent in money, in their respective cases, the term of twenty months for the first case, and that of sixty months for the second.

§ 978. *Chaplaincies Excluded.*—61. Are excluded from the disentailment (desunculacion) and the power of redeeming according to article 11 of the law of the thirteenth of July, 1859, the chaplaincies which have the charge of rendering ecclesiastical service in the cathedrals, parishes, or convents of religious persons which still subsist, and which will remain as they are to-day until the supreme government thinks that that service is no longer necessary for the extinction of the convent, or for any other motive, in which case the supreme government will dispose of the capitals. The chaplaincies which have no more charge than to celebrate or order to be celebrated a certain number of masses, although they be in a determined church, are not included in the exception.

§ 979. *Right of Censatario to Redeem.*—62. The right of the censatario to make the redemption in conformity with the law is free in the vacant chaplaincies. The chaplaincies of blood which may be now in litigation to be decided who must be the chaplain, and that he who should be appointed will enjoy the benefits and terms conceded to the present ones, are not considered vacant.

§ 980. *List of Chaplains to be Made.*—63. After the publication of this law three months, a detailed list of the chaplains, whether of blood or not, and of the censatarios, which have proceeded from the disentailment, shall be remitted to the department of the treasury by all the offices of redemption. All the chaplaincies not comprehended in that list will be denounceable for the purpose that the denouncer may be substituted in place of the chaplain or censatario.

## Title X. Of the Establishments of Beneficence.

§ 981. *Establishments of Beneficence, What are.*—64. Under the name of establishment of beneficence is comprehended houses of charity, hospitals (hospicios), insane asylums, houses of orphans, houses of maternity, and in general all those which acknowledge as a basis public charity, as well as those destined to primary, secondary, and professional instruction.

§ 982. *List of Establishments to be Made.*—65. A detailed and nominal list will be formed in the district and in the states of the establishments to which has been imparted the favor of having invested in their improvement the dotal properties destined to their subsistence. Publicity will be given to the mentioned list.

§ 983. *Capitals of the Establishments.*—66. The capitals belonging to the establishments of beneficence, from whatever cause they may proceed, are not comprehended in article 11 and the following ones of the law of the thirteenth of July, 1859.

§ 984. *Establishments to be Secularized.*—67. The establishments of beneficence which were administered by ecclesiastical corporations or bodies, independent of the government, will be secularized and put under the immediate inspection of the public authority, for which purpose will be appointed by the respective government, and in the states by their governors, the directors and administrators which may be esteemed necessary.

§ 985. *Regulations of Establishments.*—68. The general government and the governors will regulate all that concerns said establishments in the directive, administrative, and economic affairs, taking care especially that their dotal funds be managed with all purity, and invested in their preferred objects, and that an examination of their accounts be made monthly, in order to punish severely those who misapplied funds in the management of properties consecrated to ends so important. Publicity will be given in the periodicals of the cash balance sheets.

### Title XI. Of the Monks.

§ 986. *Number of Nuns—Their Dower—Sums to be Applied.* 69. Having already transpired, with an excess, the term fixed by article 32 of the law of the thirteenth of June, 1859, for the mayordomos or chaplains to present a notice of the number of nuns who have introduced their dower, and of the amount of these, as well as of the estimate of the expenses of which article 18 of the same law speaks, they will proceed immediately in the district, through the department of the treasury, and in the states through their respective governors, to fix the sum which ought to remain with each community for both objects, and to designate the impositions which must be applied to them.

§ 987. *Designation of Capitals.*—70. The designation once made of the capitals which must remain reserved to the communities of persons, they will proceed to make the redemption of all the others which before belonged to the same communities, and which should remain free.

§ 988. *Division of Capitals.*—71. The capitals reserved to communities of religious persons will be divided into two classes, some being destined to the repair of buildings, festivities, and other expenses of worship, and the others representing the dowers of the nuns. It will be obligatory to select for these last those of the quickest realization.

§ 989. *Extinguishment of Convents.*—72. As soon as a convent becomes extinguished, the capitals of the first class shall enter into the dominion of the nation, and they will be redeemed with three fifth parts in bonds or credits, and two in effective money.

§ 990. *Capitals of Second Class.*—73. In the capitals of the second class will be observed the provisions in article 24 of the law of the thirteenth of July, 1859.

§ 991. *Heirs of Nuns.*—74. The heirs by will or *ab intestato* of the nuns who die in the cloister or out of it will be subrogated in their place.

§ 992. *Repayment to Novices.*—75. To the novices who are separated from the novitiated shall be returned at the same time by the offices of redemption what they may have delivered to the convent.

§ 993. *Reduction of Convents.*—76. The convents of nuns shall be reduced to those which may be esteemed necessary by the government in the district, and by the governors in the states, observing for this the principle that the sums belonging to the same order remain united.

§ 994. *Regulations to be Made in Fifteen Days.*—77. The regulation spoken of in the preceding article shall be made in the term of fifteen days from the publication of this law.

§ 995. *Application of the Products of Sales of Convents.*—78. The half of the products from the public sales of the suppressed convents shall be destined to the capitalization of pawn-shops (monte pios) and pensions of widows and female orphans, and the other half to the improvement of public instruction and establishments of charity.

## Title XII. Of the Friars.

§ 996. *One Month to Solicit the Five Hundred Dollars.*—79. In order that the regular ecclesiastics, or those who may not live in any class of religious community, may receive the five hundred dollars offered in article 8 of the law of the twelfth of July, 1859, they will have to present themselves within the unprorogable term of one month to solicit it.

§ 997. *Physical Disability.*—80. The physical impediment of those who by infirmity or advanced age can not exercise their ministry shall be proved by certificates of two doctors, one of whom will be appointed by the respective department in the district, and by the governors in the states.

## Title XIII. Of the Responsibilities of the Nationalized Properties.

§ 998. *Responsibility of the Nation for Charges.*—81. The nation, to the dominion of which the properties called ecclesiastical have reverted, is responsible for the charges which they bore up to the seventeenth of December, 1857, provided these are not a lien on the properties or capitals reduced to private dominion.

§ 999. *Continuation of Charges.*—82. The charges of the latter class will be continued on the footing on which they now are found, and those of which the nation is responsible will be recognized by the treasurer of the nation, crediting them with annual interest at six per cent.

§ 1000. *Debts must be Undoubted.*—83. In order that the provisions in the preceding article may have effect, it will be necessary that the debts be clear and undoubted, and that they be already liquidated.

§ 1001. *Doubtful Debts Settled by the Courts.*—84. The doubtful or unliquidated debts will not be recognized until their validity and amount be sifted in the respective court. The tribunals of the federation are the only ones competent to decide all questions of this class by final judgment.

§ 1002. *Punishment for Fraud.*—85. If in the respective courts there should appear concealment or fraud of any kind, the authors thereof will be punished with all the severity of the laws, and they will be considered as defrauders of the public treasury.

§ 1003. *Ecclesiastical Property Belongs to the Nation.*—86. The properties called ecclesiastical are and have been always of the dominion of the nation; and consequently, all the contracts and transactions made by the clergy without the knowledge and approbation of the constitutional government are null and of no value.

## Title XIV.—Of the Relations between the Governments of the States and the General Government of the Nation.

§ 1004. *Approval of Contracts.*—87. The contracts and transactions already consummated, in virtue of which the nationalized properties have been encumbered, and which have been made by the governors of the states, are definitely approved.

§ 1005. *Power of Governors to Encumber Property Limited.*—88. From the date of the publication of this law, no governor can now, whatever may be the powers which were formerly conceded to him, make any transaction which will encumber the nationalized properties for more than twenty per cent, which the same law concedes to each state.

## Title XV. Of the Inspectors and Commissioners.

§ 1006. *Appointment of Commissioners.*—89. The department of the treasury in the district, and in the states the governors, will appoint, if there are already none, the commissioners necessary for the inspection of the ecclesiastical corporations which have administered the nationalized properties.

§ 1007. *Commissioners must be Faithful.*—90. The faithful and punctual compliances of the obligations which articles 2, 3, and 4 of the law of the thirteenth of July imposed upon the commissioners will be required of them.

§ 1008. *Payment of Commissioners.*—91. The commissioners will receive in remuneration for their services the sums which the department of the treasury in Mexico, and in the states the governors, shall designate, taking into consideration the work which they performed, the special merits of each one, and the importance of their discoveries.

§ 1009. *Punishment of Commissioners for Crimes.*—92. The commissioners who shall commit the crimes of concealment, supplanting, falsification, peculation, or any other in the performance of their charge, shall be punished with all severity, as defrauders of the public treasury.

## Title XVI. General Provisions.

§ 1010. *Generals in Chief.*—93. The provision in article 86 is made to extend to the generals in chief, who shall have made transactions for those who have caused the nationalized properties to be encumbered.

§ 1011. *End of Term* —94. The term which the law of the twenty-fifth of June, 1856, conceded to the tenants is ended, provided that as a fact they have enjoyed it without suffering an alteration in the quotas which they paid.

§ 1012. *Reserved Property.*—95. Whenever any part of the properties nationalized be reserved for objects of beneficence, it will follow the same destiny.

§ 1013. *Houses Excepted from the Law.*—96. The houses annexed to the convents of nuns, which were excepted from the desamortizacion by the law of the twenty-fifth of June, 1856, will remain enjoying the same exception, until the community shall be ended, in which case they will proceed to desamortizar them and to redeem their value in conformity with the laws.

§ 1014. *Parts of Houses.*—97. For the redemption of the parts of a house which may be dependent on some public establishment, although they may have divers entrances, the same rules will be observed which for their adjudication were dictated on the twenty-third of September, 1856.

§ 1015. *Delivery of Titles.*—98. As soon as the redemption is formalized, the primitive titles thereof shall be delivered to the owner of each property, for the questions which may be offered on the boundaries, servitude, and others of this kind.

§ 1016. *Payment of Interest.*—99. What may be owing as interest by the adjudicatarios, bidders, or conventional purchasers shall be accumulated with the two fifths which must be delivered in money for the redemption, thus forming a whole, which will be divided into the number of monthly installments conceded to each one.

§ 1017. *Houses Excepted.*—100. The government concedes the houses of curates and the episcopal places, or of the chiefs of any worship, declaring them excepted from desamortizacion and redemption, while they remain destined to their object.

§ 1018. *Laws Abrogated.*—101. In matters of desamortizacion and redemption, only the laws of the twenty-fifth of June, 1856, and relative posterior circulars, the laws of the twelfth and thirteenth of July, 1859, the decree of the twenty-fourth of October, 1860, and the present law, remain in force; and in virtue thereof are derogated all the other dispositions concerning both points, whether they have been dictated by the governments of the states or by the general government of the nation.

Wherefore I order that it be printed, published, and observed. Given in the national palace of Mexico, on the fifth of February, 1861. Benito Juarez. To the citizen Guillermo Prieto, minister of the treasury and public credit. And I communicate it to your excellency for your understanding and consequent ends. God, liberty, and reform. Mexico, etc. Prieto,

§ 1019. *February* 12, 1861—*Circular of the Department of the Treasury—Reasons for Issuing the Decree of the Fifth of the Present Month, on Adjudications.*—Most Excellent Señor: I have the honor to remit your excellency copies of the law issued on the fifth of the present month, with the object of resolving the divers doubts, and to remove the grave difficulties which have presented themselves in the practice, to make effective the nationalization of the properties called ecclesiastical. Although only fifteen days transpired from my ingress into the department until the issuing of the law, the questions were already much debated which enter into the matter, and I consecrated myself with preference and with so much application to resolve them, that I can not say I lack time or study to do so with effect. So conscientious has been that modest and obscure work, in which I have resisted all that has been easy with the ostentation of an innovator, that there is not a single article on which I could not enter into frank and loyal explications. Up to the compilation I have scrupulously cared to give it all clearness, which is the first requisite of the laws as to their reform. It not being possible for me to enter into such details in this communication, I shall confine myself to touching, although summarily, the capital points of the business.

The basis on which it entirely rests is that the properties called ecclesiastical are and have always been of the dominion of the nation. To depart from this principle would be to sing the palinode of the laws of reform, to incur a frightful contradiction, to justify all the charges made to the liberals by the reactionists. On the contrary, to adopt that rule as invariable was and is the most expeditious road to make it all plain, in the extreme of which the dispositions of the last law, on which already criticism has most fed, are in reality but the logical consequences of that same rule. It would have been violated openly by taking as a point of departure the law of the twelfth of July, 1859. Those who thus pretend have forgotten that that law, as declaratory, has and ought to have a retroactive effect. An inexplicable aberration would be that of sustaining the proposition that the ecclesiastical properties belong to the nation only from the date cited, converting thus this date into a dividing line for the sales, contracts, and business done before or after it. No, the right of the nation was the same in one epoch as another, and the confusion of ideas so simple would put us in an epoch of errors and contradictions.

The simple application of the principle mentioned leads us, as by the hand, to the resolution of the most difficult point of those comprehended in the law of the fifth of the present month—that of the purchases made with the clergy. The inflexibility of the rule being supposed, the termination is obvious; the nullity of such contracts appears immediately to the eye; but the basis falsified with distinctions of time, a uniform disposition would not be possible, necessitating for each case special legislation.

The notable thing in this part is, that the same persons who agree to the nullity wish to bring things back to the state which existed before celebrating the contract, presenting this solution as legal and unquestionable. In thus sustaining it, they forget that the clergy were simply the administrators of some national property; that the clergy as well as the purchasers knew of their certain knowledge that the sale was made, not only without the consent, but against the express prohibition of the legitimate owner of those same properties; that the latter had already declared the consummation of such offense a crime, for which it had imposed penalties; and that the price of those illicit contracts was employed, also with full knowledge of the contractors, in prolonging the civil war. So that what presents itself as so clear, as so out of dispute, as so fixed by the laws, is nothing less than the return of what was stupidly and maliciously given to an unfaithful administrator, to attack the rights of the owner of the properties over which he wishes to be thrown to-day so strange an obligation.

There were purchasers among those who were accomplices of the clergy, who preserved their rights as adjudicatarios, or made themselves owners of those rights belonging to those persons who were so, in order thus to meet all eventualities. Their calculation was very simple: if the reactionists triumph, they said to themselves, we will appear as purchasers of the venerable clergy, as religious persons, as enemies of the robbers of the properties of the church; and if the liberals triumph, we will turn coats; we go to the palæstra as adjudicatarios; we recognize the right of the nation to the properties called ecclesiastical; we acknowledge the robbers as legitimate owners. He who thus plays, by tossing up the coin, does not play very fairly, in truth. Notwithstanding, in declaring that those who observed such conduct lost their rights as adjudicatarios, the illegality of that conduct has been more considered than its indecorousness.

From the twenty-fifth of June, 1856, it was declared that the clergy could not hold real estate, even as administrator of the properties which it managed. The constitution of 1857 ratified that prohibition, raising it to the height of a basis of the fundamental code. They openly defaulted to the law of June and to the constitution, those who purchased properties from the clergy, in whom they recognized by that act legal capacity to execute what was expressly prohibited. And as their titles as adjudicatarios came to them precisely from that law, from that constitution which they infringed, the truth is, they broke them with their own hands, and which none to-day can reclaim.

The preceding considerations being supposed, one can not be ignorant of the justice which has been practiced in respect to the above-expressed purchasers. Far from the last law having treated them, however, with severity, it has rather tempered the preceding dispositions, in which they were subject to severe punishments. To-day the penalty is reduced in substance to the increase of twenty per cent on the primitive capital of the adjudication; it being observed that, as this twenty per cent is redeemable with three fifths part in paper and two in money, the extra is truly from eight to nine per cent. This is naturally understood when there is no prejudice to third persons; that is to say, when the purchasers have not lost their primitive titles as adjudicatarios, for some of the causes mentioned in the law. This gives me an occasion to speak of that point, which is also grave.

The law has been amplified in such matters as far as it has been possible, giving room to all the exceptions in which it could be considered that there was no voluntary act on the part of the interested party, or who conceded to an irresistible force. Beyond this, the law could not pass. Those who spontaneously renounced their titles, or consented to lose them, can complain of themselves only for the consequences of their own acts.

The question of denouncers, difficult in itself, has been resolved in a manner that neither are unduly favored those who, without venturing more than the four reals (fifty cents) on the sheet of paper on which they made their denouncement, wished from night until morning to convert themselves into the owners of rich fortunes; nor will those who had acquired a legal and respectable right come out unjustly injured. In this, as in all, no more than a general basis could be fixed, leaving to the tribunals the trial and decision of all those cases in which would be disputed the right of property in nationalized effects.

The objection to the law has already been made that it has subjected the social and political advantages to the attainment of resources, which ought to have been considered of preference. It appears that all the foundation of so grave an accusation rests on the rules dictated on the concessions on terms for the delivery of money and credits, and on the manner of making effective the collection of the notes. I have the conviction that the extensions already granted, and those which may be granted according to the true necessities, make the redemption attainable for all. And as to the arbitrations selected to make effective the payment, it was necessary to stop the abuses in this part, unless it should be preferred at once to give away the nationalized properties. Such a thing would be, without doubt, the most popular; thus the reproach would be saved that the social and political affairs of nationalization are neglected; but it is not permitted to carry the reform that far.

It is not permitted, because one would commit a deplorable

error in considering the monetary question as accessory, or of a secondary class. It is only by ignoring the terrible obligations of the present condition of affairs that one can admit to be deprived of a resource, or to squander an income, without which there would be, at present, no possibility of covering the most pressing wants, considering the bankrupt condition of the public exchequer. It would be an unpardonable madness to give away what to-day is the symbol of the public necessities of the greatest importance. On the other hand, the monetary question is intimately connected with the others. The social and the political affairs would be endangered, or at least would be of slow and difficult realization, if the government had to cross it arms for want of the indispensable elements to consummate the holy work of reform.

Further, the ample concessions which the law makes in favor of the establishments of beneficence, they now may recognize as the basis of charity, or they may be destined to primary, secondary, or professional instruction; the express determination that a part of the nationalized properties which have that same beneficent character may follow its own destiny; the favor it grants to the debtors of interest, that these are accumulated with what is redeemable in money in order to divide the whole into the number of monthly payments conceded to each one; the application of the half of the products of the suppressed convents of nuns to the capitalization of the pawn-shops (monte pios) and pensions of widows and female orphans; the order already given that it shall be liquidated with all the pensioners of the exchequer in order that it may be easy for them to place their respective titles of recognized debt; and other various dispositions too extensive to enumerate, prove in an inevitable manner, that something rather more than the question of resource has been seen; that not one moment has it been forgotten that the reform is essentially political and social.

Respecting the general government, the contracts and business celebrated by the generals in chief and the governors of the states, it has sealed them with its definite approbation, although it does not ignore the heavy encumbrances which it is going to carry for such reason. It has estimated more the public peace than the loss of some money, and it has not wished that interests created by the functionaries to whom were conceded extraordinary powers should remain vacillating and insecure. The exceptional situation in which the republic was found obliged it to make sacrifices in order not to lack resources which the campaign required; to-day, as things have returned to the normal order, a new rule of conduct is adopted.

The principal foundations are indicated on which rests the law of the fifth of the present month; equally are answered the objections clearer than they have been presented. I doubt too much my scanty lights to believe I have made a work in which errors do not abound. One thing I can assure your excellency, and it is, that after having meditated the law again, after having given myself in charge of all that I have known that has been published against it, I have gone to the bottom of my conscience, and I have found nothing to vary substantially, because neither have I favored, knowingly, any spurious interest, nor have I thought, indeed, to tread upon any legitimate right.

On manifesting to your excellency what has occurred to me in this business, I reiterate to you the protests of my distinguished considerations. God and liberty. Mexico, etc. Guillermo Prieto.

§ 1020. *February* 18, 1861—*Explanation of Article* 86 *of the Law of February 5th.*—Department of the treasury. On account of the petition of Jesus Benaridez to have it declared that the contracts to which article 86 of the law of the fifth of the present month refers are only those translative of property, or any others relative to ecclesiastic properties, his excellency the president has been pleased to declare that the law mentioned refers to all burdens imposed upon ecclesiastical properties without the authorization of the constitutional government, and that this is the natural and genuine understanding of article 86 of said law. I say it to you for its publication. God, liberty, and reform. Mexico, etc. Prieto.

§ 1021. *February* 23, 1861—*Decree of the Government—How Pardons Conceded to Persons Who Returned Adjudicated Properties ought to be Understood.—Explanation of Articles* 4 *and* 5 *of the Law of the Fifth of the Present Month.*—His excellency the constitutional provisional president has been pleased to address me the decree following: The C. Benito Juarez, constitutional provisional president of the Mexican United States, to all the inhabitants thereof, know ye:

1. The pardon conceded to certain persons in articles 4 and 5 of the law of the fifth of the present month must be applied to them without prejudice to third parties.

2. There is prejudice to a third party whenever there exists a valid denouncement in conformity with the rules established in article 19.

3. These rules will be constantly observed for the qualification of the denouncements, save any private agreement made before the cited law between the government and the denouncer.

4. Those which shall be made or have been made after said law shall not prejudice the persons favored in it.

Palace of the federal government, in Mexico, February 23, 1861. Benito Juarez. To the C. Guillermo Prieto, minister of the treasury and public credit. Which I communicate to you for your knowledge. God, liberty, and reform. Mexico, etc. Prieto.

§ 1022. *February* 23, 1861—*Decree of the Government on Contracts of Rent Made before the Adjudication or Public Sale of Nationalized Properties—Leases to be Respected.*—1. The adjudicatarios, bidders, and any other persons who, in conformity with the laws, have acquired property in the effects which the clergy were administering, and which have been nationalized, will respect the existing leases on country and city properties in the terms which the present decree orders.

§ 1023. *Leases must Run their Terms.*—2. The leases contracted for a fixed term will last until the term expires, without the proprietors increasing the rent until the expiration of the term.

§ 1024. *Leases of Indefinite Terms.*—3. If the leases which have no certain term should be altered in their rates by the new proprietors, the latter can not eject the tenants unless by a judicial order given in conformity with the laws; and in the country properties the tenant will enjoy the working year.

§ 1025. *Construction of Leases.*—4. The duration which article 2 imposes on leases is obligatory for the proprietors, but the tenants may voluntarily renounce it.

§ 1026. *March* 4, 1861—*Decree of the Government—Term Conceded to the Persons Who may have Rights of Property to Allege on Properties of the Clergy—How They ought to Proceed in Court—Rights Settled by the Courts.*—1. Every person who may have rights of property to allege on properties called the clergy's will be obliged to go to the tribunals, for which is conceded the term of eight days.

§ 1027. *Summary Trials.*—2. The judge, on receiving the demand, shall proceed immediately to cite the parties, in order to have a meeting before him, in which he shall try to have the parties agree; and if they can not agree, a summary trial will take place, which shall terminate within a month at the latest, the terms being peremptory at the judge's discretion, and without appeal or other recourse, and under his strictest responsibility.

§ 1028. *March* 6, 1861—*Decree of the Government on Voluntary Impositions of Capitals on Properties of the Clergy, and Provisions about the Dowers of Nuns and Expenses of Worship—The Treasury will Continue to Receive Impositions.*—1. The seventh section of the department of the treasury shall continue to receive the impositions which the adjudicatarios and bidders of the properties called the clergy's voluntarily make, under the conditions which the circular of the twenty-first of February last establishes, as well as those of the chaplaincies, pious works, and capitals which are recognized on estates of private property.

§ 1029. *Persons Who Wish to Acknowledge Capitals.*—2. The adjudicarios or bidders who have free their right of domain in said properties, and who wish to acknowledge three fifth parts of the capital of the total value of the estate, paying two in bonds or recognized credits, will go to said section, which will draw the corresponding writing of acknowledgment for the term of from five to nine years, and will receive one third in advance of the interests at the rate of six per cent annually, besides ten dollars as the established fees. The bonds will be delivered into section 6, as heretofore.

§ 1030. *Reception of Acknowledgments Discontinued, when.*—3. As soon as the one million nine hundred and eighty thousand dollars, the amount of the capital of the dowers of the nuns, has been completed, the section will not receive any acknowledgment under its strictest responsibility, making immediately the applications of which the relative circulars speak.

§ 1031. *Capital for Worship.*—4. The government will designate opportunely the capital which must be used for the expenses of worship, in conformity with the law of the thirteenth of July, 1859, using in the mean while what the general treasury furnishes.

§ 1032. *Redemptions not Impeded.*—5. The preceding dispositions will not impede the redemption of capitals, in conformity with the laws in force.

§ 1033. *Estimate of Dowers.*—6. The governors of the states will make the estimates of the dowers of the nuns and expenses of worship within the term of fifteen days, in order that, being approved by the general government, they may proceed with the application of this law.

§ 1034. *March* 14, 1861—*Provision of the Department of the*

*Treasury—The Term to Solicit the Imposition of Capitals Extended —Extension of Time to Verify Impositions.*—His excellency the president has thought proper to extend for eight days the term to go to section 7 of this department to verify the impositions of capitals on the same terms as heretofore, the interests due being condoned, provided they were to be paid to any private individual. Prieto.

§ 1035. *March* 15, 1861—*Provision of the Department of the Treasury that Interests, Although Due, must not be Paid, when.* His excellency the president orders that the interests due shall not be paid on the capitals imposed on estates of private property for pious works, convents, dowers of nuns, and chaplaincies vacant without successors, provided they were not to be paid to a private individual.

§ 1036. *March* 18, 1861—*Provision of the Department of the Treasury—Extension of the Term to Admit the Imposition of the Capitals Which It Expresses.*—The terms being about to expire within which the owners of private properties must present themselves to section 7 for the imposition of capitals belonging to vacant chaplaincies, pious works, dowers of convents of nuns, his excellency the president has thought proper to extend it as the last and peremptorily until the fifth of the coming April, which being passed the interests due will not be condoned, and the general inspector will proceed to require promptly the capitals and interests of time completed. His excellency equally orders that the redemption of all or part of the capital will be admitted at the time of making the imposition in section 7, it being done in effective money, which will be delivered to the nuns if they so wish to receive it, or it will be imposed on other property with the necessary securities to pass to them the writings in the manner which it has been executed heretofore.

§ 1037. *March* 25, 1861—*Circular of the Department of the Treasury—Extension of the Term Conceded to the Adjudicatarios and Bidders of Property of the Clergy in Order that They may Recognize the Capitals Imposed on Them.*—His excellency the provisional president has thought proper to order that the term conceded to the adjudicatarios and bidders of properties called the clergy's shall be extended to the fifth of the coming April, in order that they may recognize in section 7 of this department the capitals imposed on them, on the terms of which the circulars of the twenty-first of February and the sixth of the present month speak.

§ 1038. *March* 27, 1861—*Provision of the Department of the*

*Treasury—Order that on the Death of One of the Nuns the Lady Superior shall Give a Report thereof to the General Inspector.*—Department of state and that of the treasury and public credit. Section 7. Circular. In order to avoid the abuses which may be committed on the death of a nun, by accumulating again in the convents the capitals which form the dower of each one of them, and when for want of relatives in the legal degree it must enter the exchequer in possession of the inheritance, his excellency the president orders that on the death of a nun a report thereof shall be given by the superior of the convent to the inspector-general, remitting to him the title of dower, who will announce it to the public and proceed to collect the interests, in order to deliver them with the title to those who may be declared heirs.

§ 1039. *April* 19, 1861—*Circular of the Department of the Treasury—The Properties Which the Clergy Manage in the State of Puebla, and Which have not yet Passed into Private Hands, are Sold to Said State.*—His Excellent Sir: His excellency the president having been informed of the proposition made by the commissioners of that state about the proper destiny of the remaining properties which the clergy were managing on the completion of the legal terms, he has been pleased to resolve: 1. A part of the properties which the clergy in the state of Puebla was administering, and which at this date have not passed into private hands, in conformity with the laws of the twenty-fifth of June, 1856, and the eighteenth of February, 1859, are sold to the state itself on the terms which the following articles order. 2. Taking as a basis the values established for each house in said laws, the state shall pay for them to the general government with seventy-five per cent in credits against the exchequer of the federation, and with twenty-five per cent in money. 3. Of the total amount of credits and money, twenty per cent will be deducted as belonging to the state, and the balance will be delivered in sixty monthly installments, to be executed for that purpose, by the treasury of the states, promissory notes, payable to the bearer, for the part payable in money. The credits will be paid accordingly as the sales are made. 4. The government will reserve the power to except from article 1 the estates which in its judgment ought to have another destiny with more public utility, to which end notice will be remitted to you of the properties which must be comprehended within this regulation. Which I have the honor to say to your excellency for your knowledge and as a result of the proposition cited by the commission. And I transcribe it to your excellency, in case that it should suit you to accept the arrangement in question which the supreme government is disposed to make. I reiterate to your excellency the protestations of my consideration and appreciation. Liberty and reform. Mexico, etc. Francisco de P. Gochicoa.

§ 1040. *May* 5, 1861—*Circular of the Department of Relations—The Articles Which are Cited in the Laws of July* 23 *and* 28, 1859, *are Explained.*—To-day I say to his excellency the governor of the state of Tabasco, the following: His excellency—Sir: In answer to your official letter No. 55, of April last, in which you show the mistake which is found in the law of reforms of the twenty-eighth of July, 1859, by citing this in the conclusion of article 3, the forty-fifth of the multiform law issued by the department of justice on the twenty-third of said month and year; when this only comprehends thirty-one articles. His excellency the president orders me to say to your excellency that the article which is cited in article 3 of said law of the twenty-eighth of July, 1859, is the fifteenth and not the forty-fifth of the law of the twenty-third of said month, and by error appears cited. Likewise I must manifest to your excellency that the said law of the twenty-third of July, in article 4, cites the twentieth, which ought to be the twenty-first of the same. And I have the honor to communicate it to your excellency for your knowledge. God and liberty. Mexico, etc. Zarco.

§ 1041. *July* 17, 1861—*Circular from the Department of the Treasury on Estates not Adjudicated.*—His excellency the president orders that, various estates existing which have not been adjudicated, redeemed, nor denounced up to this time, it is provided as a general point that those which are found in this state can remain to be recognized in section 7 of this department as dowers of the nuns, and in favor of the first who may make the denouncement, although it may not be the tenant or the possessor of them, care being taken in said section that the facts be ascertained. Which I communicate to you for your knowledge. God, liberty, and reform. Mexico, etc. José H. Nuñez.

§ 1042. *October* 10, 1861—*Order of the Department of the Treasury that the Tribunals shall Give the Notices Which the Order Indicates Relative to the Judgments of Preference of Adjudications.* The notices being incomplete and insufficient for their object, which have been furnished by the respective functionaries to the special office of redemptions in virtue of the provisions in the circular of the eleventh of last September, which by an error of the printer was placed in it the date of the tenth, in the edition which was made, in circular form, in order that this may have its punctual fulfillment, and so that any doubts upon the understanding of those provisions may be removed, the citizen president has ordered to be observed the rules which are herein expressed:

§ 1043. *Contents of Notices.*—1. The notices which in fulfillment of provision 5 of the circular referred to the departments of the superior tribunals and judges of first instance ought to order their secretaries to form, and to remit to the respective offices, must contain: 1. The names of the litigants; 2. The location of the estates and the ecclesiastical corporation which managed them; 3. The basis on which the adjudication is claimed by each one of the claimants, with an expression of the price which follows, and whether a title of adjudication has been executed in favor of any person or persons, by what authority and on what date; and 4. The names of those who in fact possess the estates in case of its not being any of the litigants, the titles by which they hold them, since when, if they pay any rent, and who receives it, or if it has been ordered to be deposited, where, or in whose possession, and what the sums received or deposited up to date amount to. If there should be no such cases of this kind filed in any department of the superior tribunals or courts of first instance, it will be so communicated to the respective office.

§ 1044. *Collection of Facts for the Notices.*—2. In order to furnish the detailed notices to which the preceding article refers, the tribunals and judges will order collected immediately, using force, and under the strictest responsibility of the executors, the respective proceedings (autos) which exist in the possession of any of the parties, and which shall be returned to the said party after the necessary points shall have been extracted for the notice. The judges, besides, in conformity with the provision in article 17 of the decree of the preceding September, which regulates the civil courts of this capital, shall dictate the proper orders in order to collect from the notaries the expedientes which they may have in their possession.

§ 1045. *Penalty for not Giving Notices.*—3. If within eight days counted from the date of this circular the notices shall not have been received to which the preceding articles refer, the department of the treasury shall pass to the department of justice a statement of the functionaries who have incurred the penalty imposed by the fifth provision of the circular of the eleventh of the month last past, in order that it may be made irremissibly effective.

§ 1046. *Responsibility of Possessors of Estates.*—4. The litigants who are possessors of the estates which are the subject of a trial of preference are obliged to bind themselves for the first provision of the circular of the eleventh of the preceding September, even when other persons have presented themselves to make the redemption of the estates and have made the respective monthly payments, as the first are receiving in fact the products of the estates; and that to the second, in case of its resulting that they are redeemed without a right, the sums which they shall have paid must be returned to them by the public treasury, and in the kind in which they paid them, according as the law of the fifth of February of the present year provides in article 24.

§ 1047. *Possessors Who Claim Right in the Property must Pay Rents.*—5. If the estates upon which the litigation turns should be in the possession of persons who allege to have property in them or any other rights derived from contracts made with the clergy, subsequent to the sixteenth of December, 1857, and consequently without authorization from the constitutional government, such contracts being null and of no value according to the provisions in article 22 of the law of the twelfth of July, 1859, and articles 10 and 86 of that of the fifth of February of this year, payment will be required of those persons of the rents for all the time which they have possessed and continue possessing the estates. A like collection will be made from all those who, although they allege other prior titles, have entered into the possession of the estates by virtue of or in consequence of such contracts.

§ 1048. *Rents Calculated at Six per Cent.*—6. In all cases in which, according to the circular, rents must be collected, these will be calculated, at the rate of six per cent annually on the price of adjudication, which must be considered in conformity with the third provision of the circular of the eleventh of September, and compensation for them will not be admitted with credits which he who ought to pay the rents alleges to have against the nation or against the corporation which was administering the estate.

Which I say to you, by supreme order for your understanding and fulfillment, it being understood that I have to-day directed the corresponding communication to the department of justice in order that it may dictate the provisions within its jurisdiction. God, liberty, and reform. Mexico, etc. Nuñez. To the citizen chief of the sixth section of this department and special office of redemption.

§ 1049. *December* 18, 1861—*Circular from the Department of the Treasury that the Denouncements of Capitals or Estates Made by the Employees shall Give Them No Right.*—The citizen president of the republic has thought proper to declare that any denouncement of capital or houses which the employés of the administration should make shall not give to them any right. Consequently he orders that the chiefs of the offices shall have care to examine if by such denouncements the denouncers have abused their office, and in this case they shall pass the corresponding *data* to the judge of the respective district, immediately notifying this department for its final dispositions. And I communicate it to you for your knowledge and consequent ends. Liberty and reform. Mexico, etc. Gonzalez.

*June* 30, 1862—*Decree of the Government.*—The citizen constitutional president of the republic has been pleased to direct to me the decree which follows: Benito Juarez, constitutional president of the Mexican United States, to the inhabitants thereof, know ye: That in use of the full powers with which I find myself vested, I have thought proper to decree the following:

§ 1050. *Person and Time Noted on Titles.*—Art. 1. All persons who, in conformity with the law, have had adjudicated to them, or who have redeemed estates or capitals of civil or ecclesiastical corporations, which have entered the dominion of the nation by virtue of the said law, shall present themselves in the public offices to note on their respective titles the person and the time at which the adjudication or redemption was made, so that this *data* may expressly appear; and if they do not do so within the term of eight days counted from the publication of this decree, by this omission alone they will lose all right, and the estates or capitals will return to the dominion of the supreme government. Wherefore I order it to be printed, published, circulated, and observed. Given in the national palace of Mexico the thirtieth of June, 1862. Benito Juarez. To the citizen Manuel Doblado, minister of relations and government. And I communicate it to you for your understanding and consequent ends. Liberty and reform. Mexico, etc. Doblado.

§ 1051. *July* 7, 1862—*Order of the Department of Relations*

—*Explanation of the Decree of the Thirtieth of June Last, as to Cancellation of Title.*—Doubts having been raised relative to the understanding of the decree of the thirtieth of June last past, which orders to be canceled or noted in the public offices the respective titles by the adjudicatarios or redeemers of nationalized properties, the citizen president, in order to fix the sense of the decree referred to, has thought proper to declare that those only are obliged to cancel or note their titles who have not done it, and who, in conformity with said decree, shall lose all right to the capitals or estates, whether they are redeemed, adjudicated, or imposed with recognition. And I communicate it to you so that you may order its immediate publication. Liberty and reform. Mexico, etc. Doblado. To the citizen governor of the federal district.

*August* 2, 1862—*Circular of the Department of the Treasury—Provisions in Respect to Nationalized Estates and Capitals.*—The citizen president orders that for greater security and guaranty for the persons who acquire property which was managed by the clergy, the following provisions shall be observed:

§ 1052. *Titles to be Executed and Instruments Canceled.*—1. Immediately after the operations of the redemption of any nationalized estate or capital shall have been consummated, a title (escritura publica) shall be executed by the respective office in the name of the nation in favor of the redemptioner, and all public instruments which there may be in favor of the clergy or of the corporations which held said property before shall be ordered canceled, blotted out, or effaced; and a title shall be delivered to the interested party, and any documents of which said offices may have knowledge, and which exist therein relative to said property.

§ 1053. *Mortgages, Registry of.*—2. In order that the exchequer may never fail to be secured, the mortgages which the estates have which ought to remain affected by any payment within the term designated by the common laws shall be registered in the book of mortgages; and those who shall not have it done shall lose all their rights, and the estate may be again denounced by any person, to be redeemed again.

§ 1054. *Mortgages to be Given to Secure Obligations.*—3. Those who acquire capitals by redemption, and shall execute obligations or promissory notes, shall always give a mortgage bond for the part of money corresponding to said notes, without which requisite the orders to collect all the capital can not be issued to the censatarios, as the part of said capitals which cover the value of those obligations or notes must be left reserved in the possession of the censatarios until the redemptioners shall have satisfied all their obligations.

Which I communicate to you by supreme order for your most exact fulfillment. Liberty and reform. Mexico, August 2, 1862. José H. Nuñez. To the citizen governor of the federal district. Present.

*August* 4, 1862—*Resolution of the President of the Republic—Provisions Respecting Capitals Imposed in Section* 7 *for the Worship and Dower of the Nuns.*—The citizen constitutional president, in use of the ample faculties with which he finds himself vested, has thought proper to resolve that the following provisions be observed:

§ 1055. *Revision of Titles.*—1. All persons who imposed capitals in section 7 for the worship and dower of nuns shall present their titles, within the term of sixty days, before the chief auditor's office, in order that the operations which they made may be revised, and the defects which they might have be corrected.

§ 1056. *Rights Lost by Non-presentation of Titles for Revision.*—2. The persons who shall not present their titles within the term designated shall lose all right to the capitals, which may be redeemed according to law.

§ 1057. *Erroneous Titles Made Anew.*— 3. Every title which may lack the requisites of direct registry in the book of mortgages, and which is not drawn on the corresponding sealed paper, shall be made anew, and shall be executed in favor of the nation before the chief auditor, who shall accept them, taking care not to divide the capitals except in cases highly indispensable.

§ 1058. *Capitals Already Imposed Have Preference.*—The capitals which are already imposed in a stable manner, by virtue of this decree, shall enjoy the preference and age which belongs to them by their primitive imposition, and for that purpose the dates of the old titles shall be cited in the new.

§ 1059. *Capitals and Interests to be Secured.*—5. On executing every title of imposition for dowers of nuns or worship, the chief auditor's office shall have scrupulous care that the capitals and interests are well secured and guaranteed in conformity with the law; and it shall be established that the terms shall be reputed concluded immediately that for any reason said interests fail to be paid with punctuality.

§ 1059 *a*. *Terms for Impositions.*—6. The terms for the impositions shall never exceed five years nor be less than one.

§ 1060. *Redemption of Excess of Capital.*—7. All the excessive capitals which shall result in favor of the public treasury, proceeding from the rectification which the chief auditor's office is charged to make by the present supreme provision, shall be redeemed according to the laws, the present censatarios being preferred, provided that they make the operations within the thirty days following the publication which section 6 of this department will make with such object.

§ 1061. *Titles may be Ordered by Auditor.*—8. The chief auditor's office is also authorized to order titles of property of the estates drawn to the persons who lack them, provided it is proved that they have acquired them according to the laws.

And I communicate it to you by a resolution of the said citizen president for your knowledge and consequent ends. Liberty and reform. Mexico, August 4, 1862. José H. Nuñez. To the governor of the federal district.

*August* 28, 1862—*Provision of the Department of the Treasury —The Provision Ordered to be Observed by this Department on the Fourth of the Present Month, is Modified in the Third Article, and Repealed in the Fourth.*—The citizen constitutional president, in use of the ample faculties with which he finds himself vested, has thought proper to resolve that the third provision of those ordered to be observed in the order of the fourth instant, which provides that every title of those executed in the extinguished section 7 which should lack the mortgage registry, and which should not be drawn on sealed paper, should be made anew, etc., is modified in the following terms:

§ 1062. *Revised Impositions to be Registered.*—3. The chief auditor's office, once that each title of imposition be revised, shall order that it be registered in the book of mortgages, and the annotations or cancellations which correspond in the respective protocols be made.

§ 1063. *Repeal of Prior Provisions.*—The said citizen president has thought proper to repeal the fourth provision contained in the order referred to of the fourth instant, relative to this, that the capitals which shall be imposed shall enjoy the preference (prelacion) and age which correspond to them by their primitive imposition.

I communicate it to you for your knowledge and consequent ends. Liberty and reform. Mexico, etc. Nuñez.

§ 1064. *Certain Acts of the Clergy Annulled.*—The citizen constitutional president, in his supreme resolution of yesterday, has been pleased to declare by a general rule that all the acts which the clergy exercised since the seventh of December, 1857, thenceforth up to the twenty-eighth of the said month of 1860, were null and of no value, whether it was that of admitting redemptions of capitals at maturity, or whether it was in making any operation relative to the said properties which the clergy were managing. Liberty and reform. Mexico, August 29, 1862. Nuñez. To the citizen governor of the federal district.

§ 1065. *Trials of Desamortizacion of Nationalized Properties.*—The citizen minister of the treasury and public credit, with date of the twenty-first instant, directed to this department the supreme disposition which follows: Your official letter of the eighteenth instant having been reported to the constitutional president, in which you transcribe that of the second civil judge addressed to you on the twelfth of September last, relative to trials of nationalized properties, the president himself has thought proper to resolve that I shall answer you, that he agrees with the opinion of the respective section of that department, and the dispositions being clear and positive relative to the trials of nationalized properties, whether of property or possession, that they shall be terminated brief and summarily within the term fixed by law, you will be pleased to so manifest it to the tribunals by the means of a circular. And I communicate it, etc. Independence, liberty, and reform. Mexico, January 30, 1863. Teran.

§ 1066. *The Effective Force of the Titles (Testimonias de Escrituras) of Capitals Nationalized.*—Section of desamortizacion. The citizen president has thought proper to declare that the titles (testimonias de las escrituras) of nationalized capitalists ordered to be issued by the supreme government in favor of any private party to whom has been subrogated its rights (llevan aparejada ejecucion [1]), and shall produce the same effect as the first copies (testimonios) (meaning original titles) extended in favor of the corporations, and which have been secreted or maliciously retained. Mexico, March 18, 1863. F. Mejia.

§ 1066 *a*. *November* 12, 1864—*Decree of the Government—The Adjudications or Alienations of Nationalized Properties Made in the State of Chihuahua are Validated.*—Department of state and that of the treasury and public credit. The citizen president of the republic has thought proper to direct to me the decree which follows: Benito Juarez, constitutional president of the Mexican United States, to the inhabitants thereof, know ye: That in order to carry forward the purpose of allaying the

[1] Needs no further proof, and judgment may be entered upon it.

difficulties which have successively arisen since the supreme government was consulted on the nullity of the redemptions made in this state with the infraction of the law of the fifth of February, 1861, and considering that said difficulties will remain definitely terminated with the adoption of the bases proposed by a board of enlightened persons and representatives of many of the parties interested in the affair, I have thought proper to decree the following:

§ 1067. *Chihuahua Titles Validated.*—1. All the adjudications or alienations of nationalized properties made in the state of Chihuahua, according to the provisions dictated by the authorities of the same, in contravention of the general laws, remain definitely validated in virtue of the present decree, without the necessity of any revision, with the only exception of those alienations against which has been formalized up to this date any protest or reclamation by persons who are considered prejudiced in their rights.

§ 1068. *Revision of Titles.*—2. The alienations or adjudications protested or reclaimed shall be revised by the department of the treasury, in order that may be given thereon the resolution which the government shall believe just.

§ 1069. *Payment of Validation.*—3. All the adjudicatarios whose acquisitions are validated, or shall be validated in the future, shall pay to the government, in the offices of the federation which the latter may designate, four per cent in effective money on the total valuation of the alienations or adjudications.

§ 1070. *Payment in Two Installments.*—4. This imposition of four per cent shall be paid in two installments: the first shall be complied with in fifteen days from the publication of this decree in each canton, and the second within the fifteen following days.

Wherefore I order it to be printed, published, circulated, and that due compliance be given it. Given in the palace of the general government in Chihuahua, the twelfth of November, 1864. Benito Juarez. To the citizen José Maria Iglesias, minister of justice, public works, and public instruction, and charged with the department of the treasury and public credit. And I communicate it to you, for your knowledge and corresponding effects. Independence, liberty, and reform. Chihuahua, November 12, 1864. Iglesias. To the citizen governor and military commander of this state. Present.

*November* 15, 1864—*Communication from the Department of*

*the Treasury—Provisions for the Fulfillment of the Foregoing Decree.*—Department of state and that of the treasury and public credit. Section 2. According to the provisions in the decree of the twelfth instant, the citizen president has thought proper to resolve that that chief office (jefatura), and the administrations of rents of the state, shall be the offices that are charged with the collection of the four per cent, which the adjudicatarios must pay whose redemptions have been or shall be in the future revalidated, observing the following rules:

§ 1071. *No One Exempt.*—1. The payment shall be made by all the adjudicatarios, without any one being exempt, on account of its being communicated to him by the special commissioner of the federation that his business was terminated.

§ 1072. *Collection of the Four per Cent.*—2. For the collection of the four per cent, the presentation of the titles shall be required, in which the total amount of the adjudication shall appear.

§ 1073. *Special Account of the Fund.*—3. A special account of the products of this fund shall be separately kept in each of the offices charged with the collection.

§ 1074. *Receipts as Proof of Payment.*—4. For the proof of the payments which shall be made within the first term of those designated in the law, provisional receipts shall be given to the causantes,[1] in which shall be expressed the amount of the sum delivered.

§ 1075. *Second Payment—Note on Title, how Made.*—5. The second payment being made, the provisional receipt shall be taken up, and a note shall be placed at the bottom of the respective titles (escrituras), under the seal of the office, conceived in these terms: "In fulfillment of what is ordered in the decree of the twelfth of November, 1864, and the previous delivery which the citizen —— has made of the sum of ——, the amount of four per cent on the capital of ——, the adjudication contained in this title (escritura) is definitely validated." This note shall bear the date of the day on which it is made, and the signature of the chief of the office.

§ 1076. *The Four per Cent, how Paid.*—6. The adjudicatarios who wish to pay the four per cent in that chief office can do so, by themselves or by their attorney, although the latter may not be the place of their residence.

§ 1077. *Failure of Payment—Property Seized.*—7. The property of the adjudicatarios who do not pay the four per cent

[1] The person from whom one derives the right of anything.

within the terms designated shall be seized to an amount equivalent thereto, with all the extra charges which the laws in force may impose.

And I communicate it to you by supreme order for its fulfillment, and in order that this communication may circulate among the administrations of revenue of the state. Independence, liberty, and reform. Chihuahua, November 15, 1864. Iglesias. To the citizen chief of the treasury of this state. Present.

*May* 11, 1865—*Decree of the Government.*—The decree issued by the government of the empire on the twenty-sixth of February last is declared null, and all the operations of nationalized properties made according to the laws are definitely approved. Department of state and that of the treasury and public credit. The citizen president of the republic has been pleased to direct to me the decree which follows: Benito Juarez, constitutional president of the Mexican United States, to the inhabitants thereof, know ye: That in use of the ample faculties with which I find myself vested, I have thought proper to decree the following:

§ 1078. *Emperor's Acts Void.*—1. The so-called decree of the twenty-sixth of February last, and its regulation of the ninth of the following March, issued by the entitled emperor of Mexico, being null and of no value, as are equally so for want of legitimate authority all his other acts; also are null and of no value the revision to which the so-called decree and its regulation refer, and the other dispositions which these comprehend.

§ 1079. *Approval and Validity of Acts.*—2. All the operations of the desamortizacion and redemption of nationalized properties, made according to the laws on the subject, or definitely approved by the federal government, even when affected with any irregularity, have been and are perfectly and irrevocably valid in whatever concerns the rights of the fiscal department; and the only questions which remain alive are those concerning the preference of the rights between private parties, deducible before the tribunals according to the said laws.

§ 1080. *Parties Despoiled of Property.*—3. Those who should be despoiled of property which they have legitimately acquired of nationalized estates, by virtue of the so-called decree of the twenty-sixth of February, and its regulation of the ninth of the following March, have their right free to require the return of the profits received and which ought to have been received, as well as the indemnification for all damages and losses which they may suffer from the detainers of said property, who are responsible for the return and indemnification with their properties, of whatever derivation they may be.

§ 1081. *Property Denounceable, What—Rights of Denouncers.* 4. The nationalized properties which have not been legitimately entered into private dominion, on account of concealment or other motives, are denounceable, according to the laws in force. The denouncers of such properties, in whose favor the corresponding adjudication shall be made, are also free to require from those who make themselves detainers of those properties, by adjudication, sale, public sale, proceeding from the so-called decree of the twenty-sixth of February and its regulation, the delivery of the profits which they ought to have received, as well as the amount of the damage which they may suffer in the use of the thing detained.

§ 1082. *Responsibility of Traitors in Office.*—5. For the indemnification mentioned in the preceding articles, the pecuniary responsibility of the functionaries of the entitled Mexican empire, who intervened in any character in the execution of the so-called decree of the twenty-sixth of February and its regulations, is likewise affected with the part of their properties which for any cause shall fail to be comprehended in the confiscation to which they are found subject by the law of the sixteenth of August, 1863.

Wherefore I order it to be printed, published, circulated, and that due compliance be given it. Given in the national palace in Chihuahua the eleventh of May, 1865. Benito Juarez. To the citizen José Maria Iglesias, minister of justice, public works, and public instruction, and charged with the department of the treasury and public credit. And I communicate it to you for your knowledge and consequent ends. Independence, liberty, and reform. Chihuahua, May 11, 1865. Iglesias. To the citizen governor of the state of ——.

§ 1083. *May* 11, 1865—*Circular of the Department of Justice, on the Matter of the Foregoing Decree—Construction.*—Department of justice, public works, and public instruction. Circular. The entitled emperor of Mexico has issued, with the date of the twenty-sixth of February last, a so-called decree, in which it is proposed to subject to a revision all the operations of desamortizacion and redemption of nationalized properties.

The Archduke Maximilian of Austria lacks all legitimate title to reign over the destinies of this country. Called by a few traitors, imposed by Napoleon, supported by apocryphal manifestations of the popular will, sustained by the protection of foreign bayonets, detested by the majority of the nation, fought with armed bands in every place and at every hour, his power is a flagrant usurpation.

The acts emanating from it are null and of no value, for want of all legitimate authority. Vitiated in their origin, they will never prevail, nor will they be admitted by the people who desired them. The so-called decree of the twenty-sixth of February, and its regulation of the eleventh of the following March, are comprehended in the general rule, and the nullity with which they are effected being so patent in them that this simple consideration would be sufficient to take from them all legal value. But even supposing that they had been issued by a legitimate authority, a monstrous contradiction would have been committed in pretending to have operations revised which had already merited the approval of a fully empowered administration. The said Archduke Maximilian has recognized the existence of the faculties which the federal government exercised, holding them valid in all their acts up to the thirty-first of May, 1863. Not to recognize them now, in the operations of desamortizacion and in the redemption of nationalized properties, is consequently an inconsistency for which there is no possible explication.

The federal government, vested with complete faculties, as it could issue laws of desamortizacion and redemption, could equally dispense with them in determined particular cases. All the affairs which obtained its approbation remained definitely terminated by an act valid and unquestionable of the depositary of the national sovereignty.

On the Austrian Archduke's pretending to-day that the revision ordered made in his so-called decree shall have a definite character, is a part of the principle that he is empowered to declare it so in virtue of the sovereign attributes which he tries to usurp. It is certainly not comprehended how he attacks the validity of provisions emanating from a complete power recognized by all the world, including the said archduke, when he does not put in doubt the validity of his own acts, emanating from a false authority, not recognized by the country in which he wished to illegally exercise it.

The revision which the entitled sovereign of Mexico proposes to execute has for its principal object to cause to be completed the quotas of what was delivered at least in some affairs, not made according to the laws on the subject. In such pretensions is made to appear still more the inconsistency with which it proceeds. The supreme national authority which fixed the legal quotas of what ought to have been delivered in money and credits had power to have designated other quotas entirely distinct, and this is what it did in determined particular cases, without their provisions, notoriously perfect and valid, being attacked therefor.

It would be easy to make many other observations about the bases established in the so-called decree of the twenty-sixth of February and its regulation; but the supreme government wishes to limit itself alone to the capitals, which are already examined.

With the explanations which precede are assigned the grounds of each one of the articles of the law which I have the honor to transmit you. The nullity of all the acts of the entitled emperor of Mexico involve that of the so-called decree of the twenty-sixth of February and its regulation; that of the revision which in them is ordered to be practiced, and that of the other provisions which they comprehend.

The plenitude of power with which were vested the governments which approved definite operations of desamortizacion and redemption made them perfect and irrevocably valid even when they were effected with some irregularity. What the exchequer should have received, in case that they had been subjected strictly to the laws on the subject, was validly condoned by the sovereign authority vested with the right to do it.

The only things which are pending are the questions between private individuals relative to the right of preference, ventilated before the tribunals to which it belongs to resolve them, according to the said laws. The validity of the rights acquired by those who have legitimately obtained the ownership of nationalized properties constitutes by a true spoliation the deprivation of that validity, without their detainers being able to allege any other title than that of force. Such detainers and possessors in bad faith being notorious, as they enter into the enjoyment of what appears to them to belong to another, they are obligated by the principles of common law for the return, not only of the profits which they received, but also of those which they might have received, and for the indemnification of all the damages and losses which the parties despoiled may suffer. The consequent responsibility can and ought to be made effective, in the properties, from whatever source, of those possessors in bad faith.

There are motives for supposing that there yet exist concealed properties of those nationalized, which have not entered legitimately into private domain. All those which should be discovered are denounceable, according to the laws in force. The detainers who obtained them in consequence of the provisions contained in the so-called decree of the twenty-sixth of February, and its regulation, are also possessors in bad faith, obligated in justice to return to the denouncers in whose favor the corresponding adjudications were made, the profits received and those which they should have received, not less than the amount of the loss which the thing detained suffers.

It might well happen that the rights of the parties despoiled and of the new adjudicatarios would be burlesqued, if they could only exercise them against the detainers of their property, on account of these being in many cases insolvent debtors; and the indemnification would be impossible for the former, for which the latter are obligated. Therefore for this reason, as well as by its being notoriously the pecuniary responsibility of the functionaries of the entitled Mexican empire, who intervened with any character in the execution of the so-called decree of the twenty-sixth of February, and its regulation, it is but justice to declare that responsibility in favor of the injured.

In this part the consideration has been borne in mind that those imperial functionaries are comprehended in the penalty of confiscation, established by the law of August 16, 1863. Their confiscated property ought not to bear the responsibility in question, because it would then make itself effective against the national exchequer. For this reason it has been declared that it will only take place, in the part of the property of the responsible functionaries, which for any cause should fail to be comprehended in the confiscation.

The citizen president recommends to you that the greatest care be taken for the exact fulfillment of the annexed law, the provisions of which will be applied as far as possible in their execution, in the part of the republic submitted to-day by force to the Austrian archduke.

I have the honor to communicate it to you by supreme order for the consequent ends. Independence, liberty, and reform. Chihuahua, May 11, 1865. Iglesias. To the citizen governor of the state of ——

*August* 31, 1866—*Decree of the Government Relative to Denouncements of Estates and Capitals of Nationalized Properties.*—Department of the treasury and public credit. Section 21. The citizen president of the republic has been pleased to direct me the decree which follows: Benito Juarez, constitutional president of the Mexican United States, to the inhabitants thereof, know ye: That in use of the ample faculties with which I find myself vested, I have thought proper to decree the following:

§ 1084. *The General Government is the Only Authority.*—1. The denouncements of estates or capitals which can be made according to the laws and provisions relative to desamortizacion or nationalization of properties of corporations must be made exclusively before the general government, the only competent authority to admit them or dispatch them.

§ 1085. *Admissibility of Denouncements.*—2. Said denouncements will only be admissible when at the time of making them the respective redemption is immediately proceeded with.

§ 1086. *Illegal Denouncements, What are.*—3. The denouncements in which it is claimed to reserve the redemption for future epochs have no effect, nor will they have any, for want of all legal value.

Wherefore I order it to be printed, published, circulated, and that due compliance be given it. Palace of the general government in Chihuahua, the thirty-first of August, 1866. Benito Juarez. To the citizen José M. Iglesias, minister of justice, public works, and public instruction, and charged with the department of the treasury and public credit. And I communicate it to you; for the consequent ends. Independence, liberty, and reform. Chihuahua, August 31, 1866. Iglesias. To the citizen governor and military commander of the state of ——

*August* 12, 1867—*Department of the Treasury. Decree Establishing an Administration of Nationalized Properties.* Department of the treasury and public credit. Section 2. The citizen constitutional president of the republic has been pleased to direct to me the decree which follows: Benito Juarez, constitutional president of the Mexican United States, to the inhabitants thereof, know ye: That in use of the ample faculties with which I find myself vested, I have thought proper to decree the following:

§ 1087. *Administration of Nationalized Properties.*—1. A special office is established with the name of "Administration of Nationalized Properties," which will have while it lasts the character of section 7 of the department of the treasury.

§ 1088. *Attributes of Said Office.*—2. The attributes of this office will be the following: 1. To revise the proceedings (expedientes) of the so-called "Administration of the Nationalized

Properties," in order to employ all the *data* of its archives in favor of the national exchequer; 2. To have charge of all that relates to the administration and desamortizacion of the estates, and of the collection, adjudication, and redemption of the capitals which the clergy administered; 3. To have charge in the federal district of that which relates to confiscations and fines.

(The rest of this decree relates to the officers and their salaries.)

Wherefore I order it to be printed, published, circulated, and that due compliance be given it. Palace of the national government in Mexico, the twelfth of August, 1867. Benito Juarez. To the citizen José M. Iglesias, minister of the treasury and public credit. And I communicate it to you for your knowledge and corresponding effects. Independence, liberty, and reform. Mexico, August 12, 1867. Iglesias.

*August* 19, 1867—*Department of the Treasury. Decree Establishing Rules for the Denouncement and Adjudication of Nationalized Properties.*—Department of the treasury and public credit. Section 7. The citizen president of the republic has been pleased to direct to me the decree which follows: Benito Juarez, constitutional president of the Mexican United States, to the inhabitants thereof, know ye: That in use of the ample faculties with which I find myself vested, I have thought proper to decree the following:

§ 1089. *Rules.*—1. For the denouncement, adjudication, redemption, or collection of the properties which the clergy administered and which are still preserved in the national dominion, the rules contained in the following articles will be observed:

§ 1090. *Concealed Estates.*—2. In order that the denouncer may have a right to receive any part of the amount of the properties denounced, it will be necessary that the denouncement shall be of concealed estates or capitals, it being understood only of those of which no office or court, including the so-called courts and offices of the intervention party, has any notice.

§ 1091. *Denouncers' Part.*—3. The part designated for the denouncers of the liquidated sum which is received will be what the following proportion expresses: If the amount which is received of the hidden properties denounced should not exceed ten thousand dollars, thirty-three and one third per cent; if it should not exceed thirty thousand dollars, twenty-five per cent; if it should not exceed fifty thousand dollars, twenty per cent; if it should not exceed one hundred thousand dollars, fifteen per cent; if it should not exceed one hundred and fifty thousand dollars, twelve per cent; if it should not exceed two hundred thousand dollars, ten per cent; from two hundred thousand dollars upward, eight per cent.

§ 1092. *Denouncements, where Made.*—4. The denouncements of concealed properties shall be made before the chief offices (jefaturas) of the treasury in the states, and in the federal district before the department of the treasury, to which belongs in every case the declaration whether the denouncements are or are not admissible.

§ 1093. *Book of Denouncements.*—5. In the department and in each jefatura of the treasury shall be kept a book in which shall be noted, by numbered entries, and without intervals or interlineation, the day and the hour at which a denouncement is made, and there shall be issued to the denouncer the respective certificate.

§ 1094. *Denouncements to be Admitted to the Department.*—6. The chief offices (jefaturas) of the treasury shall remit to the department of the branch, the denouncements which shall have been presented to them, by the first mail following the day on which they may have been received.

§ 1095. *Formalization of Values.*—7. For the adjudication of the estates which the clergy administered, and which is still preserved in the national dominion, it is indispensable that the corresponding redemption of their value should be formalized immediately.

§ 1096. *Redemption, how Made.*—8. The redemption shall be made with forty per cent in money, and sixty per cent in bonds or credits of the federation, these values to be paid immediately.

§ 1097. *New Valuation.*—9. In order to fix the price of the estates the adjudication of which is solicited, and which shall be of those comprehended in article 7 of this law, a new valuation of them shall be made.

§ 1098. *Redemption in Part with Federal Credits.*—10. The credits of the federation, admissible for the sixty per cent of the redemptions, must necessarily be of those recognized by the general government.

§ 1099. *Nominal Value of Bonds not Admitted.*—11. In place of the bonds or credits, the nominal value which they may have in market is prohibited from being admitted.

§ 1100. *Petitions for Adjudications, where Made.*—12. The

petitions which shall be made according to the preceding bases, for the adjudication of the estates which the clergy administered, and which are still preserved in the national dominion, shall be made in the states before the chief office of the treasury (jefaturas de hacienda), and in the federal district before the administration of nationalized properties.

§ 1101. *Registry of Petitions.*—13. In the administration of nationalized properties, and in each jefatura de hacienda, shall be kept a book in which shall be noted, by numbered entries, and without intervals or interlineations, the day and hour at which is presented a petition for adjudication of one or more estates of the aforesaid, and there shall be issued to the petitioner the respective certificate.

§ 1102. *Redemptions, where Made.*—14. The redemptions shall necessarily be made before the jefatura de hacienda of the state in which the estate or estates redeemed shall be situated; and the corresponding title of adjudication shall be executed by the said jefatura.

§ 1103. *Certain Convents not to be Adjudicated.*—15. The convents and other edifices destined to public use are not to be adjudicated.

§ 1104. *Redemptions, when not Admissible.*—16. The redemption of capitals which the clergy administered, and which is preserved in the national dominion, is not admissible whenever the term shall be completed, or which should lack less than a year of the completion of the term, and which should not have the character of being concealed; and the administration of nationalized properties in the federal district, and in the states the jefaturas de hacienda, must proceed in respect to them for their collection as well as for that of the interest due and unusual.

§ 1105. *Terms of Redemption.*—17. The capitals on a term not completed, and of which there should lack less than a year for the maturity of the term, shall be redeemable on the following terms: If a year should be wanting for the maturity of the term, with seventy-five per cent in money and twenty-five per cent in bonds or credits; if two years, with sixty per cent in money and forty per cent in bonds or credits; if three years, with forty-five per cent in money and fifty-five per cent in bonds or credits; if four years and upwards, with forty per cent in money and sixty per cent in bonds or credits.

§ 1106. *Petitions, where Presented.*—18. The petitions which shall be made for the redemption of the capitals of which the preceding article speaks shall be presented in the states to the jefaturas de hacienda and in the federal district, to the administration of nationalized properties.

§ 1107. *Registry of Petitions.*—19. In the administration of nationalized properties, and in each jefatura de hacienda, a book shall be kept in which shall be noted, by numbered entries and without intervals or interlineations, the day and hour at which the petition is presented for the redemption of the said capitals, and there shall be issued to the petitioner the respective certificate.

§ 1107 *a.* *Redemptions, how Made.*--20. The redemptions shall necessarily be made before the jefatura de hacienda of the state in which may be situated the estate which recognizes the capital redeemed, and the corresponding title of adjudication shall be executed by the said jefatura.

§ 1108. *Irredeemable, What.*--21. The capitals destined to beneficence or to public instruction will have the character of being irredeemable.

Wherefore I order it to be printed, published, circulated, and that due compliance be given it. National palace in Mexico, the nineteenth day of August, 1867. Benito Juarez. To the citizen José M. Iglesias, minister of the treasury and public credit. And I communicate it to you for your understanding and consequent ends. Independence and liberty. Mexico, August 19, 1867. Iglesias.

Department of state and that of the treasury and public credit. Section 6. The citizen president of the republic has been pleased to direct to me the decree which follows: Benito Juarez, constitutional president of the Mexican United States, to the inhabitants thereof, know ye: The congress of the union decrees:

§ 1109. *Bases of Adjudication.*—1. The estates and capitals belonging to the nationalized property, and which have not been alienated, can be asked for in adjudication, including those of beneficence and public instruction which are found concealed, on the following bases:

§ 1110. *Division of Capital.*—I. The total amount of the capital and interest, or the value of the estate, shall be divided into three parts: one which shall be covered with liquidated common credits or bonds of the internal debt; another with certificates of the liquidating sections; and the last in money. In respect to the latter, no compensation will be admitted.

§ 1111. *Bidding.*—II. In case of bidding in respect to a capital or estate, the bids shall be qualified in conformity with the increase which shall be offered in money, which shall be satisfactory, as well as the third part of effective money, in the office of the respective treasury, in twenty monthly payments, counting from the date on which the public sale or adjudication shall have been made.

§ 1112. *Two or More Bidders.*—III. This shall take place whenever two or more bidders shall present themselves for a capital or estate, for which effect section 6 of the department of the treasury, or the chief offices (jefaturas) in their case, shall publish the respective notices in the official periodical for twenty days, designating what object is going to be publicly sold, and the date on which said sale is to take place.

§ 1113. *Delivery of Bonds and Certificates.*—IV. Security can be admitted in the offices of treasury for six months for the delivery of bonds and certificates of the liquidating sections, which delivery can be made in the same offices or in the general treasury.

§ 1114. *Application of Money.*—V. The part of effective money in the redemption of capitals of beneficence or public instruction will continue to be applied to the objects of their institution, and to be recognized on the estates on which they are now founded.

§ 1115. *Privileges of Censatarios.*—2. The censatarios can redeem their own debts, although they may be denounced, if they were not denounced according to the laws, or if the right of subrogation was not conceded to the denouncer; and the censatarios shall enjoy in both cases the benefits which are conceded in article 1, provided that they shall appear to formalize the redemption within the term of one month counted from the publication of this law. If they should do it within the second month, they must satisfy two thirds part of their debts in money, and the rest in certificates of the liquidating sections. The two said months having transpired, the censatarios will be obliged to satisfy their debts entirely with the exchequer, or with whomsoever may be subrogated in its place.

§ 1116. *Rights of Denouncers.*—3. The rights of the denouncers who legally prove their denouncement is understood only in order to receive the corresponding part of what in effective money comes into the exchequer, or in order that they may be credited for any redemption which they may make.

§ 1117. *Nuns not Endowed.*—4. The censatarios can acknowledge a part of the capitals which they owe to-day, in favor of the nuns who have not been endowed.

§ 1118. *Legacies, Representation of.*—5. Whenever by will any legacy is instituted for objects of beneficence, the ayuntamiento of the place in favor of which it may be made shall have the legal representation in that institution; and the place not being designated, the ayuntamiento of the place in which the property shall be found shall have said representation.

§ 119. *Payment in Notes.*—6. The promissory notes or values in bonds sold by the government, and which may result from nullified operations, shall be admitted for the half of the money which may have to be paid in the redemptions.

§ 1119 *a. Capitals, how Applied.*—7. The capitals belonging to a public institution which may have been denounced, and the redemption not being made, shall continue to be applied to to their object.

§ 1120. *Concealed Properties, What.*—8. Those properties shall be considered as concealed, for the recovery of which no formal and manifest steps have been officially made, after the nationalization shall have been decreed.

§ 1121. *Laws in Force.*—9. The laws of the nineteenth of August, 1867, and the others called laws of reform, so far as they are not modified by the present law, remain in force.

Hall of sessions of the congress of the union, Mexico, December 9, 1869. Emilio Velasco, deputy president. F. D. Macin, deputy secretary. Julio Zárate, deputy secretary. Wherefore I order it to be printed, published, circulated, and due compliance be given it. Palace of the general government in Mexico, the tenth of December, 1869. Benito Juarez. To the citizen Matias Romero, secretary of state and of the department of the treasury and public credit. And I communicate it to you for your understanding and corresponding effects. Independence and liberty. Mexico, December 10, 1869. Romero.

*Regulation of the Law Which Precedes.*—The citizen president of the republic, in use of the powers which article 85 of the constitution concedes him, has been pleased to order the following:

§ 1122. *Parties Subrogated in Place of the Exchequer.*—1. It being provided by divers provisions, and particularly by article 16 of the law of the thirteenth of July, 1859, that those who may be subrogated in place of the exchequer must give security for the part which must be paid in money by monthly payments to the satisfaction of the office of the respective treasury; section 6 of this department, and the jefaturas in their case, will require the corresponding bond, which may consist of the obligation accepted by the censatario to retain the part already expressed, while the promissory notes are not satisfied; such acknowledgment to continue with the same privileges as the capital from which it proceeds. The same will be done in treating of estates nationalized.

§ 1123. *Contents of Promissory Notes.*—2. The promissory notes which in conformity with the law of this date ought to be issued to satisfy the part which can only be covered with money, shall express the following circumstances: 1. The total amount of the capital from which they proceed, without uniting various capitals for this object; 2. The estate burdened with said capital and the name of the censatorio; 3. The date of the operation and the number of the respective liquidation; 4. The seal of section 6, or of the office which receives them; 5. The value of the promissory note, with the date on which it was issued and that of its maturity; 6. The signature of the individual who shall issue it, expressing that, without prejudice to the mortgage, he remains personally obligated for its payment, by the means of the power of attachment; 7. In cases of subrogation, the guaranty with which the operation is secured.

§ 1124. *Documents to be Remitted to the Treasury.*—3. Section 6 shall remit weekly to the general treasury a copy of the liquidations, accompanied with the corresponding promissory notes, and of the bonds and certificates of the liquidating sections which are funded. The chief offices (jefaturas) shall likewise remit a statement each month to the general treasury, accompanying the bonds or values funded.

§ 1125. *Annotations on Bonds.*—4. In case that the bonds or certificates ought to remain in the possession of the bearers on account of being of a greater sum, the respective liquidation shall be accompanied with the annotation placed on the bond or certificate.

§ 1126. *Publication of Notices.*—5. Section 6 and the jefaturas shall publish notices immediately for the term of one month, in order that the nuns who should have received dower may present themselves to claim it; and in view of the petitions which shall be presented to said offices, they shall make the assignment provided by law.

§ 1127. *Nullified Promissory Notes.*—6. The promissory notes from operations which for any reason shall be nullified shall immediately be made useless; and there shall be issued by the general treasury, or by the jefaturas in their case, provisional certificates, in which shall be stated the kinds which ought to be returned, which shall be collected when the return shall have been made.

§ 1128. *Delivery of Satisfied Notes.*—7. The promissory notes which shall be satisfied shall be delivered to the interested party, previously cutting therefrom a piece; and in case that they shall be ordered to be delivered in payment or for any other legitimate cause, as negotiable values, it shall be noted on the back of each one of them the reason of the indorsement; this shall be authorized by the chief of the office and the person in whose favor it is done, without which requisite it will have no value for the government.

§ 1129. *Copy of Liquidations to be Remitted to the Treasury.*—8. The jefaturas shall remit every fifteen days to section 6 of the department of the treasury, a copy of the liquidations which shall be made, noting the values which they may receive, with all the details of the operation to which they correspond.

And I communicate it to you for your understanding and consequent ends. Indpendence and liberty. Mexico, December 10, 1869.

# CHAPTER XIX.

## CONFISCATION OF THE PROPERTY OF TRAITORS.



§ 1130. *Confiscation Sustained by the Supreme Court.*—Notwithstanding the twenty-second article of the federal constitution prohibits the confiscation of property, nevertheless the supreme court of justice has sustained the government in its acts of confiscation. Señora Dolores Quesada de Almonte asked protection from the first judge of the district of the capital of Mexico, against the order of the government which ordered to be confiscated the house No. 10 of First San Juan street, as belonging to Don Juan N. Almonte, in virtue of his having been one of the promoters of the French invasion. The complaint was founded on articles 16, 21, 22, 27, and 50 of the constitution, which, it was said, were infringed upon by said order. The judge granted the protection; whereupon an appeal was taken to the supreme court of justice. The judgment below was given upon the ground that "the law of the twenty-seventh of May, 1863, expressly declared that the suspension of individual guaranties and the concession of extraordinary powers to the executive, should last until thirty days after the next meeting of congress, or before if the war with France was terminated;

and that as in August, 1867, not only had the French intervention ceased, but even the civil war, the executive lacked powers, constitutional order being already restored, to order on the twentieth of said August the confiscation of Don Juan N. Almonte's property." The question arose, among others, "When was constitutional order re-established in the republic, after the war of intervention? On what day did the extraordinary powers conceded to the executive by the law of May, 1863, terminate?"

§ 1131. *Re-establishment of the National Government.*—The national government re-established itself in the capital the fifteenth of July, 1867. On the thirteenth of the following August the executive appointed a provisional ayuntamiento, which exercised its functions in the capital until the end of that year, at which time the people were to elect a constitutional ayuntamiento. On the first of said month was appointed also provisionally, by the government, the supreme court of justice, with the attributes of the superior tribunal of the district, until a constitutional election was had of the persons who ought to have composed it. On the fourteenth of said month of August was issued that unfortunate letter of convocation (convocatoria) which caused so many disturbances on the said day of the triumph of the republic—a convocatoria not only for the election of federal functionaries, but even for the election of local ones. On the twenty-eighth of October the deputies were cited to the federal congress for the first preparatory meeting, which ought to have been had on the fifth of November; but congress, notwithstanding, was not installed until the eighth day of the following December. Congress decreed the declaration of a constitutional president and of the supreme court, on the nineteenth of said month of December, having delayed that of magistrates until the fourth of February, 1868; and the superior tribunal was not installed until the fourteenth of said month. Under this state of facts, was constitutional order re-established in the republic on the twentieth of August, 1867? There were no federal or local or municipal powers in being with a constitutional title.

President Juarez, in his opening discourse to the fourth constitutional congress, on the eighth of December, 1867, observed the following: "By the law of the twenty-seventh of May, 1863, the concession of powers to the executive was prorogued until thirty days after the meeting of congress, or before if the war with France was terminated. The term of the state of war could not be declared by Mexico, although in fact no hostilities exist with that nation. She it was that brought on the war, without having made up to now an express declaration not to continue it. Thus the extraordinary powers conceded to the executive ought to continue, in conformity with the law, thirty days more, counted from to-day, notwithstanding, I have believed I was acting better by declaring, as I do declare in this solemn act, that I shall no longer make use of them. * * * It is grateful to me, citizen deputies, to return to you the depository of the great sum of powers which you have confided in me." In reply thereto by the president of the house, he commenced with these words: "The nation returns to-day with the constitutional exercise of one of the most precious attributes of sovereignty, the power of legislating through the means in of its representatives, thanks to the heroic constancy of its sons the glorious struggle which it has sustained for the space of five years against foreign invasion," etc. And further on he added: "Congress has heard with pleasure that the chief of the executive power returns to its origin the authorizations which were conceded in the laws of the eleventh of December, 1861, third of May, twenty-seventh of October, 1862, and the twenty-seventh of May, 1863, because these acts signify that peace can be maintained with the constitutional powers of the government." After congress closed its sessions, on the thirty-first of May, 1863, it did not meet again until December 8, 1867. It was held by the court that the war with France was not terminated until so declared by the executive and by congress, and therefore said order of confiscation, made August 20, 1867, was valid. But, as other vital questions were involved in the power of the executive to thus decree, they were discussed by the court fully; thus: Are the extraordinary powers with which President Juarez was vested, during the war with France, constitutional? Are the laws which he issued in the use of that extraordinary power valid? Señor Ignacio L. Vallarta, the distinguished chief justice of the supreme court, rendered a very lengthy opinion in the above case in support of the constitutionality of the foregoing laws and decrees; and the said court pronounced its judgment thereon in the following terms:

§ 1132. *Judgment of the Supreme Court.*—"Mexico, February 25, 1879. Having examined the trial of protection which Senora Dolores Quesada de Almonte, as widow and executrix of D. Juan Nepomuceno Almonte, has moved before the first district court of the capital, against the order of the executive of the union, dictated through the channel of the department of the treasury, on the twentieth of August, 1867, in virtue of which, through the crime of treason, the house No. 10, situated on the first street of San Juan, belonging to D. Juan N. Almonte was confiscated, by which order, in the opinion of the complainant, the guaranties which are assigned in articles 16, 20, 21, 22, 27, and 50 of the federal constitution have been violated; having examined the written complaint which the interested party presented on the fifteenth of March of the year last past; the documents which are annexed to it, with which she proved her personality, as well as that the estate in question Almonte had by the purchase which he made of it from D. Nathaniel Davidson, on the twenty-sixth of August, 1864, by deed made before the citizen Agustin Vera y Sanchez, a notary public; the report rendered by the department of the treasury, the twenty-second of May of said year, in which it is entered that, according to the law of the twenty-seventh of May, 1863, individual guaranties remained suspended and the executive with full powers, by which he was very well able to dictate laws as that of the sixteenth of August, 1863, which designated the cases of treason and imposed the penalty of confiscation, which was carried into effect in respect to Almonte by a resolution of the twentieth of August, 1867, within the term fixed for the full powers, because congress did not meet until many months afterwards; having examined the annexed documents in said report with which it is proved that after the three legal public notices (pregones) were given, the house No. 10 of San Juan street was put up at auction and struck off to General Francisco Paz for the two thirds part of the appraised value and one dollar more; having examined the proofs rendered by the moving party, and his argument; having examined the fiscal petition in the sense that the protection which is solicited is conceded, on account of article 22 of the federal constitution having been violated, which prohibits forever the penalty of confiscation; having examined the judgment of the first instance, dated the twentieth of July of the year last past, in which, in conformity with what is asked by the moving party, the solicited protection is conceded, serving as a ground therefor, that in August, 1867, not only had terminated the French intervention, but even the civil war, and consequently the extraordinary powers which the law of the twenty-seventh of May, 1863, conceded to the executive had ceased; and having examined the rest which appears in the proceedings—

"Considering, 1. That on the twentieth of August, 1867, the

day on which the order of confiscation of the property of D. Juan N. Almonte was issued, the extraordinary powers which the law of the twenty-seventh of May, 1863, conceded to the executive had not even expired, because it ordered that these should last 'until thirty days after the next meeting of congress in ordinary sessions, or before if the war with France was terminated,' and on that day, the twentieth of August, none of these circumstances had been realized. The term marked in that law had not been completed, because after the thirty-first of May, 1863, congress was not able to perform its functions until the eighth of December, 1867; and not having had in all that epoch any period of ordinary sessions, that term of thirty days had not commenced to run on the said twentieth day of August. Neither had the condition assigned in said law been completed, because, although in that month of August no hostilities with France existed in fact, and that nation had withdrawn its soldiers from the national territory, this was not sufficient, according to the law of nations, to cause the state of war to cease between the belligerents, it being supposed that far from having been celebrated any treaty which so declared it, or having been renewed really in fact the relations of peace, the president, in his discourse at the opening of the fourth congress, manifested that our treaties with France were broken, and also that our relations with that power were broken; on the other hand, President Juarez, in the same act of the opening of congress, declared that in that moment he had ceased to make use of the extraordinary powers, a declaration which congress accepted, and it may be deduced from this that that day is that which ought to be taken as the end of the extraordinary powers;

"Considering, 2. That the extraordinary and most ample powers which the law of the twenty-seventh of May, 1863, and its concordants of the twenty-seventh of October and third of May, 1862, of the eleventh of December and seventh of June, 1861, conceded to the executive, in order to save the national independence, are constitutional, since they are authorized by part 2 of article 29 of the constitution. This truth is demonstrated with the following considerations: Part 2 of article 29 says literally that 'congress shall concede the authorizations which it may esteem necessary in order that the executive may meet the situation.' One of the cases in which the authorization to legislate ought to be considered necessary is without doubt when, in a foreign war, congress should foresee that its existence is impossible, and the question is to save the national independence, as is exactly the case which this claim presents. If the third congress, which feared it would not be able to perform its functions again on account of the occupation of the capital by the French army and through the misfortunes of war, should not have conceded to the executive in 1863 the powers to legislate, or if this supreme court should adjudge to-day that such authorization is unconstitutional, the precise consequence thereof would be, not that all that was done in the war with France defending the independence is nothing more than an attempt against the constitution, but what is more grave even, that Mexico, from the moment that its congress disappears through the machinations of its enemies, can no longer maintain its sovereign rights nor defend itself from its internal or external enemies, since the president must not impose a tax, nor increase the army, nor dispose of the national guard of the states, nor issue, at last, any law even to alter the appropriations in the time of peace; and this, although congress may give him powers for it. This *ab absurdo* argument is made manifest by the French intervention;

"Considering, 3. That the law of August 16, 1863, issued by the president in use of the powers which the law of the twenty-seventh of May of said year conceded to him, is legitimate according to what is shown in the preceding 'considering,' and consequently the recourse of protection can not proceed against it;

"Considering, 4. That article 7 of that law of the sixteenth of August, which empowered the council of ministers to resolve the questions of confiscation, does not violate article 21 of the constitution, it being supposed that by the authorizations conceded to the government the guaranties remained suspended, which this article assigns, because the law of the twenty-seventh of May, 1863, prorogued 'the suspension of guaranties ordered by the law of the twenty-seventh of October, 1862, and the concession of powers granted to the executive,' and article 4 of that law of the twenty-seventh of October only limits the extraordinary powers of the executive in judicial matters in these literal terms: 'It is declared that the executive has no power to intervene or decide in civil cases between private individuals, nor in criminal ones in which alone is a question of an offense to private rights,' and the crime or treason being of those which affect the public right, it remained, therefore, out of the limitation established by that law;

"Considering, 5. That although article 22 of the constitution orders that the penalty of confiscation is abolished forever, it can not be doubted that the guaranty which on this point this article assigns can be also suspended, since article 29 declares that the guaranties granted in this constitution may be suspended 'with the exception of those which secure the life of man;'

"Considering, 6. That the concordance of the laws of the eleventh of December, 1861, of the third of May and of the twenty-seventh of October, 1862, and of the twenty-seventh of May, 1863, prove that guaranty was also suspended, although not expressly. The first of those laws 'fully empowered the executive to dictate all provisions which he should judge proper, without any more restriction than that of saving the independence and national integrity, the form of government established in the constitution, and the laws of reform.' These ample authorizations were prorogued and extended until on the twenty-seventh of May, 1863, the president was even empowered to celebrate diplomatic treaties, and all this with the end of saving the national independence threatened by the French war. And in this amplitude of powers must be comprehended that of dictating proper measures against the traitors who united themselves with the foreign enemy—measures which would not have greater restriction than that which the law expresses, of saving the independence, the constitution, and the reform. To understand, then, that the constitutional precept which prohibits confiscation remained alive for traitors is not now to disown the spirit which those laws dictated, but to deny their literal tenor which took away all restriction out of that expressed in the measures which the government should believe proper to take in order to combat the foreign enemy and his allies;

"Considering, 7. That although those laws which conceded such ample powers to the executive should not be interpreted in this sense, neither can the enemies of the republic in a foreign war invoke in their favor article 22, for the effect that their property shall not be confiscated, because, although this article declares confiscation abolished 'forever,' this must be considered as an ordinary penalty in our penal codes, and without such precept governing in international matters, and limiting the rights which the law of nations gives to the belligerents. This truth, above all the reasonings which might be deduced in its support, demonstrates with evidence fraction 15 of article 72 of the constitution, which sanctions privateering, recognizes the legitimacy of seizures on the sea and on land, and accepts, as it could do no less than accept, the precepts of international law in respect to the right of peace and war;

"Considering, 8. That the constitution of the republic not being able to establish international precepts, but only to fix the internal public law of Mexico, it would be absurd to apply it to matters and affairs which the law of nations only regulates, because such application would serve only to limit the rights of Mexico, recognized by that law, without, indeed, the hope of reciprocity on the part of foreigners, whom our constitution does not obligate; the necessary consequence from this absurdity being, that Mexico in her international relations would be in very unequal conditions in respect to foreign governments;

"Considering, 9. That the right of confiscation being recognized by the constitution, as international law sanctions it, when the question is of affairs in which this and not that law ought to be applied, although the guaranty of article 22 may not be suspended, the property of the enemy may be confiscated in the republic, according to fraction 15 of article 72 cited, and on the terms and in the manner defined by the law of nations;

"Considering, 10. That in the war which Mexico sustained with France, it is not the constitution but the law of nations which defines the rights and duties of the belligerents, and that among those rights that of capture and confiscation of the property of the enemy on the sea or land is recognized, without counting in the limitations which in the exercise of that right the philosophical theories of modern publicists have established, that of the property of the enemy that personally makes war, and whose property may be captured by the other belligerent; all this being a consequence which, although the constitutional guaranty relative to confiscation should not have been suspended, the government of Mexico might impose, in the exercise of the war power which international law requires for it, and in representation of the sovereign rights of the republic;

"Considering, 11. That this supreme court, in its final judgment of the second of July, 1869, adjudging a similar case, declared that the penalty of confiscation imposed on traitors by the law of the sixteenth of August, 1863, did not violate the individual guaranties, because these were suspended during the war, and that that law is legitimate, as emanating from the ample powers which the law of the twenty-seventh of May, 1863, and its concordants, conceded to the executive.

"For these reasons, and on the ground of article 101 and 102 of the constitution, it is declared that the judgment pronounced by the first court of the district of this capital on the twentieth of July, 1878, be revoked, and it is revoked, and it is declared that the justice of the union does not maintain nor protect Doña Dolores Quesada de Almonte against the order of the twentieth of August, 1867, issued by the department of the treasury, and in virtue of which the house number 10 of the first street of San Juan was confiscated. Let the proceedings be returned to the judge of the district, who sent them up for revision, with a copy of this judgment annexed, for the consequent effects; and let the appeal be published and registered in its turn.

"Thus, by a majority of votes, the citizen chief justice and magistrates who formed the full tribunal of the supreme court of justice of the Mexican United States decreed and signed. Ignacio L. Vallarta, Ignacio M. Altimirano, Ezequiel Montes, Manuel Alas, José Maria Bautista, Juan M. Vasquez, Eleuterio Avila, Simon Guzman, José Manuel Saldaña, José Eligio Munoz. Enrique Landa, secretary."[1]

*August* 16, 1863—*Decree of the Government—It is Declared Who is Guilty of Treason, and the Penalties with Which They must be Punished.*—The citizen president has been pleased to address to me the decree which follows: Benito Juarez, constitutional president of the Mexican United States, to the inhabitants

[1] The case referred to by the court in the foregoing decision was that moved by D. Jacobo Sanchez Navarro for himself, and in representation of his mother, Señora Doña Apolonia Berain, and by D. José de Jesus Cuevas, attorney, in representation of D. Carlos Sanchez Navarro, against an order of confiscation on the twenty-ninth of July, 1868. The judgment therein was rendered by the said supreme court on the second of July, 1869. The constitutionality of the laws of confiscation was likewise sustained therein. That the laws of confiscation, issued during the said war with the French forces and those of Maximilian, are constitutional and binding, is not now an open question in Mexico. Whatever may have been the individual opinions of the members of the legal profession, and there were two, the doctrine has become settled, and is so considered by both bench and bar. It has been said that large estates of land have been confiscated, without the conditions of the law having been followed; and if so, it may appear in the investigation thereof that the proceedings are insufficient to be supported by said laws. If fraud can be proved, the titles issued under said proceedings may perhaps be set aside. But the first question to be considered is, Are the original owners barred by the statute of limitation, or what is known under the civil law as the law of prescription? The foregoing laws and decrees governing confiscation are set forth in this chapter; also some of the circulars. There were some other circulars relative to the construction of the laws, which have not been deemed essential to be included herein.

thereof, know ye: That in use of the ample powers with which I find myself vested, I have thought proper to decree the following:

§ 1133. *Traitors, Who are.*—Art. 1. They will be considered guilty of treason, and will suffer confiscation of their property, besides other punishments which the law affixes to this crime: 1. The public functionaries of the intervention, with pay or without it. 2. The employés of the same in the civil, municipal, or military order, and the agents or commissioners in any of those branches. Responsibility does not follow for services given in primary education, nor for the gratuitous acts for the public beneficence. 3. The functionaries of constitutional order, by the simple act of remaining, without permission of the corresponding supreme power, in places submitted to the intervention, unless they can prove within the term which is fixed for them their impossibility to change their residence. 4. The public employés of any branch who without the permission before referred to shall remain in said places, save the exception which the preceding fraction determines. 5. Those who receive subventions, titles, or decorations from the French government, or from the so-called government of the intervention. 6. Those who with their writings defend it and solicit the destruction of the national institutions. 7. Foreigners who by their conduct with the invaders of the country, or with their allied traitors, shall break the neutrality to which they are obligated, and damage the republic or its legitimate government. 8. In general, all those who serve or help, directly or indirectly, the cause of the intervention.

§ 1134. *Appointment of Employés.*—Art. 2. The general government will appoint or designate, by itself or through the medium of the governors of the states, the employés who in each one of them must engage in the confiscation.

§ 1135. *Duties of Employés.*—Art. 3. As soon as employés shall receive their appointment, they will ask any authority, office, or person for the *data* which they can furnish them about the properties which ought to be confiscated, and they will proceed immediately to secure it, appointing under their responsibility administrators to manage said properties, and experts to value the same. They will give an account, without delay, of each proceeding (expediente) to the department of gobernacion, in order that it may communicate to them the supreme resolution on the sale or return of the property.

§ 1136. *Property, how Sold.*—Art. 4. If the resolution should be in favor of a sale, the following provisions will be observed: 1. Treating of personal property, or of urban property, they shall be sold to the best bidder, and of the liquidated product, the expenses of administration and sale having been discounted, they will be made into three parts: one for the public treasury; another which will be deposited at the disposition of the war department, to reward those who shall have become mutilated in the war, or otherwise shall have become distinguished, and to give to the widows and orphans of those killed in the campaign; and a third part to indemnify those who have suffered by embargo, or confiscation of their interests on the part of the intervention. 2. The country estates will be divided into halves: the first will be sold to the best bidder, and the product will be distributed as is said in the preceding fraction; the second will be apportioned in kind, among the inhabitants of the respective district which shall have taken arms to defend the independence. Even persons must be comprehended in this apportionment who, without being citizens of the district, may solicit that participation, doing valuable services of the nature expressed. 3. In every case of public sale the publications (pregones) shall be given in half of the terms which the common law fixes. 4. When there shall be no bidders for the two thirds part of the appraised value, the employés of which this law speaks can reduce the value to one third part, or either rent out the country property or the part thereof the sale of which shall have been frustrated; and the rents which in this manner those properties may produce shall be adjudicated, in due proportion, to the exchequer and to the persons among whom the price should have been distributed.

§ 1137. *Publication of Confiscated Property.*—Art. 5. Thirty days after these employés shall have commenced to perform their commission, they shall publish a list of all the properties existing in the territory of the respective state, and to which the confiscation ought to be extended. This list being once published, denouncements of said properties can be admitted.

§ 1138. *Denouncements, how Made.*—Art. 6. These denouncements will be made before the department of government (gobernacion), directly, or through the medium of the respective employés in each state. To the denouncer will be applied the quarter part of the product of the properties denounced, which shall be deducted from them immediately after the expenses.

§ 1139. *Grounds of Confiscation.*—Art. 7. The questions as

to the motive for confiscation, and to the dominion or preference in the property sequestered, will be resolved by a board of ministers, and the determination hereon will be executed without recourse.

§ 1140. *Alcabala not Required.*—Art. 8. The transfer of the dominion which shall be made in virtue of this law shall not require the tax on sales (alcabala), nor can the alienation be suspended for want of proof of the payment of the taxes being in current money.

§ 1141. *Rebels.*—Art. 9. Those who shall resist the execution of this decree shall be considered as rebels.

Wherefore I order it to be printed, published, circulated, and that due compliance be given thereto. Palace of the federal government, in San Luis Potosí, the sixteenth day of August, 1863. Benito Juarez. To the citizen A. de la Fuente, minister of foreign relations and gobernacion. And I transcribe it to you for your understanding and compliance. San Luis Potosi, August 16, 1863. To the citizen governor of the state of ——. Fuente.

§ 1142. *Chiefs of the Treasury—Their Attributes.*—Department of foreign relations and government. Section 1. The citizen president of the republic has thought proper to order that for the present the chiefs of the treasury or the employés who perform their duties shall perform the attributes and duties which are detailed in articles 3, 4, 5, and 6 of the decree issued on the sixteenth of this month; said employés can commit, under their direction and responsibility, to other persons the proceedings of sequestration and valuation of properties existing out of the central districts of the respective states. Liberty and reform. San Luis Potosi, August 19, 1863. Fuente, citizen minister of the treasury.

§ 1143. *Questions to be Determined by the Treasury.*—Department of foreign relations and government. Section 1. The decree of the sixteenth of August last, on confiscation having been dictated by this department, it was resolved on the nineteenth of the same month that the chiefs of the treasury should be charged to execute said decree as well as not to create unnecessary new employés, because the operations relative thereto properly belong to that department; and taking this into consideration, the citizen president of the republic, in order to avoid the consequent delays from having two departments to try the particular cases, and with the object that the decree may have immediately the quickest and most efficacious completion, he has been pleased to resolve that, the provision of article 7 subsisting, about the questions which ought to be resolved in the board of ministers, that belongs to the cases which may occur, shall be determined by that department of the treasury, and it shall dictate all the new orders which may be necessary. Independence, liberty, and reform. San Luis Potosi, September 15, 1863. Lerdo de Tejada. To the citizen secretary of state and of the treasury and public credit.

§ 1144. *November* 10, 1863—*Circular of the Department of the Treasury—Distribution of the Result of Sales.*—Department of the treasury and public credit. Section of sequestrations. Circular. In consideration of the labores and responsibilities which weigh upon the offices charged with the execution of the decree of the sixteenth of August last, on the confiscation of properties of traitors to the country, the citizen president thinks proper to resolve that the five per cent which by circular dated the second of September last past was assigned for the commissioned executors of the decree, which must be separated from the net result of the sales, fines, or transactions which shall be made of said confiscations, resolved in the board of citizen ministers, shall be distributed in the following manner: three per cent to the commissioners whom the chiefs of the treasury shall appoint to carry out the proceedings of sequestration; one per cent to the office of the chiefs of the treasury of the states to which the estates sequestered belong, if they have taken part in the respective business; and one per cent to the chiefs and employés of the section which in this department has charge of what relates to said decree of the sixteenth of August last past. I introduce it to you for your understanding and corresponding effects. Independence and liberty. San Luis Potosi, November 10, 1863. Nuñez.

§ 1145. *March* 5, 1864—*Decree of the Government Declaring Traitors to the Country Those Who Met at the Meetings Called by Santiago Vidaurri.*— After citing several considerations, the president decrees as follows: I have thought proper to decree the following: Article 1, only. The provision of General Santiago Viduarri on the second of this month, calling the inhabitants of the state of Nuevo Leon to meet to vote for war, or for peace and submission to the plans of the invader, being an act of manifest treason, all those who form bodies for voting, or meet to vote, or in any manner sustain or favor the fulfillment of that provision, shall be considered as accomplices of Vidaurri in treason, and shall be subject in their persons and properties to the penalties established by the laws. Wherefore I order that it be printed, published, circulated, and that due fulfillment be given it. Given in Saltillo, on the fifth of May, 1864. Benito Juarez. To the citizen Sebastian Lerdo de Tejada, minister of foreign relations and government. And I communicate to you for your understanding and consequent ends. Independence, liberty, and reform. Saltillo, March 5, 1864. Lerdo de Tejada.

§ 1146. *October* 24, 1866—*Communication from the Department of the Treasury—Rules Which must be Observed in Matters of Confiscation.*—Department of the treasury and public credit. Section of sequestrations. The circular has reached the knowledge of the citizen president, issued by that government and military commandency on the nineteenth of September last past, providing that, in order that the decree of the sixteenth of August, 1863, shall have its due fulfillment, the satisfaction and sale of the properties subject to that penalty shall be made by the office of the chief of the treasury of that state, the effect of which will fix divers rules on the matter.

As the aforementioned provision would be contrary to what is established in the said law of the sixteenth of August, 1863, it is proper to recollect what it has provided, with the object that it may be duly observed.

Article 2 of said law expresses that the general government shall appoint or designate through itself or through the medium of the governors of the states the employees who in each one of them must carry out the confiscation decreed in article 1.

Article 3 orders that said employés, as soon as they shall have received their appointment, shall ask authority, office, or person for the *data* which they can furnish them about the properties which ought to be confiscated; and they shall proceed immediately to the security thereof, appointing under their responsibility administrators, who shall manage said properties and experts who shall value the same; and they shall give an account, without delay, of each proceeding (expediente) to the department of government, in order that it may communicate the supreme resolution on sale or the return of the properties.

And article 7 established that the questions as to the motive for the confiscation, and as to the dominion or preference in the properties sequestrated, shall be resolved in the board of ministers, and the determination which shall be declared shall be executed without recourse.

By the literal tenor of the articles cited, it is perfectly comprehended that it is the exclusive power of the general government, or of the board of ministers, or of the department of the treasury alone, which was substituted for that of the government by a special order of September 15, 1863, to resolve in each case on examination of the respective expediente, if there is an occasion or not for the confiscation, as well as the other questions which are mentioned.

In consequence, for the cases of confiscation which may be offered in that state, the provisions of the law of the sixteenth of August, 1863, must be observed; that government being empowered to appoint the employés that must carry out the said confiscation; and the expedientes which may be formed shall be remitted opportunely to this department, in order to resolve in each case upon the sale or return of the properties which ought to be secured.

By a supreme order, I communicate it to you for the consequent ends.

Independence, liberty, and reform. Chihuahua, October 24, 1866. Iglesias, citizen governor and military commander of the state of Sonora. Ures.

§ 1147. *November* 21, 1866—*Rules as to Interventions by Third Parties—Kelly's Case.*—To-day I say to the citizen governor and military commander of the state of Sonora what follows: With your official letter of the twenty-fifth of October last, I have received the annexed copies concerning the intervention instituted by the English subject Louis Kelly, in the name of the Mazatlan house of Messrs. Kelly, Myrtle & Co., for credits which it is said the house of Hermosillo of Messrs. Camou Brothers has pending. The citizen president has resolved that the rules shall be fixed which ought to be observed in the case cited, it being understood that they are applicable to the others which may occur of the same nature. Said rules are the following:

1. The proceedings concerning the investigation and security of the properties confiscated, in the cases which ought to have them, according to the provision in the circular relative thereto of this date, will not be embarrassed nor suspended by the fact of there having been instituted any claim or intervention for the mentioned properties.

2. During the time which is employed in the formation of the proceeding (expediente) in the investigation and security expressed, the third parties, opponents, can present their claims, with the *data* and necessary vouchers, to the respective offices

(jefaturas) of the treasury, which at the time will be sent from said offices to the general government, the only authority competent to solve them.

3. The proceedings on the expressed investigation and security being once concluded, it will be remitted to the department of the treasury without any delay, together with the proofs which there may be on the rights of the third party; notifying those who may have intervened that in the future they must communicate exclusively with said department, and that any delay with which they shall proceed to formalize and prove their claims will end to their damage.

Which I transcribe to you in order that it may serve you as a rule for your operations. Independence and liberty. Chihuahua, November 21, 1866. Iglesias. To the citizen chief of the treasury of the state of ——

§ 1148. *November* 21, 1866—*Circular from the Department of the Treasury—Rules Which ought to be Observed in Confiscation—Recitals and Explanations of Decree of August* 16, 1863.—Department of the treasury and public credit. Section of sequestrations. Circular. In decreeing on the sixteenth of August, 1863, the confiscation of the property of traitors, the rules were fixed which ought to have been observed in order to fulfill such a provision.

In article 2 of the law issued on the date cited, it was expressed that the general government would appoint or designate itself or through the medium of the governors of the states the employés who in each one of them should attend to the confiscation decreed in article 1.

In article 3 it was ordered that said employés, as soon as they should receive their appointment, should ask any authority, office, or person for the *data* which they could furnish them about the properties which ought to be confiscated, and they should proceed immediately to their security, appointing under their responsibility administrators to manage them and experts to appraise them; and that they should report, without delay, each expediente to the department of government, in order that the supreme resolution might be communicated to them relative to the sale or return of the property.

In article 7 it was established that the questions relative to the reason for the confiscation, and relative to the dominion or preference of the sequestered property, should be resolved by a board of ministers, and that the determination at which it arrived should be executed without recourse.

By a provision of the fifteenth of September, 1863, the department of the treasury was substituted for that of government in the dispatch of the expedientes relative to confiscated property. Since the nineteenth of August, 1863, it had been determined that the chiefs of the treasury, or the employés who should act in their stead, should perform the attributes and duties which articles 3, 4, 5, and 6 of the law issued the sixteenth day of the said month and year detailed. That said employés could commend, under their direction and responsibility, the acts of sequestration and appraisement to other persons, when the question was property existing out of the central districts of the respective states. On the fifteenth of September, 1863, the resolution was repeated that the chiefs of the treasury were those who should be charged with executing the law of the sixteenth of August. And in the circular of the tenth of November, 1863, it was resolved that the five per cent assigned on the second of the preceding September for the executing commissioners of the law, and which ought to be separated from the net result of the sales, fines, settlements, or property confiscated, should be distributed, giving three per cent to the commissioners whom the chiefs of the treasury shall appoint; one per cent to the chief offices of the respective treasuries, if they have attended to the business, and the other one per cent to the section of sequestrations of the department of the treasury.

From the whole of the provisions cited, two principal consequences are deduced; the first is, that it is the exclusive power of the general govenment, either through the department of the treasury alone, or through a board of ministers, to resolve in each case, with a consideration of the respective expediente, if there is or not a ground for confiscation, as well as the other questions mentioned; so that, only in virtue of a special and express delegation relative to that point, can any other authority exercise such power, on the terms and to the degree which is conceded to it. The second consequence is, that the chiefs of the treasury are those charged to execute the law of the sixteenth of August, 1863, by themselves, or through the means of the commissions which they shall appoint, both enjoying the assignment designated for them.

In entering into the preceding explications, the object has not been solely to bring to mind what in the matter of confiscation the legislation in force orders, of which in some states there is no perfect knowledge, on account of the circumstances in which the country is found; but also it has been wished to compel what is proper to do by choice, in order that there may be uniformity in the execution of the legal provisions, avoiding at the same time any grave inconveniences which might occur in the practice of what is commanded. With this end, then, not to give place to delays, difficulties, and complications, the citizen president has been pleased to order the following provisions:

§ 1149. *Rules to be Observed in Confiscations.*—1. The chiefs of the treasury shall proceed to the investigation and security of the properties which ought to be confiscated, without respect to the persons which the governors of the states or the generals in chief who may exercise superior command over a state, at least in respect to those who may be comprehended in their demarkation; and said governors and generals in chief shall limit themselves provisionally, to order the investigation and security of the properties of the traitors to be proceeded with, in whom may concur aggravating circumstances, on the principal part which the crime of treason imposes upon them.

2. The chiefs of the treasury, in order to proceed with the investigation and security of the properties of the traitors in whom may not concur specially aggravating circumstances, shall await the respective order of the general government, to which they shall remit opportunely, the same as the expressed governors and generals in chief detailed reports of the persons who may be considered comprehended in the law of the sixteenth of August, 1863.

3. The general government will resolve in each case, after an examination of the respective expediente, the questions which may be offered, and it will resolve opportunely also what it may estimate as justice about the traitors comprehended in the reports which may be remitted to it, and against whom.

I communicate it to you, for your understanding and fulfillment, in the part which concerns you. Independence, liberty, and reform. Chihuahua, November 21, 1866. Iglesias.

# CHAPTER XX.

## SUSPENSION OF CONSTITUTIONAL GUARANTIES.



*June* 7, 1861—*Decree of Congress on the Suspension of Guaranties.*—His excellency the provisional president of the republic has been pleased to direct to me the decree which follows: The citizen Benito Juarez, provisional constitutional president of the Mexican United States, to the inhabitants thereof, know ye: That the sovereign congress of the union has thought proper to decree the following:

§ 1150. *Personal Services.*—1. The first part of article 5, section 1, title 1 of the constitution shall remain in these terms:

"In case of national public interest, every individual may be obliged to give personal services, for a just compensation."

§ 1151. *Suspension of Article* 7, *Section* 1, *Title* 1.—2. The guaranty which article 7 of the same title and section concedes is suspended. The liberty of the press will be subject for the present to the law of the twenty-eighth of December, 1855, in that which may not be opposed to the laws of reform; but in respect to writings which directly or indirectly affect the national independence, the institutions, public order, and the prestige of the powers, the government may provide a judicial decree, imposing on the authors of the writings a fine which shall not exceed a thousand dollars, which shall be imposed on the owner of the press, in case it is not known who the author is, or when the latter has nothing with which to satisfy the fine. The said government may, instead of a pecuniary penalty, impose that of imprisonment or confinement for six months. The governors of the states can apply the same penalties; but in case of confinement they shall report to the general government in order that it may designate the place, the prisoner being in the mean time completely secured. The deputies to the congress of the union are subject, the same as the other citizens, to the precepts of this article.

§ 1152. *Permission Required.*—3. In order to exercise the guaranty conceded by article 9, in political affairs, the permission of the authority is necessary.

§ 1153. *Carrying of Arms.*—4. The governors of the state, that of the district, and political chiefs of the territories shall immediately issue a regulation relative to the carrying of arms, wherein shall be designated those prohibited, and the conditions with which those permitted can be carried; under the conception that in no case can any pecuniary burden be imposed with this pretext. In this sense the guaranty which article 10 concedes is limited.

§ 1154. *Suspension of Articles* 13, 18, and 19.—5. The guaranties of which the first part of article 13 speaks are suspended, as well as that conceded in the second part of article 18, and in the first and second parts of article 19.

§ 1155. *Article* 16 *Limited.*—6. The first part of article 16 is limited in these terms: "Nobody can be molested in his person, domicile, or possessions, except in virtue of a writ by competent authority."

§ 1156. *Article* 21, *as to Political Crimes.*—7. The guaranty conceded in article 21 in respect to political crimes is suspended.

The general government only, and in case of a political crime, can impose administrative penalties, which shall not exceed one year of seclusion, confinement, or banishment. These penalties will only be applied in cases in which the offenders shall not have been assigned to the judicial authority.

§ 1157. *Political Crime, What is not.*—8. From the moment in which one begins to act with arms in his hands in the sense of any political opinion, the crime fails to be merely political, and enters into the sphere of a common one.

§ 1158. *Article* 26 *Limited.*—9. The second part of article 26 is limited in these terms: "In time of war the military may require lodgings and personal service on the terms which the ordinance provides."

§ 1159. *Conspirators.*—10. It is declared that the law of conspirators of the sixth of December, 1856, has been and is in force.

Given in the hall of sessions of the congress of the union, in Mexico, the seventh of June, 1861. Francisco de P. Cendejas, deputy vice-president. E. Robles Gil, deputy secretary. G. Valle, deputy secretary. Wherefore, and with the consent of the council of ministers, I order it to be printed, published, circulated, and observed. Given in the national place of Mexico the seventh of June, 1861. Benito Juarez. To the citizen Leon Guzman, minister of relations and government. And I communicate it to your excellency for your understanding and consequent ends. God and liberty. Mexico, etc. Guzman.

*Decree of Congress.*—The congress of the union has thought proper to decree the following:

§ 1160. *Repeal of the Law of June 7th in Part.*—1. The law of the seventh of last June, which suspended some of the constitutional guaranties, with the exception of articles 8 and 11, is repealed.

§ 1161. *Provisions of Article* 5 *Remain.*—2. The provisions of article 5, in which the first and second part of article 19 of the constitution are referred to, limiting the suspension only to political crimes, without prejudice of continuing the judicial proceedings until their conclusion, shall subsist until the seventh of December next.

Given in the hall of sessions of the congress of the union, the twelfth of October, 1861. Vicente López, deputy president. Remigio Ibañez, deputy secretary. Juan N. Guzman, deputy secretary. Wherefore I order it printed, published, circulated, and that due fulfillment be given it. Palace of the national government in Mexico, the fourteenth of October, 1861. Benito Juarez. To the citizen Joaquin Ruiz, charged with the department of government. And I communicate it to you for your understanding and consequent ends. God and liberty. Mexico, etc. Ruiz.

*Decree of Congress.*—The citizen constitutional provisional president of the republic has been pleased to direct to me the decree which follows: The citizen Benito Juarez, constitutional president of the Mexican United States, to the inhabitants thereof, known ye: That the congress of the union has thought proper to decree the following:

§ 1162. *Law of June 7th Declared in Force.*—1. The law of the seventh of June of the present year, which suspended some of the guaranties which the constitution grants, is declared to be in force, making the suspension which it establishes extend to those which articles 11 and 27 concede in their first part.

§ 1163. *Power of Executive.*—2. The executive is fully empowered to make all the provisions he may judge proper under the present circumstances, without more restrictions than that of saving the independence and integrity of the national territory, the form of government established in the constitution, and the principles of the laws of reform.

§ 1164. *Term of Suspension.*—3. These suspensions of guaranties and the authorization conceded to the executive by the present law shall last until thirty days after the meeting of congress, to which he shall report the use he shall have made of these powers.

Given in the hall of sessions of the congress of the union in Mexico, the eleventh of December, 1861. Vicente Riva Palacio, deputy president. Juan N. Guzman, deputy secretary. M. M. Ovando, deputy secretary. Wherefore I order it to be printed, published, and observed. National palace of Mexico, the eleventh of December, 1861. Benito Juarez. To the citizen Francisco J. Villalobos, chief assistant charged with the office of government. And I communicate it to you for your understanding and consequent ends. Liberty and reform. Mexico, etc. Francisco J. Villalobos.

*Decree.*—The citizen constitutional president of the republic has been pleased to direct to me the decree which follows: Benito Juarez, constitutional president of the Mexican United States, to the inhabitants thereof, know ye: That in use of the ample faculties with which I find myself vested, and with the end to determine the law to which the press ought to be subject, I have thought proper to decree the following:

§ 1165. *Law of June 7th Declared in Force.*—Article 1, only. The decree passed by the congress of the union on the seventh of June of the prior year, on the suspension of guaranties, is declared to be in force, in all which it is not opposed to the extraordinary powers issued by the said congress on the eleventh of December of the year last past. Wherefore I order it to be in printed, published, and observed. National palace of Mexico, the twenty-second of April, 1862. Benito Juarez. To the citizen Jesus Teran, charged with the department of relations and government. And I communicate it to you for your knowledge and other ends. Liberty and reform. Mexico, etc. Teran.

*May* 3, 1862—*Decree of Congress on the Suspension of Guaranties and the Faculties Accorded to the Executive.*—The citizen president of the republic has been pleased to direct to me the decree which follows: Benito Juarez constitutional president of the Mexican United States, to the inhabitants thereof, know ye: That the congress of the union has thought proper to decree the following:

§ 1166. *Guaranties Continue Suspended.*—1. The guaranties which were suspended by the law of the eleventh of December, 1861, continue suspended.

§ 1167. *Executive Re-empowered.*—2. The executive is reinvested with the powers which the terms of said law express, with the same limitations which mark the same, and also, that of not interfering in affairs of a judicial kind which arise or may arise between private parties.

§ 1168. *Term of Suspension.*—3. The suspension of guaranties and the authorization to be executive of which this law speaks shall last until the meeting of congress on the sixteenth of next September; and if then its meeting should not be possible on account of the foreign war, or on account of not having elections, they shall last until the first meeting of the next national congress shall take place.

§ 1169. *Elections.*—4. In case the next elections for deputies can not be had in any of the districts on the days marked by the law, the government will have care to designate other days on which they shall take place, so that a meeting of congress may succeed with the possible opportunity.

§ 1170. *Report to Congress by the Executive.*—5. The executive will report the use which he shall make of the faculties which this law concedes to him, within the first fifteen days after the meeting of the national congress.

Given in the hall of the sessions of the congress of the union, in Mexico, the third of May, 1862. José Linares, deputy president. Remigio Ibañez, deputy secretary. M. M. Ovando, deputy secretary. Wherefore I order it to be printed, circulated, and that due compliance be given it. National palace, Mexico, May 3, 1862. Benito Juarez. To the citizen Manuel Doblado, minister of foreign relations and government. And I communicate it to you for your knowledge and proper ends. God and liberty. Mexico, etc. Doblado.

*October* 27, 1862—*Decree.*—The congress of the union has thought proper to decree the following:

§ 1171. *Law of May 3d Renewed.*—1. The provisions contained in articles 1 and 2 of the law of the third of last May are declared to be in force.

§ 1172. *Term of Suspension.* 2.—The suspension of guaranties and the authorizations conceded to the executive by the present law shall last six months, provided that peace with France shall not be established before. If the war last more than six months, said suspensions and authorizations shall last until thirty days after the meeting of congress.

§ 1173. *Report by Executive.*—3. The executive shall report the use which he shall make of these powers within fifteen days after his authorizations shall have ceased.

§ 1174. *Executive No Power over Private Right.*—4. It is declared that the executive has not the power to intervene nor decide in civil cases between private persons, or criminal in which only is involved an offense against private right.

§ 1175. *Limit of Power.*—5. In the powers conceded by this decree is not comprehended that of contradicting in any manner the provisions of title 4 of the constitution.

Given in the hall of sessions of the congress of the union, in Mexico, the twenty-seventh of October, 1862. José Gonzales Echeveria, deputy president. Felix Romero, deputy secretary. Joaquin M. Alcalde, deputy secretary. Wherefore I order it to be printed, published, and complied with. Given in the national palace of the federal government in Mexico, etc. Benito Juarez. To the citizen Juan Antonio de la Fuente, minister of foreign relations and government. And I communicate it to you for your understanding and fulfillment. Liberty and reform. Mexico, etc. Fuente.

*May* 27, 1863—*Decree of Congress—The Suspension of Individ-*

*ual Guaranties and the Concession of Powers to the Executive.*— The citizen president of the republic has been pleased to direct to me the decree which follows: Benito Juarez, constitutional president, etc., know ye: That the congress of the union has thought proper to decree the following:

§ 1176. *Continuance of Powers.*—1. The suspension of individual guaranties, ordered by the law of the twenty-seventh of May, 1862, is prorogued, and the concession of powers which by it was granted to the executive, until thirty days after the next meeting of congress in ordinary sessions, or before if the war terminates with France, continuing also in force the conditions and restrictions imposed on the executive by the law before cited.

§ 1177. *Diplomatic Affairs.*—2. In that order which relates to treaties, agreements, or diplomatic conventions which the government may make, it will be held as understood that it can not admit any kind of intervention.

Hall of the sessions of congress of the union, in Mexico, the twenty-seventh of May, 1863. S. Lerdo de Tejada, deputy president. Francisco Bustamante, deputy secretary. M. M. Ovando, deputy secretary. Wherefore I order it to be printed, etc. Mexico, May 27, 1863. Benito Juarez. To the citizen Juan A. de la Fuente, minister of foreign relations and government. And I communicate it, etc. Liberty and reform. Mexico, May 28, 1863. Fuente.

*November* 8, 1865—*Decree of the Government—The Powers of the President of the Republic and of the Person Who may have the Character of President of the Supreme Court of Justice.*—Department of foreign relations and government. Department of Government. Section 1. The citizen president of the republic has been pleased to direct to me the decree which follows: Benito Juarez, constitutional president of the Mexican United States, to the inhabitants thereof, know ye: That in use of the ample faculties which the national congress conferred on me, by the decrees of the eleventh of December, 1861, of the third of May and twenty-seventh of October, 1862, and of the twenty-seventh of May, 1863; and considering:

§ 1178. *Reasons for This Decree.*—1. That in the articles 78, 79, 80, and 82 of the federal constitution, the only ones which treat of the periods of the functions of the president of the republic, and of the manner of substituting one in his place, as only was foreseen the case of its being possible to make a new election for president, an act which can not be done; without having foreseen the case of a war like the present, in which republic, while the enemy occupy a great part of the national territory, it is impossible that general elections be had in the ordinary periods.

2. That in these articles of the constitution, in order to substitute one in the default of the president of the republic, it was provided to confide in the chief justice of the court of justice the executive power only provisionally, in the only case which was foreseen, that they might proceed immediately to a new election.

3. That when it is impossible to have an election on account of war, the fact that the chief justice of the court of justice should commence to exercise the functions of government for an indefinite time would mean to prorogue and extend his powers beyond the literal prescriptions of the constitution.

4. That by the supreme law of the necessity to preserve the government, the prorogation in the present case of the powers of the president and of his substitute is the most in conformity with the constitution, because in order to avoid the danger of a headless government, it was established in the constitution that there should be two functionaries, of whom one could be substituted for the other; and because in conformity with votes of the people, the president of the republic was elected first and directly to exercise the functions of the government, while the chief justice of the court was elected first and directly to exercise judicial functions, not being confided to him the government, except secondarily and provisionally, in case of absolute necessity.

5. And condsidering that the present case not being provided for in the constitution, the power to declare what is most in conformity with its spirit and prescriptions belongs exclusively to the legislative power, which by the law of the eleventh of December, 1861, confirmed by other repeated votes of confidence of the national congress, was delegated to the president of the republic, in order that without being subject to the ordinary constitutional rules, he should be "fully empowered to dictate all the provisions he might judge proper in the present circumstances, without any more restrictions than those of saving the independence and integrity of the national territory, the form of government established in the constitution, and the principles and laws of reform"—I have thought proper to decree the following:

§ 1179. *Powers of the President Prolonged.*—1. In the present state of the war, the functions of the president of the republic ought to be prorogued, and they shall be prorogued for all necessary time beyond the ordinary constitutional period, until the government can be delivered to the new president which shall be elected, as soon as the condition of war permits that a constitutional election be had.

§ 1180. *Powers of Chief Justice Prolonged.*—2. In the same manner ought to be prorogued and shall be prorogued the powers of the person who has the character of chief justice of the court of justice, for all necessary time, beyond his ordinary period in order that in case of the default of the president of the republic, he may be substituted for him. Wherefore I order it to be printed, published, circulated, and that due compliance be given it. Given in El Paso del Norte, the eighth of November 1865. Benito Juarez. To the citizen Sebastian Lerdo de Tejada, minister of foreign relations and government. And I communicate it to you for the consequent ends. Independence and liberty. Paso del Norte, November 8, 1865. Lerdo de Tejada. To the citizen governor of the state of ——.

# CHAPTER XXI.

## STATE AND CHURCH.



*Law of December* 14, 1874.—Department of state and that of government. Section 1. The citizen president of the republic has been pleased to direct to me the decree which follows: Sebastian Lerdo de Tejada, constitutional president of the Mexican United States, to the inhabitants thereof, know ye: That the congress of the union has thought proper to decree the following: The congress of the union decrees:

### Section First.

§ 1181. *State and Church are Independent, how Far.*—Art. 1. The state and the church are independent between themselves. They can not dictate laws establishing or prohibiting any religion; but the state exercises authority over all of them in that which relates to the preservation of public order and to the observance of the institutions.

§ 1182. *Every Class of Worship Guaranteed.*—Art. 2. The state guarantees in the republic the exercise of every worship. It will only prosecute and punish those acts and practices which, although authorized by some worship, shall import an offense or crime according to the penal laws.

§ 1183. *Meetings for Worship, What not Allowed.*—Art. 3. No authority nor corporation nor formed troop can meet with an official character for the acts of any worship; nor with a motive of religious solemnities shall demonstrations by the state be made of any kind. Consequently all those are permitted on holidays which shall not have as an exclusive object to solemnize events purely civil. Sundays are designed as days of rest for public offices and establishments.

§ 1184. *Religious Instructions in Public Establishments not Allowed.*—Art. 4. Religious instruction and official practices of any worship are prohibited in all the establishments of the federation of the states and of cities. Morality shall be taught in those which by the nature of their institution shall permit it, although without reference to any worship. The infraction of this article shall be punished with an administrative fine of from twenty-five to two hundred dollars, and with deprivation of office of the culpable ones, in case of repetition. The persons who live in public establishments of any class can, if they solicit it, meet at the temples of their worship, and receive in the said establishments, in case of extreme necessity, spiritual auxiliaries of the religion which they profess. In the respective regulations the manner shall be fixed of serving this authorization without injury to the object of the establishments, and without violating the provisions in article 3.

§ 1185. *Public Religious Services not Allowed, except in Temples.*—Art. 5. No religious act can be publicly performed, unless it is in the interior of the temples, under the penalty of the act being suspended and the authors thereof punished with an administative fine of from ten to two hundred dollars, or reclusion from two to fifteen days. When to the act should be given, besides a solemn character by the number of persons which shall meet it, or by any other circumstance, the authors of it, the same as the persons who shall not obey at the intimation of the authority for the act to be suspended, shall be reduced to prison and assigned to the judicial authority, incurring the penalty of two to six months imprisonment. Outside of the temples, neither can the minister of worship nor the individuals of either sex who profess the worship use special or distinctive dresses which characterize them, under the administrative penalty of ten to two hundred dollars fine.

§ 1186. *Use of Bells Limited.*—Art. 6. The use of bells shall be limited to that which shall be strictly necessary to call to religious acts. In the regulations of police shall be dictated the measures conducive to that use which shall not molest the public.

§ 1187. *Notice to the Political Authorities of the Existence of Churches.*—Art. 7. In order that a temple may enjoy the prerogatives as such, in conformity with articles 969 and those relative thereto, of the penal code of the district, which for the purpose are declared in force in all the republic, notice must be given of their existence and installation to the political authority of the locality, who, keeping a registry of those which may be found in the case, shall send it to the government of the state, and the latter to the department of government (ministerio de gobernacion). As soon as a temple be not dedicated to the exclusive exercise of the worship to which it may belong, acts of another kind being verified in it, it shall be erased from the registry of the temples, for the effects of this article.

§ 1188. *Ministers of Worship, when can not be Made Heirs or Legatees.*—Art. 8. The institution of heirs or legatees which shall be made in favor of ministers of worship by their relatives within the fourth civil degree, and by those who live with said ministers, is null; when the latter shall have given any kind of spiritual auxiliary to the testators during the sickness of which they shall have died, or shall have been directors of the same.

§ 1189. *Fraud.*—Art. 9. The institution of heirs or legatees, which, although made in favor of persons capable, should it be in fraud of the law in order to infringe upon fraction 3 of article 15, it is likewise null.

§ 1190. *Ministers can Have No Extra Privileges.*—Art. 10. Ministers of worship shall not enjoy, by reason of their character, any privilege which shall distinguish them before the law from the other citizens, nor are they subject to more prohibitions than those which in this law and in the constitution are designated.

§ 1191. *Unlawful Discourses.*—Art. 11. The discourses which the ministers of worship may pronounce counseling disobedience of the laws, or provoking any crime or offense, shall constitute the meeting in unlawfulness in which they were pronounced, and the meeting relinquishes the right to enjoy the guaranty which article 9 of the constitution assigns, and may be dissolved by the authority. The author of the discourse shall be submitted in this case to the provisions in title 6, chapter 8, book 3, of the penal code, which is declared to be in force in the case for all the republic. The offenses which shall be committed by instigation or suggestion of a minister of any worship, in the cases of the present article, shall constitute him in the category of the principal author of the act.

§ 1192. *All Church Service must be Public.*—Art. 12. All meetings which take place in the temples shall be public; they shall be subject to the vigilance of the police, and the authority can exercise in them the functions of its office, when the case may demand it.

§ 1193. *No Official Titles to be Used by the Clergy in Addressing the Authorities.*—Art. 13. Religious institutions are free to organize themselves hierarchically as shall appear best to them; but this organization does not produce before the state greater legal effects than that of giving personality to the superiors thereof in each locality for the effects of article 15. No minister of any worship can, therefore, by title of his character, address himself officially to the authorities. He shall do it in the form and with the requisites with which every citizen may do it in the exercise of the right of petition.

### Section Second.

§ 1194. *Church can not Acquire Real Estate—Exceptions.*—Art. 14. No religious institution can acquire real estate, nor capitals imposed thereon, with the exception of the temples destined immediately and directly to the public service of worship, with dependencies annexed thereto which may be strictly necessary for that service.

§ 1195. *Rights of Religious Associations.*—Art. 15. The rights of religious associations, represented by the superior thereof, in each locality, are: 1. That of petition; 2. That of property in the temples acquired according to the preceding article, the right of which shall be governed by the particular laws of the state in which the edifices may be found, the association being extinguished in each locality, or when the property shall have been abandoned; 3. That of receiving charities or donatives, which can never consist of real estate, recognitions thereon, nor of obligations or promises of future fulfillment, whether by title of testamentary institution, donation, legacy, or any other class of obligation of that kind, since all shall be null and inefficacious; 4. The right of receiving those charities in the interior of the temples by the means of collectors which they shall appoint, under the conception that outside thereof the appointment of such collectors is absolutely prohibited, and those who shall be thus appointed are comprehended in article 413 of the penal code of the district, which article is declared in force in all the republic; 5. The right which is assigned in the following article. Outside of the rights mentioned, the law does not recognize any other in religious societies with their character of corporation.

§ 1196. *The Fee in Church Property is Vested in the Nation.*—Art. 16. The fee in the temples, which in conformity with the law of the twelfth of July, 1859, were nationalized, and which were left to the service of catholic worship, as well as that of those which subsequently shall have been ceded to any other religious institutions, shall continue belonging to the nation, but their exclusive use, preservation, and improvement shall be of the religious institutions to which they shall have been ceded, while the consolidation of the property shall not be decreed.

§ 1197. *Exemption from Taxation.*—Art. 17. The edificios of which the two preceding articles speak shall be exempt from the payment of taxes, save when they shall be constructed or acquired nominally and determinedly for one or more private persons who shall preserve the property thereof, without transmitting it to a religious society. That property, in such a case, shall be governed in conformity with the common laws.

§ 1198. *Edifices to be Sold, What.*—Art. 18. The edifices which shall not be private property, and which according to this section and that which follows may be retaken by the nation, shall be sold in conformity with the laws in force relative to the matter.

### Section Third.

§ 1199. *Monastic Orders not Permitted.*—Art. 19. The state does not recognize monastic orders, nor can it permit their establishment, whatever may be the denomination or object with which they claim to be erected. The clandestine orders which may be established shall be considered as unlawful meetings which the authorities may dissolve, if their members shall live together, and in every case the chiefs, superiors, and directors thereof shall be tried as criminals attacking individual guaranties, in conformity with article 993 of the penal code of the district, which is declared to be in force in all the republic.

§ 1200. *Religious Societis Unlawful, What.*—Art. 20. The individual members of the religious societies shall live under certain rules peculiar to themselves, by means of promises or temporal or perpetual vows, and with subjection to one or more superiors, even when all the individuals of the order shall have distinct habitation. The first declaration and those relative thereto of the circular of the department of government of the twenty-eighth of May, 1861, shall remain, therefore, without effect.

SECTION FOURTH.

§ 1201. *No Religious Oath Required — Promise to Tell the Truth.*—Art. 21. The simple promise to tell the truth, and that of fulfilling the obligations which shall be contracted, shall be substituted for the religious oath, in its effects and penalties; but both are only legal requisites when the question is of affirming an act before the tribunals, in which case the first and second shall be taken when possession of an office or employment shall be taken. This latter shall be taken by making a formal protest, without any reserve, to support and to cause to be supported in its case the political constitution of the Mexican United States, with its additions and amendments, and the laws which emanate therefrom. All those who shall take possession of an employment or public charge, whether it be of the federation of the states or the municipalities, must make such a protest. In the other cases in which, according to the laws, the oath produced some civil effects, the protest fails to produce it, even when it shall be given.

SECTION FIFTH.

§ 1202. *Marriage is a Civil Contract.*—Art. 22. Matrimony is a civil contract, and it as well as the other acts which shall fix the civil state of persons are of the exclusive jurisdiction of the functionaries of civil order in the terms provided by the laws, and they shall have the force and validity which the same shall attribute to them.

§ 1203. *Civil State of Persons.*—Art. 23. It shall belong to the states to legislate upon the civil state of persons, and to regulate the manner in which the relative acts must be celebrated and registered; but their provisions must be subject to the following bases:

1. The offices of civil registry shall be as many as shall be

sufficient in order that all persons may conveniently meet in them who are required to do so, and said offices shall always be in charge of employés of aptitude and tried honesty.

2. The registry of the acts of the civil state shall be kept with due exactness and separation, in books which shall be under the inspection of the political authorities. The inscription shall be made with all the requisites and formalities which guarantee their fidelity and the authenticity of the acts. These can not contain erasures, interlineations, nor amendments, and whatever error may be committed shall be immediately entered therein correctly in a note before being signed.

3. The service of the civil state shall be entirely gratuitous for the public, and tariffs can only be established for the collection of fees for those acts which could be done in the offices, but at the solicitation of the interested parties shall be done in their houses; for the issuing of certified copies of the acts, and for the interments which in the public cemeteries shall be made in privileged places.

4. The officials of the civil registry shall keep a copy of their books, without any interruption between the acts. Every six months they shall remit this copy, attested at the bottom with an expression of the leaves which it contains, rubricated on the margin, to the archives of the government of their state. They shall besides remit monthly a notice of the acts which in the month shall have been registered.

5. All the acts of the civil registry shall have a public character, and nobody can be denied a certified copy of any of the acts which he may solicit.

6. The acts of the registry shall be the only proof of the civil state of persons, and they shall make full proof in court until their falsity shall be proved.

7. Civil marriage can not be celebrated except by one man with one woman, bigamy and polygamy being crimes which the laws shall punish.

8. The will of the contracting parties, freely expressed in the form which the law shall establish, shall constitute the essence of civil marriage; consequently, the laws shall protect the emission of said will and shall impede all compulsion thereof.

9. Civil matrimony shall not be dissolved except by the death of one of the conjugal parties; but the laws may admit the temporary separation for grave causes, which shall be determined by the legislator, without any of the consorts being able by the separation to unite themselves with any other person.

10. Civil matrimony can not be celebrated by persons who by physical incapacity can not fulfill the ends of its state; nor by those who by moral incapacity can not manifest their consent. A marriage which in these cases shall become celebrated must be declared null on petition of one of the parties.

11. The relation of consanguinity or affinity between ascendents and descendents in a right line, and of consanguineous or uterine brothers of the flesh, shall also be causes which shall impede the celebration of marriage, and which being contracted shall dissolve it.

12. All the trials which married parties shall have to move relative to the nullity or validity of marriage, relative to divorce, and others concerning this state, shall be prosecuted before the civil tribunals which the laws shall determine, without the resolutions having any legal effect which may be dictated by the ministers of worship relative to these questions.

13. The law shall not impose nor proscribe religious rites respecting marriage. Married parties are free to receive or not benedictions from ministers of worship, which shall neither produce any legal effects.

14. All the cemeteries and places in which bodies are buried shall be under the immediate inspection of the civil authority, even when they may belong to private enterprises. No enterprise of this kind can be established without license from the respective authority. Inhumations or exhumations can not be made without a permission or order in writing from the competent functionary or authority.

§ 1204. *Civil State Recognized through the Republic.*—Art. 24. The civil state which a person shall have in conformity with the laws of a state or district shall be recognized in all of the others of the republic.

SECTION SIXTH.

§ 1205. *Personal Service must be Voluntary.*—Art. 25. Nobody can be obligated to give personal services without their full consent and without a just compensation. The want of consent, even when a compensation may intervene, shall constitute an attack on the guarantee, the same as the want of compensation when the consent has been tacitly or expressly given on condition of obtaining it.

§ 1206. *Personal Liberty or Banishment can not be Bartered.*—Art. 26. The state can not permit any contract, pact, or agreement to be carried into effect, which shall have for its object the diminution, the loss, or the irrevocable sacrifice of liberty, whether it be on account of work, education, or of religious vow, nor in which a man shall agree to his proscription or banishment. All these stipulations which shall be made in contravention to this article are null, and obligate always him who shall accept them for the indemnification for the damages and losses which he shall cause.

GENERAL PROVISIONS.

§ 1207. *Penalties Imposed by Political Power.*—Art. 27. It is within the power of the political authorities of the states to impose the administrative penalties of which this law speaks. The same authorities shall incur before the governors of the states double those penalties, in case that they shall authorize or knowingly tolerate the infringement of the law. The governors of the states are responsible, in their turn, for the infraction of the present law, and for the omissions which they shall commit, or the authorities and employés who are subject to them.

§ 1208. *Offenses, Federal Character of.*—Art. 28. The offenses which may be committed by the infraction of sections 1, 2, 3, and 6 of this law have the character of federal, and are of the jurisdiction of the tribunals of the federation; but the judges of the states shall try them officially in the places in which the district judges shall not reside until ready for judgment, and shall then remit them to the district judge having jurisdiction for his judgment. The other offenses which may be committed by the infraction of sections 4 and 5 the competent authorities shall try, in conformity with the common law of each locality.

§ 1209. *Laws of Reform.*—Art. 29. The laws of reform are included in this law, which shall be observed in that which relates to the civil registry, while the states shall issue those which they must pass in conformity with section 5. Said laws are also in force in all that refers to nationalization and alienation of eccleiastical properties and payment of dower to ladies excluded from the cloisters, with the modifications which for this are introduced in article 8 of the law of the twenty-fifth of June, 1846.

Palace of the legislative power, Mexico, December 10, 1874. Nicolas Lémus, deputy president. Antonio Gómez, deputy secretary. Luis G. Alvírez, deputy secretary. J. V. Villada, deputy secretary. Alexander Prieto, deputy secretary. Wherefore I order it to be printed, published, circulated, and that due fulfillment be given it. Given in the palace of the national government in Mexico, on the fourteenth of December, 1874. Sebastian Lerdo de Tejada. To the citizen Lic. Cayetano Gómez y Perez, first assistant, charged with the department of state and of that of government. And I communicate it to you for the consequent ends. Independence and liberty. Mexico, December 14, 1874. Cayetano Gómez y Perez, first assistant. To the citizen ——

# CHAPTER XXII.

## MINES IN GENERAL.

§ 1210. *Roman Law.*—By the Roman law, gold and silver and valuable or precious stones found upon public land were held to be the property of the sovereign. The owners of private property were deemed owners of all substances found within the same. But the proprietor who worked mines on his own land was bound to pay one tenth of the product thereof to the sovereign. If he rented his land to others for mining purposes, the latter were compelled to pay one tenth to the crown and another tenth to the proprietor.[1]

§ 1211. *Civil Code Modified.*—This rule was subsequently changed in the countries governed by the civil law, which declared that all the precious metals found in the earth should belong to the sovereign. Spain declared in the laws of the partidas as follows: "Law 5, title 15, partida 2. And mines, if there be any; and although it be not mentioned in the grant that the king retains to himself the things above mentioned, yet it is not, therefore, to be understood that he to whom the grant is made acquires a right to them; moreover, if the king should make over all these things to him by grant, even then he can not hold or use them, except during the life of the king who made the grant, and of any other who may please to confirm it."

§ 1212. *All Metals the Property of the Sovereign.*—It was thereafter provided by Don Alfonso XI., in the ordenamiento real, law 8, title 1, book 6, that all metals were the property of the sovereign, and that a permission was required to work them. This law was embraced within the Nueva Recopilacion or collection of Castile.

§ 1213. *Modification of the Law.*—The strictness of the foregoing law was subsequently relaxed by King John I. Under the laws created by him, the owner of mining land could work the same; and any person could dig for mines upon the land of others by a license from the owner thereof. The privilege was allowed with a heavy burden. The miner was to pay to the

[1] Lagunez, de Fructib., 1 p., c. 10, n. 51, usque ad 54; Gutierrez, Pract., p. 4, quæst. 36, n. 59.

crown two thirds of the profits. By this law, private property could not be worked without permission from the proprietor thereof. Philip II. saw that the mines were not worked to the extent that they might be, under the decrees of King John. The decrees of John were repealed or modified, so that the owners of the soil could not restrict the working thereof for mining purposes; nor were the people compelled to obtain licenses from the crown. But the owner and crown received their proper proportions from the profits of the miner. The new law of Philip II. repealed the foregoing laws, except as to the vesting of the metals in the crown.

§ 1214. *Collection of the Indies.*—The order of the ninth of December, 1526, made by Emperor Charles, gave a right to all subjects to work mines. On this order was founded the laws of the collection of the Indies.

§ 1215. *Civil Code.*—By article 829 of the Mexican civil code, the proprietor of a tract of land is owner of the superfice and all that is below it, "with subjection to the provisions in the special legislation on mines and of those of police regulations." This language is rather indefinite. It relates, however, to the mining ordinance (ordenanza de mineria) and any special legislation on the subject.

§ 1216. *Ordinances of* 1783.—This ordenanza was issued at Aranjuez on the twenty-second of May, 1783, by the king, and promulgated in Mexico on the fifteenth of January, 1784. It was framed by Don Francisco Xavier de Gamboa, a distinguished jurisconsult, who had paid much attention to mining jurisprudence. It has been generally considered one of the most just and equitable codes of mining laws ever made, united to a body of commentaries exhibiting great learning and talent. But it contains many articles not in harmony with a republican form of government. This ordinance has universally governed the mining interest in the whole republic of Mexico, until the last few years. The supreme court of justice of the union held, in the case of Alexander Willard against the administrator of revenue, May 8, 1880, that the several states had power to legislate upon the subject of mining.

§ 1217. *State of Hidalgo.*—The state of Hidalgo, therefore, availing itself of that doctrine, promulgated its own mining code, on the tenth of October, 1881. The states generally have made some legislative enactments, such as extending the time for working or non-working the mines, so that the claimants may hold their claims without being governed by rule in the ordinances.

§ 1218. *The States.*—The states have also legislated upon the mode of denouncing mines, so far at least as the officers are concerned before whom the denouncements are to be made. The states of Guanajuato, Zacatecas, and some others have continued the practice of having mining deputations, and have in consequence thereof followed, in the main, the provisions of title 2 of these ordinances, when not in conflict with the constitution and laws. In some states there are three deputies instead of two. These deputations have no jurisdiction of judicial questions; and the very moment such a case arises the parties must seek the ordinary courts for the solution thereof. The supreme court decided this point in the case of Juan Sotres against the acts of the mining deputation of the capital of the state of Guanajuato, June 24, 1880. The deputation had given more ground to the denouncer, and at a less price, than the owner thought was just. The court held that under article 13 of the federal constitution there could exist no special tribunals for deciding litigious questions, and that the said questions were of that character. The state of Mexico passed a law, which was promulgated May 1, 1875, giving jurisdiction to the judge of first instance of the district over the proceedings of denouncements. Some other states have vested the same powers in the said named judge. In the state of Guerrero, the petition of denouncement must be addressed to the prefect of the district, who refers the same to the governor, and he orders the proper proceedings to be carried out. In the state of Vera Cruz, the petition must be first addressed to the governor, who orders the prefect to perform the necessary duties to complete the denouncement. The state of Hidalgo has its own special mining code, by virtue of which the prefect must be petitioned. It is thus easy to ascertain in any state the proper authority to whom the denouncer must appeal in order to obtain his rights and title by virtue of a denouncement.

§ 1219. *Mines, by Whom Worked.* — Mines may be owned and worked by private individuals, whether citizens or foreigners, by partners, or by corporations; and although these ordinances divide mines into twenty-four varras, yet the owners may divide them into as many shares as they may deem proper. Shares of stock in a mine are personal property, and may be seized for debt. As the fee in mines is not granted to the denouncer, they can not be seized nor sold on judgment and execution. But a receiver may be appointed to take possession for the benefit of creditors of the mines, upon a proper showing.

§ 1220. *Forfeiture.*—A mine may be forfeited and denounced by another, if not worked according to these ordinances. But the time for non-working the same may be extended by the state legislature, and thereby save the forfeiture. By presenting a petition showing good reasons why a delay of work is requisite for the owners, the same will be granted.

§ 1221. *Measurement.*—By the law of September 10, 1857, the meter is used in all measurements, instead of the vara.

§ 1222. *Elimination of the Ordinances.*—The ordinance of 1783 contains much that is inapplicable to a republic, and much that is in conflict with the constitution and laws of Mexico. The author has endeavored to eliminate therefrom such extraneous matter, and presents it thus shorn, as follows:

TITLE II. OF THE JUDGES AND DEPUTIES OF MINING DISTRICTS.

§ 1223. *Enrollment of Miners.*—Art. 2. All those who for more than one year shall have worked one or more mines, expending on them as owner thereof, in whole or in part, their capital, labor, or personal attention and care, shall be enrolled as miners of that place (lugar), and their names shall be entered in the books of enrolled miners, which shall be kept by the judge and notary of that mining place.

§ 1224. *Election of Deputies.*—Art. 3. The miners so enrolled, and the suppliers (aviadores), being miners, the millers (maquileros), and the proprietors of haciendas for grinding and smelting ores in each place, shall assémble in the beginning of January of each year, according to the custom, at the house of the judge of mines, for the purpose of electing the persons who are to exercise the office of deputy for such place; and who must be or must have been mine proprietors of great experience and intelligence in them, men of good conduct, trustworthy, and possessed of all qualifications requisite for such offices.

§ 1225. *Manner of Voting—Eligibility as Deputy.*—Art. 4. Every one of the miners thus enrolled shall have one vote at such elections; moreover, of the mine suppliers (aviadores), being miners as aforesaid, millers, and the proprietors of haciendas mentioned in the preceding article, every two persons shall have one vote, and they shall not themselves be eligible as deputies, unless they are also miners, and possess the necessary qualifications.

§ 1226. *Where Voters are Numerous, Electors to be Chosen.*—

Art. 5. Where there is a great number of voters, as in Guanajuato, the same practice which has hitherto prevailed shall be continued in such place, namely, of choosing beforehand the electors who are to proceed to the election of the deputies.

§ 1227. *Administrators of Mines may Vote, when.*—Art. 6. The administrators of mines may vote instead of their principals, provided the latter do not reside in that neighborhood (territorio), and provided such administrators be fully authorized by their principals for that purpose, and such administrators shall be eligible as deputies if their occupations permit, and they have the necessary qualifications.

§ 1228. *Presiding Officers at Election.*—Art. 7. The judge of mines of each mine-town or establishment, together with the deputies of the preceding year, shall preside at and regulate the election, and shall have voted at the same, and in case of dispute, the vote of the judge shall be decisive, and those persons who have the greater number of votes, qualified and computed as before determined, shall be considered as duly elected.

§ 1229. *Deputations.*—Art. 8. In each real, or mine-town or establishment, there shall be a deputation consisting of two deputies; and to the end that those employments may be for the duration of two years, and that one of such deputies may be a person well qualified for the office, in the first year alone of carrying this ordinance into effect, two deputies shall be appointed, but in every succeeding year only one, who is to replace the deputy then oldest in office, and as this provision can not be complied with at the second election (*i. e.*, at the end of the first year), the deputy of the two first elected shall remain in office during the second year, who at the first appointment was elected by the greatest number of votes, so that the other of the two first elected deputies will be in office only for one year.

§ 1230. *Substitutes.*—Art. 9. There shall also be elected in the same manner in each mine-town or establishment four substitutes (substitutos) who are to supply the place of the deputies in the case of their refusal to serve, their death, illness, necessary absence, or other just impediment, and to assist at the several courts of appeal in such cases and circumstances as may occur, and which will be treated of in their proper place; but in districts where the electors are to be nominated, according to the fifth article of this present title, those four who shall have the greater number of votes are to be the substitutes for the first year, and it is to be understood that these offices are to be also for the duration of two years, and in each successive year only two new substitutes are to be chosen, observing with regard to them the same rule which has been laid down for the election of deputies in the preceding article; and for the sake of greater perspicuity, and to present all arbitrary acts in the succession, either to the said offices of substitutes or to those of advisers, as directed by several articles of these ordinances, those persons shall always be preferred who shall have had the greatest number of votes at their respective elections, when the elections have been on one and the same day; but in other cases, those who have been longest in office shall be preferred.

§ 1231. *District Attorneys.*—Art. 10. The said substitutes shall also be district attorneys (procuradores síndicos) of their respective mine-towns; and shall represent, demand, and procure whatever may appear necessary for the common interests of the miners in their neighborhood, and by virtue of this office, shall have a superior claim to be elected as deputies, or to other offices connected with the mines.

§ 1232. *Persons Elected must Accept.*—Art. 11. The persons elected as deputies must accept the office within three days of the time of their election under a penalty of one thousand dollars, which penalty is to go to the fund of that mine-town, and the person refusing to accept shall be obliged to serve the office, notwithstanding the payment of such penalty; and even though there may appear a just cause for his refusal, he must accept the office notwithstanding, and serve it until such cause shall have been admitted by the royal tribunal general of the miners, to which body it must be submitted.

§ 1233. *Re-election of Same Person, when.*—Art. 12. It is forbidden to re-elect any person to any one of the beforementioned offices until the expiration of two years from his last serving in such office, and the person re-elected after such interval must accept the same office under a penalty of five hundred dollars, which penalty is to be paid to the general fund of the mine-town, and he shall be obliged to serve the office, notwithstanding the payment of such penalty, without prejudice, however, to any sufficient cause of exemption which he may have; but this must be submitted to the royal tribunal general of Mexico, and he must serve the office in the mean time, as directed by the preceding article.

§ 1234. *Powers of Deputies.*—Art. 13. All the miners, mine-suppliers, millers, and owners of haciendas of the respective places shall confer on the new deputies power to promote their interests and pretensions, and for all the usual purposes, and shall swear to obey them in all that relates to the exercise of their offices; and the deputies themselves shall take upon them their office according to law, and swear to observe these ordinances (which are to be read at every election at the time of their entering into office), and to maintain secrecy in the causes which come under their cognizance.

### Title V. Of the Ownership of Mines.

§ 1235. *Property of Mines in the Sovereign.*—By article 1, the mines are the property of the sovereign. So it is now considered in Mexico; but under the control of the sovereign state in which the mines may be situate.

§ 1236. *Owners may Sell.*—By article 2, the owners are authorized or empowered to sell or pass by will, by inheritance, or legacy, or in any other manner to dispose of all their property in said mines, upon the terms on which they themselves possess them, to any person legally capable of acquiring them.

§ 1237. *Mines Held on Conditions.*—By article 3, the mines are granted on two conditions: 1. That the grantees pay whatever may be demanded of them by the sovereign for the privileges received; and 2. That they shall carry on their operations in the mines subject to the provisions of these ordinances, on failure of which, at any time, the mines of persons so making default shall be considered as forfeited, and may be granted to any person who shall denounce them accordingly.

### Title VI. Of the Manner of Acquisition—New Discoveries—Register of Veins—Denouncement of Abandoned Mines.

§ 1238. *Rights of Discoverer.*—Art. 1. The discoverers of one or more mineral mountains (cerros minerales), wherein no mine or shaft has been opened, acquire in the principal vein as much as three portions (pertenencias), together or separate, where it best pleases them, according to the measures hereafter signified; and that on having discovered more veins, they shall acquire a portion in each vein, fixing on and making the said portions within the term of ten days.

§ 1239. *Discoverer Entitled to Two Pertenencias, when.*—Art. 2. The discoverer of a new vein in a mountain known and worked in other parts may hold in it two portions (pertenencias) together, or separated by other mines, on condition that he specifies them within ten days, as mentioned in the preceding article.

§ 1240. *Discoverer, Who is not.*—Art. 3. He who proposes

for a new mine in a vein already known and worked in part is not to be considered a discoverer.

§ 1241. *Manner of Denouncing.*—Art. 4. The persons referred to in the preceding article must present a written statement to the deputation of miners, prefect, or other officer of the district qualified to act, or in case there should not be one in that district, to the nearest thereunto, specifying in it his name, those of his associates, if he has any, the place of his birth, his place of habitation, profession, and employment, together with the most particular and distinguishing features of the tract, mountain, or vein of which he claims the discovery; all which circumstances, as well as the hour in which the discoverer shall present himself, must be noted down in a register kept by the deputation and notary, if they have one, or other officer having authority, such as the prefect, etc.; and after this, the said written statement shall, for his due security, be restored to the discoverer, and notice of its object and contents shall be affixed to the doors of the church, the government houses, and other public buildings of the town, for the sake of general notoriety. And I order, that within the term of ninety days, the discoverer shall cause to be made in the vein or veins so registered a pit of a yard and a half in diameter or breadth, and ten yards (varas) in depth, and that immediately on the existence of the vein being ascertained, one of the deputies in person (or other officer qualified) shall visit it, accompanied by the notary (if there be one), or if there be no notary, by two assisting witnesses, and by the mining expert (perito facultivo) of that district, in order to inspect the course and direction of the vein, its size, its inclination on the horizon, called its falling or declivity, its hardness or softness, the greater or less firmness of its bed, and the principal marks and species of the mineral; taking exact account of all this, in order to add the same to the entry in the registry, together with the act of possession, which must immediately be given to the discoverer in the name of the government, measuring him his portion (pertenencias), and making him inclose it by stakes at the limits, as hereafter declared; after which an authentic copy of the proceedings shall be delivered to him as a corresponding title.

§ 1242. *Summary Trial.*—Art. 5. If, during the above ninety days, any one should appear asserting a right to the said discovery, a brief judicial hearing shall be granted, and judgment in favor of him who best proves his claim; however, if this should happen after the stated time, he (the new claimant) shall not be heard.

§ 1243. *Restorers of Ancient Mines.*—Art. 6. The restorers of ancient mines which have been abandoned and left to decay shall enjoy the same privileges as discoverers, of choosing and possessing three portions (pertenencias) in the principal vein, and one in each of the others, and both revivers and discoverers shall, as a special reward, be on all occasions preferred to other persons, under parity of circumstances.

§ 1244. *Who Considered Discoverer.*—Art. 7. If there arises any question as to who has been the first discoverer of a vein, he shall be considered as such who first found metal therein, even though others may have made an opening previously; and in case of further doubt, he who first gets it registered shall be considered as the discoverer.

§ 1245. *Denouncement of Abandoned Mines.*—Art. 8. Whoever shall denounce, in the terms hereafter expressed, any mine that has been deserted and abandoned, shall have his denouncement received, if he therein sets forth the circumstances declared in article 4 of this title, the actual existence of the mine in question, the name of its last possessor—if he is acquainted with the same—and those of the neighboring miners, all of whom shall be lawfully summoned; and if within ten days they do not appear, the denouncement shall be publicly declared on the three following Sundays; this meeting with no opposition, it shall be signified to the denouncer that within sixty days he must have cleared and reinstated some work of considerable depth, or at least of ten yards perpendicular, and within the sides of the vein, in order that the mining expert may inspect its course and inclination and all its peculiar circumstances, as is declared in the above-named article 4. The said expert should, if it be possible, examine the pits and works of the mine, and see if they are decayed, destroyed, or inundated; whether they contain a draft-pit or adit, or are capable of such; whether they have an ore-shed (galera), a whim (malacate), machines, rooms for habitation, and stables; and an account and register of all these circumstances must be entered in the corresponding book of denouncements, which should be kept separately. And the said examination being made, the portions (pertenencias) being measured and bounded by stakes in the ground, as shall hereafter be explained, possession of them shall be given to the denouncer without regard to any opposition, which can not be attended to unless made within the term before described; however, if during that time any opposition is brought forward, the parties shall have a brief judicial hearing, and the cause be determined accordingly.

§ 1246. *Opposition to Denouncement.*—Art. 9. If the former mine-owner should appear in order to oppose the denouncement, when the three public proclamations are over and while the denouncer is already enjoying the sixty days allowed for reinstating the pit of ten varas, he shall not be heard as to the possession, but only as to his right in the property, and if he succeeds in establishing this, he must make good the expenses incurred by the denouncer, unless the latter is proved to have acted fraudulently, in which case he must lose such expenses.

§ 1247. *Denouncer may Lose his Right, when.*—Art. 10. If the denouncer does not make or complete the shaft as prescribed, nor taken possession within the sixty days, he loses his right, and any other person has the power of denouncing the mine. If, however, owing to the ground being entirely broken up, or otherwise difficult and impracticable, or for any other real and serious obstacle, he has been unable to complete the same within the said sixty days, he must have recourse to the respective territorial (state) deputation, or other person having authority, when, his difficulties being examined and proved, the period may be prolonged for as long a time as the deputation, or person having authority, may think necessary for the purpose, and no more; no opposition to his claim being admitted after the ordinary term of sixty days.

§ 1248. *Denouncement of Forfeited Mine.*—Art. 11. If any one denounce a mine as forfeited, on account of the non-observance of any of these ordinances which bear that penalty, such claim shall be allowed him, provided he can lawfully establish any such cause of forfeiture.

§ 1249. *Former Possessor's Rights.*—Art. 12. If the former possessor of the mine, or any person claiming in right of him, shall declare the having left therein any exterior or movable works made at his expense, such as covering of outer courts (galeras), machines, or other things of this class, and of which the denouncer may usefully avail himself, he shall be paid for them according to the valuation of experts.

§ 1250. *Intermediate Spaces, Denouncement of.*—Art. 13. If any one shall denounce any intermediate space (demasia) in the vicinity of mines already occupied, it can be only granted him in case the owners of the adjoining mines, or any one of them, should not desire it for themselves; however, if these persons have not occupied it, or shall not do so within the time which the deputations (or other proper authority of that district), after considering the circumstances of the case, shall prescribe, it shall be adjudged to the denouncer.

§ 1251. *Denouncements may be Made on Any Property.*—Art. 14. Any one may discover and denounce a vein, or mine, not only on common land, but also on the property of any individual, provided he pays for the extent of surface above the same, and the damages which immediately ensue therefrom, according to the valuation of experts of both sides, and arbitration in case of disagreement; the same is to be understood with regard to denouncing convenient places for erecting establishments, and also waters for moving the machines employed for the reduction of ores, commonly called reducing establishments (haciendas), provided in each case that no more of the land or water be used than is necessary for such purposes.

§ 1252. *Denouncements in Towns.*—Art. 15.—If, however, any one denounces a mine or establishment (hacienda) within a town or village, whereby its principal edifices might be injured, or other similar inconvenience might arise, the denouncement shall not be admitted without previous application to the royal tribunal general of Mexico, in order that they, after consulting with the supreme government, may determine the case with all due prudence and circumspection.

§ 1253. *Haciendas may be Denounced.*—Art. 16. Any one may denounce the ancient site of an establishment (hacienda) without paying anything for the same, although there may be found thereon walls, drains, yard, washing places, furnaces, chimneys, dwelling-house, etc., provided they are totally deficient in roofs, machines, tools, and timber work; if these latter exist, the former proprietor must have notices sent him to re-establish, sell, or let them within the space of four months, and on his failure to do so, they shall be granted to the denouncer, on condition of his paying the said proprietor for useful movables according to the appraisement and judgment of experts.

§ 1254. *Two Contiguous Denouncements not Allowed—Exception.*—Art. 17. I prohibit any one (not being the discoverer) from denouncing two contiguous mines upon one and the same vein; but I permit any person to acquire and possess one by denouncement, and another or more by purchase, gift, inheritance, or other just title.

§ 1255. *Placers.*—Art. 18. Beds of ore (placeres) and all other depositories (criaderos) of gold and silver, on being discovered, shall be registered and denounced in the same manner as mines or veins, the same being understood of all species of metal.

§ 1256. *What may be Denounced.*—Art. 22. I likewise grant that in the prescribed form may be discovered, claimed, registered, and denounced not only mines of gold and silver, but also those of precious stones, copper, lead, tin, quicksilver, antimony, zinc, bismuth, rock-salt, or other fossils, whether perfect metals or half minerals, bitumen, or jugos de la tierra,[1] they being given to him for his enjoyment, benefit, and working, according to the particular circumstances of the cases. (The remainder not in force.)

## TITLE VII. OF PERSONS WHO MAY OR MAY NOT DISCOVER, DENOUNCE, AND WORK MINES.

§ 1257. *Employés can not Denounce, where.*—Art. 4. Nor shall administrators, stewards (mayordomos), watchmen (veladores), tallymen (rayadores), miners, or mine-keepers, and generally any servants or workmen of owners of mines, whether regularly or temporarily employed, register, denounce, or in any other manner acquire mines within a thousand varas around those of their masters (amos); but I permit them to denounce any mine for their said masters, although they have no authority from them, provided the latter shall ratify the denouncement within the terms prescribed in article 8, title 6 of these ordinances, without prejudice to the course of procedure.

§ 1258. *Fraud.*—Art. 5. No one shall denounce a mine under any circumstances of concealment or fraud for another, nor even publicly, unless he has his power or letter of attorney for that purpose, according to established usage.

§ 1259. *Partners Protected.*—Art. 6. Neither shall any one denounce a mine for himself alone, if he has previously had

---

[1] "Jugos de la tierra" is translated by Charles Thompson, and used by Rockwell in his work on Spanish and Mexican Law, as "other production of the earth;" and by Halleck as "mineral tar." The expression in the original with the prior word is "bitumenes ó jugos de la tierra." The word "bitumenes" is in the plural, and it is followed by the disjunctive particle "or," that marks an alternative corresponding to either; meaning either bitumen or "jugos de la tierra." The word "jugos" is also in the plural. The literal meaning of the word is juice or sap; hence indicating something in the nature of a liquid. Its signification from the sentence indicates that it has reference to anything analogous to bitumen. The derivation of bitumen is from the Greek *pitus*, the pine or pitch tree. The name of bitumen is assigned to several inflammable mineral substances, as mineral pitch, naphtha, mineral tar, asphaltum, elastic bitumen, etc. As the word "jugos" is used, as before said, in the plural, it means anything in the nature of tar, pitch, asphaltum, etc., which the earth produces. Thompson's translation is too extended, and that of Halleck too limited, unless it be said that "mineral tar" embraces all the substances in the nature of a liquid bitumen.

partners in the transaction; and I order that the denouncer shall declare his partners in his written statement, under penalty of losing his share thereof if he fail to do so.

TITLE VIII. OF PROPERTIES, AND INTERMEDIATE SPACES BETWEEN PROPERTIES BELONGING TO EITHER; AND OF THE MEASURES HENCEFORWARD TO BE USED IN THE MINES.

§ 1260. *Extent of Ground Granted.*—Art. 2. On the course and direction of the vein, whether gold, silver, or other metal, I grant to every miner, without any distinction in favor of the discoverer, whose reward has been already specified, two hundred varas, called measuring varas, taken on a level, as hitherto understood. (By the law of 1857, meters are used for varas.)

§ 1261. *Rules for Measurement.*—Art. 3. To make it what they call a square (cuadra), that is, making a right angle with the preceding measure, supposing the descent or inclination of the vein to be sufficiently shown by the opening or shaft of ten varas, the portion (pertenencia) shall be measured by the following rule:

§ 1262. *Perpendicular Veins.*—Art. 4. Where the vein is perpendicular to the horizon (a case which seldom occurs), a hundred level varas shall be measured on either side of the vein, or divided on both sides, as the miner may prefer.

§ 1263. *Inclined Veins.*—Art. 5. But where the vein is in an inclined direction, which is the most usual case, its greater or less degree of inclination (dip) shall be attended to in the following manner:

§ 1264. *Inclination of One Vara.*—Art. 6. If to one vara perpendicular the inclination be from three fingers (dedos) to two palms (palmos), the same hundred varas shall be allowed for the square, as in the case of the vein being perpendicular.

§ 1265. *Degrees of Inclination.*—Art. 7. If to the said perpendicular vara there be an inclination of—

| | | | | | | | |
|---|---|---|---|---|---|---|---|
| 2 | palms and | 3 | fingers, | the square | shall be of | 112½ | yards. |
| 2 | " | 6 | " | " | " | 125 | " |
| 2 | " | 9 | " | " | " | 137½ | " |
| 3 | " | 0 | " | " | " | 150 | " |
| 3 | " | 3 | " | " | " | 162½ | " |
| 3 | " | 6 | " | " | " | 175 | " |
| 3 | " | 9 | " | " | " | 187½ | " |
| 4 | " | 0 | " | " | " | 200 | " |

So that if to one perpendicular vara there correspond an inclination of four palms, which are equal to a vara, the miner shall be allowed two hundred varas on the square on the declivity of the vein, and so on with the rest.

§ 1266. *Two Hundred Varas Square not to be Exceeded.*—Art. 8. And supposing that in the prescribed manner any miner should reach the perpendicular depth of two hundred varas without exceeding the limits of his portion, by which he will commonly have much exhausted the vein, and that those veins which have greater inclination than vara for vara, that is to say, of forty-five degrees, are either barren or of little extent, it is my sovereign will that although the declivity (dip) may be greater than the above-mentioned measures, no one shall exceed the square of two hundred level varas; so that the same shall be always the breadth of the said veins extended over the length of the other two hundred varas as declared above.

§ 1267. *Veins of Contrary Direction.*—Art. 9. However, if any miner, suspecting a vein to run in a contrary direction to his own (which rarely happens), should choose to have some part of his square in a direction opposite to that of his principal vein, it may be granted to him, provided there shall be no injury or prejudice to a third person thereby.

§ 1268. *Placers and Pockets.*—Art. 10. With regard to the banks (placeres), pockets (rebosaderos), or any other accidental depositories of silver or gold, I order that the portions (pertenencias) and measures shall be regulated by the respective territorial deputations of miners, attention being paid to the extent and richness of the place, and to the number of applicants for the same, with distinction and preference only to the discoverers; but the said deputations must render an exact account thereof to the royal tribunal general of Mexico, who will resolve on the measures which they, in their judgment, may consider the most efficacious, in order to avoid all unfair dealing in these matters.

§ 1269. *Boundaries to be Defined.*—Art. 11. The portions (pertenencias) being regulated in the manner described above, the denouncer shall have his share measured at the time of taking possession of the mine, and he shall erect around his boundaries stakes or landmarks, such as shall be secure and easy to be distinguished, and enter into an obligation to keep and observe them forever without being able to change them; though he may allege that his vein varied in course or direction (which is an unlikely circumstance); but he must content himself with the lot which providence has decreed him, and enjoy it without disturbing his neighbors; if, however, he should have no neighbors, or if he can, without injury to his neighbors, make an improvement, by altering the stakes and boundaries, it may be permitted him in such case, with the previous intervention, cognizance, and authority of the deputation of the district, who shall cite and hear the parties, and determine whether the causes for such encroachment are legitimate.

§ 1270. *Boundaries to be Retained — When Extended.*— Art. 12. In the mines already opened and worked, the old measures of the portions (pertenencias) shall be retained; but they may be extended to the limits prescribed in these ordinances, whenever such change can take place without prejudice to third persons.

§ 1271. *Old Limits to be Observed.*—Art. 13. The immutability of the stakes or boundaries already defined in article 11 of this title shall also be observed henceforth in those mines which are in a course of working, or which shall be denounced as deserted or lost, the limits being ascertained in those cases where there are none at present, and each being attended to in its order, beginning with the oldest; and as to any intermediate spaces (demasias), they shall be regulated according to the provisions of article 13 of title 6.

§ 1272. *One Miner not to Enter the Property of Another.*— Art. 14. As it has been found that the license or permission of following a vein by working lower down and within the vein, and having enjoyment thereof until the owner himself has bored it, has been and is the most fruitful cause of bitter dissensions, litigations, and disturbances among the miners, and further considering that such intrusion is more generally the result of fraud or chance than of the merit and industry of the intruder, and that the consequences thereof occasion, for the most part, nothing but serious detriment to or the total ruin of the two mines and the two neighboring miners, to the great prejudice of the public and of my royal treasury, I order and command that no miner shall enter the property of another, even though merely by continuing his own vein at a greater depth; but that every one shall keep and observe his own boundaries, unless he makes an agreement and stipulation with his neighbor to be permitted to work in his property.

§ 1273. *Following a Vein into Another's Claim.*—Art. 15. But if any miner, pursuing his operations fairly, comes to the property of another while in pursuit of a vein which he is working, or discovers it at that time without the owner of the property being aware of its existence, he shall be obliged to give such proprietor immediate notice thereof; and the two neighbors shall thenceforward divide the costs and profits equally between them, one for the merit of discovery and the other as owner of the property, all which shall be observed until there shall be a communication effected between the mines, either by the principal vein or a cross-lode, or in any manner that may be most convenient; whereupon, after erecting a mutual boundary (guarda raya), each proprietor shall remain within his own boundaries. But if any one so discovering and following a lode into the property of his neighbor fails to give immediate notice thereof to such neighbor, he shall not only lose his right to the half of all the metal that may be extracted, but also shall pay double the value of what he has already extracted, it being understood that before exacting this penalty, fraud and misconduct of persons so encroaching must be proved in the plainest and most satisfactory manner, according to the form prescribed in title 3.

§ 1274. *Veins Extending beyond the Owner's Boundary.*—Art. 16. And in case a miner shall have advanced so much in his subterranean operations as to have passed beyond the limits of his own property, whether in length or width, I declare that he shall not on this account be obliged to turn back or suspend his work, provided the ground he has entered be unclaimed (terreno virgen) or within the limits of a deserted mine; he must, however, denounce this new property, which shall be granted him, observing always that such new portion must not exceed its former size, and that he must move his boundary marks to his new limits, in order that they may be generally known.

§ 1275. *Miners Entitled to All Veins within their Limits.*—Art. 17. The miner shall not only possess a portion of the principal vein which he denounced, but likewise of all those which, in any form or manner whatever, are to be found in his property; so that if a vein takes its rise in one property, and passing on terminates in another, each proprietor shall enjoy that part of it which passes through his particular limits, and no one shall be entitled to claim entire possession of a vein having its source in his portion, or on any other pretense whatever.

## TITLE IX. OF WORKING, SUPPORTING, AND PROTECTING THE MINES.

§ 1276. *Mines must be Kept in a Secure Manner.*—Art 1. It being of the greatest importance that the lives of workmen and other persons obliged continually to enter and go out of the mines should not be endangered, and that the mines should be kept in the state of security and convenience necessary to their being successfully worked, even although they may have been judged useless and impracticable by their first possessors, and abandoned accordingly; and it not being possible to establish any general and absolute rule on the subject, on account of the variety of circumstances of each mine, the greater or less hardness, tenacity, and adherence of the sides (respaldos), and of the substance of the vein itself; its greater or less inclination, width, and depth, inducing much diversity in the size and number of the pillars, arches, beams (testeras), cross-beams (intermedias), and other props which may be left or constructed to support the sides, and also in the distribution of the works necessary to proper ventilation and the convenient removal of the substances extracted from the mine; all which can not be effected without true practical skill and science in the working of mines, I order and command as follows:

§ 1277. *Assistance of Expert Required.*—Art. 2. It shall not be permitted to any one to work the mines without the assistance and direction of one of those able and intelligent experts, who are called in New Spain miners (mineros) or mine-watchers (guardaminas), who must have been examined, qualified, and approved by the mining professor (perito facultativo) appointed to be in every mine town or district, of whom mention will be made hereafter: Title 17, art. 1. However, in the very poor and remote mine-towns, where there may be neither mining professor nor qualified and approved expert, they may be allowed to proceed under the direction of the most accredited and intelligent surveyors who can be found there, until these or others shall be examined and licensed; the same being understood in all cases which require the direction or intervention of an expert, in order that, in judicial proceedings, they may meet with the confidence and credit they deserve.

§ 1278. *Mining Professors must Visit the Mines.*—Art. 3. For the design and conception of shafts (tiros), levels (contraminas), or adits (socabones), and the great and difficult works, which if they do not turn out successfully render useless the great expenses which have been bestowed upon them, the direction of one or more of the guardaminas shall not be sufficient, but the inspection or intervention of one of the aforesaid professors of mining shall be necessary, with the obligation on his part of visiting the work once every month, or once in two months, as the progress of it may require, in order that, if he perceives any error in the execution, he may amend it in time, and before it occasions further expense.

§ 1279. *Mines to be Secured and Supported with Timbers.*—Art. 4. In mines opened on veins of which the sides and interior substance are soft, and have so little tenacity or adhesive property that on being exposed to the air they molder away, and open into cracks and crevices, or which from any other causes are perceived to be insufficient by themselves to maintain the security and firmness of the mine, I order and command that the works shall be lined and secured with large solid timber of known durability, and such as is least liable to decay under ground, cut and prepared according to the rules of art; or with good masonry of stone and mortar, if the value and other circumstances of the mine permit or require it; for which purpose there must be in all the mining places, towns, and districts a certain number of these artificers, carpenters, and masons, who are called liners (ademadores), and these must have journeymen and apprentices, in order to preserve and continue the exercise of this important business, which ought to be well paid and encouraged.

§ 1280. *Experienced Men to be Employed.*—Art. 5. In order to prevent the introduction of artificers who have not the requisite experience and intelligence in subterranean architecture, none shall be admitted, in any place, who have not been examined and approved by the mining professor of that place or some other.

§ 1281. *Pillars, Removal of.*—Art. 6. If any miner, in consequence of the great richness of the metallic substance in his vein, is desirous of substituting for the pillars, beams, or sufficient and necessary supports, made of the metallic substance itself, others constructed with masonry of stone and mortar, he may be permitted to do so, under the inspection of one of the deputies of the district, assisted by the notary, and with the approbation of the mining professor.

§ 1282. *Supports not to be Weakened.*—Art. 7. I strictly prohibit any one from taking away, or in any degree weakening and diminishing the pillars, beams, and necessary supports of the mines, under pain of ten years imprisonment, to be inflicted according to the form prescribed by title 3 of these ordinances, by the respective judge in each case, upon any workman, searcher (buscon), or investigator (cateador), who shall have committed such offense, and the same upon the miner or mine-watcher who has permitted it; and the master of the mine shall lose the same, together with half of his property, and be forever excluded from all mining employments.[1]

§ 1283. *Mines to be Kept Clean, and Ventilated.*—Art. 8. I order and command that the mines shall be kept clean and unobstructed, and that the works necessary or useful for the circulation of air, the carriage and extraction of the metal, or other purposes, although they may contain no more metallic matter than such as may remain in the pillars and partitions (intermedias), shall not be encumbered with rubbish (atierres), and clods of earth (tepetates), but that all these must be carried out, and thrown by each person on the earth mound of his own property, but on no account upon that of another person, without his express leave and consent.

§ 1284. *Step-ladders must be Safe.*—Art. 9. In the mines there must be proper and safe steps or ladders, such and as many as are considered necessary by the mining expert, for the purpose of ascending and descending to the furthermost works, so that the lives of persons employed in the mines may never be endangered by their being weak, insecure, rotten, or much worn.

§ 1285. *Mines to be Visited and Made Secure if not so.*—Art. 10. In order to avoid the violation of the provisions of any of the articles contained in this title, it is my sovereign will that the deputies of the miners, accompanied by the mining professor of the district, and by the notary, if there be one, or in default of him, by two witnesses in aid, shall once in every six months, or once in every year, in places where the former is impracticable, visit all the mines in their jurisdiction which are in a course of actual working; and if they find any failure in the points referred to in the above-mentioned articles, or in any others whatever, which regard the security, preservation, and better working of the mines, shall provide immediately a remedy for such defect, and take means to assure themselves that such remedy is carried into effect. And if the remedy be not applied, or if the same failure shall occur again, the proper penalties must be exacted, multiplying and aggravating them even to the extent of dispossessing the person so offending, of the mine, which shall then belong to the first person who may denounce it; provided the deputies proceed in the form prescribed by title 3 of these ordinances.

§ 1286. *Water and Drainage.*—Art. 11. I most rigorously prohibit all persons from piercing through adits or cross-levels

[1] The above article in relation to punishment is evidently unconstitutional and void.

(cruceros), or other subterraneous passages, from works which are higher and full of water, or from leaving between them and others such slight supports as may allow the water to burst through; on the contrary, persons owning such works must have them drained by engines before they shall attempt to communicate with new ones, unless the mining professor should judge that such piercing through will not be attended with danger to the workmen engaged in it.

§ 1287. *Noxious Vapors.*—Also I prohibit all persons from introducing workmen into any works containing noxious vapors until they have been properly ventilated according to the rules of art.

§ 1288. *Failure to Work for More than Four Months—Forfeiture.*—Art. 13. Whereas the mines require incessant and continual working in order to procure the metals, certain operations being indispensable, which can not without much time be accomplished, and which, if interrupted, generally require as great expenses in their re-establishment as they did in their original undertaking; wherefore to remedy such inconvenience, and also to prevent owners of mines, who either can not or will not work them, from keeping them in a useless state for a length of time by pretending to work them, and thus depriving them of the real and effective labor which others might bestow upon them, I order and command that whosoever, during four successive months, shall fail to work any mine with at least four paid workmen (operarios rayados), occupied in some exterior or interior work of real utility, shall by so doing lose all his right in the said mine, which shall belong to any person denouncing it, upon his satisfactorily proving, according to the provisions of title 6, such act of desertion on the part of the owner.

§ 1289. *Four Months Time Construed.*—Art. 14. Experience having shown that the provisions of the preceding article have been eluded by the artful and fraudulent practice of some owners of mines who cause their mines to be worked during some days in each interval of four months, keeping them in this manner many years in their possession, I order that whosoever shall fail to work his mine in the manner prescribed by the said article during eight months in the year, counting from the day of his coming into possession, even though the said eight months should be interspersed with some days or weeks of labor, shall by such labor forfeit the mine; and it shall be adjudged to the first person who denounces the same, and satisfactorily proves this second species of desertion; unless for this or the one mentioned in the preceding article, there be just cause assigned, such as pestilence, famine, or war in that same mining place, or within twenty leagues thereof.

§ 1290. *Four Months Disuse not of Itself a Forfeiture.*—Art. 15. Considering that many miners who have formerly worked their mines with ardor and diligence, expending large sums in shafts, adits, and other undertakings, may often be obliged to suspend their operations while soliciting supplies, or for want of workmen, or necessary provisions, and other just and sufficient causes which, combined with their former merit, render them worthy of equitable consideration, I declare that any such mine-owner, keeping his mine in disuse in the manner and for the time above mentioned, shall not forfeit it at once in the manner described above, but his mine shall nevertheless be liable to denouncement before the respective new tribunals of miners, in order that both parties having been heard, and alleged merits and causes considered and proved, justice may be done between the parties.

§ 1291. *Notice of Abandonment to be Given.*—Art. 16. Since many miners abandon their mines, either for want of the capital necessary for carrying on operations therein, or because they do not choose to consume that which they may have already acquired from them, or because they have not spirit to venture on the difficultfes of those undertakings from which they have conceived great hopes, or for other causes; and since persons are not wanting who might be desirous of taking such mines if they were informed of their intended abandonment; and as it is much easier to maintain a mine when in a course of working than to reinstate it after it has suffered the injuries of time, it is my will that no person shall abandon the working of his mine or mines without making the deputation of the district acquainted therewith, in order that the deputation may publish the same by fixing notices on the doors of churches and other customary places for the information of all persons.

Art. 17. In order to avoid the false or equivocal reports which are often spread concerning deserted mines, the consequence of which reports is to augment the distrust in which this profession is ordinarily held, deterring many persons from engaging therein who do not otherwise want inclination to abandon it, I order:

§ 1292. *No One to Abandon without Giving Notice.*—Art. 18. That no one shall abandon the working of his mine without giving notice to the respective deputation, in order that an inspection may immediately be had thereof by the deputies, accompanied by the notary and experts, who must examine and measure the mine, particularizing all its circumstances, and draw up a map describing its plan and outlines, which, together with all the necessary information, must be preserved in the archives, with liberty of access to all persons who may wish to see them or to take a copy thereof.

### Title X. Of Drains in Mines.

§ 1293. *Mines must be Kept Drained.*—Art. 1. As in most of the mines, springs and currents frequently occur, whence the water issues continually, and in such abundance as might in a short time inundate and overwhelm the works, to the hinderance of all progress in the extraction of the metals, I desire and command that the owners of such mines shall keep their works constantly drained and evacuated, so that at all times the operations may be carried on and the metals extracted without interruption.

§ 1294. *Adits must be Made.*—Art. 2. As it is much the most convenient and least expensive method of draining to countermine (contraminar) the veins by means of adits, I order that in all those mines which require draining, and the situation of which will admit of it, and where benefit is likely to arise therefrom, according to the judgment of the mining professor of the district, the owners be obliged to make an adit sufficient for the draining and clearing of the works, provided the riches and abundance of the ores are likely to repay such expense.

§ 1295. *Expenses to be Divided among Those Benefited.*—Art. 3. Whereas several mines may sometimes be drained and cleared by one and the same adit, though each of them singly might be insufficient to support the expense thereof, I declare that the adit shall be made and completed, and the expense divided among all the proprietors in proportion to the benefit they will each derive from it; and if the proportion can not at the time be ascertained, the expense shall be divided among them in the mean time in equal parts, such parts being fixed according to the sum which the poorest of them can afford to pay; and should this one improve in condition, then the said parts shall be regulated according to what the poorest of the others can pay, so that the works of the adit may not be suspended; and all these points must be estimated and regulated by the deputation of the district, according to the judgment of the respective mining professor.

§ 1296. *Offers for Making Adits.*—Art. 4. If any individual should offer to make an adit by which one or more veins, or the mines opened in them, might be drained and cleared, although he be not the proprietor of any of them, either entirely or in part, his denouncement shall be received in due form, and immediate notice given to the owner of the said mines, who, if they will undertake such work themselves, are always to have the preference; but on their refusal, it shall be assigned to the adventurer under the following conditions:

§ 1297. *Adit Made according to Judgment of Mining Professor.* Art. 5. That the adit be really useful, and its formation practicable, according to the judgment of the mining professor, who must be charged with tracing out and determining the plan of the work, and directing its execution in the manner above expressed.

§ 1298. *Counter-mine.*—Art. 6. That the counter-mine shall be drawn, as far as it is possible, in a right line, and at the least possible distance from the vein or veins intended to be drained and cleared, or in the line and direction of one of them.

§ 1299. *Circulation of Air.*—Art. 7. That the necessary openings for the admission of air be constructed, or that a counter-level (contra canon) be made, or some other means adopted to preserve a free circulation of air for the health and advantage of the workmen.

§ 1300. *Judgment of Mining Professor as to the Adit.*—Art. 8. That its size (the size of the adit) must depend on the judgment of the mining professor, which will be regulated by circumstances; but that it shall never exceed two varas in width and three in height, and that it be properly secured and lined (ademado).

§ 1301. *Rights of an Adventurer.*—Art. 9. That if the adventurer, in the progress of this work, meets with one or more new veins, he shall therein enjoy the right of a discoverer, and the reward which is assigned to him as such by these ordinances; but if they are already known and opened in other places, I grant him the liberty of acquiring one portion (pertenencia) in each of them, and if there be not sufficient space remaining for that purpose, he shall have the enjoyment of all that may remain, until he enters upon the property of another.

§ 1302. *Deserted Mines.*—Art. 10. That if the work shall pass through any deserted mine, the adventurer shall thereby become owner of the same, and may denounce them as soon as he projects the work; it being understood that he should maintain these and his new portions during the progress of his operations as far as lies in his power. But I declare that as soon as his work is concluded he must have them distinctly portioned out, under the penalty of losing them, as before enjoined.

§ 1303. *Adits Running into Mines Occupied.*—Art. 11. And finally, that if the adit should pass through mines already occupied and situated in the direction of the vein, half of the metals thence extracted should belong to the adventurer and half to the owner of the property; but the costs are to be all defrayed by the adventurer; and he must not exceed in his adit the dimensions before prescribed, nor may he undertake any other works, unless with the consent of the owner, in which case the expenses must be divided between them. But if the adit should pass across the vein, the adventurer may open other works in pursuit of the same, and the metals, as well as the expenses, shall be divided equally between them, until there shall be some communication established with the works of the master of the mines, and if the adventurer does not give notice immediately on discovering the metal, he shall not only lose his right to the half thereof, but shall be obliged to make restitution of all he may have already extracted, and to pay double its value; proof of such fraud and malice having been previously made out, according to the form declared by title 3.

§ 1304. *Provisions of This Title, how Understood.*—Art. 12. All things contained in the present title, from the fifth article inclusive, with regard to adventurers, is likewise to be understood, as far as it is capable of being adapted, in cases where mine-owners shall be disposed to attempt the clearing of their own mines or those of others, by means of an adit or countermine in common, whether the work is undertaken by all jointly, or by some without the rest, or in company with adventurers; in all of which cases the stipulations which they have made must be punctually observed, provided they do not interfere with the injunctions and objects of these ordinances.

§ 1305. *Mines that do not Admit Adits.*—Art. 13. The owners of mines which require draining, but are in a situation which will not admit of the formation of an adit, must work them by means of a general and continued shaft, which in New Spain is called tiro, and serves by means of machines and engines to draw off the water, and extract the ore and other materials from the mines; and which must be made in such situation and of such dimensions, and be secured in such manner, as the mining professor of the district may determine and direct. And the territorial deputations are enjoined to take special notice concerning this matter in their visits, inflicting and increasing the corresponding penalties in proportion to the offenses which may be proved to have been committed.

§ 1306. *Shaft, how Made.*—Art. 14. Inasmuch as experience has shown the general utility of the above-mentioned works, as well as the omission and inattention by which they are sometimes made of a less depth than the other works, in order to avoid the expense of such undertakings, which become much more serious and expensive by the delay; and if the owners have not sufficient capital they are obliged to clear the lower works by interior drains, carrying up the water to the tiro, by means of engines moved by men, with great expense and little effect, and at times with an intolerable waste of human strength, I order and command that all owners of mines which require draining shall be obliged to make the base or foundation of the tiro deeper than the lowest works, so that sufficient support may remain for their being worked, and enough room in the tiro for the water; the observance of all which must be watched with particular care in the visits of the territorial deputation, the proper penalties being imposed, as enjoined in the preceding article.

§ 1307. *Draining the Lower Works.*—Art. 15. If any owner of mines requiring drains does not choose to keep them up, contenting himself with working in the upper parts of the mines which the inundation does not reach, and any person shall denounce the said mine or mines, offering to drain and clear the lower works, immediate information thereof shall be given to the owner, in order that if he be either unwilling or unable to drain them effectually, within the period of four months, they may be adjudged to the denouncer, he giving security for the expenses of the drain, according to the estimate of experts, and the satisfaction of the deputies of the district.

§ 1308. *Owners of Higher Mines.*—Art. 16. If the owner of any mine, of which the works are lower than those of the mines belonging to his neighbors, whether from its situation or from the circumstance of greater progress having been made in the works thereof, should be put to extraordinary expense by his neighbors not draining such higher mines, or draining them insufficiently, in such manner that the waters from the higher works shall descend upon the lower, I order and command that the owners of the higher mines shall keep up all the draining which they require; or on failure thereof, shall pay respectively to the owners of the lower mines, in silver or good money, the value of all the damage they may have sustained, estimated by experts, who shall first of all inquire and make all possible experiments to ascertain the real truth and circumstances of the case.

§ 1309. *Drainers of Desert Mines.*—Art. 17. To all persons who will take upon themselves the expense of draining and cleaning several mines, by making shafts (tiros) in common, or other works, and of constructing and maintaining costly machines (where an adit is not practicable), I grant the ownership of all the deserted mines and portions which they shall effectually clear, even though they may be contiguous, and upon one and the same vein; and I command that the viceroy, at the representation of the royal tribunal general of Mexico, shall dispense to them all the customary privileges, exemptions, and aids; but I declare that the owners of occupied mines, deriving benefit in any manner from such works, shall be obliged to contribute to the expenses of the same, only in proportion to the advantage their mines have received, according to the valuation of experts, with the approbation of the deputies of the district.

### Title XI. Of Mines Worked by Companies.

§ 1310. *Companies to be Encouraged.*—Art. 1. Inasmuch as mines are often worked by miners joined in companies, from the time of the denouncement of such mines, or according to contracts entered into subsequently in various ways, to the great advantage and improvement of the operations in mines, since it is much easier to engage therein where many persons unite together, each subscribing a part of his capital, and as where the wealth of one alone is not sufficient for great undertakings, that of a united company may be ample; in such cases, I desire and command that such companies, whether public or private, may be encouraged, promoted, and protected by all convenient measures, my viceroy granting to those who may form themselves into such companies every favor, aid, and exemption which can be granted them, according to the judgment and discretion of the royal tribunal of miners, and without detriment to the public or my royal treasury.

§ 1311. *Four Pertenencias Granted to Companies.*—Art. 2. Although by these ordinances I prohibit any individual miner working within the ordinary limits from denouncing two adjoining mines on the same vein, yet, notwithstanding, to those who work in companies, although they be not the discoverers, and without prejudice to the right which they might derive from becoming discoverers, I grant the right of denouncing four new portions (pertenencias), or four deserted mines, even though they should be contiguous and on the same course (rumbo).

§ 1312. *Barras.*—Art. 3. The accustomed usage in New Spain of dividing a mine into twenty-four imaginary equal parts, commonly called barras, subdividing also each of these into suitable smaller parts, shall continue to be observed, as heretofore, without any alteration.

§ 1313. *All Joint Owners of the Whole.*—Art. 4. Consequently no one of the partners may claim or have a right to work the part A, or any determinate part of the mine, or any other to work the part B, or place therein fixed numbers of workmen; but they must work in common, as far as it is possible, and make a division of expenses, by showing the amount of the same in equal proportions among all the partners, and there shall be the like division of the produce in metals of all kinds and qualities, whether in a rough state, or after they have been wrought, as may have been agreed upon by the parties.

§ 1314. *Questions Determined by Plurality of Vote.*—Art. 5. In order to avoid the disputes and differences which usually occur in mining companies about the direction of the works, applications for supplies, the administration, and other points connected with the operations, I order and command that all the measures necessary to be taken shall be determined by plurality of votes, with the intervention of one of the deputies of the district, who shall always endeavor to preserve harmony among the parties.

§ 1315. *Votes, how Counted.*—Art. 6. The votes shall be valued and counted according to the shares (barras) which each partner shall possess in the mine; so that if one or more shall be owners of one and the same share, they shall have only one vote, and he who holds two shares shall have two votes, and so on for the rest; but if one partner alone possesses twelve or more shares, the owner of such a number of shares shall have a number of votes less by one than half the number of such shares.

§ 1316. *Tie Vote.*—Art. 7. In all cases where any dispute may arise, either from an equality in the number of votes, or from any other cause, the mining deputy who shall preside at the junta or meeting shall decide the same as above declared, and I charge the said deputy to attend always to justice, and the common interest of all the partners.

§ 1317. *Refusal of Any One to Pay Expenses.*—Art. 8. If, in the course of operations, a mine should be worked which produces no profit, or which does not repay, either entirely or in part, the expenses which have been bestowed upon it, and any one of the partners does not choose to contribute his share of the expense, in this case the others shall give notice to the respective deputations, in order that the day may be noted down on which he ceased to contribute; and if he persist in this conduct during the continuance of four months, I declare thereby he forfeits, reckoning from the day on which he ceased to contribute, all his share in the mine, which shall go to increase the portions of those who have contributed their contributions, without any obligation on their part to denounce the same; but if, before the expiration of the four months, he shall contribute his share of the expenses, he shall be still a partner, provided he pays all arrears that shall have accrued from the time when he ceased to contribute, to the satisfaction of the parties concerned.

§ 1318. *Refusal to Pay for Dead Works.*—Art. 9. If, while any mine is in a course of profitable working, any partner should refuse to concur in the expenses of the dead works (faenas muertas) (established according to the forms before prescribed), upon the ground that such dead works would consume a part or the whole of the produce of the mine, the rest of the partners may retain and devote to this purpose a part or the whole of the produce which falls to his share.

§ 1319. *Each may Sell his Right.*—Art. 10. If one or more mines are worked by two partners, and they desire to break up the partnership, on account of disagreement or other cause, they shall not be reciprocally obliged to sell or buy their shares to or from one another, but each of them has the right of selling his share to a third person, giving his partner, however, the first offer thereof.

§ 1320. *Death does not Terminate the Company.*—Art. 11. The company is not be considered as broken up by the death of one of the partners; but the obligation devolves on his heirs, who have, however, the privilege of selling their share, according to the terms prescribed in the preceding article.

§ 1321. *Lesion Enorme does not Apply.*—Art. 12. If any share in a mine, or any entire mine, should be sold, after having been appraised and valued by experts according to its condition at the time of the sale, and it should afterwards become of great value, I declare that the sale shall not on that account be rescinded, on allegation of the great loss sustained (lesion enorme), nor on demand of being restored to his former situation (*i. e.*, on the part of the seller), nor of any similar privilege.

## Title XV.—Of the Contractors for Supplying Mines with Money and Other Articles.

§ 1322. *Supplies by Aviadores.*—Art. 1. It often happens that miners carry on the works in their mines with the capital of other persons, either because they have not at first sufficient funds of their own, or from having exhausted their own funds in various operations before the extraction of sufficient metal to make them a return, and in such cases they are in the habit of agreeing with contractors for supplies (aviadores), in one of two methods: either by letting the aviadores have the gold and silver which they may extract at a price somewhat below the real value, leaving the said aviadores the benefit of the difference, which method is called allowing a premium upon the metals (aviar á premios de platas); or by giving the aviador a share in the mine, making a perpetual proprietor thereof, or of the metals for a certain time, by a species of partnership; and whereas the necessities of the miners, and the facility of some of the aviadores, often lead to contracts which, being unjust or usurious, or ill understood from the beginning, or appealed against by one or other of the parties, give rise to litigation, which suspends the supplies, and occasions injury to the mines, and the loss of capital laid out upon them; it is my sovereign will and pleasure that no miner shall conclude any agreement for supplies without a regular signed contract, leaving it his option to complete the same or not, before a notary or witnesses; and no agreements that may be entered into without such signed contract shall be capable of being enforced, but such cases to be determined according to the general rules of law.

§ 1323. *Value of Metal to be Considered.*—Art. 2. In all agreements of the first-mentioned kind (á premios de plata), attention and consideration must be given to the number of marks[1] in each delivery, and how often such deliveries take place, so that if, through any accidental circumstances in the mine, the number of deliveries should increase or diminish considerably, either of the contracting parties may be allowed to increase or diminish the premium upon the metals, without violating the original contracts in other respects; for which purpose, in the instrument as originally drawn up, the number of annual deliveries shall be specified, and the number of marks in each delivery; or the parties, if they please, may renounce altogether any right to avail themselves of such accidents as are

[1] Eight ounces to a mark.

above mentioned, in which cases the original contracts shall remain in force for all purposes.

§ 1324. *Where Security is Given.*—Art. 3. If the miner shall secure the supplies (avios) up to a certain sum, either by deposit or security to the satisfaction of the contractor (aviador), the latter shall not receive in the way of premium more than would amount to five per cent per annum on the capital advanced.

§ 1325. *Supplies, how Furnished.*—Art. 4. The contractor (aviador) shall furnish the supplies in ready money, or in bills payable without discount or loss, or if the miner should prefer having goods and effects, such shall be delivered to him of a good quality, and in a good condition, and at the price at which they could be bought for ready money at the place where the contractor (aviador) resides, and in no other manner whatsoever.

§ 1326. *Transport of Supplies.*—Art. 5. Risks and accidents happening upon the road in the transport of supplies and the freight and excise duties payable upon the supplies shall be at the expense of the miner, where the contract is by premium upon the metals; but where the contract is in the way of partnership, such costs shall be at the expense of both, unless any other mode be particularly expressed in the deed of agreement.

§ 1327. *Mining Property only Liable for Supplies.*—Art. 6. In case of the capital supplied (caudal de avios) being entirely expended, or of a part of it not being covered by the remaining effects, the miner shall not be responsible for the same in his person nor in any other property which he may possess, excepting only that connected with the mine and the establishment (hacienda), supposing this latter to be erected out of the capital advanced; but the mine and the effects and profits thereof, after deducting the expenses, shall go to the payment of the contractors (aviadores), one after another, beginning with the last or most recent; it being understood, however, that this being a privilege granted by the law only to creditors who advanced second supplies for the restoring and refitting of mines, it is necessary that the three qualifications should all concur, in order to its being enjoyed; but if the miner, from actual necessity, shall abandon the mine, without any fraudulent intention, and having given notice thereof to the creditors, it shall not remain liable for former claims when it is in the hands of the new possessor; and it is further declared, that if the capital supplied to such mines, and in regard to which such deficiency occurs, has not been furnished in the way of partnership between the contractor (aviador) and miners, in which case the profit or loss is to be common between them, but in the way of loan, and the miner shall have made his property answerable, either by choice or because the contractor required it for greater security; under such circumstances the said obligation shall remain complete in all its parts, notwithstanding the general provisions of this article.

§ 1328. *Where No Agreement is Made for Supplies.*—Art. 7. If no agreement shall have been made at first as to the mode of securing the advances contracted for, when they are supplied in the way of premium upon the metal, the contractor (aviador) shall not require the same in any manner prejudicial to the miner in the working of his mine, by cutting off the supplies; nor shall he be obliged to receive back from the miner in small sums the supplies he may have advanced.

§ 1329. *Unobserved Mixture of Metal Discovered by Contractor Belongs to the Minor.*—Art. 8. Although the miner may not have observed at any time that his silver contains a mixture of gold, the separation of which from the silver would be expensive; or that there be silver amongst the gold of a baser quality, and the contractor should have discovered the same, either by assaying or other method; be it understood that the profit thereof shall not go to the said contractor, but shall be placed to the credit of the miner or proprietor of the metal, in the account kept between him and such contractor.

§ 1330. *Profits, how Divided.*—Art. 9. When the contract of supply is made in the way of partnership in the property of the mine, be it understood that the capital invested, until the time when there shall be a surplus profit over and above the expenses, is not to be immediately deducted from the profits, with preference to the contractor, but the profits are to be divided, the capital remaining so invested during the continuance of the partnership (mientras no se separe la compania).

Art. 10 not in force.

§ 1331. *Balances and Scales.*—Art. 11. Merchants of mining districts are required to keep a correct and light balance and scales; and gold and silver shall not be weighed with steelyards.

§ 1332. *Preservation of Tools.*—Art. 12. All the working mines must keep their tools and utensils marked, and if any one shall purchase them from any workman, or receive them in pledge, he shall pay for them double the value.

§ 1333. *Heating the Amalgam by the Contractor.*—Art. 13.

The aforesaid merchants and contractors may, for their satisfaction and that of the owner, heat the blocks or ingots of silver (mixed with quicksilver) over a charcoal fire, but not over a flame, or in any manner by which it might be reduced to a state of fusion, except in crucibles; and they may also be allowed to separate them so as to examine them within; but this must be done, as well as trying its quality, by heating it upon a counter, or in such manner that the owner may be able to collect and carry away all the waste and refuse fragments of his silver.

§ 1334. *Appointment of Inspector.*—Art. 14. Every contractor has the right of appointing at any time an inspector (interventor) to any miner whom he contracted to supply, although it be not so expressed in the contract; but be it understood that such interventor is only to attend to the correctness of the accounts, and to have power over the money and effects; but not to interfere with or obstruct the working of the mine, which belongs entirely to the miner; he may, however, defer the carrying on of the operations, by presenting an account to the deputies, requesting the appointment of experts, but this only in cases which will admit of such delay.

§ 1335. *Contractor's Neglect in Furnishing Supplies.*—Art. 15. Whereas the operations of mines in a course of working, particularly where they relate to the draining thereof, can not be impeded without great injury, I command that if the supplier advancing supplies from time to time shall neglect to provide them in such manner that at the proper time of paying the wages (rayas) there shall not be sufficient to pay them, and the miner, foreseeing this event, shall have called upon the contractor accordingly and given notice thereof to the deputation, then not only the wages shall be paid from what is best supplied to the mine, and even with the implements and utensils, but the miner shall be entitled to demand immediate execution against the contractor for what is due to him, and to apply for money to any other person, or treat with a new contractor (aviador), whose claim shall be preferred to that of the preceding one, whenever the mine begins to yield a profit.

§ 1336. *Misapplication of Supplies.*—Art. 16. Those who, under pretense of obtaining supplies (avios) for mines, shall in any way misapply the capital and effects furnished to them for that purpose, shall not only be bound in their person and all their property for the repayment of the same, and for all damages done or interest due to the party, without being allowed the privileges of miners or any other whatever, but shall be punished in manner suitable to the nature, heinousness, and circumstances of the offense; more particularly so if they shall have received the advances in confidence or trust, all this being regulated by the provisions of article 29 of title 3.

§ 1337. *Obtaining Supplies by Fraud.*—Art. 17. The triers of veins (cateadores), searchers (buscones), or operatives, and other persons who shall offer stones and specimens, falsely pretending that the same are the produce of a mine, thereby soliciting supplies for such supposed mine, with intent to defraud and deceive the unwary, shall be punished with all the rigor of the law, according to the circumstances, heinousness, and maliciousness of the offense, to be proved before the proper court, according to the provisions of article 29 of title 3 of these ordinances.

COAL MINES.

§ 1338. *Question of Titles.* The discoveries of coal mines within the last few years have presented, and will doubtless in the future present many important questions of law. The main question which will arise, and which already has arisen, is, whether the denouncer of a coal mine on the land of another can be the owner of the mine, contrary to the will and consent of the proprietor of the land upon which the mine is found. In short, does the mining ordinance govern coal mines? To determine this question, it becomes necessary to examine critically the language of the said ordinance, and the subsequent legislation, decrees, cédulas, and orders.

First. Article 22, title 6, of said ordinance, is the principal part thereof bearing upon the question. So much thereof as is essential is as follows:

§ 1339. *Substances to be Denounced.*—"I likewise grant that in the prescribed form may be discovered, claimed, registered, and denounced, not only mines of gold and silver, but also those of precious stones, copper, lead, tin, quicksilver, antimony, zinc, bismuth, rock salt, or other fossils, whether perfect or mixed metals, bitumen or other production of the earth, the denouncers thereof receiving grants of the same, according to the circumstances." A royal order of the twenty-eighth of November, and cédula of the twenty-sixth of December, 1789, became law 2, title 20, book 9, of the Novisima Recopilacion. It reads as follows, so far as it bears on the question of coal rights: "In order to remove the difficulties which have occurred in the use of the minerals of coal, and to simplify the method of working them without prejudice to the proprietors and with public utility, I have resolved to declare and order as a fixed and general rule the following:

§ 1340. *Coal not a Metal.*—"1. Coal not being a metal nor semimetal, nor of any of the other things comprehended within the laws and ordinances which declare the mines the property of the royal patrimony, the working thereof shall be free, and its traffic by sea and land for all the kingdom, and its extraction, shall not be impeded in order to trade with it in foreign countries."

§ 1341. *Proprietors of Land, Owners of Coal Mines.*—"2. These mines ought to belong to the proprietors of the lands where they are, it being understood by proprietor the owner of the fee, and not the lessee or emphyteuta; without the necessity of asking any justice or tribunal in order to work them, rent, or sell them; but once being discovered, if the proprietor should refuse to use his property in any of the said modes, in order to have the effect of working them follow, my council and intendente of the province, or the corregidor of the partido (county), shall have the power to adjudicate the working thereof to the discoverer, the latter giving the proprietor the fifth part of the product thereof."

§ 1342. *Owners of Land may Rent or Sell the Mines.*—The royal cedula of the twenty-fourth of August, 1792, declared: "That the owners in fee of lands where there may be coal mines, whether they be councils, communities, or private individuals, can discover, work, and beneficiate for themselves, or permit others to do so, by renting or selling them according to their discretion, without any more license or formality than that which is necessary to work, lease, or sell the land which contains them."

§ 1343. *Coal Mines Considered as Other Products of the Land.*—Also the royal cedula of the fifth of August, 1793, which reproduced the same provision, explaining it in the sense that "the usufruct and profits of the mines of coal ought to belong to the council, parish, place, community, or person to whom should belong the usufruct and profits of the other things which the land produces in which the mines are found, without any difference."

Both of the foregoing cedulas are subsequent in date to that of the mining ordinance; and they form laws 4 and 5 of title 20, book 9, of the Novisima Recopilacion.

§ 1344. *Decree of Juarez*, 1863.—On the twenty-second of August, 1863, the president of the republic declared, in San

Luis Potosi, "that the veins of coal are subject to the same proceedings which the mining ordinances establish for the denouncement, adjudication, and possession of mines."

§ 1345. *Case of Garza* v. *Milmo.*—As has been observed herein, that an important question has arisen relative to the title to coal mines, and the question has been already ventilated before the courts of the country. Don Abraham de la Garza, for himself and in representation of other persons, denounced a vein of coal existing on the hacienda of the "Alamo," which, although undivided, belongs in its greater part to Don Patricio Milmo. The latter opposed the denouncement before the judge of Monclova, state of Coahuila, alleging that the veins of coal belong to the owner of the ground in which they are found. The judge decided, on the twenty-fifth of June, 1881, in favor of the denouncer, and on the twenty-seventh of said month ordered him to be placed in possession of the mine.

On the second of the following July the delivery of the possession took place. Milmo sued out a writ of protection (amparo) before the federal district judge of Coahuila, alleging that the article 27 of the federal constitution had been violated, and that the compiled laws were in derogation of that part of the mining ordinance relating to the subject. The district judge decreed the protection. The denouncers appealed to the supreme court of justice of the union. On a review of the case, the supreme court reversed the decision of the judge below, holding that the owner of the land was not the owner of the mine discovered thereon by another party. The judgment of the court was rendered on the first day of July, 1882, and is as follows:

Mexico, July 1, 1882. Having examined the trial of amparo, moved in the district court of Coahuila, by Manuel Z. de la Garza, attorney, in representation of Patricio Milmo, against the resolutions which on the twenty-fifth and twenty-seventh of June, of the year last past, the judge of first instance of Monclova dictated, relative to a vein of coal situated on the lands belonging to the complainant, denounced by Abraham de la Garza and associates; by which acts the mover believes that the guaranties assigned in articles 14, 16, and 27, of the federal constitution have been violated as to the person represented by him:

The judgment of the district judge, dated the nineteenth of December last, having been examined, in which protection was conceded against the decree which the judge of first instance of Monclova dictated on the twenty-fifth of June, 1881, declaring that the opposition to the denouncement of the vein of which reference has been made, had no grounds, and against the act by which possession was ordered to be given of the said vein to the denouncers.

It resulting: That Abraham de la Garza and other persons denounced before the judge of Monclova a vein of coal, situated on the lands of the hacienda de los Alamos; that to this denouncement Milmo was opposed as proprietor of the land; the trial of opposition was summarily prosecuted on the twenty-fifth of June, 1881, and the claim of Milmo was rejected; that on the date of the twenty-seventh of said month and year possession was ordered to be given to the denouncers, which proceedings were carried into effect on the second of the following July; it being stated therein that the act of possession was without prejudice to third parties, and with that of indemnification for the land to those who may be the owners.

It resulting: That against these acts has been interposed the present recourse, Milmo alleging to found it: 1. That the trial was prosecuted in a summary way, when it ought to have been in the ordinary way, as by that manner he was deprived of the ample defense which he might have used in the second case; that the act of possession was determined and executed without his citation and audience; and 2. That having the fee in the vein denounced, in conformity with laws 3, 4, and 5, title 20, book 9, of the Novisima Recopilacion, which are in force in the matter, and not the mining ordinance, the adjudication could not be made without taking it by expropriation[1] from that dominion; adding that he does not recognize in the judge competent jurisdiction to dictate that expropriation, not even when the interest is reputed public; and,

Considering first: That in the decree claimed of the twenty-fifth of June, 1881, the guaranty which the second part of articlo 14 of the constitution grants was not violated, because, as well from the literal text as from the spirit thereof, it is rightly deduced that it does not refer to the exact application of the laws in trials of civil order, but in those of the criminal: 1. Because the pronoun "nobody" and the words "tried" and "sentenced" can only be relative to persons; 2. Because if it is a guaranty that no accused can be sentenced by analogy, by a greater reason, etc., it is not that in civil cases the judicial arbitration can not be used, without which the administration of jus-

[1] Taking the property under the right of eminent domain.

tice in civil matters would be impossible; 3. That this interpretation is fully proved by the order in which the fractions of article 14 were discussed, which in the project (or bill) of the constitution were articles 4 and 16 (Garco, History of the Constituent Congress, vol. 1, pages 417 and 695); and 4. That the federal tribunals can not, without attacking the independence of the judicial power, convert themselves into revisers of the acts of all the civil tribunals, which would also be a violation of the sovereignty of the states in their internal régime, as the supreme court has resolved in many final decisions.

Considering second: That also it is decided in various final judgments that article 16 has no application in trials merely civil, under the pretext that the judge does not establish and give reasons for his proceedings who does not apply the law well, because the same reasons which persuade that article 14 can not be applied to those trials, equally convince that the sixteenth article has not that construction, because the error, abuse, or fault of a judge is only the infraction of a civil law, and not the violation of the fundamental law; and finally, because it would be absurd that this article should convert all civil questions into constitutional ones, by the sole fact that a litigant should believe that a law had not been well interpreted.

Considering third: That although the doctrine that the amparo had no place in civil trials for the bad application or interpretation of the laws, it permits some exceptions, as when therein a real individual guaranty is violated, obliging a man to render personal service against his will, giving the laws retroactive effect, etc. The present case is not comprehended in those exceptions, it being supposed that the mover makes the violation of the guaranty consist in this, that the judge of Monclova applied in his judgment a repealed law, as in the opinion of the mover the mining ordinance is, by which his proceedings are not established with reason; because far from constituting that act such a violation, it is no more than the exercise of the attributions of a judge who, in the cases which he decides, has to declare according to his criterion, and under his responsibility, which is the law in force, and which is repealed between two which are presented in conflict; because article 16 does not confer on the federal tribunals the exclusive power of making that declaration, thus amplifying their jurisdiction even against the independence of the ordinary tribunals, and reducing the jurisdiction of the latter even to the nullification thereof; and lastly, because nobody can affirm that the interpretation of the civil law is always and in all cases a constitutional question.

Considering fourth: That even supposing that the decision on the force of the ordinance, in spite of the provisions of the compiled laws, may assume a constitutional character by virtue of the subterraneous property being defined in a sense contrary to those laws, and that this once accepted with the extension which the compiled laws give it, the denouncement which the ordinance permits is an attempt against that property so defined. Even on that hypothesis, the present writ of protection (amparo) would lack foundation, because it is not certain that these laws have repealed our mining code; because they being dictated exclusively for the Spanish peninsula, accordingly as is seen in their own text, they were never applied to Mexico during Spanish domination, nor was it pretended at any time that they had repealed the ordinances specially issued for New Spain; because, after the independence, the general opinion has been that this code was not modified by those laws, and it has always been applied to the veins of pit coal; because the same jurisconsult who has pretended to affirm the contrary opinion, not only contradicts that general opinion which has always existed, but his own, since that, in the publication which he made of the Spanish laws in force in Mexico, he suppressed, as repealed, all the recopilacions which refer to coal mines; and because, finally, our legislators have always considered these mines subject to the ordinances.

Considering fifth: That in respect to the act in which, without previous indemnification, possession of the land was given in which the vein denounced was found, it results that article 27 of the constitution was violated, since although it is indispensable before the indemnification to fix the value of the land, to authorize the preparatory proceedings, as the measuring of the pertenencias, the designation of the superficial part of the ground which the denouncer requires for the working of his mine, the appointment of experts, etc., never, nor for any reason, can any one be deprived of his possession without that previous indemnification, in conformity with the prescription in said article.

For these considerations, and according to articles 101 and 102 of the general constitution, the judgment of the district judge is modified in the following terms:

1. The justice of the union does not sustain nor protect Patricio Milmo, represented in this trial by his attorney, Manuel

Z. de la Garza, against the decree of the judge of first instance of Monclova, by which he declared denounceable the vein of coal situated on the land of the complainant.

2. The justice of the union sustains and protects the complainant against the act of the said judge, who without previous indemnification, gave possession of the superficial land in which the denounced vein is; consequently, all the acts prior to that of possession are valid and will remain.

Let the proceedings be returned to the original court, with a certified copy of this judgment, for their legal effects; and the proceedings on appeal be published and registered.

Thus, by a majority of votes as to the first point, and by a unanimity as to the second, the chief justice and magistrates who formed the full bench of the supreme court of justice of the Mexican United States decreed and signed. I. L. Vallarta, Manuel Alas, Miguel Blanco, José Maria Bautista, Eleuterio Avila, Jesus Maria Vasquez Palacios, M. Contreras, M. Auza, Guillermo Valle, F. J. Corona, José Eligio Muñoz, Eduardo Ruiz. Enrique Landa, Secretary.

§ 1346. *Case of A. Diaz.*—The same question arose subsequently as to the several rights of the owner of the soil and the denouncer of coal mines in the case of Alberto Diaz and Ignacio E. de Betancourt, against the order dictated by the governor of the state of Michoacan, on appeal from the district court of that state. The governor declared that coal mines belonged to the owner of the soil in which they were discovered. The supreme court, on the fifth of August, 1882, held in this case the same views as in the preceding one. It will be observed that the magistrates were not unanimous in their opinions.

§ 1347. *Amparo.*—By article 102 of the federal constitution, the judgment in a case of amparo is limited to the case in which it is rendered, and the court can give therein no general declaration in regard to the laws brought in question.

§ 1348. *Diversity of Opinion.*—There have been considerable diversity of opinion and much ingenious speculation on this important question of the relative rights to coal mines. In the first case cited, Chief Justice Vallarta gave his views in a very lengthy opinion, which, however, in the humble opinion of the compiler of this work, are not tenable.

§ 1349. *Reasons of the Court.*—The reason assigned by the court, and the main one expressed by the chief justice, is, that the laws of the Novisima Recopilacion, which had not been communicated and promulgated in New Spain, had no application to this country. That the mining ordinance had been promulgated here, and that they were not repealed or modified by any law of said recopilation, which had not been so promulgated.

He assigns as another reason why the said laws are not applicable to Mexico, that they show on their face that the king did not so intend them. In support thereof, he quotes the following language: "Bearing in mind the abundance of coal mines which there are in these dominions, and the considerable advantages which may result to my vassals from the working thereof, on account of the scarcity of forests and the increase in the consumption of wood which every day experiences in the manufactures and towns which are increasing, coal for this reason may be counted among the commodities of first necessity," etc. The chief justice asks if there can be any doubt that the king referred alone to Spain, when it was a well-known fact that coal had not been discovered in Mexico, and that then there was sufficient wood, and no manufactures.

§ 1350. *Various Possessions of the Sovereign.*—It was absolutely impossible for the king to foresee where and when coal would be discovered in his various possessions, and when and where the same reasons would as justly apply as to Spain proper. Why, then, should he favor his home subjects by declaring the proprietors of land there to be likewise the owner of the coal discovered therein?

§ 1351. *Inducements of the Sovereigns.*—The various sovereigns of Spain had held out inducements to their home subjects to immigrate to New Spain in order that the vast extent of wild domain there might become settled; and in recompense therefor gave them extensive grants of land. Is it possible to suppose that those new settlers who had battled with the elements were to be denied the rights granted to the home subjects? Certainly not.

§ 1352. *Fossils.*—The chief justice also cited the opinions of several scientific men to show what coal was; that the word "fossil" used in the ordinance embraced minerals, and that the words therein, "all other fossils," were equivalent to "all other minerals," including mineral coal.

§ 1353. *Meaning Declared by the Sovereign.*—May it not with reason be asked, of what avail can the opinion of scientific men be, on the signification of terms, when the law-maker declared the meaning thereof, in connection with the proprietary rights pertaining to the subject-matter?

§ 1354. *Charles III.*—The chief justice suggests that Charles III. was led into an error by his counselors in regard to the signification of terms. The king had time for reflection, as he evinced the same opinion in laws 2, 3, 4, and 5, title 20, book 9, of the Novisima Recopilacion, which are composed of cédulas of different dates. But it can hardly be credited that the king was ignorant of his own act when he declared that the proprietor of the soil ought to be the owner of the coal mines found therein.

§ 1355. *Coal not Included in the Ordinances.*—The king not only decreed that coal was not a metal nor semi-metal, but that it was none of the things comprehended in the laws and ordinances which declare the mines to be the property of the royal patrimony. Now does not this alone settle the question? The mining ordinance of 1783, promulgated in Mexico, January, 15, 1784, declares in article 1, title 5: "The mines are the property of my royal crown, as well by their nature and origin as by their reunion, declared by the fourth law of the thirteenth title of the sixth book of the new compilation (of laws and statutes)." Coal is none of the things comprehended in the ordinances, said the king. How can the said ordinance be construed to embrace coal, when the king declared to the contrary?

§ 1356. *Novisima Recopilacion.*—Another point seems fatal to the doctrine laid down by the supreme court. Whether the foregoing laws of the Novisima Recopilacion became of universal application in all of the possessions of the king or not, by being inserted in said recopilacion, they were royal cédulas, in which the king, who was vested with the power of making and interpreting laws, did therein interpret the language of the then existing mining laws. Can it be possible for a court of judicature to solemnly declare that when a sovereign, acting within the sphere of his powers, places an interpretation upon certain phraseology, that interpretation is not to be received as legal and valid upon the same phraseology in every land within the territorial jurisdiction of that sovereign? These royal declarations were not to be considered as new laws merely, but valid interpretations of former ones.

§ 1357. *Manner of Interpreting Laws.*—Under the civil and Spanish law there were three ways of interpreting laws, namely, the authentic, usual, and doctrinal. The authentic is that which the same legislator makes, who is the only one that has authority to solve the doubts and fix the sense of the words by means of a decision which shall be obligatory for all: Law 14, title 1, partida 1; and law 3, title 2, book 3, Novisima Recopilacion. It would seem that the words "shall be obligatory for all" mean for all persons under the control and jurisdiction of the sovereign who made the laws.

§ 1358. *Novisima Recopilacion—What Force in Mexico.*—In Mexico, there is a question of great importance, which is still an open one; and that is, whether the civil laws embraced within the Novisima Recopilacion (compiled in 1805) were and are in force in this country, by the mere fact of being compiled therein as a code of general observance; or was it essential for that purpose and effect that all the laws made by the king should have been communicated by his authority to the viceroy, to be promulgated by the latter in his viceroyalty? The supreme court of the union has never settled the question fully, but did decide in the case of Milmo, *supra*, that it was necessary in that case.[1] Eminent jurists and legislators have been and are arrayed on both sides of the question. If the views hereinbefore expressed by the compiler be correct, it would seem that the question of the promulgation of the said laws was not altogether essential in order to determine the relative rights to coal mines as between the proprietor of the soil and the denouncer.

§ 1359. *Decree of Juarez*, 1863.—As to the decree of Juarez in August, 1863, it is held, at least by many, that the extraordinary powers which he claimed were vested in him to repel the French invasion did not warrant him in legislating on a subject so foreign to those extraordinary powers. And if the coal mines by previous legislation had become vested in the proprietor of the land the decree of Juarez could hardly deprive them of that right. And further, as the supreme court of the union has decided that the several states have the power to legislate on the subject of mines, the decree of Juarez must necessarily have no effect.

The state of Coahuila has availed itself of the doctrine laid down by the supreme court through its congress by the enactment of a law on coal mines.[2]

---

[1] In case of an amparo, the decision does not extend beyond the case in which it is rendered.

[2] Evaristo Madero, constitutional governor of the free and sovereign state of Coahuila de Zaragoza, to the inhabitants thereof, know ye: That the congress of the same has decreed the following:

The seventh constitutional congress of the free, independent, and sovereign state of Coahuila de Zaragoza decrees, No. 478:

Art. 1. The decree of February 25, 1828, and the mining ordinances, in the part which declares coal mines denounceable, are repealed.

Art. 2. The horizontal veins or tables (mantos) of coal (ulleras), peats (turbas), criaderas, or deposits of petroleum and mineral coal which may be discovered, shall be the private

§ 1360. *Coahuila.*—It thus appears, that so far as the state of Coahuila is concerned, the owners of land therein are the owners of the coal which may be contained therein. This is the only state which has passed such a law.

§ 1361. *Federal Constitution Amended.*—Since the passage of said law the federal constitution has been amended, so as to vest the power in the federal congress, to enact laws governing the mineral wealth of the republic.

It is expected that a federal mining code will be made in virtue of said amendment. It is not difficult to foresee that the titles to coal mines may present in the future important questions for solution.

This subject has been treated of only in limited manner by writers on the civil law of Mexico. It is, indeed, one of modern growth, and can not be said to be defined with entire accuracy. And we must likewise remember that precedents, neither in the courts of continental Europe nor in those of Spanish America, have the same force and authority as in the courts of England and of the United States.

---

property of the owner of the soil in which they may be found.

Art. 3. From the net products which the owners of carboniferous lands shall obtain by the working of this combustible and of petroleum, the state shall receive five per cent, in the character of an impost, to pay the expenses of public administration. If the working should be made by the said owner of the land, the product of the capital shall be taken as a basis for the collection of this impost, considering it as worked by the means of a pension, contract, or rent, according to the custom.

Art. 4. The executive shall regulate the manner of receiving the five per cent of which the preceding article treats, conciliating the fiscal interests with those of the private individuals who may put in working operation their veins of fossil coal or petroleum.

Art. 5. The denouncers and grantees of coal mines who, prior to this law, shall have acquired definite rights, but who may have incurred or shall incur any of the faults of not taking possession in a legitimate manner, abandonment of work, defect of work, or others of those which the ordinance determines as sufficient for the forfeiture of the right acquired, shall lose the dominion of the pertenencias of land which was conceded to them, and it shall return to the former owner of the soil, without the mines being in the future the object of denouncement.

Given in the hall of sessions of the congress of the state, in Saltillo, on the twenty-fifth of August, 1882. J. Juan Rodriguez, deputy president. E. Davila, deputy secretary. R. Azuela, deputy secretary.

Wherefore I order it to be printed, published, circulated, and that due compliance be given it. Palace of the government, in Saltillo, on the twenty-fifth of August, 1882. Evaristo Madero. Julio Martinez, chief secretary.

# PART SECOND.

## OF INDIVIDUAL RIGHTS, UNDER SPAIN AND MEXICO, RELATIVE TO REAL PROPERTY, PRIOR TO THE CODE OF 1871.

---

## CHAPTER I.

### WATER AND RIPARIAN RIGHTS.

§ 1362. Spanish Law.
§ 1363. Ordinances of Lands and Waters.
§ 1364. Opinions of Escriche.
§ 1365. The Laws, where Found.
§ 1366. Civil Code.
§ 1367. Contents of Chapters 5 and 6.
§ 1368. Manner of Treating the Subject.
§ 1369. Lower Estates.
§ 1370. Upper Estates.
§ 1371. Application of the Laws—To What Waters.
§ 1372. Rain-water on Upper Estates.
§ 1373. Lower Estates.
§ 1374. Obligations of Owner of Lower Estate.
§ 1375. Upper Proprietor can not Change Natural Descent of Water.
§ 1376. Springs.
§ 1377. Ponds Formed by Rains.
§ 1378. Damages by Constructions on Lower Estates.
§ 1379. Rights of Proprietor.
§ 1380. Exceptions to the Rule.
§ 1381. Third Parties.
§ 1382. Prescription.
§ 1383. Fountains.
§ 1384. Service not Sold without the Estate.
§ 1385. Not Necessary that the two Estates should Join.
§ 1386. Aqueducts.
§ 1387. Second Exception.
§ 1388. Public Water.
§ 1389. Municipal Law.
§ 1390. Water Running from Springs.
§ 1391. Water Running between Estates.
§ 1392. Owner of Both Banks.

§ 1362. *Spanish Law.*—This part contains the laws of Spain which continued in force in Mexico, until the adoption of the civil code, March 1, 1871, pertaining to real estate; that is to say, the laws which are deemed essential for this work. As but a few years have elapsed since the adoption of the civil code by the several states, it must necessarily follow that many rights have grown up which had their origin under the old Spanish laws. Having thus had their origin, any question which may arise pertaining to the legal construction of those rights must be interpreted by those same laws. Hence their title to a place herein.

§ 1363. *Ordinances of Lands and Waters.*—The ordinances of land and water (ordenanzas de tierras y aguas) are not laws or decrees, and have no binding effect. They are nothing more than the opinions of learned jurisconsults, wherein the various laws pertaining to land and water are cited and explained. They are what the civilians call doctrines (doctrinas), or opinions, which may be followed or not by a judge or court, as the latter may think proper. In other words, they are but the opinions of commentators. These ordinances will be found published separately, and also in the work of Escriche, a dictionary of legislation and jurisprudence, of great value and reputation, and considered of standard authority, when not found in conflict with the laws themselves.

§ 1364. *Opinions of Escriche.*—As to water rights, I have given herein the laws themselves relating to the subject; and also the opinions of Escriche, taken from the following heads:

"Water" (agua), "Ditch" (acequia), "River" (rio), and "Shore or Bank" (ribera). In his opinions he cites the laws, herein found, which support his views. His opinion under the head of "Water" may be of value in the construction of water rights, under both the old Spanish and modern Mexican law. For he lays down what he considers the principles of natural justice and equity which ought to govern in the absence of positive law or custom.

§ 1365. *The Laws where Found.*—The laws on this subject are to be found in titles 31 and 32, of partidas 3, under the head of "Service," chapter 2, and "New Works," chapter 3, herein; also in the Novisima Recopilacion, and referred to herein.

§ 1366. *Civil Code.*—The laws relating to this subject now in force will be found in part 3, taken from the civil code; that is, so far as the former are repealed. Chapter 4 embraces the law as to things which may be acquired and how they are acquired.

§ 1367. *Contents of Chapters* 5 *and* 6.—Chapter 5 states the law of sale and purchase. Chapter 6 contains the law on limitation or prescription.

## WATER.

§ 1368. *Manner of Treating the Subject.*—Water is the liquid substance of which the seas, rivers, streams, springs, ponds, and lakes are formed. As water on the one hand is capable of occasioning grave damage, and on the other is the blood of the earth and the life of the fields, it gives place to questions of much importance for agriculture, which we are going to develop in this article, treating first of the service or burden which lower estates have to receive the waters which naturally come down from the estates above; in the second place, of the right which one proprietor has over the water which rises on his land; in the third, of the waters which belong to the public; and in the fourth, of the use of the waters which pass between the banks or through an estate.

### I. Of the Service or Charge Which Lower Estates have to Receive the Waters from Upper Ones.

§ 1369. *Lower Estates.*—Lower estates have the service or burden to receive the waters, stones, and earth which naturally and without the intervention of hand of man run or come down from higher ones, without the owners of the former having any right to require of those of the latter any compensation for the damages which the waters shall occasion them: Law 14, title 32, partidas 3. The owner of the lower estate can not raise the wall, fence, inclosure, nor any other dike which may impede the current and cause the water to flow back, to the damage of the upper estate or to any intermediate field; and in case of a contravention, he will have to tear down the works at his cost and satisfy the damages which by the cause of them shall have been originated: Law 13, title 32, partidas 3.

§ 1370. *Upper Estates.*—The owner of the upper estate can not do anything to increase the service of the estate below, so that he will incur the said penalty of tearing down the work and of paying the damages in case of contravention; since "although a man has the power to do what he pleases upon his own ground, yet he ought to do it in such a manner as to cause no damage or harm to any other person:" Laws 13, 14, title 32, partidas 3.

§ 1371. *Application of the Law, to What Waters.*—These provisions, which our legislation has taken from the title of the digest, "De aqua et aquæ pluviæ arcendæ," ought to be applied, not only to the rain-waters and those which come from infiltration or proceed from the melting of the snows, but also to the running waters which run from the upper to the lower estates by the act of nature or of time; but not to the waters of domestic service, nor to those which are drawn or united by artificial means, nor even to those rain-waters which fall on the roofs, because in all these the hand of man has intervened. The law 2, title 13, and law 13, title 32, partidas 3, mean that every proprietor shall arrange his roofs in such a manner that the rain-waters shall fall and run on his own land or on the public road, and not on the edifice or land of his neighbor, unless that he shall acquire this service.

§ 1372. *Rain-water on Upper Estates.*—The owner of the upper estate can retain on it the rain-waters and others similar, in order to give them the destination which most suits him, although the owner of the lower estate should have always availed himself of them, and should have opened a ditch or made any other work to receive them and give them direction through his field, unless the latter should have a title constitutive of service which would give him the right to take them on going out of the upper estate, because the service or subjection of the lower estate to receive the waters of the upper one is found generally established in favor of the latter, the owner of which may renounce it, and because prescription does not run in respect to said waters; since it must be supposed, if the owner has not retained them formerly, it was only by considering them useless then, and in use of the power which he had to retain them or let them go, without by that wishing to despoil himself of this right—as the proprietor who lets many years pass without building on his land preserves always the power to do so whenever it may suit him, without a neighbor being able to prevent him by claiming that he has gained by prescription the right of view. This doctrine ought to be applied also to the rain-waters which run through the public road; and so the proprietor of the upper estate may intercept them and take them exclusively for himself, although the lower one may have constantly carried them to his field, since said waters are of the first one who occupies them; and it is likewise understood that the proprietor of the lower estate did not avail himself of them except in consequence of the power of the proprietor of the upper one to take or not take them.

§ 1373. *Lower Estates.*—It has been said above that the lower proprietor is obliged to receive the waters which naturally come down from the upper estate, without the hand of man having contributed to it, and that he can not make any work which shall impede this current; and now it is added that if the ditch or place where said waters pass through or on the boundary of his estate is naturally stopped or embarrassed by the mud, sand, stones, or any other thing, so that the waters are checked and flow back upon the upper estate, he is obliged to clean the ditch or permit that the owner of the latter cleans it in order that the waters may follow their course: Law 15, title 32, partidas 3. A ditch (acequia) being of many persons, the place in which the water is stopped, each one ought to clean it in front of his estate: Id. On the contrary, if the margin of the upper estate is destroyed so that the descent of the waters causes greater ravages on the estate below, the owner of the latter will have the right to repair it at his expense, provided the repairing does not injure the upper proprietor—upon the general rule that nobody is prohibited from doing a good to himself which does no injury to another.

§ 1374. *Obligation of Owner of Lower Estate.*—The obligation imposed on the lower proprietor to do no work which may impede the running of the waters from the upper estate does extend to the waters of rivers, streams, and torrents; since any person may make, on his own estate, dikes, mounds, or other works which may preserve it from inundations and overflows, provided he does not alter nor obstruct the drain or ordinary course of the waters, although the waters by the effect of the works flow back upon the neighbor's estates, the owners of which may take on their part like precautions. But if the question is of a lake or swamp, the waters of which are stopped, and increasing with the rains or melting of the snows, they extend and spread over a field, the Roman laws do not permit the owner of the latter estate to raise dikes to preserve it in prejudice to the upper or lateral estates.

§ 1375. *Upper Proprietor can not Change Natural Descent of Water.*—As the upper proprietor can not on his part do anything which shall injure the condition of the lower one, accordingly as has been established above, it is clear that he can not construct on his estate any work which shall change the natural descent of the waters, whether by uniting them in one single point and giving them by this manner a more rapid course, or whether by directing in a large quantity on a site of the lower estate so that they shall cause greater ravages: Law 13, title 32, partidas 3. But he may make the necessary or simply the profitable works for the cultivation of his estate, as to open furrows in sowed ground, and ditches in a vineyard, or in a meadow in order to prevent too much moisture or for irrigation, although the drainage of the furrows or of the ditches on the lower ground can not be called the natural course of the waters without the intervention of the hand of man; because the interest of agriculture so requires it, which otherwise could not progress.

§ 1376. *Springs.*—Neither can the upper proprietor change the direction of the waters of a spring which runs from his estate to that of another, in order to make them run to that of another without his consent; because this change not being a work of nature, but that of the hand of man, the latter would not be obliged to suffer it. And if a proprietor should open anew a spring on his estate, would he have a right to throw the overplus water on the lower estates? Although there are not wanting those who sustain the affirmative, the negative is more in conformity with reason and the law, because it is evident that the opening of the spring and the course of the waters is not the work of nature.

§ 1377. *Ponds Formed by Rains.*—For the same reason, if a proprietor should make on his estate a pond formed by the rains, infiltrations, meltings of snows, or by any subterraneous veins, he could not flow his waters over the neighboring fields; but if he should form and maintain it with the waters of any stream which already previously existed, he could continue directing the overplus through the drain or channel of the stream, and even let all out through the same place, when the question should be of draining the pond; provided that it would not cause more damage to the lower estates than that which they would suffer before the construction.

§ 1378. *Damages by Constructions on Lower Estate.*—When the owner of the lower estate constructs dikes or other works in order to impede the natural descent of waters, or when the owner of the upper estate makes them fall with more injury to the other by means of works which were not necessary or profitable for his cultivation, he who feels himself injured has a right, as indicated already above, to cause the things to be placed in their primitive state, and to claim satisfaction for the damages which the new works shall have occasioned him: Law 3, title 32, partidas 3. If the author of the new works is unknown, it shall be reputed to be he whom they profit, by the rule, Is fecit cui prodest; but if it is proved to have been another person, for whom the benefited party is not responsible, the latter is not obligated, except only to permit the destruction of the works. The action of the injured party does not last always, as it is extinguished by the course of time which prescription causes; so that if he lets ten years pass from the construction of the new work, being present, and twenty years, being absent, without making any claim, he can not thenceforth complain, and will have to continue suffering the work and the damage: Law 14, title 32, partidas 3. The action of which we are speaking, while it lasts, always goes actively and passively with the dominion; so it is, that if the owner of the field which receives the damage should sell it to a third party before making the complaint, the purchaser could ask that the work be torn down; and if the author of the work should sell the field in which he made it before being demanded (sued), the purchaser can be forced to tear it down, or to let it be torn down, although the vendor must pay him for the expenses which he shall make for this reason: Law 16, title 32, partidas 3. If the persons who made the new work were many, the damaged party may sue all, or any of them, to have them demolish it; but as for the recompense for the damages, he must ask each one for the part which corresponds to him, and not all; and if on the contrary the work should damage many, any one of them can ask for all its demolition, but not for the satisfaction of the damages entirely, but only for his part, unless he shall have power from the others to collect all: Law 17, title 32, partidas 3.

## II. Of the Right Which a Proprietor Has over the Water Which Rises on his Estate.

§ 1379. *Rights of Proprietor.*—Every proprietor may open in his house or on his estate a fountain or well of water, although by this cause all the water of his neighbor is diminished or fails, who, notwithstanding, will have an action to impede the work, or demand that it be stopped or destoyed when the former shall make unnecessarily, and with an intention to damage him: Law 19, title 32, partidas 3. He who has a spring of water on his estate may make that use of it which best suits him, because the spring is his as a part of the property, and as law 1, title 28, partidas 3, says, "Man has power over the things that belong to him to do with them as he thinks fit, according to the laws of God and man." Thus it is that he can use his waters to irrigate his land or make ponds, and even he can also stop them if he considers them useless or hurtful.

§ 1380. *Exceptions to the Rule.*—This principle has two exceptions: the first is when a third party has acquired a right to the water of the spring; and the second is when the spring furnishes water to the inhabitants of a town. The third party may have acquired a right to the spring by title or by prescription. The right may consist in the power of the third party to carry the water from the spring through a drain, ditch, canal, tube, or other conduit, for his lands or industrial establishments, which among the Romans was called service of aqueduct (servitus aquæductus); or in that of drawing water out of the spring or well, for the consumption of his family or of the workmen of his fields or of his beasts and cattle (servitus aquæ haustus); or in that of introducing his beasts or cattle into the estate to water them at the spring—service of watering (servitus pecoris ad aquam appulsus).

§ 1381. *Third Parties.*—The third party acquires by title a right to the spring, when the owner of this concedes it to him by a gratuitous or onerous agreement, or by a testament or other last will, or when the judge adjudicates it to him in divisive trials (trials for division). He acquires it by precription when he has used the water in good faith, with the knowledge and sufferance of the owner of the spring, and during the legal time, without any interruption: Law 15, title 31, partidas 3. The good faith consists in the persuasion of the third party that he has a right to make use of the water by way of service, without the use which he makes of it, owing to its origin to force or clandestineness, nor even to the mere favor which, at his request, and as his neighbor, the owner of the spring might have granted to him (said law 15); and this good faith must last until the completion of the prescription, according to what the authors establish. The knowledge and sufferance of the owner of the spring serves as a just title and of delivery, as well as the use of the third party serves as occupation or a taking of the possession of the right; since the owner sees or knows that the third party makes use of the water by way of a service and is silent, and tolerates it without opposition during the legal time, it shows that his will is to tacitly grant the right of service. Although the law deems the knowledge and sufferance of the owner necessary, Antonio Gomez and Gregorio Lopez do not think it necessary in the case that the third party should support his use by a just title, as would happen, for example, of holding it, as owner of the fountain without being it, he should have purchased the service on it, as then he would really gain by the means of use and good faith, although the true owner would be ignorant of it. The legal time is that of ten years between parties present and twenty between absent ones in the continuous service, and immemorial in the discontinuoses; that is to say, that if the use which the third party makes of the water of the fountain is daily or continuous, as it usually happens in the service of an aqueduct, it is necessary for the prescription that the third party may be in uninterrupted possession of the enjoyment of the water for the space of ten years, the owner of the fountain being in the province, and for the space of twenty years being out of the province; and if the use is not continuous, except by intervals, as happens in the service of watering of animals, in that of drawing water for the workmen in the field, and even in that of aqueduct when the water comes only once a week, a month, or a year, and not every day, then the possession of ten and twenty years is not sufficient, but that of time immemorial is indispensable: Law 15, title 31, partidas 3. Although Gregorio Lopez and Antonio Gomez limit the necessity of immemorial possession to that of the case where the third party does not have a just title, meaning that in the case of having it from some one who believed he was the owner without being so, the ordinary ten and twenty years would be sufficient.

§ 1382. *Prescription.*—We have said, and we repeat according to law, that in order to acquire a right to water by prescription it is necessary to make use of it by way of service, and not by force, nor clandestinely, nor by mere favor, which the owner of a fountain may have granted in a precarious manner. In truth, neither force nor clandestine use can serve as a ground for the acquisition of a right. What matters it that for ten, for twenty or more years, you come suddenly by day, or stealthily by night, to take the water from my field to carry it to yours? While I do not intervene with my tacit or express consent, your acts do not further anything, however multiplied they may be; and you can not say certainly that my consent is for you when you proceed in your acts with violence or in a manner which I do not know of. But not even the express permission which I might give you to use the water ought to be considered sufficient so that you can convert at the end of a certain time my favor into a debt, if I did not give it to you with the intention of acknowledging a right in you, and of imposing a service on myself. The familiarity which there usually is between neighbors, the friendship, the desire of pleasing each other, and the necessity in which they many times see themselves of asking for and doing mutual services, cause the owner of a fountain to concede, permit, or tolerate another to draw water for his people to drink, or to water his cattle in it, principally if it comes in abundance, without by that wishing to deprive himself of the liberty which he has of causing the effects of his tolerance to cease when it does not suit him to continue it, whether by diminishing the copiousness of the spring, whether by changing the proprietor of the immediate estate, or whether for any other reason. Thus, if I let the water run from my fountain because I do not want it for my irrigations nor other uses, and you gather it as it goes out of my field to irrigate yours, you can not claim that by the course of time you have acquired the right of having it, and availing yourself of it always in the same manner, and that I have lost that of doing anything on my estate which shall impede the running out of the water, and the use which you make of it. I have had the power to employ it or not employ it; I could let it run out of my estate, because to me it was useless; I could let you avail yourself of it, because I had abandoned it; I could permit you to make works in your field to gather it, because I had no right to stop them, since each one may do on his own estate that which most suits him; but not by that have you acquired any right to the water which still has not run out of my field, but only to that which is already out of my dominion; and thus it is that I can retain it, invert it to new uses, and even close up the fountain which perhaps may be prejudicial to me. When will it be said then, you will ask me, that I can acquire by prescription a right to the water of your fountain? When you or your ancestor shall have made on my estate an aqueduct, or other manifest work which shall have for an object to facilitate the course and descent of the water toward your field, because then it is presumed that these works were constructed in virtue of an agreement made with me or with my ancestor; and when, by the act of my permitting you the use of the water, I should have experienced any considerable damage, then it is to be supposed that my sufferance was not the effect of complacency or good neighbor, but of a right which you had, and in the exercise of which I could not stop you.

§ 1383. *Fountains.*—The owner of a fountain who has granted to his neighbor, or has let him acquire by prescription, the use of the water has not deprived himself of the right to enjoy it himself for the necessities of his estate, since he has only contracted the obligation of not doing anything which may impede the exercise of the service. But if the owner, changing the cultivation or the employment of his field, should absorb in it all or most all of the water, the neighbor could sue him to have him use it with moderation, and that he should leave him the accustomed amount, or at least sufficient for his farm, because the right of service must not be illusory. The owner of a fountain who has conceded to his neighbor, or has let him acquire by prescription, the power to carry water for the irrigation of his lands can not grant afterwards like power to another neighbor without the consent of the first, unless the water shall come in such abundance as shall be sufficient for the estates of both: Law 5, title 31, partidas 3.

§ 1384. *Service not Sold without the Estate.*—Although as a general rule the service can not be sold without the estate in favor of which it is constituted, notwithstanding, law 12, title 13, partidas 3, provides that if the service were of water which rises on an estate and irrigates another, the owner of the latter can cede the water to that of the immediate estate after it shall come to his. But this provision must be understood without prejudice to the owner of the fountain, since the latter conceded to his neighbor the use of the water for the necessities of his estate, and not that he should sell it; and thus the grantee can not dispose of the water in favor of a third party except when he who imposed the service on himself shall not have to suffer by that a greater burden.

§ 1385. *Not Necessary that the Two Estates should Join.*—In order to acquire the service or right to take water from one estate in favor of another, it is not necessary that the two estates shall be so near as to touch each other; and so one proprietor may bring water from an estate of another by way of service to irrigate his, although he shall have to pass through a road or through an intermediate estate, although he will have to obtain a competent license from the authority if it is a road which separates the two estates, or of the proprietor of the intermediate estate if it were not of himself. In this last case there will be two services: that of taking the water on the estate where the fountain rises, and that of conducting it through the intermediate estate, servitus aquæ ductus. The owner of this intermediate estate can not use the water which passes through it without a private concession from the owner of the fountain, consented to by the owner of the dominant estate, unless, as we have just said, the water is sufficient for the two estates, since, in such a case, will be sufficient the concession of the owner of the fountain or serving estate without the necessity of the approbation of the owner of the dominant estate.

§ 1386. *Aqueducts.*—He who has in his favor the service of an aqueduct, or whether it may be the right of conducting water through the estate of another, must keep and maintain the drain, ditch, canal, or tube, or other conduit, so that it can not widen, rise, nor lower, nor do any damage to the estate through which it passes. If it were a drain of water for a grist-mill or a ditch for irrigation, he must sustain and guard it with stakes without putting stones or great rocks, which shall cause hinderances or obstructions on the farm; and the quantity of water not being of so much consideration, he ought to conduct it through earthen conduits or lead pipes under ground or by canals, so that he may avail himself of it without loss or diminution of the estates which it crosses: Law 4, title 31, partidas 3.

§ 1387. *Second Exception.*—The second exception or limitation which we put above to the liberty which the owner of the fountain has to make the use of it that most suits him, or when the fountain furnishes or may furnish water to the inhabitants of a town which has no other means to provide itself with this article so necessary; in which case the owner can not dipose at his discretion of the fountain with damage to the town, nor resist to facilitate the town in availing itself of it, upon the great principle that private interest must cede to the general interest. But as nobody can be dispossessed of his things nor of his rights, not even for the cause of public utility, without competent indemnification first being given him, so that it be paid according to the judgment of good men, accordingly as it is provided in law 2, title 1, partidas 2, and in law 51, title 10, partidas 3, the owner of the fountain may ask that he be compensated by the town for the damage which it shall cause him, if it is that the town has not freed itself of the obligation of compensation by having acquired the use of the water by the means of a title or prescription. Besides, the owner always preserves the property in the fountain, not having sold all of it; and although he should have been compensated, he may use it in favor of his estate, provided he does not prejudice the use of the town.

### III. Of Waters that Belong to the Public.

§ 1388. *Public Waters.*—Waters which are not nor can not be private property belong to the public. Such are the waters of the rivers which by themselves or by accession with others follow their course to the sea. These may be navigable or not navigable. If they are navigable, nobody can avail himself of them so as to hinder or embarrass navigation; but if they are not, the owners of the land through which they pass may use the waters thereof for the utility of their farms or their industry, without prejudice to the common use or destiny which the towns on their course shall have given them, and with the modifications provided in the laws, orders, and decrees which are spoken of under the word "acequia." Who, how, and when they can fish in the waters which belong to the public, will be seen under the word "fish" (pesca).

### IV. Of the Use of the Waters Which Pass along the Border of or through an Estate.

§ 1389. *Municipal Law.*—The use of the running waters which are not of those which anybody can avail himself without a license from the authority, must be regulated by the provisions of the municipal ordinances, or by the uses and customs of the country; but in default of ordinances and customs, equity and the interest of agriculture dictate the following rules:

§ 1390. *Running Water from Springs.*—The waters of fountains and springs are property of the owners of the lands in which they rise, or of the lower fields which have acquired a right to their utility, while they remain within their precinct; but as they go out of it they make running waters, aqua profluens, and belong as common things to the first who occupies them as far as he has a necessity for them. The first who can occupy them are the owners of the estates which they bathe or cross.

§ 1391. *Water Running between Estates.*—If running water passes between estates of different owners, each one of these can use it for the irrigation of his estate or for any other object, but not the whole of it, but only the part which corresponds to him, because both have equal rights, and the one can consequently oppose the use of it all by the other, or even a part considerably more than his own.

§ 1392. *Owner of Both Banks.*—When the water passes through the interior of an estate the owner can use it at his discretion; as the two banks are his, he has not to subject himself for the interest of another riparian proprietor; but on its going out of his land, he ought to return it to its natural or ordinary course, without being able to absorb it or consume it entirely or give it another direction, because it is not his own as to property, but only as to the use which he can make of it in its passage.

§ 1393. *Canals and Cuts.*—Since every riparian proprietor can use the water which passes by the border of his estate to irrigate it, it is clear that he can open cuts, canals, or gutters, and even construct a dam, flood-gate, or other work, in order to take it and carry it to his estate, provided that he does not make it flow back on the upper fields against the will of their owners, or inundate the lower ones, or to go down in a manner which shall cause ravages, nor detain it in such a manner that the neighbors shall be deprived of the accustomed irrigation: Law 13, title 32, partidas 3.

§ 1394. *Constructions on the Estate of Another.*—None of the riparian owners can construct works on the estate of the other without his consent, nor even support on it a dam or flood-gate to make the water enter more abundantly on his own; since all have the same rights, they must not make the works except in a manner that the water will be divided equally.

§ 1395. *Agriculture.*—But this principle of equality in the division of the waters is subordinate to the interest of agriculture, which generally requires a greater quantity to be destined to the estates of the greatest extension, as the Roman law determined. Notwithstanding, as the field of the greatest extension does not always need the most water, the maxims of the law of the Romans must not be applied except with certain restrictions. So as the upper proprietors can not absolutely deprive the lower ones of the use of the water, since that they must restore it to its natural course after having used it, save the inevitable loss caused by irrigation; in the same manner, in an inverse sense, the owners of grist-mills, water-mills, fulling-mills, manufactories, or other industrial establishments, have no such right to all the water necessary for the movement of their machinery that they can totally deprive the proprietors of the upper estates of it. Notwithstanding, when it is a question of grist-mills in a country where there are few, and on account of the dryness need all of the water, the irrigation of meadows and other grounds must be suspended in their favor for the public good while the state of dryness lasts.

§ 1396. *Alienation of Rights.*—A riparian proprietor can alienate the right to take water by renunciation, cession, sale, or in any other manner, in favor of the proprietor of the other side or the lower proprietor; and if, holding two estates, he gives one away, he may reserve the exclusive right of using the water for that which he preserves, or to concede it for that which he alienates. A riparian owner can likewise acquire with respect to another the exclusive right to the water by the means of prescription.

§ 1397. *A Riparian Owner and Third Party.*—A riparian owner can not, without the consent of the other riparian owners interested, concede to a third party, to the injury of the former, the power to take water in the same current or on his estate; nor use himself the water to irrigate other lands which belong to him, but which are not situated on the same bank; although this right may be acquired by prescription. When one riparian estate is divided between co-owners or joint owners, so that the parts which are designed or adjudicated to some of them, and which form now so many other estates not bounded by the stream, both preserve notwithstanding their right to the water in the same form which they held it before the division, although nothing should have been stipulated on this matter.

§ 1398. *Acquisition of Contiguous Estates.*—A proprietor who increases the extension of his riparian estate with the acquisition of contiguous lands, which he adds to it, can not take more water than before for his irrigation, in detriment to the others interested; since if he had such power, he could in time make the rights of the other riparian owners illusory.

§ 1399. *Beds of Streams.*—The bed, mother, or ground where the running waters go must be divided between the riparian proprietors according to the frontage of their estates, in case of remaining dry through the effect of the weather, by any event of *vis major*, act of God, or by the change of the course of the water: Law 31, title 28, partidas 3.

§ 1400. *Artificial Channels.*—The rules which we have established are applicable to running waters which do not belong to any one, and which go through natural beds or drains; but not the acequias or canals which the hand of man has constructed. So that, if by the border or through my estate passes an acequia belonging to a grist-mill or other establishment, I can not use the water for my farm, except in the case of having acquired a right to it by title or prescription; although if the owner of the establishment does not enjoy the acequia by right of property, except only by right of service imposed upon my property, as must be presumed until the contrary is proved, although I can not do anything that will diminish the use of the service as to the object for which it is found established, I can at least avail myself of the overplus water, whether it be when the establishment is stopped, or whether it be when the water shall come in great abundance. (See Ditch or Channel—Acequia.) We have spoken here of waters so far as the serve for irrigation. In the article "Fishing," those who have a right to avail themselves of it will be spoken of, and of the manner and time in which they can exercise it.

## DITCH OR CHANNEL (ACEQUIA).

§ 1401. *An Acequia, a Ditch or Channel where Water is Conducted for Irrigation and for Other Uses—Navigation not to be Embarrassed.*—Nobody can open into a navigable river an acequia or channel which embarrasses navigation; and that one which may now be made, whether new or old, must be closed up or destroyed at the cost of the owner, because public utility must be preferred to that of a private person: Law 8, title 28, partidas 3. But not being a navigable river, any resident of the town where it passes may extract a part of its water and construct an acequia in order to irrigate his lands or to run his mill or water-mill or for any other object which interests him, provided he may do it without injury to the common use or destiny which the town shall have given the water; under the supposition that if the acequia should have to cross the ground of another, or the crown lands, or the ground of the pueblo lands (concejil), a license from the owner, or of the king or council, would be indispensable. It is thus deduced from law 8, title 28, and from law 18, title 32, partidas 3; and so the authors commonly judge, forming their opinion on said laws and on the Roman laws.

§ 1402. *Ditches from the Rivers.*—In the instructions of mayors of the fifteenth of May, 1788 (law 27, title 11, book 7, Novisima Recopilacion), they are ordered, article 48, that in order to facilitate the fertility of the fields with the utility of all the water which can be applied to their benefit, they shall try to make ditches from the rivers draining them through the parts most convenient without prejudice to their course and to their lower limits and districts, and taking care likewise to discover the subterraneous structure in order to use them, as well in the use of flour-mills, fulling-mills, and other necessary or convenient machinery for grinding, and for the working of wool, as to work at less cost stone and wood.

§ 1403. *Canals for Agriculture—Recompensation for.*—In the royal decree of the thirty-first of August, 1819, with the object of promoting agriculture, favors are conceded to the ayuntamientos, communities, companies, corporations, or private individuals who, with the previous corresponding permission from the government, shall construct at their expense ditches or canals anew for irrigation, whether they shall take them from the waters of large rivers, or shall unite those of many streams or springs at one point, or extract them from the cavity of high mountains. These favors are reduced to the exemption from all increase of tithes and of first fruits (primicias) for the crops for twelve years on the lands which shall receive effectively the benefit of irrigation. By increase of tithes and of first fruits is understood that which shall result after being deducted that which was paid to the legitimate receivers when the lands were found dry; which regulation must be made in conformity with the brief of his holiness of the thirty-first of October, 1816, for three years prior, computed the fertile with the sterile, remaining uninjured said tithes and first fruits with their legitimate owners. The twelve years must commence to be counted on the grain, vegetables, and any other plants of which their vegetation is concluded in one year from which the earth commences to be irrigated; in a vineyard, concluded in the seventh year of their planting; in those of olives and carob trees, concluded in twenty years; and in that of mulberry, concluded the twelfth; the king reserving the right to dictate the rules for other classes of trees or shrubs, if the utility and necessity of their improvement in any provinces of the kingdom should present themselves to him. Those who should inclose these lands of new irrigation with walls of solid make, raised at least six Castilian palms above the level of the ground, shall enjoy for two crops more the exemption of the said increase of tithes and of first fruits, and for one crop more if the inclosure should be of a dry stone wall or natural hedges. The exemption conceded to those who plant on lands newly irrigated vines, olives, carob trees, or mulberries is understood in the provinces of Andalusia, Estremadura, Murcia, or Cartagena, Valencia, Isles Baleares, Pithiusis, and Canarias; as in the rest of the provinces of the kingdom in which vegetation is retarded, one year more is conceded in the plantations of the vine and mulberry, and two in those of olive and carob trees. These same favors are extended to any community or private person who shall give to one or many lands the benefit of irrigation by any other of the means which do not require special permission from the government.

§ 1404. *Good Condition of Acequias to be Kept.*—He who enjoys the waters of a ditch (acequia) which passes through the ground of another must keep and maintain the drain so that it can not widen, rise, nor sink, nor do damage to the serving estate: Law 4, title 31, partidas 3. And it is likewise of his charge to clean it without the owner of the estate through which it passes preventing him from so doing: Laws 7, 15, title 31, partidas 3. When the acequia belongs to many, each one must assist in repairing and cleaning the part in front of his estate: Law 15, title 31, partidas 3.

§ 1405. *Acequias Made to Run Grist-mills.*—If the acequia which crosses an estate belongs to the owner of a grist-mill or of another establishment on another estate, for the benefit of which the acequia is constructed, the owner of the former estate can not avail himself of the passage of the water for the irrigation of his lands, because the water of the acequia has become private property; but he may acquire this right either by contract or other title, or by prescription. We are speaking on the hypothesis that the owner of the establishment is also the owner of the acequia; since, if he should not enjoy this, by right of property, except only by right of service, as is to be supposed, provided the contrary is not proved, then the proprietor of an estate burdened with a simple service of aqueduct can avail himself of the water which may not be necessary for the grist-mill or establishment. (See Water.)

## RIVERS.

§ 1406. *River, What is—Uses thereof—Their Banks.*—A river is a mass of water united between two banks, which runs perpetually from time immemorial. It differs from a torrent in that this is the effect of the abundant rains or extraordinary meltings of snow, so that it runs only a certain time and leaves its bed dry the greater part of the year. Rivers, as law 6, title 28, partidas 3, says, belong to all men generally, so that even those who are of other foreign lands may use them as the natives and residents of the territory which they bathe. As private good must cede to the public good, no edifice can be made in the rivers nor on their banks which will hinder navigation or restrain their common use; and if it should be made, or already be made, it must be destroyed within thirty days, at the cost of him who made it, unless the latter should have obtained a competent privilege for that purpose: Law 8, title 28, partidas 3. If any timber for the construction of vessels should have to be sent to any sea-ports, by the rivers, every impediment which there may be in them must be removed at the cost of the author thereof, in favor of the marine service, the object of which is of so much importance for the state: Law 7, title 26, book 7, Novisima Recopilacion. Any citizen may build a grist-mill or water-mill on the bank or in the river, if no injury shall result to the community, without the owner of any other grist-mill already built having a right to stop him on the ground that his rents will be diminished, provided that he does not impede the course of the water on account of the new construction, on the supposition that if the bank belongs to the king or the town council, the corresponding license must precede: Law 18, title 32, partidas 3. On the same terms may be drawn out of a public river by means of a canal the water which any one may need, unless that the town or council shall destine it to their own use: Cur. Felip., com. naval, lib. 3, cap. 1; and when a river which is not navigable becomes so after uniting with another, use of its waters must be made so that then there shall be no lack thereof for navigation.

§ 1407. *Bridges.*—All the towns, and even any person may at his cost, build bridges on the rivers, without establishing impositions or tributes; and if any one should wish to impede it by alleging to have barks or other rights in the river, he shall incur the penalty of confiscation of property, being a layman, and that of losing forever the right of being considered a native of the town (la naturaleza), and temporalities, being an ecclesiastic: Law 7, title 20, book 6, Novisima Recopilacion. The construction or repairing of bridges which the towns intend to make must be made at the costs of their lands of the town (propias); and in default of them, or they not being sufficient, at the cost of the residents, who must contribute in proportion to their power, without the ecclesiastics or other persons, however privileged they may be, being excused, since to all, without exception, these works are beneficial: Law 20, title 32, partidas 3; and law 6, title 9, book 1, Novisima Recopilacion. If the ground on which the town should wish to build a bridge should be of another, it must be purchased from the owner for a just price, or he must be otherwise indemnified. But when a toll is charged on the passage of a bridge, it is clear that the repairs thereof must run on the account of him who receives this right: Law 16, title 20, book 6, Novisima Recopilacion. For the construction or repair which the towns may wish to make of any bridge, the approbation of the authority is indispensable, who will concede it in consideration of the necessity or utility of the work, and of the reports of the academy of San Fernando on the plans.

§ 1408. *Change of the Course of the River—Overflows—Increase of Land.*—If a river changes its course for a new place, leaving the old one dry, this will be of the owners of the immediate estates, each one taking so much thereof as may be equal to the frontage of his estate; and the owners of those where it newly runs lose the dominion of the new bed, by its being made public as the river, and as the bed which is abandoned was: Law 31, title 28, partidas 3. The estates covered by water by overflows of rivers remain the properties of their owners, who can use them as before as soon as they are uncovered: Law 32, title 28, partidas 3. When rivers with their overflows take away little by little, so that it is not observed, any of the grounds of a bank, and they increase those of another, the owners of the latter acquire said grounds; but if the river should carry a part of an estate with its trees or without them to another, the owner of the latter does not gain the dominion thereof, except it is that it remains so long a time that the trees shall take root; and in such case he must give to the other for the diminution what experts shall appraise: Law 26, title 28, partidas 3.

BANK OR SHORE.

§ 1409. *Banks.*—A bank is the margin and shore of the sea or river, that is, the place or space which their waters cover at the time when they swell most with their periodical flood-tide and ebb-tide, whether in winter or summer, without going out of their bed. The shores of the sea belong as to property to the nation that is owner of the country of which it is a part, and as to the use, they belong to all men. The banks of the rivers belong to the owners of the contiguous estates as to property, and to all men as to use. Hence it is that, as on the shores of the sea as on those of rivers, any one can build a house or cabin to take shelter, or other building which may suit him, provided that he does not embarrass the common use; to make nets and to dry them, to repair ships and to fasten them to the trees which may be there, to expose and sell his comodity and fish, and to do other like things, without anybody hindering him; but if on the shores of the sea a house or other edifice is found, nobody can tear it down nor use it without the power from the owner, although if the sea should wash it down or if it should fall, any person can build anew on the same site: Laws 3, 6, title 28, partidas 3. The trees existing on the banks of rivers belong to the owners of the immediate estates, and these can consequently cut them and do with them what they may wish; but if by chance at the time of cutting one, there should be a vessel tied to it, or another should be about to be tied which had arrived, the cutting must be suspended, by being contrary to the common right which all men have to make use of the shores: Law 7, title 28, partidas 3.

§ 1410. *Laws of the Novisima Recopilacion Referred to.*—Law 7, title 20, book 6, treats of the free permission of the towns and of persons to construct bridges without the imposition of tribute. Law 7, title 26, book 7, speaks of the prohibition from closing or impeding canals or rivers of which the residents of towns avail themselves for navigation, fishing, and other uses. Law 6, title 9, book 1, relates to the rights of tolls, and the application of the product of them to the roads; by instructions of June 8, 1794. Law 16, title 20, book 6, declares the cases in which the clergy ought not to enjoy the exemptions from imposts and tribute. As the above laws do not seem essential for the object of this work, they are not cited at length herein.

# CHAPTER II.

## OF THE SERVICES (SERVIDUMBRES) WHICH SOME THINGS HAVE UPON OTHERS, AND HOW THEY ARE CREATED.

### PARTIDA 3, TITLE 31.

§ 1411. What a Service is, and the Kinds.
§ 1412. Urban Services.
§ 1413. Rural Services.
§ 1414. Services of Drawing Water.
§ 1415. Grant of Said Service to a Third Party.
§ 1416. Right of Watering Cattle at Another's Well.
§ 1417. Right to Take Earth from Another's Estate.
§ 1418. Right of Service Held, although the Property is Sold.
§ 1419. Each Heir may Demand the Whole of the Service.
§ 1420. In Granting a Service, All Co-proprietors must Concur.
§ 1421. Service on Property Held by Feudal Tenure.
§ 1422. Service can not be Sold Separately from the Property.
§ 1423. Upon What Things Service may be Granted.
§ 1424. How Many Ways a Service may be Imposed.
§ 1425. Service Acquired by Prescription.
§ 1426. Service, how Lost by Non-usage.
§ 1427. Service may be Extinguished by Purchase, How.
§ 1428. A Partner may Acquire a Service.
§ 1429. Service as to Height of a House, how Lost.
§ 1430. Service Called Usufruct.
§ 1431. Manner of Enjoying a Service on Certain Things.
§ 1432. Duties of Usufructuary.
§ 1433. How Many Ways a Usufruct may be Extinguished.
§ 1434. Usufruct is Extinguished when the Thing is Destroyed.
§ 1435. Usufruct to a City, how Long It Endures.
§ 1436. A Grant of the Right of Habitation—Its Duration.

### LAW 1.

§ 1411. *What a Service is, and how Many Sorts there Are.*—The sages have properly said that a service (servidumbre) is the right and use which one man has in the buildings and estates of another, to use them for the benefit of his own. There are two kinds of service: the first is that which one house has on another, and which in Latin is called urbana; the second is that which one estate has on another, and is called in Latin rustica. There are likewise other services which a man has in the things of another, for his personal advantage, and not for the particular advantage of his estate; as where he has the usufruct of gathering the products of another's estate, or the use of the house in which he dwells, or of the houses of another, or of the work of slaves, who are artisans or laborers. We shall speak of each in the laws of this title.

LAW 2.

§ 1412. *What are Denominated Urban (Urbana) Services, and how Many Kinds there Are.*—We have said in the preceding law that the service called in Latin urbana was that which one building has on another; as where one house has to sustain the weight of another, when neighbor places thereon a pillar or column to support a beam of the roof or story of his house, or any other like superstructure; or where one has a right to pierce his neighbor's wall to insert a beam, or to open a window to let the light enter his house, or where one house is obliged to receive the water falling from the roof of another and coming through troughs, pipes, or otherwise; or where one house enjoys such a service over another that the latter can never be raised higher than it was at the time the service was created, so as to shut out the view or light from the other, or to discover what is done in it; or where a man enjoys the service of entering by the house or yard of another, to his own house or yard, or any other like service established for the benefit of buildings.

LAW 3.

§ 1413. *What are Denominated Rural (Rustica) Services, and how Many Kinds there Are.*—We have said that a rural service was that which one estate has in another; as where a man has a path, road, or way through another's estate to pass in or out of his own. And we say that when one grants the right of a path (senda) through his estate, the grantee may pass through the place where it was designated, either on foot, horseback, or alone, or with other persons, provided they go the one before the other, and not abreast; but he can not pass there with carriages, nor lead packed horses by hand. And if one grants the right of a carriage-way (carrera), the grantee may pass there with carriages, and the other things mentioned above. And if a man grant a road (via) through his estate, then we say the grantee may pass there on foot, on horseback, either alone or in company; or he may convey along there carts, wood, stone, or any other thing necessary for the benefit of the estate, for which the service was created. And the road to be of the width and in the place agreed upon between the parties at the time it was granted; and if no agreement had been made in this respect, then we say it ought to be eight feet wide. And if it should not be straight, on account of the windings or angles, it ought to be sixteen feet wide in those places, in order that carriages may turn.

### Law 4.

§ 1414. *That a Man may have the Service of Draining Water from the Estate of Another.*—Estates may serve one another by entrance or ways running through them, as we have said in the preceding law. They may, moreover, serve one another in a different manner, as by receiving aqueducts or other conduits for water to pass to mills, or to water gardens or other estates of other persons. Wherefore we say that they who have a right to such services must watch over and maintain in good order the aqueduct, canal, or conduit, or place in which the water runs, so that neither becomes wider, nor higher, nor lower, nor do any damage to the person through whose estate it passes. And if it be a canal or ditch that conveys the water to a mill, or for the purpose of watering a garden, or other lands, it ought to be lined with pallisades, and not with stone (cantos), which encumber the estate. And if the quantity of water be small, it ought to be conveyed through aqueducts made of earth, or leaden pipes under ground, so that the water may be used without loss to those through whose estates it passed, or without prejudicing them by the construction of new works there.

### Law 5.

§ 1415. *That the Right of Service Which a Man has of Drawing Water from Another's Fountain can not be Granted to a Third Person without his Consent.*—If a man has acquired the service of drawing water from a fountain which rises in another's estate, for the purpose of watering his own, and the owner of the fountain wishes to grant to a third person the right of taking water therefrom, he can not do it without the consent of him to whom the first service was granted, unless the water be in sufficient abundance for both estates.

### Law 6.

§ 1416. *In what Manner a Man ought to Use the Service He has of Watering his Cattle at Another's Well or Fountain or Pool.* If there be a fountain or well on the estate of another, or a pool contiguous to it, and the owner grant a right to any one to water his cattle and laborers there, he ought, as a consequence of such grant, to permit the grantee to enter or go out from the water as often as he had need. We also say that where a man grants to another the right of always putting his oxen or beasts of labor upon his meadow or pasture, by such grant the grantee acquires the right of service in the meadow or pasture, and he may enjoy it, both he and those who own the estate in favor of which the service is granted; and though the meadow or pasture should be sold or alienated, he to whom it passed can not prevent the use of such service.

LAW 7.

§ 1417. *Of the Right of Service Which a Man has to Take Earth from Another's Estate, to Make Vessels, to Put his Wine or Oil in, and how He ought to Use Such Service.*—If a man should want earth to make vessels to contain the oil he extracted from his olive garden; or if he should have any other estate upon which he wished to erect buildings, to contain the fruits growing on it, and any one should own an adjoining estate upon which were materials fit for such buildings, as earth proper for making jars or tiles, or stones suitable for building or for making lime, or sand or other like thing, and the owner of such adjoining estate grant him the right of always taking any of the things herein enumerated therefrom, the grantee may avail himself of such grant, so far as is necessary for the preservation of the fruits gathered from the estate in favor of which the service is granted, and no more.

LAW 8.

§ 1418. *That a Man does not Lose the Right of Service He had in the Thing of Another Person, though It should be Sold, or Transferred in Any Other Manner Whatever.*—The property in estates is often transferred from one person to another. We therefore say that in whatever manner a house or building may be alienated, or an estate or other thing which owed a service to another in one of the ways mentioned in the preceding law, or in other the like, it will ever remain burdened with the service in favor of the estate or person to which it was before due. We likewise say that to whomsoever the estate entitled to the service may pass, it will always preserve its right of service which it had before had over the other estate, and it will be in no wise impeded or lost by such transfer, unless the service were imposed for a certain time, or for the life of a certain person. For services that are perpetual are not created on account of the persons whose they are, but on account of the things to which they are due, and those who use them, and are not therefore affected by the transfer.

LAW 9.

§ 1419. *That Each of the Heirs may Demand the Whole of the Service Which had been Granted in Favor of the Estate of Which He is Co-heir.*—If a man grant a service upon his house or estate in favor of the house or estate of another, and the grantee afterwards die, each of his heirs, however numerous they may be, may demand the whole of the service; for it is indivisible, and they can not therefore claim their parts separately. And so we say that where the grantor dies, leaving many heirs, the whole of the service may be demanded of either of them, and they will be bound therefor in the same manner as was the ancestor from whom they inherited.

LAW 10.

§ 1420. *That All the Co-proprietors of a Building or Estate must Concur in Granting a Service thereon.*—Each proprietor may grant a service upon his house or estate. But where there are several proprietors who are willing to grant a service upon a house or estate belonging to them in common, they must all concur in granting it. If, however, some only of them make the grant, they can not afterwards contest the right of the grantee; but the others who did not consent may contest such right, each for his own part, as well as for the part of every one who did not concur in the grant, as they will not be bound, nor can they be prejudiced, by the agreement of those who did consent. Yet if they who opposed the grant afterwards consent to it, the effect will be the same as if all of them had concurred in the first instance.

LAW 11.

§ 1421. *That a Man may Impose a Service upon a Thing Which he Holds by Feudal Tenure, or on Paying a Certain Rent.*—Men sometimes hold estates, houses, or other buildings in such way that, though they possess, they are not the true proprietors of them; such are the estates which they hold by feudal tenure, or during their lives, or the lives of their heirs, by paying a certain rent or rendering a certain service. Wherefore we say that if any one who holds such an estate grant a service upon the same in favor of a third person, or if such third person grant him a service upon his own estate in favor of the estate held by the former, both such services would be forever valid, in the same manner as if the grantors had made them upon their own estates. We likewise say that where a man buys a house or other building, or an estate, and the buyer and seller agree that the thing sold shall be subject to a service in favor of another's house or edifice, or estate, which belonged to the seller or any other person, the service so agreed to by the purchaser, though the thing bought had not yet passed under his power, will be as valid as if it had been granted upon any estate of which he was already owner and possessor.

LAW 12.

§ 1422. *That the Service can not be Sold Separately from the Thing to Which It Belongs.*—Where one house or estate owes a service to another house or estate, the proprietor of such service can not sell it separately from the thing to which it belongs; for it is of such a nature that it can not be separated from the estate or edifice upon which it is imposed, unless the owner thereof should consent, or unless the service be the use of water which rises in one estate and runs into another; for the proprietor of such a service may grant the use of the water already come upon his estate to a third person to water his fields or vineyards.

LAW 13.

§ 1423. *Upon What Things Service may be Granted.*—A man may impose services upon his own estate, or upon one which he holds in the manner mentioned as above. And such services are here understood as men impose upon their estates for the benefit of the estates or houses of third persons, and not their own. For a man should not use that which belongs to him as if it were a service only, but as his own property. We likewise say that services can not be imposed upon things holy, sacred, or religious; nor those which are used for the common benefit of a city or town, as the market and other public places, and public threshing-grounds, and others of a similar nature.

LAW 14.

§ 1424. *In how Many Ways a Service may be Imposed upon Things.*—Every service that we have mentioned in the laws of this title, which one house or thing can owe another, may be imposed in the three following ways: the first, where the proprietor of a thing voluntarily imposes upon it a service in favor of another person, either through affection or for a price which he receives of him; the second is that which is granted by will, as where the testator says, "I consent that the house of such a one enjoy a service upon my house, which shall never be raised higher than it now is; or that he may put the beams of his house upon the walls of mine;" or where he grants any other similar service; as the right of way to enter and pass out of his estate, or to draw water for the purpose of watering the lands of the grantee, or other the like; the third is where one acquires a service upon the estate or house of another by prescription, as we shall hereafter show.

LAW 15.

§ 1425. *In how Long a Time a Man may Acquire by Prescription a Service Which he has upon the Estate of Another.*—If the service be of such a nature that it is daily used, without labor on the part of the person who enjoys it—as if it be an aqueduct conveying water from a fountain which rose in another's field, or the like; and a neighbor make use of it during ten years to water his estate, while the owner is in the country, without his making any opposition; or during twenty years while he is out of it; acting in good faith, believing he had a right to do it, using no force nor acting under the permission he had obtained from the owner of the fountain, or field through which it passed—he will then acquire a service in such an aqueduct by prescription. And so it would be where any one had put a beam upon his neighbor's wall, or had opened a window in it for the admission of light into his house; or had opposed his raising his house any higher, that it might not exclude the light; or where he had extended the roof of his house over that of his neighbor, so as to cause the rain-water to fall on it: these and all other similar services which may be enjoyed without daily labor may be acquired in the same manner as the service of the aqueduct above mentioned. But with respect to other services which men make use of for the benefit and cultivation of their estates, or for working on their buildings, and which they do not use daily, but by intervals and particular acts; such as the use of a path, way, or road through another's lands; or the use of water which they resort to only once a week, or month, or year, and not daily: these and such like services can not be prescribed for by the above-mentioned time, and can only be acquired by being used by those who claim them, or by those from whom they are derived, during so long a time that the memory of man runneth not to the contrary.

LAW 16.

§ 1426. *In how Long a Time a Man Loses a Service, when It is not Used by Himself or Another Person for Him.*—Men are liable to lose services which they had acquired, by neglecting to use them themselves or causing them to be used by others in their names. But here a distinction must be made between services which belong to buildings and those which belong to estates. For if a man have the right to place a beam on another's wall, or of opening a window in it for the admission of light into his house, such and other like services may be lost by the owner's ceasing to use them during ten years while he was in the country, or twenty years while he was out of it; if the person who owed the service had for that length of time removed the beam from his wall or stopped up the window where the light entered, or prevented the use of the service in any other way, in good faith, believing he had a right to do so; otherwise the owner of the service would not lose it, though he had ceased to use it, during the above-mentioned time. But services due on estates, if they be of such a nature as to be enjoyed without any actual labor, can not be lost, unless by such a long disuse of them as that they shall be obliterated from the memory of men. And if they be of such a nature as to be used at intervals, and not daily, as we have said in the preceding law, they may then be lost by disuse during twenty years, whether the owner were in or out of the country.

## LAW 17.

§ 1427. *That a Service is Extinguished by being Joined to a Purchase Reciprocally Made, either of the Service Itself or of the Thing upon Which It was Imposed.*—A service may be lost in two other ways than those above mentioned: the first is where it is abandoned by the sole proprietor of the thing to which it is due; but if the house or estate to which it is due belong to several proprietors, one of them can not release it without the consent of the others; the second is where the owner of the estate which owes the service buys that to which it is due. For by the union of the two things in the same proprietor, the service is extinguished, so that though he should afterwards alienate the estate upon which it was imposed, or retain it himself, the service could not be claimed in future, nor will the thing so purchased be subjected thereto, unless it had been afterwards renewed.

## LAW 18.

§ 1428. *That One Partner may Acquire a Service by Using It Alone, and without the Other Partner.*—Where men own in common a house or an estate, to which a service is due from another house or estate, and they divide the thing they owned in common, and afterwards one of them only use the service which before belonged to them both, and the other cease to use it for so long a time that it might be lost, according to what we said in the preceding law, he will then lose it by prescription; and he can not avail himself of the time it was enjoyed by the former joint owner, who neither used it for him nor as his attorney. If, however, they do not divide the thing they possess in common, to which the service belonged, then the use which one of them makes of such service will avail the other; for until the thing be divided the service is entire. But it would be otherwise after it was divided, and therefore, he who did not then use his part of the service would lose it, as is said above.

### Law 19.

§ 1429. *He Who has a Service, whereby He can Hinder Another from Raising his House above a Certain Height, will Lose it if He Permits the House to be Raised above That Height.*—If one house owe another a service whereby the former can not be raised any higher, or if the soil of one man be subjected to receive the water which falls from the roof of another's house, and the owner of the house to which such services are due grants to the proprietor of the house or ground from which they are due the right to raise the former house higher than it was before, or the right to erect any buildings upon the ground where the water fell, he will thereby lose all claim to such services; for he will be presumed to have relinquished his right thereto, by consenting that new works be erected upon the place.

### Law 20.

§ 1430. *Of Services Called Usufruct, or Simply Use.*—We have fully treated, in the preceding laws, of the services which one house or building, or estate, may owe another. We shall now speak of the third sort of services mentioned in the second law of this title: that is to say, the service which a man enjoys in the house or estate of another for his personal advantage, and not for the particular advantage of his estate. And we say there are three ways in which one may have a personal service upon the things of another: the first is where one man grants to another, for the whole of his life, or for a certain time, the usufruct of his estate, house, slaves, or cattle, or other things which afford a revenue or fruits. This usufruct may be granted either by contract or by will. But the grantee ought to gather the fruits in good faith, first giving security that the thing of which he has the usufruct shall not be lost or deteriorated by his fault, or by gathering therefrom more than it is proper he should take; and that in case he should die, or the time of his usufruct expire, in any other manner, the thing shall be restored to the grantor, or to the person to whom he might order it to be restored, or to his heirs if he be dead. And the usufructuary will acquire a right to all the fruits and resources of the thing upon which the usufruct is granted, and may turn them to his own profit, or sell them if he choose; but he can not sell or pledge the thing itself. The second is where a man grants the use only of his house, or estate, or other thing; in that case, the grantee can not enjoy the thing of which the use is granted so fully as the usufructuary can do. For he who has the use only of a thing can not gather more of its fruits than are necessary for his support. As where the use of a garden is granted to him, he may take of its fruits or plants so much as is necessary for his consumption, and that of his family; but he can not take any to give to others or to sell. And so we say it would be where any one had granted to another the use of his meadow, vineyard, or other thing. And we moreover say that a man can not sell or pledge the thing of which he has the use; and that he ought to give good security that he will use the thing in good faith as a prudent man, and that it shall not be damaged, or deteriorated, or lost by his fault.

### Law 21.

§ 1431. *In What Manner a Man ought to Enjoy the Use Which has been Granted Him upon Another's House, Slave, or Beast.*— Where a man has the simple use of another's house, he may dwell therein with his wife, children, and household; and he may even receive guests there if he choose. And where one man grants another the use of his slaves or beasts, the grantee may employ them in laboring only for himself or in his service; but he can not hire or lend them to others. We likewise say, where one grants to another the use of his cattle, the grantee may conduct them upon his estate that they may manure his ground and make it yield more abundantly; and he may use their milk or convert it into cheese; or he may make use of their wool or young for the maintenance of himself and household, but not to give or sell to others.

### Law 22.

§ 1432. *What the Usufructuary ought to Do for the Thing the Usufruct of Which is Granted to Him; and that He ought to Preserve, Improve, Repair, and Cultivate It.*—It is but right and just that the usufructuary of a house, or an estate, or cattle, since he enjoys the profits thereof, should appropriate all he could to improve, preserve, and faithfully keep the thing itself; so that, if it be a house, he should repair and preserve it, that it might not fall or be deteriorated by his fault; or if it be an estate, vineyard, or garden, he ought to cultivate and improve it, and if he took any trees therefrom he ought to plant others in their place; or if the usufruct be of cattle, and some of them die, he ought to replace them by their increase, and rear others in their place. And if the thing itself be subject to the payment of tithes, or other tribute or impost, they ought to be paid by the usufructuary out of the fruits it yielded, so that the thing remain to the owner entire and unencumbered. But one who enjoys the use only of a thing is not bound to do what is above mentioned for the benefit of the thing to the use, unless the thing be so inconsiderable that the whole of its fruits were consumed in the enjoyment of the use; for then he will be obliged to improve, preserve, and pay for it, in the manner above prescribed.

### Law 23.

This law relates to what is acquired by the grantee of the usufruct or labor of a slave, and is not in force.

### Law 24.

§ 1433. *In how Many Ways the Usufruct Which One Man has of the Things of Another may be Extinguished.*—It is in the course of nature that everything which man promises by word, or executes by deed, should cease to have effect, however firmly it may have been done. Since, therefore, we have shown in the preceding laws the manner in which a usufruct as well as a simple use may be established, we will now speak of the manner in which they may be extinguished or destroyed. And we say that if the grantee of a usufruct or simple use die, or be perpetually banished to some island; or if he had been enfranchised, and afterwards fall again into slavery for some crime he had committed; or if, being free, he had himself consented to be sold as a slave, the usufruct or use which he enjoyed in any thing would thereby be lost, and the thing itself would be restored to the original proprietor; and so it would be where neither the grantee, nor any person in his name, make use of the usufruct or use during ten years while he was in the country, or twenty years while he was out of it; he would then lose both by prescription, and the thing would be again restored to the original proprietor. We likewise say that if the grantee sell to another the right he had to the thing, only the use and usufruct will be thereby extinguished, and the thing will return to the original proprietor, so that neither the grantee nor his vendee can afterwards enjoy them. For the grantee may lease to another his right of usufruct of a thing; nevertheless he can not alienate that right. We likewise say that when he who has the right of usufruct in a thing acquires the property in the thing itself, the usufruct is thereby extinguished, as the property and the usufruct of the thing are united in the same person.

### Law 25.

§ 1434. *That the Usufruct is Extinguished when the Thing upon Which It was Granted is Burned, or Otherwise Destroyed.*—If the house or building upon which was granted the usufruct or use only be entirely burned, or wholly destroyed by an earthquake, or in any other manner, the usufruct or use will be thereby extinguished. And notwithstanding the grantee may wish to rebuild the house or edifice upon the same ground on which it before stood, he can not do it. unless with the consent of the owner of the property.

### Law 26.

§ 1435. *How Long a Usufruct Endures Which is Granted to a City or Town without Mention of Any Specific Time.*—When the usufruct of a building or an estate, or other thing belonging to another person, is granted to a city or town, the usufruct will endure a hundred years, and no more if no specific time had been stipulated in the grant; after which it will revert to the owner of the estate or his heirs. And the reason is, that a usufruct granted expressly to the commons of any place is extinguished by the death of all its inhabitants; for the ancient sages have conceived that after the lapse of a hundred years all those would be dead who were born at the time the usufruct was granted. And we also say that the usufruct would expire if the town or place in favor cf which it was granted should be destroyed, so that the ground be cultivated on which it stood, or the place become a desert. Yet if all or a part of the inhabitants of such place afterwards establish themselves in another place, they will thereby preserve the usufruct, notwithstanding they had abandoned the soil of the town where they dwelt at the time they acquired the usufruct.

### Law 27.

§ 1436. *How Long a Grant of the Right of Habitation will Endure.*—*Habitatio* in Latin means dwelling in common speech, and relates only to houses and other buildings. And we say that if one man confer on another the right of dwelling in his house, either by grant or last will, and no mention be made of the specific time such right is to endure, it shall be understood to endure during the life of the grantee or legatee. And the person enjoying the right of habitation ought to make use of it, in good faith, by preserving, and not deteriorating or destroying the building. He ought, moreover, to give good security to restore the house to the owner or his heirs after his death, or at the time agreed upon between the parties. And the grantee of such right may dwell in the house with the family, or he may if he choose let or hire it to others; but only to such persons as are good neighbors. And a man can not lose his right of habitation unless by his death, or by abandoning it, without compulsion, during his life.

# CHAPTER III.

## OF NEW WORKS AND WATER RIGHTS.

### PARTIDA 3, TITLE 32.



### LAW 1.

§ 1437. *What is Meant by New Works—Who may Forbid their Erection—Who may be Forbidden, and in What Manner.*—By new works (labor neuva) is understood every sort of building newly erected and founded upon the ground, or begun anew upon the foundation of an old wall or other edifice, by which the form and fashion it before had is changed. And this may take place where one or more persons build, or add to, or take something from the ancient work, by which an alteration is produced therein. And any one who apprehends injury from such new works may forbid and prevent them being made. And so may his children, slaves, attorney, or steward; or the guardians or friends of minors, in their name. But they ought to give security that the persons in whose names they interpose shall ratify what they do. And the construction of such new works may be forbidden in three ways; the first: verbally, where the person who forbids says, "I summons you, such a one, to have this work pulled down, and not to make it; and I tell you it is a new work, built upon my ground and against my rights, and I therefore prohibit you from working for the future;" the second, by taking a stone in his hand, and throwing it against the work, and uttering the same expressions mentioned in the first case; the third is where the person wishing to forbid the construction of the new work is afraid to go in person to the place where it is building, because of the power of those who order it to be made; in that case he ought to present himself to the judge, and petition him to prohibit those who order, as well as those who execute the work, from doing it, as he is injured thereby; the judge ought then to go in person, or send some one, to tell them to desist, until the dispute can be decided by a judgment of court. And in whichsoever of these three ways the construction of new works is forbidden, it ought to be done in the place where they are constructing. And if their construction be going on in several places, then it must be done in each of those places. And it will be sufficient to forbid the owner of the works, or those who oversee them, or the master workman and those who labor there, when none of the above-mentioned persons be found on the place.

### Law 2.

§ 1438. *How Several Persons Engaged Together in the Construction of a New Work may be Forbidden to Erect the Same; or where Several Persons Think They will be thereby Aggrieved.*—Sometimes several persons commence jointly to erect a new work, and he who is aggrieved thereby can not find them all together that he may forbid them from erecting it. In that case, we say it will be sufficient if he speak to, and notify any one of them, in either of the ways mentioned in the preceding law, without saying anything to the others unless he choose. But if several persons think themselves aggrieved by such new work, and one only of them forbid, in his own name, those who are engaged in it, from erecting it; such forbidding will suffice for him only, and for no other person. But if he forbids one of them engaged in the building, in the name of all those who are aggrieved, it will suffice for them all, and they ought to desist from their work in the same manner as if they had been forbidden by each person aggrieved, provided he who acts in their names will give security that they will ratify what he does.

LAW 3.

§ 1439. *Every Person may Forbid the Erection of a House or Other Edifice in the Public Places, or Threshing-grounds (Exidos) of a Town.*—If a man begin to erect a new edifice in the public places or street, or common threshing-grounds (exidos) of any place, without the permission of the king or of the council, upon whose ground he builds it, then any one of the inhabitants may forbid him to continue the work, unless the person forbidding be an orphan, a minor of fourteen years of age, or a woman; for they can not do it, except where some new work is constructing upon their own property.

LAW 4.

§ 1440. *That a Man Who has the Usufruct of the Thing of Another may Forbid Anything being Done to It.*—If a man have the usufruct of a field, garden, or other place belonging to another, and anybody but the owner begins to erect new works thereon, the usufructuary may forbid him from making any more. And so may he who holds such field, garden, or other place as a pledge, or by feudal tenure, or under a rent; and although he may so forbid a stranger, he can not the owner of the soil; yet he may demand of the latter to indemnify him for all the damage he sustained in his usufruct by reason of the new works he had begun there; and the owner will be bound to do it.

LAW 5.

§ 1441. *That He Who has a Right of Service upon the House or Estate of Another may Forbid the Erection of Any New Works there.*—The enjoyment of services is sometimes hindered by new works being erected upon places from which they are due. We therefore say, if any one to whom a service is due from a house or other edifice feel himself aggrieved by the construction of new works there, by which his service may be impeded, he may forbid their erection in the ways mentioned above. But if the service be such as one estate may owe another, as the use of a path, carriage road or way, or any aqueduct, then the person to whom the service is due can not forbid the construction of the new works erected in opposition to his service in the manner we mentioned above. But he may complain to the judge of those who order the works to be made; and if the judge finds them wrongfully made, he may order them to be pulled down, and that the owner of the service receive the amount of the damages he had sustained on that account.

### Law 6.

§ 1442. *That where Any One is Notified not to Proceed in the Erection of a New Work, and He Afterwards Alienate It, He ought to Inform the Purchaser that He had been so Notified.*—If a man be forbidden in any of the ways above mentioned to construct a new work, and he afterwards alienate the place upon which he was constructing it to another person, such forbidding will prejudice the purchaser as well as the seller. The latter ought, therefore, to inform the purchaser that he had been forbidden to work there; and if he does not, he will be bound to pay the purchaser all the loss and damage he may sustain on that account. If, however, at the time of the sale, he give information of such forbidding to the purchaser, who nevertheless continued the work, the latter must pay for all the damage arising therefrom, as it happened through his fault; nor can he claim any indemnification or amends of the seller.

### Law 7.

§ 1443. *That No One can Forbid a Man from Making New Works for the Purpose of Repairing or Cleaning out the Canals, or Earthen Troughs, that are Necessary for the Use of their Houses.*—When a man repairs or cleans the canals or aqueducts which receive the water from his houses or estate, and his neighbors be aggrieved by the offensive smell caused thereby, or by stones, or bricks, or earth, or other thing necessary for the work, being thrown into the streets, or upon the ground of any person near the canal, or by stopping up the streets in uncovering the canal with wood or otherwise until the work be finished, yet no one can forbid or hinder him from executing such work; for it is for the benefit and convenience of houses, and conducive to health, that the canals should be kept well cleaned and repaired. But they who do such works ought to take care to do them in such way that when finished the right of no person shall be impaired or injured thereby in any manner, and that the place be left in the same situation it formerly was.

### Law 8.

§ 1444. *What is the Effect of Forbidding the Erection of a New Work.*—When the forbidding is made in any of the three ways above mentioned, it ought to be obeyed, whether made to the owner of the new work, to his overseers, or to a workman; so that the work ought not to be continued, unless by order of the judge of the place where it is making. For the forbidding has such force, whether made legally or not, that if the person who executes the work be obstinate and unwilling to desist, after being forbidden, he ought to be compelled by the judge to pull down everything he does thereafter, at the cost and expense of him who ordered the work to be made.

### Law 9.

§ 1445. *What ought to be Done by the Judge when a Suit is Brought before Him Relative to Forbidding the Erection of New Works.*—Men sometimes prohibit and prevent the erection of new works in one of the afore-mentioned ways, and afterwards both parties appear on that account before the judge. We therefore say that the judge ought to put the party forbidding under his oath that he does not do it maliciously, but because he believes he has a right to do it, as the works are erecting on his ground (en lo suyo), or to his prejudice. And if he be unwilling to take the oath, he ought to permit the other to go on with the work he had begun, and to order the former not to molest him. But if he be willing to take the oath, the judge ought to receive it, and to hear what both parties have to say and prove; and in the mean time the work ought to be suspended three months. And if the suit can not be determined in that time, the judge may grant to the party who had begun the work the power to go on with it, taking from him good securities, conditioned that should it appear, he could not lawfully erect the work, because he had not a right to the place where he was erecting it, that he would pull it down at his own expense; then the judge ought to grant him permission to go on with the work. We also say that if he wish to give such security before the expiration of the three months, the party forbidding the work can not be compelled to take it. Yet if the latter does take the security before coming before the judge, or if without such security he grant the other the power to go on with the work after forbidding him, the owner may then proceed with the work he had begun.

LAW 10.

§ 1446. *That Both New and Old Works Which Threaten to Fall ought to be Repaired or Pulled down.*—New works sometimes open and break because they had been badly bounded or feebly and unfaithfully constructed. Likewise ancient buildings decay and threaten to fall, through age, so that the next neighbors are afraid of sustaining injury from them. In that case, we say that the judge of the place may and ought to order the owners of such buildings to repair or demolish them. And the better to do this, he should take with him master workmen skilled in the art, and go to the place where the buildings are which the neighbors are afraid will fall; and if he finds from the report of the workmen that the buildings are in such bad condition that they can not be repaired, or that their owners are unwilling to repair them, and that they may easily fall and cause damage, he ought then to order the owners to pull them down. If, however, the workmen do not find them in such bad condition, the judge ought to compel the owners to repair them, and to give good security to the neighbors that they shall suffer no damage thereby. And if the owner be unwilling to give such security, or if he be contumacious by being unwilling to make the repairs, the neighbors who complain against him ought to be put in possession of the buildings which threaten to fall, and the property thereof given to them if the owner continue obstinate during the time in which he is commanded by the judge to repair or pull them down. We likewise say that if the owner of the building give security to the neighbors who are in fear of it that he will pay the damage they may suffer thereby, and the building afterwards fall through its own weakness, and not by accident, he will then be bound to pay the damage for which he had obligated himself. But if the building be overthrown by an earthquake, lightning, heavy winds, an inundation, or by any other similar cause, he will not be bound to pay the damages done thereby.

LAW 11.

§ 1447. *If the Buildings of Any One Fall upon the House of Another before Any Complaint had been Made to the Judge, the Owner of Such Building is not Bound to Repair the Damages Caused thereby.*—If one man's building fall upon the house of another before the latter had complained of it to the judge, the owner will not be bound to pay for the damage, if any be caused thereby. Yet if the owner wish to take away the tiles, timbers, and bricks which had fallen upon his neighbor's house or ground and leave the rubbish and earth, he can not do it. For he ought to remove at his own expense and costs everything that had fallen, or leave all for the benefit of him who had sustained the damage.

LAW 12.

§ 1448. *That Walls or Trees may be Pulled down when Any One Fears Damage from Them, in Case They should Fall on his Own Walls.*—Weak walls and tall trees badly rooted in the ground stand sometimes contiguous to others' estates and houses, so that the neighbors are afraid that if they fall they may do them damage. We therefore say that if a complaint of that nature be made to the judge he ought to take with him good men, skilled in such matters, and see if the walls or trees were in such bad condition that they might soon fall and do damage; and if they be found in such condition, he ought to have them cut or pulled down.

LAW 13.

§ 1449. *That the Troughs may be Destroyed Which Any One has Newly Constructed in his House, to Convey the Water thither, when his Neighbors are thereby Prejudiced, as Also the Trenches by Which the Water is Prevented from Running in its Usual Channels upon their Estates.*—Men sometimes erect strong works upon their own ground, and though they may be such that the neighbors are not afraid of their falling, yet they may suffer some other damage or inconvenience from them. As when one builds a town or other edifice, and collects rain-water there by means of troughs, which project so far out that the water falls upon the roofs of his neighbors' houses. When, therefore, such or any other like complaint be laid before the judge, we ordain that he cause the work to be so rectified and amended that they who complain shall not be prejudiced by them. We likewise say that if a man make a wall or an intrenchment, or put up palisades or any other work upon his own estate, in order to form a pond there, by which the water is diverted from its usual channel, and injury is done to his neighbor's estate; or if he erect any work in the place where the water takes its rise, by which its course is changed, and it made to fall from so great a height as to excavate holes and trenches in his neighbor's ground; or by which its course is impeded or stopped up so that they who were before accustomed to enjoy it can not use it to water their estates, as they usually had done; all these and the like works newly erected, by which damage is done to the neighboring estates, ought to be demolished at the expense and cost of the person erecting them, and things restored to their former condition; and he ought, moreover, to pay his neighbors for all the damage he had thereby caused them. For, as was said by the ancient sages, although a man has the power to do what he pleases upon his own ground, yet he ought to do it in such a manner as to cause no damage or harm to any other person.

LAW 14.

§ 1450. *For What Reasons the Owner of One Estate, Which does Damage to Another, is not Bound to Pay the Proprietor of the Latter for Such Damage.*—There are three ways in which a man may sustain damage from the estates of others, but which he is obliged to suffer, and can not lawfully complain of the owners of such estates: the first is that which is caused naturally, as where one man has an estate situated below that of another—for if the water run from the higher estate upon the lower, or stones or earth be carried there by the force of the waters, or in any other way, so that it is not done maliciously by the act of man, and do damage, the owner of the higher estate is not culpable, nor is he bound to pay therefor; the second is that which is caused by works anciently made—for although the owner of the estate below suffer damage from the other upon which the works are, yet, if ten years had elapsed since the works had been erected, the owner of the estate sustaining the damage being all that time in the place, and making no opposition, or twenty years while he was absent and in another country (enotra parte), he must then suffer the damage, and can not afterwards complain of it; the third is that which is caused by the service which one estate has upon another—for although the subjected estate receive damage by reason of the service for which it is bound, yet the owners can not complain, on that account, of him to whose estate the service is due.

LAW 15.

§ 1451. *What He ought to Do, on whose Estate the Water is Stopped by Stones, Wood, or Sand Which It had Carried thither.*—Where the water runs through the estates of several persons, though none of them raise any works to impede its course, yet the stream itself may do it naturally, by accumulating, little by little, wood, mud, stones, and other things, so as to dam up the water and direct it from the channel where it usually run. If any neighbor be thereby aggrieved or suffer any loss, he may compel him upon whose estate the water is stopped up to do one of two things: either to clean out and open the place where the water formerly run and cause it to flow there as usual; or to suffer the person aggrieved to do it himself; and the owner of the estate will be obliged to do one or the other, though he should be unwilling. But if the place where water is accumulated be a canal which belongs to many persons, each of them is bound to aid in cleaning it out along the limits of his estate, so that the water may run where it formerly did, that they may make use of it.

LAW 16.

§ 1452. *That a Work Erected to the Prejudice of Another Person ought to be Demolished, notwithstanding Both the Estate upon Which It was Erected and That Which was thereby Prejudiced should be Afterwards Sold.*—When a man erects upon his estate new works which detain or dam the water that ordinarily runs there, and which causes damage or loss to the owner of a neighboring estate, and the person receiving such damage sell his estate to another, before he had required that the works should be demolished; then we say the purchaser may sue for the demolition of the works, unless the person erecting them had acquired them by prescription. We also say that if he who erected the works sell the estate upon which they were erected before he had been judicially demanded to pull them down, the purchaser may be compelled to let them be demolished by those who sustain damage from them, or to demolish them himself; and he can not excuse himself by saying that he is not in fault because he had not erected the works. But he may claim of the vendor the amount of the damages (lesion) done to his estate, by the demolition of the works, and the vendor may be compelled to pay them, notwithstanding he should be unwilling to do so.

LAW 17.

§ 1453. *When Many Persons Erect Any New Work Which Causes Damages to Another, Each of Them may be Required to Demolish It.*—If many persons erect any new work by which the water that any man had a right to use is dammed up or lost, he may require such persons, either separately or jointly, as he chooses, to demolish the work they had constructed; though he can not demand reparation of any one of them separately, for the whole of the damage he had thereby sustained, but of each one his proportional part only. We likewise say that if the work had been erected to the prejudice of many persons, each or all of them may require that it be demolished; nevertheless, each one separately can not demand reparation for the whole of the damage or deterioration, though he may for his part only.

LAW 18.

§ 1454. *That One Mill may be Erected Near Another, Provided the Water be not thereby Taken from the Latter, nor Impeded in its Course.*—If a man have a water-mill for making flour or for fulling cloth, and any one desire to build another near it on the same stream, he may do it, upon his own estate, or within the limits of the king's domain, with his consent, or with the consent of the common council of the place where he wishes to build. But it ought to be built in such a manner as not to obstruct the current of water to the other mill, and to leave it to run freely, in its accustomed channel. If he build in this manner the owner of the other mill can neither prohibit nor trouble him, notwithstanding he should allege that his own produced less revenue, on account of the newly erected mill; and so it would be with respect to an oven (forno) which had been newly erected.

LAW 19.

§ 1455. *That a Man may Make a New Well or Fountain on his Estate.*—Where a man has a fountain or well in his house, and his neighbor wishes to make one in his house likewise, in order to procure water for his use, the latter may do it and the former can not prevent him, notwithstanding the water in the first well or fountain may be thereby diminished, unless the person wishing to make the new well has no need of it, and acts maliciously, with an intention of doing harm to the other, by stopping up or diminishing the veins of water that run to his well or fountain. For then the latter may prevent him from making it; or if he had already made it, he may compel him to destroy or fill it up. For the sages have said that neither the laws nor the king should permit or overlook the wickedness of men, but ought always to repress it.

LAW 20.

§ 1456. *That Castles, the Walls of Towns, and Other Fortresses, as also their Causeways, Fountains, and Canals, ought to be Repaired and Kept in Order.*—The good order and dignity of the empire require that its castles, the walls of towns and other fortresses, and causeways (calcadas), bridges, and canals of towns, should be maintained in such a state that they neither decay nor fall to ruin; and though they appertain to the good of all, yet the care and reparation of them belong to the king. He ought therefore to appoint certain diligent men, skillful in such works, to oversee them and make the necessary repairs;

and he ought, moreover, to furnish them with the requisite means for that purpose; but if it be necessary to erect any such works in cities or towns which enjoy a separate revenue, such revenue ought to be first expended for that purpose; and if it be not sufficient, or there be none, then the inhabitants of the place ought to pay in common, each in proportion to his estate, until a sum be raised sufficient to erect the work; and no one, whether a military man, ecclesiastic, widow, or orphan, or any other person whatever, can be excused from paying his part on account of any privilege he enjoys; for since all are alike benefited by the works, it is but just and right that every one should contribute to them, as much as he is able.

LAW 21.

§ 1457. *What Penalty They Deserve Who Commit Fraud in the Works Which They are Appointed to Oversee.*—They who are appointed to oversee any works ought to have them constructed with great fidelity and diligence, so that there be no deception (falsedad) in them through their fault or neglect; and if they act otherwise, they will be responsible therefor to the king, in both their persons and property. And if peradventure any newly erected work fall or totter before it is finished, or within fifteen years afterwards, the ancient sages ascribed the defect to the fault or fraud of those who were employed to construct it; and therefore, they and their heirs are bound to rebuild it, at their own cost and expense; unless it were destroyed by accident (ocasion), as by an earthquake, or lightning, or by great inundations of rivers, of aqueducts, or other extraordinary accidents of a similar nature.

LAW 22.

§ 1458. *That a House or Other Building ought not to be Erected Near the Walls of a Town or Castle.*—The roads near the walls of towns, cities, and castles ought to be left unobstructed and free: therefore, no house or other building ought to be erected there, to encumber them, or to lean against the walls. And if any one wish to erect a new house there, he ought to leave a space of fifteen feet between the building and the wall. And the ancient sages thought this a wise measure, for two reasons: the first, that men may freely pass and guard the walls in time of war; the second, that no damage might arise to the town or castle from the proximity of the house, or treachery be thereby practiced.

### Law 23.

§ 1459. *That No House or Other Building ought to be Erected in the Public Places, or Roads, or Threshing-grounds of Towns (Exidos).*—No one ought to erect a house, or other building or works, in the public places, or threshing-grounds (exidos), or roads which are common to cities, towns, or other places. For, as they are left open for the sake of regularity (apostura) and the common good of all who come there, no one ought to take possession of them, or labor there for his own particular benefit. And if any one contravene this law, that which he builds there ought to be pulled down and destroyed. And if the corporation of the place where the works are constructed choose to retain them, for their own use, and not to pull them down, they may do so; and they may make use of the revenue they derive therefrom, in the same manner as of any other revenue they possess. And we moreover say that no man who has erected works in any of the above-mentioned places can or ought to defend himself by alleging that he had acquired them by prescription.

### Law 24.

§ 1460. *That Houses, Towers, or Other Buildings ought not to be Erected Near the Church.*—Men enjoy in common the use of churches, there to pray God to pardon their sins: therefore neither houses, nor shops, nor other buildings ought to be erected near them, as is prescribed with respect to the walls of castles and towns; and because, moreover, a church is the holy house of God, and no shop of merchandise, or of other things, should be erected round about them, unless they relate to works of piety and grace. And if any building should be constructed there, it ought to be pulled down. We moreover say that they who have the care of churches ought to keep them in order and repair them, so that they neither decay nor fall down.

### Law 25.

§ 1461. *That Every Person is Bound to Repair and Keep in Order his House or Any Other Building Belonging to Him; but He is not Bound to Build Them Anew, except in Certain Cases.*—When a man has a house, tower, or any other building whatever, in a town, or other populous place, he ought to keep it in good order and repair, so that it does not fall through his fault or neglect; but he is not bound to build it anew if he does not choose; unless he had agreed, or made a contract to build a house or tower, in any place, or had inherited the estate of any one who had ordered him to build one. For then he will be bound to comply with his contract or the order of the testator. We likewise say that any one who chooses may build a new house or tower upon his own ground, provided he leave as much space on the side next the road as is usually left by others, his neighbors in the place; and provided always, he does not raise it so high as to discover much of what is doing in his neighbor's house.

LAW 26.

§ 1462. *That He Who Repairs a House or Other Building Which he Owns in Common with Others may Recover from his Co-proprietors the Expenses the Repairs Cost Him, or He will Acquire their Part of the Building.*—If many persons own in common, a tower, house, or other building which is in a bad state of repair, as to threaten to fall; and if one of the co-proprietors cause work to be done upon it, or repair it, from his own resources, in his own name or in the name of his co-proprietors, having first given them notice thereof, they will be bound, each for his part, to reimburse him the expenses he incurred for the benefit of such building. And this they ought to do within four months from the day the work was finished and payment had been demanded of them; and if they fail so to do they will lose their part of the thing upon which the work was done, and it will remain free and entirely to him who had repaired it at his expense. But if he who made the repairs had made them in bad faith, without giving any notice to his co-proprietors; repairing and doing work upon the thing held in common between them, or making some new work there, in his own name, as if the whole belonged to him; in that case he ought to lose the expenses the work cost him; and the new work he had put there will remain in common to all the co-proprietors.

# CHAPTER IV.

## THINGS OF WHICH ONE MAY ACQUIRE THE PROPERTY, AND HOW IT IS ACQUIRED.

### PARTIDA 3, TITLE 28.

### Law 1.

§ 1463. *What is Meant by Dominion, and how Many Kinds there Are.*—Dominion (sonoric) is the power which one has over the things that belong to him, to do with them as he thinks fit according to the laws of God and man. There are three kinds of dominion: the first is the absolute power enjoyed by kings and emperors to punish malefactors and to do justice to every one in the kingdom—of this we have spoken sufficiently at large in the second and in many laws of the fourth partida, in this book; the second is the power which a man has during his life over the movable and immovable things of this world, and which passes at his death to his heirs, or to those to whom he transfers it while living; the third is the right which a man has to the fruits and revenues of a thing during his life, or for a certain time, or which he has to a castle or a land which he holds by feudal tenure, as is said in the laws of this code which speak of that matter.

### Law 2.

§ 1464. *That there is a Distinction between the Things of This World; that Some of Them Belong to All Creatures Living, and Others not.*—There exists a great distinction between the things of this world. For some of them appertain to birds and beasts and all other living creatures, which use them in common with men. There are others which appertain to men only; others, to the commons of towns and cities, or to castles, or other places inhabited by men. There are others which belong to individuals particularly, and of which they may acquire or lose the dominion or property. And there are others, the dominion of which appertains to no one, nor are reckoned among his property, as we shall hereafter show.

### Law 3.

§ 1465. *What Are the Things Which Belong in Common to All Creatures Living.*—The things which belong in common to all the living creatures of this world are the air, rain, water, the sea, and its shores; for every living creature may use them according to his wants. And therefore every man may enjoy the use of the sea and its shores, either for the purpose of fishing or navigation, or doing there whatever else he may conceive advantageous to him. Nevertheless, if there be a house on the sea-shore belonging to any one, it ought not to be pulled down or used in any manner without the consent of the builder or owner. If, however, it be destroyed by the sea or otherwise, or fall to ruin, then any person may build another in its place.

LAW 4.

§ 1466. *What Are the Things a Man may Do upon the Sea-shore.*—Every man who chooses may build a house or cabin upon the sea-shore as a retreat, and he may erect there any other edifice whatever to serve his purposes; provided he does not thereby interfere with the use of the shore, which every one has a right in common to enjoy. He may also build galleys there, or any other vessel whatever; or stretch and mend his nets; and when he is there, or employed for these or other purposes of a similar nature, no one has a right to disturb him. And by the sea-shore is understood all that space of ground covered by the waters of the sea in their highest annual swells, whether in winter or summer.

LAW 5.

§ 1467. *That He Who Finds Gold, Pearls, or Precious Stones on the Sea-shore Acquires the Property of Them.*—Gold, pearls, and precious stones are sometimes found in the sand of the sea-shore. We therefore say that every one who finds and first takes possession of these things becomes the owner of them. For as things found in such places belong to no one, it is proper and just that they should belong to the first finder, who may take them away, and nobody can oppose or hinder him.

LAW 6.

§ 1468. *That Every One may Make Use of Ports, Rivers, and Public Roads.*—Rivers, ports, and public roads belong to all men in common; so that strangers coming from foreign countries may make use of them, in the same manner as the inhabitants of the place where they are. And though the dominion or property (senorio) of the banks of rivers belongs to the owner of the adjoining estate, nevertheless, every man may make use of them to fasten his vessel to the trees that grow there, or to refit his vessel, or to put his sails or merchandise there. So fishermen may put and expose their fish for sale there, and dry their nets, or make use of the banks for all like purposes which appertain to the art or trade by which they live.

LAW 7.

§ 1469. *That Trees Growing on the Banks of Rivers Belong to the Owners of the Adjacent Estate in Front of Them.*—All the trees growing on the banks of rivers belong to the owners of the adjoining estate, who may cut or cause them to be cut down, or do with them whatever they think fit. Yet, if at the time they are about to cut them down they find any vessel fastened or about to be fastened to such trees, they can not immediately cut them down, otherwise they would interfere with the rights which every man has to use the banks of rivers, as is above said. But if there is no vessel fastened nor about to be fastened to such trees by any one, then they may be cut down and converted to the owner's use.

### Law 8.

§ 1470. *That No One has a Right to Build a Mill or Other Edifice on a River, by Which the Navigation of Vessels may be Obstructed.*—No man has a right to dig a new canal, construct a new mill, house, tower, cabin, or any other building whatever, in rivers which are navigated by vessels, nor upon their banks, by which the common use of them may be obstructed. And if he does, whether the canal or edifice be newly or anciently made, if it interfere with such common use, it ought to be destroyed. For it is not just that the common good of all men generally should be sacrificed to the interest of some persons only.

### Law 9.

§ 1471. *What are the Things that Properly Belong to the Commons of Cities and Towns, and Which Every One may Use.*—The things which belong separately to the commons of cities or towns are the water-fountains, the places where fairs and markets are held, or where the city councils meet; the sandy places on the banks of rivers; the threshing (exidos) and race grounds; the forests and pastures; and all other similar places which have been appropriated and granted for the common use of each city, town, castle, or other place. For every person living there may use these things, they being common alike to every man, to the poor as well as to the rich. But they who reside in other places can not use them against the consent or prohibition of those who live there.

### Law 10.

§ 1472. *What are the Things Common to Cities and Towns, Which Each One has not the Right to Use.*—Cities and towns may possess vineyards, gardens, olive fields, and other estates, or cattle, or slaves, or other things which produce fruits or revenue. And though they belong in common to all the inhabitants, nevertheless each one can not make a particular use of them. But the fruits and revenues they produce ought to be applied to the common good of the city or town to which they belong, as for the repairs of the walls, bridges, fortifications, or the maintenance of cattle, or to pay the judges who preside at the gates (aportellados), or for other like purposes which appertain to the common good of the whole city or town.

Law 11 relates to the revenue of the ports.

Laws 12, 13, 14, and 15 relate to sacred things.

Law 16 relates to the city of Rome.

Law 17 relates to wild beasts.

Law 18 relates to the causes for which a man may enter upon the estate of another; supplied by the civil code.

Law 19 relates to the manner of losing property in wild beasts.

Law 20 relates to the enemy of the faith.

Laws 21, 22, 23, 24, and 25 relate to personal property.

LAW 26.

§ 1473. *To Whom Belongs the Increase Which a River Makes to an Estate.*—Rivers sometimes swell to such a height that they carry away a portion of one estate, and join it to another situated elsewhere on their banks. Wherefore we say that the earth which a river carries away from an estate, little by little, and imperceptibly, because not all in a body, becomes the property of him to whose estate it is carried, and he who lost it has no claim whatever to it. But if the river carries away part of an estate all at once in a body, whether with or without its trees, the earth so carried away will not become the property of him to whose estate it is joined, unless a sufficient time had elapsed for the trees to take root there; for then this new portion of earth becomes the property of the owner of the lands where the trees thus take root; but in that case he will be obliged to pay the former proprietor the damage he had sustained, according to the estimation of good men, skilled in cultivating lands.

LAW 27.

§ 1474. *How Islands Formed by Rivers are to be Divided.*—Islands sometimes rise in rivers, and men dispute about the right property in them. We therefore say that if the island rise in the middle of the river, the owners of the estates on the opposite banks ought to divide it in the middle, each one taking as much of the half towards his estate as equals the extent of his lands upon the bank. But if it rise entirely in one half of the river, towards one side, it ought to be divided as is above said, by the owners of the adjacent lands on that side. But if it does not rise entirely in one half of the river and towards one of its shores, nor in the middle, but so that the greatest part of it be rather on one side than the other, then a cord must be taken and measured out, as long as the river is wide, and after having measured it, of the same length with the width of the river, so that it be neither more nor less, it must be doubled, and the place marked on the island to which the half of the cord extends; from that point a division must be made between the proprietors of the adjacent banks, agreeably to what is above said, each taking a portion of the island, according to the extent of his estate opposite thereto.

### Law 28.

§ 1475. *If a River Form an Island within the Estate of Any One, he does not Lose his Right in It.*—Rivers are sometimes so swelled by the increase of waters that they enter upon people's estates, traverse them, and form islands there. And, notwithstanding we prescribed in the preceding law the manner in which islands formed in rivers are to be divided, yet it is not to be understood that those formed in the way here spoken of are to be so divided; for with respect to these, no one can have any right to them except the owner of the estate within which they are formed, he preserving the dominion or property which he before had in his estate unimpaired by such event.

### Law 29.

§ 1476. *To Whom the Islands Belong that are Newly Formed in the Sea.*—It seldom happens that islands are newly formed in the sea. Yet if one should be so formed, we say it will belong to the first occupant; and he or they who first occupy it will owe obedience to the sovereign within whose dominions it is formed.

### Law 30.

§ 1477. *To Whom the Island Belongs that is Formed in Front of an Estate Which is Held by a Tenant or Usufructuary.*—A man may have the usufruct for life of an estate situated on the bank of a river; or he may hold it by feudal tenure. And though we have said in the fourth preceding law that islands which are formed in rivers ought to be divided between the owners of the lands on the opposite banks in the manner we have therein prescribed, yet they who have the usufruct of such lands, or hold them by feudal tenure, can have no claim whatever to these islands; but they will respectively belong, as well as the usufruct of them, to the owners of the adjoining estates. Yet if an estate of which one has the usufruct, or which he holds by feudal tenure, is increased by the alluvion or the river, the usufruct of what is thus added will belong to him, in the same manner as the usufruct of the estate itself to which it was added.

LAW 31.

§ 1478. *When a River Changes its Course, to Whom will Belong the Bed where It Formerly Run.*—Rivers sometimes take new courses, abandoning their former beds and leaving them dry. And as disputes may arise about the right of property to the ground thus left, we say it will belong to the owners of the adjoining lands, in proportion to the extent of their estates upon the banks. And the owners of the lands through which the river makes its new bed will lose the property in the soil it covers, which will now be of the same nature of the former bed, and will, like the river itself, vest in the public.

LAW 32.

§ 1479. *That One does not Lose the Property in his Estate though Covered with Water.*—Lands are sometimes covered with water by the inundation of rivers, and remain so covered for many days; and though the owner during that time loses the possession of them, he nevertheless preserves his right to the property; for as soon as the waters retire to their former channel and leave the lands uncovered, he will enjoy them as before.

Laws 33, 34, 35, 36, 37, and 38 relate to personal property.

LAW 39.

§ 1480. *To Whom Belongs the Fruits of an Estate from Which a Man had been Ejected by a Judgment.*—A man may buy a house or an estate of another in good faith, believing it to be the property of the seller, and that he had a right to alienate it; and afterwards the true owner may claim it and evict him by judgment. In that case, we say that the fruits of the estate which he had gathered and consumed previous to issue joined in the cases will belong to him for the work and labor he had done thereon; and he will not be obliged to restore them to the successful party, though he will the estate itself as well as the fruits he had not yet consumed; first deducting the expenses he had incurred on that account. We likewise say that if the fruits he had gathered be of a nature that did not arise from the labor of man, but were yielded by the estate itself, as pears, apples, cherries, nuts, or similar fruits which trees naturally produce without the labor of man; these he will be obliged to restore with the estate, though he had made use of them in good faith. But if he had bought or had acquired the estate in any other way, in bad faith, knowing it did not belong to him who alienated it, then he will be bound to pay the price of the fruits he had gathered therefrom, notwithstanding he had already consumed them, deducting always the expenses he had incurred on their account.

### LAW 40.

§ 1481. *That he Who Possesses a Thing in Bad Faith, and is Ejected by a Judgment, must Restore the Fruits He had Gathered.*—There are two ways in which a man may acquire an estate or other property in bad faith: the first is where he obtains it by theft or robbery, or enters upon it without any right whatever: if such a person be evicted by a judgment he will be obliged to restore the estate, together with all the fruits he had gathered from it, as well as those which might have been gathered by the owner himself; the second is where he acquires it by purchase, donation, or other just title, knowing, however, that the person from whom he obtained it had no right to alienate it. If then he be evicted by a judgment, he will be obliged to restore all the fruits he had gathered from the estate, but not those which might have been gathered by the owner had he retained the possession of it; except, however, in four cases; the first is where a person had sold his estate to defraud his creditors, the purchaser knowing of the fraud; the second is where the estate is sold by force or through fear; the third is where the estate has been acquired contrary to the laws of this code; the fourth is where any one purchases fraudulently any of those things which are ordered to be sold by an officer of our court, contrary to the custom which ought to be observed in selling the same. For whoever acquires an estate in either of these four ways will be obliged to restore it with all the fruits he had gathered from it, as well as those which might have been gathered by the proprietor himself.

### LAW 41.

§ 1482. *That a Man ought to Recovey the Expenses He had Incurred, on Account of an Estate Which he had Bought in Good Faith, and from Which He had been Evicted by a Judgment of Court.* A man may purchase or acquire another's estate in good faith, and erect new buildings thereon; such as a house, a town, or other edifice; or plant trees there or make a vineyard, or do other similar things, as upon his own lands; and the true proprietor may then come and evict him by a judgment of court. And as a question may arise whether the purchaser ought to be reimbursed the expenses such additional labor had cost him, we say that before the house or estate be delivered to the successful party, he shall pay the other all the expenses he had incurred on account of the new works he had put there; and it is but just that he should be so paid, since he had acquired the estate in good faith and labored thereon, as upon his own. Yet inasmuch as he sought to be reimbursed such expenses, it is likewise just that he should account to the owner of the estate for any rents, fruits, or crops he had gathered from it. Nevertheless, if the owner be so poor that though he were willing to sell all he had, he could not then pay the expenses: in that case, we say he will not be obliged to pay them; but the person to whom they are due may carry away from the house or estate the additional works he had put there, and convert them to his own profit. Nevertheless, we think proper, and we do ordain, that if the owner be willing to pay the other for the objects he was about to remove the same price he could get for them after they were carried away, then he shall take the price, and shall not carry them away. And so we say it would be where the purchaser who had made the additional works to the house or estate acquired it in good faith, but before he had begun to construct the works there acted in bad faith, knowing that the person from whom he acquired the property had no right to alienate it; for then, if the true owner evict him by a judgment of court, he can not recover the expenses he had incurred; though he may remove the works themselves he had constructed on the estate, in the manner above mentioned.

## Law 42.

§ 1483. *That a Man can not Recover the Expenses He had Incurred on Account of a Thing Which He Held in Bad Faith.*—If a man construct an edifice, or sow seed in bad faith, upon another's lands, knowing he had no right to do it, and he be afterwards evicted by the owner, he will lose what he had so built or sowed; they will belong to the owner, and he can not recover the expenses he had incurred on their account. But when he delivers the fruits by the estate, or their estimated value to the owner, he may deduct therefrom the expenses they had cost him.

### Law 43.

§ 1484. *What Penalty a Man Incurs Who in Bad Faith Plants Trees or Vines upon Another's Lands.*—Where a man knowingly, in bad faith, plants trees or makes a vineyard upon another's land, he will lose the property in them immediately they take root, or are nourished from the ground. And so we say it would be if he had planted another man's trees or made a vineyard from the branches of another man's vines upon his own lands, that he will acquire the property in them immediately they take root, whether he planted them in good or bad faith; though he will be bound to their estimated value to the person to whom they belonged. We likewise say that if a man plant a tree on his own estate, and it afterwards extend the principal roots by which it is nourished into the lands of an adjoining proprietor, the tree will become the property of the latter, notwithstanding it extended its branches over the estate of him who planted it. But if a part of the principal roots of the tree were in the lands of him who planted it, and a part in the neighboring lands, then the property of the tree will be common to the proprietors of both estates.

### Law 44.

§ 1485. *What are and What are not the Expenses a Man may Recover for the Repairs He had Made to Another's House or Estate.* Men may incur expenses on account of other persons' houses or lands, not by erecting new works there, but by making necessary repairs, or doing other things there by which the estate is benefited. In that case we say that if such expenses were necessary, they who incurred them may and ought to recover them back while in possession of the estate upon which they expended them, whether they held in good or bad faith; and though the owner may evict them by a judgment of court, they will not be obliged to deliver him the house or estate until he shall have paid the expenses incurred on account of the same. Yet if the party cast out had gathered any fruits or rents from the house or estate, he ought to deduct their value from such expenses; for it is but just that since he sought to be reimbursed, the latter, should be on account of the revenues. We likewise say that if a man incur expenses for the advantage of another's estate or house, while he held it, acting in good faith, believing the property to be his own, he may recover the amount, whether they are necessary or not; but if he acted in bad faith, knowing that the estate or house belonged to another person, and the owner who evicted him be unwilling to reimburse him, he may then carry away the additional works he had put there. We likewise say that if a man who holds another's house or estate incurs on their account expenses which are not very useful, but rather ornamental, such as for paintings, or water-spouts, or other works, intended more for pleasure than utility, if he held the estate or house in good faith, believing them to be his own, then he may carry away the additional works he had put there. Nevertheless, if the owner be willing to pay him what would be their value, after they were taken away, then he should leave them with the owner. But if the party incurring such expenses held the house or estate in bad faith, he will lose what he had expended, nor can he carry away the additional works he had put there.

LAW 45.

§ 1486. *To Whom Belongs the Treasure Which a Man Finds in his Own or Another Man's Estate.*—A man sometimes finds a treasure in his house or lands by chance, or by searching for them. And as doubts may arise to whom it belongs, we say that if it be of such a nature that no one can know who put it there or whose it is, it will belong entirely to the person who found it in his house or lands. But if peradventure any one had hid it there, or could prove that it belonged to him, then it will not become the property of him who found it on his estate. But if a man happen to find a treasure in another's house, or on his estate, whether by laboring there or otherwise, provided he found it by chance, and not by express search, then one half will belong to him, and the other half to the owner of the house or estate where he found it. But if he had found it by expressly searching for it, and not by chance, then the whole will belong to the proprietor of the estate, and no part whatever to the finder. And so we say it would be if the treasure had been found in a house belonging to the king, or the commons of a city or town. (See the civil code, articles 854 to 866 inclusive. *Quære*, would not the rights to the treasury of Montezuma and other anciently hidden treasures, if found, be governed in some measure by the preceding ancient law, rather than by the present code?)

LAW 46.

§ 1487. *That the Property in the Thing Sold does not Pass to Him to Whom it is Delivered until He has Paid the Price.*—Men sometimes deliver their property into the possession of other persons by selling it to them, or by giving it in dowery or otherwise, or by exchange, or under any other just title. Wherefore we say that by such delivery which a man makes himself, or which another makes by his order, the property in the thing passes to the person to whom it is delivered. Nevertheless, if a man deliver a thing into the possession of one to whom he had sold it, and the buyer had not paid the price nor given any security or pledge, nor stipulated any term for the payment of it, the property in the thing sold will not pass to the buyer until he had paid the price thereof. But if he had given any security or pledge for the payment of the price, or has stipulated a term therefor, or if the seller had trusted to him for the payment of it, then the property in the thing will pass by delivery, notwithstanding the price had not been paid, and the purchaser will remain bound to pay it thereafter.

### Law 47.

§ 1488. *That a Man Acquires the Property in a Thing Which He had Hired if He Afterwards Buy It of the Person Who Let It.*—If a man hire anything belonging to himself to another person, or lend it to him, or put it in his keeping, and afterwards sells or gives it to him, though the thing be not in view of the parties at the time, nor any delivery of it be made, nevertheless the person to whom it is given or sold will acquire the property therein. We likewise say that by whatever way or means the possession of a thing can pass from one man to another, though no corporeal delivery thereof be made, according to what was said in the title which spoke of the manner in which one may acquire the possession of things, that by the same way and means the property of a thing will pass to him to whom it is sold or exchanged, or given in dowery, or otherwise; or who acquires it by any other just title, though no corporeal delivery were made of the thing itself. We likewise say that where men enter into a partnership among themselves, stipulating that all they possess or shall thereafter acquire shall belong in common to each partner, that so soon as the partnership is formed or signed or agreed upon between the parties, the property of everything each of them owns shall pass to the others in the same manner as if each had made a corporeal delivery of all he had to the others. Nevertheless, if a debt be due to either of the partners, or he be possessed of any other right whatever previous to forming the partnership, the other partners can not claim or demand it unless by his order, though he will be obliged to give them power to that effect, and what they derive thereby will be in common to them all. We also say that the property of everything that is gained by any of the partners will vest in the others in the same manner as if acquired by themselves.

LAW 48.

*That the Property is Acquired in Things Which are Thrown by Kings or Emperors in the Streets when They are Crowned or Knighted.* (Not in force.)

Law 49 relates to personal property.

LAW 50.

§ 1489. *When a Man Abandons an Immovable Thing Belonging to Him, the First Person Who Takes Possession of It will Acquire the Property therein.*—If a man be dissatisfied with his immovable estate and abandons it, immediately he departs from it corporeally, with an intention that it shall no longer be his, it will become the property of him who first enters thereon. But if he does not leave it, though he were to declare that he did not wish any longer to retain it, yet as long as he remains there no person can enter, and if any one were to enter, he would not acquire the property thereof until the owner had personally departed from it and ceased to have possession of it. We likewise say that if any one abandon his estate, and does not enter upon it through fear of enemies or robbers, no one else can take possession of it, and if he does he would not acquire the property thereof; for although the owner had not corporeal possession of his estate, he would nevertheless retain the property of it in his mind, and therefore no other person ought or can enter upon it.

# CHAPTER .V.

## OF SALE AND PURCHASE.

### PARTIDA 3, TITLE 5.

§ 1490. What a Sale is.
§ 1491. Who are and are not Capable of Selling.
§ 1492. No Person can be Compelled to Sell his Property.
§ 1493. Guardians can not Buy the Estates of Minors under their Care.
§ 1494. In What Manner Sale and Purchase should be Made.
§ 1495. Who Gains the Earnest on a Sale Broken.
§ 1496. A Sale may be Made between Absent Parties.
§ 1497. The Price should be Expressed with Certainty.
§ 1498. In What Way a Sale may be Valid, though No Certain Price be therein Expressed.
§ 1499. How a Man may Sell the Right He Expects to have in the Estate of Another.
§ 1500. Valid Sale of Houses Demolished, how Made.
§ 1501. Sacred Things and Public Places can not be Sold.
§ 1502. Fixtures not to be Sold Separately.
§ 1503. The Purchase by a Man of his Own Property not Valid.
§ 1504. A Man may Sell the Property of Another.
§ 1505. The Object and Price in a Sale must be Agreed on.
§ 1506. Fraudulent Sale Invalid.
§ 1507. As to Increase or Loss on Property Sold.
§ 1508. Amelioration or Damage on Conditional Sales.
§ 1509. Damages from Delay of Delivery by Seller.
§ 1510. What should be Done by Buyer and Seller.
§ 1511. Things Attached to the Ground Belong to the Buyer.
§ 1512. Fish in Ponds and Other Animals Belong to the Seller.
§ 1513. Olive Presses, Mills, Cellars, etc., Belong to the Seller.
§ 1514. Seller is Bound by Warranty.
§ 1515. The Owner may Take his Property Wherever Found.
§ 1516. Warranty of the Seller of the Inheritance of a Third Party.
§ 1517. The Seller is Bound to Guarantee Buildings Sold.
§ 1518. When Seller is not Bound to Guarantee.
§ 1519. What Agreements may be Validly Made between Seller and Buyer.
§ 1520. Loss before Delivery, Agreements as to.
§ 1521. Stipulation of the Seller Annexed to Conditional Sales.
§ 1522. Sales on Condition of Resales.
§ 1523. Sales on Condition that the Buyer will not Sell to Certain Persons.
§ 1524. Sales Forbidden by Wills.
§ 1525. Purchase in the Name of Another.
§ 1526. Estates Purchased by the Money of Another in the Hands of the Purchaser.

### Law 1.

§ 1490. *What a Sale is.*—Sale is a species of convention in use among men effected by the consent of the parties, for a price certain, agreed upon between the buyer and seller.

### Law 2.

§ 1491. *Who are and Who are not Capable of Selling.*—We say that those persons are capable of buying and selling, who can reciprocally obligate themselves to one another. Therefore, a sale from the father to the son, whom he has under his power, or from the son to the father, will not be valid, because they can not contract the one with the other; for though they are naturally two persons, they are considered in law as one only. But if the son has made any of those acquisitions called "castrense" or "quasi castrense," according to what we have said in the title which treats of paternal power, such things as these he may lawfully sell to his father.

### Law 3.

§ 1492. *That No Person can be Compelled to Sell What Belongs to Him.*—Neither force nor violence should be used to compel a man to sell or to buy anything against his will; and if he does either through fear, the contract will not be valid. (The rest of this law relates to the sale of slaves.)

### Law 4.

§ 1493. *That Guardians can not Buy Anything Belonging to Minors Whom They have under Their Care.*—They who are guardians of minors under fourteen years of age are in Latin called *tutores;* as such they can not sell the estates of their pupils, unless in cases of indispensable necessity, or to obtain some great advantage for them; and then not until after the fullest consideration of the matter, and under the authorization of the judge of the place. And we say that no guardian can purchase anything belonging to the estate of his pupil, unless authorized to that effect by the local judge, or some other guardian who has a joint care of the minor with himself. It is further necessary that such purchase be beneficial and not injurious to the minor; for if he be prejudiced by the sale, he may have it rescinded at any time within four years after he has become of age, as we have said in the laws which treat of the guardianship of minors and their estates.

### Law 5.

*That Presidents of Provinces and the Ordinary Judges can not Buy Anything within the Limits of their Jurisdiction.* (Not in force since the independence of Mexico.)

### Law 6.

§ 1494. *In What Manner Sale and Purchase should be Made.* Sale and purchase may be effected in two ways: the one in writing, and the other without. In writing, when the buyer says to the seller, "I wish to have this sale reduced to writing." A sale made in this manner is not perfect, although the parties are agreed upon the price, until the writing is made and executed; for until then, either of them may retract. But after the writing is once made and perfected, in presence of witnesses, neither party can recant and sue for the rescision of the sale. Without writing, when the seller and buyer have mutually agreed upon the price; the one being pleased with the price and the other with the thing, without mentioning any writing. We say that a sale thus made would be perfect although no earnest had been given by the buyer to the seller, as they would be both bound for the fulfillment of the contract they had made.

### Law 7.

§ 1495. *Who Gains the Earnest Given on Account of the Sale if It should not be Perfected.*—Earnest is sometimes given upon a purchase being made, and it then happens that one of the parties recant. Therefore we say that if it be the buyer that recants, let him lose the earnest he had given; but if it be the seller, let him return to the buyer the double of the earnest, and the sale will be null. But if the buyer, at the time he gave the earnest, declared that he gave it both as earnest and as a part of the price, or as a token of the perfection of the bargain, then neither party can recant and rescind the contract. (And this is laid down in Law 2, title 10, book 3, of the Fuero Real.)

LAW 8.

§ 1496. *That a Sale may be Effected, though neither the Buyer nor Seller be Present when It is Made.*—A sale may be made when the buyer and seller are present; and also when they are in different places, by letter or by attorney, both consenting thereto: the buyer to take the thing, and the seller the price. We moreover say that the sale may be made, though the thing sold should not be in the presence of the buyer or seller, provided they agree, as is above said.

LAW 9.

§ 1497. *That the Price should be Expressed with Certainty in the Sale.*—It is necessary for the validity of the sale that the price agreed upon between the buyer and seller should be certain. For if the seller should say, "I sell you this thing for as much as you choose to give, or for as much as I choose to take," such a sale would not be valid. But if they both agree upon a third person, to whom they present the thing, that he may fix the price for which it is to be sold, and he fix it accordingly, the sale will be valid; and if he fix an unreasonable price, either too much above or below the value of the thing, it ought to be corrected by discreet men. But if such third person, to whom the price was referred, should die before he had fixed it, the sale would not be valid.

LAW 10.

§ 1498. *In What Manner a Sale may be Valid, though No Certain Price be therein Expressed.*—If the vendor agree to sell a thing to the buyer for as much money as the latter has in a certain chest, sack, portmanteau, or in any other place, the sale would be valid, if any money should be found therein, whatever might be the sum, although it should not be equal to the value of the thing. But if no money happen to be found therein, the sale would not be valid; for there can not be a sale without a price. Moreover, we say that if a man sell anything, and the buyer agree to give what it cost the seller, the sale would be valid, if it should turn out that the buyer had really bought it. But if it appear that he had acquired it by donation or inheritance, or in any other way than by purchase, then the sale would not be valid.

Laws 11 and 12 relate to personal property.

### Law 13.

§ 1499. *How a Man may Sell the Right He Expects to Have in the Estate of Another.*—Men sometimes hope to inherit the estates of others; and this may happen in two ways: the one, when a person expects to inherit from a relation so nearly akin to him that he will succeed to the whole of his estate if he die without a will; the other, where he expects to be made the heir of any person. And as there are some who may wish to sell such hope or right to inherit, we say they can not do it, if they mention by name the person from whom they expect to inherit; unless it were done with the consent of the person himself, in which case, the sale would be valid if he continued in that intention until his death. But if he be not mentioned by name, the sale may be made by declaring that they sell for so much and to such a person all the advantages and rights from whomsoever derived to them by inheritance. And the reason we declare void such sales wherein are named the persons from whom the inheritance is expected is that the purchaser of such hope or claim may not, through a desire to enjoy it, attempt the life of the owners. (Article 2961 of the civil code, now in force, prohibits the sale of the right to the inheritance of a living person, even with the consent of the latter.)

### Law 14.

§ 1500. *In What Manner is Made Valid a Sale of a Mill, or House, or Other Building Demolished, or of Trees Torn up by the Roots.*—Where a man sells a house, or mill, or any other building, at a time when it was demolished, burned, or destroyed in any other manner, without the knowledge of the buyer, the sale would not be valid, although the seller at the time believed it to be sound and entire. And so we say it would be if he had sold trees under similar circumstances, which were at a distance; that the sale would not be valid if at the time he sold them they were cut down, burned, or torn up by the roots. And so we say it would be if the greater part of the thing sold were burned or destroyed; but if burned or destroyed in the least considerable part only, then the sale would be valid. But in that case the price ought to be reduced as much as the thing might be estimated to be diminished in value on account of the part burned or destroyed at the time of the purchase. But if the seller declared the thing to be entire when he knew it were burned or destroyed, the sale would not be valid; as a thing which does not exist can not be sold; and he would then be bound to pay the buyer all the damages he had sustained for fraudulently and knowingly selling him a thing not in existence. But if the thing thus knowingly sold were burned or destroyed in part, and not entirely, the sale would be valid, and the vendor would be bound to pay the buyer the loss and damages he had thereby sustained, for the amount of which he ought to be believed upon his oath, at the discretion of the judge. And we moreover say that if a man sell a thing burned or destroyed in part and entirely, and the buyer knew it at the time, while the seller was ignorant of it, the buyer would be bound to pay the whole price. But if he had sold it, burned or destroyed, such as it was, informing the buyer of it, the sale would be valid.

### Law 15.

§ 1501. *That a Free Man, a Thing Sacred or Holy, or a Public Place, can not be Sold.*—A free man, a thing religious, sacred, or holy, a public place, as public squares, roads, threshing-grounds, rivers and other waters which belong to the king, or the commons of any city, can not be sold or alienated. But though we here say that a thing sacred or religious can not be sold, yet there is a case in which it may be; as where a village or any other place is sold with all its dependencies. For though the church in the village, or anything belonging to it, could not be separately sold, yet by selling the village, they would pass with all other things, and the sale would be valid, as we have said in the first part of our book, under the title which treats of things belonging to the church, and of those that can and can not be alienated.

### Law 16.

§ 1502. *That the Marble Pillars, Stone, or Any Other Thing Fixed to a House, can not be Torn away and Sold*—The marble, or other stone, or the timbers, or anything whatever, employed in the construction of any house, whether for its use or ornament, can not be separated from it and be sold; and if they should be, the sale thereof will be void. Nevertheless, if any one contravene this law and sell these things, and they be delivered to the buyer, they shall remain with him; but he will be bound to pay the price to the king's court, and as much more out of his own estate. And if he had already paid the price, it must be restored to him; and the seller shall moreover pay out of his own effects, a sum equal to that which he had taken. And we further say that a man can not sell his fugitive slave during his flight.

Law 17 relates to the selling of poison.

### Law 18.

§ 1503. *That the Purchase Which a Man Makes of his Own Property is not Valid.*—A man can not buy a thing that is his own, and if he does through ignorance he may recover back the price he had given, if the thing belonged entirely to him. For if another owned a part of it, the sale would be good as to that part, but not as to his own. But if a man had in his power or possession anything belonging to another, the owner might buy the possession, and the sale would be valid. And we also say that if a man who is the possessor of a thing purchase of another his right or service in it, the sale would be valid.

### Law 19.

§ 1504. *That One Man may Sell the Property of Another.*—If a man sell anything belonging to another, the sale will be valid. But he who makes such a purchase either knew that the thing did not belong to the seller or believed that it did; if he knew that it was the property of another person, and should be compelled to restore it by a judgment of court, nevertheless the seller would not be obliged to return the price, unless he had obligated himself to do so at the time of the sale in case the owner should claim and recover the thing. But if the buyer did not know that it belonged to another person, in that case the seller would be bound not only to return the price he had received, but to pay the damages he had caused by the sale. (According to article 2959 of the civil code, the sale of the property of another is void.)

### Law 20.

§ 1505. *That the Sale is not Valid when the Parties do not Agree upon the Price or the Thing Which is the Object of the Sale.* The buyer and seller must agree upon the price; for if they disagree, the seller declaring it to be greater than the buyer is willing to admit, the sale would not be valid; as where the seller should say that he sold the thing for a hundred maravedis, and the buyer should say for no more than fifty, and there were no other means to discover the truth; but if they disagree, the seller saying the price was less than the buyer contended for, then the sale would not be valid. We also say that the sale would not be valid if they disagree about the thing which was the object of it; as if the seller should say that he sold a vineyard or piece of land, which he designates to be in such a place, and the buyer should say he did not understand that to be the piece of land, but another, which he designates to be in a different place; or if he should say that he sold such a slave, mentioning him by name, and the buyer should say he did not understand it to be that slave, but another, of a different name.

LAW 21.

§ 1506. *That a Sale is not Valid where One Thing is Fraudulently Sold for Another.*—(This would apply to real or personal estate. The illustrations in the law are made with personal property.)

LAW 22.

*That Christians ought not to Sell Arms of Wood nor of Iron to the Enemies of the Faith.* (Not in force.)

LAW 23.

§ 1507. *To Whom Belongs the Profit, or Who Suffers the Loss on the Thing Sold when It is Ameliorated or Deteriorated.*—A sale may be made in two ways, as we have said in the beginning of the present title of this book: the one in writing, and the other without. When it is made without writing, the buyer and seller having agreed, the one upon the thing, and the other upon the price; from that moment the loss happening to the thing will be on account of the buyer. We also say that when the sale is made in writing, as soon as it is finished and signed by witnesses, from that time the loss will be on account of the buyer, although the thing had not yet passed under his power; as where a man buys a slave, or any animal whatever, and after the sale is perfected it fall sick, so as to lose a limb or die, without the fault of the seller; or if he had bought anything else, and it be destroyed by fire, or thrown down in whole or in part, or otherwise deteriorated, without the fault of the vendor; and so we say it would be if the thing be lost or deteriorated in any other similar manner without the fault of the seller. In these and like cases, the loss which happens to the thing bought will be on account of the buyer alone. We likewise say that after the sale is perfected in one of the ways above mentioned, the amelioration of the thing bought will be for the benefit of the buyer, though it had not yet passed under his power; as where a man had bought a field or vineyard, and after the sale it were increased by the inundation of a river that added thereto a portion of earth, with trees or other thing upon it, by which the thing sold was ameliorated; or where the thing was worth at the time of the sale a hundred maravedis, and afterwards by a change in the circumstances of the times comes to be worth two hundred, or more. For how much soever it may be ameliorated, after the sale is perfected, in any of the foregoing ways, or in other the like, all the amelioration will be for the benefit of the buyer. For it is but just, that as the loss belongs to him, according to what we before said, in case the thing be lost or deteriorated, so should any amelioration that may happen to it.

Laws 24 and 25 relate to personal property, which is to be counted, weighed, or measured.

### Law 26.

§ 1508. *To Whom Belongs the Profit, or Who Sustains the Loss of Things Which are Sold under Condition and are afterwards Ameliorated or Damaged.*—Where a condition is annexed to the sale, and the thing sold be deteriorated or ameliorated before the happening of the condition, then the loss or profit will be on account of the buyer. But if the thing be lost or wholly destroyed, in whatever way it may happen, the loss will be on account of the seller, though the condition should be afterwards accomplished. We also say that where a sale is made under condition, and before its accomplishment the buyer or seller, or both of them, die, and the condition be afterwards accomplished, the sale will be valid, and their heirs will be bound to observe it.

### Law 27.

§ 1509. *On whose Account is the Damage Happening to the Thing Sold, when It is Deteriorated through the Delay of the Seller to Deliver It.*—Where the seller delays to give or to deliver to the buyer the thing sold, after they had agreed upon the price, and the buyer summons him before witnesses, to deliver it and receive the price which he presents and invites him to accept, if he should not then deliver it, and it be afterwards lost or deteriorated, the risk will be his, on account of his delay. Yet if afterwards the seller should wish to deliver it, before it were lost or deteriorated, and the buyer should be in fault, being unwilling to receive it, and then the thing be lost or deteriorated, the risk will be on account of the buyer, because the ultimate delay was caused by his fault.

### Law 28.

§ 1510. *What Things ought to be Done, and What Stipulations Observed, by Those Who Buy and Sell.*—The buyer ought to pay the seller the price he promised; and the seller ought to deliver to the buyer the thing sold, with all the appurtenances. Therefore we say that where a man sells a house, it is not understood that he sells a house only, but the wells, canals, aqueducts, and all other things which are generally appropriated to the use of the house, whether they are within or without. So we say the seller can not take away the brick, stones, tiles, or wood which has been detached from the house sold, or were then employed therein, if they made a part of the house. But if he had bought lime, bricks, tiles, timbers, or other like things, or had borrowed them, or if they had been given to him, although he may have brought them there with the intention to use them in the construction of the house, yet he may take away those he had not used for that purpose.

LAW 29.

§ 1511. *That the Granaries and Jars Sunk in the Ground, Which are in the House Sold, Belong to the Buyer.*—The seller can not take away the granary which is affixed to the house sold, or which was so large as not to be moved; nor the oil jars also affixed to the house, or sunk in the ground, or any like thing; for such things as these are understood to appertain to the house, and therefore belong to the buyer. But all other movable things, not affixed nor appertaining to the house, belong to the seller, who may take them away and do what he pleases with them, as the cupboard, casks, and unburied jars, and similar things.

LAW 30.

§ 1512. *That the Fish Bred in the Ponds appertaining to the House Sold and Other Animals Raised about It Belong to the Seller.*—The fish bred and found in a reservoir or fish-pond, appertaining to a house or estate at the time of the sale, belong to the seller, as also do the chickens and other fowls raised about the house. And what we here say of animals usually raised about houses, and what we said in the preceding law of houses themselves, apply also to castles, farms, or any other plantation that is sold.

LAW 31.

§ 1513. *That the Olive Presses or Mills, or the Cellars (Bodegas) Containing Jars, Which are in the Fields, Vineyards, or Olive Gardens that are Sold, do not Belong to the Buyer, unless They have been Expressly Mentioned in the Deed of Sale.*—When an olive orchard, a field, vineyard, or garden is sold, in which there is a wine or an olive press or mill, or other separate thing, as a granary or cellar containing jars to hold wine, none of them are considered as a part of the purchase unless so stipulated in the sale, or unless they had been purposely erected to receive and preserve the fruits of the estate sold. We also say that if a man sell a vineyard or vine arbor which is in need of props to support the vines, and the seller had already cut or bought some for that purpose, yet if he had not placed them under the vines they would not be considered as a part of the purchase. But if he had once placed them, although he had again taken them away to replace them the ensuing year, they will still belong to the buyer.

### Law 32.

§ 1514. *That the Seller is Bound in Warranty to the Buyer for the Thing Sold.*—The thing sold ought to be delivered to the purchaser free and clear of all encumbrances, so that if any one disturb him, or bring a suit therefor, the seller will be bound to guarantee him. But as soon as the suit is commenced, the buyer ought to notify the seller of it; or at least before the depositions of the witnesses produced against him in court are published. And if he does not notify him, and he be afterwards cast in the suit, he can not then demand the price of the thing, neither of the seller nor his heirs. But if he does inform him, and the seller would not or could not defend him in the suit, then the seller will be bound to restore the price he had received for the thing sold, and pay all the damages consequent thereupon. And if at the time of the sale the seller had bound himself in a double penalty to guarantee the buyer, it is then understood that he is bound not only to return double the price but double the value of the thing, although it may have since increased.

### Law 33.

§ 1515. *If Anything Belonging to Another be Sold, the Owner may Reclaim It of Him in whose Power He Finds It.*—Where a man sells the property of another, the owner may reclaim it of the buyer with whom he finds it. But if the buyer require the seller to come into court to defend him, and answer to the suit brought for the thing sold, and the seller consent to appear against the plaintiff, obligating himself to defend the thing in the same manner as if he were in possession of it himself, then the plaintiff will have no right to demand it of the buyer, but rather of the seller, and should let the buyer go in peace. But if the seller will not appear and contest the suit, then the plaintiff may demand the thing of the buyer. Nevertheless, the buyer will retain unimpaired the right to sue the seller in warranty for the thing sold.

LAW 34.

§ 1516. *In What Manner the Seller is Bound in Warranty when He Sells his Right to the Inheritance of a Third Person to Whom He has been Instituted Heir.*—If a man who had been instituted heir of another sell all his right to the estate or inheritance of him who instituted him, and the purchaser be afterwards evicted by a judgment of court of any part of the estate, the seller will not be bound to guarantee that part of which he was so evicted. But if he were evicted of the whole, he would be then bound to indemnify the buyer, or to pay back the price he had received, with all the loss and damages sustained. And so it would be where a man had bought all the revenues of certain customs, or of an estate, and were afterwards evicted by a sentence of court of any part of the same, the seller would not be bound to indemnify him or account therefor. But if he were evicted of the whole or of the greater part of the revenues, he would then be bound to indemnify the buyer, or to return him the price, with all the damages and loss he thereby sustained.

LAW 35.

§ 1517. *That a Man is Bound to Guarantee the House, Ship, or Sheep-fold Which He Sells.*—Where one sells a house, ship, or sheep-fold, or any like thing, together with their appurtenances, and the purchaser be evicted of any part thereof by a judgment of court, the seller will be bound in warranty therefor, in the same manner as if the buyer had been evicted of the principal object of the sale.

LAW 36.

§ 1518. *In What Cases the Seller is not Bound to Guarantee the Thing Sold to the Buyer.*—According to what we have above said, the seller is bound to guarantee the buyer for the thing sold; or if he does not, to return the price and pay all the losses and damages sustained by him on that account. But there are cases where it is not so. The first is, where the buyer delays to inform the seller of the suit commenced for the thing sold, until after the publication of the depositions of the witnesses. The second, where the cause is submitted to arbitrators, without the knowledge of or order of the seller, and they give sentence against him. The third, where the buyer, by his fault, loses possession of the thing sold. The fourth, where he has abandoned the thing and thereby loses it. The fifth, where the thing sold is a female slave, and the buyer put her in a brothel; for on that account she may claim her freedom; and if she in fact do, and obtain it, the seller will neither be bound in warranty nor to return the price. And so we say if the buyer be contumacious at the time the court is about to pronounce sentence against him for the thing he had bought, and refuse to appear and hear the judgment, and on account of his contumacy he lose the thing, that then the seller would not be bound in guaranty, nor to return the price he had received. The sixth, where the buyer had been so long in possession of the thing bought that when he is sued for it he might have defended himself by pleading prescription, but did not do it. The seventh, where sentence is rendered relative to the thing bought, the seller not being present, nor notified by the buyer of the time where it was rendered. And so we say, if a man play at draughts or dice, and while at play he sell or lose anything, and the purchaser or winner be afterwards evicted thereof by a judgment of court, the seller will not be bound either in warranty or to restore the price. And so it would be where the buyer consented that the thing he had bought should be made sacred, or made no opposition to it. And we say also, that if a judge knowingly pronounce an unjust sentence against the buyer for the thing he had bought, then the judge and not the seller will be bound to indemnify him, out of his own effects, for having wrongfully deprived him of it; for the seller is not bound to guarantee otherwise than according to law.

### Law 37.

*That the Seller is not Bound to Guarantee the Estate Sold, if the King Take It Away from the Buyer.* (Not in force.)

### Law 38.

§ 1519. *What are the Agreements or Stipulations that can be Validly Made between the Buyer and Seller.*—Every agreement or stipulation entered into between the buyer and seller must be observed, unless they be contrary to good morals, or the laws of our code; so we say, if they were to stipulate that the buyer should pay the price on a certain day, and in case he did not the sale should be dissolved, such a stipulation would be valid, and the sale will accordingly be dissolved; and the seller will then acquire the earnest, or the part of the price that had been paid him, unless he had received the whole, or the greater part of it, on the day fixed. Nevertheless, the seller has the choice either to demand the whole of the price and the performance of the sale, or to revoke it, and retain, as is above said, the earnest on the part of the price he had received. But when he has selected one of these alternatives, he can not afterwards abandon it and choose the other. We also say that if the buyer had gathered any fruits from the thing bought, he ought to return them to the seller, unless the seller were unwilling to return the earnest, or the part of the price he had received, for then he would not be entitled to the fruits. But if the seller choose to take the fruits, he will be obliged to reimburse the buyer the expense he had incurred in gathering them. We also say that if the sale be dissolved, and the thing had been deteriorated through the fault of the buyer, while in his possession, he will be obliged to indemnify the seller therefor.

LAW 39.

§ 1520. *Of the Agreement Which the Seller Makes with the Buyer concerning the Loss Happening to the Thing Sold before its Delivery.*—When the seller makes an agreement with the buyer that if the thing sold be deteriorated or lost before delivery, such loss or deterioration shall be borne by the seller, then we say the risk will be on account of the seller. And so it would be if the thing sold were wine, and he should tell the buyer that it was of such a place or of such a quality that he might keep it a long time without spoiling; for if it spoil or be deteriorated before it is delivered, the risk will be on account of the seller, and not of the buyer. And so we say it would be if the seller knew the wine were of a nature to spoil, and had concealed that circumstance.

LAW 40.

§ 1521. *Of the Stipulations Which the Seller Annexes to a Conditional Sale.*—Other agreements are sometimes annexed to sales, as where the seller says to the buyer, "I sell you my vineyard for such a price, upon condition that if before such a day I find any one who will give me more I may sell it to him." And we say that where a sale is made in this manner, if before the day appointed the seller find some person who will give him a greater price for the vineyard, or who offered him greater advantages than the other had promised him, he ought to inform the first purchaser what those advantages are, for if he offers the same the seller ought to accept and leave the vineyard to him, on his paying the price agreed upon, with what the other had offered in addition; but if the first purchaser will not consent to this, the sale will not be valid, and he will be obliged to deliver up the vineyard, with all the fruits he had gathered from it, first deducting the expenses he had incurred in gathering them. But if the person who offered to increase the price, as is above said, were the son or slave of the seller, or any one else who did it fraudulently, by his advice, then the buyer would not be obliged to return the vineyard, nor to observe the condition.

Law 41 relates to pledges of personal property.

### Law 42.

§ 1522. *Of Those Who Sell a Thing at a Certain Price on Condition that the Seller or his Heirs may Take It Back on Reimbursing the Price.*—Where a man sells anything for a certain price, stipulating in the sale that whenever the seller or his heirs shall return the price to the buyer or his heirs, that the latter should restore the thing bought, we say that if such a condition be contained in the sale, it ought to be observed. But if the buyer or his heirs be not willing to perform this agreement, nor to restore the thing, as is above said, they ought to pay the penalty, if any had been annexed to the contract. And if the seller or his heirs are willing to take the penalty, they ought to abandon the thing sold; but it would be otherwise if the condition had been that they should restore the thing and pay the penalty. And if no penalty were annexed, the buyer will, at any rate, be obliged to restore the thing if it were in his power; and if it were not, to pay the seller all the loss and damages he had sustained on account of its not being restored.

### Law 43.

§ 1523. *If the Seller Stipulate with the Buyer that He shall not Sell or Pawn the Thing Sold to Certain Persons, the Contract ought not to be Observed.*—If a man sell a castle, tower, house, or anything else, under condition that neither the buyer nor his heirs should ever sell or alienate it to certain persons whom he designates by name, and if they did, that the thing should again become the property of the seller or his heirs; such a contract we say will not be valid. And therefore though the buyer or his heirs should contravene the condition, neither the seller nor his heirs can on that account reclaim the thing of him to whom it had been sold. But if a penalty had been annexed to the contract, he who had bound himself therein would be obliged to pay it as well as the consequent loss and damage, which ought to be ascertained by the oath of the seller, under the discretion of the judge.

LAW 44.

§ 1524. *Of Those Who by their Wills Forbid the Sale of their Castle, Tower, House, Vineyard, or Any Other Part of their Estates.*—When a man by his will prohibits the sale of his castle, tower, house, vineyard, or any part of his estate, alleging some good reason therefor, as if he should say, "I desire that such a thing," expressly designating it, "should in no wise be alienated, but remain always with my son or heir, that he may be the more honored and better supported;" or if he should say, "Let it not be alienated until my heir come of age or until he has returned home, if he were gone to a foreign country;" for these and other like justifiable reasons it ought not to be sold. But if he had only said, "Let it not be sold," without alleging any good reason therefor; or had not designated any particular person or thing as the object of such a disposition; if then it were sold, the sale would be valid, although he had forbidden it.

Laws 45, 46, and 47 relate to the sale of slaves.

LAW 48.

§ 1525. *Of the Purchase Which a Man Makes with his Own Money in the Name of Another; and Whether the Condition Annexed be Valid.*—When a man buys anything with his own money in the name of another, and he in whose name it was bought ratifies the purchase when he is informed of it, then he who made the purchase will be obliged to deliver over the thing to him in whose name he made it, with all its fruits and appurtenances. We also say that he in whose name it was made will be bound to reimburse the price to the purchaser, with all the expenses he had incurred either in gathering the fruits or otherwise, for the benefit of the thing sold. And so we say, if a man send his messenger, saying to him, "Go to such a person and tell him that if he will sell me such a thing belonging to him, I will give him such a price for it;" if the person to whom the message is sent consent to sell the thing for the price proposed, the sale will be valid, although the messenger may not have had a letter of attorney authorizing him to make the purchase. Moreover, he in whose name the purchase was effected will be obliged to observe all the conditions annexed to it by him who made it in his name; for as he has ratified the bargain, he will be bound to fulfill its conditions. And so it would be where one man constituted another his attorney in fact, with power to buy or sell anything in his name, fixing the price which he should take or give; if the attorney then signed the sale or purchase in the name of his constituent, the latter will be obliged to ratify it, and is as effectually bound thereby as if he had personally signed it.

### Law 49.

§ 1526. *That the Estate Which a Man Buys with Another's Money Which He has in his Care Belongs to Him, except in Certain Cases.*—Men sometimes have the money of third persons in their care, and with it buy estates or other things they need; and as doubts have arisen whether the thing so bought belonged to the buyer or to those whose money he used, we will explain ourselves in this respect; and we say that the thing belongs to him who made the purchase in his own name, unless the money he had used belonged to a military man then employed at the king's court or other place in the service of the king; or to a minor under twenty-five years of age, then under the guardianship of the buyer; or to a church, and the prelate who then had the care of it, used the money to make the purchase, or was the dotal money of a wife whose husband had made the purchase with her consent. For in these cases, although the buyer bought in his own name, yet the thing becomes the property of those whose money was employed to pay the price. But they will, each of them, have the choice either to take the thing bought or demand the money.

### Law 50.

§ 1527. *Which of the Two Purchasers ought to have the Thing that has been Sold to Both of Them at Different Times.*—Where a man sells the same thing to two persons at different times, if the first purchaser were put in possession of it and had paid the price, it will belong to him, and not to the second. But then the seller will be obliged to return the price to the second purchaser, if he had received it, and pay him for all the loss and damage he had sustained by the fraudulent sale. We also say, if the second purchaser had come to the possession of the thing and had paid the price, it will belong to him, and not to the first. And then the seller would be, in like manner, obliged to return the price to the first purchaser, and pay him for all the loss and damage he had sustained on that account. We likewise say that if a man sell anything belonging to a third person to two men at different times, and the two purchasers dispute about it, whichsoever of them first gets possession of it will have the best right to it, and it ought to remain with him, though he had not paid the price. But if the owner come and claim the thing, he will nevertheless preserve all his right thereto.

### Law 51.

§ 1528. *Which of Two Purchasers ought to have the Thing Belonging to a Third Person that has been Sold to Them Both at Different Times.*—Where a man sells anything belonging to a third person and immediately delivers possession, and he afterwards acquire the property of the thing, as if the owner had instituted him heir, or had given it to him in any other way, and he then sell it to another, who sues the first purchaser for it, we say that the first purchaser will have the better right to it, on account of his prior possession, notwithstanding the second purchaser should allege he has a better title, inasmuch as when it was sold to the first the seller had not the property in the thing, and that he had sold it to the second after he had acquired that property. But if a man sell anything that does not belong to him, and afterwards the owner sell it to another person, the second purchaser, who bought it of him who had a better right to it, ought to have it, unless he who first sold it had a just cause for so doing; as if it had been pledged to him on condition that he might sell it if it were not redeemed before a day fixed, or if he were the attorney in fact of the owner, and in his letter of attorney power had been given him to sell, and he had accordingly sold it before he knew the owner wished to sell it to another.

### Law 52.

§ 1529. *That Judges Who have the Right, in Virtue of their Offices, to Order Seizures, may Sell Things Belonging to Third Persons.*—Judges who have power to make seizures in virtue of their offices may cause the thing seized to be sold to satisfy the judgment rendered, and the right of property will pass to any one who buys it. And we say that the collectors of the royal taxes have the same power to sell what they receive or seize for the collection thereof. But each of the above persons who have the right to sell the thing seized must do it publicly, and not in secret, by putting it up and crying it off at auction; nor ought it to be sold until after the expiration of ten days, when it may be sold to the highest bidder. And if it be sold for more than the sum for which it were seized, the overplus must be returned to the owner. And if any judge or other officer sell the property of another person in any other manner, the sale will not be valid.

LAW 53.

*Of the Things Which the King Sells or Gives as his Own when It Belongs to Another.* (Not in force.)

LAW 54.

§ 1530. *Of Him Who Sells a Thing Belonging to Another in the Name of the Owner.*—Where a man sells anything belonging to another in the name of the owner, who afterwards ratifies the sale, it will be valid, and the property of the thing will pass to the vendee, although the sale was not at first made with the consent or knowledge of the owner. But if he had sold it in his own name, and not in that of the owner, and the vendee knew that it was not his property, then it would not pass to the vendee, nor could he acquire it by prescription; but the owner might, on the contrary, sue for and recover it. But if the vendee acted in good faith when he bought the thing, not knowing it belonged to another, but believing it to be the property of the vendor, he might then acquire it by prescription; and the vendor will, in any event, be obliged to return the price to the owner. We also say that if a man sell, as his own, the property of another, and it be lost or perish after the sale, the owner of the thing may confirm the sale and claim the price of the vendor, whether it were sold in his name or not.

LAW 55.

§ 1531. *That the Sale of a Thing Common to Several is Valid, although It had not been Divided.*—Where two or more persons possess anything in common, we say that each of them may sell his part, though the thing had not been divided, either to one of his co-proprietors or to a stranger. Yet if one of the co-proprietors will give as much for it as the stranger, he ought to have the preference. But it is here understood that the sale can only be made to a stranger before an action is brought for a partition of the thing; for after the suit is begun it can not be sold to him until the partition is made, unless with the consent of the other co-proprietors.

LAW 56.

§ 1532. *Of Him Who, through Fear or Force, Buys or Sells Anything above or below its Just Value.*—If a man buy or sell anything through force or fear, the purchase or sale will not be valid; but may, on the contrary, be rescinded, if it be proved that the force was so great that he acted against his will. And though the sale was made under oath or a penalty, or with a pledge or security, it would not be valid. For inasmuch as the sale or purchase, the main object of the parties, is void, so will be that which was annexed to it as an accessory. We likewise say that the sale may be rescinded which is made for less than half the just price of the thing at the time of the sale. And if the vendor can prove this, he may compel the vendee to pay him over and above what he had given for the thing, the balance of what it was really worth at the time of the sale; and if the vendee be unwilling to do it, he ought to abandon the thing to the vendor and take back the price he had given. And a thing is said to be sold for less than its just value when it was worth ten maravedis and was sold for less than five. We also say that if the vendee can prove that he gave the just value of the thing at the time of the sale and more than half as much more, he may cause the sale to be rescinded or the price reduced as much as he had given over its just value; as where he had given more than fifteen maravedis for a thing worth only ten. And this rescission the vendor and vendee may sue for while the thing is not lost, has not perished, or been deteriorated; but afterwards they can no longer bring such action. We likewise say that if the vendee or vendor swear, at the time of the purchase or sale, that although the thing was worth more or less than they gave or took, they nevertheless renounce the right to sue for the rescission of the sale. If the vendor at the time he took the oath were above fourteen years of age, he ought to observe it, and can not thereafter rescind the sale on that account. But if he were a minor under fourteen years of age the oath would not be binding, and he might annul the purchase or sale, as though he had not taken it.

### Law 57.

§ 1533. *That a Fraudulent Sale may be Annulled.*—If a man own an estate, a house, vineyard, or anything else in another place than where he lives, and being ignorant of its value, having never seen it, nor wishing to sell it, and any person, through fraudulent motives, should prevail on him to sell it, we say that such a sale will not be valid, but may be rescinded, whether it were made for more or less than the value of the thing. But if the owner wished to sell it, and the vendee acted fraudulently, by concealing something that belonged to the estate or the thing sold, or fraudulently induced the owner to believe that although certain things belonged to the estate, yet they were in the power of another, were difficult to recover, or were lost, then we say the sale would be valid, because the vendor wished to sell. But the vendee would be obliged to indemnify him for the fraud he had practiced upon him, in such way that the seller should receive the just price for the thing sold, together with its appurtenances that had been fraudulently concealed.

### Law 58.

§ 1534. *That a Sale may be Dissolved if the Vendee does not Observe the Conditions Annexed to It.*—Men are sometimes induced, on account of the condition of a sale or of something promised them, to sell property which they would not otherwise part from. Wherefore we say, if any one sell anything belonging to him in consideration of such condition, that they must at any rate be observed according to their tenor, otherwise the sale may be rescinded. But if the sale were made differently and not on account of any specific condition, and after the vendor and vendee had agreed thereupon they had then annexed a condition, the sale would be valid, and could not be rescinded though the condition were not observed. Yet the obligor would be obliged to perform the condition annexed to the sale and pay all the loss and damage which the other sustained on account of the non-performance thereof.

### Law 59.

§ 1535. *Of Him Who Secretly and Fraudulently Buys the Property of a Person Subject to Pay Taxes, with a View to Deprive the King of his Revenue.*—Where a man liable to pay taxes, or where the debtor of the king secretly and fraudulently sells his property with a view to deprive the king of the revenue, or rents, or debts that were due him, such sale would not be valid, but ought in any event to be annulled; and if the vendee made the purchase with a knowledge of the fraud, he would be obliged to pay the king out of his own estate a sum equal to the price for which he had bought the said property.

### Law 60.

§ 1536. *That the Sale Made by a Slave of the Property of his Master may be Rescinded.*—Where a man had constituted another his attorney, with power to administer all of his estate, and had afterwards instituted such attorney his heir without his knowledge while he was yet his attorney; if then the person who had thus made him his attorney and heir should die, and one of the slaves of the deceased had sold any part of the estate, such sale would not be valid and the heir might annul it as soon as he knew it, before the thing had passed into the power of the buyer. And this he may do notwithstanding he were present at the sale, and had been called as a witness to sign the deed. And the reason is that he did know he had not been instituted heir, for had he known it he might not have consented to the sale. But if the slave from the station he held in the life-time of his master had been in the habit of selling for him, though the heir may rescind the sale for the reasons above mentioned, yet he would be obliged to reimburse the buyer for all loss and damage he had sustained on account of the sale, out of the peculium of the slave if any he had.

LAW 61.

§ 1537. *That Persons Who Repent of Sales They had Made, can not Annul Them, although They may have Obtained from the King Letters to That Effect.*—We also say that though the seller may repent after the sale is made, and offer the buyer double the price he had given to return the thing, yet the sale can not be rescinded on that account, nor can the buyer be compelled to it against his wish.

LAW 62.

§ 1538. *Of Those Who Wish to Rescind the Sales They had Voluntarily Made, alleging They were Made through Want.*—If a man wish to rescind a sale which he had made of his own free will, alleging he did it through necessity, while pressed by hunger, or burdened with heavy taxes, which he was obliged to pay on account of the thing sold, or for any other like cause, we say such would not be sufficient reason for rescinding the sale. So we say, where one wishes to rescind a sale, alleging that he had sold the thing for less than its value, it can not on that account be rescinded. But it would be otherwise where the sale had been made for less than half the just value of the thing, as was before observed in the laws of this title; or where it could be proved it had been made through fraud, knowingly practiced by the buyer, when the seller was ignorant of the true value of the thing, having never seen it, as we have above said.

LAW 63.

§ 1539. *Where a Man Sells a House or Tower Subject to a Service or Tribute, and Conceals It from the Buyer, the Sale may be Rescinded.*—Where the seller is silent and does not make known to the buyer that the house or tower which he sells him is subject to a service or tribute, the buyer may on that account rescind the sale, and the seller will be obliged to restore the price, and pay him all the loss and damage he had thereby sustained. So we say, where a man sells a field or meadow which he knew produced noxious herbs, destructive to beasts that grazed on them, and he concealed this circumstance from the buyer at the time of the sale, the seller will be obliged to restore the price to the buyer, and pay him all the loss and damage he had sustained on that account. But if the seller were ignorant of that circumstance at the time of the sale, then he would be obliged to restore the price only.

The four remaining laws of this title relate to personal property.

# CHAPTER VI.

## OF PRESCRIPTION OR LIMITATION.

### PARTIDA 3, TITLE 29, AND THE LAWS OF TORO.



### LAW 2.[1]

§ 1540. *Who can Acquire Another's Property by Prescription.* Any man of sound mind, though a minor, may acquire a thing by prescription. But a madman or an idiot can begin neither to acquire nor lose by that means, from the moment he is deprived of his reason; because he has not the necessary desire or understanding for either, notwithstanding he be in possession of the thing. Nevertheless, if before he had lost his reason he, or the person whose estate he inherited, had begun to acquire a thing by prescription, he may then acquire it, as well after he is deprived of his reason as before.

### LAW 7.

§ 1541. *The Public Places, Roads, Pastures, or Threshing-ground, or Other Like Places Belonging in Common to the People, can not be Lost by Prescription.*—No public place, street, road, pasture, or threshing-ground, nor other similar place used in common by the inhabitants of any city, town, or castle, or other place, can be acquired by prescription. But things of a different nature, as slaves, flocks, cattle, or ships, or the like, though they

[1] Laws not cited herein refer to personal property.

belong in common to any city or town, may nevertheless be acquired by a prescription of forty years. For notwithstanding they are held in common by all the inhabitants, yet they are not used in common by all of them, as are the other things before mentioned. If, however, the city or town, or other place that had last any such thing by the prescription of forty years, petition within four years thereafter, either the king or president, or judge of the place, praying that they may not be prejudiced by the time elapsed, and that they might not lose the thing thereby, the prayer of their petition ought to be granted, and the prescription of forty years will not prejudice them. But if they do not petition within four years next after the forty, they can not do it afterwards, and he who held the thing will acquire it by the forty years' prescription.

### Law 8.

§ 1542. *A Minor under Twenty-five Years of Age, or a Son under the Power of his Father, or a Married Woman, do not Lose their Property by Prescription.*—A minor under twenty-five years of age can not lose his property by prescription. Yet where prescription had begun to run against him after he became of full age, his property may be acquired in that way, like every other person. We likewise say that no one can acquire the property of a child while he remains under paternal authority, for the father may sue for the property of the child, whereas the child can not bring suit himself unless by the father's command. And we moreover say that the property which the wife brings in dowery to her husband can not be acquired by prescription until after the marriage is dissolved. Nevertheless, if the husband dissipate his estate, and his wife, though she knew of it, does not sue for her dowery, if thereafter any one should acquire the dotal effects by prescription, it will be the fault of the wife, and she will sustain the loss.

### Law 18.

§ 1543. *In how Long a Time Things Immovable and Incorporeal are Acquired by Prescription.*—Hitherto we have shown how movable things may be acquired by prescription; we shall now speak of things immovable and incorporeal, and show how and in what manner they also may be acquired by prescription. We therefore say that if one person receive of another an immovable thing, in good faith, either by purchase or exchange, or as a donation or legacy, or by any other just title, and keep possession of it during ten years, while the owner was in the country (tierra), or twenty years while he was out of it, such person will acquire the thing by prescription, notwithstanding he received it from one who was not the true owner; and he will not be obliged afterwards to answer therefor to any person who should say he could prove he were the true proprietor of the thing, and that he was ignorant the other had acquired it by prescription. And what we say in this law applies where he who alienates and he who receives the thing act in good faith, believing they had a right to do so, and the latter retains peaceable possession of it, so that it is not demanded of him during the whole time necessary to acquire it by prescription.

### Law 19.

§ 1544. *If He Who Sold the Thing Knew that He had No Right to Alienate It, the Person Who Received It could not Acquire It by Prescription in Less than Thirty Years.*—If a man who alienated an immovable thing knew, or had reason to believe, that he had not a right to do so, then the person who received it can not acquire it by prescription in less than thirty years, unless the owner knew of the alienation, and did not demand it within ten years from the day he knew it, if he were in the country, or within twenty years if he were out of it; for then the person who received the thing might acquire it by prescription in one of the aforementioned periods of ten or twenty years. And the owner would be out of the country when he was not in any part of the province where the thing was which is acquired by prescription; and he would be considered as in the country when he was in any part of the provinces, though he were not in the place where the thing was which is acquired by prescription.

### Law 20.

§ 1545. *How the Time for Prescription ought to be Counted, when either the Possessor or Owner of the Thing Absents Himself from the Country.*—A man sometimes begins to acquire another's property by prescription while the owner is in the country, and before the time is completed either he or the owner leaves the country. We therefore say that the time elapsed since the period the possessor of the thing began to acquire it by prescription, until he or the owner departed from the country, ought to be computed in the same manner it is, to enable one to acquire a thing by the ten years' prescription when the owner is in the country. And the time that either of them is absent from the country ought to be doubled and counted in the manner we have said it should be, in order to enable one to acquire a thing by the prescription of twenty years in the absence of the owner; so that if the possessor of the thing hold it during five years while both he and the owner are in the country, and ten years during the absence of either of them, he will acquire it by prescription.

LAW 21.

§ 1546. *Anything, Whatever be its Nature, may be Acquired by a Prescription of Thirty Years, whether Held in Good or Bad Faith.*—If a man have continued possession of a thing during thirty years or more, no matter how he obtained it, and no suit be brought against him for it during the whole of that time, he will acquire it by prescription, although it had been stolen or obtained by violence or robbery; and notwithstanding the owner may wish to claim it, he will not be obliged to respond thereto, but may avail himself of his prescription. But if the owner had been dispossessed of the thing, whether by losing it or otherwise, he can not bring a suit for it against the person in whose possession he finds it, unless the latter had himself stolen it or obtained it by violence or robbery, or had borrowed or hired it, for then the owner may reclaim and recover it. And so we say it would be when the plaintiff had been put into possession of anything by the judge, because the defendant, who had acquired it by prescription of thirty years, had failed to answer to a suit brought against him; for then if the defendant appear within one year afterwards, and be willing to answer to the suit and pay the costs, he may recover the thing. We likewise say that if a man possess an immovable thing in good faith during thirty years or more, believing that it belonged to him, or that it had belonged to his father, or that he held it by any other just title, he will in that time acquire it by prescription, and may thereby defend himself against every suit brought for such thing. And if he happen to lose possession of it, he may reclaim it wheresoever he finds it, unless he had found it in the possession of the true owner; for then if the latter had recovered possession of it, without force or fraud, and can prove his right of property in it, he will not be obliged to restore it.

LAW 22.

§ 1547. *A Man may, by Thirty Years' Prescription, Lose the Debts That are Due Him; though He will not in That Time Lose the Things He had Hired out.*—If a man has it in his power to make a judicial demand of what is due him, and neglects to do it during thirty consecutive years, if he afterwards make the demand, the debtor may defend himself by pleading prescription, and can not be compelled to pay unless he choose. Nevertheless, if a man held a house, vineyard, or other estate, which he had hired or leased of another, at a specific rent, payable at a certain time in every year, he could not acquire it by the prescription of thirty or more years, because he did not possess it for himself, but in the name of the person from whom he had hired or leased it.

LAW 26.

§ 1548. *In What Time the Chvrch may Lose its Property by Prescription.*—No immovable thing belonging to a church or religious place can be lost by a prescription of less than forty years. But their movable property, if of such a nature as to be lost by prescription, may be acquired of them in three years, in the same manner we have said it may be acquired of other persons. But those things which belong exclusively to the Roman church can not be prescribed for by any one in a less time than one hundred years.

LAW 27.

§ 1549. *The Pawnee may Lose by Prescription his Right to the Thing Pledged.*—When a thing, whether movable or immovable, has been pledged, and afterwards transferred by sale or other just title to a third person, who keeps possession of it in good faith during ten years, while the pawnee was in the country, or twenty years while he was out of it, if during the whole of that time it had not been judicially demanded of such third person, he will acquire it by prescription, and the pawnee will lose his right to it. Nevertheless, if the person to whom it had been so transferred received it in bad faith, knowing it was pledged, and that he from whom he received it had no right to alienate it, he can not then prescribe for it in a less time than thirty years; but after that time, if it had so long remained in his possession without being demanded by the pawnee, he will acquire it by prescription, and the pawnee will lose the right he had to it. But if the thing pledged had remained in possession of the owner, or his heirs, or of another person to whom he had since pledged it a second time, neither of them can acquire it by a prescription of less than forty years.

### Law 28.

§ 1550. *Who They are That do not Lose their Property by Prescription in their Absence.*—If a man be absent in the army, or be sent on a mission by the king or his council, or had fallen into captivity, or were in the public schools learning any science, or had gone on a pilgrimage, or the like, and any one had begun to acquire his property by prescription during his absence, we say that he may at any time within four years after his return petition the judge of the place, praying that the time by which his property had begun to be acquired shall not prejudice him; and the judge shall grant his request. But if he does not so petition the judge within four years after his return, or if it is not done by his heirs within four years from the day they knew of his death in either of the above-mentioned places to which he had gone, he can not do it afterwards; and the third possessor will be protected in what he had so acquired by prescription.

### Law 29.

§ 1551. *How the Prescription by Which a Man has Begun to Acquire a Thing is Interrupted or Destroyed.*—The prescription by which a man had begun to acquire a thing is interrupted or destroyed by abandoning the thing or losing possession of it before the time is completed in which it may be acquired; so that, though he recover possession of it again, he can not add the time past to that which is to come, in order to make out the prescription; but he must begin to count anew from the day he recovered possession of it. We likewise say that where a man had begun to acquire a thing by prescription, and the owner against whom he began to prescribe summon him therefor by letters from the king or judge, or by a constable (portero), or bring a suit against him for it, from that time the prescription will be interrupted and destroyed. Likewise we say that if a man owe another anything which he was bound to give him, and the creditor remains so long without demanding it that the other began to acquire the debt by prescription, if then the debtor renew the obligation by executing an act, or giving security or a pledge for it, or by paying something by way of damages or as a part of the debt, or by doing anything else of a similar nature after he had begun to prescribe for it, the prescription will be thereby interrupted, and the time lost during which it had already run. And so we say it would be if the creditor demand the debt in the presence of friends or of arbitrators.

LAW 30.

§ 1552. *Where the Possessor of a Thing Departs from the Country or Dies, Leaving a Child under Seven Years of Age; or where He is a Man of Great Rank and Power—What the Owner of the Thing ought to Do in That Case to Prevent its Loss by Prescription.*—Where a man had begun to acquire a thing by prescription, and then departs from the country, or becomes mad, or dies leaving an orphan under seven years of age to whom no guardian is appointed, if on that account the person against whom the prescription had begun to run could not bring a suit for the thing in a court of justice, then we say it will be sufficient for him to make a declaration before the judge of the place, or before the bishop if there be no judge, or before the neighbors of the person who had begun to prescribe for the thing, saying that he wished to bring a suit for it, but could not on account of the causes before mentioned; for by such declaration the prescription which had begun to run in favor of the other will be interrupted and destroyed, in the same manner as if the thing had been claimed by judicial demand. And so we say it would be where the person who had begun to acquire the thing by prescription were a man of such great power that the proprietor was afraid to bring a suit against him for it.

Law 63 of Toro, which is law 6, title 15, book 4 of the Recopilacion; and also law 5, title 8, book 11, Novisima Recopilacion.

§ 1553. *Judgment and Mortgage.*—The right to execute by a personal obligation is prescribed in ten years; and a personal action, and the final judgment given thereon, is prescribed in twenty years, and no menos; but where there is a mortgage on an obligation, or where the obligation is mixed, personal and real, the debt is prescribed in thirty years, and no less; which shall be observed, notwithstanding the law of the King Don Alonso, our progenitor, who established that a personal action should be prescribed in ten years.

Law 65 of Toro, which is law 7, title 15, book 4, Recopilacion; and also law 6, title 8, book 11, Novisima Recopilacion.

§ 1554. *Interruption in Possession.*—An interruption in the possession interrupts the prescription in the property; and on the contrary, interruption in the property interrupts prescription in the possession.

# CHAPTER VII.

## SALES AND INSTRUMENTS IN WRITING.



§ 1555. *Verbal Sales.*—A verbal sale of real estate was valid under the Spanish and Mexican law. The validity of contracts, except certain classes specified in the law, do not depend upon any external formality. The word "heir" was never essential in a deed to vest the fee in the heirs. There was no statue of frauds in Spain or Mexico. By virtue of law 6, title 5, partidas 5, a sale of anything, whether personal or real estate, could be made verbally or in writing, as the parties might agree; as when the buyer said to the seller: "I wish to have this sale reduced to writing." A sale made in this manner was not perfect, although the parties agreed upon the price, until the writing was made and executed, for until that time either of them might retract. If no writing was mentioned, then none was required to make the sale valid. Law 23, title 5, partidas 5, says: "We likewise say that after the sale is perfected in one of the ways above mentioned, the amelioration of the thing bought will be for the benefit of the buyer, though it had not yet passed under his power; as where a man had bought a field or vineyard, and after the sale it were increased by the inundation of a river that added thereto a portion of earth with trees or other things upon it by which the thing sold was ameliorated."

There was an ancient law which bound all parties who made mutual promises with the intention of obligating themselves one with the other. This was law 2, title 16, book 5, of the Recopilacion de Castille, which is the same as law 1, title 1, book 10, of the Novisima Recopilacion, which was compiled and went into operation in 1805. Said law is as follows: "The fulfillment of an obligation and contract in the manner it should be done, notwithstanding that a defect of the stipulation may be put in it and other exceptions. If it should appear that any one wished to obligate another by promise or by any contract, or in any other manner, he should be held to fulfill that for which he obligated himself; and he can not put an exception, that the stipulation was not made, which means a promise with certain solemnity of law, or that the contract or obligation was made between absent ones, or that it was not made before a notary public, or that it was made to a private person in the name of another between absent ones, or that some one obligated himself that another would give or do something; we command that said obligation and contract is still valid, which should be made in any manner by which it may appear that one wished to obligate another." This law was in force in Mexico until the adoption of the civil code in 1871, and the spirit of the same is the law of the code, although clothed in different language. The foregoing law is as familiar to every Mexican lawyer as are the first rudiments of Roman jurisprudence. For a long time in California it was a vexed question whether a parol sale of real estate, under Spanish and Mexican law, was valid or not. And not altogether without reason, for the learned authors Escriche and Febrero mislead the reader when they declare that a sale of real estate should be made by a public writing (escritura publica). Their language needs a qualification. It is true there was a decree issued by the king to the effect that such sales should be by escritura publica; but that was a fiscal law. It was created for the purpose of collecting the alcabala, or tax on sales. The law did not declare that sales made otherwise should be null and void. This decree of September 30, 1791, states that whereas frauds have been committed on the revenue by making secret parol sales of real estate, it is ordered that the alcabala be collected on such sales, because "the contracts became perfect by the mere consent of the parties." This decree will be found under the head of "Instruccion de Alcabales," page 208, paragraph 3, volume 3, of the Mexican Pandects, by Roderiguez de San Miguel. Sales of real estate or contracts in relation thereto, made in the territory ceded by Mexico to the United States, and subsequent to the concession, could not possibly have been effected by such a fiscal law. There was no law in force in the United States authorizing the collection of an alcabala, and no officer had power to collect such an impost. Such a fiscal law could not have been carried into execution in said territory. "When the reason ceases the law itself ceases," is a well-established legal maxim. The supreme court of Mexico cited the said law as being in force in 1860, and reported in volume 1, pages 724, 725, of the Gaceta de los Tribunales, A. D. 1860. Under the Roman, Spanish, and Mexican law, three things were requisite to make a valid contract: 1. A thing or subject-matter of the contract; 2. A price; 3. The consent of the parties. This law related as well to real as to personal property. Such is the present law of Mexico under the civil law.

§ 1556. *The Manner of Making Public Instruments, Such as Deeds, Mortgages, etc., by Notaries.*—According to law 9, title 19, partidas 3, the notaries were to have a register, in which they were to write the minutes of every act as prescribed by the judge, or as required by the contracting parties. After which, they were to draw up the public act itself, observing the form peculiar to each, according to what is said in a preceding title, without substantially changing or altering anything contained in the register; and then deliver it to the person entitled to it, notwithstanding he had been forbidden to do so by the other party, except he were prohibited by the judge for some good cause shown by such party. By said law the notaries were commanded to transcribe all their acts in a register, in order that if any of them be lost, or any doubt should arise concerning their contents, reference might be had to the record. By a decree in 1503, this law was modified, and the notaries were required to draw up on their registers the original act in full, and not by notes or minutes. A copy is then furnished the party from the register, to serve him instead of the act itself, which was formerly made out from the notes. This method is now in practice. The parties sign the instrument in the register, and then a certified copy thereof is given to the party entitled thereto, and this is called the original; and is proof in court, and not the register. The register of each year is kept by itself, and certified to by the notary at the end of the year.

§ 1557. *Records of Deeds, Wills, and Contracts.*—Titles, wills, and contracts executed prior to the adoption of the civil code will be found on the registries of the notaries before whom they were executed.

§ 1558. *Records of Mortgages.*—In all cities and capitals or heads of districts (partidos) there were offices for the registry of mortgages under the care of the ayuntamientos. Pragmatics or edicts were issued on the subject in 1539, 1558, and others subsequently. The one of January 31, 1768, was an extensive one, giving in detail the manner of keeping the registries. It declared that a mortgage should be recorded within six days from the day of execution, if made in the town or place where the registry was kept, and if executed out of that place and in the same partido, within a month; and if at a greater distance, greater time was allowed, in proportion thereto. On the twentieth of May, 1821, rules were established at Madrid for the regulation of offices for the registry of mortgages, as follows: 1. There shall be established an office for the registry of mortgages in every town which was the head of a partido. 2. The provisional deputation shall form, print, and publish a list of the heads of partidos. 3. The office of mortgages shall be under the charge of the secretary of the ayuntamiento whenever he should be a notary public. 4. When the secretary of the ayuntamiento may not be a notary public, the ayuntamiento shall appoint for the office of mortgages another person who has said qualities, under the provisions contained in the pragmatic of January 31, 1768. Ever since that time, and until the adoption of the present civil code, the registry of mortgages has been in the office of mortgages, under the charge of the ayuntamientos of the head towns of the partidos.

# PART THIRD.

## CIVIL CODE—PERSONAL RIGHTS, REAL PROPERTY, CONTRACTS, AND INHERITANCE.

## CHAPTER I.

### COMMENTARY—EFFECTS OF THE LAWS—PERSONS, DOMICILES, ASSOCIATIONS, AND CORPORATIONS.

§ 1559. Civil Code.
§ 1560. New Code, 1884.
§ 1561. Contents of Part Third.
§ 1562. Amendments.
§ 1563. Preliminary Parts.
§ 1564. Equality.
§ 1565. Promulgation.
§ 1566. When Laws Take Effect.
§ 1567. Day of Promulgation, What.
§ 1568. No Retractive Laws.
§ 1569. Renouncement.
§ 1570. Acts against Laws.
§ 1571. Repeal.
§ 1572. Custom—Disuse.
§ 1573. Exceptions to Laws.
§ 1574. Conflict of Rights.
§ 1575. Judicial Capacity.
§ 1576. Capacity of Persons.
§ 1577. Real Property.
§ 1578. Form of Instruments.
§ 1579. Laws.
§ 1580. Mexicans in Foreign Lands.
§ 1581. Foreigners.
§ 1582. Foreign Laws.
§ 1583. General Principles of Law.
§ 1584. Ignorance.
§ 1585. Mexicans.
§ 1586. Nationality.
§ 1587. Jurisdiction of Person.
§ 1588. Absent Persons Holding Property.
§ 1589. Domicile.
§ 1590. Employés.

§ 1559. *Civil Code.*—The civil code of the federal government of Mexico was adopted on the eighth day of December, 1870, to take effect on the first of March, 1871, as will be observed by the decree herein relative thereto. This code is in force in all of the states of the union, except those of Vera Cruz and Tlaxcala. The state of Vera Cruz formed its own code December 18, 1868. Tlaxcala adopted this federal civil code, but soon thereafter repealed the act of its adoption, and left in force the ancient laws of Spain. A list of the states which have adopted the federal civil code, with the dates of the adoption thereof respectively, will be found in Appendix No. 2. The following is the decree of the congress of the union adopting the civil code: "The congress of the union decrees: Art. 1. The civil code which for the federal district and territory of Lower California, a commission composed of the citizens Mariano Yañez, José Maria Lafragua, Isidro Montiel, and Raphael Dondé, formed by order of the minister of justice, is approved. This code shall commence to govern the first of March, 1871. Art. 2. From said date, all ancient legislation on the matters contained in the four books of which said code is composed, shall be abolished. Hall of the session of the congress of the union. Mexico, December 8, 1870. José Maria Lozano, deputy president. Guillermo Valle, deputy secretary. Protasio P. Tagle, deputy secretary. Wherefore I order that it be printed, published, and circulated, in order that due compliance be given it. Palace of the national government in Mexico, on the eighth of December, 1870. Benito Juarez." As is seen by the said decree, it only has force in the federal district and Lower California by virtue of said decree; and only in the several states by the adoption thereof by their respective congresses or legislatures.

§ 1560. *New Code,* 1884.—The congress of the union adopted a new code in 1884, which is in the main the old code with various amendments.[1]

§ 1561. *Contents of Part Third.*—This part contains so much of the laws of the civil code as relates to real property in any manner; also all of the laws pertaining to inheritance, and the greater part of those governing contracts. These seem essential, for the laws of inheritance have woven all through them, in woof and web, the rights of real property; and the laws of contracts, in every part nearly, may effect real as well as personal property. A mere verbal promise and consent of parties may bind them as to certain real rights. As the laws pertaining to dowers and marriage settlements are in force, they necessarily form a part of this work; but as a matter of fact, they are rarely if ever put in practice in Mexico. The same may be said of the old Spanish laws of dowers—they were seldom carried into effect in Mexico.

§ 1562. *Amendments.*—As the amendments in the new code of 1884 are now in force in the federal district and Lower California, they are absolutely essential parts of this work, and are embraced herein in the form of notes.

§ 1563. *Preliminary Parts.*—The preliminary parts of the civil code relating to the effects of the laws, and to the laws of natural persons, domiciles, and artificial persons, are as follows:

### Of the Laws and their Effects, with the General Rules of their Application.

§ 1564. *Equality.*—Art. 1. The civil law is equal for all, without distinction of person or of sex, more than in the cases specially declared.

§ 1565. *Promulgation.*—Art. 2. The laws, regulations, circulars, or any other provisions of general observance, emanating

[1] The transitory articles of the new code of 1884 are as follows: "1. This code shall commence to govern the first day of June next. 2. From said date the civil code of the eighth of December, 1870, shall remain abolished, as well as all prior civil legislation. Wherefore I order that it be printed, published, circulated, and that due compliance be given it. Palace of the national government, in Mexico, the thirty-first of March, 1884. Manuel Gonzales."

from authority, obligate and have their effects from the day of their promulgation, in the places in which that must be made.

§ 1566. *When Laws Take Effect.*—Art. 3. If the law, regulation, circular, or general provision fixes the day on which it ought to commence to be observed, it will obligate from that day, although it may have been published before.

§ 1567. *Day of Promulgation, What.*—Art. 4. In order that the law, regulation, circular, or general provision may be reputed, promulgated, and obligatory in the places in which the authority does not reside, which makes the promulgation, the time shall be computed at the rate of one day for each five leagues of distance; if there shall be a fraction which may exceed the half of the distance indicated, one day more shall be computed.[1]

§ 1568. *No Retroactive Laws.*—Art. 5. No law nor administrative provision shall have a retroactive effect.

§ 1569. *Renouncement.*—Art. 6. Any renouncement of the laws in general has no efficacy, nor any special renouncement of prohibitive laws or laws of public interest.

§ 1570. *Acts against Laws.*—Art. 7. The acts executed against the tenor of prohibitive laws shall be null if the said laws do not otherwise provide.

§ 1571. *Repeal.*—Art. 8. A law is not abrogated or repealed except by another posterior.

§ 1572. *Custom—Disuse.*—Art. 9. Against the observance of the law, disuse, custom, or practice to the contrary can not be alleged.

§ 1573. *Exceptions.*—Art. 10. The laws which establish exceptions to the general laws are not applicable to any case which may not be expressly specified in said laws.

§ 1574. *Conflict of Rights.*—Art. 11. He who, in exercising his own right, solicits his interest, ought, in a case of conflict and want of a special decree, cede to him who tries to avoid injuries.[2]

§ 1575. *Judicial Capacity.*—Art. 12. Judicial capacity is ac-

[1] "Five leagues" is changed to "twenty kilometers" in the code of 1884.

[2] This is modified by article 21, code of 1884.

Article 18 is a new one of the code of 1884, which reads: "The initiation and formation of laws are governed by the provisions in the political constitution of the republic."

"Art. 21. In case of a conflict of rights and a want of express law for the special case, the controversy shall be decided in favor of him who tries to avoid injuries, and not in favor of him who pretends to obtain lucre. If the conflict should be between equal rights of the same kind, it shall be decided by observing the greatest possible equality between the interested parties.

quired by birth; but from the moment in which an individual is procreated, he enters under the protection of the law, and he is considered as born for the effects declared in the present code.

§ 1576. *Capacity of Persons.*—Art. 13. The laws concerning the state and capacity of persons are obligatory for the Mexicans of the federal district and of California, even when they reside in a foreign country, in respect to the acts which must be executed in the whole or in part of the mentioned demarkations.

§ 1577. *Real Property.*—Art. 14. In respect to the immovable property situated in the federal district, and in California, the Mexican laws shall govern, although it may be possessed by foreigners.

§ 1578. *Foreigners—Form of Instruments.*—Art. 15. In respect to the form or external solemnities of contracts, wills, and all other public instruments, the laws of the country in which they shall have been executed shall govern. Notwithstanding, Mexicans or foreigners residing out of the district, or out of California, are at liberty to subject themselves to the forms and solemnities prescribed by the Mexican law in the cases in which the act must be executed in those demarkations.

§ 1579. *Laws.*—Art. 16. The laws in which the public right and good custom are interested can not be altered or nullified as to their effects by an agreement celebrated between private persons.

§ 1580. *Mexicans in Foreign Lands.*—Art. 17. The obligations and rights which may arise from contracts or wills executed in a foreign country by Mexicans of the district, and of California, shall be governed by the provisions of this code, in case that said acts must be fulfilled in the said demarkations.

§ 1581. *Foreigners.*—Art. 18. If the contracts or wills of which the preceding article speaks should be executed by a foreigner, and should have to be executed in the district of California, the maker shall be free to elect the law which the internal solemnity of the act may have to be subject to, as to the interest which may consist of movable property. As to what respects real estate, the provision in article 14 shall be observed.

§ 1582. *Foreign Laws.*—Art. 19. He who founds his rights on foreign laws must prove their existence, and that they are applicable to the case.

§ 1583. *General Principles of Law.*—Art. 20. When a judicial controversy can not be decided, either by the text or by the natural sense or spirit of the law, it must be decided according to the general principles of law, taking into consideration all the circumstances of the case.

§ 1584. *Ignorance.*—Art. 21. Ignorance of the law serves as no excuse, and it avails no one.[1]

### Of Persons.

§ 1585. *Of Mexicans and Foreigners—Mexicans.*—Art. 22. Mexicans are those whom article 30 designates; foreigners are those whom article 33 designates; and citizens are those whom article 34 designates, of the political constitution of the Mexican United States.

§ 1586. *Nationality.*—Art. 23. The change of nationality produces no retroactive effects.

§ 1587. *Jurisdiction of Person.*—Art. 24. Mexicans as well as foreigners, residents of the district or of California, may be summoned before the tribunals of the country for the obligations contracted with Mexicans or with foreigners within or without the republic.

§ 1588. *Absent Persons Holding Property.*—Art. 25. They may be also summoned before said tribunals, although they do not reside in said places, if they have therein property which may be affected by the obligations contracted, or if these must have their execution in said places.

### Of Domiciles.

§ 1589. *Domicile.*—Art. 26. The domicile of a person is the place where he habitually resides; for want of this, that in which he has the principal seat of his business; for want of both, the reputed domicile of a person is the place in which he is found.

§ 1590. *Employés.* —Art. 27. Public employés have their domicile in the place where they serve their profession.

§ 1591. *Transient Persons.*—Art. 28. Those who accidentally find themselves in a town performing some commission do not acquire a domicile therein by this fact alone.[2]

§ 1592. *Military Persons.*—Art. 29. Military persons in ac-

[1] Article 21 is amended by the code of 1884 by inserting the words "duly promulgated" after the word "law."

[2] Articles 27 and 28 are united in the code of 1884, and amended to read as follows: "Art. 28. Public employés have their domicile in the place where they serve their profession. Those who accidentally find themselves in a town performing some commission do not acquire a domicile therein by this fact alone; but they will preserve that which belongs to them in conformity with the first part of article 27 (26 old code), if they should have no fixed place for the performance of their charge."

tive service have their domicile in the place in which they are stationed.

§ 1593. *Minors.*—Art. 30. The domicile of a minor not emancipated is that of the person in whose paternal power he is found.

§ 1594. *Minors under Tutors.*—Art. 31. The domicile of a minor who is not under paternal power, and that of a person incapacitated, is that of the tutor.

§ 1595. *Married Women.*—Art. 32. The domicile of a married woman, if she is not legally separated from her husband, is that of the latter; if she should be separated, she will be subject to the rules established in article 26.[1]

§ 1596. *Domestics.*—Art. 33. Those who serve a person and live in his house, whether they be of the age of majority or minors, have the domicile of the person whom they serve; but if they are minors and possess property which may be under the charge of a tutor, in respect to the property the domicile shall be that of the tutor.

§ 1597. *Condemned Persons.*—Art. 34. The domicile of those who are extinguishing a condemnation is the place where they are extinguishing it, as to what belongs to juridical relations posterior to the condemnation; as to the preceding relations, they will preserve the last domicile which they shall have had. Those condemned to banishment simply will preserve their prior domicile.[2]

§ 1598. *Family of a Condemned Person.*—Art. 35. The wife and children of a party sentenced to confinement, who should not accompany him to the place of his confinement, will not have the domicile of the husband and father, but their own, in conformity with the rules established in the preceding articles.

§ 1599. *Corporations.*—Art. 36. The domicile of corporations, associations, and establishments recognized by the law is the place where their direction or administration is situated, save what may be provided in their by-laws or special laws, provided that the domicile which therein shall be determined is within the territorial demarkation subject to this code.

§ 1600. *Persons in the Navy.*—Art. 37. The individuals who serve in the navy of the republic have their domicile in the Mexican place in which they may be found.

---

[1] Article 32 is amended by the code of 1884 by inserting the words "in the preceding articles" after the word "established."

[2] Art. 34 is amended by the code of 1844 by suppressing the words "those condemned to banishment simply will preserve their prior domicile."

§ 1601. *Merchant Marine.*—Art. 38. Those who serve in the merchant marine of the republic shall be considered domiciled in the place of the matriculation of the ship; but if they be married, but not separated, and the wife should have a house in another place, the latter shall be the reputed domicile of the husband and wife.

§ 1602. *Unmarried Sailors.* — Art. 39. When, not being married, they should have any establishment in a place distinct from that of the matriculation of the ship, they shall be considered domiciled therein; but if they should be married, the place of the establishment shall be the domicile in respect to the acts relative to the business, and in respect to the others that of the habitation of the wife.[1]

§ 1603. *Foreign Navy.*—Art. 40. The Mexican citizens who without license from the government serve in a foreign navy or in any armed cruiser for a foreign government lose their Mexican citizenship and domicile, and can only recover them according to the rules established for those who serve foreign powers.

§ 1604. *Foreign Merchant Marine.* — Art. 41. Those who serve in a foreign merchant marine, if they have not renounced Mexican citizenship, preserve the domicile which they had on entering the service of said marine.[2]

§ 1605. *Obligations.*—Art. 42. The rules on domicile established in the preceding articles do not deprive the parties of the right which they have to fix the place in which an obligation ought to be fulfilled, or in which they may be considered as domiciled, provided that the designation be not contrary to the law.

## Of Moral Persons.

§ 1606. *Corporations.*—Art. 43. The associations or corporations, temporal or perpetual, founded with any end or for any motive of public utility, or of public and private utility jointly, which in their civil relations represent a juridical entity, are called moral persons.[3]

§ 1607. *Legal Authorization.*—Art. 44. No association or corporation has juridical entity if it is not legally authorized.[4]

[1] Articles 37, 38, and 39 are suppressed in the code of 1884.

[2] Articles 40 and 41 are suppressed in the code of 1884.

[3] Article 43 is amended to read in the code of 1884 as follows: "Art. 38. They are moral persons, and with such character have a juridical entity: 1. The nation, the states and the municipalities; 2. Temporal or perpetual associations or corporations founded for some end or for some motive of public utility, or public and private utility jointly; 3. Civil or mercantile partnerships formed according to law.

[4] Article 44 is article 39 in the code of 1884, and is amended by adding, "or permitted."

§ 1608. *Juridical Entity.*—Art. 45. The associations or corporations which enjoy juridical entity can exercise all the civil rights relative to the legitimate interest of their institute.

§ 1609. *Restitution.*—Art. 46. Neither the state nor any other corporation or public establishment enjoys the privilege of restitution *in integrum.*[1]

§ 1610. *Private Interests.* — Art. 47. The associations of private interest are subject to the rules of the contract of partnership.

---

[1]Article 46 is article 41 in the code of 1884, and reads: "No moral person enjoys the privileges which the laws concede to persons incapacitated."

# CHAPTER II.

## IMMOVABLE PROPERTIES.



§ 1611. *Immovable Property, What is.*—Art. 782.—Immovable properties are: 1. Lands and edifices, and other constructions which can not be transported. 2. Plants and trees while they are united to the earth, and the fruit hanging on said trees and plants while they are not separated from them by harvest or regular felling. 3. All that is united to an edifice in a fixed manner, so that it can not be separated without irreparable deterioration of the said edifice, or of the object to which it is adhered. 4. The statues placed in niches constructed in the edifice exclusively for them. 5. Any artistic object incrusted in the edifice. 6. Reservoirs of fish, dove-cotes, beehives, and other abodes of animals. 7. The machinery, vases, instruments, or utensils[1] destined by the proprietor of an estate for the proper use of the industry which is carried on upon said estate; and the pipes of any kind which are used to conduct water to the estate, and to extract it therefrom. 8. The services and other real rights upon the immovable.[2]

§ 1612. *Certain Property, when Personal.*—Art. 783. The

[1] An amendment is made in the code of 1884, by inserting after the word "utensils," "and animals."

[2] Fraction 8 reads as follows in new code: "8. The animals which form breeding stock on rural estates destined wholly or partially to stock-raising."

things referred to in fractions 3, 4, and 5 of said preceding article shall be considered as personal property when the said owner shall separate them from the edifice; save the case when in the value of the latter has been computed the value of the former, in order to constitute a real right in favor of a third party.

### Of Properties Considered according to the Persons to Whom They Belong.

§ 1613. *Public or Private.*—Art. 795. Properties are either public or private.

§ 1614. *Public Property.*—Art. 796. Are public properties: 1. The territory of the district, and of California, which is not under private dominion in conformity with the laws. 2. Those which form the federal exchequer in conformity with the laws. 3. The properties of the municipalties, and those of the public offices or establishments which belong to the general government or the local government of the district, or that of California. 4. The things which have no owner, and the properties which persons leave who die without heirs, or whose succession must be considered abandoned according to the laws.[1]

§ 1615. *Special Laws.*—Art. 797. Public properties will be governed by the dispositions of this code, as far as it is not determined by special laws, being subject in every case to the rules which are established in it for prescription.

§ 1616. *Private Property.*—Art. 798. All things the dominion of which legally belongs to private individuals, and those which can not be used without the consent of the owner, are private property.

§ 1617. *Corporations.*—Art. 799. Corporations are not capable of acquiring property, except in the terms fixed in article 27 of the constitution, and by special laws on the subject.

§ 1618. *Public Property.*—Art. 800. Public property is divided into property of common use and bienes propios.

§ 1619. *Property of Common Use.*—Art. 801. Property of common use is that which may be used by all of the inhabitants, with the restrictions established by law, or by administrative regulations.

§ 1620. *What is Property of Common Use.*—Art. 802. In the preceding article are comprehended: 1. The shores of the sea:

[1] Article 796 is article 698 of the new code, and reads thus: "Art. 698. Public property is that which belongs to the federation, to the states, and to the municipalities."

it being understood by such those parts of land which the water covers in its greatest ordinary flux. 2. The ports, bays, roads, and coves. 3. The rivers, although not navigable, their bed, source, mouths, and the creeks of the sea (esteros). 4. The bridges, causeways, roads, and canals constructed and preserved at the expense of the state. 5. The shores of navigable rivers, as far as their use may be indispensable for navigation. 6. The lakes and ponds which are not private property. 7. The streets, squares, fountains, and pleasure-grounds of the towns. 8. The palaces, monuments, and national edifices destined for offices and other public establishments.[1]

§ 1621. *Obstruction.*—Art. 803. Those who obstruct the common use of public property are subject to the established penalties, to pay all the damage and injury caused, and to suffer the loss of the works they shall have made.

§ 1622. *Propios.*—Art. 804. The properties which in conformity with the laws are exclusively destined to cover the public expenses of cities or towns are propios.

§ 1623. *Propios, how Used.*—Art. 805. No one can use or avail himself of the propios without a special concession from the authority. The infraction of this article will be considered and punished in conformity with the prescriptions of the penal code, or by the regulations of the police in such a case.

§ 1624. *Public Lands.*—Art. 806. Everything relative to the occupation and alienation of public lands will be regulated by the provision of the organic law in faction 24, of article 72, of the constitution.

§ 1625. *Denouncement of Properties without Owners.*—Art. 820. He who has notice of any immovable property having been found, and wishes to acquire the part which in conformity with the law may belong to him, must make a denouncement thereof before the political authority of the place where the property is situated.

§ 1626. *Denouncer.*—Art. 821. In this case the provisions of this chapter relative thereto shall be observed, and the denouncer shall receive the fourth part of the price.[2]

---

[1] Article 802 is suppressed in the code of 1884.

A new article entirely is given in the code of 1884, as follows: "Art. 707. When in conformity with the law can be and is sold a public way, the proprietors of the adjoining estates shall enjoy the right of preference (tanto) as purchaser of the part which corresponds to them, for which effect notice of the sale shall be given. The right which this article concedes must be exercised precisely within eight days following the notice. When this has not been given, the adjoining owners may ask for the rescission of the contract within six months, counted from the celebration thereof."

[2] Article 821 is amended in the new code of 1884 to read as follows: "Art.

§ 1627. *Auction.*—Art. 824. All sales shall be made at public auction.

---

723. In this case the provisions of this chapter relative thereto shall be observed, except those of articles 711 and 718, and the denouncer shall receive the fourth part of the price. The valuation by the experts and the publication of the notices shall be made at the cost of the denouncer, and the deposit of the estate shall not be ordered except when, the legal terms having transpired, no reclamation shall have been presented, or when the thing shall have been judicially declared abandoned. If any one should present himself claiming the real estate denounced as abandoned, the political authority shall make known the claim to the denouncer, and if the latter shall insist on his denouncement, he shall prove on a trial with the claimant the fact of the thing being abandoned. If he should not prove it, he shall be condemned or the payment of the costs, damages, and losses."

# CHAPTER III.

## PROPERTY IN GENERAL.

## Of Property in General.

§ 1628. *Property.*—Art. 827. Property is the right of enjoying and disposing of a thing without any more limitations than those which the laws fix.

§ 1629. *Public Use.*—Art. 828. Property is inviolable; it can not be occupied except for a cause of public utility, and a previous indemnification.

§ 1630. *Rights of Proprietor.*—Art. 829. The proprietor of land is the owner of the superfice thereof, and of what is under it. Therefore he can use it, and make thereon all the works, plantations, or excavations which he may wish, save the restrictions established in the title of services, and with subjection to the provisions in the special legislation of mines and in the regulations of police.

§ 1631. *Undivided Property.*—Art. 830. Those who by any

legal title have the common dominion of a thing can not be obliged to preserve it undivided, except in the cases in which, on account of the nature of the thing or by the determination of the law, the dominion is indivisible.

§ 1632. *Sales.*—Art. 831. If the dominion is not indivisible, but the thing does not admit of a convenient division, and the participants do not agree that it shall be adjudicated to any one of them, the sale thereof shall be proceeded with, and a partition of the value shall be made to the interested parties.

§ 1633. *Division of Property.*—Art. 832. The division of immovable properties is null if not made in public writing (escritura publica).[1]

### Of the Appropriation of Animals.

§ 1634. *Hunting on Public Land.*—Art. 833. The right of hunting and the appropriation of the products thereof are entirely free on public land.

§ 1635. *Private Property.*—Art. 834. The right to which the foregoing article refers can not be exercised on the land of private proprietorship, either by commencing the chase on said land, or by continuing one commenced on public land, unless by permission of the owner.

§ 1636. *Hunting, Regulation of.*—Art. 835. The exercise of the right of hunting shall be governed by the police regulations and by the following bases:

§ 1637. *Hunter.*—Art. 836. The hunter is made owner of the animal which he hunts by the act of obtaining possession of it, save the provisions in article 838.

§ 1638. *Game.*—Art. 837. The animal is considered caught which has been killed by the hunter during the venatic act, and that one which is caught in his nets.

§ 1639. *Owner of Game.*—Art. 838. If the wounded game should die on the land of another, the proprietor, or whoever represents him, must deliver it to the hunter, or permit him to enter to seek for it.

§ 1640. *Penalty.*—Art. 839. The proprietor who infringes upon the foregoing article shall pay the value of the game; and the hunter shall lose the game if he enter to seek for it without the permission of the former.

§ 1641. *Responsibility.*—Art. 840. In every case the hunter is responsible for the damages which he may cause.

---

[1] Article 832 is amended by the new code of 1884 to read as follows: "Art. 735. The division of immovable properties is null if not made with same formalities which, for the sale thereof, articles 2921 and 2924 (3057 and 3060 old code) require public writing (escritura publica)."

§ 1642. *Joint Responsibility.* — Art. 841. When there are more than one hunter, all shall be jointly responsible.

§ 1643. *Hunting-dogs.*—Art. 842. The fact of the hunting-dogs entering the lands of another, independently of the will of the hunter, will only obligate the latter for the mere reparation of the damages caused.

§ 1644. *Prescription.*—Art. 843. The action to ask for reparation may be answered by the plea of prescription, after thirty days, counted from the day on which the damage was caused.

§ 1645. *Wild Animals.*—Art. 844. It is lawful for the farmers to destroy at any time wild animals which injure their sowed grounds and plantations.

§ 1646. *Domestic Birds.*—Art. 845. The farmers have the same right in respect to domestic birds, in the fields where there are lands sown with cereals, or where there are hanging fruits which those birds might injure.

§ 1647. *Destruction of Nests, etc.*—Art. 846. The destruction of nests, eggs, or the young of birds of any kind upon the lands of another is absolutely prohibited.

§ 1648. *Public Waters.*—Art. 847. Fishing and the hunting for pearls are entirely free in public waters and waters of common use, save what administrative regulations provide.

§ 1649. *Private Waters.*—Art. 848. The right of fishing in private waters belongs exclusively to the owners of the lands through which those waters run.

§ 1650. *Wild Animals, Ownership.*—Art. 849. It is lawful for any person to appropriate to himself wild animals in conformity with the police regulations.

§ 1651. *Bees.*—Art. 850. It is lawful for any person to appropriate to himself the swarms of bees which have not been inclosed in hives, or which having been so inclosed, have abandoned the hives.

§ 1652. *Ownership of Bees.*—Art. 851. It is not understood that the bees have abandoned the hive when they have rested on the land of the owner of them, or when he follows them, keeping them in sight.

§ 1653. *Ferocious Animals.*—Art. 852. Ferocious animals which escape from their inclosure in which their owners confine them can be destroyed or taken by any one.

§ 1654. *Possession of Domestic Animals.*—Art. 853. The possession of domestic animals is governed by the provisions contained in the title of properties with unknown owners.

### Of Treasures.

§ 1655. *Hidden Treasure.*—Art. 854. Hidden treasure belongs to him who discovers it in a place on his property.

§ 1656. *Treasure on Public or Private Property.*—Art. 855. If the place should be public property, or should belong to a private person who is not the said discoverer, one half shall be applied to the discoverer, and the other to the proprietor of the place.

§ 1657. *Objects of Science.*—Art. 856. When the objects discovered shall be interesting to the sciences or to the arts, they will be applied to the nation for their just price, which will be distributed in conformity with the provisions of articles 854 and 855.

§ 1658. *Discovery, Casual.*—Art. 857. In order that he who discovers a treasure in the soil of another may enjoy the right declared, it is necessary that the discovery should be casual.

§ 1659. *Excavations.*—Art. 858. Nobody on his own authority can make excavations or boring or any work on the land or edifice of another to seek for treasure.

§ 1660. *Consent of the Owner.*—Art. 859. The treasure which shall be discovered in the land of another by works performed without the consent of the owner belongs wholly to the latter.

§ 1661. *Penalty.*—Art. 860. He who, without the consent of the owner, should do work on the land of another, in order to discover treasure, will be obliged in every case to pay the damage and losses, and besides to replace, at his own cost, the things in their original condition; he shall lose the right as a tenant, if he should have it on the ground, although the term of the lease may not have expired, when the owner shall so ask it.

§ 1662. *Distribution.*—Art. 861. If the treasure should be sought for with the consent of the owner of the ground, the stipulations shall be observed which shall be made for the distribution; and if there should be none, the expenses and the treasure discovered shall be equally distributed.

§ 1663. *Owner and Usufructuary.*—Art. 862. When one shall have the property and another the usufruct of an estate in which treasure may have been found, if he who found it was the same usufructuary, the part which shall belong to him shall be determined according to the rules which are established for the extraneous discoverer.

§ 1664. *Owner not the Discoverer.*—Art. 863. If the discoverer is not the owner nor usufructuary, the treasure will be divided between the owner and the discoverer, observing in this case the provisions in articles 859, 860, and 861.[1]

§ 1665. *Owner Being Finder.*—Art. 864. If the owner himself finds the treasure on the estate or land, the usufruct of which belongs to another person, the latter will have no part of the treasure; but he will have a right to require from the proprietor an indemnification for the damage and losses by the interruption of the usufruct on the part occupied or demolished in seeking for the treasure. The indemnification shall be paid even when no treasure shall have been found.

§ 1666. *Treasure, What is.*—Art. 865. For the effects of the foregoing articles, it is understood by "treasure" the hidden deposit of money, jewelry, or other precious objects, the legitimate source of which does not appear. A treasure shall never be considered as the fruit of an estate.

§ 1667. *Usufructuary.*—Art. 866. If the treasure is found on land given in emphyteusis, the emphyteuta shall be considered the usufructuary for the effects of the preceding articles.

### Of Mines.

§ 1668. *Mines.*—Art. 867. The denouncement, adjudication, the working, and everything concerning mines, shall be governed by the special mining ordinance, and other laws relative thereto.

### Of Woods, Pastures, and Woodlands.

§ 1669. *Woods and Pastures.*—Art. 868. Everything relative to the cutting of timbers and the preservation of woods, pastures, and woodlands shall be governed by special ordinances.

### Of the Right of Accession.

§ 1670. *Accession.*—Art. 869. The ownership of properties gives a right to all which they produce or which is united to or incorporated into them, naturally or artificially. This right is called accession.

§ 1671. *Proprietor's Rights.*—Art. 870. In virtue of it, shall belong to the proprietor: 1. The natural fruits; 2. The industrial fruits; 3. The civil fruits.

---

[1] Articles 862 and 863 are amended and united in one article as follows: "Art. 767. When one shall have the property and another the usufruct of an estate in which treasure may have been found, if he who found it was the same usufructuary, the part which shall belong to him shall be determined according to the rules which are established for the extraneous discoverer. If the discoverer is not the owner nor usufructuary, the treasure will be divided between the owner and the discoverer, with the exclusion of the usufructuary."

§ 1672. *Natural Fruits.*—Art. 871. Natural fruits are the spontaneous productions of the earth; the young, skins, and other products of animals.

§ 1673. *Young Animals.*—Art. 872. The young of animals belong to the owner of the mother, and not to the owner of the father, save a prior agreement to the contrary.

§ 1674. *Industrial Fruits.*—Art. 873. Industrial fruits are those which estates of any kind produce through the benefit of cultivation or work.

§ 1675. *When Rights to Fruits Begin.*—Art. 874. Natural or industrial fruits are not reputed as such, except from the time they are manifest or propagated.

§ 1676. *Animals.*—Art. 875. In order that animals may be considered fruits, it is sufficient that they may be in the belly of the mother, although they have not been born.

§ 1677. *Civil Fruits.*—Art. 876. The rents of movable properties; the rents of immovables; the interests of capitals, and all those which, not being produced directly by the same thing, come from it by contract, by last will, or by the law, are civil fruits.

§ 1678. *Animals on One's Land.*—Art. 877. Animals without another's mark, found upon the lands or properties, are presumed to be the property of the owners of said lands or properties, until the contrary is proved.[1]

§ 1679. *Things United to Another.*—Art. 878. All that which is united to or incorporated into a thing; that which is built, planted, and sown; and the repairs and improvement on lands or the estate being the property of another, belong to the owner of the land or estate, with subjection to what is provided in the following articles.

§ 1680. *Improvements.*—Art. 879. All the works, sowing and planting, as well as improvements and repairs made on the land, are presumed to have been made by the proprietor at his cost, until the contrary is proved.

§ 1681. *Contiguous Estates.*—Art. 880. The proprietor of the tree or bush contiguous to the land of another has a right to require of the latter permission to make the collection of the fruits which can not be gathered on his own side; but he is responsible for any injury which he may cause the other on account thereof.[2]

---

[1] Article 877 is amended by the code of 1884, by adding thereto the following: "Unless the proprietor of the lands has no breeding animals of the race to which the animals belong," and is numbered article 736.

[2] Article 880 is amended by the code of 1884, and reads as follows:

§ 1682. *Trees Held in Common.*—Art. 881. The fruits of a tree or bush held in common, and the expenses of cultivation, shall be divided into equal parts among the proprietors.

§ 1683. *Land Sown with Seed of Another.*—Art. 882. He who sows, plants, or builds on his own estate with seeds, plants, or materials of another acquires the property of both, but with the obligation of paying in every case to compensate for the damage and losses if he has proceeded in bad faith.

§ 1684. *Owner of the Seed.*—Art. 883. The owner of the seeds, plants, or materials shall never have the right to ask for the return thereof to him, thereby destroying the work or planting; but if the plants have not taken root, and can be taken up, the owner of them has a right to ask that it be done.

§ 1685. *Claim of Seed.*– Art. 884. When the seeds or the materials are not applied to their object nor confounded with others, they may be claimed by the owner.

§ 1686. *Land Sowed in Good Faith.*—Art. 885. The owner of land on which shall be built, sown, or planted in good faith, will have the right to make the work, sowing, or planting his own by the previous indemnification prescribed in article 882, or of obliging him who built or planted to pay him the price of the land, and he who sowed only the rent.

§ 1687. *Land Sowed in Bad Faith.*—Art. 886. He who builds, plants, or sows in bad faith on the land of another shall lose what is built, planted, or sown, without having the right to reclaim any indemnification from the owner of the soil or of retaining the thing.

§ 1688. *Demolition of Work.*—Art. 887. The owner of the land on which has been built in bad faith, can ask for the demolition of the work and the replacing of the things in their primitive state at the cost of the builder.

§ 1689. *Bad Faith in Both Parties.*—Art. 888. When there is bad faith, not only on the part of him who builds, but on the part of the owner, this circumstance will be understood as compensated, and the rights of both will be regulated in conformity with what is resolved for the case where the proceedings were in good faith.

§ 1690. *Bad Faith, What is, in the Builder.*—Art. 889. It

"Art. 783. The proprietor of the tree or bush contiguous to the land of another has a right to require of the latter permission to make the collection of the fruits which can not be gathered on his own side, provided he has not used or does not use the right which articles 1019 and 1020 (1125 and 1126, old code) concede; but he is responsible for any injury he may cause the other on account thereof."

is understood that there is bad faith on the part of the builder, planter, or sower when he makes the planting or sowing, or permits without reclamation that another may do so on land which he knows is another's, not asking the owner previously his consent in writing.

§ 1691. *Bad Faith in the Owner.*—Art. 890. It is understood that there is bad faith on the part of the owner whenever the building, sowing, or planting shall be made within his view, knowledge, and endurance.

§ 1692. *Third Parties.*—Art. 891. If the materials, plants, or seeds belong to a third party who has not proceeded in bad faith, the owner of the land is responsible in a subsidiary manner for the value of these objects whenever the two following circumstances concur: 1. That he who in bad faith employed the materials, plants, or seeds shall not have property with which to respond for their value; 2. That what is built, planted, or sown benefits the owner.

§ 1693. *Force of Article Preceding.*—Art. 892. The provisions in the foregoing article shall not have force if the proprietor uses the right which article 887 concedes to him.

§ 1694. *Riparian Owners.*—Art. 893. To the owners of estates bounded by the banks of rivers belongs the increase which those estates receive slowly and insensibly by the effect of the current of the waters.

§ 1695. *Estates on Lakes.*—Art. 894. The owners of estates bounded by lakes or ponds do not acquire the land uncovered by the natural diminution of the waters, nor lose that which is inundated by extraordinary flows.

§ 1696. *Lands Washed Away.*—Art. 895. When the force of the river washes away a considerable and recognizable portion of a riparian field, and carries it towards another below, or to the opposite bank, the proprietor of the portion washed away may reclaim his property, doing so within two years counting from the event; this term having passed, he will lose his right of property unless the proprietor of the field to which the washed-away portion was united shall not have taken possession of the same.

§ 1697. *Trees Washed Away.*—Art. 896. If the force of the river washes away trees only, the proprietor of them preserves the right of reclaiming them and of carrying them to his estate in the same period of two years; but he can not use the rights of proprietor of them in the field of another on which they are found.

§ 1698. *River-beds.*—Art. 897. When a river varies its course, the owners of the fields or estates newly covered with the waters lose the space which the river occupies; and the riparian proprietor of the abandoned bed acquires the part which remains in front of his land to the middle of the bed or course of the river.

§ 1699. *Islands.*—Art. 898. The islands which are formed in the seas adjacent to the coasts of Lower California are public domain, and no one can acquire property in them, except by concession from the government.

§ 1700. *Islands in Rivers Navigable.*—Art. 899. The provision in the foregoing article is also applicable to the islands which are formed in navigable rivers, and even in those which are floatable, which are those in which are navigated tow-boats and rafts.

§ 1701. *Islands in Rivers not Navigable.*—Art. 900. The islands which are formed in rivers not navigable or floatable, belong to the proprietors of both banks, proportionally with the extension of their front of each estate along the river, drawing a dividing line through the middle of the bed.

§ 1702. *Divided Rivers.*—Art. 901. When the current of the river is divided into two arms or branches, leaving isolated one estate or a part of it, the owner does not lose his property, except in the part occupied by the waters, although the divided river be navigable.

# CHAPTER IV.

## POSSESSION.

§ 1703. *Possession.*—Art. 919. Possession is the tenancy of a thing or the enjoyment of a right by ourselves or by another in our name.

§ 1704. *Good or Bad Faith.*—Art. 920. The possession, as a means of acquiring, is either in good or bad faith.

§ 1705. *Capability to Acquire.*—Art. 921. Those who are capable of acquiring are capable of possessing. Incapacitated persons possess through the means of their legitimate representatives, in conformity with the law.

§ 1706. *Presumption.*—Art. 922. The possessor has in his favor the presumption of possessing for himself.

§ 1707. *Possession for Another.*—Art. 923. He who possesses in the name of another is not the possessor in law.

§ 1708. *Continuation of Presumption.*—Art. 924. It is presumed that he who commenced to possess in the name of another continues possessing in the same character.

§ 1709. *Presumption of Proprietorship.*—Art. 925. Possession gives to him who has it the presumption of prcprietorship for all legal effects.

§ 1710. *Intermediate Possession.*—Art. 926. The actual possessor who proves he has possessed in a former time has in his favor the presumption of having possessed in the intermediate time.

§ 1711. *Good Faith, What is.*—Art. 927. He who possesses or fundamentally believes he possesses in virtue of a title sufficient to transfer the dominion is a possessor in good faith.

§ 1712. *Possessor in Good Faith.*—Art. 928. He is also a possessor in good faith who is ignorant of the viciousness of his title. Ignorance is presumed in this case.

§ 1713. *Possessors in Bad Faith.*—Art. 929. He who possesses knowing he has no title, he who without any grounds believes he has a title, and he who knows that his title is insufficient or vicious, are possessors in bad faith.

§ 1714. *Presumption of Good Faith.*—Art. 930. The possessor has in his favor the presumption of passing in good faith, save the provision in article 959.

§ 1715. *Fruits.*—Art. 931. The possessor in good faith makes the fruits he receives his while the good faith is not interrupted.

§ 1716. *Interruption.*—Art. 932. Good faith is interrupted by the same means as prescription, in conformity with what is provided in article 1232.

§ 1717. *Suspension of Good Faith.*—Art. 933. By the suspension of good faith the possessor does not lose the right of receiving the fruits, only in the cases expressly determined in the laws; but he is obliged to return those which he may have received after that, or their value, if it shall be declared by a final judgment that he possessed in bad faith.

§ 1718. *Fruits, when Received.*—Art. 934. Natural or industrial fruits are understood as received from the time they are gathered or separated. Civil fruits are produced day by day, and belong to the possessor in this proportion, as soon as they are due, although they may not have been received.

§ 1719. *Pending Fruit.*—Art. 935. The possessor in good faith has a right to a credit for the expenses made by him for the production of the natural and industrial fruits, which do not become his on account of being pending at the time of the interruption of the possession.

§ 1720. *Legal Interest.*—Art. 936. He has also a right to legal interest on the amount of the expenses from the day on which they have been respectively made, to that on which the payment thereof shall be made.

§ 1721. *Possession by Robbery.*—Art. 937. A possessor in bad faith, whenever he has acquired the tenancy by robbery, is obliged to restore all the fruits which the thing has produced, and those which it has failed to produce by the culpable omission of the possessor in the ordinary cultivation of the estate.

§ 1722. *Title, Possession by.*—Art. 938. A possessor in bad faith, who has acquired the tenancy by a title translative of the dominion, will only be obliged to restore the fruits which he has received; and he will have no responsibility for those which the estate or thing might have produced, unless he shall have acquired the thing sold knowingly by force or fear, or against the prescriptions of this code; since in these cases the possessor in bad faith is considered the same as he who acquires the thing by robbery.

§ 1723. *Expenses.*—Art. 939. Every possessor ought to be credited with the necessary expenses; but only he who of good faith has a right to retain the thing until the payment thereof is made.

§ 1724. *Useful Expenses.*—Art. 940. A possessor in good faith ought to be credited with the useful expenses; and he also has a right to retain the thing until the payment thereof be made.

§ 1725. *Improvements.*—Art. 941. A possessor in bad faith may withdraw the useful improvements if the owner does not pay him for them, and they can be separated without detriment from the thing improved.

§ 1726. *Voluntary Expenses.*—Art. 942. The voluntary expenses are not to be credited to any possessor; but the possessor in good faith may withdraw these improvements, if no detriment is caused thereby to the thing improved, or by repairing the detriment thereby caused, in the judgment of experts.

§ 1727. *Necessary Expenses.*—Art. 943. Necessary expenses are those which are prescribed by law, and those without which the thing would be lost or damaged.

§ 1728. *Useful Expenses, What are.*—Art. 944. Useful expenses are those which, without being necessary, increase the price or product of the thing.

§ 1729. *Voluntary Expenses, What are.*—Art. 945. Voluntary expenses are those which serve only as an ornament to the thing, or as a pleasure or convenience to the possessor.

§ 1730. *Proof of Expenses.*—Art. 946. The possessor ought to prove the amount of the expenses to which he has a right. In case of doubt, they will be taxed by the means of experts.

§ 1731. *Indemnification.*—Art. 947. When the possessor ought to be indemnified for expenses, and has received fruits to which he had no right, there shall be compensation.

§ 1732. *Improvements.*—Art. 948. The improvements or increase in value proceeding from nature or time always belong to the proprietor.

§ 1733. *Possessor in Good Faith.*—Art. 949. A possessor in good faith shall not respond for the deterioration or loss of the thing possessed, although they may have occurred by his own act; but he shall respond for the profit which he himself may have obtained from the loss or deterioration.

§ 1734. *Possessor in Bad Faith.*—Art. 950. A possessor in bad faith shall respond for all loss or deterioration which may have happened through his fault or by a fortuitous case, unless he shall prove that this would have taken place if the thing had been possessed by the owner.

§ 1735. *Losses, Natural.*—Art. 951. Neither shall he respond for the loss which naturally and inevitably happens solely through the course of time.

§ 1736. *Possession Lost.*—Art. 952. Possession is lost: 1. By the abandonment thereof; 2. By concession with an onerous or gratuitous title; 3. By the destruction or loss of the thing, or by its being out of commerce.

§ 1737. *Possession for More than a Year.*—Art. 953. Possession is also lost when another possesses the thing for more than a year, which shall be counted from the day on which the new possession publicly commenced, or from that day on which notice thereof reached him who possessed prior thereto, if the new possession commenced secretly.

§ 1738. *Heirs.*—Art. 954. Possession is transmissible by inheritance; the heirs of the possessor continue the possession commenced by him.[1]

§ 1739. *Right of Possessor.*—Art. 955. A possessor has a right to be maintained in his possession whenever he shall be disturbed in it.

§ 1740. *Restoration.*—Art. 956. A possessor has a right to be restored to his possession, if he requires it, within a year, counted in conformity with the provision in article 953.

§ 1741. *Possession Less than a Year.*—Art. 957. If the possession is less than a year, no one can be judicially maintained in or restored to the same, except against those whose possession shall be no better.

§ 1742. *Possession and Title.*—Art. 958. A possession credited with a legitimate title is better than any other; for want of this, or the titles being equal, the oldest shall be preferred; if both possessions should be doubtful, the thing in litigation shall be placed in trust.

§ 1743. *Forcible Ejectment.*—Art. 959. Bad faith is always presumed in him who ejects another forcibly from the possession in which he is found.

§ 1744. *Judicial Possession.*—Art. 960. He who was judicially maintained in or restored to the possession of a thing is never reputed as disturbed or despoiled thereof.

§ 1745. *Payment for Losses.*—Art. 961. He who has judicially been maintained in the possession, or restored to it, has a right to be indemnified for the losses which may have followed him thereby.

§ 1746. *Presumptions.*—Art. 962. In the cases comprehended in articles 922, 924, 925, 926, 928, 930, and 959, the presumption will subsist until the contrary shall be proved.

[1] Article 954 is suppressed in the code of 1884.

# CHAPTER V.

## USUFRUCTS IN GENERAL—USE AND HABITATION.

§ 1747. Usufruct.
§ 1748. Usufruct, how Constituted.
§ 1749. One or More Persons.
§ 1750. Various Persons.
§ 1751. Successively Constituted.
§ 1752. Corporations.
§ 1753. Conditions.
§ 1754. For Life.
§ 1755. Creditors.
§ 1756. Title of Usufruct.
§ 1757. Actions.
§ 1758. Fruits.
§ 1759. Hanging Fruit.
§ 1760. End of Usufruct.
§ 1761. Beginning and End of Usufruct.
§ 1762. Usufructuary—Right to Fruit.
§ 1763. Mines.
§ 1764. Third Party.
§ 1765. Accessions.
§ 1766. Rights of Usufructuary.
§ 1767. Perpetual Services.
§ 1768. Interest.
§ 1769. Deterioration.
§ 1770. Forests.
§ 1771. Cutting Wood.
§ 1772. Trees, how Cut.
§ 1773. Vivaries.
§ 1774. Improvements.
§ 1775. Alienation of Property.
§ 1776. Tanto.
§ 1777. Before Entering into Enjoyment of the Property.
§ 1778. Donor.
§ 1779. Exemption.
§ 1780. Contract.
§ 1781. Onerous Title.
§ 1782. Right to Fruit.
§ 1783. Losses.
§ 1784. Cattle.
§ 1785. When Cattle Perish.
§ 1786. When Cattle Perish in Part.
§ 1787. Trees.
§ 1788. Gratuitous Title.
§ 1789. Losses from Natural Causes.

### Of Usufructs in General—Use and Habitation.

§ 1747. *Usufruct.*—Art. 963. A usufruct is the right of enjoying the property of another without altering its form or substance.

§ 1748. *Usufruct, how Constituted.*—Art. 964. A usufruct is constituted by law, by an act among the living (entre vivos), or by a last will, and by prescription.

§ 1749. *One or More Persons.*—Art. 965. A usufruct may be constituted in favor of one or many persons simultaneously or successively.

§ 1750. *Various Persons.*—Art. 966. If it is constituted in favor of various persons simultaneously, either by inheritance or by contract, the right of one of the persons ceasing, the usufruct inures to the others.

§ 1751. *Successively Constituted.*—Art. 967. If it is constituted successively, the usufruct will not take place except in favor of the persons who exist at the time in which the right of the first usufructuary commences.

§ 1752. *Corporations.*—Art. 968. Civil corporations can not acquire or administer real estate, neither can they have a usufruct constructed on property of this kind.

§ 1753. *Conditions.*—Art. 969. A usufruct may be constituted from or until a certain day purely and under a condition.

§ 1754. *For Life.*—Art. 970. A usufruct is for life, unless the contrary is expressed in the title constituting the same.

§ 1755. *Creditors.*—Art. 971. Creditors of the usufructuary may seize the products of the usufruct, and oppose every concession or renouncement of the latter whenever they are made in fraud of their rights.

§ 1756. *Title of Usufruct.*—Art. 972. The rights and obligations of the possessor of the usufruct and of the proprietor are arranged in every case by the title constituting the usufruct.

### Of the Rights of the Usufructuary.

§ 1757. *Actions.* Art. 973. The usufructuary has a right to institute all possessory, personal, or real actions, and exceptions, of being considered a party in every litigation, although it be prosecuted by the proprietor, whenever the usufruct is interested in said litigation.

§ 1758. *Fruits.*—Art. 974. The usufructuary has a right to receive all the natural, industrial, and civil fruits of the property enjoyed as a usufruct (usufructuados).

§ 1759. *Hanging Fruit.*—Art. 975. The natural or industrial fruits hanging at the time of the commencing of the usufruct shall belong to the usufructuary, save the obligations by which the thing may be affected by priority.

§ 1760. *End of Usufruct.*—Art. 976. The natural or industrial fruits hanging at the time of the extinguishment of the usufruct belong to the proprietor.

§ 1761. *Beginning and End of Usufruct.*—Art. 977. Neither the usufructuary nor the proprietor must be paid anything by reason of labor, seed, or other like expenses. This provision shall not prejudice the colonists or tenants who have a right to receive any portion of the fruits at the time of the commencement or extinguishment of the usufruct.[1]

§ 1762. *Usufructuary—Right to Fruit.*—Art. 978. The civil fruits belong to the usufructuary in proportion to the time which the usufruct lasts, even when they are not collected.

§ 1763. *Mines.*—Art. 979. The products of mines do not belong to the usufructuary which are acquired by denouncement, and which are found in a working condition, unless they are expressly conceded to him in the title which constitutes the usufruct or that it be universal; but if the usufructuary should discover and denounce a mine during the usufruct it will make it entirely his, with the obligation of paying the proprietor at the termination of the usufruct what the land should amount to according to the provisions of the mining ordinances.

§ 1764. *Third Party.*—Art. 980. If a third party or the said proprietor should be the one who should discover or denounce the mine, the payment of the indemnity for the land will be made to the usufructuary according to the provisions for the case of the discovery of a treasure in article 864.

§ 1765. *Accessions.*—Art. 981. Equally belongs to the usufructuary the fruit of the increase which the things receive by the accession and the enjoyment of the services which they may have in their favor, and generally the other rights inherent to the mines.

§ 1766. *Rights of Usufructuary.*—Art. 982. The usufructuary may enjoy by himself the thing possessed as a usufruct, rent it to another, alienante, rent, and encumber the exercise of the right of the usufruct, although it be by a gratuitous title; but all the contracts which he shall make as such usufructuary shall terminate with the usufruct.

§ 1767. *Perpetual Service.*—Art. 983. The usufructuary can not constitute perpetual services on the estate which he possesses as a usufruct. Those which he shall legally constitute will cease at the termination of the usufruct.

§ 1768. *Interest.*—Art. 984. If the usufruct is constituted

[1] Articles 975, 976, and 977 are united into one article in the code of 1884, which reads as follows: "Art. 877. The natural or industrial fruits hanging at the time of the commencement of the usufruct shall belong to the usufructuary. Those hanging at the time of the extinguishment of the usufruct belong to the proprietor. Neither the latter nor the usufructuary must be paid anything by reason of work, seed, or other like expenses. The provision in this article shall not prejudice the farming partners (aparceros) or lessees who may have a right to receive any portion of the fruits at the time of the commencement or extinguishment of the usufruct."

upon capital drawing interest, the usufructuary only makes the latter his, and not the former; and even when the capital is redeemed, it must again draw interest to the satisfaction of the usufructuary and the proprietor.

§ 1769. *Deterioration.*—Art. 985. If all or any of the things on which the usufruct is constituted wear out or deteriorate slowly by use, the usufructuary has a right to use them like the good father of a family for the uses to which they are found destined, and he is only obliged to return them on the extinguishment of the usufruct in the condition in which they are found; but he is responsible for the payment of the deterioration which happens by his fraud, fault, or negligence.

§ 1770. *Forests.*—Art. 986. The usufructuary of a forest enjoys all the products of which it may be susceptible, according to its nature.

§ 1771. *Cutting Wood.*—Art. 987. If the forest should be of fire-wood or of timber for building, the usufructuary can make of it the ordinary felling or cutting which the owner would do, accommodating himself in the manner, portion, and epochs, according to the special ordinances or the constant customs of the country.

§ 1772. *Trees, how Cut.*—Art. 988. In other cases the usufructuary can not cut the trees at the foot, as it may not be in order to replace or repair any of the things possessed as a usufruct, and in this case he must previously prove to the proprietor the necessity of the work.

§ 1773. *Vivaries.*—Art. 989. The usufructuary can make use of the vivaries without injury to their preservation, and according to the customs of the country.

§ 1774. *Improvements.* — Art. 990. The usufructuary can make useful and purely voluntary improvements, but he has no right to reclaim payment therefor, although he may withdraw them, provided that it be possible to do so without detriment to the thing on which the usufruct is constituted.

§ 1775. *Alienation of Property.*—Art. 991. The proprietor of property on which another has the usufruct may alienate it upon condition that the usufruct be preserved, and in no other manner.

§ 1776. *Tanto.*—Art. 992. The usufructuary enjoys the right of tanto, or the right of buying the property at the same price which the owner offers it to any other person, or is willing to take from another.

### Of the Obligations of the Usufructuary.

§ 1777. *Before Entering into the Enjoyment of the Property.*—Art. 993. The usufructuary before entering into the enjoyment of the property is obliged: 1. To form at his expense, with citation of the owner, an inventory of all the property, causing the personal property to be valued and the condition in which the immovable property is found to appear; 2. To give the corresponding security that he will take care of the things as a good father of a family and restore them to the owner with their accession, on the extinguishment of the usufruct, not impaired nor deteriorated by his negligence, save the provision in article 408. (This relates to the usufruct of property of the child conceded to the father.)

§ 1778. *Donor.*—Art. 994. The donor who reserves the usufruct of the property donated is exempt from giving the required security, unless he has expressly obligated himself to give it.

§ 1779. *Exemption.*—Art. 995. He who reserves the property can exempt the usufructuary from the obligation of giving security.

§ 1780. *Contract.*—Art. 996. If the usufruct should be constituted by contract, and he who contracted should be proprietor, and should not require in the contract the security, the usufructuary will not be obliged to give it; but if the proprietor should be a third party the latter can ask for it, although it has not been stipulated in the contract.

§ 1781. *Onerous Title.*—Art. 997. If the usufruct be constituted by an onerous title, and the usufructuary does not give the corresponding security, the proprietor has the right to intervene in the administration of the property in order to procure its preservation, subjecting himself to the conditions prescribed in article 1033, and receiving the recompense which is conceded to him in it.

§ 1782. *Rights to Fruits.*—Art. 998. The usufructuary, having given the security, will have a right to all the fruits of the thing from the day on which, in conformity with the title constituting the usufruct, he ought to commence to receive them.

§ 1783. *Losses.*—Art. 999. In the cases designated by article 982, the usufructuary is responsible for the loss suffered by the property through the fault or negligence of the person whom he substituted in his place.

§ 1784. *Cattle.*—Art. 1000. If the usufruct is constituted

on cattle, the usufructuary is obliged to replace with the young the heads of cattle that may be wanting through any cause.

§ 1785. *When Cattle Perish.*—Art. 1001. If the cattle on which the usufruct was constituted all perish without the fault of the usufructuary, through the effect of an epizootic or other uncommon event, the usufructuary will fulfill his duty by delivering to the owner the remains which he may have saved from that misfortune.

§ 1786. *When They Perish in Part.*—Art. 1002. If the flock perish in part, and without the fault of the usufructuary, the usufruct will continue in the part which remains.

§ 1787. *Trees.*—Art. 1003. The usufructuary of fruit trees is obliged to replant those which die naturally.

§ 1788. *Gratuitous Title.*—Art. 1004. If the usufruct has been constituted by a gratuitous title, the usufructuary is obliged to make the indispensable reparations in order to maintain the thing in the state in which it was found when he received it.

§ 1789. *Losses from Natural Causes.*—Art. 1005. The usufructuary is not obliged to make said reparations, if the necessity of these arise from old age, intrinsic vice, or grave deterioration of the thing prior to the constitution of the usufruct.

§ 1790. *Consent.*—Art. 1006. If the usufructuary wishes to make the said reparations he must beforehand obtain the consent of the owner; and in no case has he a right to require indemnification of any kind.

§ 1791. *Reparations by Proprietor.*—Art. 1007. The proprietor in the case of article 1005 also is obliged to make reparations; and if he makes them he has no right to require indemnification.

§ 1792. *Onerous Titles—Obligations.*—Art. 1008. If the usufruct has been constituted by an onerous title, the proprietor is under obligation to make all the proper reparations in order that the thing, during the time stipulated in the agreement, may produce the fruits which ordinarily are obtained from it at the time of delivery.

§ 1793. *Notice.*—Art. 1009. If the usufructuary wishes to make in this case the reparations, he must give notice to the proprietor; and prior to this requisite, he will have a right to collect the amount at the end of the usufruct.

§ 1794. *Omission of Notice.*—Art. 1010. The omission of opportune notice to the proprietor makes the usufructuary responsible for the destruction, loss, or deterioration of the thing for want of reparations; and it deprives him of the right of asking for indemnification, if he makes them.

§ 1795. *Taxes.*—Art. 1011. All diminution of the fruits which arise from the imposition of taxes, or ordinary charges on the estate or thing possessed as a usufruct, is on account of the usufructuary.

§ 1796. *Diminution of Usufruct.*—Art. 1012. The diminutions which through proper causes are made, not in the fruits, but in the said estate or thing possessed as a usufruct, will be on account of the proprietor; and if the latter, in order to preserve the thing whole, makes the payment, he has a right to have the interest on the sum paid credited to him through all the time which the usufructuary continues enjoying the thing.

§ 1797. *Interest.*—Art. 1013. If the usufructuary makes payment of the sum, he has no right to collect interest, he being compensated for this with the fruits which he receives.

§ 1798. *Usufruct by Succession.*—Art. 1014. He who acquires by succession the universal usufruct is obliged to pay the entire legacy of life-rent or pension of allowance.

§ 1799. *Aliquot Part.*—Art. 1015. He who by the same title acquires an aliquot part will pay the legacy or pension in proportion to his quota.

§ 1800. *Forced Heirs.*—Art. 1016. The provisions in the two preceding articles are understood as excepting the right of forced heirs.[1]

§ 1801. *Mortgage.*—Art. 1017. The special (particular) usufructuary of a mortgaged estate is not obliged to pay the debts for the security of which the mortgage was constituted.

§ 1802. *Judicial Sale of Estate.*—Art. 1018. If the estate is attached or sold judicially for the payment of the debt, the proprietor shall respond to the usufructuary for what he loses on this account, if he has provided something else on constituting the usufruct.

§ 1803. *Inheritance.*—Art. 1019. If the usufruct is of some inheritance or of an aliquot part of it, the usufructuary can advance the sums which for the payment of the hereditary debts correspond to the property held in usufruct; and he shall have the right to require from the proprietor restitution thereof, without interest, on the extinguishment of the usufruct.

§ 1804. *Sale.*—Art. 1020. If the usufructuary should refuse to make the advancement of which the preceding article speaks,

[1] Article 1016 is suppressed in the code of 1884.

the proprietor can cause to be sold a part of the property which may be sufficient for the payment of the sum which that ought to satisfy, according to the established rule in said article.

§ 1805. *Interest on Advancement.*—Art. 1021. If the proprietor should make the advancement on his account, the usufructuary shall pay the interest on the money, according to the rule established in article 1012.

§ 1806. *Third Party.*—Art. 1022. If the rights of the proprietor are disturbed by a third party, in whatever manner or for whatever reason, the usufructuary is obliged to give information thereof to the former; and if he does not do it, he is responsible for the damages which result, as if they had been occasioned by his fault.

§ 1807. *Expenses of Suits.*—Art. 1023. The expenses, costs, and judgments of suits sustained on the usufruct are on account of the proprietor if the usufruct has been established by an onerous title, and on account of the usufructuary if it has been constituted by a gratuitous title.

§ 1808. *Expenses Joint, when.*—Art. 1024. If the suit interests at the same time the owner and the usufructuary, they shall contribute to the expenses in proportion to their respective rights if the usufruct was constituted by a gratuitous title; but the usufructuary in no case will be obliged to respond for more than what the usufruct produces.

§ 1809. *Citation.*—Art. 1025. If the usufructuary, without citation of the proprietor, or the latter without citation of the former, has prosecuted a suit, a favorable judgment avails the party not cited, and an adverse judgment does not injure him.

### Of the Manner of Extinguishing the Usufruct.

§ 1810. *Extinguishment of Usufruct.*—Art. 1026. A usufruct is extinguished: 1. By the death of the usufructuary, save the provision in article 1028;[1] 2. By the expiration of the term for which it was constituted; 3. By the fulfillment of the condition imposed in the constitutive title, for the cessation of this right; 4. By the union of the usufruct and the property in one person; but if the union is made in one thing only, or in a part of the property held in usufruct, in the rest the usufruct will subsist; 5. By prescription, in conformity with what is provided in respect to real rights; 6. By the renouncement of the usu-

[1] The words "save the provision in article 1028" are suppressed in the code of 1884.

fructuary, save the provision in respect to the renouncements made in fraud of creditors; 7. By the total loss of the thing which was the object of the usufruct; if the destruction is not total, the right continues on what remains of the thing; 8. By the cessation of the right of him who constituted the usufruct, when having a revocable dominion, the case of revocation arises; 9. By the usufructuary not giving security for a gratuitous title, if the owner has not exempted him from that obligation.

§ 1811. *Corporation.*—Art. 1027. A usufruct constituted in favor of corporations or partnerships (sociedades), which can acquire and administer real estate, will only last thirty years; ceasing in case said partnerships or corporations are dissolved.

§ 1812. *Concession for Time.*—Art. 1028. A usufruct conceded for the time which awaits a third party to arrive at a certain age lasts the number of years prefixed, although the third party dies before.

§ 1813. *Destruction of the Estate.*—Art. 1029. If the usufruct is constituted upon an edifice, and this is ruined by fire, or by old age, or by any other accident, the usufructuary has no right to enjoy the land nor the materials; but if it were constituted upon a hacienda, country seat (quinta), or rancho, of which the ruined edifice formed a part, the usufructuary may continue to possess the land and materials in usufruct.

§ 1814. *Reconstruction of Buildings.*—Art. 1030. If the edifice is reconstructed by the owner or by the usufructuary, it will be subject to the provisions in articles 1006, 1007, 1008, and 1009.

§ 1815. *Vis Major.*—Art. 1031. The temporary impediment by a fortuitous case or *vis major* (fuerza mayor), does not extinguish the usufruct, nor give a right to require indemnification from the proprietor.

§ 1816. *Impediment.*—Art. 1032. The time of the impediment will be held as run for the usufructuary, from whom will be the fruits which the thing may produce during the impediment.

§ 1817. *Extinguishment.*—Art. 1033. The usufruct shall not be extinguished by the bad use which the usufructuary may make of the thing held in usufruct; but if the abuse is grave, the proprietor may ask that he be put in possession of the property, obligating himself under a bond to pay annually to the usufructuary the net product of the same, for the time which the usufruct lasts, deducting the premium of administration which the judge may adjudge to him.

§ 1818. *Contracts.*—Art. 1034. The usufruct having terminated, the contracts which respecting the same the usufructuary may have made, do not obligate the proprietor, and the latter will enter into the possession of the thing without those who contracted with the usufructuary having any right against him to ask him for indemnification for the dissolution of their contracts, or for the stipulations in the contracts which only can be made valid against the usufructuary and his heirs.[1]

### Of Use and Habitation.

§ 1819. *Cestui que Use.*—Art. 1035. The rights and obligations of the person having the sole use of a thing (usuario cestui que use), and of him who has the enjoyment of a habitation, are governed by their respective titles, and in default thereof by the following dispositions:

§ 1820. *Reference.*—Art. 1036. The provisions of articles 975, 976, 977, 993, 1022, 1023, 1024, 1025, 1026, 1027, 1028, 1029, 1030, 1031, 1032, and 1033 are applicable to the rights of use and habitation.

§ 1821. *Use.*—Art. 1037. The use gives a right to receive so much of the fruits of a thing of another as is sufficient for the necessities of the usuario (cestui que use) and his family, although the latter increases.

§ 1822. *Habitation.*—Art. 1038. He who has a right of habitation may inhabit all the rooms which are destined for this effect; but not to use the other parts of the edifice, nor collect the fruits of it. He can besides receive other persons into his company.

§ 1823. *Can not Sell or Rent.*—Art. 1039. The usuario, and he who has the right of habitation in an edifice, can not alienate nor rent wholly nor in part their rights to another; nor can these rights be seized by the creditors of the usuario.

§ 1824. *Use of Cattle.*—Art. 1040. He who has a right of use on cattle may avail himself of the young, milk, and wool, so far as is sufficient for his consumption and that of his family.

§ 1825. *Obligations.*—Art. 1041. If the usuario consume all the fruits of the property, or he who has the right of habitation occupies all the rooms of the house, they are obligated with all the expenses of cultivation, reparations, and payment of taxes the same as a usufructuary; but if the first only consumes part

[1] In the code of 1884, the words "save the provisions in article 877" (975 to 977 old code) are added thereto, and the article is 933.

of the fruits, or the second occupies only a part of the house, they ought to contribute nothing, provided there remains to the proprietor a part of the fruits or benefits sufficient to cover the expenses and charges.

§ 1826. *Expenses—Deficit.*—Art. 1042. If the fruits which remain to the proprietor do not amount to enough to cover the expenses and charges, the deficit will be covered by the usuario, or by him who has a right to the habitation.

# CHAPTER VI.

## SERVICES (SERVIDUMBRES).

§ 1827. Service, What is.
§ 1828. Service Consists in Doing or Tolerating.
§ 1829. Object of Services.
§ 1830. Kinds of Services.
§ 1831. Continuous Services.
§ 1832. Discontinuous Services.
§ 1833. Apparent Services.
§ 1834. Services not Apparent.
§ 1835. Inseparable.
§ 1836. Change of Owners.
§ 1837. Indivisible.
§ 1838. How Services Arise.
§ 1839. Right to Inclose Property.
§ 1840. Legal Services.
§ 1841. Chapter 11 Applicable.
§ 1842. Lower Estates.
§ 1843. Owners.
§ 1844. Defensive Works.
§ 1845. Disencumbering Estates.
§ 1846. Participants in Profits Liable for Expenses.
§ 1847. Springs, Wells, etc.
§ 1848. Overplus Water.
§ 1849. Rights within Limits of Property.
§ 1850. Right of the State does not Prejudice.
§ 1851. Navigation not to be Prejudiced.
§ 1852. Use of River Banks.
§ 1853. Proprietor of Waters.
§ 1854. Prior Rights.
§ 1855. Courses not to be Changed.
§ 1856. Wells.
§ 1857. Intermediate Grounds.
§ 1858. Exceptions.
§ 1859. Passage of Water.
§ 1860. New Canals, when not Allowed.
§ 1861. Convenience Considered.
§ 1862. Passage across Public Roads.
§ 1863. Police Regulation.
§ 1864. Trespassers.
§ 1865. Claimant's Duty.
§ 1866. Claimant to the Passage of Waters, his Obligations.
§ 1867. Limitation on Quantity of Water.
§ 1868. Aqueducts.
§ 1869. Right of Transit.

### Of Provisions Common to All Services.

§ 1827. *Service, What is.*—Art. 1043. A service is a burden imposed upon an estate or inheritance for the benefit or for the service of another estate or inheritance belonging to a distinct owner. The estate or inheritance in favor of which the service is constituted is called the dominant estate (predio dominante); the estate or inheritance which suffers it is called the serving estate.

§ 1828. *Service Consists in Doing or Tolerating.*—Art. 1044. The service consists in not doing or in tolerating. In order that the execution of an act can be required of the owner of the serving estate, it is necessary that it be expressly determined by the law or in the act by which the service is constituted.

§ 1829. *Object of Services.*—Art. 1045. Services are constituted for the subsistence or convenience of an edifice, and of the object to which the edifice is destined, or for the convenience and use of an agricultural object; the first are called urban (urbanas), and the second rustic (rusticas), without considering whether the estate be in a town or in the country.

§ 1830. *Kinds of Services.*—Art. 1046. Services are continuous or discontinuous, apparent or not apparent.

§ 1831. *Continuous Services.*—Art. 1047. Those are continuous, the use of which is or may be incessant without the intervention of any act of man, as are the services of lights and others of the same kind.

§ 1832. *Discontinuous Services.*—Art. 1048. Those are discontinuous the use of which requires some actual act of man; as are those of a path or cart-way, and others of this class.

§ 1833. *Apparent Services.*—Art. 1049. Those are apparent which are announced by works or exterior signs, arranged for their use and advantage, such as a bridge, a window, drain, or other like things.

§ 1834. *Services not Apparent.*—Art. 1050. Those are not apparent which present no exterior signs of their existence, as the obligation of not building in a certain place, that of not raising an edifice except at a determined height, and others similar.

§ 1835. *Inseparable.*—Art. 1051. The services are inseparable from the estate to which they actively or passively belong.

§ 1836. *Change of Owners.*—Art. 1052. If the estates change owners, the service continues, whether actively or passively, on the estate or object on which it was constituted until it is legally extinguished.

§ 1837. *Indivisible.*—Art. 1053. Services are indivisible. If the serving estate is divided among many owners, the service is not modified, and each one of them must tolerate it in the part which belongs to him. If it is the dominant estate which is divided among many, each participant can use the service entirely, not varying the place of its use nor burdening it in any other manner.

§ 1838. *How Services Arise.*—Art. 1054. Services arise from the contract or the last will of the proprietors and from the law, whether they be expressly established or whether they be authorized in virtue of prescription.

§ 1839. *Right to Inclose Property.*—Art. 1055. Every proprietor has a right to lock and inclose his property in whole or in part, at his cost, in the manner which he deems convenient, save the service of public or private use, which it owes by a just title, including that of prescription.

### Of Legal Services in General.

§ 1840. *Legal Services.*—Art. 1056. Legal service is that which exists without the necessity of an agreement or prescription, and which as a natural consequence of the respective positions of the estates the law recognizes whether for the public or common utility, or whether for the benefit of private persons.

§ 1841. *Chapter* 11 *Applicable.*—Art. 1057. The provision in chapter 11 of this title, with the exceptions of articles 1146 and 1149, is applicable to legal services in all cases in which in respect to them no special precept is established.

### Of the Legal Service of Waters.

§ 1842. *Lower Estates.*—Art. 1058. The lower estates are subject to receive the waters which naturally and without the act of man fall from the estates above, as well as the stones and earth which are carried in their course.

§ 1843. *Owners.*—Art. 1059. Neither the owner of the lower estate can make works which will impede said service, nor the owner of the upper estate works which will enlarge it.

§ 1844. *Defensive Works.*—Art. 1060. The owner of an estate on which exist defensive works to restrain the water, or on which, through the variation of the course of the water, it shall be necessary to construct new ones, is obliged, at his election, either to make reparations or constructions, or to tolerate the owners of estates which experience or may be imminently exposed to experience damages, to make them, without injury to himself, unless the special laws of police impose upon him the obligation of making the works.

§ 1845. *Disencumbering Estates.*—Art. 1061. The provision in the foregoing article is applicable to the case in which it may be necessary to disencumber any estate from the materials the accumulation or fall of which impedes the course of the water, with damage or danger to a third party.

§ 1846. *Participants in Profits Liable for Expenses.*—Art. 1062. All the proprietors who participate in the benefits arising from the works of which the foregoing articles treat are obliged to contribute to the expense of their execution in proportion to their interest and according to the judgment of experts. Those who through their fault shall have occasioned the damage will be responsible for the expenses.

§ 1847. *Springs, Wells, etc.*—Art. 1063. The owner of an estate on which there is a natural spring, or who has constructed an overflowing well, reservoir, or dam to detain the rain-water on his own ground may use and dispose of the water freely.

§ 1848. *Overplus Water.*—Art. 1064. If there is an overplus of water which passes to the estate of another, the property in the overplus of water may be acquired by the owner of the ground which receives it through the course of twenty years, which shall be counted from the time at which the owner of said estate shall have constructed the works destined to facilitate the fall or the course of the water.[1]

§ 1849. *Rights within Limits of Property.*—Art. 1065. The provision in the foregoing article does not deprive the owner of the spring, reservoir, or dam of the power to obtain all possible advantage from the waters, within the limits of his property.

§ 1850. *Right of the State does not Prejudice.*—Art. 1066. The property which over waters belongs to the state does not prejudice the rights which corporations or private individuals may have acquired over them by a legitimate title, according to what is established in the special laws over the rights of public property. The exercise of the right of property in waters is subject to what is provided in the following articles.

§ 1851. *Navigation not to be Prejudiced.*—Art. 1067. Nobody can use the water of rivers in a manner prejudicial to navigation, nor make in them works which shall impede the free passage of barks or rafts or the use of other means of fluvial transportation; nor can they avail themselves of prescription or other title therefor.

§ 1852. *Use of River Banks.*—Art. 1068. In like terms they are prohibited from impeding or embarrassing the use of the river banks so far as they may be necessary for the same ends.

§ 1853. *Proprietor of Waters.*—Art. 1069. The proprietor of water, whatever may be his title, can not impede the use of that which may be necessary for the supply of the persons or cattle of a possession or rustic estate, nor oppose the indispensable works in order to satisfy this necessity in the manner the least injurious to the proprietor; but he shall have a right to indemnification, save the use of the water which the inhabitants shall have acquired by prescription or by other legal title.[2]

---

[1] The word "twenty" in the article 1064 is changed to "ten" in the code of 1884.

[2] Articles 1067, 1068, and 1069 are united in one article in the code of 1884, which reads as follows: "Art. 966. No one can use the water of the rivers, nor their banks, in a manner prejudicial to navigation, nor make works which shall impede the free passage of barks or rafts or the use of other means of fluvial transportation, nor can they avail themselves of prescription or other title therefor. He who, in conformity with the preceding article, may be using the water of a

§ 1854. *Prior Rights.*—Art. 1070. The provisions of this code about the services of waters make no innovation in any manner upon the rights legally acquired up to this time.

§ 1855. *Courses not to be Changed.*—Art. 1071. The proprietor of waters can not change their course in a manner which may cause damage to a third party, because they overflow, or for any other reason.

§ 1856. *Wells.*—Art. 1072. If any one should make a well on his property, although it should diminish the water in the one opened on the ground of another, he is not obliged to indemnify the latter.

§ 1857. *Intermediate Grounds.*—Art. 1073. Every one who wishes to use water of which he may dispose has a right to cause it to pass through intermediate grounds, with the obligation of indemnifying their owners, as well as also those who own the estates below over which the waters filter or fall.

§ 1858. *Exceptions.*—Art. 1074. The edifices, courts, gardens, and other dependencies are excepted from the service which the foregoing article establishes.

§ 1859. *Passage of Water.*—Art. 1075. He who has to use the right of causing waters to pass which are treated of in article 1073 is obliged to construct the necessary canal on the intermediate estates, although there are canals on them for the use of other waters.

§ 1860. *New Canals, when not Allowed.*—Art. 1076. He who has on his estate a canal for the coursing of waters which belong to it may impede the opening of a new one by offering to give passage through his own canal, provided it causes no injury to the claimant.

§ 1861. *Convenience Considered.*—Art. 1077. Also must be conceded the passage of waters across the canals and aqueducts in the most convenient manner, provided the course of waters conducted through the latter, and their volume, suffer no alteration, and that the waters of both aqueducts do not mix.

§ 1862. *Passage across Public Roads.*—Art. 1078. In the case of article 1073, if it were necessary to cause the aqueduct to pass through a public road, river, or torrent, it will be indispensable to previously obtain permission of the authority under whose inspection the road, river, or torrent is.

---

river, whatever may be his title, can not impede the use of that which may be necessary for the supply of the persons of a town, possession, or rural estate, nor oppose the indispensable works to satisfy this necessity in the manner the least burdensome to the proprietor; but he will have a right to indemnification, save that the inhabitants should have acquired the use of the water by prescription or by other legal title."

§ 1863. *Police Regulations.*—Art. 1079. The authority will only concede the permission with entire subjection to the police regulations, and obliging the owner of the water to cause it to pass in its transit without narrowing or deteriorating the road, nor embarrassing nor obstructing the course of the river or torrent.

§ 1864. *Trespassers.*—Art. 1080. He who, without previous permission, shall run the water or let it flow over the road shall be obliged to replace things in their former state, and to indemnify any one who is damaged thereby, without prejudice to the penalties imposed by the regulations of police.

§ 1865. *Claimant's Duty.*—Art. 1081. He who claims to use the right assigned in article 1073 must previously: 1. Prove that he can dispose of the water which he claims to convey; 2. Prove that the passage which he solicits is the most convenient and the least onerous for the third party; 3. Pay the value of the land which the canal must occupy, according to the estimate of experts, and ten per cent more; 4. Make recompense for the immediate damages, including those which result from dividing into two or more parts the serving estate, and any other deterioration.

§ 1866. *Claimant to the Passage of Waters—His Obligations.* Art. 1082. In the case to which the prescription of article 1076 refers, he who claims the passage of the waters must pay in proportion to the quantity of the same, the value of the land occupied by the canal in which the waters are introduced, and the necessary expenses for their preservation, without prejudice to the indemnification due for the land which may be necessary to occupy anew, and for the other expenses which the passage that is conceded to him occasions.

§ 1867. *Limitation on Quantity of Water.*—Art. 1083. The quantity of water which can be made to pass through an aqueduct established on the estate of another will have no other limitation than that which results from the capacity which by the dimensions agreed upon have been fixed by said aqueduct.

§ 1868. *Aqueducts.*—Art. 1084. If he who uses the aqueduct should need to enlarge it, he must pay the expenses of the necessary works, and pay for the land which he newly occupies, and the damages which he causes, in conformity with the provisions in Nos. 3 and 4 of article 1081.

§ 1869. *Right of Transit.*—Art. 1085. The legal service established by article 1073 carries with it the right of transit for the persons and animals, and that of the transportation of the necessary materials for the use and repair of the aqueduct, as well as for the care of the water which is conducted through it; observing in respect to it the provisions in articles 1093 to 1098.

§ 1870. *Swamp Lands.*—Art. 1086. The provisions concerning the passage of waters are applicable to the case in which the possessor of swamp land wishes to drain it, or give an outlet by the means of drains to the waters obstructed.

§ 1871. *Previous Rights.*—Art. 1087. The concessions of waters which shall be made by competent authority are presumed to be made without prejudice to other rights previously acquired.

§ 1872. *Protection to Third Parties.*—Art. 1088. Every one who uses an aqueduct, whether it passes through his own field or that of another, must construct and preserve the bridges, canals, aqueducts, subterraneous structures, and the other necessary works, in order that the rights of others may not be injured.

§ 1873. *Joint Users.*—Art. 1089. If those who should use them should be various, the obligation would fall upon all in proportion to their use, if there is no prescription or agreement to the contrary.

§ 1874. *Duties of Users.*—Art. 1090. The provisions in the two preceding articles comprehend the cleaning, construction, and repairs in order that the course of water may not be interrupted.

## Of the Legal Service of Passage.

§ 1875. *Outlet and Passage-way.*—Art. 1091. The proprietor of an estate or land inclosed between other lands of other persons, without an outlet to the public way, has a right to require a passage for the use of said way through the neighboring lands without the respective owners claiming anything more than an indemnification equivalent to the injury this burden may occasion them.

§ 1876. *Prescription.*—Art. 1092. The action to reclaim this indemnification is prescriptible; but although one pleads prescription, the passage obtained does not cease for this reason.

§ 1877. *Serving Estate.*—Art. 1093. The owner of the serving estate has a right to designate the place where the service of passage must be constituted.

§ 1878. *Passage-way being Impracticable, how Changed.*—Art. 1094. If the judge qualifies the place designated as impracticable or very grievous to the dominant estate, the owner of the serving estate must designate another.

§ 1879. *Conciliation of Two Estates.*—Art. 1095. If this place is qualified in the same manner as the first, the judge will designate that which he believes the most convenient, and try to conciliate the interest of the two estates.

§ 1880. *Shortest Distance.*—Art. 1096. If there should be various lands through which passage can be given to the public way, the one obligated to the service shall be that where the distance would be the shortest. If the distance should be equal through two estates, the judge shall designate which of them shall give the passage.

§ 1881. *Width of Passage.*—Art. 1097. In the service of passage the width of it shall be that which is sufficient for the necessities of the dominant estate in the judgment of the judge; but it shall not exceed five meters nor be less than two, unless by agreement of the interested parties.

§ 1882. *Prior Passage-way.*—Art. 1098. If there should have been a communication before between the estate of land and public way, the passage can only be required from the land or estate where it had lately been.

§ 1883. *Survey.*—Art. 1099. Every proprietor has a right to ask of him who is proprietor of the contiguous lands for the survey, marking, or the fixing of monuments of those lands which respectively belong to him, if the marking has not been done before, or if the boundary by time has been obliterated.

§ 1884. *Expenses.*—Art. 1100. The expenses of the survey shall be paid *pro rata* by him who asks for it and the adjoining proprietors; but the judge can in his discretion exempt from the obligation of contributing to the expenses the adjoining proprietors who are notoriously poor.[1]

Of the Legal Service of Partition Walls (Medianeria).

§ 1885. *Partition Wall, Whose.*—Art. 1101. When there is proof which shows who made the wall which divides estates, he who paid for it is the exclusive owner thereof; if it appears that it was made by the contiguous owners, or it does not appear who made it, it is joint property (medianeria).

§ 1886. *Joint Ownership.*—Art. 1102. The jointure is presumed while there are no exterior signs which show the contrary: 1. In the dividing walls of contiguous edifices to the common point of elevation; 2. In the dividing walls of gardens or yards (corrales) situated in a town or in the country; 3. In the inclosures, fences, and hedges which divide rustic estates.

[1] This article 1100 is suppressed in the code of 1884.

If the constructions do not have the same height, there is only a presumption of jointure up to the height of the least elevated construction.

§ 1887. *When Joint Ownership is not Presumed.*—Art. 1103. There is a contrary sign to jointure: 1. When there are windows or open spaces in the dividing walls of the edifices; 2. When evidently all the wall, fence, inclosure, or hedge are constructed on the land of one of the estates, and not half on one and half on the other of two contiguous estates; 3. When the wall supports the weight of the girders, passage, and frames of one of the possessions and not of the contiguous one; 4. When the dividing wall between courts, gardens, and other lands is constructed so that the coping of the wall (albardilla) falls towards only one of the properties; 5. When the dividing wall, constructed of stone and mortar (anamposteria), presents stones called stepping-stones (pasaderas), which at certain distances project out of only one side thereof, and not the other; 6. When the dividing wall is between an edifice of which it forms a part and a garden, field, corral, or a place without an edifice; 7. When a ground is found inclosed or defended by pickets, fences, or hedges, and the contiguous grounds are not; 8. When the fence which completely incloses a ground is of a distinct kind from that which the neighboring estate has on the sides contiguous thereto.

§ 1888. *Presumption.*—Art. 1104. In general, it is presumed in the cases designated in the preceding article the property in the walls, fences, pickets, or hedges belongs exclusively to the owner of the estate or ground who has in his favor these exterior signs.

§ 1889. *Ditches.*—Art. 1105. The open trenches or ditches between grounds are also presumed to be held in joint ownership, if there is no title or sign which shows to the contrary.

§ 1890. *Signs of a Single Owner.*—Art. 1106. There is a contrary sign to joint ownership when the earth or rubbish taken from the trench or ditch to open or clean it is found only on one side; in this case it is presumed that the property in the trench or ditch is exclusively of the owner of the ground which has in its favor this exterior sign.

§ 1891. *Cessation of Presumption.*—Art. 1107. The presumption which the preceding article establishes ceases when the inclination of the land obliges the earth to be thrown on one side.

§ 1892. *Care of Joint Property.*—Art. 1108. The owners of

estates are obliged to take care that the wall, ditch, or hedge held in joint ownership are not deteriorated; and if by the act of any of their dependents or animals they are deteriorated, they must replace them, paying the damages and losses which shall have been caused.[1]

§ 1893. *Expenses, Joint.*—Art. 1109. The repair and construction of the walls held in joint ownership, and the maintenance of the picket fences, living hedges, trenches, or ditches also held in joint ownership, shall be paid proportionally by all of the owners who have in their favor this joint ownership.

§ 1894. *Renouncement.* — Art. 1110. The proprietor who wishes to free himself from the obligations which the preceding article imposes can do so by renouncing the joint ownership; save the case in which the dividing wall sustains his edifice.

§ 1895. *Owners of Dividing Walls.*—Art. 1111. The proprietor of an edifice which is supported on a dividing wall can, on its being torn down, renounce or not the joint ownership. In the first case the necessary expenses to avoid or to repair the damages which the demolition causes will be on account of all. In the second, besides this obligation, he is subject to those which articles 1108 and 1109 impose on him.

§ 1896. *Proprietors of Contiguous Estates.*—Art. 1112. The proprietor of an estate contiguous to a dividing wall, not held in joint ownership, can only give it this character in whole or in part by a contract with the owner of it.

§ 1897. *Dividing Wall.*—Art. 1113. Every proprietor can raise the wall held in joint ownership, doing it at his own expense, and indemnifying for the injuries which are occasioned by the work, although it be temporarily.

§ 1898. *Preservation of the Wall.*—Art. 1114. All the works for the preservation of the wall on the part which he has increased in height or thickness shall equally be on his account, and the works on the part held in joint ownership which may be necessary, provided the deterioration thereof arises from the greater extension which he has given to the height or thickness of the wall.

§ 1899. *Reconstruction of Wall.*—Art. 1115. If the wall held in joint ownership can not resist the greater elevation, the pro-

[1] Article 1108 is amended by the code of 1884, and reads as follows: "Art. 1003. The owners of estates are obliged to take care that the wall, ditch, or hedge held in joint ownership be not deteriorated; and if by the act of any of their dependents or animals, or by any other cause which depends on them, they are deteriorated, they must replace them, paying the damages and losses which shall have been caused."

prietor who wishes to raise will be under obligation to reconstruct it at his cost; and if it were necessary to give it greater thickness, it must be given from the ground.

§ 1900. *Ownership of Walls.*—Art. 1116. In the cases designated by articles 1113 and 1115 the wall continues to be held in joint ownership up to the height where it formerly was, even when it has been built anew at the expense of one alone; and from the point where the greater height commenced, it is exclusively the property of him who built it.

§ 1901. *Extended Walls.*—Art. 1117. The other proprietors, who have not contributed to give greater elevation or thickness to the wall, can notwithstanding acquire in the part newly elevated the rights of joint ownership by paying proportionally the value of the work and the half of the value of the ground upon which rests the greater thickness given.

§ 1902. *Use of Wall.*—Art. 1118. Each proprietor of a wall held in joint ownership can use it in proportion to the right he has in the community property; he can therefore build, supporting his work on the wall held in joint ownership, or by introducing beams to the middle of its thickness, but without impeding the common and respective use of the other joint owners.

§ 1903. *Disagreements.*—Art. 1119. In case of resistance on the part of the proprietors, they shall regulate by the means of experts the necessary conditions in order that the new work shall not prejudice the rights of the former.

§ 1904. *Separate Owners of Separate Parts of a Houses—Rule of Contribution.*—Art. 1120. When the different stories of a house shall belong to distinct proprietors, if the titles to the property do not regulate the terms in which they must contribute to the necessary works, the following rules shall be observed: 1. The main walls, the roof or top of the house, and the other thing in common use shall be at the charge of all the proprietors in proportion to the value of their story; 2. Each proprietor shall pay the cost of the floor of his story; 3. The pavement of the porch (portal), entrance door, common court, and works of police common to all shall be paid for pro rata by all the proprietors; 4. The stairs which lead to the first story shall be paid pro rata by all except the owner of the lower story, that which leads from the first story to the second shall be paid by all except by the owners of the first and lower story, and so successively.

### Of the Distances Which in Conformity with the Law is Required for Certain Constructions and Plantings.

§ 1905. *Distances between Certain Properties.*—Art. 1121. Nobody can build or plant near the squares (plazas), forts, fortresses, and public buildings, without subjecting himself to the conditions required by the special regulations of the matter.

§ 1906. *Public Ways and Rivers.*—Art. 1122. The services established for public or common utility, in order to maintain the navigation of rivers in proper condition (expedida), and the construction or repair of the public ways, and for the other common works of this class, are regulated and determined by special laws and regulations, and for want of these, by the rules established in this code.

§ 1907. *Constructions must not Injure Others.*—Art. 1123. Nobody can construct near the wall of another, or wall held in joint ownership, wells, drains, aqueducts, ovens, forges, chimneys, stables, deposits of corrosive materials, steam-engines, or other works destined to uses which may be dangerous or hurtful, without keeping the distance prescribed by the regulations, or without constructing the works with the necessary safety, and with subjection in the manner as to the conditions provided in the said regulations, or which in default thereof shall be determined by skillful judgment.

§ 1908. *Planting Trees.*—Art. 1124. Nobody can plant trees near the ground of another, except at the distance of two meters from the dividing line, if the planting is made with large trees, and one meter if the planting is of bushes or small trees.

§ 1909. *Trees to be Taken up.*—Art. 1125. Every proprietor can ask that the trees planted at a less distance than that designated in the preceding article be torn up, and even when the distance is greater, if the damage which they cause him is evident.

§ 1910. *Extending Branches.*—Art. 1126. If the branches of any trees extend over the land of another, or a neighboring garden or court, the owner of the trees shall have a right to claim that they be cut so far as they extend over his property; and if the roots of the neighboring trees should extend into the ground of another, he in whose ground they are introduced can cause them to be cut by himself within his ground, but with a previous notice to the neighbor.

§ 1911. *Partition Trees.*—Art. 1127. The trees existing in a partition fence are also joint property, as well as the fence, and any of the owners have a right to ask for their demolition; but if the tree is a landmark of boundary, it can not be cut nor substituted for another, except by consent of both parties.[1]

### Of the Lights and Views Which in Conformity with the Law can be Had in the Property of a Neighbor.

§ 1912. *Consent.*—Art. 1128. No owner in a dividing wall can without the consent of the other open a window nor any space in said wall.

§ 1913. *Openings for Light.*—Art. 1129. The owner of a wall not held in joint ownership, continguous to the estate of another, can open in it windows or spaces to receive light, at such a height that the lower part of the window shall be distant from the floor of the apartment to which it gives light three meters at least, and in every case with bars of iron placed in the wall, and with a wire net, with spaces between the threads thereof, at the most three centimeters.

§ 1914. *Owner of Contiguous Estate.*—Art. 1130. Notwithstanding the provisions in the preceding article, the owner of the estate or property contiguous to the wall in which there may be open windows or spaces can construct a wall contiguous to it, or if he acquires the dividing wall, rest the wall on the said dividing wall, although in either way he covers the spaces or windows.

§ 1915. *Projections.*—Art. 1131. Windows can not be had to appear in, nor balconies or other similar thing projecting over, the property of a neighbor, prolonging them beyond the limits which separate the grounds. Neither can there be side or oblique views over the said property if there is not a distance of six decimeters.

§ 1916. *Measure of Distance.*—Art. 1132. The distance of which the foregoing article speaks is measured from the line of separation of the two properties.

### Of the Legal Service of Drainage.

§ 1917. *Manner of Constructions.*—Aft. 1133. The proprietor of an edifice is obliged to construct his roofs or house-tops in

[1] Article 1127 is amended by the code of 1884 to read: "Art. 1021. The trees existing in a partition fence, or which designate the line, are also partition trees, and can not be cut nor substituted for others without the consent of both proprietors, or by a judicial decision pronounced on a trial issue, in case of disagreement of the proprietors."

such a manner that the rain-water will not fall on the ground of his neighbor.[1]

§ 1918. *Passage through Exterior Property.* — Art. 1134. When a rural or urban estate is found inclosed between others, in such a manner that it has no direct communication with any road, canal, or public streets, the owners of the surrounding estates shall be obliged to permit to run through these the drainage of the central one. The dimensions and direction of the conduit of the drain shall be fixed by the judge, with a previous report of experts and an audience of the interested parties, and as far as possible shall be observed the rules given for the service of passage.

### Of Voluntary Services in General.

§ 1919. *Services, What may be.*—Art. 1135. Every proprietor of an estate or ground can establish on it as many services as he think proper, and in the manner and form which appears to him best, provided they be not contrary to public order.

§ 1920. *Service, What is its Nature.*—Art. 1136. The constitution of a service is reputed as an alienation in part of the property in the serving estate; therefore those who can not alienate their things, except with certain solemnities or conditions, can not without them impose services on the same.

§ 1921. *Joint Ownership.*—Art. 1137. If the proprietors of an estate are various, a service can not be imposed upon it without the consent of all.

§ 1922. *Joint Services Acquired by One.*—Art. 1138. If being various the proprietors, one of them alone acquires a service on another estate, in favor of the common estate, all the proprietors can avail themselves thereof; but by obligating themselves for the natural burden it brings with it, and for the agreements with which it may have been acquired.

### How Voluntary Services are Acquired.

§ 1923. *How Acquired.*—Art. 1139. Continuous and apparent services are acquired by any legal title, including that of prescription.

§ 1924. *Prescription, when not Available.*—Art. 1140. Continuous services not apparent, and discontinuous ones, whether apparent or not, can not be acquired by prescription, except by other legal title.

[1] The words "or edifice" are added after the word "ground" in the code of 1884.

§ 1925. *Proof of Service.*—Art. 1141. To him who claims to have a right to a service, it belongs to prove, although he be in possession thereof, the title by virtue of which he enjoys it.

§ 1926. *The Want of a Title.*—Art. 1142. The want of a title constitutive of services, which can not be acquired by precription, can only be supplied by judicial confession or recognition made in a public writing (escritura publica) by the owner of the serving estate, or by a final judgment which declare the service to exist.

§ 1927. *Signs of a Service.*—Art. 1143. The existence of an apparent sign of service between two estates, established or preserved by the proprietor of both, is considered as a title for which the service continues actively and passively, when the estates pass to the property of different owners, unless at the time of the division of the property the contrary is expressed in the title of alienation of any of them.

§ 1928. *Accessory Rights.*—Art. 1144. On constituting a service, all the necessary means are understood, and that being extinguished, these accessory rights also cease.

§ 1929. *Independent Means.*—Art. 1145. The provision in the final part of the foregoing article does not comprehend those means which have been obtained by a title independent of the service.

Rights and Obligations of the Proprietors of the Estates between Which is Constituted Some Voluntary Service.

§ 1930. *Regulations of Uses.*—Art. 1146. The use and the extension of the services established by the will of the proprietor shall be regulated by the terms of the title in which they have their origin, or in default thereof by the following provisions:

§ 1931. *Necessary Works.*—Art. 1147. The owner of the dominant estate can make at his cost all the necessary works for the use and preservation of the service.

§ 1932. *Obligatory Works.*—Art. 1148. He is obliged also to make at his cost the works which should be necessary in order that to the owner of the serving estate shall not be caused by the service more burden than that consequent to it; and if by his neglect or omission other damage should be caused, he will be obliged to make indemnification therefor.

§ 1933. *How Freed from Obligation.*—Art. 1149. If the owner of the serving estate should be obligated in the title constitutive of the service to do anything or to pay the expenses of any work, he will be free from this obligation by abandoning his estate to the owner of the dominant one.

§ 1934. *Deterioration.*—Art. 1150. The owner of the serving estate can not deteriorate in any manner the service constituted on this estate.

§ 1935. *Inconveniences.*—Art. 1151. The owner of the serving estate, if the place originally designated for the use of the service should present grave inconveniences, can offer another which may be convenient to the owner of the dominant estate, who can not refuse it, if it does not prejudice him.

§ 1936. *Owner of Serving Estate.*—Art. 1152. The owner of the serving estate can execute the works which will make the service less onerous, if from it no prejudice results to the dominant estate.

§ 1937. *Prejudice to Dominant Estate.*—Art. 1153. If from the preservation of said works shall follow any prejudice to the dominant estate, the owner of the serving estate shall be obliged to re-establish the things in the former state and to indemnify for the damages and losses.

§ 1938. *Judge's Decision.*—Art. 1154. If the owner of the dominant estate opposes the works of which article 1152 treats, the judge shall decide, prior reports by experts being made.

§ 1939. *Doubts.*—Art. 1155. Any doubt upon the use and extension of the service shall be decided in the sense least onerous for the serving estate, without making impossible or very difficult the use of the service.

§ 1940. *Joint Owners.*—Art. 1156. If the dominant estate should be divided between divers proprietors, the service shall remain in favor of all and each one, without altering the form of it in prejudice to the serving estate. But if the service was established in favor of only one of the parties of the dominant estate, only the owner of this part can continue to enjoy it.

### Of the Extinction of Voluntary and Legal Services.

§ 1941. *Extinguishment.*—Art. 1157. Voluntary services are extinguished: 1. By uniting in the same person the property of both the dominant and serving estates, and not reviving them by a new separation, save the provision in article 1143; but if the act of reunion was resolvable by its nature, and the case of a resolution arrives, all the services are renewed as they were before the reunion. 2. By non-use: when the service should be continuous and apparent by non-use for ten years if there should be good faith, and fifteen if there should not be good faith, counting from the day on which the apparent sign of the service failed to exist.[1] When it should be a discontinuous or not apparent service, by the non-use for twenty years if there should be good faith, and thirty if there should not be good faith, counting from the day on which it failed to be used on account of the owner of the serving ground having executed an act contrary to the service, or through having prohibited it to be used. If there was no contrary act or prohibition, although the service may not have been used, or if there were such acts, but the use continues, the time of prescription does not run. 3. When the estates reach, without the fault of the owner of the serving one, such a condition that the service can not be used. If in the future the estates are re-established in such a manner that the service may be used, it will revive, unless that from the day on which it might have been used again sufficient time for prescription shall have run. 4. By the gratuitous or onerous remission made by the owner of the dominant estate. 5. When constituted in virtue of a revocable right the term is completed, the condition is fulfilled, or the circumstances arise which ought to put an end to that.

§ 1942. *Use of Service.*—Art. 1158. The mode of using the service may be prescribed in the time and manner as the service itself.

§ 1943. *Prescription.*—Art. 1159. If the dominant estate belongs to various owners undivided, the use by one of them avails the others to prevent prescription.

§ 1944. *Prescription not Available, when.* — Art. 1160. If between the proprietors there should be any against whom by special laws prescription can not run, it can not run against the others.

§ 1945. *Non-user.*—Art. 1161. Legal services established for public or common utility shall be lost by the non-use of twenty years, if it is proved that during this time another service has been acquired of the same nature for a distinct place, by him who enjoyed them.[2]

§ 1946. *Failure of Service.*—Art. 1162. If the estates between which is constituted a legal service pass into the possession of the same owner, the service fails to exist; but the

[1] Art. 1157 is amended by the code of 1844, by inserting "five years" in the place of "ten years," and "ten years" in the place of "fifteen years."

[2] Article 1161 is amended by the code of 1884, by inserting "ten" in the place of "twenty."

properties being again separated, the service revives, even when no apparent sign has been preserved.

§ 1947. *Services, how Lost.*—Art. 1163. The legal service of lights and views may be lost by non-use in the terms which fraction 2 of article 1157 establishes, with the following distinctions: 1. If the owner of the dominant estate voluntarily closes the space or window, the provision in the fraction cited shall be observed, and he shall lose the right of opening it again; 2. If the window or space has been covered by the owner of the serving estate, in virtue of the right which article 1130 concedes to him, the owner of the dominant estate can open the window through another place which may be free; and if the work is destroyed which obstructs the first window, he shall immediately recover the use of it.

§ 1948. *Release from Service.*—Art. 1164. The owner of an estate subject to a legal servitude may through the means of an agreement free himself from it, with the following restrictions: 1. If the service is constituted in favor of the whole of a municipality or town, the agreement will have no effect in respect to the whole town, unless it has been made by the intervention of the sindic of the town council (ayuntamiento); but it will produce an action against each one of the private individuals who have renounced said service; 2. If the service is of public use, as that constituted on the margin of riparian estates, the agreement is null in every case; 3. If the service is of lights or views, the agreement in virtue of which it is renounced shall be reputed as a new service not to act on the part of him who before enjoyed the lights and views; and the estate shall be considered as dominant which before was a serving one, and *vice versa;* 4. If the service is of passage or drainage, the agreement shall be considered as made with the condition that the owners of the surrounding estates shall approve it, or at least he of the estate where the service is newly constituted; 5. The renunciation of a legal service of drainage will only be valid when it is not opposed to the regulations of police.

# CHAPTER VII.

## PRESCRIPTION.

§ 1949. Prescription, What is.
§ 1950. Positive Prescription.
§ 1951. Things Prescriptible.
§ 1952. Who can Acquire.
§ 1953. Negative Prescription.
§ 1954. Can not be Renounced, What.
§ 1955. Renounced, What may be.
§ 1956. Time Commenced.
§ 1957. Express or Tacit.
§ 1958. Who can not Renounce.
§ 1959. Creditors.
§ 1960. Possession in Name of Another.
§ 1961. Change of Possession.
§ 1962. Joint Possessors.
§ 1963. Exceptions.
§ 1964. Creditors and Debtors.
§ 1965. Sureties.
§ 1966. Effect of Prescription.
§ 1967. Prescription to be Pleaded.
§ 1968. What Persons may Plead Prescription.
§ 1969. Time.
§ 1970. Provisions of This Title.
§ 1971. Rules for Positive Prescription.
§ 1972. Just Title, What is.
§ 1973. Proof of Title.
§ 1974. Good Faith.
§ 1975. Pacific Possession.
§ 1976. Continuous Possession.
§ 1977. Public Possession.
§ 1978. Twenty and Thirty Years.
§ 1979. Real Rights and Actions.
§ 1980. Restitutions.
§ 1981. Minors.
§ 1982. Twenty Years against Minors.
§ 1983. Minors at the Beginning of the Time.
§ 1984. Age of Eighteen.
§ 1985. Restitution.
§ 1986. From What Time.
§ 1987. Time to the Age of Eighteen.
§ 1988. Incapacitated Persons.
§ 1989. End of Impediment.
§ 1990. Prodigals.
§ 1991. Among Whom Prescription can not Run.

§ 1949. *Prescription, What It is.*—Art. 1165. Prescription is a means of acquiring the dominion of a thing, or of freeing one's self from a charge or obligation, by virtue of the course of certain time, and under the conditions established by law.

§ 1950. *Positive Prescription.*—Art. 1166. The acquisition of things or rights in virtue of possession is called positive prescription; the exoneration of obligations by not requiring their fulfillment is called a negative prescription.

§ 1951. *Things Prescriptible.*—Art. 1167. The things, rights, and obligations which are in commerce can only be prescribed, save the exceptions established by law.

§ 1952. *Who can Acquire.*—Art. 1168. All those who are capable of acquiring by any other title can acquire by positive prescription; minors and others incapacitated can do so by means of their legitimate representatives.

§ 1953. *Negative Prescription.*—Art. 1169. Negative prescription avails all, even those who by themselves can not be obligated.

§ 1954. *Can not be Renounced, What.*—Art. 1170. The right of acquiring by positive prescription can not be renounced beforehand.

§ 1955. *Renounced, What may be.*—Art. 1171. The right of freeing one's self from an obligation by negative prescription may be renounced, but the renunciation will only produce the effect of duplicating the terms, provided that, being duplicated, they shall not exceed in any case thirty years. The terms shall be counted from the day on which the renunciation has been made.[1]

§ 1956. *Time Commenced.*—Art. 1172. The prescription which has commenced to run, and that already consummated,

[1] The word "twenty" is inserted in the place of "thirty" in the code of 1884.

may be renounced; but in these cases the renunciation must be considered as a true donation of the rights which in each one of them may have been acquired, and will be subject to the rules established for that contract.

§ 1957. *Express or Tacit.*—Art. 1173. The renunciation of prescription is express or tacit, this latter being that which results from an act which imports the abandonment of the right acquired.

§ 1958. *Who can not Renounce.*—Art. 1174. He who can not alienate can not renounce a prescription pending nor that which is consummated.

§ 1959. *Creditors.*—Art. 1175. The creditors, and all those who may have a legitimate interest in what the prescription subsists, can make it available, although the debtor or the proprietor may have renounced the rights acquired in its virtue.

§ 1960. *Possession in Name of Another.*—Art. 1176. He who possesses in the name of another can not acquire by prescription the thing possessed, unless the cause of the possession has been legally changed.

§ 1961. *Change of Possession.*—Art. 1177. The cause is said to be legally changed when he who possesses in the name of another commences to possess in good faith and with a just title in his own name; but in this case the prescription does not run, only from the day on which the cause has been changed.

§ 1962. *Joint Possessors.*—Art. 1178. If various persons possess in common anything, neither of them can prescribe against his co-proprietor or co-possessor; but he may prescribe against a stranger; and in this case the prescription avails all the participants.

§ 1963. *Exceptions.*—Art. 1179. The exception which by prescription a co-debtor *in solidum* acquires does not avail the others, only when the time required by law has duly run in the same manner for all of them.

§ 1964. *Creditor and Debtor.*—Art. 1180. In the case provided by the preceding article the creditor can only require of the debtors who do not prescribe the value of the obligation, deducting the part which corresponds to the debtor who prescribed.

§ 1965. *Sureties.*—Art. 1181. The prescription acquired by the principal debtor always avails his sureties.

§ 1966. *Effect of Prescription.*—Art. 1182. The prescription once perfected can be deduced as an action and be opposed as an exception.

§ 1967. *Prescription to be Pleaded.*—Art. 1183. The judges can not officially consider prescription.[1]

§ 1968. *What Persons may Plead Prescription.*—Art. 1184. The Union, the District, and California, in their cases, as well as the ayuntamientos, and all public establishments, and moral persons (companies or corporations), shall be considered as private individuals for the prescription of their properties, rights, and actions, which may be susceptible of being private property.

§ 1969. *Time.*—Art. 1185. He who prescribes may complete the necessary term for his prescription, by uniting with the time which he may have possessed that which the person who transmitted the thing to him possessed, provided that both possessions have the legal requisites.

§ 1970. *Provisions of This Title.*—Art. 1186. The possessions of this title, relative to the time and other necessary requisites for prescription, shall only fail to be observed in the cases in which the law expressly provides otherwise.

§ 1971. *Rules for Positive Prescription.*—Art. 1187. The necessary possession in order to prescribe must be: 1. Founded on a just title; 2. Of good faith; 3. Pacific; 4. Continuous; 5. Public.

§ 1972. *Just Title, What is.*—Art. 1188. That which is sufficient to transfer the dominion is called a just title.[2]

§ 1973. *Proof of Title.*—Art. 1189. He who alleges prescription must prove the existence of the title on which his right is founded.

§ 1974. *Good Faith.*—Art. 1190. Good faith is only necessary at the moment of acquisition.

§ 1975. *Pacific Possession.*—Art. 1191. Pacific possession is that which is acquired without violence; useful possession commences only after it has been juridically declared that violence has ceased.

§ 1976. *Continuous Possession.*—Art. 1192. Continuous possession is that which has not been interrupted in any of the modes enumerated in chapter 7 of this title.

§ 1977. *Public Possession.*—Art. 1193. Public possession is that which is enjoyed in a manner which may be known by those who have interests in interrupting it.

---

[1] Articles 1182 and 1183 are suppressed in the code of 1884.

[2] Article 1188 is amended by the code of 1884 so as to read: "Art. 1080. That which is, or is fundamentally believed, sufficient to transfer the dominion is called a just title."

### OF THE PRESCRIPTION OF IMMOVABLE THINGS.

§ 1978. *Twenty and Thirty Years.*—Art. 1194. All immovable properties are prescribed with good faith in twenty years, and with bad faith in thirty; save what is provided in article 1176.[1]

§ 1979. *Real Rights and Actions.*—Art. 1195. In the same terms, and with the same conditions which the preceding article establishes, real rights and actions are acquired by prescription, including those of voluntary servitudes.

### OF THE SUSPENSION OF PRESCRIPTION.

§ 1980. *Restrictions.*—Art. 1219. Prescription may commence and run against any person, save the following restrictions:

§ 1981. *Minors.*—Art. 1220. Prescription can not commence nor run against minors, and those incapacitated for want of intelligence, only when their guardianship has been appointed in conformity with the laws.

§ 1982. *Twenty Years against Minors.*—Art. 1221. The prescription of twenty years only runs against a minor, if they have commenced to run against the person from whom the minor inherits, or from whom he has had the thing by another legal title.[2]

§ 1983. *Minors at the Beginning of Time.*—Art. 1222. Said prescriptions do not run against a minor if they have commenced to run directly against him during his minor age.

§ 1984. *Age of Eighteen.*—Art. 1223. The prescriptions of more than twenty years run against one of eighteen years of age.[3]

§ 1985. *Restitution.*—Art. 1224. In the case of the article 1221, the minor may, within the legal term of four years, ask restitution from the time which has run against him, but not from that which has run against the person from whom he received the property (causante).

§ 1986. *From What Time.*—Art. 1225. In the case of the article 1222, the minor can ask restitution from the time which has run during his minor age.

§ 1987. *Time to the Age of Eighteen.*—Art. 1226. In the case of the article 1223, the minor can only ask restitution from the

---

[1] Article 1194 is amended by the code of 1884, by inserting "ten" in place of "twenty," and "twenty" in place of "thirty."

[2] Article 1221 is amended by inserting "ten" in the place of "twenty" in the code of 1884.

[3] Article 1223 is amended by the code of 1884, by inserting "ten" in place of "twenty."

time which has run up to the completion of the age of eighteen years.

§ 1988. *Incapacitated Persons.*—Art. 1227. Prescription does not run against those who are incapacitated for want of intelligence, unless it has commenced to run against their persons from whom they received the property (causantes), or against themselves before their impediment.

§ 1989. *End of Impediment.*—Art. 1228. The person incapacitated can only ask restitution from the time the impediment ended.

§ 1990. *Prodigals.*—Art. 1229. Any prescription runs against the prodigal, but his rights shall remain safe against his tutor.[1]

§ 1991. *Among Whom Prescription can not Run.*—Art. 1230. Prescription can not commence nor run: 1. Between ascendants and descendants during the parental power (patria potestad), in respect to the properties to which the latter may have a right in conformity with the law; 2. Between consorts; 3. Between minors and persons incapacitated, including prodigals, and their tutors and curators, while the tutelage lasts; 4. Against those absent from the district and from California, in the public service; 5. Against military persons in active service in time of war, as well out of the district and California as in them.[2]

§ 1992. *Married Women and Third Parties.*—Art. 1231. Neither can prescription commence nor run between a third party and a married woman: 1. In respect to dotal properties, unless it has commenced before the marriage; 2. In respect to immovable properties of the matrimonial estate, alienated by the husband without the consent of the wife, but only the part of the properties which belongs to the wife; 3. In the cases in which the action of the wife against a third person may have a reversion against the husband.

## Of the Interruption of Prescription.

§ 1993. *Interruption.*—Art. 1232. Prescription is interrupted: 1. If the possessor is deprived of the possession of the thing, or of the enjoyment of the right during a year; 2. By a judicial demand, the possessor being notified, or the debtor in his case, or by attachment, save if the creditor desist from the action instituted or the defendant should be absolved from the demand, or the judicial act should be null for want of formality (solemnidad); 3.

---

[1] Articles 1224, 1225, 1226, 1228, and 1229 are suppressed in the code of 1884.

[2] Art. 1830 is amended by the code of 1884, by suppressing the words "including prodigals," in fraction 3.

By citation for a conciliatory act, judicial protest, or the securing of properties made in virtue of a precautionary decree, from the day on which these acts occur, if within one month the plaintiff institutes his action of a contentious suit;[1] 4. If the person in whose favor the prescription runs expressly recognizes, by word or writing, or tacitly by indubitable acts, the right of the person against whom he prescribes.

§ 1994. *Debtors in Solidum*—Art. 1233. The causes which interrupt the prescription in respect to one of the debtors *in solidum* interrupts it in respect to the others.

§ 1995. *Division of Debt.*—Art. 1234. If the creditor who consents to the division of the debt in respect to one of the debtors *in solidum* shall only require of him the part which corresponds to him, the prescription in respect to the others shall not be held as interrupted.

§ 1996. *Heirs.*—Art. 1235. The provisions in the two preceding articles are applicable to the heirs of the debtor whether or not he be debtor *in solidum.*

§ 1997. *Interruption—Sureties.*—Art. 1236. The interruption of prescription against the principal debtor produces the same effects against his surety.

§ 1998. *Joint Debtors not in Solidum.*—Art. 1237. In order that the prescription of an obligation shall be interrupted in respect to all the debtors not *in solidum,* the recognition or citation of all shall be required.

§ 1999. *Creditors in Solidum.*—Art. 1238. The interruption of the prescription in favor of any of the creditors *in solidum* avails all.

Art. 1239. The effect of the interruption is to render useless for prescription all time which has run before it.

### Of the Manner of Counting the Time for Prescription.

§ 2000. *Time.*—Art. 1240. The time for prescription is counted by years, and not from moment to moment, except in the case in which the law expressly determines it to be so.

[1] Article 1232 becomes article 1117 in the code of 1884, and fraction 3 thereof is amended to read as follows: "3. By citation for a prejudical act, or the security of property in virtue of a precautionary decree from the day on which these acts shall occur, if the plaintiff institutes his action in a contentious suit within the term fixed for each case in the code of civil procedure, or in default thereof within a month. For the effects of this fraction and the preceding one, neither the notification nor citation, nor the sequestration of property, is necessary to be practiced within the term for prescription, and their effects will take place even when they are practiced out of it, if the motion shall have been made in time, and there should be no fault nor omission of the plaintiff."

§ 2001. *Months.*—Art. 1241. The months shall be regulated by the number of days which correspond to them.

§ 2002. *Days.*—Art. 1242. When the prescription is counted by days, there shall be understood as twenty-four natural hours, counted from twelve to twelve of the night.

§ 2003. *Day of Beginning and End.*—Art. 1243. The day on which the prescription commences is counted entire, whether it be so or not; but that on which the prescription terminates must be complete.

§ 2004. *Holidays.*—Art. 1244. When the last day is a holiday, the prescription shall not be held as complete, but the next day, shall make it complete if it should be a working day.

# CHAPTER VIII.

## PARTIES TO SALES, LEASES, ETC.

§ 2005. Age of Majority.
§ 2006. Rights of Men and Women over Age.
§ 2007. Property of Minors—Tutors—Sales.
§ 2008. Tutors, their Relatives.
§ 2009. Nine Years' Lease.
§ 2010. Payment in Advance Limited.
§ 2011. Compromises.
§ 2012. Restitution.
§ 2013. Marriage—Death.
§ 2014. Emancipation after the Age of Eighteen.
§ 2015. Public Writing.
§ 2016. Effect of Emancipation.
§ 2017. Marriage Settlement.
§ 2018. Husband is Administrator.
§ 2019. Settlement, when to be Made.
§ 2020. Revocation.
§ 2021. Public Writing.
§ 2022. Alteration.
§ 2023. Common Property.
§ 2024. Alienation.
§ 2025. Consent of Judge.
§ 2026. Husband, his Will.
§ 2027. Sales by Husband.
§ 2028. Conjugal Parties' Rights.
§ 2029. Wife can not Alienate.
§ 2030. Void Agreements.
§ 2031. Wife can not Burden.
§ 2032. Dotal Property.
§ 2033. Power of Attorney.
§ 2034. Private Instrument.
§ 2035. Powers.
§ 2036. General Power.
§ 2037. Absent Parties.
§ 2038. Power of Public Writing.
§ 2039. Private Writing.
§ 2040. Married Women and Minors.
§ 2041. Change of Attorney.
§ 2042. Death of Principal.
§ 2043. Heirs.
§ 2044. Death of Attorney.
§ 2045. Renouncement by Attorney.
§ 2046. Obligations.
§ 2047. Firm Name.

PARTIES TO SALES, LEASES, ETC.

§ 2005. *Age of Majority.*—The age of majority commences after twenty-one years complete, with both male and female: Art. 694.

§ 2006. *Rights of Men and Women over Age.*—A party of age may dispose of his person and property freely. But women over twenty-one years and under thirty years can not leave the paternal house without the license of the father or mother, except to be married, or when either of the former shall have contracted a new marriage: Art. 695.

MINORS.

§ 2007. *Property of Minors—Tutors—Sales.*—The immovable property of a minor, the rights annexed thereto, and precious movables can not be burdened nor hypothecated by the tutor, except for a cause of absolute necessity or evident utility of the minor, duly justified, and with the previous consent of his curator and judicial authority: Art. 613; nor the individual property of the child by the father, except for the aforesaid reasons: Art. 409.[1] A sale of real estate of a minor is null if it is not made by a judicial sale at public auction: Art. 615.

§ 2008. *Tutors and their Relatives.*—A tutor can not sell or lease the property of the minor, nor make any contract relative thereto for himself, for his wife, children, or brothers by consanguinity or affinity, even with judicial license, nor at public auction, or otherwise: Art. 616.

§ 2009. *Nine Years' Lease.*—A tutor can not rent the property of a minor for more than nine years, except in a case of necessity or utility, with a previous consent of the curator and judicial authorization: Art. 621.[2]

---

[1] The following is a new article of the code of 1884: "Art. 519. When the question is of selling, burdening, or mortgaging, by an onerous title, property which may belong to an incapacitated person as proprietor, the operation shall be made if the majority of the co-participants calculated by the amounts so determine; and they shall not subject themselves to the rules established for the property of persons incapacitated, except when said majority shall be represented by one or more persons subject to tutorship."

[2] Article 621 becomes article 525 in the code of 1884, and is amended by adding after the words "judicial authorization," "observing in case thereof the provisions in article 519."

§ 2010. *Payment in Advance Limited.*—A lease made in conformity with the preceding article shall subsist for the time agreed, although the tutorship shall have ceased; but all payments for rent or hire in advance for more than three years shall be null: Art. 622. A tutor can not make donations in the name of a minor.

§ 2011. *Compromises.*—A tutor can not compromise affairs of the minor without judicial approbation: Art. 627.

§ 2012. *Restitution.*—There is no restitution of property to be made to a minor for sales thereof made by his tutor and curator, which have been judicially approved: Art. 686.

EMANCIPATION OF MINOR.

§ 2013. *Marriage—Death.*—The marriage of a minor produces in law his emancipation. The death of either conjugal party does not replace the survivor under paternal power: Art. 689.

§ 2014. *Emancipation after the Age of Eighteen.*—A minor over eighteen years and under twenty-one may be emancipated by him who has the minor under his paternal power, provided he give his consent to his emancipation, and the judge approves the same with a knowledge of the cause: Art. 690.

§ 2015. *Public Writing.*—The act of emancipation must be reduced to a public writing (escritura publica): Art. 691.

§ 2016. *Effect of Emancipation.*—An emancipated party has the free administration of his property; but he always requires during his minority the authorization of him who emancipated him, and in default thereof, of the judge, to alienate, burden, or mortgage real estate.

MARRIED PARTIES.

§ 2017. *Marriage Settlement.*—A marriage settlement may determine the manner of controlling and administering the property: Art. 2099.

§ 2018. *Husband is Administrator,*—The husband is the legitimate administrator of the conjugal partnership, unless there is an express agreement or judgment to the contrary: Arts. 2109, 205.

§ 2019. *Settlement, when Made.*—Marriage settlements may be made before or during the marriage, and may include the property possessed at the time of the making thereof, and that acquired thereafter: Art. 2113.

§ 2220. *Revocation.*—They can not be altered nor revoked

after the marriage except by an express agreement or by a judicial sentence: Art. 2114.

§ 2021. *Public Writing.*—Marriage settlements must be executed by public writing (escritura publica).

§ 2022. *Alterations.*—Alterations must be noted in the protocols, and in the certified copies given thereof: Art. 2117.

§ 2023. *Common Property.*—The dominion and possession of the common property resides in both conjugal parties while the partnership subsists: Art. 2156.

§ 2024. *Alienation.*—The real estate belonging to the social fund can not be obligated nor alienated in any manner by the husband without the consent of the wife: Art. 2158.

§ 2025. *Consent of Judge.*—In cases of unfounded opposition, the consent of the wife may be supplied by a judicial decree: Art. 2159.[1]

§ 2026. *Husband, his Will.*—The husband can by will dispose of only one half of the ganancial property: Art. 2162.[2]

§ 2027. *Sales by Husband.*—No sales which the husband shall make of the ganancial property, in contravention of the law or in fraud of the wife, shall prejudice the latter or her heirs: Art. 2163.

§ 2028. *Conjugal Parties' Rights.*—The conjugal parties preserve the property and administration of their movables and immovables, and the enjoyment of their products: Art. 2208.

§ 2029. *Wife can not Alienate.*—The wife can not alienate the immovable property nor real rights without the express consent of her husband, or of the judge if the opposition is unfounded: Art. 2210.

§ 2030. *Void Agreements.*—Any agreement which contravenes the preceding article is null: Art. 2211.

§ 2031. *Wife can not Burden.*—The wife can not, without a judicial license, burden nor sell the immovable property which in virtue of a separation shall belong to her, or the administration of which she has been charged with: Art. 2226.

§ 2032. *Dotal Property.*—As to any disposition of dotal property, see the law regulating the same, under the head thereof, commencing with article 2280. Husband and wife can not sell to each other unless separated as to their property: Art. 2968.

---

[1] Article 2159 is amended by the code of 1884, by adding thereto "and her previous audience."

[2] Article 2162 is amended by the code of 1884, and reads as follows: "Art. 2029. The conjugal partners can by will dispose of only one half of their ganancial property."

### Attorneys in Fact.

§ 2033. *Power of Attorney.*—A power of attorney may be by a public writing (escritura publica) or by a private instrument: Art. 2478.

§ 2034. *Private Instrument.*—A private instrument is one that is written by the principal and signed by him; or one written by another and signed by the principal, with two witnesses: Art. 2479.

§ 2035. *Powers.*—A power may be general or special. The first comprehends all the business of the principal; and the second is limited to certain and determined affairs: Art. 2481.

§ 2036. *General Power.*—A general power only comprehends the acts of administration. In order to alienate, mortgage, and to do any other act of strict dominion, the power must be special: Art. 2482.

§ 2037. *Absent Parties.*—A power may be made between absent parties; and it will be understood in this case as tacitly accepted if the attorney shall execute the charge: Art. 2483.

§ 2038. *Power by Public Writing.*—A power must be made by a public writing: 1. When it is general; 2. When the interest in the affair for which it is conferred exceeds a thousand dollars; 3. When in virtue of it the attorney has to execute in the name of the principal any act which in conformity with the law must appear in a public instrument; 4. When it is executed for judicial affairs which must be prosecuted in writing in conformity with the code of procedure: Art. 2484.

§ 2039. *Private Writing.*—A power may be by a private writing when the interest in the affair for which it is conferred exceeds three hundred dollars but does not reach one thousand dollars: Art. 2485.

§ 2040. *Married Women and Minors.*—A wife, and minors who are over eighteen years, may be attorneys in fact; but in order that the contract shall have effect, the wife requires the express authorization of her husband, and the minor that of the father or tutor: Art. 2489.

§ 2041. *Change of Attorney.*—The constitution of a new attorney for the same business imports the revocation of the first from the day on which he is notified of the new appointment: Art. 2527.

§ 2042. *Death of Principal.*—Although the power terminates by the death of the principal, the attorney must continue in the administration of the affairs until the heirs provide for themselves, whenever any loss would otherwise result: Art. 2528.

§ 2043. *Heirs.*—In that case the attorney may ask the judge to designate a short time to the heirs, in order that they shall present themselves to take charge of the business: Art. 2529.

§ 2044. *Death of Attorney.*—If the power should terminate by the death of the attorney, his heirs must give notice to the principal, and perform, until the latter resolves what to do, only the acts which are indispensable to avoid any loss: Art. 2530.

§ 2045. *Renouncement by Attorney.*—An attorney who renounces is under obligation to follow the business until the principal provides for the attorneyship, if any loss would otherwise follow: Art. 2531.

§ 2046. *Obligations.*—What an attorney, knowing his power has ceased, shall do with a third party who is ignorant of the terms of the power, shall obligate the principal and attorney personally with the third party; but the attorney is responsible to the principal for all damages and losses which shall have happened, even by a fortuitous case: Art. 2532.

### Copartners.

§ 2047. *Firm Name.*—When in the contract of copartnership it has been stipulated who must administer the affairs, only he who is designated can use the firm name: Art. 2433.

§ 2048. *Obligation of Company.*—The administering partner can not obligate the company in making a contract, except when he employs the firm name; unless he proves that the contract has been made in favor of the partnership: Art. 2434.

§ 2049. *Authority to Act.*—The administering partner requires express authorization in writing from the other copartners: 1. To sell the things of the company if it has not been established with this object; 2. To pawn, mortgage, or burden said things with any other real right; 3. To borrow capital.

### Executors.

§ 2050. *Sales.*—Executors can not sell without the consent of the heirs, or judicial approbation: Art. 3720. They can not lease without the consent of the heirs: Art. 3722. They can not mortgage without the consent of the heirs: Art. 3724. They can not arbitrate without said consent: Art. 3725.

§ 2051. *Co-proprietors.*—The co-proprietors of an indivisible thing can not sell to extraneous persons their respective part, if the other co-owners will pay the same price: Art. 2973.[1]

[1] Articles 2973 and 2974 are united in the code of 1884, and read as follows: "Art. 2843. The owners of an undivided thing can not sell to ex-

§ 2052. *Co-heirs.*—A co-heir can not sell or burden any of the hereditary property: Art. 4086.

§ 2053. *Corporations.*—Associations or corporations which enjoy juridical entity may exercise all the civil rights relative to the legitimate interests of their institutions: Art. 45. They may purchase or sell through their agents legally authorized by their charters, by-laws, or resolutions legally made.

§ 2054. *Corporations, What Are.*—*Quære,* What is a corporation under Mexican law? The law of the twenty-fifth of June, 1856, in article 3, defines a corporation as follows: "Art. 3. Under the name of 'corporations' are comprehended all religious communities of both sexes, * * * and in general every establishment or foundation which may have the character of perpetual or indefinite duration." Article 430 of the code says: "Associations or corporations, temporal or perpetual, * * * are called moral persons." No judicial construction has been given yet on the language of these two conflicting articles.

---

traneous persons their respective part if the participant wishes to make use of the right of preference (tanto). For this purpose, the co-proprietor who shall sell shall notify the others by means of a notary, or judicially, of the sale which he shall have agreed on, in order that within the days following they shall make use of the right of privilege (tanto). The eight days having passed, by the sole lapse of the term, that right is lost. Until the notification shall have been made, the sale shall produce no legal effect."

# CHAPTER IX.

## PURCHASE AND SALE.

§ 2098. Transfer.
§ 2099. Giving the Property.
§ 2100. Expenses.
§ 2101. Payment.
§ 2102. Insolvency.
§ 2103. Credit.
§ 2104. Condition.
§ 2105. Profits after Sale.
§ 2106. Quantity.
§ 2107. Reduction.
§ 2108. Fixed Price.
§ 2109. Boundaries.
§ 2110. Restoration.
§ 2111. Several Sales of Same Thing.
§ 2112. Personal Property.
§ 2113. Responsibility of Vendor.
§ 2114. Real Estate.
§ 2115. Valued by Experts.
§ 2116. Rescission.
§ 2117. Eviction.
§ 2118. Obligations.
§ 2119. Payment.
§ 2120. Doubts.
§ 2121. Interest.
§ 2122. Sales on Time.
§ 2123. When Interest to be Paid.
§ 2124. Disturbed Possession.
§ 2125. Want of Payment.
§ 2126. Delay in Payment.
§ 2127. Resale.
§ 2128. Real Estate.
§ 2128 *a*. Five Years.
§ 2129. Irrevocable, when.
§ 2130. Condition of Resale.
§ 2131. Damages.
§ 2132. Fortuitous Case.
§ 2133. Vendor's Rights.
§ 2134. Second Contract.
§ 2135. Purchaser's Rights.
§ 2136. Creditors.
§ 2137. Agreement of Resale.
§ 2138. Joint Vendors.
§ 2139. Heirs.
§ 2140. Obligation of Vendors.
§ 2141. Retraction.
§ 2142. Various Heirs.
§ 2143. Division of Inheritance.
§ 2144. Free of Burden.
§ 2145. Growing Fruit.
§ 2146. Fruit at the Time of Retraction.
§ 2147. Contract of Sale.

GENERAL PROVISIONS.

§ 2055. *Purchase and Sale, What is.*—Art. 2939. A purchase and sale is a contract by which one of the contracting parties obligates himself to transfer a right or to deliver a thing and the other to pay a certain price and in money.

§ 2056. *Sale or Exchange.*—Art. 2940. If the price of the thing sold has to be paid part in money and part with the value of another thing, the contract will be one of sale when the part in money is equal or greater than that which is paid with the value of another thing; if the part in money should be less, the contract will be one of exchange.

§ 2057. *Price, how Fixed.*—Art. 2941. The contractors may agree that the price shall be that which is current of the day or of a determined place, or that which a third party shall fix.

§ 2058. *Price—Third Party.*—Art. 2942. The price having been fixed by the third party, it can not be rejected by the contracting parties, unless by common consent.

§ 2059. *Price not Designated.*—Art. 2943. If the third party does not wish or can not designate the price, the contract shall be without effect, save an agreement to the contrary.

§ 2060. *Persons not Merchants.*—Art. 2944. The price of fruits or cereals sold on credit to persons not merchants, and for their consumption, can not exceed the greatest which those kinds shall have in the place in the period run from the delivery to the end of the following crop.

§ 2061. *One Party.*—Art. 2945. The designation of the price can not be left to the arbitration of one of the contracting parties.

§ 2062. *When Sale Perfect.*—Art. 2946. The sale is perfect and obligatory for the parties by their sole agreement for the thing and for the price, although the first may not have been delivered nor the second satisfied.

§ 2063. *Simple Promise.*—Art. 2947. In order that a simple

promise of a purchase and sale shall have legal effects, it is necessary that the thing sold shall have been designated, if it is real estate or personal property not fungible. In fungible things it shall be sufficient that the kind and quantity be designated. In every case the price must be fixed.

§ 2064. *Pledges.*—Art. 2948. If the purchase and sale should not be realized, and pledges (arras) should have intervened, the purchaser shall lose those which he shall have given when by his fault the contract shall not have effect.

§ 2065. *Fault of Vendor.*—Art. 2949. If the fault should be that of the vendor, the latter shall return the pledges (arras) with as much more.

§ 2066. *Perfection of Sale, Rights thereof.*—Art. 2950. From the moment that the sale is perfect in conformity with articles 1392, 1552, and 2946, the thing belongs to the purchaser and the price to the vendor, each one of them having a right to require from the other the fulfillment of the contract.

§ 2067. *Third Parties.*—Art. 2951. In respect to a third party a sale will not produce its effects, it being of real rights or of real estate only after it shall be registered in the terms provided in the respective title.

§ 2068. *Risk.*—Art. 2952. As to the risk of the thing sold, the provisions in chapter 3, title 3, of this book shall be observed.

§ 2069. *Expenses.*—Art. 2954. The contracting parties shall pay by halves the expenses of title and registry, save an agreement to the contrary.

§ 2070. *Public Utility.*—Art. 2955. A forced sale, on account of public utility, shall be governed by the organic law of article 27 of the constitution.

### Of the Effects of a Purchase and Sale.

§ 2071. *Objects of Sale.*—Art. 2956. All things which are in commerce, and which may not be excepted by the law or by administrative regulations in conformity with it, can be objects of purchase and sale.

§ 2072. *Manner of Sale.*—Art. 2957. The following can only be sold in the cases and form which the law establishes: 1. The property of minors and persons incapacitated, and any other which is found in administration; 2. Dotal property; 3. Public property; 4. Property pledged or mortgaged.

§ 2073. *Property not One's Own.*—Art. 2958. No one can sell except what is of his own property, or that to which he has a legitimate right.

§ 2074. *Void Sale.*—Art. 2959. A sale of a thing belonging to another is null; and the vendor is responsible for the damages and losses if he shall proceed with fraud or bad faith.

§ 2075. *Revalidation.*—Art. 2960. In the case of the preceding article, the contract will be revalidated, and the vendor free from penal responsibility which he may have incurred, if before eviction or accusation shall have taken place he shall acquire by any legitimate title the property to the thing sold.

§ 2076. *Inheritance.*—Art. 2961. The right to an inheritance of a living person can not be the object of a purchase and sale, even when that person shall give his consent; nor the allowance due by family right.

§ 2077. *Litigious Rights.*—Art. 2962. The sale of a litigious right or thing is not prohibited; but the vendor who does not declare the circumstance of the thing being found in litigation is responsible for the damages and losses, if the purchaser shall suffer eviction; being besides subject to the penalties imposed for the crime of fraud.

§ 2078. *Non-existence.*—Art. 2963. The sale of a thing which does not exist or which can not exist is null; and the vendor is responsible for the damages and losses, if there should be fraud with bad faith.

§ 2079. *Damage.*—Art. 2964. If the thing sold only be damaged in part, the purchaser will have the election to rescind the contract, or to accept the remaining part, reducing the price proportionally in the judgment of experts; save an agreement to the contrary.

OF THOSE WHO CAN SELL AND PURCHASE.

§ 2080. *Who can Sell.*—Art. 2965. All persons can sell who are not legally prohibited from disposing of their property, either by reason of their condition, or on account of the nature of the thing itself.

§ 2081. *Who can Purchase.*—Art. 2966. All persons may purchase who may contract, save the following exceptions:

§ 2082. *Corporations.*—Art. 2967. Neither public establishments nor corporations can purchase real estate, under the penalty of losing what is purchased in favor of the nation.[1]

---

[1] Article 2967 becomes article 2839, new code, and is amended to read as follows: "The persons enumerated in fractions 1 and 2 of article 38 (43) can not buy real estate except when it may be in order to destine it immediately and directly to the service or object of their institutions. In case

§ 2083. *Consorts.*—Art. 2968. Consorts (man and wifé) can not celebrate between themselves a contract of purchase and sale, unless they shall be legally separated as to property.

§ 2084. *Purchasers—Exceptions.*—Art. 2969. Those who can not be grantees according to the provision in article 1737 can not purchase things in litigation, except in the case of a sale of hereditary shares, being co-heirs, or in that of responsibility for the mortgaged property which they may possess.[1]

§ 2085. *Lawyers.*—Art. 2970. Lawyers can not purchase the property and rights which shall be an object of litigation in which they may intervene through their profession.[2]

§ 2086. *Parent and Child.*—Art. 2971. The children of a family may sell to their father any property[3] comprehended in the fifth class of those mentioned in article 401.[4]

§ 2087. *Sale by a Father to Children*—Art. 2972. The father who has several children can not sell to one of them any class of property without the express consent of the others if they should be of age, nor without judicial authority if they should be minors.[5]

§ 2088. *Co-Proprietors.*—Art. 2973. Co-proprietors of an indivisible thing can not sell to strangers their respective part if the participant wishes to make use of the privilege of buying in preference.

§ 2089. *Rescission.*—Art. 2974. In case of a violation of the provision in the preceding article, the preferred co-proprietor can ask for the rescission of the contract; but only within six months counted from the celebration of the sale.

§ 2090. *Who can not Buy.*—Art. 2975. The following persons can not purchase the property, the sale or administration of which they are charged with: 1. Tutors and curators; 2. Attorneys in fact; 3. Testamentary executors, and those who may be appointed in case of an intestate; 4. Intervenors appointed by the testator or by the heirs; 5. Representatives, ad-

---

of an infraction of this precept, the property purchased will enter that of national domain."

[1] Article 2969 becomes article 2841, and is amended by suppressing the word "responsibility," and all after it; and by inserting in place thereof "a sale of the rights by which may be affected their property."

[2] Article 2970 is by the code of 1884 suppressed.

[3] Property which the child may acquire by honest work, whatever it may be.

[4] Article 2971 becomes article 2842, new code, and is amended by inserting "sixth" in place of "fifth."

[5] Article 2972 is suppressed by the code of 1884.

Article 2844 is a new article of the code of 1884, and reads as follows: "If various co-proprietors of an undivided thing should make use of the right of preference (tanto), he will be preferred who represents the greater part, and being equal, that designated by chance, save an agreement to the contrary."

ministrators, and intervenors, in case of absence; 6. Public employés.

§ 2091. *Brokers.*—Art. 2976. Experts and brokers can not buy property in the sale of which they have intervened.

§ 2092. *Void Purchase.*—Art. 2977. Purchases made in contravention to the provisions in this chapter shall not produce any effect, whether they have been directly made, or through the interposition of a third party.

§ 2093. *Third Person—Who is.*—Art. 2978. By a third person (interposita) shall be understood the consort or any other of whom the purchaser shall be a presumptive heir.[1]

§ 2094. *Fraud.*—Art. 2979. If the thing should have been acquired with fraud, the purchaser shall be besides responsible for the damages and losses.

§ 2095. *Public Sales.*—Art. 2980. Sales made at public auction shall be governed by the provisions of the code of procedure.

### Of the Obligations of the Vendor.

§ 2096. *Vendor's Obligations.*—Art. 2981. The vendor is obliged: 1. To deliver to the purchaser the thing sold; 2. To guarantee the qualities of the thing.

### Of the Delivery of the Thing Sold.

§ 2097. *Delivery.*—Art. 2983. If the thing sold is real estate, it is said to be delivered as soon as the title (escritura publica), is executed, or if there is no writing, as soon as the titles to the estate are delivered.

§ 2098. *Transfer.*—Art. 2984. The provision in the preceding article shall be observed also for the transfer (translacion) of rights.

§ 2099. *Giving.*—Art. 2985. In any case the delivery shall be considered made if the purchaser gives the thing as received.

§ 2100. *Expenses.*—Art. 2986. The expenses of the delivery of the thing sold are on account of the vendor, and those of transportation or transfer of the charge of the purchaser, save an agreement to the contrary.

§ 2101. *Payment.*—Art. 2987. The vendor is not obliged to deliver the thing sold, if the purchaser has not paid the price or has not designated in the contract a term for the payment.

§ 2102. *Insolvency.*—Art. 2988. Neither is he obligated for the delivery when he has conceded a term for the payment, if

[1] Article 2978 becomes article 2848, new code, and is amended by adding thereto "or partner in a universal partnership."

after the sale it is discovered that the purchaser is found in a state of insolvency, so that the vendor runs imminent danger of losing the price, save if the purchaser gives him security to pay at the time agreed upon.

§ 2103. *Credit.*—Art. 2989. If the sale should be made on credit, the vendor can require the price with interest thereon in case of delay, but he can not ask for a rescission of the contract.

§ 2104. *Condition.*—Art. 2990. The vendor must deliver the thing sold in the condition in which it was found on perfecting the contract.

§ 2105. *Profits after Sale.*—Art. 2991. The vendor must also deliver all the fruit produced since the sale was perfected, and the rents, accessions, and titles of the thing.

§ 2106. *Quantity.*—Art. 2992. When the thing shall be sold by number, weight, or measure, with an expression of these circumstances, the purchaser can ask for the rescission of the contract if in the delivery there should be a default which the vendor can not or does not wish to supply, or an excess which can not be separated without injury to the thing.

§ 2107. *Reduction.*—Art. 2993. If the purchaser wishes to sustain the contract, he may require a reduction of the price in proportion to the default, and he must increase it in proportion to the excess.

§ 2108. *Fixed Price.*—Art. 2996. If the sale of one or more immovable properties should be made for a fixed price, and without estimating specially their parts or measures, there shall be no ground for a rescission, although in the delivery there should be a default or excess.

§ 2109. *Boundaries.*—Art. 2997. If, in the sale of an immovable property, the lines have been designated, the vendor will be obliged to deliver all that is comprehended within them, although there may be an excess in the measure expressed in the contract.

§ 2110. *Restoration.*—Art. 2998. The contract being rescinded, according to the provisions in the preceding articles, the vendor will be obliged to restore the price which he may have received, and to satisfy all the expenses which the purchaser may have made in order to fulfill his obligation.

§ 2111. *Several Sales of Same Thing.*—Art. 3000. If the same thing shall be sold by the same vendor to several persons, the following shall be observed:

§ 2112. *Personal Property.*—Art. 3001. If the thing sold were personal property, the sale first in date shall prevail; and if it should not be possible to prove the priority thereof, the sale shall prevail made to him who shall be found in possession of the thing.

§ 2113. *Responsibility of Vendor.*—Art. 3002. In every case the vendor shall respond for the price which he shall have unduly received, as well as for the damages and losses; and he may be accused of deceit by those who were injured or deceived.[1]

§ 2114. *Real Estate.*—Art. 3003. If the thing sold were real estate, the sale shall prevail which shall have been first registered; and if neither shall have been, the provisions in article 3001 shall be observed.

§ 2115. *Valued by Experts.*—Art. 3022. A contract of purchase and sale can not be rescinded in any case under pretext of damage whenever the estimation of the thing shall have been made by experts at the time of making the contract.

§ 2116. *Rescission.*—Art. 3023. If the thing has been valued by experts prior to the making of the contract, the contract may be rescinded if from their decision it results that any one of the parties has suffered damage in the terms which article 1772 establishes.

### Of Eviction.

§ 2117. *Eviction.*—Art. 3024. The vendor is obliged to guarantee the property and the possession of the purchaser, and to defend and pay for the eviction in the terms declared in chapter 5 and title 3 of this book. (See article 1604, and following.)

### Obligations of the Purchaser.

§ 2118. *Obligations.*—Art. 3025. The purchaser must comply with all that for which he has obligated himself, and especially to pay the price of the thing at the time, place, and manner agreed.

§ 2119. *Payment.*—Art. 3026. If no time and place have been fixed, the payment shall be made at the time and place in which the thing is to be delivered.

§ 2120. *Doubts.*—Art. 3027. If a doubt shall occur as to which of the contracting parties must make the first delivery, both shall make the deposit in the hands of a third party.

§ 2121. *Interest.*—Art. 3028. The purchaser owes interest for the time which runs between the delivery of the thing and the payment of the price in the three following cases: 1. If it has been so agreed; 2. If the thing sold and delivered produces

[1] Article 3002 is amended by the code of 1884, by inserting "fraud" in place of "deceit."

fruit or rent; 3. If there shall have been made a delay according to articles 1539 and 1548.

§ 2122. *Sales on Time.*—Art. 3029. In the sales on time without stipulating interest, the purchaser does not owe any by reason thereof, although in the mean time he may receive fruits of the things, as the time made a part of the contract, and it ought to be presumed that in consideration of this the price of the sale was increased.

§ 2123. *When Interest to be Paid.*—Art. 3030. If the concession of the time was subsequent to the contract, the purchaser will be obliged to give interest, save an agreement to the contrary.

§ 2124. *Disturbed Possession.*—Art. 3031. When the purchaser on time or with a stay in the payment of the price shall be disturbed in his possession and right, or shall have a just fear in being so, he can suspend the payment, even if it has not been done, until the vendor shall secure him the possession or shall give him a bond, save if there is an agreement to the contrary.

§ 2125. *Want of Payment.*—Art. 3032. The vendor of the thing, whether it be personal or real estate, can not rescind the contract after the delivery for want of payment of the price.[1]

§ 2126. *Delay in Payment.*—Art. 3033. Although in the sale of immovables it should have been stipulated that for want of payment of the price at the time agreed, a dissolution of the contract shall take place in full right, the purchaser may pay even after the expiration of the time, if, in the mean time, no delay has been made by virtue of an injunction; but if this has been done, the judge can not concede him a new term.[2]

[1] Article 3032 is suppressed by the code of 1884.

[2] The following four articles are new ones, of the code of 1884:

"Art. 2926. Judicial sales at auction (en almoneda), or at public auction (subasta ó remate publica), shall be governed by the provisions of this title as to the substance of the contract and the obligations and rights of the buyer and of the seller, with the modifications which the following articles contain. As to the terms and conditions on which they have to be verified, they shall be governed by what is provided in the code of procedure.

"Art. 2927. The judge himself nor through a third person, the secretary, and others employed by the court, the judgment debtor, the attorneys in fact, the executors, administrators, tutors, curators, sureties, and attorneys of the judgment debtor, nor the experts who may have appraised the property which is the object of the sale, can not make public auction sales.

"Art. 2928. As a general rule, judicial sales shall be made in effective money and for cash down; and when the thing shall be immovable, it shall pass to the purchaser free of all burden, unless by an express stipulation to the contrary, for which effect the judge shall order the respective conciliation or conciliations to be made on the terms which the code of procedure provides.

"Art. 2929. In judicial sales which

### Of a Resale.

§ 2127. *Resale.*—Art. 3035. A sale made with the condition that within a fixed time the contract may be rescinded, and the thing and price be respectively returned, is called a resale.

§ 2128. *Real Estate.*—Art. 3036. A resale can only take place with real estate.

§ 2128 *a.* *Five Years.*—Art. 3037. A resale can not be stipulated for a longer time than five years, counted from the date of the contract.

§ 2129. *Irrevocable, when.*—Art. 3038. If the vendor does not make use of the right of retraction within the term agreed, and for want of this within the five years, the sale shall remain irrevocably consummated.

§ 2130. *Condition of Resale.*—Art. 3039. A vendor who wishes to effectuate a resale must reimburse the purchaser: 1. For the price received; 2. For the expenses of the contract; 3. For the necessary expenses and improvements made on the thing sold.

§ 2131. *Damages.*—Art. 3040. The purchaser shall respond for the damages and deteriorations which the thing may have suffered by his fault or negligence.

§ 2132. *Fortuitous Case.*—Art. 3041. If the thing perishes by a fortuitous case or *vis major*, within the time fixed for the resale, both shall be on the account of the vendor.

§ 2133. *Vendor's Rights.*—Art. 3042. The vendor may demand the thing, although it may be found in the possession of a third party; save the right of the latter against him who sold it.

§ 2134. *Second Contract.*—Art. 3043. The provision in the preceding article shall have place, although in the second contract no mention shall have been made of the agreement of a resale.

§ 2135. *Purchaser's Rights.*—Art. 3044. The purchaser has relative to the thing, until the resale is realized, all the rights of the vendor, except those which import injury to the right of retraction.

§ 2136. *Creditors.*—Art. 3045. The creditors of the vendor can not exercise the right of retraction against the purchaser, except after having exhausted all the property of the vendor.[1]

§ 2137. *Agreement of Resale.*—Art. 3046. If a purchaser with

---

may have to be verified in order to divide a common thing, the provisions in article 2316 (2448) of this code and the provisions of the code of civil procedure in respect to the partition of hereditary property, shall be observed."

[1] Articles 3041 and 3045 are suppressed in the code of 1884.

an agreement of resale of an undivided part of an estate has obtained the whole of it, by buying at a public sale moved against him, he may oblige the vendor to redeem the whole if the latter wishes to make use of the right of retraction.

§ 2138. *Jo nt Vendors.*—Art. 3047. If many conjointly and in one sole contract sell an undivided estate, with an agreement of resale, no one of them can exercise this right more than for his respective part.

§ 2139. *Heirs.*—Art. 3048. The same shall be observed, if he who has sold by himself a sole estate has left many heirs; in this case one of these alone may redeem the part which he shall have acquired.

§ 2140. *Obligation of Vendors.*—Art. 3049. In the cases of the two preceding articles, the purchaser may require from all the venders or co-heirs that they shall agree on the redemption of the whole of the thing sold; and if they should not do so, he can not be obliged to consent to a partial retraction.

§ 2141. *Retraction.*—Art. 3050. If each one of the co-proprietors of an undivided estate has sold his part separately, he can exercise with said separation the right of retraction for his respective portion, and the purchaser can not oblige him to redeem the whole of the estate.

§ 2142. *Various Heirs.*—Art. 3051. If the purchaser shall have left many heirs, and the thing should be indivisible, the action of retraction shall be exercised against all of them.

§ 2143. *Division of Inheritance.*—Art. 3052. If the inheritance should be divided, the action will be exercised against the heir or heirs to whom the thing shall have been adjudicated.

§ 2144. *Free of Burden.*—Art. 3053. The vendor who recovers the thing sold acquires it free of all charge or mortgage imposed by the purchaser; but he is obliged to submit to the leases which the latter shall have made in good faith, and according to the custom of the place.

§ 2145. *Growing Fruit.*—Art. 3054. If on making a sale there should be on the estate growing or grown fruits, credit shall not be made, nor a division of those which there may be at the time of the resale.

§ 2146. *Fruit at the Time of Retraction.*—Art. 3055. If there was none at the time of the sale, and there is at the time of the retraction, they shall be divided between the retractor and the purchaser; giving to the latter the part corresponding to the time which he possessed the estate in the last year, which shall commence to be counted from the term fixed for the resale.

### Of the Form of the Contract of Purchase and Sale.

§ 2147. *Contract of Sale.*—Art. 3056. A contract of purchase and sale does not require for its validity any special formality, except when it pertains to immovable property.

§ 2148. *Value of Five Hundred Dollars.*—Art. 3057. A sale of an immovable property, the value of which does not exceed five hundred dollars, shall be made by a private instrument, which the vendor and purchaser shall sign before two known witnesses.

§ 2149. *Ignorance of Writing.*—Art. 3058. If any of the contracting parties should not know how to write, another person with legal capacity shall sign it in his name and at his request; but none of the witnesses can sign with that character.

§ 2150. *Two Originals.*—Art. 3059. Two originals shall be formed of said instrument, one for the vendor and the other for the purchaser, the same being drawn on the corresponding sealed paper.[1]

§ 2151. *Excess over Five Hundred Dollars.*—Art. 3060. If the value of the immovable property exceeds five hundred dollars, the sale shall be reduced to a title made before a notary (escritura publica).

§ 2152. *Third Parties.*—Art. 3061. A sale of real estate shall not produce any effect in relation to a third party, except after being registered in the terms prescribed in this code.

### Of Exchange.

§ 2153. *Exchange.*—Art. 3062. An exchange (cambio ó permuta) is a contract by which one thing is given for another.

§ 2154. *Sale or Exchange.*—Art. 3063. Giving a thing and money for another thing shall be a sale or exchange accordingly as is provided in article 2940.

§ 2155. *Identity of Property.*—Art. 3064. If one of the contracting parties has received the thing which was promised him in exchange, and he proves that it was not the property of him who gave it, he can not be obliged to deliver that which he offered in exchange, and he complies by returning that which he received.

§ 2156. *Eviction*—Art. 3065. An exchanger who suffers eviction from the thing which he received in exchange can recover what he gave, if it is found even in the possession of the other

[1]Article 3059 is amended by the code of 1884, by inserting the words "and another for the public register," after the word "purchaser."

exchanger, or he can require its value and the damages and losses.

§ 2157. *Third Parties*—Art. 3066. The provision in the preceding article does not prejudice the rights which a third party may have acquired by an onerous title to the thing which he claims who suffered an eviction.

§ 2158. *Rules of Construction.*—Art. 3067. With exception to what relates to the price, the rules of a purchase and sale are applicable to this contract, so far as they are not opposed to the foregoing articles.

# CHAPTER X.

## ANTICRESIS AND MORTGAGES.

§ 2159. *Anticresis, What is.*—Art. 1927. A debtor may give as security for his debt any immovable which belongs to him; the creditor having the right to enjoy the use of it on account of the interest due, or of the capital if there is no interest due; this is what is called anticresis.

§ 2160. *Public Writing* —Art. 1928. The contract (of anticresis) is null if not made by a public writing (escritura publica).

§ 2161. *Contents of Writing.*—Art. 1929. In the writing it shall be declared if the capital bears interest, and the terms must be fixed in which the creditor must manage the estate (finca). Otherwise it will be understood that there is no interest, and that the creditor must manage it in the same manner as an attorney in fact with a general power, in conformity with article 2482. (See said article.)

§ 2162. *Time of Contract.*—Art. 1930. The contracts which the creditor makes as manager of the thing are valid; but they can not extend beyond the time for which the anticresis is to run, save by an express contract to the contrary.[1]

§ 2163. *Rights of Creditor.*—Art. 1931. The anticresis confers on the creditor the right: 1. Of retaining the immovable until the debt be wholly paid, save the special right acquired by a third party over the immovable through the effect of a mortgage registered prior thereto; 2. Of transferring to another under his responsibility the usufruct and management of the thing if there should be no stipulation to the contrary; 3. Of defending his rights by possessory actions.

§ 2164. *Rights of Creditor and Liability.*—Art. 1932. The anticretic creditor must give an account of the products of the thing. He has the same obligations as the creditor of a pledge, and responds: 1. For the fruits and income which may be lost by his fault; 2. For the taxes and other predial charges, save the right of deducting them from the rents or income.

§ 2165. *Expenses.* —Art. 1933. The creditor is equally obliged to pay the necessary expenses for the preservation of the thing, deducting them from the amount of the fruits.

§ 2166. *Value of Fruits.*—Art. 1934. When through any cause the fruits can not be exactly known, they will be regulated by experts as if the immovable were rented.

§ 2167. *Accounts.*—Art. 1935. If in the writing the term for the accounts is not designated, the creditor must render them once a year.

§ 2168. *Ten Years' Possession.*—Art. 1936. If the creditor shall have preserved in his power the thing given in anticresis more than ten years without giving accounts, the capital and interests will be presumed paid, save proof to the contrary.

§ 2169. *Intervenor.*—Art. 1937. If the creditor who manages the thing does not give accounts within three months after the term in which he ought to give them, an intervenor may be put in possession of the thing at the creditor's cost if the debtor ask for it.

§ 2170. *Want of Payment.*—Art. 1938. The want of pay-

[1] Article 1930 is amended by the code of 1884, by adding thereto "celebrated between the creditor and the debtor."

ment does not authorize the creditor to remain with the thing; but he must proceed as articles 1917 to 1922 provide in respect to a pledge.

§ 2171. *Things of Another.*—Art. 1939. In respect to the thing of another given in anticresis, the provisions in articles 1902 and 1903 will be observed.

### Of Mortgages in General.

§ 2172. *Mortgage, What is.*—Art. 1940. A mortgage is a real right which is constituted upon immovable property or real rights, in order to guarantee the fulfillment of an obligation and its preference in payment.

§ 2173. *Third Parties.*—Art. 1941. Property mortgaged remains subject to the burden imposed, although it may pass into the hands of a third possessor.

§ 2174. *Real Estate.*—Art. 1942. A mortgage can only rest upon certain and determined immovable property, or upon real rights which are constituted upon them.

§ 2175. *Prior Burdens.*—Art. 1943. Whenever estates subject to real burdens shall be mortgaged, the mortgage shall only comprehend the value of said estates after deducting that of the real burden, or the corresponding service for five years if the obligation should be of annual rents or pensions.

§ 2176. *Extent of Mortgage.*—Art. 1944. A mortgage of lands comprehends: 1. The naked area or superfice which serves as a basis to the edifices; 2. The edifices or any other constructions executed upon the area; and it is understood with the improvements and natural accessions, and with the movable objects which the proprietor adds for perpetuity to the estate mortgaged.[1]

§ 2177. *Buildings.*—Art. 1945. A mortgage of a construction raised on the land of another does not comprehend the area.

§ 2178. *Movables.*—Art. 1946. If the movables which are spoken of in article 1944, fraction 2, should be sold before the constitution of the mortgage, the mortgage creditor will have no action against the owner of the thing, nor against the third possessor.

---

[1] Article 1944 is amended by the code of 1884, and reads: "Art. 1827. A mortgage of land only comprehends: 1. The naked area or superfice which serves as a basis to the edifices; 2. The edifices and any other constructions existing at the time of the constitution of the mortgage, or executed by the owner subsequent thereto; 3. The accessions and permanent improvements which the land shall have, and which increases the area and the edifices and constructions; 4. The objects comprehended in fractions 3 to 7 of article 684, which the proprietor has added to the mortgaged estate; 5. The animals which in the constitutive mortgage title have been fixed as breeding ones on the estates to which fraction 8 of article 684 refers (782)."

§ 2179. *Usufructs.*—Art. 1947. The naked property may be mortgaged; in which case, if the usufruct be consolidated with the property in the person of the proprietor, not only will the mortgage subsist, but it will extend also to the same usufruct.

§ 2180. *Second Mortgages.*—Art. 1948. Property which is already mortgaged may be mortgaged, although it be with an agreement not to mortgage it again, save in every case the rights of preference which this code establishes.

§ 2181. *Free Disposition.*—Art. 1949. Properties belonging to persons who have not the free dispcsition of them can not be mortgaged except with the formalities which for their respective case this code establishes.

§ 2182. *Real Rights.*—Art. 1950. A mortgage constituted upon real rights will only last while said rights subsist; but if the rights on which they shall have been constituted have been extinguished through the fault of him who was enjoying them, the latter will be obliged to constitute a new mortgage, to the satisfaction of the creditor, and in a contrary case to pay all the damages and losses.

§ 2183. *What can not be Mortgaged.*—Art. 1951. Can not be mortgaged: 1. Pending fruits and rents, separately from the land which produces them; 2. Movable objects placed permanently in the edifices, either for adornment or convenience, or either for the service of any industry, unless they are jointly mortgaged with said edifices; 3. Services, unless they are mortgaged jointly with the dominant estate, and excepting in all cases that of water, which may be mortgaged; 4. The right to receive the fruits in the usufruct conceded by this code to the ascendants on the property of their descendants; 5. The use and habitation; 6. Property sold with an agreement of resale, while the sale is not irrevocably consummated or dissolved; 7. Mines, until the title of a definite concession has been obtained; although they may be situated on one's own land; 8. Property in litigation.

§ 2184. *Emphyteuta.*—Art. 1952. When the emphyteuta has constituted a mortgage upon the estate without the consent of the owner, the provisions in article 3271 shall be observed.

§ 2185. *Various Estates.*—Art. 1953. When various estates are jointly mortgaged for only one credit, the sum or part of the burden for which each one must respond shall be determined.[1]

[1] Article 1953 is amended by the code of 1884 to read: "Art. 1836. When various estates are jointly mortgaged for only one credit, the creditor may make the obligation effective on any of them or on all, simultaneously or successively, until he has obtained the whole payment, unless in the

§ 2186. *How Long to Exist.*—Art. 1954. A mortgage shall wholly subsist, until it is canceled upon the whole of the property mortgaged, although the obligation guaranteed shall be reduced, and on any part of the said property which is preserved, although the rest shall have disappeared; but without prejudice to what is provided in the two following articles.

§ 2187. *Division of Property.*—Art. 1955. If a mortgaged estate shall be divided into two or more, the mortgage credit shall not be distributed between them, except when the creditor and the debtor voluntarily agree to it.

§ 2188. *Distribution.*—Art. 1956. The distribution not being made in the terms established in the preceding article, the creditor can claim the whole of the sum guaranteed, against any of the new estates into which the first has been divided, or against all jointly at the same time.

§ 2189. *Cancellation of a Part.*—Art. 1957. A mortgage constituted for one credit being divided among several estates, the part of it with which any of them may be burdened being paid, the partial cancellation of the mortgage as to the said estate may be required by him who is interested therein.

§ 2190. *Election of Estates.*—Art. 1958. If the part of the credit paid could be applied to the liberation of one or the other of the estates burdened, on account of not being inferior to the amount of the special responsibility of each one, the debtor shall elect which must remain free.

§ 2191. *All Held till Cancellation of Debt.*—Art. 1959. When there shall be one estate mortgaged, or when, being various, the responsibility of each one has not been designated, on account of the case provided in article 1955 occurring, the liberation of no part of the properties mortgaged can be required, whatever may be the part of the credit which the debtor has satisfied.[1]

§ 2192. *Insurance—Destruction.*—Art. 1960. If the estate should be insured, and it should be destroyed by fire or other fortuitous case, not only will the mortgage subsist on the rest of the estate, but the value of the insurance will remain effected for the payment. If the credit should be of a term completed, the creditor can ask for the retention of the insurance; and if

mortgage the sum or part of the burden that each one of the estates must respond for has been determined."

[1] Article 1959 is amended by the code of 1884, and reads as follows: "Art. 1842. When there shall be one estate mortgaged, or when, being various, the responsibility of each one h s not been designated, the liberation of no part of the properties mortgaged can be required, whatever may be the part of the credit which the debtor has satisfied."

it should not be so, he can ask that said value be placed to his satisfaction, in order that the payment may be made at the completion of the term.

§ 2193. *Public Utility.*—Art. 1961. The provisions in the preceding article shall be observed with the price which shall be obtained in case of occupation for a cause of public utility.[1]

§ 2194. *Deficit in Value.*—Art. 1962. If the immovable property should be made, through the fault of the debtor, insufficient for the security of the debt, the creditor can require the payment before it is due, or the mortgage be extended to other property.[2]

§ 2195. *Diminution of Value.*—Art. 1963. When the diminution of the value shall be made without the fault of the debtor, he shall not be obliged to pay before maturity, if he extends the mortgage to other property.

§ 2196. *Who can Mortgage.*—Art. 1964. He only can mortgage who can alienate, and that property only can be mortgaged which may be alienated.[3]

§ 2197. *Void Mortgage.*—Art. 1965. A mortgage constituted by him who has no right to mortgage shall not become valid, although the maker shall afterwards acquire the right which he lacked.

§ 2198. *Sale.*—Art. 1966. If for the payment of any of the installments of the capital or of the interest it should be necessary to sell the mortgaged estate, and even other installments should remain not yet due of the obligation, the sale shall be made and the estate transferred to the purchaser with the corresponding mortgage for the part of the credit which may not be satisfied, which, with the interest, shall be deducted from the price.[4]

§ 2199. *Purchase with Condition.*—Art. 1967. If the purchaser of the estate does not wish the estate with this charge, he shall deposit the amount, with the interest which shall correspond to it, in order that the creditor may be paid at the completion of the pending installments.[5]

§ 2200. *Prescription.*—Art. 1968. A mortgage action will be

---

[1] Articles 1960 and 1961 are amended by being united, and adding thereto "or of judicial sale:" Code of 1884.

[2] Article 1962 is amended by the code of 1884, by adding thereto the words "to his satisfaction."

[3] Article 1964 is amended by the code of 1884, by adding thereto the words "save the provisions for the case of a necessary mortgage, in articles 1876 and 1877:" 2001 and 2002, old code.

[4] Article 1966 is by the code of 1884 suppressed.

[5] Article 1967 is suppressed by the code of 1884.

prescribed after twenty years, counted from the time it can be instituted according to the registered title.[1]

§ 2201. *Bankrupt.*—Art. 1969. A mortgage constituted by a bankrupt within thirty days prior to the declaration of bankruptcy is null.[2]

§ 2202. *Rent.*—Art. 1970. The proprietor of a mortgaged estate can not contract for the payment of rents in advance for a time which shall exceed the term of the mortgage credit.

§ 2203. *Rent in Advance Limited.*—Art. 1971. If the payment should not depend on a certain term, the proprietor can not stipulate for rent in advance for more than four years without the consent of the respective creditor, under a penalty of the nullity of the contract in the part which exceeds said time.

§ 2204. *Interest.*—Art. 1972. If the mortgage credit draws interest, the estate burdened shall not respond for the interest due for more than five years, unless the mortgage has been extended to said interests and entered in the respective registry, and then only from its date will it produce effect with relation to a third party.

§ 2205. *Debtor not Owner.*—Art. 1973. If the estate mortgaged should not belong to the debtor, the creditor can not require that the enlargement of the mortgage be constituted upon it of which the preceding article treats; but he can exercise an equal right in respect to any other immovable property which the same debtor possesses and which can be mortgaged.[3]

§ 2206. *Title by Creditor.*—Art. 1974. The creditor can not acquire the mortgaged estate except by an agreement with the debtor, by a public sale at auction, or by adjudication in the cases in which another bidder is not presented, and with the conditions and solemnities which the code of procedure establishes.[4]

§ 2207. *By Whom Constituted.*—Art. 1975. A mortgage may be constituted as well by the debtor as by another in his favor.

§ 2208. *Conditions.*—Art. 1976. Nobody can mortgage his property except with the conditions and limitations to which his right of property may be subjected.

§ 2209. *Presumption of Fraud.*—Art. 1977. A proprietor whose right may be conditional or in any other manner limited

---

[1] Article 1968 is amended by the code of 1884, by adding thereto: "While the action is not prescribed, the mortgage will preserve its preference according to the date of its inscription."

[2] Article 1969 is, by the code of 1884 suppressed.

[3] Art. 1973 is suppressed by code 1884.

[4] Article 1974 is amended by the code of 1884 by suppressing the words "by a public sale at auction."

must declare in his contract the nature of his property, if he knows it. The omission of this circumstance induces a presumption of fraud.

§ 2210. *Co-proprietors.*—Art. 1978. An estate in common can not be mortgaged in its totality, except with the consent of all the co-proprietors; but these can mortgage their respective portions.[1]

§ 2211. *Public Writing.*—Art. 1979. A mortgage can only be constituted by a public writing (escritura publica). The notaries must declare the hour and day on which the writing was executed, under a penalty of a loss of office.

§ 2212. *Never Tacit.*—Art. 1980. A mortgage is never tacit; in order to subsist it is necessary to be registered, and to be contracted by the will in the agreements, and by necessity in the cases in which the law subjects any person to give that guaranty on determined properties; in the first case it is called voluntary; in the second, necessary.[2]

### Of a Voluntary Mortgage.

§ 2213. *Voluntary.*—Art. 1981. The agreements between parties, or imposed by the disposition of the owner of the property upon which they are constituted, are voluntary mortgages.

§ 2214. *Pure or Conditional.*—Art. 1982. A voluntary mortgage may be constituted purely or on condition.

§ 2215. *By Attorney.*—Art. 1983. Those who can legally constitute a voluntary mortgage can do so by themselves or through the means of an attorney, with a special power to contract this kind of obligations, executed before a notary.

§ 2216. *Future Obligation.*—Art. 1984. A mortgage constituted for the security of a future obligation, or subject to suspensive conditions registered, will have effect against a third party from its registry, if the obligation becomes realized or the condition fulfilled.

§ 2217. *Mortgage to be Noted.*—Art. 1985. When a future obligation becomes demandable, or the suspensive condition shall be fulfilled of which the preceding article treats, the interested parties ought to make it so appear by the means of a note on the margin of the mortgage registry; without which requisite it can not avail or prejudice a third party with a constituted mortgage.

[1] Article 1978 is amended by the code of 1884, and reads as follows: "Art. 1885. An estate in common can not be mortgaged, except with the consent of all the proprietors."

[2] Article 1980 is amended by the code of 1884, by adding the words "nor general" next after the word "tacit."

§ 2218. *Resolutive Condition.*—Art. 1986. If the obligation secured should be subject to a resolutive (which may be rescinded) condition registered, the mortgage will not have its effect as to a third party, except from the time the fulfillment of the condition is made to appear in the registry.

§ 2219. *Mortgage may be Sold.*—Art. 1987. A mortgage credit may be alienated or ceded to a third party wholly or in part, provided it be done in a public writing (escritura publica), so that knowledge thereof may be given to the debtor, and that it be inscribed in the registry.

§ 2220. *Time.*—Art. 1988. A mortgage will last the time designated by the contractors; if no time shall have been designated, it will only last ten years.[1]

§ 2221. *Extension.*—Art. 1989. A mortgage can only be extended before the legal time, or the agreement shall have expired.

§ 2222. *Limit of Extension.*—Art. 1990. An extension executed with a term fixed shall last the time which shall be designated; that executed without any term shall only last ten years.

§ 2223. *First Extension.*—Art. 1991. During the first extension the mortgage shall preserve the preference which belonged to it from its origin.[2]

§ 2224. *Second Extension.*—Art. 1992. A mortgage extended the second or more times, whether with a fixed term or whether for an indeterminate term, shall only have the preference which corresponds to it by the date of the last registry.

### Of a Necessary Mortgage.

§ 2225. *Necessary, What is.*—Art. 1993. The special and express mortgage which by the provision of the law certain persons are obliged to constitute in order to secure the property which they administer is called necessary.

Art. 1994. The special and express mortgage, the constitution of which certain persons have a right to require by the provisions of the law in order to guarantee their credits or the administration of their property, is also called necessary.

---

[1] Article 1988 is amended by the code of 1884, and reads as follows: "Art. 1865. A mortgage will last the time designated by the contractors; if no time is designated, it will last for all that in which the obligation which it guarantees may be demanded; and if there should be no time for the maturity of the obligation, it will be understood that this has the time of ten years."

[2] Article 1991 is amended by the code of 1884, and reads as follows: "Art. 1867. During the first extension, and the terms designated for the prescription, the mortgage shall preserve the preference which belonged to it from its origin."

§ 2226. *Constitution of.*—Art. 1995. The constitution of a necessary mortgage can be required at any time, although the cause may have ceased which gave grounds for it, as marriage, tutorship, paternal power, or administration, provided the fulfillment of the obligation may be pending which ought to have been secured.

§ 2227. *Disagreement.*—Art. 1996. If for the constitution of any necessary mortgage different properties should be offered, and the interested parties should not agree to the part of the responsibility which ought to rest on each one, in conformity with the provisions in article 1953, the judge, with a previous opinion of experts, shall decide.[1]

§ 2228. *Judge to Decide.*—Art. 1997. In the same manner the judge shall decide the questions which arise between the interested parties on the qualification of the sufficiency of the properties offered for the constitution of any necessary mortgage.

§ 2229. *Registry.*—Art. 1998. The necessary mortgages registered shall subsist until the rights for the security of which they shall have been constituted are extinguished.

§ 2230. *Who must Mortgage.*—Art. 1999. They are obliged to constitute a mortgage, although it is not demanded of them: 1. The ascendants for the property comprehended in fraction 5 of the following article; 2. Tutors in conformity with fraction 6 of said article; 3. The husband for the property comprehended in fractions 7 and 8 of said article, and in conformity with articles 2001 and 2003.[2]

§ 2231. *Right to Demand Mortgage, Who.*—Art. 2000. They have a right to ask for a necessary mortgage for the security of their credits: 1. A co-heir or particeps, on the immovables partitioned, as to the amount of their respective securities or the excess of the properties which they have received; 2. A seller, or he who exchanges, on the immovable sold or exchanged, for the price or for the difference of values; 3. A donor on the immovables given, for the pecuniary charges imposed upon the donee; 4. He who loans money to buy any estate on the same estate, provided it appears in a public writing that the loan was made with that object; 5. The descendants of whose property their fathers or ascendants were mere administrators on the

[1] Article 1996 is amended by the code of 1884 to read as follows: "Art. 1872. If for the constitution of a necessary mortgage various properties should be offered, the provision in article 1836 (1953 old code) shall govern."

[2] Article 1999 by code of 1884 is suppressed.

properties of the latter, in order to guarantee the preservation and return thereof; 6. Minors and other incapacitated persons on the properties of their tutors, for those which the latter administer; 7. A married woman on the property of her husband, for the dower and paraphernal property, provided that the delivery of both appear by a public writing; 8. A married woman for the antenuptial donations which may have been made her by her husband in conformity with the law;[1] 9. Creditors who may have obtained in their favor a judgment which may have caused execution, on the property which the debtor may have free, and which the creditors themselves shall designate; 10. Legatees on the immovables of the inheritance, for the amount of their legacy, if there should be no special mortgage designated by the said testator; 11. Insurers, on the properties insured for the premiums of insurance for two years; and if the insurance should be mutual, for the two last dividends which shall have been made; 12. The state, towns, and public establishments, on the properties of their administrators or collectors, to insure the revenues of their respective offices.

§ 2232. *Preference.*—Art. 2001. If the dotal or paraphernal properties should be real estate, the wife may require that the mortgage be in preference constituted on them.

§ 2333. *Wife's Rights.*—Art. 2002. The wife enjoys the right which fraction 7 of article 2000 concedes to her, at any time in which the dower shall be constituted.

§ 2334. *Antenuptial Donations.*—Art. 2003. A necessary mortgage, by reason of antenuptial donations will only have place in the case in which they shall have been offered as an increase of dower. If they should be offered without this requisite, they will only produce a personal obligation, being in the discretion of the husband to secure it or not with a mortgage.[2]

§ 2235. *Security of Dower.*—Art. 2004. The constitution of a mortgage to secure the dower may be asked for: 1. By the wife if she be of age; 2. By him who shall have given the dower; 3. By the parents of the wife, although they may not have given it; 4. By the tutor.

§ 2236. *Public Minister.*—Art. 2005. If none of those mentioned in the preceding article shall ask for the constitution of a mortgage, the public minister shall ask for it.[3]

[1] Fraction 8 is suppressed by the code of 1884.

[2] Article 2003 is suppressed by the code of 1884.

[3] Articles 2004 and 2005, old code, become article 1878 new code, which reads as follows: "Art. 1878. The constitution of a mortgage in the

§ 2237. *Prescription.*—Art. 2006. The action of the wife to ask for the construction of the mortgage is imprescriptible.

§ 2238. *Dilapidation.*—Art. 2007. When the husband shall not have constituted the dotal mortgage and her properties commence to dilapidate, the right will remain to the wife which the law concedes, without injury, to require that those which shall subsist of her dower shall be delivered to her, deposited in a safe place, or placed in administration.

§ 2239. *Subrogation.*—Art. 2008. The wife, by herself or through the means of her legitimate representative, can require the subrogation of her mortgage on other properties of the husband at any time which she may think proper, whenever she has consented in writing to the alienation or burden of the immovables affected with dower, or as a previons condition to give said consent.

§ 2240. *Pensions.*—Art. 2009. When the dotal properties consist in perpetual rents or pensions, if they should become alienated their return shall be secured by constituting a mortgage for the capital which at legal interest shall produce the same rent or pension.

§ 2241. *Temporary Pensions.*—Art. 2010. If the pensions should be temporary, and might or ought to subsist after the dissolution of the marriage, a mortgage for the sum to which the consorts shall agree shall be constituted; and if they shall not agree, for that sum which the judge may fix.

§ 2242. *Minors.*—Art. 2011. The constitution of a mortgage for the properties of the children of the family, of minors and of the others incapacitated shall be governed by the provisions of chapters 2, title 8, 13, title 9, and 1 and 3, title 13, of book 1.

§ 2243. *Insurer.*—Art. 2012. The insurer of immovable property shall have the right to require a special mortgage on the property insured, the owner of which shall not have satisfied the premiums of the insurance of two or more years; or of two or more of the last dividends, if the insurance should be mutual.

---

cases to which fractions 5, 6, and 7 of article 1875 (2000) refer may be asked: 1. In the case of property of which the parents should be mere administrators by the legitimate heirs of the minor; 2. In the case of property which the tutors shall administer by the legitimate heirs, and by the curator of the minor or incapacitated person; 3. In the case of dower, by the wife if she should be of age, by him who shall have given the dower, by the parents of the wife, although they may not have given it, and by the tutor; 4. In case of paraphernal property, by the wife if she should be of age, by her parents, and by the tutor; 5. In every case by the public minister if the persons enumerated in the preceding fractions should not ask it."

§ 2244. *The Whole Sum.*—Art. 2013. The mortgage to which the preceding article refers can be constituted for the whole sum which may be due; and the registry shall have no effect except from its date.

§ 2245. *Insufficiency.* — Art. 2014. Those who in conformity with article 2000 have the right to require the constitution of a necessary mortgage have also that of judging of the insufficiency of that which shall be offered, and that of asking for its enlargement when the properties mortgaged shall be made by any reason insufficient to guarantee the credit.[1]

§ 2246. *Want of Real Estate.*—Art. 2015. If the party responsible for the mortgage designated in numbers 5, 6, 7, 8, 9, and 10 of article 2000 shall not have immovables, the creditor shall not enjoy more than the privilege mentioned in article 2090, fraction 5, save the provisions in chapter 13, title 9, book 1, and in articles 2306, 2307, and 2308.

### Of the Registry of Mortgages.

§ 2247. *Registry, Effect of.*—Art. 2016. A mortgage will not produce any legal effect except from the date in which it shall be duly registered.[2]

§ 2248. *Duty of Judges.*—Art. 2017. The judges before whom shall be presented wills which shall contain appointments of tutor, and those which they shall appoint to this charge in respect to minors or incapacitated persons, shall have care, under their responsibility, that the mortgages shall be registered within six days, which for the security of the administration the tutors shall constitute with their sureties.

§ 2249. *Notaries.*—Art. 2018. The notaries before whom dotal writings, or of antenuptial donations, or of paraphernal properties shall be executed, which shall be secured with mortgages constituted by the husbands, shall cause within the same term the registry of those mortgages to be made, under the penalty of indemnification for damages and losses; in case of insolvency, they shall lose the office.

§ 2250. *Tutors.*—Art. 2019. In the same term of six days the tutors shall register the mortgages constituted in favor of the minors and others incapacitated. Of the omission of the registry the restitution *in integrum* shall not have place which shall prejudice another third party, who may have registered in

[1] Article 2014 is amended by the code of 1884, by adding thereto, "In both cases the judge shall decide."

[2] Article 2016 is amended by the code of 1884, by inserting the words "and hour" after the word "date."

the intermediate time; and the tutors shall be responsible for all damages and losses which may follow from it.[1]

§ 2251. *Time.*—Art. 2020. The term designated in the three preceding articles shall be counted from the day on which the mortgage shall have been constituted, not including in it the days which shall be holidays nor those necessary for the going and coming of the mail.

§ 2252. *Prior Burdens.*—Art. 2021. The notaries before whom writings are executed in which a mortgage is constituted must commence them with an insertion of a certificate from the party charged with the registry, in which must appear the preceding burdens or the exemption of the estate.[2]

§ 2253. *Damages for Neglect.*—Art. 2022. The notaries who shall omit this requisite shall incur the penalty of paying the damages and losses which they may cause; and in case of insolvency; the suspension of office for two years.

§ 2254. *Neglect of Registry.*—Art. 2023. Whenever it shall be observed that through negligence of the judges or notaries, or through any other cause, the registry has not been made within the legal term, it can be done; but the mortgage can not take effect except from the date of the registry. Those who may become responsible are obliged to pay the damages and indemnification for losses.

§ 2255. *Registry, where.*—Art. 2024. The registry shall be made in the books of the offices of mortgages, within the district of which the mortgaged estates belong, on account of their situation.

§ 2256. *Presentation of Mortgage.*—Art. 2025. The creditor who desires to register his mortgage shall present in the respective office the original title (that is, the mortgage).

§ 2257. *Contents of Registry.*—Art. 2026. In the registry shall appear: 1. The names, domiciles, and professions of the creditor and debtor; moral persons[3] shall be designated by the official name they bear and companies by their firm name; 2. The date and nature of the credit, the authority or notary which shall subscribe it, and the hour in which it shall be pre-

---

[1] Article 2019 is amended by the code of 1884 so as to read as follows: "Art. 1892. In the same time of six days the tutors shall register the mortgages constituted in favor of the minors and others incapacitated. And the tutors shall be responsible for all damages and losses which may follow from it."

[2] Article 2021 is amended by the code of 1884, by adding thereto, "Even when the interested parties shall renounce this requisite. The certificates of registry must comprehend at least the twenty years anterior to the date of the constitution of the mortgage."

[3] Associations or corporations are called "moral persons." (See article 43.)

sented to the registry; 3. The kind of right which is constituted, transmitted, modified, or extinguished by the title (mortgage), as well as the contract, partition, or judgment from which it proceeds; 4. The amount of the credit; 5. If it draws interest, the rate of it shall be expressed and the date from which it must run; 6. The time from which the payment of the capital may be demanded; 7. The nature of the real right or of the mortgaged estates; with the situation thereof, their names, number, boundaries, and other circumstances which characterize them; 8. The payment of taxes to which the mortgaged estate shall be subject to.[1]

§ 2258. *Estimated Dower.*—Art. 2027. The immovable properties or real rights which are delivered as an estimated dower shall be registered in the name of the husband in the registry of property, in the same form as any other acquisition of dominion; but it being expressed in the entry the amount of the dower of which said properties shall make a part, the sum at which they have been estimated, and the dotal mortgage which may be constituted thereon.

§ 2259. *Dotal Mortgage.*—Art. 2028. At the time of registering the title of such properties in favor of the husband, the dotal mortgage which may be constituted thereon shall be inscribed in the corresponding registry.

§ 2260. *Estimated Dower and Paraphernal Property.*—Art. 2029. When the wife shall have inscribed as her property the immovable properties which must constitute the estimated dower, or the paraphernal properties which shall be delivered to her husband, the respective quality of both will be made to appear in the registry, placing a note which shall so express it on the margin of the same inscription of property.

§ 2261. *Contents of Inscription.*—Art. 2030. If said properties shall not be inscribed in favor of the wife, they shall be inscribed in the ordinary form, expressing in the inscription their quality as dotal or paraphernal.

§ 2262. *Duty of Recorder.*—Art. 2031. Whenever the recorder shall inscribe properties as estimated dower in favor of the husband in the registry of property, he will officially make

[1]Article 2026 becomes article 1899, new code, and is amended by inserting the words "and age," in fraction 1, after the words "professions." And it is further amended by making the fourth fraction thereof read as follows: "4. The amount of the credit which is guaranteed. If the obligation guaranteed should not be of a determined sum, the interested parties shall fix in the mortgage title the estimation which they may give it."

A new article was adopted in the code of 1884 as follows: "Art. 1906. No title can be inscribed in the registry which lacks any of the requisites established in articles 1894 and 1899" (2021 and 2026, old code).

the corresponding mortgage inscription in the registry of mortgages.

§ 2263. *Insufficiency of Title.*—Art. 2032. If the title presented for the first of said inscriptions should not be sufficient to make the second, both will be suspended, taking of both the presentative annotation which shall correspond.

§ 2264. *Void Registry.*—Art. 2033. A registry made in contravention of the provisions in articles 2021, 2024, 2025, and 2026 is null.

§ 2265. *Amendments.*—Art 2034. Any other omissions may be amended at the cost of the creditor.

§ 2266. *Annotations.*—Art. 2035. All the annotations of the registry shall be inscribed and numbered one after the other, without alterations or interlineations, nor shall they occupy more space than is necessary for them to be distinguished; and they shall always be signed by the party charged with the registry.

§ 2267. *Amendments Noted.*—Art. 2036. If it should be indispensable to make some amendment or interlineation, it shall be noted at the end, and shall be authorized also with the signature of the said official charged with the registry.

§ 2268. *Effect of Registry.*—Art. 2037. The registry shall preserve its effects until it shall be canceled or declared prescribed.

§ 2269. *Foreign Countries.* — Art. 2038. The registry of mortgages contracted in foreign countries will only produce effect in the district and in California, the respective mortgage title being found duly legalized.

§ 2270. *False Registry.*—Art. 2039. He who shall falsely cause to be registered or canceled any mortgage shall be responsible for the damages and losses, and shall suffer besides the penalties which the law imposes on forgers.[1]

§ 2271. *Access to Registry.*—Art. 2040. Persons charged with offices of mortgages are under obligation to let the registries be seen by any person who asks to see them, and to issue certificates which are asked of the exemption or burden of the estates.

§ 2272. *Responsibility of Register.* — Art. 2041. Persons charged with the registry are responsible, besides the penalties which they may incur, for the damages and losses to which they may give place: 1. If they refuse or retard the reception of the

[1] Article 2039 is amended by the code of 1884, by adding thereto, "In this case the registry or cancellation shall be null."

documents which shall be presented to them for their registry; 2. If they do not make the registry in the legal form; 3. If they refuse to issue with promptness the certificates which are asked of them; 4. If they commit omissions in drawing the certificates mentioned, save if the error raise from the insufficiency or inexactness of the declarations which may not be imputable to them.

§ 2273. *Information of Refusal.*—Art. 2042. In the cases of the numbers 1 and 3 of the preceding article, the interested parties shall make it appear immediately by judicial information of two witnesses the fact of the party charged with the registry having refused him, in order that it may serve them as proof in the corresponding trial.

### Of the Cancellation of Mortgages.

§ 2274. *Cancellation*—Art. 2043. Mortgage registries may be canceled by the consent of the creditor or by a judicial decision.

§ 2275. *How Made.*—Art. 2044. The cancellation consists or the declaration made by the person charged with the office of mortgages, on the margin of the respective registry, of the mortgage being extinct with all its effects.

§ 2276. *Declaration, how Made.*—Art. 2045. This declaration may be made in virtue of the express consent, or duly proved of the creditor, or by final judgment.

§ 2277. *Minors.*—Art. 2046. The parents, as administrators of the properties of their children, the tutors of minors and persons incapacitated, any other administrators, although empowered to receive payments and give receipts, can only consent to the cancellation of the registry relative to any mortgage of the parties represented by them.

§ 2278. *Cancellation by Judgment.*—Art. 2047. The legal cancellation of the registry through the effect of a final judgment which orders it takes place: 1. When the debt being extinguished wholly or in part, the creditor unjustly refuses to give his consent for the total or partial cancellation; 2. In the case of the nullity of the registry.[1]

§ 2279. *Action.*—Art. 2048. The action to cancel or rectify the registry shall be instituted in the court of first instance, to the jurisdiction of which the office corresponds in which that registry was entered.

---

[1] Article 2047 is amended by the code of 1884, by adding thereto another fraction, thus: "3. In the other cases which the law may establish."

§ 2280. *Registry in Various Places.*—Art. 2049. If a title shall have been registered in divers offices, the action shall be instituted in the court in the jurisdiction of which the greatest part of the burdened properties may be situated; and that being regulated by the greatest amount of the direct tax.

§ 2281. *Regulations.*—Art. 2050. The organization of the offices of mortgages, the rights and obligations of the recorders, the form of the inscriptions, and other points concerning the development of the mortgage system, shall be determined by a special regulation.

### Of the Extinction of a Mortgage.

§ 2282. *Extinguishment of Mortgage.*—Art. 2051. Mortgages are extinguished: 1. By rescission, by nullity, and by the extinction of the obligations to which they serve as a guaranty: 2. By the destruction of the mortgaged estate, save the provision in article 1960; 3. By the express remission of the creditor; 4. By the declaration of the registry being prescribed, according to the provisions in articles 1988 to 1992, 2037, and 2043 to 2045; 5. By the dissolution or extinction of the right of the debtor on the mortgaged estate; 6. By the expropriation of the mortgaged estate for the cause of public utility, without prejudice to the provision in article 1961.[1]

§ 2283. *Revival of Mortgage.*—Art. 2052. A mortgage will revive if the payment should be without effect, whether because the thing may be lost through the fault of the debtor, and being still in his possession, or whether because the creditor shall lose it in virtue of eviction.

§ 2284. *Revival, when.*—Art. 2053. In the two cases of the preceding article, if the registry should have been already canceled it will only revive after the new inscription, being always saved to the creditor the right to be indemnified by the debtor for the damages and losses which shall have followed therefrom.

### Of the Graduation of Creditors.

§ 2285. *Proof of Credit.*—Art. 2059. The mortgage creditor will prove the legitimacy of his credit in a summary suit by which he will prosecute the debtor, if the latter opposes the payment, in the terms which the code of procedure establishes.[2]

[1] Article 2051 is amended by the code of 1884, by adding another fraction thereto, thus: "7. By judicial sale of the estate in conformity with article 2028" (new code).

[2] Article 2059 becomes article 1930, new code. This article also includes article 2058 of the old code, which is not cited in this work; and the part of this article 1930 which modifies

§ 2286. *Sale.*—Art. 2060. The creditor may, in virtue of an express agreement made at the time of constituting the mortgage, cause the mortgaged estate to be sold without judicial solemnities.

§ 2287. *Sale, how Made—Presented to the Judge.*—Art. 2061. The creditor, in case of the foregoing article, must present to the judge of the concourse (of creditors) the title which proves his credit, in order that it may be registered, and to proclaim the terms in which the sale of the mortgaged estate has been made, for the effects of articles 2063 and 2076.

§ 2288. *Failure to Present.*—Art. 2062. If the creditor should not present it within the period which the concourse lasts, the concourse, before the judgment of graduation is pronounced, will cause the mortgage estate to be sold, and deposit the amount of the mortgage credit and interest, preserving the rest for the provisions relative to absent ones and those which, for the case of which it treats, the code of procedure establishes.

§ 2289. *Payment of Expenses.*—Art. 2063. From the price of the whole estate mortgaged, in the following order shall be paid: 1. The expenses of the trial of which article 2059 treats, and those which are caused by the sales spoken of in articles 2060 and 2062; 2. The expenses of the preservation of the thing mortgaged;[1] 3. The debt of insurance on the same thing; 4. The taxes which may be due on it for the last five years; 5. The mortgage creditors, in conformity with their respective registry, including in the payment the interests for the last five years.

§ 2290. *Requisites to Preference.*—Art. 2064. In order that the creditors should be paid with the designated preference comprehended in the second and third cases of the foregoing article, are indispensable requisites that those of the second have been necessary, and that those of the third appear by public writing.[2]

article 2059 of the old code reads as follows: "The mortgage creditor shall prove the legitimacy of his credit in the corresponding trial. The trials to which this article refers shall be substantiated by the debtor if he opposes the payment; by the sindic if the creditors are opposed; or by both if the debtor and creditors are opposed."

[1] Article 2063 is amended by the code of 1884, so that fraction 2 thereof reads as follows: "2. The expenses of the preservation and administration of the thing mortgaged."

[2] Article 2064 is amended by the code of 1884, by inserting "authentically," in place of "by public writing."

# CHAPTER XI.

## LEASES AND RURAL PARTNERSHIP.

§ 2291. *Lease, What is.*—Art. 3068. The contract by which a person cedes to another the use or the enjoyment of a thing for a determined time, and in virtue of a certain price, is called a lease.

§ 2292. *Who can Lease.*—Art. 3069. Those who can contract may give and receive by lease.

§ 2293. *Not Being Owner may Lease.*—Art. 3070. He who may not be the owner of a thing may lease it if he has the power to make this kind of contract, whether in virtue of an express authorization from the owner, or whether by the provision of the law.

§ 2294. *Limits in Making Lease.*—Art. 3071. In the first

case of the preceding article the constitution of the lease shall be subject to the limits which the agreement shall designate; and in the second to those which the law has fixed for the husband, the tutor, the executor, and for other administrators of the properties of others.

§ 2295. *Co-proprietor.*—Art. 3072. A co-proprietor of an undivided thing can not rent it without the consent of the other co-proprietors, or of the person who shall represent them.

§ 2296. *Usufruct.*—Art. 3073. The usufruct and service may be rented with subjection to the provisions contained in titles 5 and 6 of book 2.

§ 2297. *Officers.*—Art. 3074. Magistrates, judges, and all other public employés are prohibited from taking by lease through themselves or through the interposition of a third party the properties which must be rented by virtue of a judgment, or by distribution in which they shall have intervened.

§ 2298. *Public Establishments.*—Art. 3075. The members of public establishments are prohibited from taking by lease through themselves or through the interposition of a third party the properties which may belong to said establishments.

§ 2299. *Third Parties, Who are.*—Art. 3076. The persons declared in article 2978 are third parties.

§ 2300. *Term of Lease.*—Art. 3077. A lease may be made for the time which may suit the contracting parties, save what the law establishes for determined cases.

§ 2301. *Rent.*—Art. 3078. The rent or price of the lease may consist of a sum of money, or of any other equivalent thing, provided that it be certain and determined.

§ 2302. *Writing.*—Art. 3079. A lease must be executed in writing when the rent exceeds three hundred dollars annually.[1]

§ 2303. *Public Writing.*—Art. 3080. If the estate should be rural (in the country), and the rent should exceed a thousand dollars annually, the contract shall be executed by a public writing (escritura publica).

§ 2304. *Form of Lease.*—Art. 3081. The form of a lease of national properties and of any public establishment shall be governed by administrative ordinances.

§ 2305. *Lessor's Obligations.*—Art. 3082. The lessor is obliged, although there may not be any express agreement: 1. To deliver to the lessee the estate rented with all its appurtenances, and in a condition to serve for the use agreed; and if there were no

[1] Article 3079 is amended by the code of 1884, by inserting "one" in place of "three."

express agreement for that use to which by its own nature it may be destined; 2. To preserve the thing leased in the same condition during the lease, making therefor all the necessary repairs; 3. Not to hinder nor embarrass in any manner the use of the thing leased, unless on account of indispensable and urgent repairs; 4. To guarantee the use or pacific enjoyment of the thing for all of the time of the contract; 5. To respond for the losses which the lessee may suffer through the defects or hidden vices of the thing, prior to the lease.

§ 2306. *Delivery of the Thing.*—Art. 3083. The delivery of the thing shall be made at the time agreed, and if there should be no agreement, as soon as the lessor may be required to deliver it.

§ 2307. *Form of the Thing—No Change.*—Art. 3084. The lessor can not, during the lease, change the form of the thing leased nor interfere in the legitimate use of it, save in the case designated in fraction 3 of article 3082.

§ 2308. *Chapter 5 to be Observed.*—Art. 3085. In order to fulfill the provision in fraction 4 of article 3082, the prescriptions contained in chapter 5, title 3, of this book, shall be observed. (See article 1604, and those following it.)

§ 2309. *Third Parties.*—Art. 3086. The provision in said fraction 4 does not comprehend the embarrassments which may arise from the mere acts of a third party, nor those executed in virtue of abuse by force.

§ 2310. *Observation of Chapter 6.*—Art. 3087. In order to fulfill the provision in fraction 5 of said article 3082, the provisions in chapter 6, title 18, of this book, shall be observed. (See article 3004, and those following it.)

§ 2311. *Taxes.*—Art. 3088. The lessor shall pay the taxes imposed on the estate, save an agreement to the contrary.

§ 2312. *Taxes Paid by Lessee.*—Art. 3089. When the law imposes the taxes on the lessor, requiring payment thereof from the lessee, the latter shall pay them and charge them to the rent account.

§ 2313. *Balance in Favor of Lessee.*—Art. 3090. If, on the termination of the lease, there should be a balance in favor of the lessee, the lessor must return it immediately, unless he shall have some right to exercise against the former; in this case he shall judicially deposit said balance.

§ 2314. *Privileges of Lessor.*—Art. 3091. The lessor may enjoy the privilege of preference for the payment of the rent and other charges of the lease, relative to the furniture and utensils of the lessee existing within the thing, and relative to the fruits of the respective crops, if the estate should be a rustic one, on the terms declared in articles 2088 and 2089.

§ 2315. *Obligations of Lessee.*—Art. 3092. The lessee is obliged: 1. To satisfy the rent or price at the time and in the form agreed; 2. To respond for the losses which the thing leased may suffer through his fault or negligence, or that of his family or sublessees; 3. To use the thing solely for the use agreed, or in conformity with the nature thereof.

§ 2316. *Time.*—Art. 3093. The lessee is not obliged to pay the rent except from the day on which he receives the thing leased, save an agreement to the contrary.

§ 2317. *Payment to be Prompt.*—Art. 3094. The rent must be paid at the times agreed; and in default of an agreement, at the expiration of each month, if the estate leased is in a city (urbana); and at the end of every four months, if the estate is rural.[1]

§ 2318. *Place of Payment.*—Art. 3095. The rent must be paid in the place agreed; and in default of an agreement, in conformity with the provision in article 1634.

§ 2319. *Article 3090—Lessee.*—Art. 3096. The provision in article 3090, in respect to the lessor, shall govern in his respective case the lessee.

§ 2320. *Failure to Pay Rent.*—Art. 3097. The lessee who fails at one of the times designated for the payment of the rent has no right to require the fulfillment of the contract.

§ 2321. *Money Agreed upon.*—Art. 3098. The lessee is obliged to pay the rent in the kind of money agreed; observing in this case the provisions in article 1569.

§ 2322. *Time Paid for.*—Art. 3099. The lessee is obliged to pay the rent that shall become due up to the day on which he shall deliver the thing leased.

§ 2323. *Failure to Deliver Fruit in Payment.*—Art. 3100. If the price of the lease must be paid in fruits, and the lessee shall not deliver them at the time due, he will be obliged to pay in money the greatest price which the fruits had in all the time past.

§ 2324. *Hinderances, Effect of.*—Art. 3101. If, by a fortuitous case or *vis major*, the lessee shall be totally hindered from the use of the thing leased, it shall not cause any rent while the hinderance lasts.

§ 2325. *Partial Hinderance.*—Art. 3102. If he shall be hin-

[1] Article 3094 is amended by the code of 1884, by inserting "six" in the place of "four."

dered only in part of the use of the thing, the lessee can ask for a partial reduction of the rent, according to the judgment of experts.

§ 2326. *Agreements.*—Art. 3103. The provisions in the two preceding articles shall be observed, save an agreement to the contrary.

§ 2327. *Deprivation by Eviction.*—Art. 3104. If the deprivation of the use arises from an eviction from the estate, the provisions in article 3101 shall be observed; and if the owner is a possessor in bad faith, he shall also respond for the damages and losses.

§ 2328. *Diminution of Rent not Allowed.*—Art. 3105. The lessee of a country estate has no right to require a diminution of the rent, if during the lease he shall lose wholly or in part the fruits or harvests of the estate.

§ 2329. *Acts of Lessor.*—Art. 3106. If the deprivation of the use, or the loss of the fruits or harvests arise from the direct or indirect act of the lessor, the lessee may require the fulfillment of the provisions in articles 3101, 3102, and 3152, as well as the payment for all the damages and losses.

§ 2330. *Lessee's Responsibility.*—Art. 3107. The lessee is responsible for fire, unless it arises from a fortuitous case *vis major*, or from viciousness of construction.

§ 2331. *Loss by Fire.*—Art. 3108. Neither will the lessee respond for fire which shall have been communicated from a neighboring house, provided he shall have had the vigilance which may be required of a good father of a family.

§ 2332. *Joint Responsibility.*—Art. 3109. If the lessees are various, all are jointly responsible for a fire, unless it is proved that the fire commenced in the habitation of some one of them, who in such case will be alone responsible.

§ 2333. *Proof in Favor of Lessee.*—Art. 3110. If any of the lessees prove that the fire could not have commenced in their habitation, they will be free from responsibility.

§ 2334. *Occupancy of Lessor.*—Art. 3111. If the lessor shall occupy any part of the house he will be considered as a lessee in respect to the responsibility.

§ 2335. *Damages and Losses.*—Art. 3112. The responsibility of which the five preceding articles treat comprehends not only the payment of damages and losses suffered by the proprietor, but that of those which have been caused to other persons, provided they arise directly from the fire.

§ 2336. *Duty of Lessee.*—Art. 3113. The lessee is obliged to inform the proprietor, in the shortest time possible, of all usurpation or injurious change which another may have done or openly is preparing to do on the thing rented.

§ 2337. *Repairs.*—Art. 3114. He is also obliged to inform the owner with the same urgency of all repairs.

§ 2338. *Negligence of Lessee.*—Art. 3115. The lessee in both cases will be responsible for the damages and losses which by his negligence shall be occasioned to the proprietor.

§ 2339. *Non-user to Repair.*—Art. 3116. The lessee who on account of repairs loses the total or partial use of the thing shall have the rights which articles 3101, 3102, 3150, and 3151 concede to him.

§ 2340. *No Change in the Thing Leased.*—Art. 3117. The lessee can not without the written consent from the lessor vary the form of the thing leased; and if he does it, he must, when he returns it, re-establish it in the condition in which he received it, being besides responsible for all damages and losses.

§ 2341. *Sublessee.*— Art. 3118. The lessee can not sublease the thing wholly nor in part without the consent of the lessor; if he should do it, he with the sublessee shall jointly respond for the damages and losses.

§ 2342. *Sublessee by Authority.*— Art. 3119. If the sublease shall be made in virtue of a general authorization conceded in the contract, the lessee shall be responsible to the lessor as if he himself should continue in the use or enjoyment of the thing.

§ 2343. *Rights of Lessor.*—Art. 3120. In the case of the article which precedes, the lessor shall preserve the rights which article 3091 establishes in his favor.

§ 2344. *Subrogation.*—Art. 3121. If the lessor approves expressly the special contract of the sublease, the sublessee is subrogated in all the rights and obligations of the lessee, unless by an agreement it is otherwise agreed.

§ 2345. *Taxes.*—Art. 3122. The taxes which shall be imposed on the lessee, or on his business or affairs, shall be on his own account.

§ 2346. *Sublessee.* — Art. 3123. The sublessee who does not fulfill the obligation which fraction 3 of article 3092 imposes on him, is responsible for the damages and losses, and in this case the lessor can, besides, use the right which article 3144 concedes to him.

§ 2347. *Return of Property—Condition thereof.*—Art. 3124. If the lessee has received the estate with the express description of the parts of which it is composed, he must return it at the conclusion of the lease as he received it; save what it shall have suffered or shall have been injured by time or inevitable cause.

§ 2348. *Presumption.*—Art. 3125. The law presumes that the lessee who admitted the thing leased without the description expressed in the preceding article received it in good condition, save the proof to the contrary.

§ 2349. *Lessee must Make Redelivery of Estate.*—Art. 3126. The lessee can not refuse to make the delivery of the estate after the termination of the lease, nor even under the pretext of improvements, whether these be useful or necessary.

§ 2350. *Improvements.*—Art. 3127. The lessee can not collect for the useful and voluntary improvements without anthorization from the lessor; but he may carry them away if on separating them no deterioration to the estate follows.

§ 2351. *Country Estates.*—Art. 3128. In the lease of country estates for a determined time, the lessee must, in the last agricultural year he shall remain on the ground, permit his successor to the estate or the owner in his case, to plow the lands which he shall have left vacant, and on which he can not make a new sowing, as well as the use of the edifices and other means which shall be necessary for the preparatory labors of the following agricultural year.

§ 2352. *Time for Successor.*—Art. 3129. The permission to which the preceding article refers shall not be obligatory except in the period and for the time rigorously indispensable, in conformity with the local customs, save an agreement to the contrary.

§ 2353. *Outgoing Tenant.*—Art. 3130. The lease having terminated, the outgoing tenant shall have in his turn the right to use the lands and edifices for the time absolutely indispensable for the gathering and advantge of the hanging fruits on the termination of the contract.

§ 2354. *Joint Parties to Lease.*—Art. 3131. If there should be two or more lessors or lessees, the provisions in chapter 5, title 2, of this book, shall be observed.

§ 2355. *Partnerships.*—Art. 3132. A lease for a partnership in lands and cattle shall be governed by the provisions relative to the contract of partnership.

## Of the Manner of Terminating Leases.

§ 2356. *Termination of Leases.*—Art. 3134. A lease may be terminated: 1. By the time fixed in the contract having been fulfilled or the object satisfied for which the thing was leased; 2. By an express agreement; 3. By being null; 4. By rescision.

§ 2357. *Time Fixed.*—Art. 3135. If the lease has been fixed for a designated time, it shall be concluded on the day determined without the necessity of a dismission. If the time has been designated, the provisions in the following chapter shall be observed.

§ 2358. *Continuation of Lessee.*—Art. 3136. If after the lease shall have terminated the lessee continues without opposition in the enjoyment and use of the estate, and this is a rustic one, the contract will be considered renewed for another working year.

§ 2359. *Working Year.*—Art. 3137. The space of time necessary, according to the circumstances of the land and the conditions of the sowing, in order to harvest the fruits, whether it be less or greater than the civil year, is called a working year.

§ 2360. *Differences—Experts.*—Art. 3138. The differences which may arise relative to the provisions in the preceding article shall be decided by experts.[1]

§ 2361. *City Leases.*—Art. 3139. In the case of article 3136, if the estate should be in a city (urban) the lease will not be held as reserved; but the lessee must pay the rent which corresponds to the time which shall exceed that of the contract, according to what he was paying.

§ 2362. *Security by Third Party.*—Art. 3140. In the cases of which articles 3136 and 3139 speak, the obligations executed by a third party for the security of the lease shall cease, save an agreement to the contrary.

§ 2363. *Fulfillment of Agreement.*—Art. 3141. In the case of fraction 2 of article 3134, the agreement shall be fulfilled so far as it does not injure the rights of third parties.

§ 2363 *a.* *Nullity.*—Art. 3142. In the cases of nullity, the provisions in chapter 2, title 5, of this book, shall be observed.

§ 2364. *Rescissions.*—Art. 3143. In the cases of rescission, the provisions in chapter 1, title 5, of this book, shall be observed.

§ 2364 *a.* *Lessor may Require a Rescission.*—Art. 3144. The lessor may require a rescission of the contract: 1. For a default of the payment of the rent in the terms provided in articles 3094 and 3097; 2. For using the thing in contravention to the provisions in fraction 3 of article 3092; 3. For the subletting of the thing in conformity with the provisions in article 3118.

---

[1] Articles 3137 and 3138 are suppressed in the code of 1884.

§ 2365. *Fault of Lessee.*—Art. 3145. Whenever the contract shall be rescinded through the fault of the lessee, he will be under an obligation to pay the price of the lease for all the time which shall run until another can be made, besides the damages and losses which shall have been caused to the proprietor.

§ 2366. *Lessor can not Rescind, when.*—Art. 3146. The lessor can not rescind the contract, although he may allege that he wishes or needs the thing leased for his own use, unless the contrary shall have been agreed.

§ 2367. *Lessee may Rescind, when.*—Art. 3147. If the owner shall not deliver the thing on the terms provided in article 3083, the lessee can rescind the contract, and sue the lessor for the damages and losses.

§ 2368. *Repairs.*—Art. 3148. If the lessor shall not comply with making the necessary repairs for the use to which the thing is destined, it shall remain at the election of the lessee to rescind the lease or appear before the judge to compel the fulfillment of the obligation by the lessor.

§ 2369. *Damages.*—Art. 3149. The judge, according to the circumstances of the case, shall decide upon the payment of the damages and losses which shall be caused to the lessee for want of convenience in the repairs.

§ 2370. *Total Loss of Use.*—Art. 3150. In the cases of article 3116, the lessee can rescind the contract when the loss of the use shall be total; and even when it shall be partial, if the repairing shall last more than two months.

§ 2371. *Acquiescence by Lessee.*—Art. 3151. If the lessee should not use the right which the preceding article concedes to him to rescind the contract, the repairing being made, he shall continue in the use of the thing, paying the same rent until the time of the lease shall terminate.

§ 2372. *Lessee's Right to Ask a Rescission.*—Art. 3152. The lessee may ask for the rescission of the contract in the case of article 3106.

§ 2373. *Vis Major.*—Art. 3153. If the thing should be totally destroyed by a fortuitous case or *vis major*, the lease shall be rescinded, save an agreement to the contrary.

§ 2374. *Destruction of the Thing.*—Art. 3154. If the destruction of the thing should be partial, the provisions in article 3102 shall be observed, unless the lessor or the lessee should prefer to rescind the contract.

§ 2375. *Subletting.*—Art. 3155. If the lessor, without a

founded reason, shall cppose the subletting which the lessee rightly claims, the latter can rescind the contract.

§ 2376. *Death.*—Art. 3156. The contract of lease shall not be rescinded by the death of the lessor nor of the lessee, save an agreement of a contrary import.

§ 2377. *Transmission by Universal Title.*—Art. 3157. Neither shall the lease be rescinded by the transmission of the thing by a universal title, unless it is in a case of an agreement to the contrary.

§ 2378. *Singular Title.*—Art. 3158. When the transmission shall be a singular title, as a donation or sale, the lease shall subsist in the terms of the contract, save an agreement to the contrary.

§ 2379. *Resale.*—Art. 3159. The lease which he who purchased with an agreement of resale shall make for a term which shall exceed that designated for the exercise of the retraction, as soon as this shall take place shall remain rescinded in full right; the lessee preserving his rights against the lessor.

§ 2380. *Public Utility.*—Art. 3160. If the transmission should be made on account of public utility, the contract shall be rescinded; but the lessor and the lessee must be indemnified by the expropriator in conformity with the rules which the constitutional law establishes.

§ 2381. *Usufructuary.*—Art. 3161. If the usufructuary did not manifest his quality as such on making the lease, and the property having been consolidated with the usufruct, the proprietor may require the vacancy of the estate; the lessee having the right to sue the lessor for the indemnification of damages and losses.

§ 2382. *Rural and City Estates.*—Art. 3162. In the case of the preceding article, what is provided in articles 3136, 3137, and 3138 shall be observed, if the estate should be a rural one; and if it should be an urban estate, what article 3170 provides.

§ 2383. *Judicial Execution.*—Art. 3163. If the transmission should take place by a judicial execution, the provisions in the two following articles shall be observed.[1]

---

[1] Article 3163 is article 3029 of the new code, and is amended to read as follows: "If the transmission should take place by a judicial execution, the provisions in article 3024 (3158), unless the contract shall appear celebrated within the sixty days prior to the sequestration of the estate, in which case the lessee can be turned out immediately. In respect to the payment of the rent, the following rules shall govern: 1. The lessee is obliged to pay to the new proprietor the rent stipulated in the contract, from the date on which shall have been executed the corresponding title of property, even when he alleges that he has paid the first proprietor; 2. The rent which shall have been advanced to the first proprietor is ex-

§ 2384. *Urban Estate.*—Art. 3164. If the estate leased should be an urban one, and there should lack for the termination of the lease a year or more, that time shall be reduced to six months from the public sale or adjudication; in any other case, the contract shall be observed.

§ 2385. *Rural Estate.*—Art. 3165. If the estate should be a rural one, the lessee can not be dismissed before the working year shall have terminated, pending at the time of the public sale or adjudication.

§ 2386. *Expropriation.*—Art. 3166. In the cases of expropriation and of judicial execution, the provisions in articles 3128, 3129, and 3130 shall be observed.

§ 2387. *Fraud.*—Art. 3167. Whenever a lease shall have been made in fraud of creditors, the provisions in chapter 3, title 5, of this book, shall be observed.

SPECIAL PROVISIONS RESPECTING LEASES FOR AN INDETERMINATE TIME.

§ 2388. *Term Three Years.*—Art. 3168. All leases, whether of rural or urban estates, which have not been made for a determined time, shall last three years, at the expiration of which they shall terminate, without the necessity of a dismissal.[1]

Art. 3169. The three years shall be obligatory only for the lessor.

§ 2389. *Expiration of Term.*—Art. 3170. If, the term of three years having terminated, the parties should not again agree to continue the contract, and the estate should be urban, in order to vacate the premises the tenant shall have the term of thirty days, during which he will be obliged to put up notices and show the interior of the house to those who shall solicit to see it.[2]

§ 2390. *Third Year.*—Art. 3171. If the estate leased should

---

cepted from the provisions in the prior fraction, when the advancement shall appear expressly stipulated in the contract; 3. The lessee who, having made advancements in the rent, shall be obligated for the second payment, in conformity with fraction 1, has a right to require from the first proprietor the return of the amounts advanced."

[1] Article 3168 becomes article 3032 (new code) and reads as follows: "All leases, whether of urban or rustic estates, which may not have been celebrated for a time expressly fixed, shall conclude at the will of any of the contracting parties, by a previous judicial notification to the other party, made two months in advance if the estate is urban, and one year if it is rustic."

[2] Article 3170 is article 3033, of the new code, and reads as follows: "The notification to which the prior article refers being made, the lessee of an urban estate is obliged to put notices and to show the interior of the house to those who may wish to see it. In respect to the rustic estates, the provisions in articles 2996 and 2997 (3128 and 3129) shall be observed."

be rural, the lessee must, before gathering the crop of the third year, go to the lessor to extend the contract; and if he does not do it, and the lessor shall require an increase of rent or a vacation of the premises, the lessee shall enjoy the right which article 3130 concedes to him; and he shall never have the right to ask for an indemnification for the expenses which he shall have made for the new sowing.

§ 2391. *Two First Years.*—Art. 3172. The lessee of a rural estate for an indeterminate time, who may not wish to continue the lease, must within the two first years give notice to the lessor sixty days before the agricultural year shall terminate; and if he should not do it, he will be obliged to sustain the contract for the following agricultural year.

§ 2392. *Continuance of Lessee.*—Art. 3173. If the three years obligatory on the lessor of a rural estate shall have passed, and he makes no renewal of the contract, and the lessee continues on the premises, the contract will be considered as extended for another agricultural year.

### Of Rural Partnership (Aparceria).

§ 2393. *Rural Partnership.*—Art. 2449. Rural partnership comprehends agricultural partnership, and that of cattle or beasts of pasture.

§ 2394. *Agricultural Partnership.*—Art. 2450. Agricultural partnership takes place when any person gives another a rustic estate or part of it in order to cultivate it, ceding him a part of the fruits to which they may agree, or that may be in conformity with the custom of the place.

§ 2395. *Death.*—Art. 2451. If during the time of the contract any one of the contracting parties should die, neither he who survives nor the heirs of the deceased shall be obliged to continue in the partnership, save an agreement to the contrary.

§ 2396. *Death—Prepared Ground.*—Art. 2452. If at the time of the death of the proprietor the workman shall have prepared the ground for sowing, pruned the trees, or executed any other necessary work for cultivation, the contract shall subsist for that year, if by common consent it is not agreed to rescind the partnership.

§ 2397. *Workmen.*—Art. 2453. The workmen who may have estates on equal shares can not harvest the crops or in general gather the fruits in which they ought to have a part, without notice to the proprietor or to whoever takes his place, he being in the place or within the jurisdiction to which the land belongs.

§ 2398. *Absence of Proprietor.*—Art. 2454. If neither in the place nor within the jurisdiction the proprietor or his attorney in fact can be found, the workman can cause to be measured, counted, or weighed the fruits in the presence of witnesses above all exceptions.

§ 2399. *Failure to Act by the Workmen.*—Art. 2455. If he should not act in this manner, he shall pay double what he ought to pay; the products being valued by experts appointed, one by each party.

§ 2400. *Non-cultivation.*—Art. 2456. The partner who leaves the land without cultivation, or who does not cultivate it according to agreement, or at least in the accustomed form, will be responsible for the damages and losses which he shall cause.

§ 2401. *Copartners.*—Art. 2457. The provisions of the articles relative to the rights and obligations of a lessor and lessee are applicable to the copartners.

§ 2402. *Cattle.*—Art. 2458. A partnership in cattle takes place when one or more persons give to another or others certain animals, or a certain number of them, in order to breed them, pasture and care for them, with the object of dividing the gain and fruits in a determined proportion.

§ 2403. *Conditions of Contract.*—Art. 2459. The conditions of this contract shall be regulated by the will of the interested parties; but for want of an agreement, the general custom of the place shall be observed, save the following provisions:

§ 2404. *Copartners in Cattle.*—Art. 2460. The copartner in cattle is obliged to employ in the keeping and treatment of the animals the care which he ordinarily employs in his own things; and if he should not do so, he will be responsible for the damages and losses to which he shall give place.

§ 2405. *Guaranty by Proprietor.*—Art. 2461. The proprietor is obliged to guarantee to his copartner the possession and use of the cattle, and to substitute by others, in case of eviction, the animals lost; otherwise he is responsible for the damages and losses to which he shall give place through the want of the fulfillment of the contract.

§ 2406. *Fortuitous Case—Loss.*—Art. 2462. If the animals shall perish by a fortuitous case, the loss shall be on account of the proprietor.

§ 2407. *Dead Animals.*—Art. 2463. The benefits which can

be taken from the remains of dead animals shall belong to the proprietor, and the copartner shall be responsible for it.

§ 2408. *Agreement as to Losses.*—Art. 2464. An agreement that all the losses which may be the result by a fortuitous case shall be to the account of the working copartner in cattle (mediero) shall be null.

§ 2409. *Consent of Parties for Sales.*—Art. 2465. The copartner in cattle can not dispose of any head nor of the young without the consent of the proprietor, nor the latter without that of the former.

§ 2410. *Notice.*—Art. 2466. The copartner in sheep can not make the shearing without giving notice to the proprietor, and if he omits to do so, he shall pay double the value of the part which might belong to him, taxed by experts.

§ 2411. *Term of Partnership.*—Art. 2467. The partnership in cattle shall last the time agreed upon, and for want of an agreement, the time which shall be the custom in the place; it not being obligatory in any case to last less than a year.[1]

§ 2412. *Rescission, when.*—Art. 2468. The proprietor can ask the rescission of the contract, if the copartner shall not fulfill his obligations.

§ 2413. *Creditors of Proprietor.*—Art. 2469. The creditors of the proprietor can only seize the rights which belong to the latter; the obligations contracted with the copartner being protected, unless the latter shall have proceeded in bad faith.

§ 2414. *Creditors of Copartners.*—Art. 2470. The creditors of the copartner can not seize the head of cattle, but only the rights which the copartner shall have acquired or may acquire in virtue of the contract.

§ 2415. *Sales Unduly Made.*—Art. 2471. The proprietor whose cattle are unduly sold by the copartner has a right to recover them, even when they have been sold at public auction; but he to whom the right belongs will preserve it without diminution against the copartner, in order to collect from him the damages and losses occasioned by the want of notice.

§ 2416. *Presumption of Extension.*—Art. 2472. If the proprietor does not require his part of the profits within sixty days after the completion of the time of the contract, it will be understood as extended for another year.

§ 2417. *Right of Preference.*—Art. 2473. In case of a sale of the animals before the partnership terminates, the partners shall enjoy the right of preference (tanto).

---

[1]Article 2467 is amended by the code of 1884, by suppressing the words "it not being obligatory in any case to last less than a year."

# CHAPTER XII.

## CONTRACTS IN GENERAL.

§ 2418. Contract, What is.
§ 2419. Kinds of.
§ 2420. Unilateral.
§ 2421. Onerous.
§ 2422. Consent.
§ 2423. Persons Obligated.
§ 2424. Validity.
§ 2425. Conditions.
§ 2426. Oath.
§ 2427. Capable, Who.
§ 2428. By Attorney.
§ 2429. Authority to Contract
§ 2430. Contracts, Null, What.
§ 2431. Consent must be Clear.
§ 2432. Consent, how Shown.
§ 2433. Signs.
§ 2434. Acceptance.
§ 2435. Parties Being Present.
§ 2436. Parties Absent.
§ 2437. No Time Being Fixed.
§ 2438. Proponent.
§ 2439. Acceptance.
§ 2440. New Proposition.
§ 2441. Death.
§ 2442. Void Contracts.
§ 2443. Fraud.
§ 2444. Intimidation.
§ 2445. Intimidation, What is.
§ 2446. Compulsion.
§ 2447. Vague Expressions.
§ 2448. Nullities of the Future.
§ 2449. Ratification.
§ 2450. Impossible Contracts.
§ 2451. Physically Impossible, What.
§ 2452. Legal Impossibility, What.
§ 2453. Renouncements must be Clear.
§ 2454. Renouncements Limited.
§ 2455. Renouncements Prohibited.
§ 2456. Intention of Parties Controls.
§ 2457. Penalty Limited.
§ 2458. Nullity.
§ 2459. Penal Clause.
§ 2460. Modification of Penalty.

§ 2461. Equitable Construction.
§ 2462. Creditors.
§ 2463. Defense to Obligation.
§ 2464. Joint Obligations.
§ 2465. Co-heirs.
§ 2466. Indemnification.
§ 2467. Joint Obligations—Partial Payment.
§ 2468. Form of Contract.
§ 2469. Indefiniteness.
§ 2470. Rules of Construction.
§ 2471. Personal Obligations.
§ 2472. Real Obligations.
§ 2473. Pure Obligations.
§ 2474. Conditional.
§ 2475. Conditional Past Acts.
§ 2476. Suspensive Conditions.
§ 2477. Dissolvable.
§ 2478. Casual.
§ 2479. Potestative.
§ 2480. Fulfillment.
§ 2481. Fault of Obligated Party.
§ 2482. Succession.
§ 2483. Creditors.
§ 2484. Debtor.
§ 2485. Suspensive Condition.
§ 2486. Loss.
§ 2487. Deterioration.
§ 2488. Fault of Debtor.
§ 2489. Improvements.
§ 2490. Debtor, Usufructuary.
§ 2491. Restoration.
§ 2492. Restitution.
§ 2493. Party that Restores.
§ 2494. Implication.
§ 2495. Injured Party.
§ 2496. Failure of Payment.
§ 2497. Movable Property.
§ 2498. Rescission.
§ 2499. Void Conditions.
§ 2500. Obligation on Time, What is.
§ 2501. Certain Day.
§ 2502. Uncertainty.
§ 2503. Time.
§ 2504. Payment in Advance.
§ 2505. Presumption.
§ 2506. Insolvents.
§ 2507. Joint Debtors.
§ 2508. Joint Obligations.
§ 2509. Alternate Obligations.
§ 2510. Election.
§ 2511. What must be Delivered.

§ 2512. Election by Debtor.
§ 2513. Fault of Debtor.
§ 2514. Fortuitous Case.
§ 2515. Election by Creditor.
§ 2516. Loss without Fault of Debtor.
§ 2517. Loss by Fault of Debtor.
§ 2518. Distinction in Losses.
§ 2519. Election by Debtor—Loss.
§ 2520. Election by Creditor—Loss.
§ 2521. Loss of the Two Things.
§ 2522. Election by Debtor—Designation of Price.
§ 2523. Creditor's Obligation.
§ 2524. Obligation of Acts.
§ 2525. Performance by Debtor.
§ 2526. Right of Election.
§ 2527. Refusal.
§ 2528. Loss by Fault of Debtor.
§ 2529. Loss without Fault of Debtor.
§ 2530. Right of Debtor.
§ 2531. Fault of Creditor.
§ 2532. Construction of Fault.
§ 2533. Must be Executed.
§ 2534. Succession.
§ 2535. Judicial Enforcement.
§ 2536. What a Contract may be.
§ 2537. Responsibility.
§ 2538. Interpolation.
§ 2539. Creditor.
§ 2540. Right of Creditor.
§ 2541. Further Right of Creditor.
§ 2542. Damages for Violation.
§ 2543. Obligation of Donor.
§ 2544. Perfection—Risk.
§ 2545. Risk.
§ 2546. Performance.
§ 2547. Payment.
§ 2548. Reciprocal Obligations.
§ 2549. Giving Things.
§ 2550. Delivery.
§ 2551. When Transferred.
§ 2552. Quality.
§ 2553. Fault of Debtor.
§ 2554. Fortuitous Case—Agreement.
§ 2555. Fortuitous Case without Agreement.
§ 2556. Redemption.
§ 2557. Crime.
§ 2558. Lost Thing.
§ 2559. Proof.
§ 2560. Fault or Negligence.
§ 2561. Discretion of the Judge.
§ 2562. Reservations.

### Preliminary Provisions.

§ 2418. *Contract, What is.*— Art. 1388. A contract is an agreement by which two or more persons transfer some right to each other, or contract some obligation.

§ 2419. *Kinds of.*—Art. 1389. A contract may be unilateral or bilateral, onerous or gratuitous.

§ 2420. *Unilateral.*—Art. 1390. A contract is unilateral in which only one of the parties obligates himself; that is bilateral in which all the contracting parties are obligated.

§ 2421. *Onerous.*—Art. 1391. A contract is onerous in which reciprocal benefits and burdens are stipulated; and that is gratuitous in which the benefit is solely for one of the parties.

§ 2422. *Consent.*—Art. 1392. Contracts are perfected by the mere consent; and from then they obligate not only the fulfillment of what is expressly agreed, but also all the consequences which, according to its nature, are in conformity with good faith, with use, and with the law.[1]

§ 2423. *Persons Obligated.*—Art. 1393. Contracts only obligate the persons who execute them.

§ 2424. *Validity.*—Art. 1394. The validity and the fulfillment of contracts can not be left to the discretion of one of the contracting parties, with the exception of the cases expressly designated in the law.

§ 2425. *Conditions.*—Art. 1395. In order that a contract may be valid, it must have the following conditions: 1. Capacity of the contracting parties; 2. Mutual consent; 3. A lawful object.[2] Art. 1396. That which is not contrary to the law or good customs is lawful.

§ 2426. *Oath.*—Art. 1397. An oath shall produce no legal effect in contracts; and never in virtue of it, nor of a promise which may be substituted for it, can an obligation be confirmed if there should be no other legal cause which supports it.

---

[1] Article 1392 is amended by the code of 1884, and reads as follows: "Art. 1276. Contracts legally celebrated obligate not only the fulfillment of what is expressly agreed, but also all the consequences which, according to its nature, are in conformity with good faith, with use, and with the law."

[2] Article 1395 is amended by the code of 1884, and reads as follows: "Art. 1279. In order that a contract may be valid, it must have the following conditions: 1. Capacity of the contracting parties; 2. Mutual consent; 3. That the subject-matter of the contract shall be lawful; 4. That it shall have been celebrated with the external formalities which the law requires."

OF THE CAPACITY OF CONTRACTORS.

§ 2427. *Capable, Who.*—Art. 1398. All persons not excepted by the law are capable of contracting.

§ 2428. *By Attorney.*—Art. 1399. He who is capable of contracting may do so by himself or by the means of another legally authorized.

§ 2429. *Authority to Contract.*—Art. 1400. No one can contract in the name of another without being authorized by him or by the law.

§ 2430. *Contracts Null, What.*—Art. 1401. Contracts made in the name of another by him who is not his legitimate representative shall be null, unless the person in whose name they were made shall ratify them before they shall be retracted by the other.[1]

OF MUTUAL CONSENT.

§ 2431. *Consent.*—Art. 1402. The consent of those who contract must be clearly shown.

§ 2432. *Consent, how Shown.*—Art. 1403. The manifestation of consent must be made by word, by writing, or by acts by which it is necessarily presumed.

§ 2433. *Signs.*—Art. 1404. He only who shall have a physical impossibility to speak or write can express his consent by other unquestionable signs.

§ 2434. *Acceptance.*—Art. 1405. As soon as a proposition shall be accepted, the contract remains perfect, except in those cases in which the law requires some other formality.

§ 2435. *Parties Being Present.*—Art. 1406. If the contracting parties should be present, the acceptation shall be made at the time of the proposition, save an express contract to the contrary.

§ 2436. *Parties Absent.*—Art. 1407. If the contracting parties should not be present, the acceptation shall be made within the time fixed by the proponent.

§ 2437. *No Time being Fixed.*—Art. 1408. When no time shall have been fixed, the proposition shall not be considered accepted, if the other party does not respond within three days, besides the necessary time for the going and coming of the regular public mail, or of that time which shall be judged sufficient, there not being any public mail, according to the distances and facility or difficulty of communications.

§ 2438. *Proponent.*—Art. 1409. The proponent is obliged to

---

[1] Article 1401 is amended by the code of 1884, by adding thereto: "The ratification must be made with the same formalities which the law requires for the contract."

maintain his proposition, until he receives an answer from the other party, in the terms designated in articles 1406, 1407, and 1408. Otherwise he is responsible for the damages and losses which may result from his retraction.

§ 2439. *Acceptance.*—Art. 1410. The obligation which the preceding article imposes on the proponent shall only remain when the acceptation is plain and full; if it imports a modification of the proposition it shall be considered as a new proposition, and the proponent remains free in respect to the first, and is obliged only to answer in respect to the new one, in conformity with said articles.

§ 2440. *New Proposition.*—Art. 1411. The new proposition not being answered, the provisions of the two preceding articles shall be observed.

§ 2441. *Death.*—Art. 1412. If at the time of the acceptation the proponent shall have died, without the acceptor knowing of his death, the heirs of the former shall be obliged to sustain the contract.

§ 2442. *Void Contracts.*—Art. 1413. A contract made through error is null: 1. If the error is common to both contracting parties, whatever may be the cause from which it proceeds; 2. If the error is relative to the reason or object of the contract, the deceived party declaring or proving by the circumstances of the said obligation, equally known to the other party, that for the supposed false part, which the contract assigned, and for no other cause, was the contract made; 3. If the error proceeds from the fraud or bad faith of one of the contracting parties; 4. If the error proceeds from the fraud of a third party who may have an interest in the contract; in this case, the contracting parties also have an action against the third party.[1]

[1] Article 1413 is amended by the code of 1884, and reads as follows: "Art. 1296. An error of law does not annul a contract. A material error of arithmetic only gives place to a reparation thereof. An error of fact annuls a contract: 1. If the error is common to both contracting parties, whatever may be the cause from which it proceeds; 2. If the error is relative to the reason or object of the contract, declared in the act of celebration or proved by the circumstances of the said obligation, equally known to the other party, that for the supposed false part which the contract assigned, and for no other cause, was the contract made." (The third and fourth fractions are not amended.)

Article 1322 is a new article of the code of 1884, and reads as follows: "Art. 1322. Every contract on time for more than six months, and the interest of which exceeds two hundred dollars, requires, in order to be valid, to appear, indispensable in writing, whether by executing said contract in a private document, or whether by executing a receipt or other written proof, save the cases comprehended in special provisions. If the performance of the contract should be periodical, its quantity will be regulated by the amount of one annual payment. When the person who must sign a document does not know how to write, some other person shall sign it, at his request, before two witnesses."

§ 2443. *Fraud.*—Art. 1414. By fraud (dolo) in contracts is understood any suggestion or artifice which is employed in order to induce error, or to maintain any one of the contracting parties in it; and by bad faith, a dissimulation of the error of one of the contracting parties, once known.

§ 2444. *Intimidation.*—Art. 1415. A contract made by intimidation is null, whether this proceeds from any of the contracting parties, or from a third party.

§ 2445. *Intimidation, What is.*—Art. 1416. There is intimidation when physical force or threats are employed which import a danger of the loss of life, honor, liberty, health, or a considerable part of the property of him who contracts, of his partner in marriage (cónyuge), or of his ascendants or descendants.

§ 2446. *Compulsion.*—Art. 1417. When there is only an abuse of paternal authority, marital or other similar, it is said that there is compulsion; but this does not annul the contract.

§ 2447. *Vague Expressions.*—Art. 1418. The vague and general considerations which the contracting parties shall express relative to the benefits and losses which may naturally result from the making or not making of a contract, and which do not import deception or any threat to any of the parties, shall not be taken into consideration in judging of the fraud or force.

§ 2448. *Nullities of the Future.*—Art. 1419. It is not lawful to renounce for the future the nullity which may result from fraud or from intimidation.

§ 2449. *Ratification.*—Art. 1420. If, the intimidation having ceased, or the fraud being known, he who suffered the violence or lost by the deception ratifies the contract, he can not claim in the future for such viciousness.

Of the Object of Contracts.

§ 2450. *Impossible Contracts.*—Art. 1421. A contract the object of which is physically and legally impossible is null.

§ 2451. *Physically Impossible, What.*—Art. 1422. Only that shall be considered physically impossible in contracts which may be so in an absolute manner by reason of the thing, or when the act can not be executed by the person obligated, nor by any other in place thereof.

§ 2452. *Legally Impossible, What.*—Art. 1423. Are legally impossible: 1. Things which are out of commerce by nature, or by the disposition of the law; 2. Things or acts which can not be reduced to a value capable of being demanded; 3.

Things the species of which is not nor can not be determined; 4. Unlawful acts.

### Of the Renouncements and Clauses Which may Contain Contracts.

§ 2453. *Renouncements must be Clear.*—Art. 1424. The renouncements which contracting parties may legally make shall produce no effect, if they are not expressed in clear and precise terms, and by citing the law the benefit of which is renounced.

§ 2454. *Renunciations Limited.*—Art. 1425. Renunciations legally made can not be extended to other cases than those which are comprehended in the provision renounced.

§ 2455. *Prohibited Renunciations.*—Art. 1426. A renunciation which shall be prohibited by law shall be held as not made.

§ 2456. *Intention of Parties Control.*—Art. 1427. The contracting parties may place the clauses which they may think proper; but those which refer to the essential requisites of the contract, or shall be a consequence of their ordinary nature, shall be considered as placed although not expressed; unless the second shall be renounced in the cases and terms permitted by the law.

§ 2457. *Penalty Limited.*—Art. 1428. The contracting parties may stipulate certain service (prestacion), as a penalty for the non-fulfillment of the contract. In this case there shall be no room for claims for damages or losses.

§ .458. *Nullity.*—Art. 1429. The nullity of a contract imports that of a penal clause; but the nullity of the latter does not import that of the former.

§ 2459. *Penal Clause.*—Art. 1430. The penal clause can not exceed in value nor in amount the principal obligation.

§ 2460. *Modification of Penalty.*—Art. 1431. If the obligation should be complied with in part, the penalty shall be modified in the same proportion.

§ 2461. *Equitable Construction.*—Art. 1432. If the modification should not be exactly in proportion, the judge shall reduce the penalty in an equitable manner, taking into account the nature and other circumstances of the obligation.

§ 2462. *Creditors.*—Art. 1433. The creditor may require the fulfillment of the obligation or that of the penalty, but not both, save an agreement to the contrary.

§ 2463. *Defense to Obligation.*—Art. 1434. The penalty can not be made effective, when the party obligated to it has not been able to fulfill on account of the act of the creditor, a fortuitous case, or insuperable force.

§ 2464. *Joint Obligations.*—Art. 1435. In joint obligations with a penal clause, the contravention of one of the heirs of the debtor will be sufficient for the penalty to be incurred.

§ 2465. *Co-heirs.*—Art. 1436. The creditor can require the penalty of the contravenor in every case, or of any of the co-heirs, provided that the latter after being notified of the default of the party required, they do not redeem the penalty by complying with the obligation.

§ 2466. *Indemnification.*—Art. 1437. The contravenor must indemnify him who shall have paid.

§ 2467. *Joint Obligations—Partial Payment.*—Art. 1438. If the obligation should not be joint, the provisions in the three preceding articles shall govern; but if the creditor admitted a partial payment of the debt or obligation on the part of any of the co-heirs, he must discount the penalty, even when he shall require this from the contravenor.

### Of the External Form of Contracts.

§ 2468. *Form of Contract.*—Art. 1439. The validity of contracts does not depend upon any external formality, unless in those cases in which the law expressly provides otherwise.[1]

### Of the Interpretation of Contracts.

§ 2469. *Indefiniteness.*—Art. 1440. When by the terms in which a contract is conceived the intention or will of the contracting parties relative to the principal object of the obligation can not be understood, it is null.

§ 2470. *Rules of Construction.* — Art. 1441. If the doubt relates to accidental circumstances of the contract, and can not be solved by the terms thereof, the following rules shall be observed: 1. If the contract should be gratuitous, the doubt will be solved in favor of the least transmission of right or interests;[2] 2. If the contract should be onerous, the doubt shall be solved in favor of the greatest reciprocity of interests.

### Of the Different Kinds of Contracts.

§ 2471. *Personal Obligations.*—Art. 1442. A personal obligation is that which only binds the person who contracts it and his heirs.

---

[1] Article 1439 is amended by the code of 1884, and reads as follows: "Art. 1323. No contract requires for its validity more external formalities than those expressly provided by law."

[2] Fraction 1 of article 1441 is amended by the code of 1884, and reads: "If the circumstances, although accidental, by the nature of the contract, reveal that without them the consent of any of the parties would not have been given, it will be with the provisions in the preceding article."

§ 2472. *Real Obligations.*—Art. 1443. A real obligation is that which affects the thing and works against any possessor of the same.

### Of Pure and Conditional Obligations.

§ 2473. *Pure Obligation.*—Art. 1444. An obligation is pure when its fulfillment does not depend upon any condition.

§ 2474. *Conditional.*—Art. 1445. An obligation is conditional when it depends upon a future or uncertain event, whether it be by suspending it until the latter shall exist, or whether it be by dissolving it, accordingly as the foreseen event shall become or not become verified.

§ 2475. *Condition—Past Acts.*—Art. 1446. A conditional obligation may also be constituted by making it depend on an act passed, but unknown to the parties.

§ 2476. *Suspensive Condition.*—Art. 1447. The condition is suspensive when it suspends the fulfillment of the obligation until the event shall or shall not be verified.

§ 2477. *Dissolvable.*—Art. 1448. It is dissolvable when, being complied with, it produces the dissolution of the obligation, and replaces the things in the state which they had before that was executed.

§ 2478. *Casual.*—Art. 1449. The condition is casual when it depends entirely upon chance or of the will of a third party not interested in the contract.

§ 2479. *Potestative.*—Art. 1450. It is potestative or voluntary when it depends purely upon the will of one of the parties; and mixed when it depends jointly on an event foreign to the will of the parties and of the will of one of them.

§ 2480. *Fulfillment.*—Art. 1451. If the fulfillment of the contract depends upon any condition, positive or negative, on an act or time, which being complied with, the contract will be held as perfected from the day of its celebration; but as soon as there is a certainty that the condition can not be realized, it will be held as not verified.

§ 2481. *Fault of Obligated Party.*—Art. 1452. The condition will be held as fulfilled which fails to be realized by the voluntary act of the obligated party, unless the act may have been inculpable.

§ 2482. *Succession.*—Art. 1453. The rights and the obligations of the contracting parties who shall die before the fulfillment of the condition shall pass to their heirs.

§ 2483. *Creditors.*—Art. 1454. The creditors whose contracts shall depend upon any condition can, even before that is fulfilled, exercise the necessary lawful acts for the preservation of their rights.

§ 2484. *Debtor.*—Art. 1455. The debtor may demand what he in the same time shall have paid.

§ 2485. *Suspensive Condition.*—Art. 1456. When the obligations shall have been contracted under a suspensive condition, and pending this the things which were the object of the contract should be lost, deteriorated, or either improved, the following provisions shall be observed:

§ 2486. *Loss.*—Art. 1457. If the thing was lost through the fault of the debtor, he shall be obligated for the compensation for damages and losses.

§ 2487. *Deterioration.*—Art. 1458. When the thing shall be deteriorated without the fault of the debtor, the diminution is on account of the creditor.[1]

§ 2488. *Fault of Debtor.*—Art. 1459. It being deteriorated through the fault of the debtor, the creditor can choose between the indemnification for damages and losses, and the rescission of the contract.

§ 2489. *Improvements.*—Art. 1460. If the thing should be improved by its nature or by time, the improvements are ceded in favor of the creditor.

§ 2490. *Debtor, Usufructuary.*—Art. 1461. If it shall be improved at the expense of the debtor, he will have no other right than that conceded to the usufructuary in article 990.

§ 2491. *Restoration.*—Art. 1462. When the obligation shall have been contracted under a dissolvable condition, this being fulfilled, what shall have been received in virtue of the contract ought to be restored.

§ 2492. *Restitution.*—Art. 1463. The restitution shall be made besides with the fruits and interests by that person who shall have failed in the fulfillment of his obligation.

§ 2493. *Party that Restores.*—Art. 1464. In the case of the loss, deterioration, or improvement of the restorable thing, the provisions which in respect to the debtor the preceding articles contain shall be applied to him who ought to make the restitution.

§ 2494. *Implication.*—Art. 1465. The dissolvable condition is always implied in bilateral contracts, for the case in which one of the contracting parties should not fulfill his obligation.

[1] Article 1458 is amended by the code of 1884, and reads as follows: "Art. 1343. When the thing is lost or deteriorated without the fault of the debtor, the loss or diminution is on account of the creditor."

§ 2495. *Injured Party.*—Art. 1466. The injured party can select between requiring the fulfillment of the obligation or the dissolution of the contract, with a compensation for the damages and security of interest; and he can adopt this second means even in the case that, having elected the first, the fulfillment of the obligation was not possible.

§ 2496. *Failure of Payment.*—Art. 1467. The dissolution of a contract founded on the failure of payment on the part of the acquirer of immovable property, or other real right thereon, shall have no effect against a third party in good faith, if it has not been expressly stipulated, and has been inscribed in the public registry in the form provided in title 23 of this book.

§ 2497. *Movable Property.*—Art. 1468. In respect to movable property, whether there is or has not been any express stipulation, said dissolution will never take place against a third party who acquired them in good faith.

§ 2498. *Rescission.*—Art. 1469. If the rescission of a contract shall depend on a third party, and he should be fraudulently induced to rescind it, it will be held as not rescinded.

§ 2499. *Void Conditions.*—Art. 1470. Conditions physically or legally impossible annul a contract which depends on them.

### Of Obligations on Time.

§ 2500. *Obligation on Time, What is.*—Art. 1471. That obligation for the fulfillment of which a certain day has been designated is an obligation on time.

§ 2501. *Certain Day.*—Art. 1472. By a certain day is understood that which must necessarily arrive.

§ 2502. *Uncertainty.*—Art. 1473. If the uncertainty should consist in whether or not the day will arrive, the obligation will be conditional, and will be governed by the rules which the preceding chapter contains.

§ 2503. *Time.*—Art. 1474. The time in obligations shall be counted in the manner provided in articles 1240 to 1244.

§ 2504. *Payment in Advance.*—Art. 1475. What shall have been paid in advance can not be claimed.

§ 2505. *Presumption.*—Art. 1476. Whenever a term is designated in contracts, it is presumed to be established in favor of the debtor, unless in a contract itself, or from other circumstances, it should follow that it has also been placed in favor of the creditor.

§ 2506. *Insolvents.*—Art. 1477. A debtor declared to be in bankruptcy, he who shall be found in notorious insolvency, and he who shall have diminished by his own acts the securities executed to the creditor, may be required to fulfill an obligation on time, even when the time shall not have expired.[1]

§ 2507. *Joint Debtors.*—Art. 1478. If there should be various joint debtors, the provision in the preceding article will only comprehend him who shall be found in any of the cases which are designated therein.

### Of Joint and Alternative Obligations.

§ 2508. *Joint Obligations.*—Art. 1479. He who has obligated himself for divers things or acts jointly must give all of the first and perform all of the second.

§ 2509. *Alternate Obligations.*—Art. 1480. If the debtor has obligated himself for one of two acts, or for one of two things, or for one act or for one thing, he complies by performing any of the acts or things; but he can not against the will of the creditor perform part of one thing and part of another, or execute in part one act.

§ 2510. *Election.*—Art. 1481. In the alternative obligations the election belongs to the debtor, if it has not been otherwise agreed.

§ 2511. *What must be Delivered.*—Art. 1482. When two things have been promised in the alternative, if one of the two could not be the object of the obligation, the other must be delivered.

§ 2512. *Election by Debtor.*—Art. 1483. If the election belongs to the debtor, and any of the things are lost by his fault or a fortuitous case, the creditor is obliged to receive what remains.

§ 2513. *Fault of Debtor.*—Art. 1484. If the two things have been lost, and one has been by the fault of the debtor, he must pay the price of the last which was lost. The same shall be observed if the two things have been lost by the fault of the debtor.

§ 2514. *Fortuitous Case.*—Art. 1485. If the two things have been lost by a fortuitous case, the debtor shall be free from the obligation.

§ 2515. *Election by Creditor.*—Art. 1486. If the election be-

[1] Article 1477 is amended by the code of 1884, and reads as follows: "Art. 1361. A debtor declared to be in bankruptcy, he who shall be found in notorious insolvency, and he who without the consent of his creditors shall have diminished by his own acts the securities executed to the creditor, may be required to fulfill an obligation on time, even when the time shall not have expired."

longs to the creditor, and one of the things shall be lost by the fault of the debtor, the first may elect the thing which has remained or the value of the one lost.

§ 2516. *Loss without Fault of Debtor.*—Art. 1487. If the thing was lost without the fault of the debtor, the creditor will be obliged to receive what shall have remained.

§ 2517. *Loss by Fault of Debtor.*—Art. 1488. If both things shall be lost by the fault of the debtor, the creditor can demand the value of any of them, with the damages and losses, or the rescisssion of the contract.

§ 2518. *Distinction in Losses.*—Art. 1489. If both things shall be lost without the fault of the debtor, the following distinction shall be made: 1. If the election or designation of the thing shall have been made, the loss shall be on accouut of the creditor; 2. If the election shall not have been made, the contract shall remain without effect.

§ 2519. *Election by Debtor—Loss.*—Art. 1490. If the election is of the debtor, and one of the things is lost by the fault of the creditor, the first can ask to be discharged from the obligation, or that the contract be rescinded, with indemnification for the damages and losses.

§ 2520. *Election by Creditor—Loss.*—Art. 1491. In the case of the preceding article, if the election is of the creditor, the obligation will be satisfied with the loss of the thing.

§ 2521. *Loss of the Two Things.*—Art. 1492. If the two things are lost by the fault of the creditor, and it is from this election, it shall remain with his discretion to return the price which he may wish of one of the things.

§ 2522. *Election by Debtor—Designation of Price.*—Art. 1493. In the case of the preceding article, if the election is of the debtor, he will designate the price of one of the two things.

§ 2523. *Creditor's Obligation.*—Art. 1494. In the cases of the two preceding articles, the creditor is obligated for the payment of the damages and losses.

§ 2524. *Obligation of Acts.*—Art. 1495. If the alternative obligation should be of acts, the creditor, when he shall have the election, can demand any of the acts which shall be matter of the contract.

§ 2525. *Performance by Debtor.*—Art. 1496. If the election belongs to the debtor, he will have power to perform the act which he may wish.

§ 2526. *Right of Election.*—Art. 1497. If the obligation

should be of a thing or an act, he who may have the election can demand or give in his case the first or the second.

§ 2527. *Refusal.*—Art. 1498. If the party obligated refuses to execute the act, the creditor can require the thing or the execution of the act by a third party on the terms of article 1542.

§ 2528. *Lost by Fault of Debtor*—Art. 1499. If the thing is lost by the fault of the debtor and the election is of the creditor, the latter can require the price of the thing or the performance of the act.

§ 2529. *Loss without Fault of Debtor.*—Art. 1500. In the case of the preceding article, if the thing has been lost without the fault of the debtor, the creditor is obliged to receive the performance of the act.

§ 2530. *Right of Debtor.*—Art. 1501. Whether there has been or not fault in the loss of the thing on the part of the debtor, if the election is his, the creditor is obliged to receive the performance of the act.

§ 2531. *Fault of Creditor.*—Art. 1502. If the thing is lost or the act fails to be performed by the fault of the creditor, the obligation is considered as fulfilled.

§ 2532. *Construction of Fault.*—Art. 1503. The fault of the performance of the act shall be governed by the provisions in articles 1539 to 1543.

### Of the Execution of Contracts—General Provisions.

§ 2533. *Must be Executed.*—Art. 1535. Contracts legally made shall be punctually fulfilled, and they can not be revoked nor altered except by the mutual consent of the contracting parties, save the exceptions assigned in the law.

§ 2534. *Succession.*—Art. 1536. The rights and obligations which result from contracts may be transmitted between the living, and by succession, if they are not purely personal by their nature, by the effect of the said contracts or by the provision of the law.

§ 2535. *Judicial Enforcement.*—Art. 1537. If the obligated party in a contract should fail to comply with his obligation, the other interested party can judicially demand the fulfillment of the agreement or the rescission of the contract, and in both cases payment for the damages and losses.

§ 2536. *What a Contract may be.*—Art. 1538. A contract may consist in the performance of acts, in the giving of things, and in both.

### Of the Performance of Acts.

§ 2537. *Responsibility.*—Art. 1539. He who shall have obligated himself to perform some act, and should fail to perform it, or should not perform it in conformity with the agreement, shall be responsible for the damages and losses on the following terms: 1. If the obligation should be on time, the responsibility shall commence from the expiration thereof; 2. If the obligation should not depend upon a certain time, the responsibility shall only run from the day on which the debtor shall have been notified to comply therewith (interpelado).

§ 2538. *Interpellation.*—Art. 1540. The act by which the creditor intimates or orders it to be intimated to the debtor to fulfill his obligation is called interpelacion.

§ 2539. *Creditor.*—Art. 1541. The creditor can make the intimation before a notary or two witnesses.

§ 2540. *Right of Creditor.*—Art. 1542. The creditor of the performance of an act may ask, in place of damages and losses, for the authority to have the act which is the object of the contract performed by another, at the cost of the obligated party, where the substitution may be possible.

§ 2541. *Further Right of Creditor.*—Art. 1543. If the act has not been executed in the manner agreed, the creditor shall have the rights which the preceding article concedes to him, and besides that of requiring the work badly made to be destroyed.

§ 2542. *Damages for Violation.*—Art. 1544. He who should obligate himself not to do anything shall be subjected to the payment of damages and loss in case of a contravention thereof. If it should be a material work, the creditor can require that it be destroyed at the cost of the obligated party.

### Of the Giving of Things.

§ 2543. *Obligation of Donor.*—Art. 1545. A party obligated to give anything is likewise obligated to preserve it with the proper care of a good father of a family, and to deliver it, under the responsibility established in charter 4 of this article.

§ 2544. *Perfection—Risk.*—Art. 1546. From the time the contract is perfected by the consent of the parties, the risk of the thing is on account of the creditor, even when it has not been delivered.

§ 2545. *Risk.*—Art. 1547. The risk will be on account of the debtor, if the thing which was in possession should be lost or deteriorated by his fault.

§ 2546. *Performance.*—Art. 1548. The provisions in article

1539 in respect to the performance of acts is applicable to the giving of things.

§ 2547. *Payment.*—Art. 1549. The payment which shall be made in money without interest is excepted from the provision in said article; in which case indemnification may be had for damages and losses in the form provided in article 1567, only from the day on which the debtor shall be notified to pay.

§ 2548. *Reciprocal Obligations.*— Art. 1550. In reciprocal obligations none of the contracting parties shall incur delay, if the other does not fulfill or be found ready to duly fulfill the obligation which belongs to him.

§ 2549. *Giving Things.*—Art. 1551. The giving of things may consist: 1. In the translation of the dominion of a certain thing; 2. In the temporal alienation of the use or enjoyment of a certain thing; 3. In the restitution of the thing of another, or the payment of a thing due.

§ 2550. *Delivery.*—Art. 1552. In the alienation of certain and determined things, the translation of the property is verified between the contracting parties by the mere effect of the contract, without dependence on delivery, either natural or symbolical, save an agreement to the contrary.

§ 2551. *When Transferred.*—Art. 1553. In the alienation of any undetermined kind of property, it is not transferred until the moment in which the thing is made certain and determined with the knowledge of the creditor.

§ 2552. *Quality.*—Art. 1554. If the quality of the thing is not designated, the debtor complies by delivering a medium quality.

§ 2553. *Fault of Debtor.*—Art. 1555. There being fault or delay on the part of the debtor, he will be obligated for the indemnification according to chapter 4 of this title.

§ 2554. *Fortuitous Case—Agreement.*—Art. 1556. He will have the responsibility when he has obligated himself for the giving in a fortuitous case.

§ 2555. *Fortuitous Case without Agreement.*—Art. 1557. Although the debtor may have placed himself in delay, if he has not obligated himself to respond in fortuitous cases, the obligation will be extinguished whenever he proves that the thing would have likewise been lost in the possession of the creditor.

§ 2556. *Presumption.*—Art. 1558. The loss of the thing in the possession of the debtor is presumed to be by his fault, until the contrary shall be proved.

§ 2557. *Crime.*—Art. 1559. When the debt of a certain and determined thing shall proceed from a crime or offense, the debtor shall not be exempt from the payment of the price, whatever may have been the cause of the loss; unless that, having offered the thing to him who ought to receive it, the latter shall have placed himself in delay.

§ 2558. *Lost Thing.* — Art. 1560. The debtor of a lost thing, without his fault, is obliged to cede to the creditor all the rights and actions he may have to claim the indemnification from whoever shall be responsible for the loss.

§ 2559. *Proof.*—Art. 1561. The loss may be verified: 1. By the perishing of the thing; 2. The thing disappearing so that no notice may be had of it, or although some notice may be had, the thing can not be recovered.

§ 2560. *Fault or Negligence.*—Art. 1562. There is fault or negligence when the obligated party executes acts contrary to the preservation of the thing, or fails to execute those which are necessary therefor.

§ 2561. *Discretion of the Judge.*—Art. 1563. The qualification of the fault or negligence remains with the prudent discretion of the judge, according to the circumstances of the act, of the contract, and of the persons.

§ 2562. *Reservations.*—Art. 1564. In the contracts of alienation, with a reservation of the possession, use, or enjoyment of the thing until a certain time, the following rules shall be observed: 1. If there is an express agreement, it shall be according to the stipulation; 2. If the loss should be through the fault of any of the contracting parties, the amount will be of the responsibility of said party; 3. In default of a contract and of blame, each interested party shall suffer the loss which shall correspond to him, in the whole, if the thing totally perishes, or in part, if the loss should only be partial; 4. In the case of the preceding fraction, if the loss should be partial, and the parties should not agree in the diminution of their respective rights, experts shall be appointed who shall determine it.

§ 2563. *Second Sale.*—Art. 1565. If the thing transferred should be again sold to a third party, before being delivered by the obligated party to the first acquirer, the latter can recover it on the terms established in articles 3000 to 3003.

§ 2564. *Risk of Owner.*—Art. 1566. In the contracts in which the giving of the thing does not import the translation of the property, the risk shall always be on account of the owner, unless fault or negligence shall intervene on the part of the other.

§ 2565. *Amount of Damages.*—Art. 1567. If the giving should consist in the payment of a certain amount of money, the damages and losses which shall result from the want of the fulfillment of the contract shall not exceed the legal interest, save an express contract to the contrary.

### Of Eviction and Warranty.

§ 2566. *Eviction, What is.*—Art. 1604. There will be an eviction when he who acquired anything shall be deprived of the whole or part of it by a judgment which causes execution, on account of some right prior to the acquisition.

§ 2567. *Obligation of Vendor.*—Art. 1605. All who sell are obliged to respond for an eviction, although nothing shall have been expressed in the contract.

§ 2568. *Agreement of Parties.*—Art. 1606. The contracting parties may increase or diminish conventionally the effects of eviction, and even may agree that this shall not be warranted against in any case.

§ 2569. *Agreements Null, What.*—Art. 1607. Every agreement is null which exempts him who sells from responding for an eviction whenever there shall be bad faith on his part.

§ 2570. *Renouncements.*—Art. 1608. The renouncements of eviction and of warranty shall be made in precise terms, and specifying the rights which are renounced, in conformity with which is provided in article 1424.

§ 2571. *Knowledge of the Risk.*—Art. 1609. When he who acquires has renounced the right to warranty for the case of an eviction, this having arrived, he who sells must deliver only the price of the thing according to articles 1612 and 1613 in his case; but even he may be free from this obligation, if he who acquired did it with a knowledge of the risks of eviction and submitting himself to its consequences.

§ 2572. *Notice.*—Art. 1610. The acquirer must give notice of the suit for eviction to him who sold, before the written or verbal argument of his right which closes the trial, if the question should be simply of law; or before receiving the case for proof in the cases in which this shall be necessary.

§ 2573. *Judgment.*—Art. 1611. A judicial judgment imposes on him who sells the obligation of indemnifying on the following terms:

§ 2574. *Good Faith.*—Art. 1612. If he who sold shall have

proceeded in good faith, he will be obliged to deliver to him who suffered the eviction: 1. The whole price which he received for the thing; 2. The expenses caused by the contract, if they were satisfied by the acquirer; 3. The expenses caused in the suit for eviction and in that of the warranty; 4. The value of the useful and necessary improvements, provided that in the judgment it shall not be determined that the evictor shall satisfy the amount.

§ 2575. *Bad Faith.*—Art. 1613. If he who sold shall have proceeded in bad faith, he shall be under the obligations which the preceding article expresses, with the following aggravations: 1. He shall return, at the election of the acquirer, the price which the thing had at the time of the acquisition, or which it may have at the time in which he suffers the eviction; 2. He shall satisfy the acquirer for the amount of the voluntary improvements and of mere pleasure which may have been made on the thing; 3. He shall pay the damages and losses.

§ 2576. *Bad Faith in Both Parties.*—Art. 1614. If he who sells and he who acquires proceed in bad faith, the second shall not have in any case the right to warranty nor to indemnification of any kind.

§ 2577. *Right of Restorer.*—Art. 1615. If the acquirer should be condemned to restore the fruits of the thing, he can require from him who sold the indemnification for them or the legal interest of the price which he may have given.

§ 2578. *Fruits Received*—Art. 1616. If he who acquired should be condemned to said restoration, the interest shall be compensated for with the fruits received.

§ 2579. *Freedom from Responsibility.*—Art. 1617. If he who sells, on being summoned, shows that he has no means of defense, and assigns the price on account of the acquirer not wishing to receive it, he shall be free from any responsibility subsequent to the date of the assignment.

§ 2580. *Deterioration*—Art. 1618. The deteriorations which the thing may have suffered shall be on account of him who caused them.

§ 2581. *Profits from Deterioration.*—Art. 1619. If he who acquired shall have made any profit from the deteriorations, the amount of it shall be deducted from that of the indemnification.

§ 2582. *Improvements.*—Art. 1620. The improvements which he who sold shall have made before the sale shall pass to him on account of what he must pay, provided they were credited by the victor.

§ 2583. *Deprivation of a Part.*—Art. 1621. When the acquirer shall be deprived only of a part of the thing acquired, the rules established in this chapter shall be observed in respect to this; unless the acquirer shall prefer the rescission of the contract.

§ 2584. *One Contract for Two Things.*—Art. 1622. The provisions in the preceding article shall also be observed when in one sole contract shall have been sold two or more things without fixing the price of each one of them; and one person alone should suffer the eviction.

§ 2585. *Election of Rescission.*—Art. 1623. In the cases of the two preceding articles, if he who acquires elects the rescission of the contract, he is obliged to return the thing free of the burdens which he may have imposed upon it.

§ 2586. *Acknowledgment of Seller.*—Art. 1624. If on being notified of the suit, or during the trial, he who sold acknowledges the right of him who claims the property, and obligates himself to pay in conformity with the prescriptions of this chapter, he will only be responsible for the expenses which shall have been caused up to the time of the acknowledgment, whatever may be the result of the suit.

§ 2587. *Burdened Estate.*—Art. 1625. If the estate which was sold was found burdened without mention having been made of it in the title, with any charge or voluntary service not apparent, he who acquired can ask for the indemnification corresponding to the burden, or the rescission of the contract.

§ 2588. *Actions.*—Art. 1626. The rescissory actions, and those for indemnification, to which the preceding article refers, may be prescribed in one year (that is, limitation may be pleaded), which shall be counted for the first from the day on which the contract was perfected, and for the second from the day on which the acquirer shall have notice of the charge or service.

§ 2589. *Non-liability of Seller, when.*—Art. 1627. He who sells does not respond for the eviction: 1. If he shall have so agreed, with the conditions established in article 1608; 2. In the case of article 1609; 3. If he who acquires, knowing the right of him who institutes suit for eviction, should have fraudulently kept it secret from him who sells: 4. If the eviction proceeds from a cause subsequent to the act of transfer not imputable to him who sells, or from an act of him who acquires, whether it be prior or subsequent to said act; 5. If the acquirer does not comply with the provisions in article 1610; 6. If the acquirer and he who claims the property settle or compromise the case by arbitration without the consent of him who sold; 7. If the eviction took place through the fault of the acquirer.[1]

### Of the Rescission of Obligations.

§ 2590. *Rescinded, What Can be.*—Art. 1770. Only obligations which are in themselves valid can be rescinded.

§ 2591. *Rescission, how.*—Art. 1771. No obligation is rescinded solely by lesion[2] save the provision in article 3023.

§ 2592. *Lesion.*—Art. 1772. There is lesion only when the party who acquires gives twice as much more, or the party who sells receives two thirds less, than the just price or estimation of the thing.

§ 2593. *Rescission, when.*—Art. 1773. A rescission shall take place: 1. In cases in which in conformity with law restitution proceeds *in integrum;*[3] 2. In those in which fraud has been committed in prejudice to creditors in selling the property of the debtor; 3. In those in which the law expressly establishes it.

§ 2594. *Action for Rescission.*—Art. 1774. The action to ask for a rescission lasts four years.

§ 2595. *Governing Provisions.*—Art. 1775. A rescission which proceeds on account of restitution *in integrum* shall be governed by the provision in title 11 of book 1, and that which proceeds from fraud in prejudice to creditors, by the provisions in chapter 3 of this title.[4]

§ 2596. *Gratuitous Titles.*—Art. 1776. Alienations by a gratuitous title, made by a debtor in a state of insolvency, shall be rescinded as fraudulent, at the instance of the creditors.

§ 2597. *Insolvency.*—Art. 1777. A payment made in a state

[1] A new article is formed by the code of 1884, and reads as follows: "Art. 1490. When the thing which is the object of the eviction shall have belonged successively to divers proprietors, each one of them is obligated to the immediate acquirer, and he has right to claim warranty from the person who sold to him; all according to the provisions of this chapter."

Also a new article which reads as follows: "Art. 1499. If he who sold does not appear without a just cause in the suit of eviction in the proper time, or if he does not render any proof, or does not defend, he is obligated for the guaranty in the terms of the preceding article."

[2] "Lesion" is the damage caused in an onerous contract, and especially in a sale, on account of not having received a just price therefor, or having paid too much therefor.

[3] Article 1773 is amended by the code of 1884 by suppressing fraction 1.

[4] Article 1775 is amended by the code of 1884, and reads as follows: "Art. 1661. The rescission which proceeds from fraud in prejudice of creditors is governed by the provisions in chapter 3 of this title."

of insolvency, for an obligation for the fulfillment of which the debtor could not have been compelled to make at the time of the payment, is also subject to a rescission and may be revoked.

OF THE NULLITY OF OBLIGATIONS.

§ 2598. *Nullity—Action.*—Art. 1778. The action of nullity which results from the incapacity of the contracting parties may be instituted on the terms established in articles 516, 517, 518, and 519.

§ 2599. *Married Women.*—Art. 1779. The nullity of obligations contracted by a married woman without competent authorization may be asked for within four years, counted from the dissolution of the marriage.[1]

§ 2600. *Error.*—Art. 1780. The action of nullity founded on error may be prescribed by the lapse of five years, unless he who incurred the error shall know of it before that time shall expire. In this case the action is prescribed in sixty days, counted from that on which the error was known.

§ 2601. *Intimidation—Action.*—Art. 1781. The action to ask for the nullity of a contract made by intimidation is prescribed in six months, counted from the day on which the cause ceased.

§ 2602. *Illegitimacy of the Object.*—Art. 1782. If the nullity proceeds from the illegitimacy of the object of the contract, the provisions in the two following articles shall be observed:

§ 2603. *Crime in Both Parties.*—Art. 1783. If the object of the contract constitutes a crime or offense common to both contracting parties, none of them shall have an action to claim either the fulfillment of the contract or the return of what was given; and both shall be subject to the responsibility which they may have incurred, in conformity with the prescriptions of the penal code.

§ 2604. *One Party Culpable.*—Art. 1784. If one only of the contracting parties should be culpable, the innocent party may reclaim what he shall have given, without having an obligation on his part to comply with what he may have promised.

§ 2605. *Neither Party a Right, when.*—Art. 1785. If the object of the contract should be some act which, although morally reproved, shall not be punishable in conformity with the law, and for which both parties should be responsible, none of

[1] Article 1779 is amended by the code of 1884 so as to read as follows: "Art. 1665. The nullity of obligations contracted by a married woman without competent authorization may be asked for during the marriage and within four years, counted from the dissolution of marriage."

them can claim the fulfillment of the promise, nor the restitution of what may have been given.

§ 2606. *One Responsible.*—Art. 1786. If only one of the contracting parties should be responsible for the act reproved, the other may claim what he gave, without being obliged on his part to comply with what he may have promised.

§ 2607. *Nullity Perpetual.*—Art. 1787. The exception (defense) of nullity of a contract is perpetual.

§ 2608. *Action for Nullity.*—Art. 1788. The action and the defense of nullity belong to the principal parties and to their sureties, excepting those cases in which the law expressly provides otherwise.

§ 2609. *Nullity from Incapacity.*—Art. 1789. The nullity which arises from the incapacity of one of the contracting parties can not be alleged by the other, unless it is proved that at the time of the contract he was ignorant of the incapacity.

§ 2610. *One's Own Wrongs.*—Art. 1790. Neither can the defense be alleged which arises from error or from intimidation, by him who has contributed to the one or the other.

§ 2611. *Incapacity.*—Art. 1791. When the contract is null through incapacity, intimidation, or error, the vice or ground of nullity having ceased, and no other cause which invalidates a ratification occurring, the contract may be ratified.

§ 2612. *Voluntary Fulfillment.*—Art. 1792. The voluntary fulfillment, by the means of payment, novation, or by any other manner, executed with same circumstances, shall be considered as ratified, and it can not be reclaimed.

§ 2613. *Ratification.*—Art. 1793. The ratification and the voluntary fulfillment of an obligation null for want of form or solemnity, which shall be made at any time, extinguishes the action of nullity, excepting the cases in which the law expressly provides otherwise.

§ 2614. *Nullity.*—Art. 1794. The nullity of a contract being declared, each one of the contracting parties shall recover the thing which he shall have given, with its fruits or the value thereof, and that which it had when it was lost with the interest, if the restitution in kind should be impossible.

§ 2615. *Rules to Decide the Action of Nullity.*—Art. 1795. In order to decide whether or not the action of nullity is admissible when the thing was lost which was the object of the obligation before the term commences to run, the following rules shall be observed: 1. If the nullity proceeds from incapacity, the action can always be instituted. 2. The same shall be observed if the nullity is founded upon error, fraud, violence, or intimidation, unless the thing shall have been lost by the fault of the claimant; 3. In the other cases of nullity, if the thing shall have been in the possession of the claimant, this recourse shall cease; it shall also cease if it shall have been lost in the possession of him against whom it is claimed, without his fault or without it be constituted in delay.

§ 2616. *Non-fulfillment of One Party, Defense to the Other.* Art. 1796. While one of the contracting parties does not comply with the return of that which in virtue of the declaration of nullity of the contract he is obligated, the other can not be compelled to comply on his part.

# CHAPTER XIII.

## CONTRACTS OF MARRIAGE RELATIVE TO THE PROPERTY OF THE CONSORTS.

§ 2617. Contract of Marriage.
§ 2618. Constitution of Dower.
§ 2618 *a*. Conjugal Partnership.
§ 2619. Voluntary Partnership.
§ 2620. Voluntary and Legal Partnership.
§ 2621. Commencement.
§ 2622. Termination.
§ 2623. Dissolution—Judgment.
§ 2624. Judgments.
§ 2625. Divorce.
§ 2626. Administrator.
§ 2627. Separation.
§ 2628. Separation may be Absolute or Partial.
§ 2629. Marriage Settlements, What are.
§ 2630. Settlements, when Executed.
§ 2631. Settlements, how Revoked.
§ 2632. Public Writing.
§ 2633. Alterations.
§ 2634. Noted in the Protocol.
§ 2635. Third Party.
§ 2636. Void Agreements.
§ 2637. Contents of Voluntary Partnership Titles.
§ 2638. Agreements of Spouses.
§ 2639. Void Settlements.
§ 2640. Fixed Sum.
§ 2641. Creditors.
§ 2642. Donation.
§ 2643. Void Agreements.
§ 2644. Minors.
§ 2645. Legal Provisions.
§ 2646. The Articles Which can not be Modified.
§ 2647. Default of Settlement.
§ 2648. Out of the District and California.
§ 2649. Citizens of the District and California.
§ 2650. Individual Property.
§ 2651. Acquisition during the Partnership.
§ 2652. Donations.
§ 2653. Resales.
§ 2654. Expenses.
§ 2655. Property Exchanged—Individual.
§ 2656. Consolidated Titles.
§ 2657. Loans.

GENERAL DISPOSITIONS.

§ 2617. *Contract of Marriage.*—Art. 2099. The contract of marriage may be celebrated under the regimen of a conjugal partnership or under that of a separation of property.

§ 2618. *Constitution of Dower.*—Art. 2100. In the two cases mentioned in the preceding article, the constitution of dower make take place, which in both shall be governed by the provisions in chapters 10, 11, 12, and 13 of this title.

§ 2618 *a*. *Conjugal Partnership.*—Art. 2101. The conjugal partnership may be voluntary or legal.

§ 2619. *Voluntary Partnership.*—Art. 2102. The voluntary partnership shall be governed strictly by the marriage settlement which constitutes it; all that shall not be expressed therein in a definite manner shall be governed by the precepts contained in chapters 4, 5, and 6 of this title, which shall regulate the legal partnership.

§ 2620. *Voluntary and Legal Partnership.*—Art. 2103. The voluntary and the legal partnership shall be governed by the provisions relative to the common partnership in all that which may not be comprehended in this title.

§ 2621. *Commencement.*—Art. 2104. The conjugal partnership, whether it be voluntary or whether it be legal, commences from the time in which the marriage is celebrated.

§ 2622. *Termination.*—Art. 2105. The voluntary partnership may terminate before the marriage is dissolved if it is so agreed in the settlement.

§ 2623. *Dissolution—Judgment.*—Art. 2106. The legal partnership terminates by the dissolution of the marriage and by the judgment which declares the presumption of the death of the absent conjugal partner.

§ 2624. *Judgments.*—Art. 2107. Judgments which declare a divorce necessary, or absence, terminate, suspend, or modify the conjugal partnership in the cases designated in this code.

§ 2625. *Divorce.*—Art. 2108. A voluntary divorce and a separation of property made during the marriage may terminate, suspend, or modify the conjugal partnership according as the consorts may agree.[1]

§ 2626. *Administrator.*—Art. 2109. The husband is the legal administrator of the conjugal partnership while there is no agreement or judgment to the contrary.[2]

§ 2627. *Separation.*—Art. 2110. The separation of property is governed by the marriage settlement which expressly establishes it, and by the precepts contained in articles 2206 to 2217.

§ 2628. *Separation may be Absolute or Partial.*—Art. 2111. The separation of property may be absolute or partial. In the second case the points which may not be comprehended in the settlement of separation shall be governed by the precepts which regulate a legal partnership, unless the spouses shall constitute about them a voluntary partnership.

### Of the Marriage Settlements.

§ 2629. *Marriage Settlements, What are.*—Art. 2112. The agreements which the spouses celebrate to constitute either a voluntary partnership, or a separation of property, and to administer these in both cases, are called marriage settlements.

§ 2630. *Settlements, when Executed.*—Art. 2113. Marriage settlements may be executed before the celebration of the marriage or during the marriage; and it may comprehend not only the property of which the spouses or consorts may be the owners at the time of making the settlement, but also that which may be acquired after.

§ 2631. *How Revoked.*—Art. 2114. Settlements can not be altered or revoked after the celebration of the marriage, except by an express agreement or by judicial judgment.

§ 2632. *Public Writing.*—Art. 2115. Settlements must be executed by public writings.

§ 2633. *Alterations.*—Art. 2116. Any alteration which in virtue of the power which article 2114 concedes shall be made in the settlement must be executed by a public writing, and

---

[1] Article 2108 becomes article 1974, new code, and is amended by adding thereto as follows: "The unjustifiable abandonment of the conjugal domicile by one of the conjugal partners causes the effects of the legal partnership to cease for that partner from the day of the abandonment so far as they may favor said partner, and these can not commence again except by an express agreement."

[2] Article 2109 is article 1975, new code, and reads as follows: "Art. 1975. The husband is the legitimate administrator of the conjugal partnership. The wife shall only administer when there shall be an agreement or judgment which so establishes it, in case of absence or impediment of the husband, or when the latter may have unjustifiedly abandoned the conjugal domicile."

with the intervention of all the persons which shall be interested therein.

§ 2634. *Noted in the Protocol.*—Art. 2117. The alteration which shall be made in the settlements must be noted in the protocol in which the settlements were drawn and in the authenticated copies which shall have been given thereof.

§ 2635. *Third Party.*—Art. 2118. Without the requisite provided in the preceding article the alterations will not produce any effect against a third party.

§ 2636. *Void Agreements.*—Art. 2119. The agreements celebrated by an infraction of articles 2115 and 2116 are null.

### Of Voluntary Partnerships.

§ 2637. *Contents of Voluntary Partnership Titles.*—Art. 2120. The title of settlement which constitutes a voluntary partnership must contain: 1. An inventory of the property which each spouse carries into the partnership, with a statement of the value thereof and its burden; 2. A declaration whether the partnership is universal or only of some property or values, stating which that shall be, or the part of its value which must enter the social fund; 3. The character which the property must have which in common or individually the consorts shall acquire during the partnership, as well as the manner of proving its acquisition; 4. The declaration whether the partnership is only one of gains, stating minutely which must be the common and the part that must belong to each consort; 5. A specified schedule of the debts of each contracting party, with a statement whether the social fund must respond therefor or only for those which shall be contracted during the partnership, whether by both consorts or by any of them; 6. A definite declaration of the powers which correspond to each consort in the administration of the property and in the reception of the fruits, with a statement of the property and fruits which each one may sell, mortgage, lease, etc., and of the conditions which for those acts must be required.

§ 2638. *Agreements of Spouses.*—Art. 2121. Besides the clauses contained in the preceding article, the spouses may establish all the rules which they think proper for the administration of the partnership, provided they are not contrary to the laws.

§ 2639. *Void Settlements.*—Art. 2122. Every settlement is null in virtue of which one of the consorts must receive all the profits, as well as that which establishes that any one of them shall respond for all the losses and common debts in a part which may exceed that which proportionally corresponds to their capital or the profits which they must receive.

§ 2640. *Fixed Sum.*—Art. 2123. When it shall be established that one of the consorts alone must have a fixed sum, the other consort, or the heirs thereof, must pay the sum agreed, whether there are or are not profits in the partnership.

§ 2641. *Creditors.*—Art. 2124. The creditors who shall not have had a knowledge of the terms in which the voluntary partnership may be constituted can exercise their action in conformity with the rules of the legal partnership; but the consort who, in virtue of the settlement, ought not to respond for that debt will preserve, save by his or her rights to recover, the part which shall correspond to him or her, from the gains of the other consort, and if these shall not be sufficient, from the individual property of the latter.

§ 2642. *Donation.*—Art. 2125. Every agreement which imports a cession of a part of the individual property of each contracting party will be considered as a donation, and shall remain subject to what is provided in chapters 8 and 9 of this title.

§ 2643. *Void Agreements.*—Art. 2126. The agreements which the spouses shall make against the laws or good customs; those depressive of the authority which respectively belongs to them in the family, and those contrary to the prohibitive provisions of this code, and to the legal rules relative to divorce, whether voluntary or necessary, emancipation, tutorship, privileges of the dower, and hereditary succession, whether of themselves or whether of their forced heirs, are null.[1]

§ 2644. *Minors.*—Art. 2127. A minor who, according to law, can marry can also execute settlements, which will be valid if at their execution the same persons whose previous consent was necessary for the celebration of the marriage shall concur.

§ 2645. *Legal Provisions.*—Art. 2128. Settlements must contain a definite statement of the legal provisions which are modified thereby; and the notary, under the penalty of twenty-five to a hundred dollars fine, is obliged to make it appear in the writing that he has notified the parties of the obligation which this article imposes, and of the provision in article 2102.

§ 2646. *The Articles Which can not be Modified.*—Art. 2129. Articles 2102, 2151, 2153, 2154, 2155, 2163, 2167, 2169 fraction 1, 2173, 2174, 2181, 2182, 2183, 2184, 2185, 2186, 2189, 2191, 2192, 2193 to the words "to the marriage," 2195, 2196, 2197, 2200, 2202, and 2203, can not be modified by settlements.

[1] Article 2126 is amended by the code of 1884, by inserting the word "legitimate" before the word "heir."

§ 2647. *Default of Settlement.*—Art. 2130. In default of an express settlement, a marriage is understood to be celebrated under the condition of the legal partnership.

### Of Legal Partnerships.

§ 2648. *Out of the District and California.*—Art. 2131. A marriage contracted out of the District or out of California, by persons who may come afterwards to be domiciled therein, shall be subject to the laws of the country in which it was celebrated, save the provisions in articles 14 and 18, and without prejudice to what the consorts may agree to by subsequent settlements, executed in conformity with this code.

§ 2649. *Citizens of the District and California.*—Art. 2132. The natives or citizens of the District and of California who shall contract marriage outside of those demarkations are under obligation to subject themselves to the provisions of this title and the contents of articles 13, 14, 15, and 17.

§ 2650. *Individual Property.*—Art. 2133. Each conjugul partner is the owner of the property which he or she had at the time of celebrating the marriage, and that which each possessed before that, although not the owner thereof, if he or she shall acquire them by prescription during the partnership.

§ 2651. *Acquisitions during the Partnership.*—Art. 2134. Also is each one the owner of the property which he or she may acquire during the partnership by the gift of fortune, by donation of any kind, by inheritance, or by legacy, constituted in favor of one of them alone.

§ 2652. *Donations.*—Art. 2135. If the donations shall be onerous, the charges thereof shall be deducted from the dower, or from the capital of the husband, in their respective case, whenever they shall have been supported by the partnership.

§ 2653. *Resales.*—Art. 2136. The property belongs to each consort which was acquired by a resale (retroventa) or individual title which may be prior to the marriage, although the giving shall have been made after the celebration of it.

§ 2654. *Expenses.*—Art. 2137. The expenses which shall have been caused in order to make the title effective shall be a charge on the owner thereof.

§ 2655. *Property Exchanged—Individual.*—Art. 2138. Property acquired by purchase or exchange of real estate which may belong to the conjugal partners, in order to acquire also other real estate which shall be substituted in place of that sold or exchanged, is individual property.

§ 2656. *Consolidated Titles.*—Art. 2139. Property acquired by the consolidation of the title and the usufruct is individual property of each conjugal partner, as well are the expenses individual which said property shall have made.

§ 2657. *Loans.*—Art. 2140. If any of the conjugal partners shall have a right to a loan demandable in installments which shall not have the character of a usufruct, the sums collected for the terms completed during the marriage shall not be common property (ganancial), but the individual property of each conjugal partner.[1]

§ 2658. *Property of Legal Partnership, What is.*—Art. 2141. The property which forms the fund of the legal partnership is: 1. All the property acquired by the husband in military service, or by any of the conjugal partners in the exercise of a scientific, mercantile, or industrial profession, or by mechanical work; 2. Property which shall arise from inheritance, legacy, or donations made to both conjugal partners without designation of parts; if there should be a designation of parts, and these should be unequal, the fruits alone of the inheritance, legacy, or donation shall be common; 3. The price taken out of the mass of common property to acquire by a resale (por retroventa) or other title which may arise from an individual right of any of the conjugal partners prior to the marriage; 4. The price of the reparation (refaccion) of credits, and that of any improvements and repairs made on estates or individual credits of one of the conjugal partners; 5. The excess or difference of price given by one of the conjugal partners for the sale or exchange of individual property, in order to acquire others in place of those sold or exchanged; 6. Property acquired by an onerous title during the partnership at the cost of the common fund, whether the acquisition shall be made for the community, or whether for only one of the consorts; 7. The fruits, accessions, rents, and interest received or obtained by service during the partnership proceeding from the common property or from the individual property of each one of the consorts.

§ 2658 *a.* *Usufructs.*—Art. 2142. That acquired by reason of a usufruct belongs to the social fund.

---

[1] Article 2005 is a new article, and reads as follows: "Art. 2005. When immovable property belonging to one of the conjugal partners is sold, and its price is not invested in buying other immovables, the price acquired shall be considered as the property of the conjugal owner of the property sold, if these entered the conjugal partnership without being estimated; but if they were estimated on celebrating the marriage, or on executing the marriage settlement, the price at which they were estimated will be the property of the owner, reputing as gains or losses of the partnership the increase or diminution which they shall have had on being sold."

§ 2658 *b*. *Edifices.*—Art. 2143. The edifices belong to the social fund constructed during the partnership with the funds thereof, on the individual ground of any of the conjugal partners, to whom the value of the land shall be credited.

§2658 *c*. *Cattle.*—Art. 2144. The head of cattle only belong to the social fund which shall exceed the number of those which on the celebration of the marriage should be the individual property of any one of the conjugal partners.

§ 2658 *d*. *Mines.*—Art. 2145. The mines denounced during the marriage by one of the conjugal partners, as well as the bars or shares acquired with the common fund, belong likewise to the social fund.

§ 2659. *Fruits Pending.*—Art. 2146. Fruits pending at the time of the dissolution of the partnership belong to the social fund; and they will be divided in proportion to the time which the partnership shall have existed during the last year. The years shall be computed from the date of the celebration of the marriage.

§ 2660. *Treasure Found by Chance.*—Art. 2147. The treasure found by chance is the property of the conjugal partner who finds it. That found by industry belongs to the social fund.

§ 2661. *Mining Shares.*—Art. 2148. The bars or shares of mines which a conjugal partner shall have shall be the individual property of that partner, but the products thereof, received during the partnership, shall belong to the fund thereof.

§ 2662. *Presumption.*—Art. 2149. The property will be reputed as acquired during the partnership, which any one of the conjugal partners ought to have acquired as individual property during that time, and which was not acquired except after the dissolution, whether on account of having had notice of the property, or whether on account of having been unjustly embarrassed in its acquisition or enjoyment.

§ 2663. *After Dissolution of Partnership.*—Art. 2150. The fruits of the property to which the preceding article refers shall be of the social fund, which shall have been received after the dissolution of the partnership, and which should have been received during it.

§ 2664. *Renouncement.*—Art. 2151. The ganancials (common property) can not be renounced during the marriage; but this being dissolved, or the separation of property decreed, those acquired may be renounced, and the renouncement is valid, if made in a public writing.

§ 2665. *Presumption of Ganancial Property.*—Art. 2152. All the property which exists in the possession of any one of the conjugal partners on making the separation thereof shall be presumed ganancials until the contrary is proved.

§ 2666. *Proof.*—Art. 2153. Neither the declaration of one of the conjugal partners who affirms a thing to be his or hers, nor the confession of the other, nor both jointly, shall be estimated as sufficient proof, although they be judicial.

§ 2667. *Confession.*—Art. 2154. The confession in the case of the preceding article shall be considered as a donation, which shall not be confirmed except by the death of the donor, and which shall subsist as far as it may not be inofficious.[1]

§ 2668. *Due Proof, What.*—Art. 2155. For due proof of the property to which article 2133 refers, an inventory thereof shall be formed in the marriage settlement, or in a separate public instrument. If an inventory has not been made, proof may be admitted at any time; but in the mean time the property is presumed common.

### Of the Administration of the Legal Partnership.

§ 2669. *Common Property.*—Art. 2156. The dominion and possession of the common property resides in both conjugal partners while the partnership subsists.

§ 2670. *Movable Property.*—Art. 2157. The husband can alienate and obligate with an onerous title the movable property without the consent of the wife.

§ 2671. *Real Estate.*—Art. 2158. Real estate belonging to the social fund can not be obligated nor alienated in any manner by the husband without the consent of the wife.

§ 2672. *Judicial Consent.*—Art. 2159. In cases of unfounded opposition, the consent of the wife may be supplied by judicial decree.[2]

§ 2673. *Common Inheritance.*—Art. 2160. The husband can not repudiate nor accept the common inheritance without the consent of the wife; but the judge may supply that consent.[3]

§ 2674. *Responsibility of Acceptation.*—Art. 2161. The responsibility of the acceptation without the wife consents, or the judge authorizes it, will only affect the individual property of the husband and his half of the ganancials.

---

[1] Article 2154 is amended by the code of 1844, by suppressing the words "and which shall subsist as far as it may not be inofficious."

[2] Article 2159 is amended by adding thereto, "and her previous audience," in code of 1884.

[3] Article 2160 is amended by adding thereto, "with a previous audience of the wife."

§ 2675. *Husband's Will.*—Art. 2162. The husband can not dispose by will except of his half of the common property (ganancials).[1]

§ 2676. *Husband can not Prejudice the Wife.*—Art. 2163. No alienation which the husband shall make of the ganancial property, in contravention of the law or in fraud of the wife, shall prejudice the latter or her heirs.

§ 2677. *Wife Administers, when.*—Art. 2164. The wife can only administer by consent of the husband or in the absence or through an impediment of the latter.

§ 2678. *Wife can not Obligate.*—Art. 2165. The wife can not obligate the ganancial property without the consent of the husband.

§ 2679. *Wife may Pay Ordinary Expenses.*—Art. 2166. The wife may pay with the ganancials the ordinary expenses of the family, according to their circumstances.

§ 2680. *Wife as Surety.*—Art. 2167. A married woman who legally shall be a surety, in the cases of a separation of property shall respond with the individual property she may have; and in those of a conjugal partnership only with her ganancials, and with the part which belongs to her in the social fund.

§ 2681. *Debts during Marriage.*—Art. 2168. The debts contracted during the marriage by both conjugal partners, or by the husband alone, or by the wife, with the authorization of the latter, or in his absence or by his impediment, are a charge on the legal partnership.

§ 2682. *Exceptions.*—Art. 2169. From the provisions in the preceding article are excepted: 1. The debts which arise from an offense of any one of the conjugal partners or from any act morally reproved, although it may not be punishable by law; 2. The debts which burden the individual property of the conjugal partners, not being by a censo or pension, the amount of which may have entered into the social fund.

§ 2683. *Debts Prior to Marriage.*—Art. 2170. The debts of each conjugal partner prior to the marriage are not a charge on the legal partnership, unless in the following cases: 1. If the other conjugal partner should be personally obligated; 2. If they should have been contracted for the common benefit of both.

§ 2684. *Debts Made Effective during Marriage.*—Art. 2171. Among the debts spoken of in the preceding article are compre-

[1] Article 2162 is amended by the code of 1884, and is as follows: "Art. 2029. The conjugal partners can not dispose by will except of their half of the common property (ganancials)."

hended those which arise from any act of the consorts prior to the marriage, even when the obligation shall be made effective during the partnership.

§ 2685. *Credits Prior to Marriage.*—Art. 2172. The credits prior to the marriage, in case that the obligated conjugal partner shall not have sufficient to satisfy them, can only be paid with the ganancials which shall belong to him or her after the dissolution of the legal partnership.

§ 2686. *Creditors.*—Art. 2173. The creditors of the conjugal debtor can also make use, in respect to the property of the latter, of the right which articles 2065 and 2066 concede.

§ 2687.—*Pensions.*—Art. 2174. The arrears of pensions or interest acquired during the marriage from the obligations by which the individual property of the conjugal partners, as well as those which form the social fund, may be effected, are a charge on the partnership.

§ 2688. *Expenses.*—Art. 2175. The expenses which shall be made in the indispensable repositions for the preservation of the individual property of each conjugal partner are also a charge on the partnership.

§ 2689. *Expenses of Social Fund.*—Art. 2176. All the expenses which shall be made for the preservation of the property of the social fund are a charge on the partnership.

§ 2690. *Maintenance of Family.*—Art. 2177. Equally so are the maintenance of the family, the education of the common children, and that of the children-in-law, who shall be legitimate children and minors.

§ 2691. *Collation.*—Art. 2178. The amount given or promised by both consorts to the common children for their collation is also a charge on the partnership when they have not agreed that it shall be satisfied from the property of one of them, wholly or in part. If the donation or the promise shall have been made by one of the consorts alone, it shall be paid from his or her individual property.

§ 2692. *Expenses of Partnership.*—Art. 2179. The expenses of inventory, and others which may be caused in the liquidation and in the delivery of the property which formed the social fund, are equally charges on the partnership.

### Of the Liquidation of the Legal Partnership.

§ 2693. *Termination of Partnership.*—Art. 2180. A legal partnership terminates and is suspended in the cases designated in articles 2106, 2107, and 2108.

§ 2694. *Nullity of Partnership.*—Art. 2181. In cases of nullity of partnership, it shall be considered subsisting until a judgment shall be pronounced, which shall cause execution if the two conjugal partners proceeded in good faith.

§ 2695. *Good Faith.*—Art. 2182. When only one of the conjugal partners had good faith, the partnership shall also subsist until a judgment causes execution, if the continuance is favorable to the innocent partner; otherwise, it shall be considered null from the beginning.

§ 2696. *Bad Faith.*—Art. 2183. If the two conjugal partners shall proceed in bad faith, the partnership shall be considered null from the celebration of the marriage; leaving safe in every case the rights which a third party may have against the social fund.

§ 2697. *Necessary Divorce.*—Art. 2184. In cases of necessary divorce, they shall proceed in conformity with the provisions in articles 274, 275, 276, and those relative thereto.

§ 2698. *Voluntary Divorce.*—Art. 2185. In cases of voluntary divorce or of simple separation of property, the agreements which the consorts have celebrated, and which were approved by the judge, shall be observed for the liquidation, save the agreements in the marriage settlements and the provisions in this chapter, in their respective cases.

§ 2699. *Creditors.*—Art. 2186. The dissolution and suspension shall not produce any effect in respect to creditors, except from the date on which they shall be notified of the judicial judgment.

§ 2700. *Suspension of Partnership.*—Art. 2187. The suspension of the partnership shall cease with the completion of the term, if any was fixed for it, and with the reconciliation of the consorts in the cases of divorce.

§ 2701. *Termination Understood.*—Art. 2188. If the marriage shall be dissolved before the reconciliation, the partnership shall be understood as terminated from the time the suspension commenced, notwithstanding the provisions in articles 2106, 2107, and 2108.[1]

§ 2702. *Inventory.*—Art. 2189. The partnership being dissolved or suspended, they shall proceed immediately to form an inventory.

[1] Article 2188 is amended by the code of 1884 so as to read as follows: "Art. 2055. If the marriage shall be dissolved before the completion of the term, and before the reconciliation, the partnership shall be understood as terminated from the time the suspension commenced, notwithstanding the provisions in articles 2106, 2107, and 2108."

§ 2703. *Property of Inventory.*—Art. 2190. In the inventory shall be included specifically not only all the property which formed the legal partnership, but that which ought to be brought to the collation.

§ 2704. *Collation, Property of.*—Art. 2191. Must be brought to the collation: 1. The sums paid for the social fund, and which shall be an exclusive charge on the individual property of each conjugal partner; 2. The amount of the donations and that of the alienations which must be considered fraudulent in conformity with article 2163.

§ 2705. *Not to be Inventoried, What.*—Art. 2192. The effects which formed the bed and ordinary clothing of the consorts, which must be immediately delivered to them or to their heirs, shall not be included in the inventory.

§ 2706. *Disposition after Inventory.*—Art. 2193. The inventory being terminated, the credits which there may be against the social fund shall be paid; what each consort carried into the marriage shall be returned to him or her; and the remainder, if there should be any, shall be divided among the conjugal partners by halves. In case there should be losses, the amount of these shall be deducted by halves from what each consort shall have carried into the partnership; and if only one carried capital, from this shall be deducted the whole of the capital.

§ 2707. *Division of Ganancials.*—Art. 2194. The division of the ganancials by halves among the consorts or their heirs shall take place, whatever may be the amount of the property which each one of them may have carried to the marriage, or acquired during it, and although any one or both may have lacked property at the time of celebrating it.

§ 2708. *Bad Faith.*—Art. 2195. If the dissolution of the partnership proceeds from a nullity of the marriage, the consort who shall have acted in bad faith shall not have any part of the ganancials.

§ 2709. *Effect of Bad Faith.*—Art. 2196. In the case of the preceding article, the ganancials which ought to belong to the conjugal partner who acted in acted in bad faith shall be applied to his or her children; and if there should be none, to the innocent conjugal partner.

§ 2710. *Both Parties in Bad Faith, Effect of.*—Art. 2197. If both proceeded in bad faith, the ganancials shall be applied to the children; and if there should be none, they shall be distributed in proportion to what each consort carried into the marriage.

§ 2711. *Losses.*—Art. 2198. The losses or decay of the movable property not estimated, although they may arise from a fortuitous case, shall be paid from the ganancials, if there should be any; in a contrary case, the owner shall receive the movables in the state in which they may be found.

§ 2712. *Deterioration of Real Estate.*—Art. 2199. The deteriorations of the immovable property are not chargeable in any case to the owner, except those which may arise from the fault of the husband.[1]

§ 2713. *Mourning Expenses.*—Art. 2200. The mourning of the widow shall be taken from the estate of the husband.

§ 2714. *Rights of Survivor.*—Art. 2201. One of the conjugal partners having died, the survivor shall continue in the possession and administration of the social fund with the intervention of the representative of the execution of the will, until the partition shall be verified.

2715. *Two or More Marriages.*—Art. 2202. When there is to be executed simultaneously the liquidation of two or more marriages contracted by the same person, in default of inventories the ordinary proofs shall be admitted in order to fix the fund of each partnership.

§ 2716. *Doubt.*—Art. 2203. In case of doubt, the ganancials shall be divided between the different partnerships in proportion to the time which they may have lasted and to the value of the individual property of each partner.

§ 2717. *Inventory and Partition.*—Art. 2204. All which relates to the formation of inventories and to the solemnities of the partition and adjudication of the property shall be governed by what the code of procedure may provide.

### Of the Separation of Property.

§ 2718. *Separation, how Made.*—Art. 2205. There may be a separation of property, either in virtue of settlements prior to the marriage or during it, in virtue of an agreement of the consorts or of judicial judgment.

§ 2719. *Settlement.*—Art. 2206. In the settlements which shall establish separation of property shall be observed the provisions in articles 2111, 2113 to 2119, fractions 1, 5, and 6 of article

[1] Article 2199 is amended by the code of 1884, by inserting the words "conjugal administrator" in place of the word "husband."

2120, 2d part of 2122, 2123 to 2128, 2153 to 2155, 2173, 2185, 2186, and 2200, in all that shall be applicable to the separation.

§ 2720. *Conditions of Administration.*—Art. 2207. In settlements of this class the consorts shall establish all the conditions which they shall believe proper for the administration of their property, conforming with the provisions in the preceding article and in the ten which follow.

§ 2721. *Reservation of Rights.*—Art. 2208. The conjugal partners shall preserve the property and the administration of their movables and immovables and the enjoyment of their products.

2722. *Support of Family.*—Art. 2209. Each one of the consorts shall contribute to support the supplies, habitation, the education of the children, and other charges of the marriage, according to the agreement; and in default of an agreement, in proportion to their income. When this shall be insufficient, the expenses shall be charged to their capitals in the same proportion.

§ 2723. *Consent of Husband.*—Art. 2210. The wife can not sell the immovable property, nor real rights, without the express consent of her husband, or of the judge if the opposition is unfounded.

§ 2724. *Void Agreements, What.*—Art. 2211. Any agreement which may contravene the preceding article is null.

§ 2725. *Property Acquired during Marriage.*—Art. 2212. As to property acquired during the marriage by a title common to both conjugal partners and in which no designation of parts has been made, the provisions for the property which forms the legal partnership shall be observed, until a division of said property shall be made.

§ 2726. *Individual Rights.*—Art. 2213. A division between the conjugal partners being made, each one of them shall enjoy exclusively the portion which belongs to him or her.

§ 2727. *Debts Prior to Marriage.*—Art. 2214. The debts prior to the marriage shall be paid out of the property of the conjugal party that owes them.

§ 2728. *Debts during Marriage.*—Art. 2215. The debts contracted during the marriage shall be paid by both conjugal partners, if they shall have been jointly obligated.

§ 2729. *Separate Responsibility.*—Art. 2216. If both shall have been obligated each one shall respond for the debts which he or she shall have contracted.

§ 2730. *Husband's Enjoyment of Wife's Property.*—Art. 2217. If the wife shall have left the enjoyment of her property to her husband, he shall not respond in any case for the fruits consumed. Those existing on dissolving the marriage belong to the wife.

§ 2731. *Separation of Property.*—Art. 2218. A separation of property by an agreement can be verified, either in virtue of a voluntary divorce, or, although there may be no divorce, in virtue of any other grave cause, which the judge may qualify as sufficient, with an audience of the public minister.

§ 2732. *Voluntary Divorce.*—Art. 2219. In the case of a voluntary divorce shall be observed the provisions of articles 248, 249, 253, 2185, 2186, 2189 to 2194, 2198 to 2200, and 2202 to 2204, save marriage settlements.

§ 2733. *Judicial Decree.*—Art. 2220. A separation of property by a judicial decree will take place in the case of a divorce not voluntary, when any one of the consorts shall be condemned to the loss of family rights in conformity with the penal code, and in cases of absence.

§ 2734. *Necessary Divorce.*—Art. 2221. In the cases of necessary divorce, the provisions in articles 273 to 276, and in 2184, and the others cited in 2219, shall be observed.

§ 2735. *Absence.*—Art. 2222. In the cases of absence, they shall proceed in conformity with the provisions in chapter 4, title 13, book 1.

§ 2736. *Separation by Agreement or Decree.*—Art. 2223. In the cases of separation of property by an agreement or decree, the provisions in article 2209 shall be observed.

§ 2737. *Separation Caused by Penalty.*—Art. 2224. When the separation shall take place for a penalty imposed upon the husband, the wife shall administer her individual property; the common property and that of the husband shall be administered by an attorney in fact appointed by the latter, and in default thereof by the wife.[1]

§ 2738. *Wife as Administrator.*—Art. 2225. When the wife shall administer the property she shall have the same powers and responsibilities that the husband would have.

§ 2739. *Wife can not Burden Real Estate.*—Art. 2226. The wife can not, without judicial license, burden nor sell the immovable property which in virtue of the separation may have

[1] Article 2224 is article 2091, new code, and is amended to read as follows: "Art. 2091. When the separation shall take place for a penalty imposed upon the husband, and which disqualifies him to personally administer the property, the wife shall administer her own property and that of the community; and that of the husband shall be administered by the attorney in fact, which he shall appoint, and in default thereof by the wife."

belonged to her, or the administration of which has been charged to her.

§ 2740. *Creditors' Prior Rights.*—Art. 2227. The separation of property does not prejudice the rights acquired with priority by the creditors.

§ 2741. *Registry.*—Art. 2228. The demand for a separation, and the decree which causes execution, must be registered in the office of the public registry.

§ 2742. *Separation after It Ceases, What.*—Art. 2229. When the separtion shall cease by the reconciliation of the consorts in any of the cases of divorce, or on account of the causes having ceased in the others, the partnership shall be restored on the same terms on which they were constituted before the separation, unless the consorts wish to celebrate new settlements, which shall be executed in conformity with the law.

§ 2743. *Acts during Separation.*—Art. 2230. The provisions in the preceding article shall not prejudice in any manner the acts executed nor the contracts celebrated during the separation according to the laws.

### Of Antenuptial Donations.

§ 2744. *Antenuptial, What is.*—Art. 2231. The donations which before the marriage one spouse makes to the other are called antenuptials, whatever may be the name which custom shall have given them.

§ 2745. *Extraneous Parties, Gifts by.* — Art. 2232. Those which an extraneous party makes to any one of the spouses or to both, in consideration of the marriage, are also antenuptial donations.

§ 2746. *Between the Spouses.*—Art. 2233. The antenuptial donations between the spouses, although they should be various, can not exceed altogether the fifth part of the property of the donor. As to the excess, the donation will be inofficious.[1]

§ 2747. *Inofficious Donations.*—Art. 2234. The antenuptial donations made by an extraneous person will be inofficious on the terms on which common ones would be.

§ 2748. *Inofficious, how Determined.*—Art. 2235. In order to calculate whether an antenuptial donation is inofficious, the conjugal donee and his or her heirs have the power of electing the epoch in which the donation was made, or that of the death of the donor.

---

[1] Article 2233 is amended by the code of 1884, by inserting the word "sixth" in place of the word "fifth."

§ 2749. *Election of Time.*—Art. 2236. If on making the donation the inventory of the property of the donor was not formed, the epoch in which that was executed can not be elected.

§ 2750. *Express Acceptation not Required.*—Art. 2237. Antenuptial donations do not require for their validity an express acceptation.

§ 2751. *Not Revoked.*—Art. 2238. Antenuptial donations are not revoked by supervenient children of the donor.

§ 2752. *Not Revoked by Ingratitude.*—Art. 2239. Neither are they revoked by ingratitude, unless the donor should be an extraneous person, or that the donation shall have been made to both spouses, and that both are ungrateful.

§ 2753. *Minors.*—Art. 2240. Minors can make antenuptial donations, but only with the intervention of their parents or tutors, with judicial approbation.

§ 2754. *Failure of Marriage.*—Art. 2241. Antenuptial donations shall remain without effect if the marriage shall fail to be verified.

§ 2755. *If Marriage is Null.*—Art. 2242. If the marriage should be declared null, the donations made in favor of the conjugal partner or partners who acted in good faith shall subsist.

§ 2756. *Bad Faith.*—Art. 2243. Donations made to conjugal partner who acted in bad faith shall belong to his or her heirs; if there should be none, they shall be returned to the donor.

§ 2757. *Bad Faith in Both Parties.*—Art. 2244. If both conjugal partners acted in bad faith, the donations shall remain without effect, unless there shall be children, in which case the donations shall belong to them.

§ 2758. *Common Donations.*—Art. 2245. The rules of common donations are applicable to antenuptial donations in all that which shall not be contrary to this chapter.

### Of Donations between Consorts.

§ 2759. *Between Consorts, how Made.*—Art. 2246. Consorts may make each other donations which do not exceed the fifth part of their present property, by disposition (entre vivos), while living, or by last will, but both only are confirmed by the death of the donor, and provided that they are contrary to the marriage settlements.[1]

[1] Article 2246 is article 2114, new code, and is amended to read as follows: "Art. 2114. Consorts may make each other donations by disposition (entre vivos), or by last will; but they are only confirmed by the death of the donor, and provided that they shall not be contrary to the marriage settlements nor prejudice the right of the ascendants and descendants to receive supplies in conformity with chapter 4, title 2, of book 4."

§ 2760. *Revocation.*—Art. 2247. Donations between consorts may be freely revoked, and at all times, by the donors.

§ 2761. *Authorization not Required.*—Art. 2248. The wife does not require for this effect to be authorized by the husband or by judicial decree.

§ 2762. *Revocation, Express or Tacit.*—Art. 2249. The revocation may be made expressly or by acts which shall make it to be presumed in a necessary manner.

§ 2763. *How not Annulled.*—Art. 2250. These donations shall not be annulled by supervention of children, but they shall be reduced as inofficious if they shall exceed the disposable part of the donor.[1]

[1] Article 2250 is article 2118, new code, and reads as follows: "Art. 2118. These donations shall not be annulled by the supervention of children; but they shall be reduced on the same terms as common ones, in conformity with article 2615 (2733)."

Article 2107 is a new article of the code of 1884, and reads as follows: "Antenuptial donations are revocable and are understood revoked by the adultery or unjustified abandonment of the conjugal domicile on the part of the donor, when the donor should be the other conjugal party."

# CHAPTER XIV.

## DOWER.

§ 2764. *Dower, What is.*—Art. 2251. Dower is any thing or sum which the wife or another in her name gives the husband, with the express object of helping him sustain the charges of matrimony.

§ 2765. *When Constituted.*—Art. 2252. The dower may be constituted before the celebration of the marriage or during it.

§ 2766. *Increase.*—Art. 2253. The dower may be increased during the marriage, but the increase shall not have the dotal character except after the date of its register.

§ 2767. *Governing Articles.*—Art. 2254. In the constitution of the dower and in its increase, the provisions in articles 2114 to 2119 and in 2126 shall be observed.

§ 2768. *All Intervene.*—Art. 2255. In the articles of dower all the interested parties must intervene by themselves or through their legitimate attorney in fact.

§ 2769. *Minors.*—Art. 2256. Minors of either sex can not endow without being emancipated, and with the consent of him who emancipated them, and in default thereof with the consent of the judge. Female minors can not constitute a dower in their favor except with the authorization of the persons whose consent they require to contract matrimony; if they should be married they can not constitute said dower nor increase that which constituted without judicial approbation.

§ 2770. *It may Consist of.*—Art. 2257. The dower may be constituted with the personal and real estate which the wife possessed before contracting the marriage, and it may be increased with that acquired during the marriage.

§ 2771. *Father aud Mother.*—Art. 2258. When the father and mother constitute jointly a dower, without designating the part with which each one contributed, each one remains obligated for the half.

§ 2772. *One of the Parties.*—Art. 2259. If one of the conjugal parties constitute the dower for himself or herself alone, he or she must pay it with his or her own property.

§ 2773. *Eviction.* Art. 2260. Every one who shall give a dower will be obligated for an eviction of the property on which it shall be constituted, save an agreement to the contrary.

§ 2774. *When Dotal.*—Art. 2261. The property acquired

in legal form during the marriage is made dotal: 1. By exchange with other dotal property; 2. By the right of resale (retroventa), whether in virtue of it shall be received the property promised in dower, or whether shall be recovered the dotal property which shall have been legally alienated with that agreement; 3. By giving in payment of the dower; 4. By purchase made with the money of the dower with the previous consent of the wife.

§ 2775. *Payment from Wife's Property.*—Art. 2262. In the cases 1 and 2 of the preceding article, if the money employed should not be of the dotal property it will be paid from that of the wife, or it will be discounted from her property on making the liquidation of her estate.

§ 2776. *Requisite of Dotal.*—Art. 2263. In order that the immovable property purchased according to the fourth case of article 2261 shall be considered dotal it is necessary that the two circumstances which in it are required shall appear in the writing and in the registry.

§ 2777. *Legal Interest.*—Art. 2264. He who shall promise a dower which shall consist in money or fungible things which shall have been estimated, shall pay the legal interest from the day on which according to the contract he should make the delivery; and not having a fixed time, from the day of the celebration of the marriage.

§ 2778. *Title.*—Art. 2265. The title of dower must contain: 1. The name of the one who gives it, that of the one who receives, and of the person in whose favor it is constituted; 2. If he who endows is over or under age; and in the second case, the requisite which article 2253 requires; 3. The class of property or rights in which the dower consists, specifying both, with a statement of their value and burdens; 4. In its case the provision in the following article and that of 2316.

§ 2778 *a*. *Of Money.*—Art. 2266. If the dower shall consist in money, it may be stipulated that this shall be put at interest, and that the husband can only dispose of the latter.

§ 2779. *Fraud.*—Art. 2267. The frauds and simulations about the constitution and delivery of the dower shall be punished with the penalties established for the crimes of fraud and falsification, independently of the indemnification for the damages and losses.

§ 2780. *Daughters.*—Art. 2268. The dower shall always be imputed to the daughters; but if he who constitutes it declares that he gives it by the way of addition (mejora) to the disposable part, only the excess of the legitimate part shall be imputed to the addition made.[1]

### Of the Administration of the Dower.

§ 2781. *Administration by Husband.*—Art. 2269. The administration and the usufruct of the dower belong to the husband, with the restriction contained in article 205, and the free disposition of it with the limitations which are established in this chapter.

§ 2782. *Obligation of Husband.*—Art. 2270. The husband is under the obligation of sustaining the charges of the marriage even when he may not receive a dower; but this being constituted, the wife can not require the security which article 232 concedes to her on the property of the husband, except for want or insufficiency of the dotal property.

§ 2783. *Rights of Husband.*—Art. 2271. The husband has the rights and obligations of the usufructuary, save the provisions in this title; and can exercise all the real and personal actions which shall be necessary for the collection and administration of the dower.

§ 2783 *a.* *Capital Due the Wife.*—Art. 2272. If in the dotal property is comprehended a capital which the husband may owe to the wife, the time to pay it shall remain extended until the epoch in which the dower is to be restored.

§ 2783 *b.* *Interest.—Usufruct.*—Art. 2273. If the capital of which the preceding article treats shall produce interest, this shall be considered as a usufruct of the dower from the celebration of the marriage until the former be restored.

§ 2783 *c.* *Responsibility of Husband.*—Art. 2274. The husband is responsible with his own property for what he shall fail to collect of the capital of the dower, and for all the losses which shall follow therefrom, unless he shall prove there has been no fault nor negligence on his part.

§ 2783 *d.* *Husband's Power.*—Art. 2275. The husband may, save an agreement to the contrary, freely dispose of the common movables belonging to the dower, but he shall respond for their value.

§ 2784. *Power of Disposition.*—Art. 2276. If the dower shall consist of precious movables or of money, the husband

[1] Article 2268 becomes article 2136, new code, and is amended to read as follows: "Art. 2136. The dower constituted by one of the parents shall not be imputed to the hereditary portion of the daughters, whether there be a will or not, except when he who constituted it may have so expressly disposed, and it shall only subsist so far as it shall not prejudice the right of the other legitimate heirs, to receive supplies in legal cases."

can not dispose of it except in the terms which article 2281 provides.[1]

§ 2785. *Mortgage.*—Art. 2277. At whatever time the husband may receive the dower, and when it may become increased, he will be obliged to constitute the mortgage which article 1999 establishes.

§ 2786. *Real Estate.*—Art. 2278. If the husband has no immovables of his own, he shall mortgage the first which he may acquire of that class.

§ 2787. *Not Suspended.*—Art. 2279. The provisions in the two prior articles do not impede nor suspend the power which article 2275 concedes to the husband.

§ 2788. *Not to be Burdened.*—Art. 2280. Neither the husband nor the wife, nor the two together, can alienate, mortgage, or burden in any other manner the dotal immovables, save the exceptions contained in the following articles.

§ 2789. *Alienation.*—Art. 2281. The husband can alienate the dotal immovables, whether they are estimatod or not, provided he has previously secured the restitution of their value, with a mortgage constituted upon his property, or upon the same which he alienates; unless by the articles of dower the alienation thereof is prohibited in every case.

§ 2790. *Endowment of Children.*—Art. 2282. The wife can alienate or mortgage the dotal immovables and precious movables, when the mortgage of which article 2277 speaks is not yet yet constituted, in order to endow or establish her children and descendants who shall not be of the husband.

§ 2791. *Consent to Sell.*—Art. 2283. Both conjugal parties, by consent, can alienate or mortgage the property of which the preceding article speaks, when even the mortgage is not constituted to which article 2277 refers: 1. In order to endow or establish their descendants; 2. In order to cover the expenses of the family which can not be furnished otherwise; 3. In order to pay the debts of the wife or of the party that constituted the dower, prior to the marriage, if they appear in authentic documents and can not be paid with other property; 4. For the indispensable repairs of other dotal property; 5. When the dotal property forms a part of an inheritance or other mass of undivided property, which is not susceptible of a convenient par-

[1] Article 2276 is article 2144, new code, and is amended to read as follows: "Art. 2144. If the dower shall consist in precious movables or in money, the husband can not dispose of it without previously securing the restitution of its value with a mortgage constituted upon his property, unless that by the dotal settlement he is prohibited from making a sale of it in any case."

tition; 6. To exchange or buy other property which must remain with the character of dotal;[1] 7. In the cases of expropriation for a cause of public utility.

§ 2792. *Public Auction.*—Art. 2284. The alienations which articles 2282 and 2283 permit shall be made at public auction with judicial authority.

§ 2793. *Husband.*—Art. 2285. In the case of article 2282, the audience of the husband is also required.

§ 2794. *No Formality.*—Art. 2286. When the value of the property which must be alienated does not exceed three hundred dollars, no formality is required for the sale.

§ 2795. *Judge Limited.*—Art. 2287. The judge can not authorize the sale for more property than is necessary to cover the object in question.

§ 2796. *Mortgage.*—Art. 2288. In order to mortgage the said property, judicial authorization is also required, and the audience of the husband in its case.

§ 2797. *Governing Articles.*—Art. 2289. The provisions in article 2282, and in the fractions 1, 2, 3, 4, 5, and 6 of article 2283, is applicable to any other dotal sums and other property of the wife which in conformity with the articles of dower can not be alienated.

§ 2798. *Expenses.*—Art. 2290. The dower shall also be obligated for the usual and daily expenses of the family, caused by the wife, with the acquiescence or tolerance of the husband, if the property of the latter and the ganancials should not cover them.

§ 2799. *Wife's Indemnification.*—Art. 2291. The wife shall be indemnified for the diminution which her dower suffers by the alienations of which articles 2282 and 2283 treat, so far as they shall have benefited the husband.

§ 2800. *Remaining Sums.*—Art. 2292. The sums which remain after covering the expenses to which the amount of the property alienated must be dedicated shall be considered as dotal; and in respect to said sums, they shall proceed as in the cases in which the dower shall consist of money.

§ 2801. *Lease.*—Art. 2293. The husband can not lease the dotal property not guaranteed even with a mortgage, except for nine years at the most, and with the consent of the wife.

§ 2802. *Duration of Lease.*—Art. 2294. A lease made in con-

[1] Article 2283 becomes article 2151, new code, and is amended by adding to fraction 6 thereof the following: "Or to free any of these from the burden which they may sustain."

formity with the provisions in the preceding article shall subsist for the time agreed, although during it the marriage may be dissolved; but all payments for rents or hiring made to the husband for more than one year in advance shall be null.

§ 2803. *Responsibility of Husband.*—Art. 2295. A husband who alienates or obligates the dotal property in the cases in which he is not permitted makes himself responsible for the damages and losses, as well to his wife as to third parties to whom he shall not have declared the nature of the property sold.

§ 2804. *Prescription.*—Art. 2296. Prescription against the dotal property, immovables, or precious movables, which shall not be even guaranteed with a mortgage, does not run during the marriage. The common dotal movables may be prescribed against, but the husband is responsible for their value.

§ 2805. *Wife's Own Property.*—Art. 2297. The property which a woman married under dotal articles acquires afterwards, and which shall not be included in the dower, shall belong exclusively to her as her own.

§ 2806. *Administration.*—Art. 2298. In respect to the administration and enjoyment of the property of which the preceding article treats, the provisions relative to a legal or voluntary partnership shall be observed in their respective cases, with the separation of property and with mortgages.

### Of Dotal Actions.

§ 2807. *Actions.*—Art. 2299. The wife has a real action of dominion for her dotal immovable property, and for the movables not fungible which are found in possession of the husband at the time of the dissolution of the partnership.

§ 2808. *Rights of Wife.*—Art. 2300. The wife can, during the partnership and after its dissolution, recover the immovable property alienated in contravention of article 2283 and the following ones, although she may have consented to the alienation.

§ 2809. *Mortgages.*—Art. 2301. She can also require that the mortgages imposed thereon be annulled, although the burden shall have been constituted with her consent.

§ 2810. *Precious Movables.*—Art. 2302. When the property sold are precious movables the wife may recover them if they are found in the possession of the first acquirer, or of another who shall have proceeded in bad faith or who shall have acquired them by merely a lucrative title.

§ 2811. *Heirs.*—Art. 2303. The heir of the wife has the same rights.

§ 2812. *Mortgage Action.*—Art. 2304. The wife has a mortgage action on the property of the husband on which the latter shall have constituted a mortgage in conformity with articles 1999, 2000, and 2001.

§ 2813. *Wife's Benefit.*—Art. 2305. The wife has also the benefit which article 2090, fraction 5, concedes to her.

§ 2814. *Bad Administration.*—Art. 2306. If there should be just grounds for believing that the dotal property was in danger, by the negligence or bad administration of the husband, the wife, or her parents or brothers, can, in the case of her being unable, ask the judge that the property be secured, either by limiting the powers of the husband, or by depriving him of the administration.

§ 2815. *Duty of Judge.*—Art. 2307. The judge with an audience of the husband shall judge of the justice of the complaint, having in every case as reasons founded thereby the infractions of articles 2276, 2277, 2278, 2281, and those relative thereto, as well of this title as of that of mortgages.

§ 2816. *Subsistence.*—Art. 2308. The provisions in the two preceding articles shall also be observed when the husband shall not provide for the proper subsistence of the family.

### Of the Restitution of Dower.

§ 2817. *Restoration.*—Art. 2309. The marriage being dissolved, and in the cases provided by articles 274 and 748, the dower shall be restored to the wife or to her heirs.

§ 2818. *Lost.*—Art. 2310. Neither the husband nor his heirs are responsible for the restitution mentioned in the preceding article, if the property of the wife shall be lost by accident which can not be imputable to them.

§ 2819. *When to be Restored.*—Art. 2311. If the dower consists of real estate, or of movables not alienable, it shall be restored as soon as its delivery shall be demanded.

§ 2820. *Delivery.*—Art. 2312. If the dower consists of estimated immovables, of movables sold, or of money, the delivery can only be required six months after the dissolution of the marriage, or after the legal separation.

§ 2821. *Stay.*—Art. 2313. This stay does not take place as to the movable property of the wife, which the husband preserves in his power.

§ 2822. *Legal Interest.*—Art. 2314. The wife and her heirs

can collect notwithstanding the legal interests of the sums retained in the aforesaid form.

§ 2823. *Restoration by Judgment.*—Art. 2315. When the husband shall be deprived of the administration in conformity with articles 2306, 2307, and 2308, and when the partnership shall terminate by a voluntary divorce or by an agreement, the dower shall be restored at the times which the judgments shall respectively fix.

§ 2824. *Dower not Constituted by the Wife.*—Art. 2316. The dower, when it shall not be constituted by the wife, shall be returned to the person and at the times which shall have been expressly agreed; in default of an agreement, the provisions in this chapter shall be observed.

§ 2825. *Real Estate.*—Art. 2317. The dotal immovables shall be restored in the state in which they shall be found; and if they shall have been sold, the price for which the mortgage shall have been constituted shall be restored.

§ 2826. *Alienated Property.*—Art. 2318. The provision in the preceding article will not take place when the property shall have been legally alienated, and the price shall have been invested in the object of the alienation; but if any part of said price remained in respect to it, the restitution shall take place.

§ 2827. *Exchanged.*—Art. 2319. If the alienation was legal, and the price was invested in purchasing other property, which shall remain as dotal in place of that sold, there shall be no restitution of the latter nor of their price, except that of the former.

§ 2828. *Wife and Representatives.*—Art. 2320. Neither shall there be if the price was employed in the exclusive favor of the wife, or of her ascendants or descendants; but if it was employed in favor of the husband, the price must be paid from his property which the sold property had when he received it.

§ 2829. *Deterioration.*—Art. 2321. The husband shall respond for the deteriorations which by his fault the immovable property shall have suffered; but if they were delivered estimated, the wife or her heirs have the right to require the value, even when the property exists.

§ 2830. *Wife's Election.*—Art. 2322. The wife can exercise the actions which articles 2300, 2301, and 2302 concede to her, or require from the husband the price of the property; but if she has used one of those means, she can not use the other.

§ 2831. *Restoration of Fruits.*—Art. 2323. The husband is

obliged to restore the fruits and interest of the dotal property from the day on which he ought to restore the dower.

§ 2832. *Expenses and Improvements.*—Art. 2324. As to the expenses and improvements made on the dotal property, the provisions in respect to a possessor in good faith shall govern in respect to the husband.

§ 2833. *Movable Dotal Property.*—Art. 2325. The movable dotal property which shall exist in the possession of the husband or his heirs shall be restored in the state in which they are found; but if the husband received them estimated, the wife shall have a right to require the price which was then given them.

§ 2834. *Price.*—Art. 2326. The price which must be restored for the movables which may not exist shall be that which was given them when the husband received them; if then they were not estimated, the price for which they were sold shall be delivered; and if they have perished unestimated, that which by suppletory proofs shall be fixed for them.

§ 2835. *Fungible Property.*—Art. 2327. The restitution of fungible property shall be made by delivering the price at which they were estimated; and if they were not estimated, with as much other property of the same kind.

§ 2836. *Value.*—Art. 2328. The value of the movable property not fungible, which shall have been consumed by use or by a fortuitous case, must not be restored.

§ 2837. *Dotal Credit.*—Art. 2329. The dotal credit, or the part of it which is not restored on the same property on which the dower was constituted, must be restored and always paid in money, save an agreement to the contrary.

§ 2838. *Price, how Paid.*—Art. 2330. The price of the dotal movable property which may not exist can be paid with the same movables of the same kind.

§ 2839. *Indemnification.*—Art. 2331. In the same form designated in the preceding articles must be restored the indemnifications due the wife by the husband in the cases which the law designates.

§ 2840. *Usufructs and Rents.*—Art. 2332. If the dower consists of usufructs, censos, or rents, the restitution shall be made by returning the respective titles.

§ 2841. *Stay.*—Art. 2333. In this kind of property the stay conceded in the latter part of article 2312 shall not take place.

§ 2842. *Active Credits.*—Art. 2334. If the dower consists in active credits, the husband shall respond for the sums received.

§ 2843. *Negligence of Husband.*—Art. 2335. If any credits have been prescribed against, or shall have been lost in whole or in part by the fault or negligence of the husband, he shall respond for the relative amount.

§ 2844. *Debtor.*—Art. 2336. If the debtor should have been the father or mother of the wife, and the husband shall not have demanded them judicially, he can not for this sole cause require the amount of the credit from them.

§ 2845. *Credits not Collected.*—Art. 2337. The credits not collected without the fault of the husband shall be restored by delivering the respective title.

§ 2846. *Constitution of Dower.*—Art. 2338. When, on constituting a dower, were comprehended credits of doubtful or difficult collection, estimating them at a price less than the nominal one, if the husband responded for this price he must restore it, whatever may have been the fate of the credits.

§ 2847. *Clothing.*—Art. 2339. The bed and ordinary clothes shall be delivered to the widow, without discounting their price from the dower.

§ 2848. *Two or More Dowers.*—Art. 2340. When the restitution has to be made out of two or more dowers, each one shall be paid with the property which shall exist from their respective source; and if the amount inventoried should be sufficient to cover the rest, they shall be paid according to their dates, save the preference which may belong to them by reason of a mortgage.

§ 2849. *To be Taken from the Dower.*—Art. 2341. From the dower shall be taken the following items, if they shall have been paid by the husband: 1. The amount of the costs and expenses employed for the recovery and defense of the dotal property; 2. The debts and obligations inherent or affected with the dower, which shall not be a charge of the legal partnership; 3. The sums which shall be of the peculiar responsibility of the wife.

§ 2850. *Credit to Husband.*—Art. 2342. When the dower shall be restored, the donations shall be credited to the account of the husband, which his wife shall have legally made him.

§ 2851. *Fruits Pending.*—Art. 2343. The fruits pending on the dotal estates shall be divided in the manner established in article 2146, applying to the husband or to his heirs those which should belong to the partnership.

§ 2852. *Obligation of Wife.*—Art. 2344. If there should be

none manifested or borne, the wife will pay the expenses of cultivation.

§ 2853. *Presumption.*—Art. 2345. The dower constituted with a certain term for its delivery is presumed to be collected by the husband, or has failed to be collected through his fault, ten years after the time is completed.

§ 2854. *Responsibility of Husband.*—Art. 2346. In the case of the preceding article, the husband is responsible for the amount of the dower, unless he shall prove he has employed all the judicial and extrajudicial means necessary in order to realize the collection.

§ 2855. *Dower Constituted by the Wife.*—Art. 2347. The provisions in article 2345 shall not be observed when the dower shall be constituted by the wife or by her parents.

§ 2856. *Expenses.*—Art. 2348. The ordinary expenses and charges of the dotal property shall be compensated with the rents of the same property.

§ 2857. *Rules of Restitution.*—Art. 2349. The rules prescribed about the restitution of the dotal property are applicable to the restitution of the other individual property of the wife.

§ 2858. *Governing Provisions.*—Art. 2350. All the provisions relative to the dower shall govern, whether the marriage has been celebrated with a separation of property, or whether it is to be administered in the conjugal partnership.

# CHAPTER XV.

## DONATIONS.

§ 2859. Donation, What is.
§ 2860. General Rules.
§ 2861. Future Property.
§ 2862. Kinds of Donation.
§ 2863. Pure.
§ 2864. Onerous.
§ 2865. Excess.
§ 2866. Between the Living.
§ 2867. After Death.
§ 2868. Irrevocable.
§ 2869. Verbally or in Writing.
§ 2870. Verbal, when.
§ 2871. Value Limited.
§ 2872. Public Writing.
§ 2873. Real Estate.
§ 2874. Value Stated.
§ 2875. Acceptation.
§ 2876. Separate Acceptance.
§ 2877. Acceptance, how Made.
§ 2878. Null, when.
§ 2879. All Property.
§ 2880. Inofficious.
§ 2881. No Forced Heirs—Effect.
§ 2882. Legal Third.
§ 2883. Death without Disposition of Property.
§ 2884. Express Will of Donor.
§ 2885. Property to One, Usufruct to Another.
§ 2886. Joint Donation.
§ 2887. Responsibility of Donor.
§ 2888. Subrogation—Eviction.
§ 2889. Charge on Donation.
§ 2890. Certain and Definite Property.
§ 2891. All of the Property.
§ 2892. When No Express Declaration of Donor.
§ 2893. Who can Make Donation.
§ 2894. Who can Accept.
§ 2895. Married Women and Minors.
§ 2896. Unborn.
§ 2897. Null, What.
§ 2898. Interposing Persons.
§ 2899. Rescission.
§ 2900. Revoked, when.
§ 2901. When not Revoked.

## Of Donations in General.

§ 2859. *Donation, What is.*—Art. 2712. A donation is a contract by which a person transfers to another, gratuitously, a part or the whole of his present property.

§ 2860. *General Rules.*—Art. 2713. The general rules on contracts are applicable to a donation so far as they are not opposed to the provisions contained in this title (title 15).

§ 2861. *Future Property.*—Art. 2714. A donation can not comprehend future property.

§ 2862. *Kinds of Donations.*—Art. 2715. A donation may be pure, conditional, onerous, or remuneratory.

§ 2863. *Pure.*—Art. 2716. A donation is pure which is executed in absolute terms.

§ 2864. *Onerous.*—Art. 2717. A donation is onerous which is made by imposing any burdens; and remuneratory, that which is made in consideration of services received by the onor, and which does not import a debt.

§ 2865. *Excess.*—Art. 2718. When a donation shall be onerous, the excess there shall be in the price of the thing shall only be considered as given, deducting from it the charges.

§ 2866. *Between the Living.*—Art. 2719. Donations can take place only between the living, and they can not be revoked except in the cases declared in the law.

§ 2867. *After Death.*—Art. 2720. Donations which shall be made to take effect after the death of the donor shall be governed by the provisions relative to legacies; and those which shall be made between consorts, by the provisions in chapter 9, title 10, of this book.

§ 2868. *Irrevocable.*—Art. 2721. A donation is irrevocable from the time the donee accepts it and the acceptation is made known to the donor.

§ 2869. *Verbally or in Writing.*—Art. 2722. A donation can be made verbally or in writing.

§ 2870. *Verbal, when.*—Art. 2723. A verbal donation can not be made except of movable property.

§ 2871. *Value Limited.*—Art. 2724. A verbal donation will only produce legal effects if the value of the thing does not exceed three hundred dollars.[1]

§ 2872. *Public Writing.*—Art. 2725. If the value of the movables donated exceed three hundred dollars, the donation must be executed by a public writing.[2]

§ 2873. *Real Estate.*—Art. 2726. If the donation should be of real estate, it can only be made by a public writing, whatever may be its value; and it will take effect only from the time it is duly registered.[3]

§ 2874. *Value Stated.*—Art. 2727. In the writing shall be made to appear specifically the value of each movable, the qualities of the immovable, and the charges and obligations which are imposed on the donee.

§ 2875. *Acceptation.*—Art. 2728. The acceptation must be made in the same writing of the donation, or in another separate; but it will have no effect if it should not be made in the life of the donor.

§ 2876. *Separate Acceptance.*—Art. 2729. If the acceptation

[1] Article 2724 is amended by the code of 1884, by inserting the word "two" in place of "three."

[2] Article 2725 is amended by the code of 1884, by inserting the word "two" in place of "three."

[3] Article 2726 is amended by the code of 1884 to read as follows: "Art. 2608. If the donation should be of real estate, it can only be made by a public writing, whatever may be its value; and it will take effect against a third party only from the time it is duly registered."

should be made in a diverse writing, the donor shall be notified in due form, and the act shall be noted in the two writings.

§ 2877. *Acceptance, how Made.*—Art. 2730. The donee must, under a penalty of nullity, accept for himself, or by the means of him who shall have his special power for the case, or a general power to accept donations.

§ 2878. *Null, when.*—Art. 2731. A donation is null which comprehends the whole of the property of the giver, if he shall not reserve in property or in usufruct what is necessary for him to live according to his circumstances.

§ 2879. *All Property.*—Art. 2732. If the donor makes a donation of all his property, personal and real, all rights and actions will be comprehended.

§ 2880. *Inofficious.*—Art. 2733. Donations will be inofficious so far as they shall exceed the part which the law declares of free disposition.[1]

§ 2881. *No Forced Heirs—Effect.*—Art. 2734. If he who has no forced heirs makes a general donation of all his property for a cause of death, and reserves some to will, without other declaration, the third part of the property given will be understood as reserved.[2]

§ 2882. *Legal Third.*—Art. 2735. If the donor disposes of his legal third in the aforesaid form, the third part of that will be understood as reserved.

§ 2883. *Death without Disposition of Property.*—Art. 2736. If the donor should die without disposing of the property which has been reserved, and this shall be found in his possession, his legitimate heirs will succeed to it, and in default of these, the donee. In this case the treasury will not succeed.

§ 2884. *Express Will of Donor.*—Art. 2737. The provisions in the preceding article shall be observed, save the will of the donor expressed in the title of donation.

§ 2885. *Property to One, Usufruct to Another.*—Art. 2738. The property may be given to one and the usufruct to another; in this case the rights of the interested parties shall be governed by the provisions contained in title 5 of book 2.

§ 2886. *Joint Donation.*—Art. 2739. A donation made to various persons jointly does not produce in these the right of

[1] Article 2733 is article 2615, new code, and is amended to read as follows: "Art. 2615. Donations will be inofficious so far as they may prejudice the obligation of the donor to furnish supplies to his ascendants, descendants, and conjugal partner, in conformity with chapter 4, title 5, of book 1, and chapter 4, title 2, of book 4."

[2] Article 2734 is article 2616, and is amended by suppressing the words "has no forced heirs," after the words "if he who."

accretion, unless the donor shall have established it in an express manner.

§ 2887. *Responsibility of Donor.*—Art. 2740. The donor is only responsible for the eviction of the thing given, if he was expressly obliged to give it, save the provisions in article 2260.

§ 2888. *Subrogation—Eviction.*—Art. 2741. Notwithstanding the provision in the preceding article, the donee shall be subrogated to all the rights of the donor, if the eviction is verified.

§ 2889. *Charge on Donation.*—Art. 2742. If the donation is made with the charge of paying the debts of the donor, those will only be understood as comprehended which may exist at the time of the donation with an authentic date.

§ 2890. *Certain and Definite Property.*—Art. 2743. If the donation should be of certain and definite property, the donee shall respond for the debts of the donor, except when on the property given there may be constituted some mortgage, or in case of fraud in prejudice to the creditors.

§ 2891. *All of the Property.*—Art. 2744. If the donation should be of all of the property, the donee will be responsible for all of the debts of the donor previously contracted, but only for the sum concurring with the property given.

§ 2892. *When No Express Declaration of Donor.*—Art. 2745. The provisions in the three preceding articles shall be observed when on those points there shall have been no express declaration of the donor accepted by the donee.

### Of the Persons Who may Make or Receive Donations.

§ 2893. *Who can Make Donation.*—Art. 2746. All those who can contract and dispose of their property can make donations.

§ 2894. *Who can Accept.*—Art. 2747. All those can accept donations who are not specially prohibited by a provision of the law.

§ 2895. *Married Women and Minors.*—Art. 2748. In respect to married women, and to minors and others incapacitated, the provisions in articles 207, 624, and 626 shall be observed.

§ 2896. *Unborn.*—Art. 2749. Those not born can acquire by donation, provided that they shall have been conceived at the time in which the donation was made, and shall be alive in conformity with article 327.

§ 2897. *Null, What.*—Art. 2750. Donations made simultaneously to persons who, in conformity with the law, can not receive them, are null, whether they shall be made in a direct manner or by the interposition of another person.

§ 2898. *Interposing Persons.*—Art. 2751. The descendants, ascendants, or the conjugal partner of any of the incapable persons, shall be considered as such interposing persons.[1]

OF THE REVOCATION AND DONATION OF DONATIONS.

§ 2899. *Rescission.*—Art. 2752. Donations may be rescinded or annulled in the cases in which other contracts may be.

§ 2900. *Revoked, when.*—Art. 2753. Donations legally made by a person who at the time of executing them had no forced heirs will be revoked by the sole fact of the supervening to the donor legitimate or legitimated children, or natural or spurious recognized ones, and who may have been born with all the conditions which article 327 requires.[2]

§ 2901. *When not Revoked.*—Art. 2754. A donation will not be revoked by the supervention of children: 1. Being of less than three hundred dollars;[3] 2. Being antenuptial; 3. Being made to any one of the consorts during the marriage.

§ 2902. *Restoration.* — Art. 2755. A donation being rescinded by the supervention of children, the property donated shall be restored to the donor, or its value if they have been sold before the birth of the children.

§ 2903. *Mortgaged Property.*—Art. 2756. If the donee shall have mortgaged the property donated, the mortgage shall subsist; but the donor will have the right to have it redeemed by the former. In the cases of usufruct and service, the provisions

[1] Article 2750 is united to article 2751, and amended by the code of 1844 to read as follows: "Art. 2632. Donations made simulating another contract, to persons who in conformity with the law can not receive them, are null, whether they shall be made in a direct manner or by the interposition of another person. The descendants or ascendants, or the conjugal partner of any of the incapable persons, shall be considered as such interposing persons."

[2] Article 2753 is article 2634, and reads as follows: "Art. 2634. Donations legally made by a person who at the time of executing them had no children may be revoked by the donor when he shall have supervened to him legitimate, legitimated, recognized natural or designated spurious children, and which have been born with all the conditions which article 303 (327) requires. When, in the same case, the legitimate child shall be posthumous, the donation shall be held as wholly revoked."

Article 2635 is a new article of the new code, and reads as follows: "Art. 2635. If in the first case of the preceding article the father should have revoked the donation, this must be reduced when it is found comprehended in the provision of article 2615 (2733), unless the donee shall take upon himself the obligation of furnishing the supplies due to the supervening children, and guarantee in conformity with law the fulfillment of that obligation."

[3] Article 2754 becomes article 2636, and is amended by inserting in fraction 1 "two hundred" in place of "three hundred."

in articles 1026, fraction 8, and 1157, fraction 5, shall be observed.

§ 2904. *How Valued.*—Art. 2757. When the property can not be restored in kind, the demandable value shall be that which it had at the time of the donation.

§ 2905. *Birth of Child.*—Art. 2758. The donee makes his own the fruits of the property donated until the day of the birth of the child.[1]

§ 2906. *Revocation not Renounceable.*—Art. 2759. The donor can not renounce the right of revocation by the supervention of children.

§ 2907. *Action of Revocation.*—Art. 2760. The action of revocation by the supervention of children is only transmitted to them and their legitimate descendants.[2]

§ 2908. *Prescription.*—Art. 2761. The action to ask for the revocation by the supervention of children is lost in twenty years, counted from the date of the birth thereof.

§ 2909. *Failure of Condition.*—Art. 2762. A donation shall be revoked at the instance of the donor when the conditions with which he made it have failed to be complied with.

§ 2910. *Restitution, how Made.*—Art. 2763. In the case of the preceding article the provisions in articles 2755 and 2756 shall be observed; making the restitution of the property, with the fruits and interest, according to the determinations in articles 1462 and 1463.

§ 2911. *Ingratitude.*—Art. 2764. A donation may be revoked for ingratitude: 1. If the donee commits any crime against the person, the honor, or the property of the donor; 2. If the donee accuses the donor judicially of any crime which might be prosecuted officially, although he may prove it, unless it shall have been committed against the said donee, his or her conjugal partner, his or her legitimate[3] ascendants or descendants; 3. If the donee refuses to help, according to the value of the donation, the donor who has become poor.

§ 2912. *Registered Mortgages.*—Art. 2765. The provisions in articles 2754 to 2757 are applicable to revocations of dona-

[1] Article 2758 is amended by the code of 1884, so as to read as follows: "Art. 2640. The donee makes his own the fruits of the property donated until the day on which he is notified of the revocation, or until the day of the birth of the posthumous child, in case there be one."

[2] Article 2760 is article 2642, new code, and is amended to read as follows: "Art. 2642. The action of revocation by the supervention of children belongs exclusively to the donor and to the posthumous child; but that of reduction which article 2634 establishes is transmitted to all the descendants enumerated in the said article."

[3] Article 2764 is article 2646, new code, and is amended by the suppression of the word "legitimate" in fraction 2 thereof.

tions for ingratitude; but mortgages registered before the demand will only subsist, and the fruits received after it will only be restored.

§ 2913. *Renouncement of Action.*—Art. 2766. The action of revocation for a cause of ingratitude can not be renounced in advance, and prescription may be pleaded in one year from the time the act was known.

§ 2914. *Heirs of Donee.*—Art. 2767. This action can not be exercised against the heirs of the donee, unless within the life of the donee it shall have been instituted.

§ 2915. *No Action by Heirs.* — Art. 2768. Neither can this action be exercised by the heirs of the donor, if he, being able, shall not have instituted it.

§ 2916. *Revocation for Inofficiousness.*—Art. 2769. A donation may be revoked for inofficiousness if it imports injury to the legitimate rights of the forced heirs of the donor; and that which is made in fraud of creditors is null.

§ 2917. *Legitimate Right.*—Art. 2770. If the injury to the legitimate right does not equal the total value of the donation, this may be reduced so far as may be necessary in order that the former may be made whole.[1]

§ 2918. *Rules for Inofficiousness.*—Art. 2771. The rules to establish a donation inofficious are established in chapter 4, title 2, of book 4.[2]

§ 2919. *Reductions.*—Art. 2772. The reduction of donations between the living shall commence with the last in date, which shall be totally suppressed if the reduction shall not be sufficient to complete the legitimate right.[3]

§ 2920. *Amount of Donation.*—Art. 2773. If the amount of the latest donation should not suffice, they shall proceed in respect to the preceding one in the terms established in the preceding article, following the same order until the oldest donation is reached.

---

[1] Articles 2769 and 2770 are united into article 2651, which reads as follows: "Art 2651. A donation must be revoked when it is inofficious, in conformity with article 2615 (2733); but if the injury which by it has been caused to those who have a right to receive supplies do not equal the total value of the donation, this will only be reduced in the part which shall be necessary, observing the provisions in articles 2636 to 2639 (2754 to 2757)."

[2] Article 2771 becomes article 2652, and is amended to read as follows: "Art. 2652. Inofficious donations shall not be revoked nor reduced when, the donor being dead, the donee takes upon himself the obligation of furnishing the supplies due by the former, according to the provisions in chapter 4, title 2, book 4, and guarantees in conformity with law the fulfillment of that obligation."

[3] Article 2772 becomes article 2653, and is amended by inserting the words "the supplies" in place of "the legitimate right."

§ 2921. *Reduction pro Rata.*—Art. 2774. There being divers donations executed in the same act or on the same date, the reduction shall be made among them *pro rata.*

§ 2922. *Value.*—Art. 2775. If the donation consists of movable property, the value which it had at the time of being donated must be borne in mind.

§ 2923. *Reduction in Kind.*—Art. 2776. When the donation consists of real estate which may conveniently be divisible, the reduction shall be made in kind.

§ 2924. *Indivisible Real Estate.*—Art. 2777. When the immovable can not be divided, and the amount of the reduction exceeds the half of the value thereof, the donee shall receive the rest in money.

§ 2925. *Half the Value.*—Art. 2778. When the reduction does not exceed the half of the value of the immovable, the donee shall pay the rest in money.

§ 2926. *Donee Who is Heir.*—Art. 2779. The provisions in the two preceding articles are not applicable to a donee who is heir, who can retain the immovable donated, paying what the value thereof may exceed his legitimate right.

§ 2927. *Exoneration from Burden.*—Art. 2780. The reduction or the suppression in case thereof being made, the immovable will be fully exonerated in all or in part of the burdens and mortgages which the donee shall have imposed on it.

§ 2928. *Value at the Time of Donating.*—Art. 2781. If the immovable shall not be found at the time of the revocation or reduction in the possession of the donee, he shall be responsible for the value which it had at the time of the donation.

§ 2929. *Insolvent Donee.*—Art. 2782. When the donee shall be found insolvent, the heirs can recover the property donated if the third possessor should refuse to pay the price which he gave for it.

§ 2930. *Prescription.*—Art. 2783. This action is prescribed, not being instituted within two years, counted from the day on which the heir or legatee shall have accepted the inheritance or legacy.[1]

§ 2931. *Responsibility of Donee.*—Art. 2784. A donation being revoked or reduced on account of being inofficious, the donee shall only respond for the fruits from the time he shall have been demanded; but if he is a co-heir, he shall respond for them from the death of the donor.[2]

---

[1] Articles 2779 to 2783, inclusive, are suppressed by the code of 1884.

[2] Article 2784 is amended by the suppression of all after the words "been demanded."

# CHAPTER XVI.

## CENSOS OR ANNUAL PENSIONS OR ANNUITIES.

## Of Censos or Annual Pensions or Annuities.

§ 2932. *Censo, What is.*—Art. 3206. A censo is the right which a person acquires to receive a certain annual pension for the delivery which he makes to another of a determined sum of money or of an immovable thing.

§ 2933. *Consignativo.*—Art. 3207. The censo is called consignativo when he who receives the money assigns for the payment of the pension (or annuity) the estate, the fee in which he reserves.

§ 2934. *Emphyteutic.*—Art. 3208. The censo is called emphyteutic when the person who receives the estate only acquires the use thereof, reserving to him who receives the annuity the fee.

§ 2935. *Censualista.*—Art. 3209. In the first censo he who receives the pension (or annuity) is called annuitant (censualista), and he who pays it, censatario.

§ 2936. *Owner—Emphyteuta.*—Art. 3210. In the second censo he who receives the annuity is called owner, and he who pays it, emphyteuta.

§ 2937. *Life Rent.*—Art. 3211. If the censo is constituted for the life of one or more persons it is governed by the provisions relative to the contract of life rent.

§ 2938. *Sale on Time.*—Art. 3212. If one should give to another in fee an immovable thing, reserving to himself only a pension, the contract will be considered as a sale on time, and it can not exceed ten years, and shall be governed by the provisions of the title of a purchase and sale.

§ 2939. *Censo Consignativo.*—Art. 3213. The contract which has been called until now an irregular deposit, and every imposition of money on immovables, shall have in the future the name of censo consignativo, and shall be governed by the provisions relative to this title.

§ 2940. *Redeemable.*—Art. 3214. All censos which shall be constituted in the future shall be redeemable; any pact to the contrary shall be null.

§ 2941. *Redeemable by Agreement.*—Art. 3215. The censos existing with the character of irredeemable can be redeemed by an agreement of the parties.

§ 2942. *How Redeemed.*—Art. 3216. Censos can not be partially redeemed except in virtue of an express compact.

§ 2943. *Interest.*—Art. 3217. The interest of the censos shall be determined by the parties according to their discretion, on executing the contract; in default of an agreement, the interest shall be six per cent annually.

§ 2944. *When Demandable.*—Art. 3218. The capital of the censos is not demandable before the time fixed in the contract, unless it is through bankruptcy or insolvency of the debtor, or for want of payment of one of the annuities or pensions.

§ 2945. *Time of Payment.*—Art. 3219. The pensions shall

be paid at the times agreed, and in default of an agreement, at the end of every four months (port ercios vencidos).

§ 2946. *Written Evidence of Delivery.*—Art. 3220. The annuitant, at the time of delivering the receipt of any pension or interest, can oblige the debtor to give him a written security (resguardo), in which the payment shall appear to have been made.

§ 2947. *Prescription.*—Art. 3221. The capital of the censo may be prescribed in twenty years; the interests in the time designated by article 1212.

§ 2948. *Public Writing.*—Art. 3222. Every censo must be constituted in public writing (escritura publica), under the penalty of nullity.

§ 2949. *Action for.*—Art. 3223. The action for the collection of the pensions in every class of censos shall be instituted by verbal process, in conformity with the prescriptions of the code of procedure, and without consideration of the sum which they import.

§ 2950. *Governing Provisions.*—Art. 3224. The provisions in titles 8 and 9 of this book shall be observed in respect to the consos in all that which is not specially determined herein.

§ 2951. *Privileges.*—Art. 3225. The censos guaranteed with mortgages shall enjoy all of the privileges of this law; those which lack this guaranty, although they give a real action, have no more privilege than that which article 2094 concedes to them.

### Special Provisions in Respect to the Consignativo Censo.

§ 2952. *Interest Paid in Money.*—Art. 3226. The interest or pension of the consignativo censo shall always be paid in money, and in the class of money agreed.

§ 2953. *Terms of Redemption.*—Art. 3227. The term of the redemption of the censo remains with the discretion of the parties, but it never can exceed ten years. If it should exceed this term, it shall subsist only as a personal obligation; and if it should be guaranteed with a mortgage, the provisions in articles 1991 and 1992 shall be observed.

§ 2954. *Notice.*—Art. 3228. Neither can it be agreed that the redemption shall not be made without giving notice in advance.

§ 2955. *Provision as to Notice.*—Art. 3229. If nothing should be agreed about the notice, the provision in article 3227 shall be observed.

§ 2956. *Destruction of Estate.*—Art. 3230. If the estate assigned perishes wholly or is destroyed in part, as to the collection of the capital, with its new imposition and with the subrogation of the mortgage, the provisions in articles 1960 and 1963 shall be observed.

§ 2957. *Security of the Pension.*—Art. 3231. If the one who pays the pension (censatario) has other property, he must constitute thereon the whole of the censo or the part which the rest of the things (acensuada) leased, does not cover.

§ 2958. *Reduction of the Pension.*—Art. 3232. If the censatario is wanting in other property with which to make the reimbursement of the capital, or the subrogation of the thing leased, and a part of it exists, he can ask, if he has not been in fault in the destruction or insufficiency of the thing, for the reduction of the pensions in proportion to what shall remain of the estate, according to the judgment of experts appointed, one by each party; or to free himself from the payment of pensions, making a resignation of the thing in favor of the annuitant.

§ 2959. *Fraud or Fault.*—Art. 3233. The censatorio through whose fraud or fault the destruction or partial sterility of the thing shall have happened has no right to ask for a reduction of the pension, nor to make a resignation of the thing, except by the express consent of the annuitant.

§ 2960. *Complete Destruction.*—Art. 3234. In the case of the destruction or complete sterility of the thing, and in which, by the insolvency of the censatorio, the subrogation of which articles 1960 to 1963 and 3231 speak of can not take place, the censo as a real burden shall be extinguished, but the annuitant shall always preserve the personal action against his debtor, save a compact to the contrary.

§ 2961. *Restoration.*—Art. 3235. The estate having been restored or fertilized anew, the censo shall revive if the restoration shall have been made by the censatorio.

§ 2962. *Pensions, when Collected.*—Art. 3236. In the case of the preceding article, the pensions shall only be collected from the restoration if in the loss or sterility of the estate there was no blame or bad faith on the part of the censatorio; if there were, the pensions due can not be collected.

§ 2963. *Personal Action.*—Art. 3237. The estate having been restored or fertilized by a third party, the censo shall not revive, and the personal action, in the terms which article 3234 expresses, shall only remain subsistent.

§ 2964. *Alienation.*—Art. 3238. If the remainder of the thing has been alienated, the censo will revive in a part proportional to the price of the alienation.

### Of the Emphyteutic Censo.

§ 2965. *Quality and Amount.*—Art. 3239. The quality and amount of the emphyteusis shall be regulated by the will of the parties.

§ 2966. *Laudemio.*—Art. 3240. The burden called laudemio[1] can not be imposed on the emphyteuta; and every agreement to secure the collection of the mentioned burden, or of any other outside of the pension, is null.

§ 2967. *Pension Paid in Money.*—Art. 3241. If the emphyteusis should be of an urban estate or building site, the pension shall always be paid in money.

§ 2968. *Boundaries.*—Art. 3242. On constituting the emphyteusis, the estate must be named and described, so that their limits may not be confounded with those of the surrounding estates.

§ 2969. *Value.*—Art. 3243. The value of the estate shall be made with a deduction of the amount of the fee, capitalizing the pension, which by reason thereof must be received at so much agreed per cent, and in default of an agreement, at six per cent annually.

§ 2970. *Experts.*—Art. 3244. The valuing and marking of boundaries shall be done by experts appointed at the will of the contracting parties, and the report thereof shall be inserted in the writing of the contract.

§ 2971. *When and where Paid.*—Art. 3245. The pension shall be paid at the time and place agreed.

§ 2972. *When No Agreement.*—Art. 3246. If there should be no place agreed upon, the pension shall be paid in the house of the owner if he lives in the district where the estate is situated.

§ 2973. *Payment, where Made when Owner Absent.*—Art. 3247. If the owner shall not reside in the district or he shall not have an agent therein, the payment shall be made in the domicile of the emphyteuta.

§ 2974. *Time of Payment.*—Art. 3248. If there should be no time designated, and the pension should consist in fruits, payment shall be made at the end of the respective harvest; if

---

[1] A tax paid to the owner of the fee when lands and the possession are sold which have been given forever, or at least for a long time, in emphyteusis. It consisted of a fiftieth part of the price for which the property and possession sold for.

it should consist in money, at the end of the year counted from the date of the contract.

§ 2975. *Division.*—Art. 3249. In case of a division of the emphyteusis the provisions in articles 1955 and 1956, with the following additions, shall be observed.

§ 2976. *Division by Lots.*—Art. 3250. If the owner should consent to the division by lots, each one of these shall constitute a diverse emphyteusis, and the owner can only require the respective pension from each one of the emphyteutas, in conformity with the distribution made.

§ 2977. *Distribution.*—Art. 3251. The distribution shall be made by experts appointed by the parties, and it shall have no legal value except when the report thereof shall be made to appear in public writing (escritura publica), including in this the express consent of the owner.

§ 2978. *Pension may be Increased, when.*—Art. 3252. In case of a division, the pension may be increased which shall correspond with each one of the new emphyteutas, with the quota which the said experts shall fix in order to compensate the inconvenience which may result from the division of the collection.

§ 2979. *Hereditary.*—Art. 3253. The emphyteusis is hereditary; and when there shall have been no agreement in opposition to the distribution, it shall be distributed among the heirs according to the provision in article 3251.

§ 2980. *Agreement.*—Art. 3254. If there is an agreement in opposition to the division, the heirs can elect among themselves who is to continue in the contract; and not being able to agree, he shall be elected by chance.

§ 2981. *Sale.*—Art. 3255. If none of the heirs shall accept, the emphyteusis shall be sold and the price shall be divided among them.

§ 2982. *In Default of Heirs.*—Art. 3256. In default of testamentary or legitimate heirs of the last emphyteusis, the estate shall be returned to the owner.

§ 2983. *Alienable Estate.*—Art. 3257. Only alienable real estate can be given in emphyteusis, save the following provisions:

§ 2984. *Minors.* Art. 3258. The estates of minors and persons incapacitated can not be given in emphyteusis except by judicial authorization, solicited by the tutor with the consent of the curator, and with an audience of the public minister.

§ 2985. *Who can Concede.*—Art. 3259. All those who can contract or alienate their property can concede in emphyteusis.

§ 2986. *Emphyteusis.*—Art. 3260. Married persons can not give their property in emphyteusis except in the cases and with the conditions which the law has established to alienate it.

§ 2987. *Who can Receive in Emphyteusis.*—Art. 3261. All those who can contract may receive in emphyteusis, excepting: 1. Corporations and any other public establishments; 2. Those who can not purchase according to the provision in articles 2968, 2972, and 2975.

§ 2988. *Owner's Rights.*—Art. 3262. The owner has a right to be paid the pensions agreed upon wholly and punctually and to enjoy the privilege on the property of the emphyteusis in the terms of article 2077, fraction 6.

§ 2989. *Confiscation.*—Art. 3263. If the emphyteuta fails to pay the pension for three consecutive years, he shall lose the estate as confiscated, if the owner wishes to recover it.

§ 2990. *Not Necessary to Sue.*—Art. 3264. In order to incur confiscation, it is not required that the owner shall have demanded judicially the emphyteuta.

§ 2991. *One Quarter Loss.*—Art. 3265. If the emphyteuta deteriorates the estate so that it loses a quarter part of its value, the owner may recover it as confiscated.

§ 2992. *Usufruct.*—Art. 3266. The emphyteuta has a right to enjoy the usufruct of the estate and dispose of it as a thing of his own, save the restrictions expressed in this code.

§ 2993. *Notice of Disturbance.*—Art. 3267. If the emphyteuta should be disturbed in his rights by a third party, who disputes the title in fee and the validity of the censo, he must notify the owner of the suit; and if he should not do it, he will have no action against the latter for the damages and losses which he may suffer by the judgment of eviction.

§ 2994. *Defense.*—Art. 3268. The owner in every case can defend the suit alone.

§ 2995. *Taxes.*—Art. 3269. The emphyteuta is obliged to pay all the predial or personal taxes imposed on account of the estate.

§ 2996. *Taxes on Pension.*—Art. 3270. Notwithstanding the provision in the preceding article, the owner must pay the emphyteuta the taxes imposed on the pension itself.

§ 2997. *Burden on the Estate.*—Art. 3271. The emphyteuta can mortgage the estate and impose upon it any other charge or service without the consent of the owner; but in case of a return, the estate shall pass free to the owner if he has not consented to those burdens.

§ 2998. *Exchange or Sale.*—Art. 3272. The emphyteuta can give or exchange the estate freely; but in this case the grantee must make it known to the owner within sixty days, counted from that on which the cession was made.

§ 2999. *Grantee.*—Art. 3273. The grantee who shall not comply with the provision in the preceding article shall be responsible jointly with the emphyteuta for the payment of the pensions.

§ 3000. *Right of Preference.*—Art. 3274. The owner and the emphyteutica, whenever they wish to sell or give in payment the rights which they respectively enjoy in the thing, will have the right of preference.

§ 3001. *Notice of Sale.*—Art. 3275. He who intends an alienation must give notice to his co-proprietor of the définite price which may be offered him; and if within thirty days, counted after the required party shall receive formal notice, he should not use his privilege and pay really and effectively, the former can alienate freely his right.

§ 3002. *Extinguishment.*—Art. 3276. If the required party makes use of his privilege, and really and effectively pays, the censo is extinguished.

§ 3003. *Judicial Sale.*—Art. 3277. This right subsists even in the case of a judicial sale, and if, the estate being publicly cried, no bidder shall present himself, the owner may ask for the adjudication in the terms established in the code of procedure.[1]

§ 3004. *Void Sales.*—Art. 3278. If the emphyteuta does not comply with the provision in article 3275, the alienation is null, and the owner may recover the estate as confiscated.

§ 3005. *Damages.*—Art. 3279. If he who failed in the provision in the cited article 3275 was the owner, the emphyteuta shall have no right to recover the estate, but he will have the right to require the indemnification for the damages and losses which he may prove resulted to him by the preterition.[2]

§ 3006. *Defendants.*—Art. 3280. The emphyteuta shall institute his demand against the owner if the latter was alone culpable; and against the owner and the acquirer if both acted by consent in the preterition.

---

[1] Article 3277 is amended by the code of 1884, by adding thereto the following: "In respect to the adjudication in favor of the creditor."

[2] Article 3279 is amended by the code of 1884, by adding thereto the following: "If the owner shall not have colluded with the acquirer; in case of collusion, the emphyteuta can recover the estate."

§ 3007. *Various Estates.*—Art. 3281. The estates being various in which the emphyteusis were constituted, none of the contracting parties can choose some and reject others in case of preference, but they must do it in respect to all.

§ 3008. *Back Services.*—Art. 3282. The owner can not require back services of more than five years except by personal action, in case that the credit shall appear in writing, signed by the emphyteuta with two witnesses more, or acknowledged before a notary.

§ 3009. *Prescription.*—Art. 3283. In the emphyteusis prescription may take place in the form which is established in the respective title of book 2.

§ 3010. *Fortuitous Case.*—Art. 3284. If the estate is destroyed or made wholly useless by *vis major* or a fortuitous case, the contract shall terminate.

§ 3011. *Destruction in Part.*—Art. 3285. If the estate should be destroyed or made useless only in part, the emphyteuta can require the owner to reduce the pension; and if he should oppose it, the former can free himself by making a resignation of the emphyteusis.

§ 3012. *Confiscation—Action.*—Art. 3286. The action for confiscation in the cases of articles 3264 and 3278 may be prescribed within one year, counted from the last execution, or from the act of sale; and in the case of article 3265, within one year counted after notice has been had of the deterioration of the estate.

§ 3013. *Destruction of Fruit.*—Art. 3287. In case of extraordinary sterility, or of fortuitous destruction of fruits, so that sufficient thereof shall not remain to pay the pension, the cost of the seed and expense of cultivation being deducted, the emphyteuta will not be obliged to pay what is lacking, provided that before the gathering of the crop he shall give notice to the owner.

§ 3014. *Agreement.*—Art. 3288. The provision in the preceding article shall not be observed if it has been otherwise agreed in the contract.

§ 3015. *Rescission.*—Art. 3289. In every case in which a contract of emphyteusis shall be rescinded by confiscation or other cause, the owner must credit the improvements which shall have increased the value of the estate; but only when the increase shall subsist at the time of the rescission.

§ 3016. *Retention of the Estate.*—Art. 3290. The provision in the preceding article does not give a right to the emphyteuta to retain the estate.

# CHAPTER XVII.

## SUCCESSIONS.

§ 3158. Equal Parts.
§ 3159. Institution of Heir, how Made.
§ 3160. Heir's Obligation.
§ 3161. Individually Named.
§ 3162. Whole and Half Brothers.
§ 3163. Simultaneous Heirs.
§ 3164. Heirs, how Named.
§ 3165. Identity Sufficient.
§ 3166. Error in Name.
§ 3167. Uncertainty, Void for.
§ 3168. The Soul, the Poor, etc.
§ 3169. Subsequent Birth of Heir.
§ 3170. Natural and Spurious Children—Division.
§ 3171. Death of Children before That of Testator.
§ 3172. Forced Heirs Protected.
§ 3173. No Alteration of Legitimate Right.
§ 3174. Donations *entre Vivos.*
§ 3175. Promise to Improve.
§ 3176. Promise when Null.
§ 3177. Reputed Improvement.
§ 3178. Improvement, how Designated.
§ 3179. When not Designated.
§ 3180. Power not to be Delegated.
§ 3181. Legacies, of What They may Consist.
§ 3182. Excess in Legacy.
§ 3183. When No Forced Heirs Exist.
§ 3184. Incapable Persons.
§ 3185. Capacity of Legatees.
§ 3186. Governing Articles.
§ 3187. Legacy of Thing, Act, or Service.
§ 3188. Creditors.
§ 3189. Burden on Legacies.
§ 3190. Responsibility.
§ 3191. Charge, how Paid.
§ 3192. Acts.
§ 3193. Reduction of Charge.
§ 3194. Governing Articles.
§ 3195. Void Legacies.
§ 3196. Existence of the Thing in the Inheritance.
§ 3197. Not in Commerce.
§ 3198. Invalid Legacies.
§ 3199. Legacies without Effect.
§ 3200. Sale of the Thing.
§ 3201. Indefinite Movables.
§ 3202. Election.
§ 3203. Election, how Made.
§ 3204. Verbal Trial.
§ 3205. Immovables.
§ 3206. Restriction of Right.
§ 3207. Pledges.
§ 3208. Securities.

§ 3260. Specific Things.
§ 3261. Risk of Legatee.
§ 3262. Security.
§ 3263. Rights of Legatee for Security.
§ 3264. When Only Legatees.
§ 3265. Error in Name.
§ 3266. Delivery of Possession.
§ 3267. When in Possession of Legatee.
§ 3268. Condition of the Thing.
§ 3269. Delivery in Kind.
§ 3270. Money, Legacies of.
§ 3271. Expenses of Delivery.
§ 3272. Taxes.
§ 3273. Whole Estate in Legacies.
§ 3274. Insufficient to Cover Legacies.
§ 3275. Right of Legatee to Recover.
§ 3276. Insurance.
§ 3277. Actions under Void Will.
§ 3278. Substitutes.
§ 3279. How Appointed.
§ 3280. Heir of Substitute.
§ 3281. Simple Substitution.
§ 3282. Minors.
§ 3283. Ascendants can Appoint Substitutes.
§ 3284. Substitution, when not Valid.
§ 3285. Recovery of Capacity.
§ 3286. How Substitute shall Receive Inheritance.
§ 3287. Unequal Parts.
§ 3288. Fiduciary Substitutes Prohibited.
§ 3289. Nullity of Imports, What.
§ 3290. What is not Fiduciary.
§ 3291. Heir, Usufructuary, when.
§ 3292. When Disposition Null.
§ 3293. Prohibited Disposition.
§ 3294. Prohibition, not against the Poor.
§ 3295. Definite Property.
§ 3296. Capitalization, how Made.
§ 3297. Heirs, how Burdened.
§ 3298. May Establish Beneficence.
§ 3299. Collateral Relatives.
§ 3300. Public Beneficence.
§ 3301. Heirs and Legatees.
§ 3302. Disinheritance.
§ 3303. Cause of Disinheritance.
§ 3304. Heirs of Disinherited Parties.
§ 3305. Ascendants not to be Deprived.
§ 3306. Disinheritance, how Made.
§ 3307. Proof.
§ 3308. Disinheritance without Cause, Insufficient.
§ 3309. Support of Disinherited Parties.
§ 3310. Prescription.

## Preliminary Provisions.

§ 3017. *Inheritance, What is.*—Art. 3364. Inheritance is the succession in all the properties of the deceased, and in all his rights and obligations which are not extinguished by death.

§ 3018. *How Declared.*—Art. 3365. Inheritance is declared by the will of man, or by the provisions of the law. The first is called testamentary; the second legitimate.

§ 3019. *By Will and Law.*—Art. 3366. The inheritance of the same person may also be declared in part by the will of man, and in the other part by the provisions of the law.

§ 3020. *Heir.*—Art. 3367. The heir represents the person of the author of the inheritance.

§ 3021. *Part Distribution.*—Art. 3368. If the testator distributes a part of his property in legacies without disposing of the rest, the legitimate heir is the representative of the deceased.

§ 3022. *Legatees.*—Art. 3369. When all the inheritance is distributed in legacies, the legatees will be considered as heirs, and under this character will be representatives of the testator.

§ 3023. *Death of All.*—Art. 3370. If the author of the inheritance and his heirs or legatees should perish in the same disaster, or on the same day, without its being known who died first, it shall be considered that all died at the same time, and the transmission of the inheritance or legacy shall not take place between them.

§ 3024. *Proof of Death.*—Art. 3371. The proof that one person has died before another devolves upon the person who has an interest in proving the fact.

§ 3025. *Transmission.*—Art. 3372. The title and legal possession of the properties, and the rights and obligations of the author of the inheritance, are transmitted by the death of the latter to his heirs in the terms established in the present book.

§ 3026. *Manner of Succession.*—Art. 3373. The law calls to the succession in the order, form, and terms established in this code: the legitimate and illegitimate descendants born, or posthumous; the legitimate and illegitimate ascendants; the consort that survives; the collateral relations and the public treasury.

Of Successions by Will.—Of Wills in General.

§ 3027. *Will, What is.*—Art. 3374. The act by which a person disposes of his property or a part thereof, to take effect after his death, is called a will.

§ 3028. *Personal.*—Art. 3375. A will is a personal act, which can not be performed by an attorney.

§ 3029. *Appointment of Heirs and Legatees.*—Art. 3376. The permanence of the appointment of heirs or legatees can not be left to the discretion of a third party, nor the designation of the amounts which correspond to them when they are instituted nominally.

§ 3030. *Distribution.*—Art. 3377. A testator may commit to a third party the distribution of the quantities which he may leave to determined classes, as relatives, the poor, orphans, etc., and the election of the persons to whom they ought to be applied.

§ 3031. *Election of Objects.*—Art. 3378. A testator may also commit to a third party the election of objects or public establishments of beneficence to which he leaves his properties, and the distribution of the quantities which belong to each one.

§ 3032. *Nearest Heir.*—Art. 3379. The vague disposition of the testator in favor of relations will be understood in favor of the nearest, according to the order of the legitimate succession.

§ 3033. *False Cause.*—Art. 3380. The expression of a false cause will be considered as not written, unless it follows from the said will that the testator would not have made that disposition knowing the falsity of the cause.

§ 3034. *Illegal Cause.*—Art. 3381. The expression of a cause contrary to law, although it may be true, will be held as not written.

§ 3035. *Institution of Heir—Time.*—Art. 3382. The designation of a day or time in which the institution of an heir ought to commence or cease will be held as not written.

§ 3036. *Two or More Persons.*—Art. 3383. Two or more persons can not will in the same act, whether in a reciprocal benefit or in favor of a third person.

§ 3037. *Doubts.*—Art. 3384. In case of doubt relative to the understanding of a testamentary disposition, what appears to be most in conformity with the intention of the testator shall be observed, according to the tenor of the will and the auxiliary proof which can be rendered in this respect.

§ 3038. *Lost Will.*—Art. 3385. If an open will, whether public or private, be lost, by an event unknown to the testator or on account of having been secreted by another person, the interested parties can require its fulfillment if they duly show the fact of the loss or secreting, and the contents of said will.

Of the Conditions Which may be Put in Wills.

§ 3039. *Testator's Freedom.*—Art. 3386. The testator is free to dispose of his property upon certain conditions.

§ 3040. *Failure of Condition.*—Art. 3387. The want of the fulfillment of any condition imposed upon an heir or legatee will not prejudice them, provided they have employed all necessary means to fulfill the condition.

§ 3041. *Impossible Condition.*—Art. 3388. A condition physically or legally impossible, whether to do or not to do, is held as not put in the will.

§ 3042. *Condition Possible.*—Art. 3389. If the condition which was impossible at the time of the execution of the will should fail to be so at the death of the testator, it will be valid.

§ 3043. *Void Condition.*—Art. 3390. The institution made upon the condition that the heir or the legatee shall make in his will some disposition in favor of the testator or of another person is null.

§ 3044. *Suspensive Condition.*—Art. 3391. The condition which only suspends for a certain time the execution of the will will not impede the heir or legatee from acquiring a right to the inheritance or legacy, and from transmitting it to their heirs.

§ 3045. *Governing Articles.*—Art. 3392. In respect to the conditions placed in wills, the provisions contained in articles 1445 to 1464 shall govern in all that which is not specially determined in this book.

§ 3046. *Doubtful Events.*—Art. 3393. The disposition with

a term designated by an event which may not happen is reputed made upon the condition that that event takes place.

§ 3047. *Positive Event.*—Art. 3394. A disposition with a term designated by a fixed day, or by an event which necessarily will happen, is not conditional.

§ 3048. *Time for Condition.*—Art. 3395. When the testator shall not have designated the time for the fulfillment of the condition, the thing bequeathed shall remain in the possession of the executor; and the partition having been made, the provisions in articles 4047, 4048, and 4049 shall be observed.[1]

§ 3049. *Potestative.*—Art. 3396. If the condition is purely possible (potestativa), and to give or do something, and he who has been burdened with it offers to comply with it, but he in whose favor it is established refuses to accept the thing or the act, the condition is held as fulfilled.

§ 3050. *Potestative Condition—Fulfillment.*—Art. 3397. The potestative condition shall be held as fulfilled when the heir or legatee has given the thing or done the act before the will shall have been executed, unless the service shall be reiterated; in which case the latter will not be obligatory except when the testator may have had knowledge of the first.

§ 3051. *Proof.*—Art. 3398. In the final case of the preceding article the proof that the testator had knowledge of the first service belongs to him who ought to pay the legacy.

§ 3052. *Negative Condition.*—Art. 3399. The condition of not giving or of not doing will be held as not imposed.

§ 3053. *Casual or Mixed Condition.*—Art. 3400. If the condition should be casual or mixed, it will be sufficient that it be realized in any time, the testator being alive or dead, if he should not have otherwise disposed.

§ 3054. *Complied Condition.*—Art. 3401. If the condition had been complied with on the making of the will, the testator being ignorant thereof, it will be held as complied with; but if he knew it, it will only be held as complied with if it can not now exist or be complied with again.

§ 3055. *Void Condition.*—Art. 3402. The condition imposed upon an heir or legatee to take or to fail to take a state (condition in life) is held not imposed.

---

[1] Article 3395 is amended by the code of 1884 so as to read as follows: "Art. 3258. When the testator shall not have designated the time for the fulfillment of the condition, the thing bequeathed shall remain in the possession of the executor; and on making the partition, the right of the legatee shall be competently secured for the purpose of complying with the condition, observing besides the provisions established to make the partition when one of the heirs is conditional."

§ 3056. *Bachelor or Widower.*—Art. 3403. The usufruct, the use, the habitation, or a pension, or a periodical service, may be validly left to one for the time which he shall remain bachelor or widower.

§ 3057. *Retroactive.*—Art. 3404. The condition which has been fulfilled, the person on whom it is imposed existing, shall be retroactive from the time of the death of the testator, and from then the fruits of the inheritance or legacy ought to be credited, unless the testator otherwise expressly disposed.

§ 3058. *Resolute Condition.*—Art. 3405. The charge of doing anything is considered as a resolute condition.

§ 3059. *No Time for Fulfillment.*—Art. 3406. If no time should be designated for the fulfillment of the charge, and this should not have it by its own nature, the provision in article 3395 will be observed.

§ 3060. *Periodical Service.*—Art. 3407. If the legacy should be of a periodical service, which must conclude on a day which is uncertain whether it will arrive or not, the day having arrived, the legatee will have made his own all the services which correspond up to that day.

§ 3061. *Day Certain.*—Art. 3408. If the day on which the legacy ought to commence were certain, whether he who has to deliver the thing bequeathed shall know or not when it must arrive, he will have in respect to the thing the rights and the obligations of the usufruct.

§ 3062. *Fulfillmeut of Periodical Service.*—Art. 4009. In the case of the preceding article, if the legacy consists in a periodical service, he who ought to pay it makes his all that which corresponds to the interval, and complies by making the service, commencing the day designated.

§ 3063. *Day Certain — Conclusion of Legacy.* — Art. 3410. When the legacy ought to conclude on a day which is certain to arrive, the thing or sum bequeathed to the legatee will be delivered, who will be considered as usufructuary of it.

§ 3064. *Legatee's Rights.*—Art. 3411. If the legacy should consist in a periodical service, the legatee will make his own all the sums due up to the day designated.

### Of the Capacity to Will and to Inherit.

§ 3065. *Persons Who may Will.*—Art. 3412. The law only recognizes capacity to will in the persons who have: 1. A perfect knowledge of the act; 2. A perfect liberty to execute the act; that is, exempt from intimidation and all moral influence.

§ 3066. *Want of Certain Requisites.*—Art. 3413. For want of the first of the requisites mentioned in the article which precedes, the law considers incapable of willing: 1. A male less than fourteen years and a female less than twelve; 2. He who is found habitually and accidentally in a state of mental alienation, while the impediment lasts.

§ 3067. *Valid Will.*—Art. 3414. A will made before the mental alienation is valid.

§ 3068. *Lucid Intervals.*—Art. 3415. Also is valid a will made by a demented person in a lucid interval, provided the following prescriptions are observed.

§ 3069. *Demented Persons.*—Art. 3416. Whenever a demented person attempts to make a testament, his tutor, and in his default the family of the former, shall present a petition in writing to the judge, who, accompanied by two physicians, shall visit the house of the patient.

§ 3070. *Eamination.*—Art. 3417. The physicians shall examine the infirm person, asking him, as well as the judge, all questions which they shall believe conducent in order to ascertain his mental state.

§ 3071. *Report.*—Art. 3418. A formal act shall be drawn up, in which shall be made to appear the result of the examination.

§ 3072. *Making of Will.*—Art. 3419. If this should be favorable, they will proceed immediately with the formation of the will, the clauses of which shall be precisely drawn in writing, and with the other solemnities which are required for this class of instruments.

§ 3073. *Signing Wills.*—Art. 3420. The act being terminated, the judge and physicians, besides the witnesses, shall sign it; placing at the bottom of the will an express statement that during all the act the patient preserved a perfect lucidness of judgment; without which requisite and proof the testament will be null.

§ 3074. *Failure of Other Requisites.*—Art. 3421. For want of the second of the requisites mentioned in article 3412, the law considers incapable to will those who on executing a testament act under the influence of threats against their life, liberty, honor, or their property, or against the life, liberty, honor, or property of their consort, or of their relations in any degree.

§ 3075. *Revalidation.*—Art. 3422. The testator who is found in the case of the article which precedes can, as soon as the violence ceases and he enjoys complete liberty, revalidate his testament with the same solemnities as if he should execute it anew; otherwise the revalidation will be null.

§ 3076. *Foreigners.*—Art. 3423. Foreigner who make a will in the district and in California may select the law of their country or the Mexican law in respect to the internal solemnity of the act; as to the external solemnities, they must subject themselves to the precepts of this code.

§ 3077. *Proof of Capacity.*—Art. 3424. In order to judge of the capacity of the testator, the state in which he is found on making the will will be considered.

§ 3078. *District—California—Inhabitants of.*—Art. 3425. All the inhabitants of the district and of California, of whatever age and sex they may be, have capacity to inherit, and they can not be deprived of it in an absolute manner; but with relation to certain persons and determined properties, they may lose it for any of the following causes: 1. A want of personality; 2. A crime; 3. A presumption of influence contrary to the liberty of the testator or to the truth or integrity of the will; 4. A want of international reciprocity; 5. Public utility; 6. A renouncement or removal of any charge conferred in the will.

§ 3079. *Incapable of Acquiring.*—Art. 3426. For want of personality they are incapable of acquiring by will or intestacy, who shall not be conceived at the time of the death of the author of the inheritance, or that even when they are, are not capable of living (viable) in conformity with the provisions in article 327, or should be born after three hundred days, counted from the death of the former.

§ 3080. *Valid Will for Certain Children.*—Art. 3427. Notwithstanding the disposition will be valid made in favor of the children who shall be born of certain and determined persons living at the time of the death of the testator; but what is made in favor of descendants of the ulterior degrees will not be valid.

§ 3081. *Incapable by Crime of Acquiring.*—Art. 3428. By reason of crime they are incapable of acquiring by will or by intestacy: 1. A person condemned for having given, ordered, or attempted to kill the person whose succession is in question, or the parents, children, or consort of said person; 2. He who shall have made against said person an accusation of a crime which merits capital punishment or imprisonment, even when that is established, if it were his descendant, his ascendant, his consort, or his brother, unless that act has been necessary in order that the accuser should save his life or that of some of his descendants or ascendants, or brother or consort;[1] 3. The consort who survives and has been declared an adulterer in court, during the life of the other, or who shall be divorced, and shall have given cause for the divorce, if the question shall be of the succession of the deceased consort; 4. The wife condemned as an adulteress in the life of her husband, if the question shall be of the succession of the legitimate children had by the marriage in which she committed the adultery; 5. The father and the mother in respect to the child exposed by them; 6. He who shall have committed against the honor of the deceased, or that of his children, or of his consort, or of his parents, an attempt by which he ought to be punished criminally, if it should be so declared in court; 7. He who shall use violence with the deceased in order to cause him not to make his will or to revoke it; 8. The father or the mother in respect to his natural or spurious children, and of the descendants of the latter, if he has not recognized them; 9. Persons declared incestuous, provided the question is of the succession of the one in respect to the other; 10. He who, in conformity with the penal code, shall be guilty of suppression, substitution, or supposition of an infant, whenever the question is of the inheritance which ought to have belonged to the latter, or to the persons whom he has injured or attempted to injure by those acts; 11. The accomplice of the adulterous consort, whenever the question is of the succession of the latter, if the judicial sentence has been pronounced before the death of the author of the inheritance.

§ 3082. *Accusation, Character of.*—Art. 3429. In the case of fraction 2 of the prior article, if the deceased should not be a descendent, ascendent, nor consort of the accuser, it will be necessary that the accusation be declared calumnious.

§ 3083. *Pardon.*—Art. 3430. When the party aggrieved by any of the modes which article 3428 expresses shall pardon the offender, the latter shall recover the right to succeed the offended party by intestacy, if the pardon shall appear by an authentic declaration, or by undoubted facts.

§ 3084. *Capacity Recovered.*—Art. 3431. The capacity to succeed by will is only recovered if after the damage is known the

[1] Article 3428 is amended by the code of 1884 so as to read as follows, in fraction 2 thereof: "He who shall have made against the author of the succession, or against his conjugal partner, an accusation of a crime which merits capital punishment or imprisonment, even when that is established, if it were his descendant, his ascendant, his consort, or his brother, unless that act has been necessary in order that the accuser should save his life or that of some of his descendants or ascendants, or brother or consort."

offended party institutes the offender an heir or revalidates his former institution with the same solemnities which are required to make a will.

§ 3085. *Tutors and Curators.*—Art. 3432. By the presumption of an influence contrary to the liberty of the author of the inheritance, the tutors and curators of a minor are incapable of acquiring his property by his will, unless they are instituted before being appointed for the charge or after the age of majority of the minor, the accounts of tutorship being already approved.

§ 3086. *Incapacity, Extent of.*—Art. 3433. The incapacity to which the preceding article refers does not comprehend the ascendants and brothers of the minor, save in every case the provision in fraction 7 of article 3428.

§ 3087. *Physicians and Ministers.*—Art. 3434. For the same reason on which is founded article 3432, the physician and minister, of whatever worship, who attended the deceased in the last sickness are incapable of inheriting by will, unless they were also legitimate heirs.

§ 3088. *Notary Public—Penalty.*—Art. 3435. The notary who knowingly authorizes a will in which the preceding article is contravened shall be deprived of office. The judge to whom the will shall be presented shall officially impose this penalty summarily, and if he does not, he shall be suspended for six months. Neither relative to the deprivation nor suspension, shall be admitted any recourse in the suspensive effect; but these may be reinstated on appeal (devolutivo).

§ 3089. *Notary and Witnesses.*—Art. 3436. By the presumption of an influence contrary to the truth or integrity of a will, the notary and witnesses who shall be instituted in it, and in the execution and authorization of which they shall have intervened, are incapable of succeeding.

§ 3090. *Foreigners.*—Art. 3437. For want of international reciprocity, foreigners who, according to the laws of their country, can not will, or leave by intestacy their property in favor of Mexicans, are incapable of inheriting by will or by intestacy from the inhabitants of the District or of California.

§ 3091. *Corporations.*—Art. 3438. On account of public utility, ayuntamientos and religious corporations or corporations of public beneficence, of whatever class they may be, are incapable of acquiring real estate, either by inheritance or by legacy.[1]

[1] Article 3438 becomes article 3301, new code, and reads as follows: "Art. 3301. On account of public utility the moral persons whom the political constitution of the republic prohibits from acquiring real estate, whether by inheritance or as legatee, are incapable of holding this kind of property."

§ 3092. *Public Establishments.*—Art. 3439. A legacy which shall be left to a public establishment, imposing any burden or upon any condition, shall only be valid if the government shall approve of it.

§ 3093. *Privilege of Testator—Corporations.*—Art. 3440. A testator is free to designate the person who shall manage the capitals imposed which he may leave to public corporations and establishments.

§ 3094. *Sums Left to Corporations.*—Art. 3441. The sums which are left in money to public corporations and establishments shall be immediately imposed, and the administrators shall give a detailed notice thereof to the government.

§ 3095. *The Poor.*—Art. 3442. A disposition made in favor of the poor in general, without a designation of persons or town, shall avail only those of the domicile of the testator at the time of his death, if his will does not clearly appear to have been otherwise.

§ 3096. *Distribution to the Poor.*—Art. 3443. The qualification of the poor and the distribution shall be made by the person whom the testator may have designated; in default thereof by the executor, and in default of the latter by the judge.

§ 3097. *The Judge.*—Art. 3444. If it is the judge who makes the qualification and distribution, he must apply the funds to the hospitals or houses of charity or of education dependent upon the government.

§ 3098. *Dispositions for the Soul.*—Art. 3445. A general disposition of an aliquot part of the property which the testator may make in favor of his soul, without determining the pious or beneficent act which he wishes to be executed, shall be understood to have been made in favor of the establishments of public beneficence.

§ 3099. *Tutors, Curators, and Executors.*—Art. 3446. By the renouncement or removal from a charge, they are incapable of inheriting by a will who, being appointed in it as tutors, curators, or executors, shall have refused without a just cause the charge, or by bad conduct shall have been judicially separated from its exercise.

§ 3100. *Limit of Certain Dispositions.*—Art. 3447. The disposition in the first part of the preceding article does not comprehend forced heirs in their legitimate portion, nor those whose excuse has been thrown out by the judge, they having served the charge.[1]

[1] Article 3447 is amended by the code of 1884 so as to read as follows: "Art. 3310. The disposition in the first part of the preceding article does not comprehend those whose excuse has been thrown out by the judge, they having served the charge."

§ 3101. *Capability of the Heir.*—Art. 3448. In order that the heir may succeed, it is sufficient that he be capable at the time of the death of the author of the inheritance.

§ 3102. *Conditions.*—Art. 3449. If the institution should be conditional, it will be necessary besides that the heir be capable at the time in which the condition is fulfilled.

§ 3103. *Voluntary Heir.*—Art. 3450. A voluntary heir who dies before the testator, or before the condition is fulfilled, the party incapable of inheriting, and he who renounces the succession, do not transmit any right to their heirs.

§ 3104. *Legitimate Heir.*—Art. 3451. In the cases of the preceding article, the inheritance belongs to the legitimate heirs of the testator, unless the latter has disposed otherwise, or that the right of accretion must take place.

§ 3105. *Incapable Person's Possession.*—Art. 3452. Should he who is incapable of succeeding enter into the possession of the property, he must restore it with all its accessions, and with all the fruits and rents which he shall have received.

§ 3106. *Substituted Person.*—Art. 3453. He who inherits in place of the party excluded will have the same charges and conditions which legally had been imposed upon said party.

§ 3107. *Usufruct and Management.*—Art. 3454. The incapable party will not have the usufruct nor the management of the property which, in the cases designated in articles 3427, 3486, and 3634, belong to their descendants.

§ 3108. *Hereditary Debtor.*—Art. 3455. The hereditary debtors who should be sued, and who in no case can have the character of heirs, can not plead against him who is in possession by the right of heir or legatee the exception of incapacity.

§ 3109. *Allowances.*—Art. 3456. Incapacity does not deprive one of the allowance which by law belongs to him, except in the cases of fractions 1, 2, 3, 6, 7, 8, and 11 of article 3428.

§ 3110. *Judicial Termination.*—Art. 3457. Incapacity does not produce the effect of depriving the incapable party of what he should have received, except after it has been declared in court on the petition of some interested party; the judge not being able to move it officially.

§ 3111. *Prescription.*—Art. 3458. No action can be brought to declare the incapacity after five years shall have passed from the time the incapable person is in possession of the inheritance or legacy.

§ 3112. *Sale and After Loss by Inapacity.*—Art. 3459. If he who entered into the possession of the inheritance and lost it afterwards by incapacity should have alienated or burdened the whole or a part of the property before being cited in court for the possession, and the person with whom he contracted should have had good faith, the contract will stand; but the incapable heir will be obliged to indemnify the legitimate one for all damages and losses.

OF THE LEGITIMATE RIGHT, AND OF INOFFICIOUS WILLS.

§ 3113. *Legitimate Right.*—Art. 3460. The legitimate right is the portion of property destined by law for the heirs in a right line, ascending or descending, which for this reason is called forced.

§ 3114. *Heirs of Legitimate Right.*—Art. 3461. A testator can not deprive his heirs of the legitimate right except in the cases designated in the law.

§ 3115. *No Burdens nor Conditions.*—Art. 3462. The legitimate right does not admit burdens, nor conditions, nor substitution of any kind.

§ 3116. *Four Fifths.*—Art. 3463. The legitimate right consists in four fifths of the property if the testator only leaves legitimate or legitimated descendants, in two thirds if he only leaves natural children, and in the half if he only leaves spurious children.

§ 3117. *Legitimate and Natural Children.*—Art. 3464. If the testator should leave legitimate or legitimated and natural children, the four fifths part of the property shall be considered the legitimate right of all of them; but on distributing this among the mentioned children, shall be deducted from the divisible portion which belongs to the natural children one third, which shall be added to the divisible among the legitimate ones, and not to the fifth of which the father may dispose.[1]

[1] Articles 3460 to 3464, inclusive, are suppressed in the code of 1884.

The following twelve articles are new ones:

"Art. 3323. Every person has a right to freely dispose of his property by will, with title of inheritance or of legacy.

"Art. 3324. This right is not limited, except by the obligation of leaving supplies to the descendants, to the surviving conjugal partner, and to the ascendants, in conformity with the following rules: 1. To the male descendants of less than twenty-five years; 2. To the male descendants who may be impeded from work, and to the women who may not have contracted marriage and live honestly, both even when they may be over twenty-five years; 3. To the surviving conjugal partner, provided that being a male he is impeded from working, or that being a woman she remains a widow and lives honestly; 4. To the ascendants.

"Art. 3325. There is no obligation to leave supplies to descendants, except for want or for the impossibility of ascendants nearer in degree. Neither is there an obligation to leave supplies to ascendants, except for want and for an impossibility of nearer descendants.

"Art. 3326. There is no obligation to leave supplies when the descendants or surviving conjugal partner shall have their own property; but if

§ 3118. *Example.*—Peter, author. John and Lewis, legitimate children. Joseph and Sexton, natural children. Peter on dying leaves a capital of $15,000, and four children; two legitimate, John and Lewis, and two natural, Joseph and Sexton. The disposable part of the father will be $3,000. The $12,000 remaining shall be distributed fictitiously among the four children, and to each one will belong $3,000; but deducting $1,000, the portion of each one of the natural children, they will both receive $4,000. Adding the $2,000 which was deducted from the portion of the natural children to the $6,000 divisible among the legitimate ones, each one of these will receive $4,000, and both $8,000.

§ 3119. *Legitimate and Spurious Children.*—Art. 3465. A concurrence of legitimate children with spurious ones, the legitimate right of the four fifths belongs exclusively to the first; and the second will only have a right to support,

---

having their product does not equal the pension which belongs to them, the obligation shall be reduced to what may lack to complete it.

"Art. 3327. In order to have the right to be supplied it is necessary to be found at the time of the death of the testator in some of the cases fixed in article 3324; and that right ceases as soon as the interested party, failing to be in the conditions to which said article refers, shall observe bad conduct or acquires property of his own, applying in this case the provisions in article 3326.

"Art. 3328. The right of receiving supplies is not renounceable, nor can it be an object of transaction. The pension for living shall be fixed and secured in conformity with articles 211, 212, 214, 217, and 220 (222, 223, 225, 228, and 232) of this code, and for no reason shall it exceed the products of the portion which in case of intestate succession would correspond to him who shall have a right to said pension, nor below the half of said products. If the testator should have fixed the pension for living (pension alimenticia), his designation shall subsist, whatever it may be, provided it does not go below the minimum before established. With the exception of the articles cited in the present one, the provisions of chapter 4, title 5, of book 1. are not applicable to the supplies due by succession.

"Art. 3329. The provisions of article 3324 only comprehend the legitimate descendants and the illegitimate recognized or designated, and the legitimate ascendants or who have recognized the descendants whose succession is in question.

"Art. 3330. When the hereditary wealth shall not be sufficient to furnish supplies to all the persons enumerated in article 3324, they shall be furnished in the first place to the descendants and to the surviving conjugal partner *pro rata*, and only their pensions being wholly covered, the ascendants shall be furnished *pro rata*, and whatever may be their line or grade.

"Art. 3331. A will is inofficious in which the pension for living is not left according to what is established in this chapter.

"Art. 3332. The ascendant, descendant, or conjugal partner (preterido) omitted, will only have a right to have given him the pension which corresponds to him, the will subsisting in all that which does not prejudice that right.

"Art. 3333. The pension (alimenticia) for living is a charge on the hereditary mass, except when the testator shall have burdened with it some of the participants in the succession.

"Art. 3334. Notwithstanding the provisions in article 3332, the posthumous child shall have a right to receive entire the portion which should correspond to him as legitimate heir if there should be no will, unless the testator shall have expressly otherwise disposed."

which shall be drawn from the free fifth of the author of the inheritance, and in no case can they exceed the quota which would correspond to the spurious if they were natural children.

§ 3120. *Natural and Spurious Children.*—Art. 3466. A concurrence of natural children with spurious ones, the legitimate right will consist of all of two thirds of the property; but on making the division, one half will be deducted from the part which corresponds to the spurious, which will increase the divisible portion between the natural children, and not the third of the free disposition.

§ 3121. *Example.*—Peter, author. John and Lewis, natural children. Joseph and Sexton, spurious children. Peter dies leaving a capital of $12,000, and four children; two natural ones, John and Lewis, and two spurious ones, Joseph and Sexton. The division shall be made in this form: The disposable third of the father, $4,000. A fictitious division of two thirds remaining between the four children, which will give for each one of them $2,000; but deducting from each one of the spurious one half, both will receive $2,000. Adding the $2,000 deducted from the spurious ones to the portion divisible among the natural ones, both will receive $6,000.

§ 3122. *Descendants of Second Degree.*—Art. 3467. The legitimate right of the descendants of the second or ulterior degree will be that which ought to correspond to the person whom they shall represent, observing in respect to the descendants of the legitimate children the provisions in article 3864.

§ 3123. *Legitimate Right Two Thirds, when.*—Art. 3468. If the author of the inheritance, at the time of his death, should have no children, but if the father or mother should be living, the legitimate right of the parents will consist of two thirds of the inheritance.

§ 3124. *Legitimate Right One Haf, when.*—Art. 3469. If the author of the inheritance should only have, at the time of his death, ascendants of other degrees, the legitimate right of these will consist of the half of the property.[1]

§ 3125. *Ascendants and Legitimate Children.*—Art. 3470. By a concurrence of ascendants of any degree with legitimate children, the four fifths parts will belong exclusively to the children; and the ascendants will only have a right to a support, which will be drawn from the body of the inheritance, but without its exceeding in any case the portion of one of the children.

§ 3126. *Ascendants and Natural Children.*—Art. 3471. By a

[1] Articles 3467 to 3469, inclusive, are suppressed in the code of 1884.

concurrence of ascendants of the first degree with natural children, the legitimate right of both will consist of two thirds of the inheritance, which will be divided in equal parts between the descendants and ascendants, considering the latter as one person.[1]

§ 3127. *Example.*—Louis and Mary, parents. Antonio, author. Peter and Ann, natural children. Antonio, author of the inheritance, dies leaving living his parents, Louis and Mary, and two natural children, Peter and Ann, and a liquidated capital of $18,000, which is divided in this form: The disposable third of the author of the inheritance, $6,000, the portion of Peter, $4000, the portion of Ann, $4,000, the portion of the parents, Louis and Mary, which will be divided between them in equal parts, giving each one $2,000—$4,000.

§ 3128. *Ascendants of Second Degree with Natural Children.* Art. 3472. By a concurrence of ascendants of the second or ulterior degree with natural children, the legitimate right of the children will consist of two thirds of the inheritance, and the ascendants only will have a right to a support, which shall be deducted from the third of free disposition.

§ 3129. *Ascendants of First Degree and Spurious Children.* Art. 3473. By a concurrence of ascendants of the first degree with the spurious children, two thirds of the inheritance will be the legitimate right of both; but on making the division, one half will be deducted from the divisible portion between the children, which will increase the divisible portion among the ascendants, and not the third of free disposition.

§ 3130. *Example.*—Louis and Mary, parents. Antonio, author. Peter and Martha, spurious children. Antonio, author of the inheritance, dies leaving living his parents, Louis and Mary, and two spurious children, Peter and Martha, and a capital of $18,000. The division will be made in this manner: The disposable third of the author of the inheritance, $6,000. The portion of each one of the children, deducted one half; which produces for both $4,000. The part deducted $4,000 added to the $4,000 divisible between the parents, each one of these will have $4,000, and both $8,000.

§ 3131. *Ascendants of Second Degree with Spurious Children.* Art. 3474. By a concurrence of ascendants of the second and ulterior degree with spurious children, the legitimate right of

[1] Article. 3471 is amended by the code of 1884 so as to read as follows: "Art. 3601. By a concurrence of ascendants of the first degree with natural children, the estate will be divided in equal parts between the descendants and ascendants, considering the latter as one sole person."

all will be the half of the inheritance; which will be divided into equal parts among the ascendants and the spurious children, considering those as one person.[1]

§ 3131 *a*. *Ascendants of Any Degree with Legitimate and Natural Children.*—Art. 3475. By a concurrence of ascendants of any degree with legitimate and natural children, the provisions in article 3464 will be observed, and the ascendants will only have the right of support which shall be drawn from the body of the inheritance.[2]

§ 3132. *Ascendants of First Degree with Natural and Spurious Children.*—Art. 3476. By a concurrence of ascendants of the first degree with natural and spurious children, the legitimate right of both will be two thirds of the inheritance; but on making the division, the part corresponding to the spurious children, one half, will be deducted, which will increase the divisible portion between the ascendants and the natural children.[3]

§ 3133. *Example.*—Peter and Martha, parents. John, author. Joseph and Leon, natural children. Sexton and Maurice, spurious children. John, on dying, leaves living his parents, Peter and Martha, and four children, two natural ones, Joseph and Leon, and two spurious ones, Sexton and Maurice, and a divisible capital of $30,000. The partition will proceed in this form: The third disposable by the author of the inheritance, $10,000. The fictitious portion of each one of the descendants and of both ascendants, $4,000. The half of each one of the spurious children being deducted, these will remain with $4,000. Adding the $4,000 deducted to the $12,000 divisible between the ascendants and the natural children, $16,000 will result, distributed in this form: The portion of both descendants, $10,666.6C⅔. The portion of both ascendants, $5,333,33⅓.

§ 3134. *Ascendants of Ulterior Degree with Natural and Spurious Children.*—Art. 3477. By a concurrence of ascendants of ulterior degrees with natural and spurious children, the legiti-

[1]Article 3474 is amended by the code of 1884 so as to read: "Art. 3604. By a concurrence of ascendants of the second and ulterior degree with spurious children, the estate will be divided into equal parts among the ascendants and the spurious children, considering those as one person."

[2]Article 3475 is article 3605, new code, and is amended by inserting the words "in conformity with article 3600" (3470) in place of the words "which shall be drawn from the body of the inheritance."

[3]Article 3476 is amended by the code of 1884 so as to read: "Art. 3606. By a concurrence of ascendants of the first degree with natural and spurious children, on making the division, the part corresponding to the spurious children, one half, will be deducted, which will increase the divisible portion between the ascendants and the natural children."

mate right and the partition thereof will be those which article 3466 establishes, and the ascendants will only have the right of support, which will be taken from the free third.

§ 3135. *Legal Recognition.*—Art. 3478. The provisions of this chapter relative to natural and spurious children shall only comprehend those which shall have been legally recognized.[1]

§ 3136. *Rights of Ascendants.*—Art. 3479. The ascendants, even when they may be legitimate, shall have the rights which are conceded to them in this chapter, provided the descendants shall have been recognized whose succession is in question.

§ 3137. *Recognition after Inheritance of Descendant.*—Art. 3480. If the recognition is verified after the descendant has inherited or acquired a right to an inheritance, neither he who recognizes nor his descendants have any right to the inheritance of the party recognized, and can only ask support, which shall be conceded to them in conformity with the law.

§ 3138. *Excuse may be Accepted.*—Art. 3481. The natural children as well as the spurious can in their testamentary disposition excuse the default of recognition, and leave to their ascendants what by law would correspond to them if they had not committed the default.[1]

§ 3139. *Inofficious Wills, What.*—Art. 3482. A will is inofficious which diminishes the legitimate right in any of the cases comprehended in articles 3463 to 3477, save the provision in article 3497.

§ 3140. *Right of Forced Heir.*—Art. 3483. The right of the forced heir in the case of the preceding article is only that of asking for the complement of his legitimate right.

§ 3141. *Preterition.*—Art. 3484. The preterition of any or of all the heirs in a right line, whether they be living on the execution of the will or shall be born after, although the testator being dead, annuls the institution of heir; but the legacies and improvements (mejoras), so far as they may not be inofficious, shall be valid.

§ 3142. *Institution of Heir No Effect, when.*—Art. 3485. If the forced heirs (preteritos) omitted, shall die before the testator, the institution will have effect.

§ 3143. *Death of Forced Heir.*—Art. 3486. The legitimate right of the forced heir who dies before the testator, that of the person incapacitated from inheriting, and that of him who re-

[1] Articles 3478 and 3481 are suppressed in the code of 1884.

nounces the succession shall form a part of the hereditary mass which shall be divided in conformity with the provisions in this chapter.

§ 3144. *Value of Property Considered.*—Art. 3487. In order to fix the legitimate right, the value of the property which may have remained at the death of the testator will be considered, with the deduction of the debts and charges, without comprehending among them those imposed by the will.

§ 3145. *Donations entre Vivos.*—Art. 3488. To the liquidated value of the hereditary property will be added that of the donations *entre vivos* according to the provisions in chapter 3, title 15, book 3.

§ 3146. *Reduction of Legacies.*—Art. 3489. The legitimate right being fixed in the terms provided in the preceding article, the legacies shall be reduced in the order established in chapter 7 of this title.

§ 3147. *What Legacies to be Reduced.*—Art. 3490. If the testator designated for the reduction any legacy, the others shall not be reduced, except when the amount of that which shall have been designated shall not be sufficient.[1]

§ 3148. *Preference.*—Art. 3491. If the testator gave a preference in the payment of a legacy, this shall not suffer the reduction except when the amount of the others has not been sufficient to cover the legitimate right.

§ 3149. *Usufruct or Life Rent.*—Art. 3492. If the disposition consists of a usufruct or of a life rent, the value of which shall be considered superior to the disposable part, the forced heirs can choose between executing the disposition or abandoning the disposable part.

§ 3150. *Distribution among Legatees.*—Art. 3493. When in the case of the preceding article there should be other legacies, and the heirs should deliver the disposable part, if the testator shall not have disposed that the life rent or the usufruct may be preferred to the other legacies, the disposable part shall be distributed among all the legatees according to the judgment of the judge if they should not agree.

§ 3151. *Exercise of Rights.*—Art. 3494. If the heir or legatee to whom the right conceded in articles 2778 and 2779 belongs should not use it, the other interested party can exercise it if he should have any real right on the thing given; and if none of them shall exercise it, the immovable shall be sold at public auction.

[1]Articles 3482 to 3490, inclusive, are suppressed in the code of 1884.

§ 3152. *Insufficiency of Donations.*—Art. 3495. If the value of the testamentary donations shall not suffice to complete the legitimate right, those made *entre vivos* shall be applied to its payment, on the terms which articles 2770 to 2784 establish; the provisions of which shall also be observed in the reduction of the legacies.

§ 3153. *Renunciations of Future Rights.*—Art. 3496. Every renunciation or transaction relative to the legitimate future right is null; those who shall make it can reclaim it whenever they who shall owe it die; but they must bring to the collation what in the case they shall have received.[1]

### Of the Institution of Heirs.

§ 3154. *Conjugal Partner.*—Art. 3497. Although there are forced heirs, the testator is free to leave or not to his conjugal partner the part to which by intestacy she may have the right, in the terms and with the conditions which articles 3884 and 3885 establish; if besides the testator should leave said partner the part of free disposition, this shall not be considered among the individual properties of the conjugal partner, for the effects of the articles cited.

§ 3155. *Testator's Privilege.*—Art. 3498. He who has no forced heirs may freely dispose of his property in favor of any person who has a legal capacity to acquire it.[2]

§ 3156. *Institution of Heir.*—Art. 3499. A will legally executed will be valid although it may not contain an institution of heir, and although the party named does not accept the inheritance or be incapable of inheriting.

§ 3157. *Fulfillment of Disposition.*—Art. 3500. In the three cases designated in the preceding article the other testamentary dispositions which shall be made in conformity with the laws shall be fulfilled.

§ 3158. *Equal Parts.*—Art. 3501. Heirs instituted without a designation of the part which shall belong to each one will inherit in equal parts.

§ 3159. *Institution of Heir, how Made.*—Art. 3502. The institution of heir may be made either by assigning to the named party a certain thing or a definite sum, or an aliquot part of the inheritance.

§ 3160. *Heir's Obligations.*—Art. 3503. The heir shall not respond for the debts, for the legacies, nor for the other hered-

[1] Articles 3491 to 3496, inclusive, are suppressed in the code of 1884.

[2] Articles 3497 and 3498 are suppressed in the code of 1884.

itary and testamentary charges, except so far as the amount he inherits may suffice.

§ 3161. *Individually Named.*—Art. 3504. Although the testator may name some heirs individually and others collectively, as if he should say: "I institute for my heirs Peter and Paul and the children of Francis;" the collectively named shall be considered as if they were individually named, unless it shall be known in a clear manner that the will of the testator has been otherwise.

§ 3162. *Whole and Half Brothers.*—Art. 3505. If the testator institutes his brothers, and he has some of them only by his father, some of them only by his mother, and some by his father and mother, the inheritance will be divided as in the case of an intestate.

§ 3163. *Simultaneous Heirs.*—Art. 3506. If the testator calls to the succession a certain person and his children, all will be understood as instituted simultaneously and not successively.

§ 3164. *Heirs, how Named.*—Art. 3507. The heir must be instituted by designating him by his family and christian name; and if there should be various heirs who shall have the same family and christian name, they must be designated by other names and circumstances which shall distinguish him whom he wishes to appoint.

§ 3165. *Identity Sufficient.*—Art. 3508. Although the name of the heir may have been omitted, if the testator shall designate him in a manner that can not be doubted who he is, the institution will be valid.

§ 3166. *Error in Name.*—Art. 3509. An error in the family or christian name or qualities of the heir will not vitiate the institution if it may be otherwise known who is the person appointed.

§ 3167. *Uncertainty, Void for.*—Art. 3510. If among various individuals of the same name and circumstances it can not be known whom the testator wished to designate, no one will be heir.

§ 3168. *The Soul, the Poor, etc.*—Art. 3511. When the soul, the poor, or any public establishment shall be appointed heirs, the provisions of articles 3377, 3378, and 3488 to 3445 shall be observed.

§ 3169. *Subsequent Birth of Heir.*—Art. 3512. The appointment of heir, and the distribution of an estate in legacies made by a person who has no children, nor legitimate nor legitimated descendants will be forfeited by the subsequent birth of those heirs, and only remain valid for the part which the testator can freely dispose of.

§ 3170. *Natural and Spurious Children—Division.*—Art. 3513. If after the institution of a spurious child as heir a natural one is born; or if being instituted, the former or the latter, a legitmate one shall be born, the inheritance must be divided in conformity with articles 3464, 3465, and 3466.

§ 3171. *Death of Children before That of Testator.*—Art. 3514. If the after-born children should die before the testator the disposition will be valid.

### Of Improvements (Mejoras).

§ 3172. *Forced Heirs' Protected.*—Art. 3515. Every disposition of a testator which has for its object the diminution of the legitimate right of his forced heirs in favor of any one or any of them is null.

§ 3173. *No Alterations of Legitimate Right.*—Art. 3516. The law, save the provision in article 3497, does not consent to any more alteration in the legitimate rights assigned in chapter 4 to forced heirs than that which results from the total or partial application which to one of them the testator may make of his part of free disposition.

§ 3174. *Donations entre Vivos.*—Art. 3517. No donation by contract *entre vivos*, whether simple or for an onerous cause, in favor of forced heirs, shall be reputed an improvement (mejora), if the donor has not declared formerly his will to improve.[1]

§ 3175. *Promise to Improve.*—Art. 3518. A promise to improve made in public writing (escritura publica) and accepted by him to whom it is made is equivalent to an improvement.

§ 3176. *Promise, when Null.*—Art. 3519. If the promise should be not to improve, and it should be made in a public writing, all improvement made in contravention thereof shall be null.

§ 3177. *Reputed Improvement.*—Art. 3520. An increase which the testator makes to the legitimate right of any one of the forced heirs shall be reputed an improvement, even when in the will that name should not be given it.

§ 3178. *Improvement, how Designated.*—Art. 3521. An improvement may be designated by him who makes it in a certain thing, and it is valid if the price of the thing does not exceed the free part.

[1] Articles 3512 to 3517 inclusive are suppressed in the code of 1884.

§ 3179. *When not Designated.*—Art. 3522. When the improvement shall not have been designated in a certain thing, it shall be paid with the same hereditary property, observing, so far as can take place, articles 4071 and 4072.

§ 3180. *Power, not to be Delegated.*—Art. 3523. A testator can not commit the power to any one to improve, nor that of designating the thing or sum in which the improvement may consist.[1]

### Of Legacies.

§ 3181. *Legacies, of What They may Consist.*—Art. 3524. A testator who has forced heirs can only distribute in legacies the part which in conformity with chapter 4 of this title is not comprehended in the legitimate right.

§ 3182. *Excess in Legacy.*—Art. 3525. A legacy which exceeds the part of free disposition must be reduced and even suppressed as inofficious.

§ 3183. *When No Forced Heirs Exist.*—Art. 3526. A testator who has no forced heirs can distribute in legacies a part of his property or all of it.[2]

§ 3184. *Incapable Persons.*—Art. 3527. Those who are incapable of inheriting are incapable of acquiring by legacy.

§ 3185. *Capacity of Legatees.*—Art. 3528. In respect to the capacity of legatees, the provisions in articles 3426 to 3449 shall be observed.

§ 3186. *Governing Articles.*—Art. 3529. In respect to legatees, articles 3450, 3451, and 3452 will govern.

§ 3187. *Legacy of What.*—Art. 3530. A legacy may consist of the use (prestacion) of a thing or of an act or service.

§ 3188. *Creditor.*—Art. 3531. A creditor whose credit only appears by a will will be considered for the legal effects as a preferred legatee.

§ 3189. *Burden on Legacies.*—Art. 3532. A testator can burden with legacies, not only the heirs but the same legatees; who are not obliged to respond to the burden, except so far as the value of their legacy.

§ 3190. *Responsibility.*—Art. 3533. An heir or legatee whom the testator has expressly burdened with the payment of a legacy will only be responsible therefor in the terms which the preceding article, 3503, establishes.

§ 3191. *Charge, how Paid.*—Art. 3534. If the heir or legatee should renounce the succession, the charge which has been

[1] Articles 3518 to 3523, inclusive, are suppressed in the code of 1884.

[2] Articles 3524 to 3526, inclusive, are suppressed in the code of 1884.

imposed upon them shall be paid only with the sum to which he who renounced had a right.

§ 3192. *Acts.*—Art. 3535. If the charge consist of an act, the heir or the legatee who accepts the succession is obliged to perform the act.

§ 3193. *Reduction of Charge.*—Art. 3536. If a legatee on whom is imposed any burden does not receive all of the legacy, the charge shall be reduced proportionally; and if he suffers eviction, he can claim what he has paid.

§ 3194. *Governing Articles.*—Art. 3537. The provision in respect to heirs in articles 3504, 3505, and 3506 shall also be observed in respect to legatees.

§ 3195. *Void Legacies*—Art. 3538. The legacy which a testator makes of a thing of his own, individually determined, which at the time of his death is not found in his estate, is null.

§ 3196. *Existence of the Thing in the Inheritance.*—Art. 3539. If the thing mentioned in the preceding article exist in the inheritance but not in the sum or numbers designated, the legatee shall have whatever there may be.

§ 3197. *Not in Commerce.*—Art. 3540. A legacy of a thing not in the commerce of men is null.

§ 3198. *Invalid Legacies.*—Art. 3541. If by the act of the testator a thing be bequeathed loses the form and denomination which determined it, the legacy will produce no effect.

§ 3199. *Legacies without Effect.*—Art. 3542. A legacy remains without effect if the thing bequeathed wholly perishes, living the testator, if it is lost by eviction, or if it perishes after the death of the testator without the fault of the heir.

§ 3200. *Sale of Thing.*—Art. 3543. A legacy also remains without effect if the testator sells the thing bequeathed; but valid if he recovers it by a valid title.

§ 3201. *Indefinite Movables.*—Art. 3544. A legacy of an indefinite movable thing, but comprehended in a definite kind, will be valid, although in the inheritance there is nothing of the kind to which the legacy belongs.

§ 3202. *Election.*—Art. 3545. In the case of the preceding article, the election belongs to him who must pay the legacy; who if the things exist complies by delivering one of a medium quality; otherwise by purchasing one of that same quality, or by paying to the legatee the corresponding price, by a previous agreement, or according to the judgment of experts.

§ 3203. *Election, how Made.*—Art. 3546. If the testator

expressly conceded the election to the legatee, the latter can, if there should be various things of the definite kind, elect the best; but if there are none, he can only require one of a medium quality, or the price which may correspond to it.

§ 3204. *Verbal Trial.*—Art. 3547. Any difference which may occur relative to the fulfillment of the three preceding articles shall be decided by a verbal trial.[1]

§ 3205. *Immovables.* — Art. 3548. If the indefinite thing should be an immovable, the legacy will only be valid if there exist in the inheritance various ones of the same kind; for in the election will be observed the rules established in articles 3545, 3446, and 3547.

§ 3206. *Restriction of Right.*—Art. 3549. When the testator, the heir, or the legatee alone shall have a certain part or right in the thing bequeathed, the legacy will be restricted to that part or right, if the testator does not declare in an express manner that he knew the thing to be partially that of another, and that notwithstanding this he bequeathed the whole of it.

§ 3207. *Pledges.*—Art. 3550. A legacy of a thing received in pledge or in anticresis, as well as that of a title constitutive of a mortgage, only extinguishes the right of the pledge, anticresis, or mortgage, but not the debt, unless that it is so expressly provided.

§ 3208. *Securities.*—Art. 3551. The provisions in the preceding article will also be observed in the legacy of a security, whether made to the surety or to the principal debtor.

§ 3209. *Usufructs and Uses.*—Art. 3552. Legacies of usufruct, use, habitation, or service shall subsist while the legatee lives, unless the testator shall have expressly disposed otherwise.

§ 3210. *Limit of Thirty Years.*—Art. 3553. Legacies of which the preceding article treats will only last thirty years, if they should be left to any corporation which shall have capacity to acquire.

§ 3211. *Redemption.*—Art. 3554. If the thing bequeathed is given in pledge or mortgage, or should be after the execution of the will, the redemption will be a charge on the inheritance, unless the testator shall have expressly disposed otherwise.

§ 3212. *Deposits.*—Art. 3555. A legacy of a thing or sum deposited in a designated place will only subsist in the part which is found therein.

§ 3213. *Usufructs and Uses—Heir's Right.*—Art. 3556. If

[1] Article 3547 is suppressed in the code of 1884.

the thing bequeathed should be subjected to a usufruct, use, or habitation, the legatee must give them until they shall be legally extinguished, without the heir being under obligation of any kind.

§ 3214. *Pensions or Services.*—Art. 3557. If the thing bequeathed supports any service, pension, or any other burden, it shall pass with it to the legatee; and if there should be due back pensions or interest, they shall be paid for the account of the inheritance.

§ 3215. *Disposition of Testator.*—Art. 3558. The provisions in the two preceding articles shall be observed if the testator should not dispose otherwise.

§ 3216. *Third Parties—Credits.*—Art. 3559. A legacy made to a third party of a credit in favor of the testator will only produce effect in the part of the credit which was unpaid at the time of opening the succession.

§ 3217. *Title of Credit.*—Art. 3560. In the case of the preceding article, he who must fulfill the legacy shall deliver to the legatee the title of the credit, and he shall cede to him all the actions which in virtue of it belonged to the testator.

§ 3218. *Freedom from Obligation.*—Art. 3561. The provisions in the preceding article being complied with, he who must pay the legacy remains entirely free from the obligation of warranty, and from any other responsibility, whether it may proceed from the said title or from the insolvency of the debtor, or from that of his sureties, or from any other cause.

§ 3219. *Debts.*—Art. 3562. The legacy of a debt made to the said debtor extinguishes the obligation; and he who must fulfill the legacy is obligated not only to give to the debtor the proof of the payment, but also to redeem the pledges, to cancel the mortgages and the securities, and to free the legatee of all responsibility.

§ 3220. *Interest.*—Art. 3563. The legacies of which articles 3559 and 3562 speak comprehend the interest which by the credit or debt may be due at the death of the testator.

§ 3221. *Entry of Suits.*—Art. 3564. Said legacies shall subsist, although the testator may have judicially demanded the debtor, if the payment has not been realized.

§ 3222. *Debt, how Bequeathed.*—Art. 3565. The title of a debt being bequeathed, whether public or private, it is understood that the debt itself is bequeathed; save the provisions in articles 3550 and 3551.

§ 3223. *Generic Legacy.*—Art. 3566. A generic legacy of the freedom or pardon from debts comprehends only those existing at the time of the execution of the will, not the subsequent ones.

§ 3224. *Legacy to a Creditor*—Art. 3567. A legacy made to a creditor does not compensate the credit, unless the testator expressly declares so.

§ 3225. *Excess of Credit.*—Art. 3568. In case of compensation, if the values should be different the creditor will have a right to collect the excess of the credit or that of the legacy.

§ 3226. *Debtor may Improve Creditor.*—Art. 3569. A debtor may improve the condition of his creditor by the means of a legacy, make pure a conditional credit, a simple credit, a mortgage one, or demandable immediately that which was so on time; but this improvement shall not prejudice in any manner the privileges of the other creditors.

§ 3227. *Void Legacy.*—Art. 3570. A legacy of a thing which at the time of the execution of the will belongs to the same legatee is null.

§ 3228. *Bequest of Testator's Interest Valid.*—Art. 3571. If in the thing bequeathed the testator or a third party has any part, the former knowing it, in that part which may belong to him, the legacy is valid.

§ 3229. *Acquisition of the Thing Bequeathed.*—Art. 3572. If the legatee acquires the thing bequeathed after the execution of the will its price is understood bequeathed.

§ 3230. *Third Party.*—Art. 3573. A legacy made to a third party of a thing belonging to an heir or legatee is valid, who, if they accept the succession, must deliver the thing bequeathed or its price.

§ 3231. *Forced Heirs not Prejudiced.*—Art. 3574. The provision in the preceding article is understood without prejudice to the legitimate right of the forced heirs.[1]

§ 3232. *Void Legacy.*—Art. 3575. If the testator was ignorant that the thing was of the heir or legatee the legacy will be null.

§ 3233. *Things not Belonging to Testator.*—Art. 3576. A legacy of a thing of another, if the testator knew that it was so, is valid, and the heir is obliged to acquire it in order to deliver it to the legatee, or to give to him the price thereof.

§ 3234. *Proof by Legatee.*—Art. 3577. The proof that the testator knew that the thing belonged to another belongs to the legatee.

§ 3235. *Property of Another—When Legacy Void.*—Art. 3578.

[1] Article 3574 is suppressed in the code of 1884.

If the testator was ignorant that the thing which he bequeathed was another's, the legacy is null.

§ 3236. *Property Acquired after Execution of the Will.*—Art. 3579. A legacy is valid if the testator, after executing the will, acquires the thing which at the execution thereof was not his.

§ 3237. *Education.*—Art. 3580. A legacy of an education lasts until the legatee arrives at age.

§ 3238. *Education, Legacy of, Ceases, when.*—Art. 3581. A legacy of an education ceases also if the legatee during the age of minority has a profession or office by which he is able to subsist, or if he contracts marriage.

§ 3239. *Support.*—Art. 3582. A legacy of support (alimentos) lasts during the life of the legatee unless the testator shall have otherwise disposed.

§ 3240. *Sum not Designated.*—Art. 3583. If the testator did not designate the sum for support, the provisions in chapter 4, title 5, of book 1, will be observed.

§ 3241. *Custom as to Amount.*—Art. 3584. If the testator was accustomed in life to give to the legatee a certain sum of money by way of support, the same sum will be considered as bequeathed.

§ 3242. *Pension, Legacy of.*—Art. 3585. A legacy of a pension, whatever may be the sum, the object, and the terms, runs from the death of the testator. It is demandable at the end of each period, and the legatee makes his what he had a right to collect, although he may die before the period commenced shall terminate.

§ 3243. *Proof of Property.*—Art. 3586. When a thing is bequeathed with all that which it comprehends, it will not be understood that the documents proving the property, or the active credits are bequeathed unless they have been specially mentioned.

§ 3244. *Furniture.*—Art. 3587. A legacy of the furniture of a thing does not comprehend money, the live-stock, the books, the sculptures, the paintings, nor the personal jewelry, unless it is expressly designated.

§ 3245. *Acquisitions to Property.*—Art. 3588. If he who bequeathes a property adds to it afterwards new acquisitions, these will not be comprehended in the legacy, although they may be contiguous, if there is no new declaration of the testator.

§ 3246. *Declaration.*—Art. 3589. The declaration to which the preceding article refers is not required in respect to the necessary, useful, or voluntary improvements made on the same estate.

§ 3247. *Alternative Legacies.*—Art. 3590. In alternative legacies the election belongs to the heir if the testator does not expressly concede it to the legatee.

§ 3248. *Election of Thing.*—Art. 3591. If the heir has the election, he may deliver the thing of least value; if the election belongs to the legatee, he may elect the thing of the greatest value.

§ 3249. *Alternative Legacies.*—Art. 3592. In alternative legacies shall be observed, besides, the provisions for the obligations of that class in chapter 4, title 2, of book 3.

§ 3250. *Election, how Made.*—Art. 3593. In all cases in which he who may have the right to make the election should be unable to do so, his legitimate representative or his heir shall make it.

§ 3251. *Election by the Judge.*—Art. 3594. The judge, on petition of the legitimate party, shall make the election if in the period which he shall designate the person who has the right to do it should not do it.

§ 3252. *Irrevocable.*—Art. 3595. An election legally made is irrevocable.

§ 3253. *All or None Accepted.*—Art. 3596. A legatee can not accept a part of a legacy and repudiate the other.

§ 3254. *Heirs.*—Art. 3597. If the legatee dies before accepting the legacy and leaves various heirs, one of these may accept and the other repudiate the part which belongs to them in the legacy.

§ 3255. *Two Legacies—Acceptance.*—Art. 3598. If two legacies should be left and one should be onerous, the legatee can not renounce the latter and accept that which is not onerous.

§ 3256. *Heir Who is Legatee.*—Art. 3599. An heir who at the same time is a legatee may renounce the inheritance and accept the legacy, or renounce the latter and accept the former.

§ 3257. *Condition of Marriage.*—Art. 3600. If any sum is bequeathed for a time when a condition may be taken, it is understood as bequeathed to contract marriage.

§ 3258. *Legacies Governed by Provisions of Inheritance.*—Art. 3601. The provisions in respect to inheritances in articles 3512 to 3514 shall also be observed in respect to the legacies, which in the cases in question will only be valid as far as the part of free disposition may extend.[1]

§ 3259. *Death of Testator.*—Art. 3602. A legatee acquires a right to the legacy pure and simple, as well as that to a day

[1] Article 3601 is suppressed in the code of 1884.

certain, from the moment of the death of the testator, and transmits it to his heirs.

§ 3260. *Specific Things.*—Art. 3603. When a legacy is of a specific and definite thing of the testator, the legatee acquires his property as soon as the testator dies, and makes his own the pending and future fruits, unless the testator has otherwise disposed.

§ 3261. *Risk of Legatee.*—Art. 3604. A thing bequeathed, in the case of the preceding article, will run from the same instant at the risk of the legatee; and as to its loss, subsequent increase, or deterioration, the provisions in articles 1546 and 1547 will be observed.

§ 3262. *Security.*—Art. 3605. A legatee may demand that the heir give security in all cases in which a creditor may demand it.

§ 3263. *Rights of Legatees for Security.*—Art. 3606. Legatees may use for the security of their legacies the right which article 2000 concedes to them; save that any one of the heirs should have been specially obligated for the payment, as then only on the property of the latter can the legatee require the constitution of the necessary mortgage.

§ 3264. *When Only Legatees.*—Art. 3607. If there should only be legatees, these can require among themselves the guaranty to which the article cited in the preceding one refers.

§ 3265. *Error in Name.*—Art. 3608. An error about the name of the person or about the thing bequeathed does not annul the legacy, if it can be demonstrated what was the intention of the testator.

§ 3266. *Delivery of Possession.*—Art. 3609. A legatee can not occupy by his own authority the thing bequeathed; but must ask for its delivery and possession from the executor or the special administrator.

§ 3267. *When in Possession of Legatee.*—Art. 3610. If the thing bequeathed should be in the possession of the legatee, he may retain it without prejudice to the return thereof in case of reduction, which may correspond to it in conformity with the law.

§ 3268. *Condition of the Thing.*—Art. 3611. A thing bequeathed must be delivered with all its accessories, and in the state in which it may be found at the death of the testator.

§ 3269. *Delivery in Kind.*—Art. 3612. In a legacy of kind the heir must deliver the same thing bequeathed; in case of loss, the provisions in chapters 3 and 4, title 3, of book 3.

§ 3270. *Money, Legacies of.*—Art. 3613. Legacies in money must be paid in that kind; and if there is none in the inheritance, with the product of the property which for that purpose shall be sold.

§ 3271. *Expense of Delivery.*—Art. 3614.—The necessary expenses for the delivery of the thing bequeathed shall be at the charge of the inheritance, but without prejudice to the legitimate right.[1]

§ 3272. *Taxes.*—Art. 3615. The amount of taxes corresponding to the legacy shall be deducted from the value thereof, unless the testator disposes otherwise.

§ 3273. *Whole Estate in Legacies.*—Art. 3616. If all the inheritance should be distributed in legacies, the debts and burdens thereof shall be apportioned among all the participants in proportion to their quotas, unless the testator shall have otherwise disposed.

§ 3274. *Insufficient to Cover Legacies.*—Art. 3617. If the property of the inheritance should not suffice to cover all the legacies, the payment shall be made in the following order: 1. Remunatory legacies; 2. Legacies which the testator may have declared preferred; 3. Legacies of a certain and definite thing; 4. Legacies of support and education; 5. The others *pro rata.*

§ 3275. *Right of Legatee to Recover.*—Art. 3618. Legatees have a right to recover from any third party the thing bequeathed, whether it is personal or real estate, provided it be certain and definite.

§ 3276. *Insurance.*—Art. 3619. A devisee of an immovable, which perishes by fire after the death of the testator, has a right to receive the indemnification from the insurance if the premises were insured.

§ 3277. *Actions under Void Will.*—Art. 3620. If the will is declared null after the payment of the legacy, the action of the real heir to recover the thing bequeathed proceeds against the legatee and not against the other heir, unless the latter has made the partition with fraud.

### Of Substitutions.

§ 3278. *Substitutes.*—Art. 3621. A testator may substitute one or more persons for the heir or heirs instituted, for the case in which they may die before him, or in case that they can

[1] Article 3614 is amended in the code of 1884 to read: "Art. 3432. The necessary expenses for the delivery of the thing bequeathed shall be at the charge of the legatee, save the disposition of the testator to th contrary of the inheritance, but with out prejudice to the legitimate right.

not or do not wish to accept the inheritance; this is what is called vulgar substitution.

§ 3279. *How Appointed.*—Art. 3622. The substitutes may be appointed jointly or successively.

§ 3280. *Heir of Substitute.*—Art. 3623. The substitute of the substitute, the latter failing, is the heir of the substitute.

§ 3281. *Simple Substitution.*—Art. 3624. A simple substitution, and without expression of cases, comprehends the three designated in article 3621.

§ 3282. *Minors.*—Art. 3625. For male minors of fourteen years and for female minors of twelve years, the father or ascendant under whose power they are may appoint a substitute in case the said minors shall die before the said age; this is what is called pupillary substitution.

§ 3283. *Ascendants can Appoint.*—Art. 3626. An ascendant may appoint a substitute for a descendant of age, who in conformity with the law shall have been declared incapable by mental alienation; this is what is called exemplary substitution.

§ 3284. *Substitution, when not Valid.*—Art. 3627. The substitutions of which the two preceding articles speak are not valid when the substituted party has forced heirs.[1]

§ 3285. *Recovery of Capacity.*—Art. 3628. The exemplary substitution will be without effect if the incapacitated person recovers his reason, and it is so declared by a judicial decree.

§ 3286. *How Substitute shall Receive Inheritance.*—Art. 3629. The substitutes shall receive the inheritance with the same burdens and conditions with which the heirs should have received it, unless the testator has expressly disposed otherwise, or that the burdens or conditions should be merely personal of the heir.

§ 3287. *Unequal Parts.*—Art. 3630. If the heirs instituted in unequal parts should be substituted reciprocally, they will have the same parts in the substitution as in the institution, unless the will of the testator shall clearly appear to have been otherwise.

§ 3288. *Fiduciary Prohibited.*—Art. 3631. Fiduciary substitutions are prohibited, and any other diverse from the three assigned in this chapter, whatever may be the form in which they are clothed.

§ 3289. *Import of Nullity.*—Art. 3632. The nullity of a fiduciary substitution does not import that of the institution

[1] Article 3627 is suppressed in the code of 1884.

nor that of a legacy; the clause of fiduciary being held as unwritten.

§ 3290. *What is not Fiduciary.*—Art. 3633. A disposition in which the testator leaves the title of all or a part of the property to one person and the usufruct to another is not reputed fiduciary, unless the proprietor or the usufructuary shall be obliged to transfer on their death the property or the usufruct to a third party.

§ 3291. *Heir Usufructuary, when.*—Art. 3634. The father may leave the free part of his property to his child with the charge of transferring it to the child or children which he may or might have; in which case the heir shall be considered as a usufructuary.[1]

§ 3292. *When Disposition Null.*—Art. 3635. The disposition which the preceding article authorizes shall be null when the transmission of the property ought to be made to the descendants of the ulterior degree.

§ 3293. *Prohibited Dispositions.*—Art. 3636. Dispositions which contain a prohibition to sell, or that call a third party to what may remain of the inheritance by the death of the heir, or a charge of giving to more than one person successively a certain rent or pension, are considered fiduciary, and consequently are prohibited.

§ 3294. *Prohibition not against the Poor.*—Art. 3637. In the prohibition of the preceding article are not comprehended the obligation of any sum imposed on the heirs in favor of the indigent, to endow poor maids, or in favor of any establishment or foundation of public beneficence, keeping the prescriptions which the three following articles establish.

§ 3295. *Definite Property.*—Art. 3638. The obligation ought to be assigned by the testator on certain and definite property; but the heir burdened is at liberty to capitalize it and impose interest upon it.

§ 3296. *Capitalization, how Made.*—Art. 3639. The capitalization shall be made with the intervention of the first political authority of the place, and with an audience of the interested parties, and of the public minister.

§ 3297. *Heirs, how Burdened.*—Art. 3640. The heirs burdened in this manner do not remain burdened beyond the ful-

---

[1] Article 3634 is amended by the code of 1884 so as to read as follows: "Art. 3451. The father may leave a part or the whole of his property to his child with the charge of transferring it to the child or children which he may or might have; in which case the heir shall be considered as a usufructuary."

fillment of the charge; their particular succession is governed by the relative precepts of this code.

§ 3298. *May Establish Beneficence.*—Art. 3641. A testator may found one or more places in an establishment of beneficence or of public instruction for his descendants.

§ 3299. *Collateral Relatives.*—Art. 3642. A testator may also make a like foundation for his collateral relatives; but in this case it will not have effect outside of the eighth degree.

§ 3300. *Public Beneficence.*—Art. 3643. The persons of which the two preceding articles speak being wanting, the capital will remain destined generally for public beneficence.

§ 3301. *Heirs and Legatees.*—Art. 3644. Every disposition in this chapter in respect to heirs shall be observed also in respect to legatees.

Of Disinheritance.

§ 3302. *Disinheritance.*—Art. 3645. Disinheritance can only take place for the causes and in the cases in which the law expressly permits it.

§ 3303. *Causes of Disinheritance.*—Art. 3646. Legitimate causes for disinheritance of descendants are those contained in fractions 1, 2, 6, 7, and 10 of article 3428; and besides, the following: 1. Having denied without legitimate reason support to the ascendant who disinherits; 2. Having contracted marriage against the provisions in articles 165 and 166, unless the dissent of the ancestor has been supplied in conformity with article 173; 3. Having delivered a daughter or granddaughter to prostitution.

§ 3304. *Heirs of Disinherited Parties.*—Art. 3647. The children and descendants of the disinherited party will have the legitimate right of which their parents or ascendants were deprived of; but these will not enjoy the usufruct, nor administer the legitimate right, nor succeed to it by intestacy.[1]

§ 3305. *Ascendants not to be Deprived.*—Art. 3648. The children and descendants have in no case the right to deprive the ascendants of the legitimate right; and even when these may be omitted (preteridos), they shall not be excluded from the legitimate, if they are not incapable of acquiring it by any of the causes enumerated in article 3428.

§ 3306. *Disinheritance, how Made.*—Art. 3649. A disinheritance can only be made in a will and with an express declaration of the cause.

§ 3307. *Proof.*—Art. 3650. The cause of the disinheritance

[1] Articles 3645 to 3647, inclusive, are suppressed in the code of 1884.

being answered, the proof of it is incumbent upon the heirs of the testator.

§ 3308. *Disinheritance without Cause Insufficient.*—Art. 3651. A disinheritance made without an expression of cause, or with cause which is not proved, or for an illegitimate cause, will cause the testamentary disposition to fail only in that which prejudices the legitimate right of the disinherited.

§ 3309. *Support of Disinherited.*—Art. 3652. Those who by the exclusion of the disinherited are called to the succession of the property are under obligation to give support to the former, if he lacks means of subsistence, in proportion to the part which they may receive from the quota which should have belonged to the disinherited party.

§ 3310. *Prescription.*—Art. 3653. The action of the disinherited party against the disinheritance may be prescribed in five years, counted from the opening of the will, the disinherited person being present, and in ten if absent.

§ 3311. *Reconciliation.*—Art. 3654. A reconciliation of the offended and the offender, subsequent to the inheritance, leaves it without effect.[1]

### Of the Nullity and Revocation of Wills.

§ 3312. *Institution of Heir, when Null.*—Art. 3655. The institution of heir made en memoria[2] or secret communications are null.

§ 3313. *Duty of Person Charged with Fulfillment of Legacies.* Art. 3656. Legacies can be left by those means; but the heir or person whom the testator has left expressly charged to fulfill them is obliged to reveal them to the judge having the settlement of the estate and to the public minister, with due reserve and before the inventories are approved, in order that it may be known whether they are contrary to the law.

§ 3314. *If Contrary to Law.*—Art. 3657. If those communicated are contrary to the law, the public minister and the judge shall prevent their fulfillment; if they should be in conformity with the law, they will have care that they be complied with, and they shall require the person who shall have been charged that he sufficiently prove that he has performed the commission which the testator confided to him.

§ 3315. *Penalty for Neglect.*—Art. 3658. The heir or person

[1] Articles 3648 to 3654, inclusive, are suppressed in the code of 1884.

[2] A separate paper from the will, in which a party is instituted heir with conditions, which are not expressed in the will, but to which the will refers, naming the heir and the paper.

charged who does not comply with the prescription of article 3656, as well as he who does not prove that he has complied with the charge, shall pay a fine equal to twenty-five per cent on the amount of secret communications.

§ 3316. *Void from Violence.*—Art. 3659. A will executed through violence, or obtained by deceit or fraud, is null.

§ 3317. *Penalty.*—Art. 3660. He who, by deceit, fraud, or violence, prevents any one from making his last will, shall be punished in conformity with the penal code, losing, besides, the right which he may have to succeed by intestacy.

§ 3318. *Proof of Hinderance—Taken by the Judge.*—Art. 3661. A judge who shall have notice of any one hindering another from making a will shall present himself in the house of the second without delay, in order to secure him in the exercise of his rights, and he shall draw an act in which he shall make the fact appear which has caused his presence; the person or persons who cause the violence, and the means which they have employed for the purpose, or intend to employ, and if the person whose liberty he protects makes use of his right.

§ 3319. *Signs Insufficient.*—Art. 3662. A will in which the testator does not express completely and clearly his will, except only by signs or monosyllables, in answer to questions which are made him, is null.

§ 3320. *Limit of Testator's Power.*—Art. 3663. A testator can not prohibit a will from being impugned in the cases in which it must be null in conformity with law.

§ 3321. *Void Will.*—Art. 3664. A will is null when it is executed in contravention to what is provided in title 3 of this work.

§ 3322. *Revocable till Death.*—Art. 3665. A will is a revocable act until the last moment of the life of the testator.

§ 3323. *Renunciation of Power Void.*—Art. 3666. A renunciation of the power to revoke a will is null.

§ 3324. *Effect of Revocation.*—Art. 3667. An acknowledgment of an illegitimate child does not lose its legal force, although the will be revoked in which it was made, provided the will has been opened and executed before a notary.

§ 3325. *Void Renunciations.*—Art. 3668. A renunciation of the right to will, and the clause in which any one obligates himself not to use that right, except under certain conditions, of whatever class they may be, excepting what is provided in article 3519, are null.[1]

[1] Article 3668 is amended by the code of 1884 by suppressing the words "excepting what is provided in article 3519."

§ 3326. *Change of Testator's State—Subsequent Children.*—Art. 3669. A will does not lose its force by a change of the state of the testator, nor by the supervenience of children, who in this case may exercise the right which in respect to the legitimate right belongs to them.[1]

§ 3327. *A Second Will Revokes First One.*—Art. 3670. A prior will remains revoked, *ipso facto*, by a perfect subsequent one, if the testator does not express in the latter his will that the former shall subsist wholly or in part.

§ 3328. *Effect of Revocation when Second Will Becomes Extinct.* Art. 3671. A revocation will produce its effect, although the second will becomes extinct by the incapacity of the heir or of the legatees newly appointed, or by their renunciation.

§ 3329. *Restoration of Prior Will.*—Art. 3672. A prior will will be restored, notwithstanding its force, if the testator, revoking the subsequent one, declares it to be his will that the first shall subsist.

§ 3330. *When Dispositions are without Effect.*—Art. 3673. Testamentary dispositions become extinct and remain without effect in that which relates to the heirs and legatees: 1. If the heir or legatee dies before the testator or before the condition is fulfilled on which the inheritance or the legacy depends; 2. If the heir or legatee is made incapable of receiving the inheritance or legacy; 3. If he renounces his right.

§ 3331. *When not Extinct by Unknown Condition.*—Art. 3674. A testamentary disposition which contains a condition of a past or present event unknown does not become extinct, although the notice of the fact is acquired after the death of the heir or legatee whose rights are transmitted to their respective heirs.

---

[1] Article 3669 is suppressed by the cede of 1884.

# CHAPTER XVIII.

## EXECUTORS OF LAST WILLS.

§ 3332. *Executors, Who can be.*—Art. 3675. The law only recognizes as universal executors of last wills, when there are forced heirs, the heirs themselves, whether they be by will, whether by intestacy, or their legal representative.

§ 3333. *Special Executor, when.*—Art. 3676. The testator, when there are forced heirs, is free to select among them the executor, and to appoint an extraneous person as a special executor for a definite object.

§ 3334. *Who Represents.*—Art. 3677. For the effects of article 3675 legitimately represent: 1. The husband represents the wife under age; 2. Ascendants their descendants who are under their paternal power; 3. Tutors their minors, although they may be emancipated, and the others which may be found subject to tutorship; 4. The representative or possessor of the property of the absent; 5. Sindics, the ayuntamientos; 6. The directors, public establishments; 7. The public minister, the treasury.[1]

§ 3335. *When No Forced Heirs Exist.*—Art. 3678. When there are no forced heirs, the testator may freely appoint one or various executors.[2]

§ 3336. *Heirs may Appoint, when.*—Art. 3679. There being forced heirs or not, if the testator does not appoint an executor, the heirs by a majority of votes will appoint one.

§ 3337. *How Majority Estimated.*—Art. 3680. The majority in all the cases of which this chapter and those relative to inventory and partitions speak is calculated by the amount of the credits, and not by the number of the persons, unless the greatest credit corresponds to one single person.[3]

§ 3338. *How Selected.*—Art. 3681. In the case of article 3679, the executor must be selected precisely among the same heirs or their legitimate representative.

§ 3339. *Appointment by the Judge.*—Art. 3682. If there should not be a majority, the executor will be appointed by the judge, on the same terms provided in the preceding article.

§ 3340. *Intestate.*—Art. 3683. The provision in the four preceding articles will be observed also in the cases of an intestate, and when the executor appointed fails, whatever may be the cause.

§ 3341. *Can not be Executors, Who.*—Art. 3684. In the cases of voluntary inheritance, can not be executors: 1. Minors and others incapacitated; 2. Magistrates and judges who have jurisdiction in the place where the succession is opened; 3. Those who by a decree may have been removed before from the charge of executor.[4]

§ 3342. *Voluntary Heir.*—Art. 3685. A voluntary heir which

---

[1]Article 3677 is amended by the code of 1884 by inserting the words "for the performance of the executorship" in place of the words "for the effects of article 3675." Also by adding to the end of the article the following: "The provisions in fraction 3 shall only be observed when the laws or administrative regulations do not provide otherwise."

[2]Articles 3676 and 3678 are suppressed by the code of 1884.

[3]Article 3680 is article 3705, new code, and is amended by inserting in the place of "unless the greatest credit corresponds to one single person" the words: "In case that the greatest portion exceeds the half of the inheritance and belongs to one sole person, the representation of the latter shall be reduced to only one quarter part of the inheritance."

[4]Article 3684 is amended by the code of 1884 so as to read as follows: "Art. 3708. In the cases of voluntary inheritance they can not be executors, except in the case of being the only heirs: 1. Magistrates and judges who have jurisdiction in the place where the succession is opened; 2. Those who by a decree may have been removed before from the charge of executor."

should be the only one will be the executor if no other shall have been appointed in the will.[1]

§ 3343. *No Heirs — No Legatees — Appointment.*—Art. 3686. When there is no heir, or the one appointed does not enter into inheritance, the judge shall appoint the executor, if there should be no legatees.

§ 3344. *Appointment of Legatees.*—Art. 3687. In the case of the preceding article, if there are legatees, the executor will be appointed by them.

§ 3345. *Time of Holding Discharge.*—Art. 3688. The executor appointed in conformity with the two preceding articles will remain in his charge until legitimate heirs being declared, they make the election in conformity with articles 3679 to 3682.

§ 3346. *All in Legacies.*—Art. 3689. When all the inheritance is distributed in legacies, the legatees will appoint the executor, observing the provisions in articles 3679 to 3682 cited.

§ 3347. *Universal or Special.*—Art. 3690. In the cases in which the appointment of executor is free, he may be universal or special.[2]

§ 3348. *Jointly or Successively.*—Art. 3691. The executors may be appointed in every case jointly or successively.

§ 3349. *Joint Acts.*—Art. 3692. If the executors are joint, what they may do together, or what one may do legally authorized by the others, will only be valid.

§ 3350. *Urgency.*—Art. 3693. In the cases of extreme urgency one of the joint executors may perform, under his personal responsibility, the acts which may be necessary, reporting immediately to the others.

§ 3351. *Order of Appointment.*—Art. 3694. If the testator does not establish a jointure between the executors, nor fix the order in which they must perform their charge, they will enter the service in the natural order of appointment.

§ 3352. *The Charge is Voluntary.*—Art. 3695. The charge of executor is voluntary; but he who accepts it is constituted under an obligation to perform it.

§ 3353. *Effect of Renouncement.*—Art. 3696. An executor who renounces without a just cause will lose what the testator may have left him, save always the right which he may have to the legitimate part.[3]

---

[1] Article 3685 is amended by the code of 1884, by suppressing the word "voluntary" in the first line.

[2] Article 3690 is suppressed by the code of 1884.

[3] Article 3696 is amended by the code of 1884, by suppressing the words "save always the right which he may have to the legitimate part."

§ 3354. *Excuse within Six Days.*—Art. 3697. The executor who solicits to excuse himself, must do so within the six days following that on which he had notice of his appointment; or if this was already known to him, within six days following that on which he had notice of the death of the testator.

§ 3355. *Must Act until Excuse Decided.*—Art. 3698. The executor who may be present, until his excuse is decided upon, must perform the charge under the penalty in article 3696, and that of paying the damages and losses.

§ 3356. *Charge not to be Delegated—Exceptions.*—Art. 3699. The office of executor can not be delegated, except in virtue of a solemn power, save in every case the disposition of the testator.

§ 3357. *General Executor.*—Art. 3700. The general executor is obliged to deliver to the special one the sums or things necessary in order that he may comply with the part of the will which may be in his charge.

§ 3358. *Delivery of Legacies.*—Art. 3701. If the fulfillment of the legacy depends upon time, or on any other suspensive circumstance, the general executor can resist the delivery of the thing or sum, giving security to the satisfaction of the legatee or of the special executor that the delivery will be made in due time.

§ 3359. *Special Executor.*—Art. 3702. The special executor may also, in the name of the legatee, require the constitution of a mortgage to which fractions 1 and 10 of article 2000 refer.

§ 3360. *Transmission of Possession.*—Art. 3703. The possession of the hereditary property is transmitted by the ministry of the law to the universal executors from the moment of the death of the author of the inheritance, save the provisions in article 2201.

§ 3361. *Executor Possesses, how.*—Art. 3704. The executor possesses in his own name for the part which corresponds to him of the inheritance, and as agent (en nombre ajeno) for the part which belongs to the other heirs and the legatees.

§ 3362. *Powers of Executor.*—Art. 3705. The powers of the executor, besides those contained in this chapter, shall be those which the testator shall have expressly conceded to him, and which may not be contrary to the laws.[1]

§ 3363. *Actions.*—Art. 3706. The executor may prosecute

[1] Article 3705 is amended by the code of 1884, by inserting the words "or the heirs" after the word "testator," and also "them" in place of "him."

all the actions which belonged to the author of the inheritance, and which shall not have been extinguished by his death.

§ 3364. *Obligations of General Executor.*—Art. 3707. The obligations of the general executor are: 1. The representation of the will; 2. The security of the property of the inheritance; 3. The formation of the inventory; 4. The administration of the property and the rendition of the account of executorship; 5. The payment of the funeral, hereditary, and testamentary debts; 6. The partition and adjudication of the property between the heirs and legatees; 7. The defense in court and out of it, as well of the inheritance as of the validity of the will, in conformity with law.[1]

§ 3365. *Appointment by Will.*—Art. 3708. If the executor has been appointed by the will, and he has it in his possession, he must present it within the eight days following the death of the testator.

§ 3366. *Heirs—Copy of Will.*—Art. 3709. The executor can not oppose the giving to the heirs a full copy of the will, and to the legatees the respective clause.

§ 3367. *Intestacy.*—Art. 3710. In the case of intestacy, or when it does not appear which of the heirs ought to be the executor, the application (denuncia) made by any one of them will be admitted; but it must be presented in writing, authorized by the signature of an attorney at law. This same requisite will be required when the application shall be made by an extraneous person.

§ 3368. *Application for Executorship.*—Art. 3711. The application being admitted, the interested parties shall be cited; and the judge shall determine that he be appointed executor according to the provisions in articles 3679 to 3682.

§ 3369. *Receiver.*—Art. 3712. Until the interested parties shall present themselves, the judge can appoint a receiver, who shall have the character of a simple depositary of property, without being able to perform other administrative functions than those which may be necessary for the mere preservation of the property and those which refer to the payment of funeral debts, both by a previous judicial authorization.

§ 3370. *Judicial Receiver — Inventory.*—Art. 3713. The judicial receiver shall receive the property by a solemn inventory.[2]

---

[1] Article 3707 is amended by the code of 1884, by adding thereto the following: "8. To represent the succession in all the trials which there may be to move in in its name, or to be moved in against it; 9. The others which the law imposes."

[2] Articles 3712 and 3713 are suppressed by the code of 1884.

§ 3371. *Judicial Receiver—Cessation of Charge.*—Art. 3714. The judicial receiver shall cease in his charge as soon as an executor shall be appointed; he shall deliver to the latter the property, and can not retain it under any pretext, nor even for improvements or expenses of maintenance or repair.[1]

§ 3372. *No Delivery of Property before Inventory Formed.*—Art. 3715. The executor, before forming the inventory, shall not permit the extraction of anything, unless it is that it appears to be the property of another by the will, by a public writing, or by the books of the house kept in due form, if the author of the inheritance shall have been a merchant.[2]

§ 3373. *Property of Third Parties.*—Art. 3716. When the property of another appears by divers means of the enumerated articles which precede, the executor shall limit himself to putting on the margin of the respective items a note which indicates the ownership of the thing, in order that the property may be discussed in the corresponding court.

§ 3374. *Damages.*—Art. 3717. An infraction of the two preceding articles makes the executor responsible for the damages and losses.

§ 3375. *Excuse from Inventory.*—Art. 3718. The provisions by which the testator shall excuse the executor from the obligation of making an inventory or that of rendering accounts are null absolutely, save the case of a sole heir, and he a forced one, and there being no legatees.[3]

§ 3376. *Payment of Expenses.*—Art. 3719. The executor, within the first month of exercising his charge, shall fix with the consent of the heirs the sum which must be employed in the expenses of the administration and the number and salary of clerks.

§ 3377. *Sale by Consent of Heirs.*—Art. 3720.—If, for the payment of a debt or other urgent expense, it should be necessary to sell any property, the executors must do so with the consent of the heirs; and if this should not be possible, with the approbation of the judge.

§ 3378. *Tutors.*—Art. 3721. The provisions in articles 616 and 617 in respect to tutors shall also be observed in respect to executors.

---

[1] Article 3714 is suppressed by the code of 1884.

[2] Article 3731 is a new article and reads as follows in the code of 1884: "Art. 3731. The creditors and legatees can not require the payment of their credits and legacies only after the inventory shall have been formed and approved, save the cases provided in articles 3775 and 3778 (3997 and 4000), and those debts on which there may be a trial pending at the opening of the succession."

[3] Article 3718 is article 3739, code of 1884, and is amended by suppressing the words "and he a forced one."

§ 3379. *Can not Lease the Property.*—Art. 3722. The executor can not lease the property without the consent of the heirs.

§ 3380. *Consent of Devisees.*—Art. 3723. The property specially devised can not be burdened, mortgaged, nor leased without the consent of the devisees.

§ 3381. *Consent of Heirs.*—Art. 3724. An executor can not burden nor mortgage the property without the consent of the heirs.

§ 3382. *Arbitration.*—Art. 3725. An executor can not settle disputes nor compromise by arbitration the affairs of the inheritance without the consent of the heirs.

§ 3383. *Obligation of Heirs.*—Art. 3726. The obligation which the executor has to render accounts passes to his heirs.

§ 3384. *Settlement within a Year.*—Art. 3727. The executor for whom the testator may not have fixed a time must fulfill his charge within a year counted from his acceptation, or from the the time the litigations shall have terminated which shall have been moved relative to the validity or nullity of the will.

§ 3385. *Extended Time.*—Art. 3728. If the testator shall prolong the legal term, he must expressly designate the time of the prolongation.

§ 3386. *Extension by Heirs and Legatees.*—Art. 3729. A majority of the heirs and legatees may also prolong the term in which the executor must perform his charge, observing the provisions in the two preceding articles.

§ 3387. *Approval by Heirs.*—Art. 3730. The account of the administration must be approved by all the heirs; he who dissents can prosecute at his cost the respective trial on the terms which the code of procedure may establish.

§ 3388. *Public Minister.*—Art. 3731. When the treasury shall be interested, the public minister shall intervene in the approbation of the accounts.

§ 3389. *After Settlement of Accounts.*—Art. 3732. The accounts being approved, the interested parties may celebrate relative to the result the agreements which they may wish and which shall not be contrary to the laws.

§ 3390. *Expenses.*—Art. 3733. The expenses made by the executor in the fulfillment of his charge, including the fees of lawyers and attorneys in fact who may have been employed, shall be paid from the mass of the inheritance.

§ 3391. *Compensation.*—Art. 3734. The testator may designate what he wishes as the compensation for the executor, not exceeding his disposable part.[1]

§ 3392. *Compensation of Two per Cent, when.*—Art. 3735. If the testator should not designate the recompense, the executor will collect two per cent on the net and effective amount of the inheritance. If he himself should make the partition, he will collect also the fees of the established regulations (arancel).

§ 3393. *When Executor is Heir.*—Art. 3736. The executor who is heir, and who has been improved by the disposable part, or to whom has been assigned any legacy by reason of his charge, has no right to collect other recompense.

§ 3394. *Joint Executors—Recompense.*—Art. 3737. If there should be various and joint executors, the recompense shall be divided among all of them; if they should not be joint, the distribution will be made in proportion to the time which each one may have administered, and the work which each shall have had in the administration.

§ 3395. *Verbal Trials.*—Art. 3738. Whatever differences may arise relative to the provisions in the foregoing article shall be decided in a verbal trial.[2]

§ 3396. *Bequests to Executors Jointly.*—Art. 3739. If the testator bequeathed jointly to the executors anything in order that they perform their charge, the part of those who shall not receive the charge shall be added to those who shall exercise said charge.

§ 3397. *Receiver.*—Art. 3740. The testator may freely appoint a receiver.

§ 3398. *Appointment by Heirs.*—Art. 3741. The heirs who do not administer have a right to appoint by a majority of votes an inspector, who shall watch over the estate in the name of all.

§ 3399. *When Heirs Disagree.*—Art. 3742. If the heirs should not agree in the election, the judge shall appoint the inspector, selecting him from among the persons who may have been proposed by the heirs.

§ 3400. *Inspector.*—Art. 3743. The inspector can not take possession, not even temporarily, of the property.

§ 3401. *When Inspector must be Appointed.*—Art. 3744. An inspector must necessarily be appointed: 1. When among the heirs appointed there may be any married woman of minor age, or

[1] Article 3734 is amended by the code of 1884, by suppressing the words "not exceeding his disposable part." A new article is added to the code of 1884, as follows: "Art. 3760. An executor who may not represent in legal terms shall lose all right to be compensated."

[2] Article 3738 is suppressed by the code of 1884.

whose husband shall have been separated judicially from her or from the administration of the property; 2. Whenever the heir may be absent or may not be known; 3. When the amount of the legacies equal or exceed the portion of the heir who is executor; 4. When legacies shall have been left, whatever may be their amount, for objects or establishments of public beneficence.

§ 3402. *Functions of Inspectors.*—Art. 3745. The functions of the inspector shall be limited to watch over the exact fulfillment of the charge of the executor; but on doing it, he must associate himself always with the person whose interest he believes to be prejudiced; and in the name of this person, and with his express consent, perform any judicial or extrajudicial act.

§ 3403. *Inspector—Copy of Will.*—Art. 3746. The inspector has a right to ask for a full copy of the will, unless the testator has disposed otherwise.

§ 3404. *Age of Majority.*—Art. 3747. The inspectors must be of the age of majority, and capable of contracting obligations.

§ 3405. *Governing Provisions.*—Art. 3748. In respect to the inspector, the provisions in articles 3695 to 3698 shall govern.

§ 3406. *When Charges Finished.*—Art. 3749. The charges of executor and inspector are finished: 1. By the natural term of their charge; 2. By death; 2. By legal incapacity declared in form; 4. By an excuse which the judge shall qualify as legitimate with an audience of the interested parties, and of the public minister when minors or the public treasury are interested; 5. By the lapse of the term designated by the testator or by the law; 6. By removal, which shall not take place except by a decree pronounced on petition of a legitimate party, and with an audience of the interested party.

# CHAPTER XIX.

## OF THE FORM OF WILLS AND SUCCESSION.

§ 3450. Withdrawal.
§ 3451. Power of Attorney.
§ 3452. Judge's Duty.
§ 3453. Opening of Closed Will.
§ 3454. When All the Witnesses can not Appear.
§ 3455. Absence of Witnesses.
§ 3456. Recognition of Signatures.
§ 3457. Protocolization.
§ 3458. When Will is without Effect.
§ 3459. Possessor of a Will—His Duty.
§ 3460. Private Will, when Permitted.
§ 3461. Declaration of Testator.
§ 3462. Writing not Necessary.
§ 3463. Three Witnesses Sufficient, when.
§ 3464. Governing Provisions.
§ 3465. Effect of Private Will.
§ 3466. Public Writing, when Required.
§ 3467. Death of Testator.
§ 3468. Declaration of Witnesses.
§ 3469. Amount of Proof—Decision of the Judge.
§ 3470. Witnesses, when Some are Dead.
§ 3471. Absence of One or Several Witnesses.
§ 3472. Examination by Deposition.
§ 3473. Military and Employed Persons.
§ 3474. On the Field of Battle.
§ 3475. Closed or Sealed Will.
§ 3476. Prisoners.
§ 3477. Delivery of Will—Death of Testator.
§ 3478. Verbal Will.
§ 3479. Military Persons.
§ 3480. On the High Seas.
§ 3481. Maritime Will.
§ 3482. Commander as Witness.
§ 3483. Duplicates.
§ 3484. Deposit with Counsel.
§ 3485. Deposit with Maritime Authority.
§ 3486. Receipt of the Deposit.
§ 3487. Proof of Delivery and Will Sent to Department of Relations.
§ 3488. Legal Effect, when.
§ 3489. As to Death, when Doubted.
§ 3490. Made in Foreign Countries.
§ 3491. Officers in Place of Notaries.
§ 3492. Copies of Wills Sent to Department of Relations.
§ 3493. Act of Execution.
§ 3494. Wills in Keeping of Officers.
§ 3495. Seals of Legation or Consulship.
§ 3496. Legitimate Inheritance Opened, when.
§ 3497. Legatees, when not to be Reduced.
§ 3498. Part Disposition by Testator.
§ 3499. Origin of Property not Considered.
§ 3500. Legitimate Succession, when Conceded.

### General Provisions.

§ 3407. *Form.*—Art. 3750. A will as to form is public or private.

§ 3408. *Public Will.*—Art. 3751. A public will is that which is executed before a notary and proper witnesses, and is drawn on paper with the corresponding seal.

§ 3409. *Private Will.*—Art. 3752. A private will is that which is executed before proper witnesses without the intervention of a notary, and which may be or not drawn on sealed paper.

§ 3410. *Open or Closed.*—Art. 3753. A public will may be open or closed; a private will can only be open, save the provisions in articles 3818, 3819, and 3820.

Art. 3754. A will is open when the testator manifests his last will in the presence of the persons who must attest the act.

§ 3411. *When Closed.*—Art. 3755. A will is closed when the testator, without revealing his last will, declares that this is found contained in the sheet of paper which he presents to the persons who must attest the act.

§ 3412. *Sealed Paper.*—Art. 3756. The sealed paper in which wills are executed will be that which the law may determine in the matter.

§ 3413. *Military Persons.*—Art. 3757. Wills of military and maritine persons may be drawn on common paper.

§ 3414. *Witnesses.*—Art. 3758. They cannot be witnesses to a will: 1. The amanuensis of the notary who draws the will; 2. Blind persons, and those who do not understand the language of the testator; 3. Those who are dumb or mute; 4. Those who are not of sound judgment; 5. Those who may not have the quality of persons domiciled, save in the cases excepted by the law; 6. Women; 7. Males under age; 8. Those who have been condemned for the crime of falsity.

§ 3415. *Inability, Time of.*—Art. 3759. In order that a witness may be declared unqualified, it is necessary that the inability shall have existed at the time of the execution of the will.

§ 3416. *Ignorance of the Language.*—Art. 3760. When the testator is ignorant of the language of the country, two interpreters appointed by the testator shall meet at the time of the act and shall sign the will, besides the witnesses and the notary.

§ 3417. *Testator must be Known.*—Art. 3761. The notary as well as the witnesses who intervene in any will must know the

the testator, or certify in some manner his identity, and that he was found in his sound mind and free from any compulsion.

§ 3418. *Identity of Testator.*—Art. 3762. If the identity of the testator can not be verified, this circumstance will be declared by the notary or by the witnesses in their case, all adding all the signs which may characterize the person of the testator.

§ 3419. *Proof of Identity.*—Art. 3763. In the case of the article which precedes, the will shall have no validity until the identity of the testator shall be proved.

§ 3420. *Blank Leaves.*—Art. 3764. Notaries and other persons who shall have to draw provisions of a last will are prohibited from leaving blank leaves, and using abbreviations or figures, under the penalty of five hundred dollars fine on the notaries, and the half thereof on those who are not notaries.

§ 3421. *Death of Testator—Notary's Duty.*—Art. 3765. A notary who shall have drawn an open will, or delivers a closed one, must inform the interested parties with as much brevity as possible as soon as he shall know of the death of a testator; if he does not do so, he is responsible for the damages and losses which the delay may occasion.

§ 3422. *Possessor of a Will.*—Art. 3766. The provisions in the preceding article shall be observed by any one who shall have in his possession a closed will.

§ 3423. *Absent or Unknown Parties.*—Art. 3767. If the interested parties are absent or unknown, the notice shall be given by the judge.

### Of an Open Public Will.

§ 3424. *Open Will, how Made.*—Art. 3768. A public open will shall be dictated in a clear and definite manner by the testator, in the presence of three witnesses and a notary; the latter shall draw in writing the clauses, and shall read them in a loud voice, in order that the testator may manifest if he is suited with it; if he is, all shall sign the instrument, putting down the place, the hour, the day, the month, and the year in which it shall have been executed.

§ 3425. *Witnesses Unable to Write.*—Art. 3769. If any of the witnesses should not know how to write, another witness shall sign for him; but at least the entire signatures of two witnesses must appear.

§ 3426. *When Testator can not Write.*—Art. 3770. If the testator can not or does not know how to write, one more witness must intervene, who shall sign at his request.

§ 3427. *Extreme Urgency.*—Art. 3771. In a case of extreme urgency, and another witness can not be called, one of the instrumental witnesses shall sign for the testator; and this circumstance must be made to appear.

§ 3428. *Deaf Persons.*—Art. 3772. He who is entirely deaf, but who knows how to read, must read his will; if he does not know how or can not do so, he shall designate a person who shall read in his name.

§ 3429. *Certificate of Notary.*—Art. 3773. All the formalities shall be observed thereafter; and the notary shall certify that all have been fulfilled.

§ 3430. *Void Will.*—Art. 3774. If any of the said solemnities shall be wanting, the will shall be without effect, and the notary shall be responsible for the damages and losses, and shall incur the penalty of losing his office.

### Of a Sealed Public Will.

§ 3431. *Sealed Will.*—Art. 3775. A sealed will may be written by the testator, or by another person at his request, and on common paper.

§ 3432. *Rubrication of the Leaves.*—Art. 3776. The testator must rubricate all the leaves and sign at the end of the will; but if he does not know how or can not do it, another person may rubricate and sign for him at his request.

§ 3433. *Declaration of Testator.*—Art. 3777. In the case of the article which precedes, the person who shall have rubricated and signed for the testator will meet with him at the presentation of the sealed sheet; at that time the testator shall declare that that person rubricated and signed in his name; and both shall sign on the cover with the witnesses and the notary.

§ 3434. *Closed and Sealed.*—Art. 3778. The paper on which the will is written or that which is used as the cover must be closed and sealed, and the testator will cause it to be closed and sealed in the act of the execution; and he shall exhibit it to the notary in the presence of three witnesses.

§ 3435. *Declaration of Last Will.*—Art. 3779. The testator on making the presentation shall declare that in that parcel is contained his last will.

§ 3436. *Certificate of Notary — Cover of Will.*—Art. 3780. The notary shall certify to the execution, with a statement of the formalities required in the preceding articles, that proof must be drawn on the cover of the will, which shall be of the corresponding sealed paper, and must be signed by the testator, the witnesses, and the notary, who shall put on his seal besides.

§ 3437. *Witnesses Who can not Sign.*—Art. 3781. If any one of the witnesses does not know how to sign, another person shall be called who shall do it in his name and in his presence, so that there shall always be three signatures.

§ 3438. *Testator Who can not Sign.*—Art. 3782. If on making the presentation of the will the testator can not sign, another person shall do it in his name and in his presence; but none of the witnesses can do it.

§ 3439. *Extreme Urgency.*—Art. 3783. Only in a case of extreme urgency can one of the witnesses sign, whether for him who does not know how to do it, or whether for the testator. The notary shall make this circumstance expressly appear, under the penalty of a suspension of office for three years.

§ 3440. *Incapability.*—Art. 3784. Those who do not know how or can not read are incapable of making a closed will.

§ 3441. *Deaf and Dumb Persons.*—Art. 3785. A deaf and dumb person can make a closed will, provided that it is all written, dated, and signed by his own hand, and that on presenting to the notary before five witnesses he shall write in the presence of all on the cover, that in that parcel is contained his last will, and that it was written and signed by himself. The notary shall declare at the time on the cover that the testator so wrote it, observing besides the provisions in articles 3778, 3780, and 3781.

§ 3442. *When Testator can not Sign on the Cover.*—Art. 3786. In the case of the preceding article, if the testator can not sign on the cover, the provisions in articles 3782 and 3783 shall be observed, the notary certifying of the election which the testator shall make of one of the witnesses to sign for him.

§ 3443. *Mute or Deaf.*—Art. 3787. He who may be only mute or only deaf may make a closed will, provided that it be written with his own hand; or if it has been written by another, the testator shall so note it, and shall sign the note with his own hand, subjecting himself to the other precise solemnities for this class of wills.

§ 3444. *Will without Effect.*—Art. 3788. A closed will which lacks any of the aforesaid formalities shall be without effect; and the notary shall be responsible in the terms of article 3774.

§ 3445. *Delivery of Will.*—Art. 3789. The will, being closed and certified, shall be delivered to the testator; and the notary shall make an entry in the protocol of the place, hour, day, month, and year in which the will was certified and delivered.

§ 3446. *Penalty.*—Art. 3790. By the infraction of the preceding article the will shall not be annulled; but the notary will incur the penalty of suspension for six months.

§ 3447. *Testator may Keep the Will or not.*—Art. 3791. The testator may preserve the will in his possession, or give it in keeping to a person of his confidence, or deposit it in the judicial archives.

§ 3448. *Deposit in the Archives.*—Art. 3792. The testator who wishes to deposit his will in the archives shall present himself with it before the keeper thereof, who shall cause to be entered in the book which must be kept for this object, a memorandum of the deposit and delivery, which shall be signed by said functionary and the testator, to whom shall be given a certified copy.

§ 3449. *Deposit, by Whom Made.*—Art. 3793. The presentation and deposit may be made by an attorney in fact, spoken of in the preceding article, and in this case the power shall be annexed to the will.

§ 3450. *Withdrawal.*—Art. 3794. The testator can withdraw his will whenever he wishes; but the return shall be made with the same solemnities as the delivery.

§ 3451. *Power of Attorney.*—Art. 3795. The power for the delivery and for the extraction of the will must be executed by a public writing; and this circumstance shall be made to appear in the respective note.

§ 3452. *Judge's Duty.*—Art. 3796. As soon as the judge shall receive a closed will he shall cause the notary and the witnesses who met at the execution thereof to appear before him.

§ 3453. *Opening of Closed Will.*—Art. 3797. A closed will can not be opened except after the notary and instrumental witnesses shall have recognized their signatures before the judge, and that of the testator or of the person who shall have signed for the latter, and they shall have declared that in their opinion it is closed and sealed as it was at the time of the delivery.

§ 3454. *When All the Witnesses can not Appear.*—Art. 3798. If on account of death, sickness, or absence, all of the witnesses can not appear, the recognition by the greater part of them and the notary will be sufficient.

§ 3455. *Absence of Witnesses.*—Art. 3799. If for like causes the notary, the greater part of the witnesses, or any of them can not appear, the judge shall make it so appear by information, as also the legitimacy of the signatures, and that on the date which the will bears they were at the place in which it was executed.

§ 3456. *Recognition of Signature.*—Art. 3800. In every case those who shall appear shall recognize the signatures.

§ 3457. *Protocolization.*—Art. 3801. What is prescribed in the five preceding articles being complied with, the judge shall decree the publication and protocolization of the will.

§ 3458. *When Will without Effect.*—Art. 3802. A closed will shall be without effect whenever the interior parcel shall be found broken, or that sheet which forms the cover open, or the signatures which attest it found effaced, erased, or amended, although the contents be not vitiated.

§ 3459. *Possessor of a Will—His Duty.*—Art. 3803. Every person who shall have in his possession a closed will, and shall not present it as is provided in articles 3765 and 3766, or shall fraudulently subtract of the property of the deceased, shall incur the penalty, if he is an intestate heir, of losing the right which he may have, without prejudice to what shall correspond to him in conformity with the penal code.

§ 3460. *Private Will, when Permitted.*—Art. 3804. A private will is permitted in the following cases: 1. When the testator is attacked with an infirmity so violent that it threatens his life in an imminent manner; 2. When it is executed in a town having no intercourse by reason of an epidemic, although the testator shall not be found attacked with it; 3. When it is executed in a place besieged; 4. When there is no notary in the place, nor a judge who can act in place thereof.

§ 3461. *Declaration of Testator.*—Art. 3805. A testator who shall be found in the position to make a private will shall declare in the presence of five proper witnesses his last will, which one of them shall put down in writing.

§ 3462. *Writing not Necessary.*—Art. 3806. It shall not be necessary to put the will in writing when none of the witnesses know how to write, and in the case of great urgency.

§ 3463. *Three Witnesses, when Sufficient.*—Art. 3807. In the case of great urgency, three proper witnesses shall be sufficient.

§ 3464. *Governing Provisions.*—Art. 3808. On executing a private will, the provisions contained in articles 3768 to 3773 shall be observed.

§ 3465. *Effect of Private Will.*—3809. A private will shall only have its effects if the testator shall die with the sickness or in the danger in which he was found, or within a month after the former or the latter shall have ceased.

§ 3466. *Public Writing, when Required.*—Art. 3810. A private will requires besides for its validity that it shall be drawn in a public writing by judicial declaration, which shall be done by virtue of the depositions of the witnesses who signed or heard in case thereof the will of the testator.

§ 3467. *Death of Testator.*—Art. 3811. The reduction to a public writing shall be asked for by the interested parties immediately after they may know of the death of the testator and the form of his disposition.

§ 3468. *Declaration of Witnesses.*—Art. 3812. The witness who attests a private will must declare circumstantially: 1. The place, the hour, the day, the month, and the year in which the will was executed; 2. If they recognized, saw, and heard the testator distinctly; 3. The tenor of the disposition; 4. If the testator was in his right mind and free from all compulsion; 5. The reason why there was no notary; 6. If the testator died or not of the infirmity or from the danger in which he was found.

§ 3469. *Amount of Proof—Decision of the Judge.*—Art. 3813. If the witnesses were proper ones, and agreed in all and each one of the circumstances enumerated in the preceding article, the judge shall declare the statements of them to be a formal will of the person who is in question; he shall order it to be protocolized, and shall order that the respective certified copies shall be drawn for the persons who had a right therein.

§ 3470. *Witnesses, when Some are Dead.*—Art. 3814. If, after the death of the testator and before drawing what is said to be his last disposition into a formal will, any of the witnesses should die, the legalization shall be made with the remainder, provided that they be not less than three, perfectly agreeing and above all exceptions.

§ 3471. *Absence of One or Several Witnesses.*—Art. 3815. The provisions in the preceding article shall be observed also in the case of the absence of one or several of the witnesses, provided that in the default of the appearance of the witnesses there shall be no fraud.

§ 3472. *Examination by Deposition.*—Art. 3816. The place of the witnesses being known, they shall be examined by deposition.

### Of the Will of a Military Person.

§ 3473. *Military and Employed Persons.*—Art. 3817. Military persons and civil employés in the army, as soon as they enter the field, can will in a private form, subjecting themselves to the formalities prescribed for this class of wills.

§ 3474. *On the Field of Battle.*—Art. 3818. If a military person or civil employé makes his disposition at the time of entering an action of war, or being wounded on the field of battle, it shall be sufficient that he declares his will before two proper witnesses, or that before the same he shall present a closed parcel which contains his disposition, written and signed, or at least signed by his hand.

§ 3475. *Closed Will.*—Art. 3819. If the will is closed, the witnesses shall sign on the cover, the testator doing so, if he can.

§ 3476. *Prisoners.*—Art. 3820. The provisions in the preceding articles shall be observed in case thereof respecting prisoners.

§ 3477. *Delivery of Will—Death of Testator.*—Art. 3821. Wills executed in writing in conformity with this chapter must be delivered as soon as the testator dies, by him in whose possession they shall have remained, to the immediate chief of the deceased, who shall remit them to the department of war, and the latter to the competent judicial authority for the legal effects.

§ 3478. *Verbal Will.*—Art. 3822. If the will shall have been executed by word, the witnesses shall immediately inform the immediate chief of the testator, who will send the information to the department of war, and he to the competent judicial authority, in order that, the witnesses being cited, it shall be proceeded with in conformity with the law.

§ 3479. *Military Persons.*—Art. 3823. The provisions contained in articles 3809 and following shall be observed in the will of a military man.

### Of the Will of a Maritime Person.

§ 3480. *On the High Seas.*—Art. 3824. Those who find themselves on the high seas on board of the national marine, whether of war or commerce, can also will under a private form, subjecting themselves to the following prescriptions.

§ 3481. *Maritime Will.*—Art. 3825. A maritime will shall be written in the presence of the two witnesses and the commander of the ship, and shall be read, dated, and signed as has been said in articles 3768 to 3773; but in every case the commander and two witnesses shall sign it.

§ 3482. *Commander as Witness.*—Art. 3826. If the commander should make his will, he who succeeds him in command shall take his place in attesting the will.

§ 3483. *Duplicates.*—Art. 3827. A maritime will must be made in duplicates, preserved among the most important papers of the ship, and mentioned in its diary.

§ 3484. *Deposit with Consul.*—Art. 3828. If the ship arrives in a port in which there is a Mexican consul or vice-consul, the commander shall deposit in his possession one of the copies of the will, dated and sealed, with a copy of the note, which must appear in the diary of the ship.

§ 3485. *Deposit with Maritime Authority.*—Art. 3829. The ship arriving at Mexican territory, the other copy shall be delivered, or both if one was not left in another place, to the maritime authority of the place, in the form declared in the preceding article.

§ 3486. *Receipt of the Deposit.*—Art. 3830. In any of the cases mentioned in the two preceding articles, the commander of the ship shall require a receipt of the delivery, and he shall cite it in a note in the diary.

§ 3487. *Proof of Delivery Sent to Department.*—Art. 3831. The consuls or maritime authorities shall draw up an act of the delivery as soon as they receive said copies, and remit them with the cited copies, with all possible brevity, to the department of relations, which will cause to be published by the periodicals the notice of the death of the testator, in order that the interested parties may move the opening of the will.

§ 3488. *Legal Effect, when.*—Art. 3832. A maritime will will only produce legal effects when the testator dies at sea, or within a month, counted from his disembarkation in any place in which, in conformity with Mexican law or foreign law, he can ratify or execute anew his last disposition.

§ 3489. *As to Death, when Doubted.*—Art. 3833. If the testator disembarks in a place where there is no consular agent, and it is not known whether he has died, nor the date of his death, proceedings will be carried on in conformity with the provisions in title 13 of book 1.

## Of a Will Made in a Foreign Country.

§ 3490. *Made in Foreign Countries.*—Art. 3834. Wills made in a foreign country shall produce effect in the district and in

California, when they shall have been formulated authentically in conformity with the laws of the country in which they were executed.

§ 3491. *Officers in Place of Notaries.*—Art. 3835. The Mexican secretaries of legation, the consuls and vice-consuls, can take the place of notaries in the execution of wills of Mexicans, conforming to the precepts of this code.

§ 3492. *Copies of Wills Sent to Department of Relations.*—Art. 3836. The functionaries referred to shall remit certified copies of open wills which shall have been executed before them to the department of relations, for the effects provided in article 3831.

§ 3493. *Act of Execution.*—Art. 3837. If the will should be closed, the functionary who authorizes it shall remit a copy of the act of execution.

§ 3494. *Legitimate Inheritance Opened, when.*—Art. 3840. The legitimate inheritance is opened: 1. When there is no will executed, or that which was executed is null or lost afterwards its force, although before it may have been valid; 2. When the testator does not dispose of all his property; 3. When the condition imposed on the heir fails, or the latter should die before the testator, or he repudiates the inheritance without having substituted or having placed the right of accretion; 4. When the heir instituted is incapable of inheriting.

§ 3495. *Legatees, when not to be Reduced.*—Art. 3841. When the will, being valid, and the institution of heir ought not to subsist, the legatees, if the legitimate heirs are not forced ones, ought not to be reduced as inofficious.[1]

§ 3496. *Part Disposition by Testator.*—Art. 3842. If the testator only disposes legally of a part of his property, the rest of it shall form the legitimate succession.

§ 3497. *Origin not Considered.*—Art. 3843. In inheritances the law does not consider the origin and nature of the property of the deceased in order to regulate the right of inheriting it.

§ 3498. *Wills in Keeping of Officers.*—Art. 3838. If the will should be confided to the keeping of the secretary of legation, consul, or vice-consul, he will make mention of this circumstance, and give a receipt of the delivery.

§ 3499. *Seal of Legation or Consulate.*—Art. 3839. The paper

[1] Article 3841 is article 3572, code of 1884, and reads as follows: "Art. 3572. When the will, being valid, and the institution of heir ought not to subsist, the other dispositions made therein notwithstanding shall subsist, and the legitimate succession will only comprehend the property which ought to correspond to the heir instituted."

on which shall be drawn wills executed before diplomatic agents or consuls shall bear the respective seal of the legation or consulate.

### Of the Legitimate Succession.

§ 3500. *Legitimate Succession, when Conceded.*—Art. 3844. Legitimate succession is conceded: 1. To the descendants and ascendants, and to the conjugal partner who survives, with the exclusion of the collaterals and of the treasury; 2. Descendants and ascendants failing to exist, to the brothers and nephews and nieces representing deceased brothers or sisters, and to the conjugal partner who survives, with the exclusion of the other collaterals and of the treasury; 3. Brothers or sisters and nephews or nieces representing deceased brothers or sisters failing to exist, to the conjugal partner who survives, although there may be other collaterals; 4. Descendants, ascendants, brothers and sisters, and conjugal partner failing to exist, to the other collaterals within the eighth degree, with the exclusion of the treasury; 5. Collaterals failing to exist, to the treasury.

§ 3501. *Affinity Gives No Right.*—Art. 3845. The relation by affinity gives no right to inherit.

§ 3502. *Nearest Relation.*—Art. 3846. The nearest relations exclude the more remote, save the right of representation in the cases in which it must take place.

§ 3503. *Relations of Same Degree.*—Art. 3847. The relations who shall be found in the same degree shall inherit per head or by equal parts.

§ 3504. *Various Relatives.*—Art. 3848. If there should be various relatives in the same degree, and any one or several should not wish or could not inherit, their part shall increase the others of the same degree, save the right of representation when it must take place.

§ 3505. *When Nearest Relation does not Succeed.*—Art. 3849. If the nearest relation repudiates or can not succeed, if he is alone, or all the nearest relations, those of the following degree in their own right shall inherit without representing the repudiating parties or incapable ones.

§ 3506. *Degrees, how Regulated.*—Art. 3850. The lines and degrees of relation shall be regulated by the provisions contained in chapter 2, title 5, book 1.

§ 3507. *Heirs of Incapacitated Persons.* — Art. 3851. The children and descendants of an incapacitated person, or of him who has been disinherited, shall not be excluded from the succession for those causes, although their parents and ascendants be living, if they were called by their own right; but if they should be only so by right of representation, they can only claim the legitimate part of the incapacitated or disinherited parties.[1]

OF THE RIGHT OF REPRESENTATION.

§ 3508. *Right of Representation, What is.*—Art. 3852. That right which belongs to the relations of a person to succeed to all the rights which that person would have if he had lived or had been able to inherit is called the right of representation.

§ 3509. *In the Descending Line.*—Art. 3853. The right of representation will always take place in the right descending line, but never in the ascending.

§ 3510. *Transversal Line.*—Art. 3854. In the transversal line the right of representation shall only take place in favor of the children of the brothers and sisters, whether they be of the father and mother, or whether by one sole line, when they meet with other brothers and sisters of the same deceased.

§ 3511. *Per Head.*—Art. 3855. The other collaterals shall inherit always per head.

§ 3512. *Division.*—Art. 3856. The representatives of the same person being various, they shall divide equally among themselves what belonged to that person.

§ 3513. *What may be and What not Represented.*—Art. 3857. That person whose succession has been repudiated may be represented; but that person whose succession has been declared incapable or disinherited ought not to be a representative.

§ 3514. *May Repudiate One Line.*—Art. 3858. He who repudiates the inheritance which belongs to him by one line is not for that reason impeded from accepting that which belongs to him by another.

§ 3515. *Between Persons Living.*—Art. 3859. Between persons living, representation does not take place, except in cases of disinheritance or incapacity.[2]

---

[1] Article 3851 becomes article 3582, and is amended by the code of 1884 so as to read as follows: "Art. 3582. The children and descendants of an incapacitated persons shall not be excluded from the succession, even when the incapacitated ascendant lives, if they themselves were called to inherit by the law in representation of the former.

[2] Article 3859 is amended by the code of 1884 to read as follows: "Art. 3590. Between persons living, representation does not take place, except in the case of article 3582" (3851, old code).

## Of the Succession of Descendants.

§ 3516. *Legitimate Children.*—Art. 3860. If at the death of the parents there shall remain only legitimate or legitimated children, the inheritance shall be divided among all in equal parts, without distinction of sex or age, and although they proceed from distinct marriages.

§ 3517. *When Only Descendants of Last Degree.*—Art. 3861. If there shall remain only descendants of the last degree, the inheritance shall be divided per stirpes; and if in any of these there should be various heirs, the portion which shall belong to them shall be divided into equal parts.

§ 3518. *Children and Descendants.*—Art. 3862. If there should be children and descendants, the first shall inherit per head and the second per stirpes.

§ 3519. *Natural and Spurious Children.*—Art. 3863. If there should be only natural children or spurious ones, both being legally recognized, they shall succeed in the same form as legitimate ones.[1]

§ 3520. *Descendants of Natural and Spurious Children.*—Art. 3864. The descendants of natural and spurious children do not enjoy the right of representation, except when they are legitimate or legitimated.

§ 3521. *Legitimate Descendants and Illegitimate Ones.*—Art. 3865. When legitimate descendants occur with illegitimate ones, or both with ascendants, the decision shall be made in the terms provided in articles 3464, 3465, 3466, and 3470 to 3477, on the liquidated whole of the inheritance.[2]

§ 3522. *Estate Absolute.*—Art. 3866. If the intestate estate should be absolute, the part which the testator shall have disposed of shall be deducted from the whole inheritance, and the rest shall be divided in the manner which the preceding articles provide.

§ 3523. *Surviving Consort and Descendants.*—Art. 3867. The

[1] Article 3863 is amended by the code of 1884, by inserting the words "or designated" after the word "recognized."

[2] Article 3865 is article 3596, new code, and is amended to read as follows: "Art. 3696. When legitimate or legitimated descendants occur with recognized natural ones, the division shall be made by deducting from the portion which corresponds to the natural ones if it should be made in equal parts, one third which shall be added to the divisible among the legitimate ones."

Article 3599 is a new article, in the code of 1884, and reads: "Art. 3599. When legitimate descendants occur with natural and spurious ones, the division shall be made between the legitimate and the natural ones, in the terms which article 3596 (3865) provides, and the spurious only shall have a right to supplies in conformity with article 3597 (3465)."

conjugal partner who survives occurring with descendants, the provisions in article 3884 shall be observed.

OF THE SUCCESSION OF ASCENDANTS.

§ 3524. *Father and Mother.*—Art. 3868. In default of descendants, the father and mother shall succeed in equal parts.

§ 3525. *Father or Mother.*—Art. 3869. If there should be a father or mother, the survivor shall succeed to all the inheritance of the child.

§ 3526. *Equal Parts.*—Art. 3870. If there should only be ascendants of the last degree by one line, the inheritance shall be divided in equal parts.

§ 3527. *Ascendants of Both Lines.*—Art. 3871. If there should be ascendants by both lines, the inheritance shall be divided into two equal parts, and shall be applied, one to the ascendants of the paternal line, and the other to those of the maternal line.

§ 3528. *Equal Division.*—Art. 3872. The members of each line shall divide among themselves in equal parts the portion which belongs to them.

§ 3529. *Surviving Consort and Ascendants.*—Art. 3873. The conjugal partner who survives occurring with ascendants, the provisions in article 3884 shall be observed.[1]

§ 3530. *Illegitimate Ascendants.*—Art. 3874. In respect to illegitimate ascendants, the provisions in articles 3479, 3480, and 3481 shall govern in inheritances without a will.[2]

OF THE SUCCESSION OF COLLATERALS.

§ 3531. *Collaterals.*—Art. 3875. In default of ascendants, descendants, and the conjugal partner, the law calls to the succession the collaterals within the eighth degree.

§ 3532. *Brothers and Sisters Only.*—Art. 3876. If there are only legitimate brothers and sisters by both lines, they will succeed in equal parts.

§ 3533. *Whole and Half Brothers and Sisters.*—Art. 3877. If should occur whole brothers and sisters and half brothers and sisters, the former will inherit a portion double that of the latter.

§ 3534. *Brothers and Nephews.*—Art. 3878. If there should occur brothers and sisters with nephews and nieces, children of

[1] Article 3873 becomes article 3615, and is amended by inserting after the word "ascendants" "the inheritance shall be divided into two equal parts, of which one shall be applied to the conjugal partner, and the other to the ascendants, in the terms of the prior articles."

[2] Article 3874 is suppressed in the code of 1884.

sisters, the first will inherit by the head, and the second per stirpes.

§ 3535. *Children of Brothers or Sisters.*—Art. 3879. In default of legitimate brothers or sisters, their children, also being legitimate, shall succeed by dividing the inheritance per stirpes, and the portion of each stirpe per capita.

§ 3536. *Natural and Spurious Brothers or Sisters.*—Art. 3880. In default of those called in the preceding article, the natural brothers and sisters shall succeed, and in default of these, the spurious, both being legally recognized; in default of them, their legitimate children; and in respect to all, the provisions in the three preceding articles shall be observed.

§ 3537. *Children of Half-brothers.*—Art. 3881. The children of the half brothers or sisters shall enjoy the right of representation, and shall succeed to the part which belongs to them, whether they are alone, or whether they occur with their uncles.

§ 3538. *Relations in Nearest Degree.*—Art. 3882. In default of those called in the preceding articles, the relations in the nearest degree shall succeed, without distinction of lives or consideration of a double tie; and they will inherit in equal parts.

§ 3539. *Conjugal Consort and Collaterals.*—Art. 3883. In a concurrence of collaterals and the conjugal partner, the provisions in articles 3866 to 3890 shall be observed.

Of the Succession of the Conjugal Partner.

§ 3540. *Conjugal Partners Surviving.*—Art. 3884. The conjugal parner who survives, concurring with descendants or ascendants, shall have the right of a legitimate child, if said partner lacks property, or if that which said partner has at the time of opening the succession should not equal the portion which must belong to each legitimate child in the inheritance.[1]

§ 3541. *Conjugal Consort Surviving shall Receive What.*—Art. 3885. In the first case of the preceding article the conjugal partner shall receive in whole the portion designated; in the second, he or she will have the right to receive what shall be sufficient to equalize his or her property with said portion.

§ 3542. *Conjugal Survivor with a Brother or Sister*—Art. 3886. If the conjugal partner who survives should concur with one brother or sister alone, the inheritance will be divided in equal parts.

[1] Article 3884 is amended by suppressing the words "or ascendants," in the code of 1884.

§ 3543. *Conjugal Partner and Two or More Brothers or Sisters.*—Art. 3887. If should concur two or more brothers or sisters, the conjugal partner shall have one third of the inheritance, and the two thirds shall be divided among the brothers or sisters.

§ 3544. *Conjugal Partner Succeeds to the Whole.*—Art. 3888. In default of brothers or sisters, the conjugal partner shall succeed to the whole of the inheritance in conformity with fraction 3 of article 3844.

§ 3545. *Conjugal Partner Having Property shall Succeed.*—Art. 3889. The conjugal partner shall receive the portions which belong to him or her, in conformity with the three articles which precede, although they shall have property of their own.

§ 3546. *Conjugal Partner and Illegitimate Brothers and Sisters.*—Art. 3890. The provisions in articles 3886 and 3887 shall only be understood in respect to legitimate brothers or sisters, and also of their legitimate children. The conjugal partner, concurring with illegitimate brothers and sisters, shall only have these rights to allowances.

### Of the Succession in the Public Treasury.

§ 3547. *Public Treasury.*—Art. 3891. In default of all the heirs called in the preceding chapters, the public treasury shall succeed, save the provisions in articles 1370, 2736, and 3256.[1]

§ 3548. *Public Treasury Equal to Heirs.*—Art. 3892. The rights and obligations of the treasury are in every point equal to those of other heirs.[2]

---

[1] Article 3891 is amended by the code of 1884 to read as follows: "Art. 3634. In default of all the heirs called in the preceding chapter, the public treasury and the public beneficence shall succeed in equal parts."

[2] Article 3892 is amended by the code of 1884 by inserting the words "and the beneficence" after the word "treasury."

The following is a new article in the code of 1884: "Art. 3635. Notwithstanding the provision in article 3301 (3438), the treasury and the public beneficence shall succeed in the case of the preceding article, even when in the inheritance there shall be real estate; but then, unless said property be destined to the public service, it shall be sold in conformity with the law before the making of the adjudication by the judge who shall have cognizance of the intestate estate, applying to the treasury and to the public beneficence the price which shall be obtained."

# CHAPTER XX.

## DISPOSITIONS COMMON TO THE TESTAMENTARY AND TO THE LEGITIMATE SUCCESSION.

§ 3549. When Widow is *Enceinte.*
§ 3550. Petition for Examination.
§ 3351. Judge may Make Orders.
§ 3552. Provision for Care of Widow.
§ 3553. Repetition of Examination.
§ 3554. Husband's Recognition of Pregnancy.
§ 3555. Support of Widow.
§ 3556. Support of Widow may be Denied.
§ 3557. Prior Expenses of Support.
§ 3558. Legitimacy of the Child.
§ 3559. Support not to be Returned.
§ 3560. Decision of the Judge.
§ 3561. Minors under Care of Widow.
§ 3562. Executor Administers.
§ 3563. Suspension of Division.
§ 3564. Widow Entitled to be Heard.
§ 3565. Conjugal Survivor.
§ 3566. Supplies Cease, when.
§ 3567. Usufructs.
§ 3568. Supplies will Last until when.
§ 3569. Amount of Supplies Taxed by the Judge.
§ 3570. Right of Accretion.
§ 3571. What is Required.
§ 3572. Actual Division.
§ 3573. Want of a Co-heir.
§ 3574. Forced Heirs.
§ 3575. Improvements.
§ 3576. Heirs whose Right is Increased.
§ 3577. Repudiation by Heirs.
§ 3578. Joint Interest in Usufructs.
§ 3579. Governing Articles.
§ 3580. Legatees.
§ 3581. Testators may Modify.
§ 3582. Inheritance without a Will.
§ 3583. Succession when Opened.
§ 3584. Where Opened.
§ 3585. Want of Domicile.
§ 3586. Where Greater Part of Real Estate is.
§ 3587. Where the Author shall have Died.
§ 3588. Where Several Persons Inherit.
§ 3589. Being No Executor Appointed.
§ 3590. Tardy Action of Executor.

### Of the Precautions Which must be Adopted when the Widow is Enceinte.

§ 3549. *When Widow is Enciente.*—Art. 3893. When on the death of the husband the widow is or believes she is *enceinte*, she must inform the judge of it within forty days, in order that he may notify the parties interested in the succession.

§ 3550. *Petition for Examination.*—Art. 3894. The interested parties can ask the judge to proceed opportunely and decorously with the examination of pregnancy.

§ 3551. *Judge may Make Orders.*—Art. 3895. Although the pregnancy shall certainly result, or the interested parties may not contest it, they can ask the judge to dictate the proper orders in order to avoid the supposition of birth, or that the child which may be born shall not pass as living, not being so in reality.

§ 3552. *Provision for Care of the Widow.*—Art. 3896. When the result of the examination shall be contrary to the certainty of the pregnancy, and the widow shall insist that it is true, she can ask the judge that with an audience of the interested parties a decent house be designated where she may be kept in sight, and with all necessary precautions, until the natural time of birth shall arrive.

§ 3553. *Repetition of Examination.*—Art. 3897. The interested parties can ask at any time that the examination be repeated.

§ 3554. *Husband's Recognition of Pregnancy.*—Art. 3898. If the husband recognized in a public or private instrument the certainty of the pregnancy of his consort, the examination can not be proceeded with; but the interested parties can ask that the proceedings of which article 3895 speaks be practiced.

§ 3555. *Support of Widow.*—Art. 3899. The widow *enceinte*, even when she has property, must be competently supported.

§ 3556. *Support may be Denied.*—Art. 3900. If the widow does not give notice to the judge, or does not observe the measures dictated by him, the interested parties can deny her support when she shall have property.

§ 3557. *Prior Expenses of Support.*—Art. 3901. If by posterior examinations the certainty of pregnancy should result, they must pay for the support which they shall have failed to pay.

§ 3558. *Legitimacy of the Child.*—Art. 3902. The omission of the mother shall not prejudice the legitimacy of the child if by other legal means it shall be proved.

§ 3559. *Support not to be Returned.*—Art. 3903. The widow ought not to return the support received, even when there shall have been an abortion or the certainty of pregnancy should not result; save the case in which there shall have been a counter-statement by the professional information (de plano).

§ 3560. *Decision of the Judge.*—Art. 3904. The judge shall decide immediately all the questions relative to the support, in a sense favorable to the widow.[1]

§ 3561. *Minors under Care of Widow.*—Art. 3905. A widow who shall be in the exercise of parental power shall continue in

[1] Article 3904 is amended by the code of 1884 to read as follows: "Art. 3648. The judge shall decide de plano immediately all the questions relative to the support in conformity with the preceding articles, deciding in case of doubt in a sense favorable to the widow."

the administration of the property which may belong to the minors.

§ 3562. *Executor Administers.*—Art. 3906. If she shall have no children, or they should be of the age of majority, the executors shall administer the property, save the provision in article 2201.

§ 3563. *Suspension of the Division.*—Art. 3907. The division of the inheritance shall be suspended until the birth shall be verified; but the creditors can be paid by a judicial mandate.

§ 3564. *Widow Entitled to be Heard.*—Art. 3908. Whatever proceeding may be practiced in conformity with the provisions of this chapter, the widow must be heard.

OF THE WIDOW'S OR WIDOWER'S PORTION.

§ 3565. *Conjugal Survivor.*—Art. 3909. The conjugal survivor, whatever may be the settlements of the dissolved marriage, who shall be found without proper means of subsistence, shall have a right to be furnished with supplies from the fruits of the property which the deceased conjugal partner may leave.

§ 3566. *Supplies Cease, when.*—Art. 3910. The concession of supplies ceases if the conjugal partner who survives shall be found in the cases designated by fractions 1, 2, 3, 6, and 10 of article 3428.

§ 3567. *Usufructs.*—Art. 3911. The provision in article 3909 does not comprehend the property of which the husband may have been the usufructuary.

§ 3568. *Supplies will Last until when.*—Art. 3912. The supplies shall last as long as the deceased's partner shall need them, and does not pass to a second marriage, or does not receive the part of the inheritance which in conformity with law belongs to him or her.

§ 3569. *Amount of Supplies Taxed by the Judge.*—Art. 3913. The supplies shall be taxed by the judge, considering the rents of the property and the necessity and circumstances of the surviving partner, unless there shall have been a friendly arrangement.[1]

OF THE RIGHT OF ACCRETION.

§ 3570. *Right of Accretion.*—Art. 3914. The right of accretion is that which the law concedes to an heir in order to add to his hereditary portion what should have belonged to another heir.

---

[1] Articles 3909 to 3913, inclusive, are suppressed in the code of 1884.

§ 3571. *What is Required.*—Art. 3915. In order that in the inheritances by will the right of accretion shall take place, it is required: 1. That two or more shall be called to one same inheritance, or to one same portion of it, without a special designation of parts; 2. That one of the so-called shall die before the testator, renounce the inheritance, or be incapable of receiving it.

§ 3572. *Actual Division.*—Art. 3916. It shall not be understood that the parts are designated, except when the testator shall have expressly ordered that they be divided, or they have been designated with physical signs; but the phrase, "by halves," or "by equal parts," or others, which, although they designate an aliquot part, do not fix this numerically, or by signs which make each one owner of a separate body of property, do not exclude the right of accretion.

§ 3573. *Want of a Co-heir.*—Art. 3917. If the want of a co-heir happens after having accepted the inheritance, the right of accretion does not take place, and his part is transmitted to his heirs, save the provision in article 3922.

§ 3574. *Forced Heirs.*—Art. 3918. If the heirs are forced, the right of accretion only takes place when the part of free disposition is left to two or more of them, or to some one of them and to an extraneous person.

§ 3575. *Improvement.*—Art. 3919. The improvement (mejora) which is left to one sole forced heir, or to various, without the requisite which is required in fraction 1 of article 3915, increases the other co-heirs.[1]

§ 3576. *Heirs whose Right is Increased.*—Art. 3920. The heirs whom the part which fails increases succeed to all the rights and obligations which he who did not wish or could not receive the inheritance would have.

§ 3577. *Repudiation by Heirs.*—Art. 3921. The heirs can only repudiate the portion which increases their own by renouncing the inheritance, unless they are forced heirs.[2]

§ 3578. *Joint Interest in Usufructs.*—Art. 3922. When in conformity with the law the right of accretion ought to take place among those called jointly to a usufruct, the portion of him who fails shall always increase the other, although the former fails after having accepted, and even has been in possession of, his part of the usufruct.

---

[1] Articles 3918 and 3919 are suppressed in the code of 1884.

[2] Article 3921 is amended by the code of 1884 by suppressing the words "unless they are forced heirs."

§ 3579. *Governing Articles.*—Art. 3923. The provisions in articles 3915, 3916, 3917, 3920, 3921, and 3922 shall be likewise observed in legacies.

§ 3580. *Legatees.*—Art. 3924. When the legatees shall not be found in the case of fraction 1 of article 3915, but in any of those designated in fraction 2, the legacy shall be gained by the heirs.

§ 3581. *Testator may Modify.*—Art. 3925. The testator can prohibit or modify, as he may wish, the right of accretion, save the legitimate rights.[1]

§ 3582. *Inheritance without a Will.*—Art. 3926. In the inheritances without a will, the provisions in articles 3848, 3849, and 3851 shall be observed.

### Of the Opening and Transmission of the Inheritance.

§ 3583. *Succession, when Opened.*—Art. 3927. The succession is opened at the moment in which the author of the inheritance dies, and when in conformity with the provisions in chapter 5, title 13, of book 1, the presumption of the death of an absent person is declared.

§ 3584. *Where Opened.*—Art. 3928. The succession shall be opened in the place where the deceased shall have had his domicile.

§ 3585. *Want of Domicile.*—Art. 3929. For want of a fixed domicile, it shall be opened in the place where the real estate that forms it shall be situated.

§ 3586. *Where Greater Part of Real Estate is.*—Art. 3930. If there should be real estate in divers places, the succession shall be opened where the greater part thereof shall be found, calculated by the payment of the greater sum of direct taxes.

§ 3587. *Where the Author shall have Died.*—Art. 3931. For want of a fixed domicile and of real estate, the succession shall be opened in the place where the author thereof shall have died.[2]

§ 3588. *Where Several Persons Inherit.*—Art. 3932. Being various the persons called simultaneously to the same inheritance, the right which they have to it shall be considered indivisible, as well as in respect to the possession of the dominion, while the partition shall not be made.

§ 3589. *Being No Executor Appointed.*—Art. 3933. There being no executor appointed, each one of the heirs can in the case

---

[1]Article 3925 becomes article 3662, new code, and is amended by suppressing the words "save the legitimate rights."

[2]Articles 3928 to 3931, inclusive, are suppressed in the code of 1884.

of the preceding article claim the whole of the inheritance which may belong to him jointly with the others, without the defendant being able to oppose the defense that the inheritance does not belong wholly to him.

§ 3590. *Tardy Action of Executor.*—Art. 3934. An executor being appointed, he must move the reclamation to which the preceding article refers; and being tardy in doing so, the heirs can ask for his removal.

§ 3591. *Prescription.*—Art. 3935. The right of reclaiming an inheritance may be prescribed in twenty years, and is transmissible to the heirs.

### OF THE ACCEPTATION AND OF THE REPUDIATION OF THE INHERITANCE.

§ 3592. *Right of Acceptation and Repudiation.*—Art. 3936. The acceptation and the repudiation of the inheritance are acts entirely voluntary and free for those of the age of majority, although they may be forced heirs.[1]

§ 3593. *Express or Tacit.*—Art. 3937. The acceptance may be express or tacit.

§ 3594. *When Express and when Tacit.*—Art. 3938. The acceptation is express if the heir accepts with definite words, and tacit if he executes any acts by which the intention of accepting is necessarily deduced, or those which he could not execute except with the quality of heir.

§ 3595. *Not to be Accepted in Part.*—Art. 3939. No one can accept or repudiate the inheritance in part, with time or conditionally.

§ 3596. *Who can Accept or Repudiate.*—Art. 3940. All those who have the free disposition of their property can accept or repudiate.

§ 3597. *Married Woman.*—Art. 3941. A married woman can not accept or repudiate an inheritance validly without the authorization of her husband or judicial license. In respect to the husband, the provision in article 2160 shall be observed.

§ 3598. *Minors.*—Art. 3942. An inheritance left to minors and others incapacitated will be accepted by the tutors.

§ 3599. *Deaf and Dumb.*—Art. 3943. Persons deaf and dumb, who shall not be in tutelage and know how to write, can accept or repudiate an inheritance by themselves or by an attorney; but if they should not know how to write, a tutor elected for the case shall accept it in his name, in conformity with the provisions in the cases of injunction (interdiccion).

---

[1] Article 3936 is amended by the code of 1884 by suppressing the words "although they may be forced heirs."

§ 3600. *Disagreement of Heirs.*—Art. 3944. If the heirs should not agree on the acceptation or repudiation, they can accept some and repudiate others; but only those who may accept shall have the character and the rights of heirs.

§ 3601. *Heirs of Heirs.*—Art. 3945. If an heir shall die without accepting or repudiating the inheritance, the right of doing so shall be transmitted to his heirs.

§ 3602. *Retroactive Effect.*—Art. 3946. The effects of the acceptation or repudiation of an inheritance shall always be retroactive to the date of the death of the person from whom it it inherited.

§ 3603. *In Writing.*—Art. 3947. A repudiation must be express, and made in writing before the judge.[1]

§ 3604. *Right to Legacies.*—Art. 3948. A repudiation does not deprive him who makes it, if he is not heir and executor, of the right to reclaim the legacies which shall have been left him.

§ 3605. *Testamentary and Intestate Rights.*—Art. 3949. If an heir appointed in the will, and who at the same time may have a right to inherit by intestacy, if he repudiates as testamentary heir, he loses the right to succeed by intestacy.

§ 3606. *Repudiation without Notice.*—Art. 3950. He who repudiates the right to succeed by intestacy, without having notice of his testamentary title, can in virtue thereof accept the inheritance.

§ 3607. *Forced Heirs.*—Art. 3951. The renunciation made by a forced heir, of the inheritance which may be left him with some condition or burden on his legitimate right, is excepted from the provisions in article 3949.[2]

§ 3608. *Succession of Living Persons.*—Art. 3952. No one can, even by a contract of marriage, renounce the succession of a living person, nor sell the rights which he eventually may have to his inheritance.

§ 3609. *Uncertainty of the Death of Testator.*—Art. 3953. No one can accept nor repudiate without being certain of the death of that person whose inheritance is in question.

§ 3610. *Under Condition.*—Art. 3954. The death of the person from whom one inherits being known, he may renounce the inheritance left under a condition, although this has not been complied with.

---

[1] Article 3947 is amended by the code of 1884 so as to read as follows: "Art. 3681. A repudiation must be express and made in writing before the judge, or by the means of a public instrument executed before a notary, when the heir is not found in the place of the court."

[2] Article 3951 is suppressed by the code of 1884.

§ 3611. *Corporations and Partnerships.*—Art. 3955. The legitimate representatives of partnerships and corporations capable of acquiring, can accept an inheritance which they shall have left them; but in order to repudiate, they require judicial approbation with an audience of the public minister.

§ 3612. *Public Establishments.*—Art. 3956. Public establishments can not accept nor repudiate an inheritance without the approbation of the government.

§ 3613. *Time.*—Art. 3957. When any one shall have an interest in that the heir may declare whether he accepts or repudiates the inheritance, he can ask that nine days having passed from the opening of the inheritance, the judge shall assign to the heir a term which shall not exceed one month, in order that within it he shall make his declaration, being warned that if he does not make it the inheritance will be held as accepted.

§ 3614. *Irrevocable.*—Art. 3958. An acceptation and a repudiation once made are irrevocable, and they can not be impugned unless in the cases of fraud or violence.

§ 3615. *Revocable from Ignorance of Facts.*—Art. 3959. An heir can revoke an acceptation or a repudiation, when by a will unknown at the time of making it the quality or quantity of the inheritance is altered.

§ 3616. *Return of Property.*—Art. 3960. In the case of the preceding article, if an heir revokes the acceptation, he shall return all that he shall have received from the inheritance; observing in respect to the fruits the rules relative to possessors in good or bad faith accordingly as that of the heir shall have been.

§ 3617. *Creditors' Rights.*—Art. 3961. If an heir repudiates an inheritance in prejudice of his own creditors, they can ask the judge to authorize them to accept it in the name of the former.

§ 3618. *Payment of Credits.*—Art. 3962. In the case of the preceding article, the acceptation alone shall avail the creditors for the payment of their credits; but if the inheritance shall exceed the amount thereof, the excess shall belong to him whom the law calls, and in no case to him who made the renunciation.

§ 3619. *Posterior Credits.*—Art. 3963. Creditors whose credits may be posterior to the repudiation can not exercise the right which article 3961 concedes.

§ 3620. *Interested Parties.*—Art. 3964. He who by the repudiation of the inheritance ought to enter into it can impede the creditors from accepting it by paying them their credits which they had against him who repudiated.

§ 3621. *Culpability of Heir.*—Art. 3965. An heir who, by a judgment, is declared culpable of having secreted or subtracted anything from the inheritance is responsible for the damages and losses, and is also subject to the prescriptions of the penal code.

§ 3622. *Adjudged Heir.*—Art. 3966. He who in the petition of a legatee or hereditary creditor shall have been declared an heir shall be considered as such by the others, without the necessity of a new trial.

§ 3623. *No Confusion Produced.*—Art. 3967. An acceptation in no case produces a confusion of the property of the author of the inheritance and of those of the heir.

§ 3624. *Presumption.*—Art. 3968. Every inheritance is understood as accepted with the benefit of inventory, although it is not expressed.

§ 3625. *Joint Obligations.*—Art. 3969. In the provision of article 3503, joint obligations which the heir and the author of the inheritance shall have contracted are not comprehended.

# CHAPTER XXI.

## INVENTORY.

§ 3626. Inventory to be Asked for.
§ 3627. Executor to Form It.
§ 3628. Heir may Form It.
§ 3629. Heir Associated with Executor.
§ 3630. After Ninety Days.
§ 3631. Care of Property.
§ 3632. Public Minister.
§ 3633. How Formed.
§ 3634. Solemn, when.
§ 3635. Citation.
§ 3636. Public Minister.
§ 3637. Conclusion.
§ 3638. Extension of Time.
§ 3639. Expert Appraisers.
§ 3640. Arbiter.
§ 3641. Duty of Experts.
§ 3642. Actual Value.
§ 3643. Divisible Objects.
§ 3644. Average Products.
§ 3645. Emphyteusis.
§ 3646. All Interests to be Included.
§ 3647. Another's Property.
§ 3648. Creditors and Legatees, when Paid.
§ 3649. Creditors and Legatees can Sue.
§ 3650. Judge as Arbiter.
§ 3651. Liquidation.
§ 3652. Funeral Debts.
§ 3653. Funeral Debts, What are.
§ 3654. Funeral Debts, how Paid.
§ 3655. Second Class of Debts.
§ 3656. Sale of Property.
§ 3657. Hereditary Debts.
§ 3658. Hereditary Debts, What are.
§ 3659. Payment by Graduation.
§ 3660. Order of Payment.
§ 3661. Legacies.
§ 3662. Creditors after Payment of Legacies.
§ 3663. Sale.
§ 3664. Application of Funds.
§ 3665. Inventory by Heir.
§ 3666. Effect of Inventory.
§ 3667. Property not Included.
§ 3668. Penalty for Fraud.

§ 3626. *Inventory to be Asked for.*—Art. 3970. Every heir, whether by will or intestacy, if he accepts the inheritance, will be under an obligation to ask for the formation of an inventory within eight days, counted from the time he shall know of his appointment or shall take part in the succession.[1]

§ 3627. *Executor to Form It.*—Art. 3971. The executor shall ask for himself in the term indicated in the preceding article, and the legal inventory which he may form shall avail the others interested.[2]

§ 3628. *Heir may Form It.*—Art. 3972. If the executor shall not ask that the inventory be made, any heir can do so, and it shall avail the others although they be not cited.

§ 3629. *Heir Associated with Executor.*—Art. 3973. The heir who shall have asked it to be made shall be considered as associated with the executor, who can not, without the consent of the former, execute any act of administration.[3]

§ 3630. *After Ninety Days.*—Art. 3974. The provisions in the two preceding articles shall be likewise observed when the ninety days and the extension which article 3983 concedes shall have passed, the executor not having concluded, and any heir shall have caused the conclusion of the inventory.

§ 3631. *Case of Property.*—Art. 3975. The judge, during the days designated in article 3970, and even immediately after the death of a person, if none of the heirs are present, shall dictate opportune orders so that the property may not be secreted or lost.

§ 3632. *Public Minister.*—Art. 3976. In the case of the preceding article, the public minister shall necessarily be heard.[4]

§ 3633. *Inventory, how Formed.*—Art. 3977. The inventory shall be formed by simple statements, without the aid of a notary, with citation of all the interested parties or of their legitimate representatives.[5]

---

[1] Article 3970 is suppressed by the code of 1884.

[2] Article 3971 is amended by the code of 1884 to read as follows: "Art. 3771. The definite executor within fifteen days after he knows of his appointment shall ask for the formation of the inventory."

[3] Articles 3972 and 3973 are united into one article in the code of 1884, and there is also added thereto the following words: "In cases of disagreement, it shall go to the judge for a resolution."

[4] Articles 3974 to 3976 inclusive, are suppressed by the code of 1884.

[5] Article 3977 is amended to read as follows in the code of 1884: "Art. 3773. The inventory shall be formed as the code of civil procedure provides."

§ 3634. *Solemn, when.*—Art. 3978. The inventory shall be solemn in the following cases: 1. If a majority of the heirs and legatees so require it; 2. When the hereditary creditors ask for a separation of patrimony, in conformity with the provisions in articles 2065 and 2066; 3. Whenever in the inheritance there should be confounded dotal property; 4. Whenever the public treasury or establishments of beneficence shall have an interest in the inheritance; 5. In those of an intestate of which articles 3710 and 3713 speak.

Art. 3779. The solemn inventory shall be formed accordingly as the code of procedure shall provide.

§ 3635. *Citation.*—Art. 3980. The executor shall cause the legatees and creditors of the deceased to be judicially cited for a term which shall not pass thirty days, in order that, if they shall wish, they may be present at the formation of the inventory.

§ 3636. *Public Minister.*—Art. 3981. Said term having passed, if the persons cited should not appear, the formation of the inventory shall continue with the presence of the public minister.

§ 3637. *Conclusion.*—Art. 3982. The executor shall be under an obligation to conclude the inventory within ninety days, counted from the time he accepted the appointment.

§ 3638. *Extension of Time*—Art. 3983. If the property should be found distributed or situated at great distances, or if by the nature of the business ninety days should not be considered sufficient, the judge can extend the term to nine months, with an audience of the interested parties and of the public minister.

§ 3639. *Expert Appraisers.*—Art. 3984. The executor on promoting the formation of the inventory shall appoint, with the consent of the interested parties, one or more expert appraisers; and if there should be no agreement in the appointment, the half of the experts shall be of the election of the executor, and the other half of that of the others interested.

§ 3640. *Arbiter.*—Art. 3985. The experts, before commencing their work, shall appoint a third party for cases of disagreement; and if they should not agree, the election shall be made by the judge.

§ 3641. *Duty of Experts.*—Art. 3986. The experts shall include their opinion in the same inventory; this being signed under a protest; and if they should be convicted of fraud or bad faith, they shall be responsible for the damages and losses.

§ 3642. *Actual Value.*—Art. 3987. All the objects must be estimated according to their state and actual value.

§ 3643. *Divisible Objects.*—Art. 3988. The experts shall declare what objects can be divided without injury.

§ 3644. *Average Products.*—Art. 3989. Rural and urban estates shall be valued by the average amount of their products in a term of five years, deducting the expenses and repairs and cultivation and any other burden.

§ 3645. *Emphyteusis.*—Art. 3990. If among the property of the inheritance there should be estates subject to emphyteusis, not valued as is provided in article 3243, the value of the useful dominion shall be calculated by the same bases established in the preceding article; and the fee shall be calculated by capitalizing the pension at so much stipulated per cent, and for want of an agreement, at six per cent annually.

§ 3646. *All Interests Included.*—Art. 3991. The inventory must comprehend all the movable and immovable property of the deceased, his rights and actions and his debts, with a statement of the origin, nature, and quality of documents in which they may appear.

§ 3647. *Another's Property.*—Art. 3992. If the deceased had in his possession borrowed property of another, on deposit, on pledge, or under any other title, they will also be made to appear in the inventory, with a statement of the cause.

§ 3648. *Creditors and Legatees, when Paid.*—Art. 3993. During the formation of the inventory the creditors and legatees can not require the payment of their credits and legacies, with the exceptions contained at the end of articles 3997 and 4000.

§ 3649. *Creditors and Legatees.*—Art. 3994. The creditors and legatees can also sue the executor on any question of dominion or possession which are founded on titles anterior to the succession, as well as the executor can sue the hereditary debtors.

§ 3650. *The Judge as Arbiter.*—Art. 3995. If the interested parties should not agree as to the inventory, the judge shall decide with an audience of all of them, on the terms which the code of procedure shall establish.[1]

§ 3651. *Liquidation.*—Art. 3996. The judicial decision being obtained, or the interested parties agreeing to the inventory, the executor shall proceed to liquidate the inheritance.[2]

---

[1] Articles 3978 to 3995, inclusive, are suppressed by the code of 1884.

[2] Article 3996 is amended by the code of 1884 so as to read as follows: "Art. 3774. The inventory having been concluded and judicially approved, the executor shall proceed to the liquidation of the inheritance."

§ 3652. *Funeral Debts.*—Art. 3997. In the first place the funeral debts shall be paid, if they should not be already, since they may be paid before the formation of the inventory.

§ 3653. *Funeral Debts, What are.*—Art. 3998. The expenses of the funeral, and those which shall have been caused by the last sickness of the author of the inheritance, are called funeral debts.

§ 3654. *How Paid.*—Art. 3999. The payment of the funeral debts shall be imputed to the free part, whether or not the testator shall have disposed of it; what shall exceed that part shall be paid from the body of the inheritance.

§ 3655. *Second Class of Debts.*—Art. 4000. In the second place shall be paid the expenses caused by the same inheritance and the provision credits, which can also be covered before the formation of the inventory.

§ 3656. *Sale of Property.*—Art. 4001. If, in order to make the payments of which the preceding articles speak, there should be no money in the inheritance, the executor shall ask for the sale of the movables, and even of the immovables, with the solemnities which are respectively required.

§ 3657. *Hereditary Debts.*—Art. 4002. Then shall be paid the hereditary debts which shall be demandable.

§ 3658. *What are Hereditary.*—Art. 4003. The debts contracted by the author of the inheritance, independently of his last disposition, and of those for which he is responsible with his property, are called hereditary.

§ 3659. *Payment by Graduation.*—Art. 4004. If there should be pending any insolvent proceedings, the executor must not pay except in conformity with the judgment of graduation.

§ 3660. *Order of Payment.*—Art. 4005. The creditors, when there shall be no insolvent proceedings, shall be paid in the order in which they present themselves; but if among those not presented there should be any preferred, the bond of a creditor of a better right (acreedor de mejor derecho) shall be required of those who shall be paid.

§ 3661. *Legacies.*—Art. 4006. The executor, having concluded the inventory, can not pay the legacies without having covered or assigned property sufficient to pay the debts; preserving on the respective property the special burdens which they may have.

§ 3662. *Creditors after Payment of Legacies.*—Art. 4007. The creditors who shall present themselves after the payment of the legatees shall only have an action against the latter when in the inheritance there shall not be property sufficient to cover their credits.

§ 3663. *Sale.*—Art. 4008. The sale of hereditary property for the payment of debts and legacies shall be made at public auction, unless the majority of the interested parties otherwise agree.

§ 3664. *Application of Funds.*—Art. 4009. The agreement of the interested parties, or the judicial authorization in case thereof, shall determine the application which must be given to the price for which the things may be sold.

§ 3665. *Inventory by Heir.*—Art. 4010. The inventory made by the heir who afterwards repudiates shall avail the substitute and the heirs by intestacy.

§ 3666. *Effect of Inventory.*—Art. 4011. The inventory prejudices those who made it and those who approved it; but not those who were not cited for it.

§ 3667. *Property not Included.*—Art. 4012. If the hereditary or testamentary creditors, on suing the heir, shall designate as belonging to the inheritance any property not included in the inventory, the corresponding proof is a charge on them.

§ 3668. *Penalty for Fraud.*—Art. 4013. If said creditors obtain a favorable judgment, and in the omission there was fraud on the part of the heirs, a fine of twenty-five per cent of the amount of their liquidated part shall be imposed upon them, besides the indemnification for damages and losses.

§ 3669. *Insufficiency of Property.*—Art. 4014. When the property does not suffice to pay the debts and legacies, the executor must report his administration to the creditors and legatees.

§ 3670. *No Reformation of Inventory, Except when.*—Art. 4015. The inventory being approved by the judge or by the consent of all the interested parties, it can not be reformed except for error or fraud declared by a final judgment, pronounced in the ordinary court.

§ 3671. *Expenses.*—Art. 4016. The expenses of the inventory are a charge on the inheritance, save that the testator may have otherwise disposed.[1]

[1]Articles 4010 to 4016, inclusive, are suppressed by the code of 1884.

# CHAPTER XXII.

## COLLATIONS.



§ 3672. *Bringing to the Collation, What is.*—Art. 4017. The amounts which the forced heirs shall have received before the death of the testator, as dower, donation, or other lucrative title, shall be considered as existing in the mass of the inheritance, for the designation of the legitimate rights and the account of partition; this is what is called bringing to the collation.

§ 3673. *When Collation does not Take Place.*—Art. 4018. The collation shall not take place among the legitimate heirs if the donor shall have so declared, or if the donee should repudiate the inheritance; save the case in which the donation ought to be reduced as inofficious.

§ 3674. *Grandchildren.*—Art. 4019. When the grandchildren shall succeed their grandfathers, representing their fathers, they will bring to the collation what their fathers shall have received, even when they may not have inherited it.

§ 3675. *When Collation not Brought by Father, Husband, or Wife.*—Art. 4020. The father is not obliged to bring to the collation in the inheritance of his ascendants the amount donated to the child by them; nor the husband or wife the amount donated to their respective consort by the father-in-law or mother-in-law, even when the donor disposes expressly to the contrary, save the limitation of article 2233.

§ 3676. *Expenses for Cure of a Child.*—Art. 4021. The expenses made by the father in the cure of a child, although they may be of great importance and extraordinary, are not subject to collation.

§ 3677. *Education.*—Art. 4022. Neither are the support and primary education, nor the secondary, which a child may receive in the house of his father, subject to collation.

§ 3678. *Professional Education.*—Art. 4023. The expenses which a father may make in giving his children a professional or artistic career, or for the payment of their debts, shall be brought to the collation, but there shall be deducted therefrom what a child shall have spent while living in the house and company of his parents.

§ 3679. *When Collation Dispensed with.*—Art. 4024. A father can dispense with a collation of which the preceding article treats, unless, although the deduction be made which is provided therein, the expenses exceed the legitimate right.

§ 3680. *Donations.*—Art. 4025. The same things donated need not be brought to the collation, but the value which they had at the time of the donation, although its just price shall not have then been made.

§ 3681. *Loss and Deterioration.*—Art. 4026. The increase or posterior deterioration, and even the total loss, whether it be casual or culpable, shall be at the charge of the donee.

§ 3682. *Dower.*—Art. 4027. In respect to the things given in dower, the wife shall elect for the computation the time in which the dower was constituted, or that of the opening of the succession.

§ 3683. *Payment in Kind.*—Art. 4028. The co-heirs of the donee shall be paid in property of the same kind and nature as that brought to the collation, if it should be possible.

§ 3684. *Payment in Money.*—Art. 4029. The co-heirs who can not be paid in kind have the right to be equaled in money, if the property brought to the collation should be real estate, in which case the property shall be sold which may be necessary for the purpose.

§ 3685. *Movables.*—Art. 4030. If the property should be

movables, the co-heirs will only have the right to be satisfied with other movables of the inheritance according to their value.

§ 3686. *Value Donated.*—Art. 4031. When the value of the property donated shall exceed the legitimate portion of the donee, and the testator or the law should not make an application of the disposable part, if the donation was by the way of dower, the wife will not have more option to preserve it whole than that which article 4027 concedes to her.

§ 3687. *Donation as Improvement.*—Art. 4032. In the case of the preceding article, if the donation should not be as dower, it will be considered as an improvement (mejora) of the free part of the testator; and what shall exceed this and the legitimate right shall be returned to the mass of the inheritance.

§ 3688. *Divers Donees.*—Art. 4033. If there should be divers donees, and the part of free disposition should not suffice to pay all, it shall be apportioned among them.

§ 3689. *Application Considered as not Made.*—Art. 4034. In the case of the preceding article, if the author of the inheritance should have applied his disposable part to another heir distinct from the donee, the application shall be held as not made.

§ 3690. *Conjugal Partners, Donation by Both.*—Art. 4035. If the donation is made by both conjugal partners, only the part with which each one contributed to the donation will be brought to the collation from the inventory of each one of them.

§ 3691. *Excess in Donation of Immovables.*—Art. 4036. When the value of the immovables donated shall exceed the fortune of the donee, and he shall have sold them, the co-heirs can only demand from the third possessor the excess, and by a previous exhaustion of the property of the donee.

§ 3692. *No Interest until Partition.*—Art. 4037. The property, by the sole fact of being brought to the collation, does not bear interest nor produce fruits for the inheritance, until a partition is made.

§ 3693. *Legal Interest, when.*—Art. 4038. If, the value of the property being computed, it results that there is any part which on account of exceeding all that could be applied to the donee ought to be returned by him, the legal interest of that part or the fruits is due to the hereditary mass from the day on which the succession is opened.

§ 3694. *No Suspension of Partition.*—Art. 4039. Although the heirs may not agree in what some one of them ought to bring to the collation, the partition of the inheritance will not be suspended, but the right claimed by them will be previously secured.[1]

[1] This chapter is suppressed by the code of 1884.

# CHAPTER XXIII.

## PARTITIONS.

§ 3695. *Partition, when Made.*—Art. 4040. The inventory and the account of administration being approved, the executor must immediately make a partition of the inheritance.

§ 3696. *Divisible.*—Art. 4041. No heir is obliged to remain with the estate undivided, not even by an express provision of the testator.

§ 3697. *Suspension.*—Art. 4042. A partition can only be suspended in virtue of an express agreement of the interested parties, and for a term which shall not pass five years.[1]

§ 3698. *Partition may be Asked for by Any Heir.*—Art. 4043. Every co-heir who shall have the free disposition of his property can ask for the partition of the inheritance at any time.

§ 3699. *Incapacitated Persons.*—Art. 4044. Persons incapacitated and absent ones must ask for the partition through their representatives.

§ 3700. *Consent of Consorts.*—Art. 4045. The husband can not ask for the partition in the name of his wife without her consent, nor the wife without the authorization of the husband; in default of either it shall be supplied by the judge.

§ 3701. *Conditions.*—Art. 4046. Heirs under a condition can not ask for the partition until that is fulfilled.

§ 3702. *Co-heirs—Conditional Heir.*—Art. 4047. The co-heirs of a conditional heir may ask for a partition by completely securing the right of him for the case of the existing condition; and until it is known that the condition has failed, or can not be verified, the partition shall be held provisional.

§ 3703. *By Executors.*—Art. 4048. The provision in the preceding article shall be observed also when the executor may make the partition in use of his powers.

§ 3704. *Provisional.*—Art. 4049. The partition shall be considered provisional only as to the part in which consists the pending right, and as to the bond with which it has been secured.

§ 3705. *Execution Levied.*—Art. 4050. A creditor of an heir or legatee who has levied execution on the right which the former has in the inheritance, and who has obtained a judgment of sale, can ask for the partition, provided the payment can not be made with other property.

§ 3706. *Grantees.*—Art. 4051. A grantee of an heir or legatee may ask for a partition.

§ 3707. *One Heir may Ask for Partition.*—Art. 4052. If before making a partition one of the co-heirs should die, leaving two or more heirs, it will be sufficient that one of these shall ask for it; but all must proceed jointly, and under the same representation.

---

[1] Article 4042 becomes article 3790 in the code of 1884, and reads as follows: "Art. 3790. A partition can only be suspended in the case of article 3651 (3970), or in virtue of an express agreement of the interested parties, There being minors among them, the tutor and public minister must be heard, and the decree in which the agreement is approved shall determine the time which the indivision must last."

§ 3708. *Absent Persons.* Art. 4053. In respect to the division of the property of an absent person, the provisions in title 13 of book 1 shall be observed.[1]

§ 3709. *Partition Made by the Owner.*—Art. 4054. The owner of property who shall have forced heirs may make a partition thereof by an act among the living, subjecting themselves to the following rules: 1. That all of the heirs shall be of the age of majority; 2. That in fact each one of them shall receive the property which corresponds to him; 3. That the partition shall be reduced to a public writing, and shall be expressly accepted by the heirs.[2]

§ 3710. *Property of Free Disposition may be Reserved.*—Art. 4055. In the case of the preceding article, the owner of the property may reserve the part which in conformity with the law is of free disposition; and in respect to the part of any other property which he shall acquire after the partition, the forced heirs shall have no right except in the case of an intestate estate.

§ 3711. *Heirs not Forced.*—Art. 4056. When the heirs are not forced ones, the provisions for donations among the living shall be observed.

§ 3712. *Partition by Last Will.*—Art. 4057. If the partition shall be made by a last will, it shall be complied with so far as it does not prejudice the legitimate right of the forced heirs.

§ 3713. *Absent Heirs.* — Art. 4058. If any of the heirs should be absent or should not have a legitimate representative, the judge shall proceed in conformity with the provisions in articles 697 to 706 and others relative thereto.

§ 3714. *Judicial Approval.*—Art. 4059. The partition in the case of the preceding article must be judicially approved; observing besides the provisions in articles 768 to 771.

§ 3715. *Separation of Property.*—Art. 4060. The executor shall separate in the first place the part which belongs to the surviving conjugal partner, in conformity with the marriage settlement, and with the dispositions which regulate dotal property and the legal partnership.

§ 3716. *Deduction.*—Art. 4061. Then the part which in conformity with the law shall be of the free disposition of the testator shall be deducted.

---

[1] Articles 4043 to 4053 are suppressed in the code of 1884.

[2] Article 4054 becomes article 3791 in the code of 1884, and reads as follows: "Art. 3791. If the author of the inheritance should make the partition of the property in his will, it must be saving the rights of third parties. Also the partition may be made by acts among the living, being subject to what this code provides on donations *entre vivos*."

§ 3717. *Payment of Legacies.*—Art. 4062. With it the legacies shall be paid; observing the order and other dispositions relative to the preference and reduction contained in chapter 7, title 2, of this book.

§ 3718. *Remainder.*—Art. 4063. What remains shall be added to the rest of the hereditary estate, which shall be divided among the heirs in parts proportional to their legitimate rights or the quotas which the testator shall have assigned them.

§ 3719. *Project of Partition.*—Art. 4064. The executor shall form the project of partition by himself, and shall charge other persons with it, with the consent of a majority of the heirs.

§ 3720. *Judge may Appoint, when.*—Art. 4065. If there should not be a majority, the judge shall appoint immediately, selecting the person among those who shall have been proposed by the executor or by the heirs.

§ 3721. *Project Subject to Rules.*—Art. 4066. The project of partition shall be snbject to the following rules: 1. If the testator made a designation of the parts, the executor shall observe it strictly, noting the excess or defect of the price of the thing designated in respect to the legitimate right or portion of the heir; 2. If there is no designation of the parts in a determined thing, they will be included in each portion of property of the same kind as far as possible; 3. If the immovables of the inheritance bear burdens, they shall be specified, indicating the manner of redeeming them or dividing them among the heirs.

§ 3722. *Approbation of All Parties* —Art. 4067. The executor shall present the project of partition with the approbation of all the interested parties or their legitimate representatives.

§ 3723. *Opposition to Partition Settled by the Judge.*—Art. 4068. If, being formed the partitions, any heir claims more than the amount which has been assigned him, the judge, after hearing immediately and summarily the computer, shall decide, confirming the partition or ordering it to be set aside.

§ 3724. *Summary Trials.*—Art. 4069. From the determination of the judge there shall be no further recourses than those which for summary trials the code of procedure establishes.

§ 3725. *Sale.*—Art. 4070. If the claim should be relative to the class of property assigned, and there should be no agreement, the property in dispute shall be sold, observing the provisions in articles 4074 to 4080.

§ 3726. *Payment to Heirs or Legatees.*—Art. 4071. Every heir or legatee of a sum has a right to ask that the property of the inheritance be applied to the payment thereof; the application thereof shall be made for the price which the property may have by the valuation.

§ 3727. *Election.*—Art. 4072. In case of the preceding article, the election shall be by him who must pay the inheritance or the legacy, unless the testator shall have disposed otherwise.

§ 3728. *Indivisible Property.*—Art. 4073. The property which may be indivisible, or which will be deteriorated by the division, may be adjudicated to one of the heirs, with the condition of paying the others the excess in money.

§ 3729. *Sale of Property.*—Art. 4074. If the provision in the preceding article can not be realized, and the heirs shall not agree in the use of the property in common or in another mode of payment, the sale thereof shall be proceeded with, the heir being preferred who shall make the best bid.

§ 3730. *Sale, how Made.*—Art. 4075. The sale shall be made at public auction, and foreign bidders shall be admitted whenever there are minors or any of the heirs shall ask it.

§ 3731. *Modification, when.*—Art. 4076. The difference which there shall be in the price shall increase or diminish the hereditary estate. In these cases the partition must be modified.

§ 3732. *Disagreement Settled by the Judge.*—Art. 4077. If in spite of the provision in article 3988, a question shall arise as to whether the property may admit of a proper division, the judge hearing a new expert which he shall appoint shall decide what is proper.

§ 3733. *Settled by Chance, when.*—Art. 4078. If three auctions shall be had, and there shall be no bidders for the property which does not admit of a convenient division, it shall be drawn for by chance, and he to whom chance shall assign it shall have it adjudicated to him for the half of its value.

§ 3734. *Adjudicated Property in Excess.*—Art. 4079. What in the case of the preceding article shall exceed the quota of the heir receiving the adjudicated property shall be acknowledged by him, save an agreement otherwise, during six years, with interest at six per cent with a mortgage on the thing adjudicated, in favor of the person to whom it belongs, according to the partition.

§ 3735. *Insufficiency of the Value of Adjudicated Property.*—Art. 4080. If the thing adjudicated should not cover the quota of the heir in adjudication, and can not be completed with other property, the difference shall be recognized on other immovables on the terms established in the preceding article.

§ 3736. *Various Claimants.*—Art. 4081. If various heirs claim the same thing of the inheritance, it shall be bid for between them, and what shall be given over the legitimate price shall enter into the common fund.

§ 3737. *Refusal to Receive.*—Art. 4082. If there should be anything which all should refuse to receive, the provisions in article 4070 and those which are cited therein shall be observed.

§ 3738. *Right of Heirs when Drawn by Chance.*—Art. 4083. Any heir may, even after lots drawn for the thing, in the cases of articles 4078 and 4082, avoid the adjudication for the half of the price by increasing the price; and if there should be various claimants, citation shall be had.[1]

§ 3739. *Obligations of Co-heirs.* — Art. 4084. The co-heirs must charge each other reciprocally the rents and fruits which each one may have received from the hereditary estate, the necessary and useful expenses, and the damages occasioned by malice or negligence.

§ 3740. *Debts before Division.*—Art. 4085. The debts contracted during the time of the indivision shall be paid in preference to others.

§ 3741. *No Burdens Allowed.*—Art. 4086. A co-heir can not alienate nor burden anything of the hereditary estate.

§ 3742. *Pensions.* — Art. 4087. If the testator shall have bequeathed any pension or life rent on account of his disposable part, without burdening with it in particular any heir or legatee, it shall be capitalized at six per cent annually, and a capital or equivalent fund shall be separated, which shall be delivered to the heir or legatee, who shall be subject to all the obligations of a mere usufructuary.[2]

§ 3743. *Insufficiency of Disposable Property.*—Art. 4088. If the property of the disposable quota shall not be sufficient, in the case of the preceding article, for the formation of the capital mentioned therein, it shall remain with the discretion of the heirs to deliver to the legatee the disposable part, or retain it by paying the whole pension.[3]

§ 3744. *Plan of Partition.*—Art. 4089. In the plan of partition shall be expressed the part of the capital affected with

---

[1] Articles 4055 to 4083, inclusive, are suppressed by the code of 1884.

[2] Article 4087 becomes article 3794, code of 1884, and is annexed by suppressing the words "on account of his disposable part."

[3] Article 4088 is suppressed by the code of 1884.

the payment of the pension which shall correspond to each one of the heirs, as soon as that shall be extinguished.[1]

§ 3745. *Public Writing.*—Art. 4090. The co-heirs agreeing to the plan of partition, it shall be reduced to a public writing; and with that requisite alone all the legal effects shall arise if the interested parties shall be of age.

§ 3746. *If Minors.*—Art. 4091. The partition shall only be judicial if any of the interested parties shall be minors, or if the majority of the heirs require it.[2]

§ 3747. *Various Minors — One Tutor.* — Art. 4092. When there shall be various minors represented by one sole tutor, the provisions for the case provided in article 535 shall be observed.

§ 3748. *Contests of Title of Partition.*—Art. 4093. The title of partition must contain: 1. The family and Christian names of all the heirs and legatees; 2. The names, measures, and boundaries of the adjudicated estates, with a statement of the part which the heir in adjudication shall have the obligation to return if the price of the thing exceeds that of his portion, or to receive if it lacks anything; 3. The special guaranty which for the return of the excess the heir shall constitute in the case of the fraction which precedes; 4. The enumeration of the movables or sums distributed; 5. Notice of the delivery of the titles of the property adjudicated or distributed; 6. A statement of the sums which any heir recognizes as due another, and the guaranty which has been constituted; 7. The signatures of all the interested parties.

§ 3749. *Delivery of Titles.*—Art. 4094. The titles which prove the property or the adjudicated right shall be delivered to the heir or legatee to whom the thing may belong.

§ 3750. *Owner of Greatest Interest Holds Title.*—Art. 4095. When in the same title are comprehended estates adjudicated to divers co-heirs, or one sole estate, but divided among two or more, the hereditary title shall remain in the possession of him who shall have the greatest interest represented in the estate or estates, giving to the others authentic copies at the cost of the hereditary estate.

---

[1] Article 4089 is article 3795, and is amended by the code of 1884, by inserting the words "or funds" after the word "capital."

Article 3796 is a new article, and reads as follows, in the code of 1884: "Art. 3796. The provisions in the two preceding articles shall be observed when the question is of pensions alimenticias to which article 3324 refers."

[2] Articles 4090 and 4091 become article 3797 in code of 1884. A new article in the code of 1884 reads: "Art. 3798. The partition shall appear in a public writing whenever there is property in the inheritance, the sale of which must be made with that formality."

§ 3751. *Original Title.*—Art. 4096. If the title should be an original, the party in whose possession it shall remain must also exhibit it to the other interested parties when it shall be necessary.

§ 3752. *Judge may Deposit the Title.*—Art. 4097. If all the interested parties should have an equal portion in the estates, the title shall remain in the possession of him whom the judge shall designate, if there should be no agreement between the parties.

§ 3753. *Cost Paid out of Common Fund.*—Art. 4098. In the title and in the relative protocols shall be made to appear the delivery of the copies at the cost of the common fund.

§ 3754. *Hereditary Creditors may Oppose Partition.*—Art. 4099. The hereditary creditors legally recognized can oppose the carrying into effect the partition until their credit shall be paid, if the time of payment should be completed, and if it should not be, until the payment be duly secured to them.

§ 3755. *Guaranty.*—Art. 4100. The guaranty of which the preceding article speaks shall be the same as secured the credit; if this was not guaranteed, what the judge shall designate shall be given, if there should be no agreement between the interested parties.

§ 3756. *Creditors under Tutorship.*—Art. 4101. If the creditor should be subject to a tutorship, the credit shall be guaranteed with a mortgage, with a previous judicial authorization.[1]

§ 3757. *Action.*—Art. 4102. The action to ask for the partition of an inheritance may be prescribed in twenty years against the co-heir who has possessed the whole or part of it in his own name.

§ 3758. *Prescription.*—Art. 4103. If all the co-heirs possess in common the inheritance or any one in the name of all, prescription does not run.

§ 3759. *Time.*—Art. 4104. The term for prescription shall be counted from the day on which the author of the inheritance died.

§ 3760. *Alienation.*—Art. 4105. The heir or legatee can not alienate his part of the inheritance except after the death of him from whom he inherits.

§ 3761. *Notice to Co-heirs.*—Art. 4106. If there should be other heirs, he who wishes to alienate his part must inform the others of the alienation and of the conditions thereof.

---

[1] Articles 4092 to 4101, inclusive, are suppressed in the code of 1884.

§ 3762. *Preference.*—Art. 4107. The co-heirs shall be preferred by the rights of preference, if they use this right within three days following the notice, and fulfill the other conditions imposed on the outside grantee.

§ 3763. *Cessation of Right.*—Art. 4108. The right conceded in the preceding article shall cease if the alienation is made to a co-heir, or when it is made to an outside party by donation.

§ 3764. *Rules.*—Art. 4109. The rules given for the partition of the principal inheritance shall be observed also in that which is made between those who succeed by the right of representation.

§ 3765. *Expense.*—Art. 4110. The expenses of the partition shall be taken from the common fund; those which shall be made for the private interest of any one of the heirs or legatees shall be imputed to his property.

OF THE EFFECTS OF A PARTITION.

§ 3766. *Partition, Effect of.*—Art. 4111. A partition legally made shall confer on the co-heirs the exclusive title to the property which shall have been distributed to them.

§ 3767. *Obligations in Evictions.*—Art. 4112. The co-heirs are reciprocally obligated to indemnify in case of eviction from the objects distributed, and can use the right which article 2000 concedes to them.

§ 3768. *Cessation of Warranty.*—Art. 4113. The obligation of warranty shall only cease in the following cases: 1. When the same author of the inheritance shall have made the partition in his life; 2. When on making this an express agreement has been made; 3. When the eviction shall proceed from a cause subsequent to the partition, or should be occasioned by the fault of him who suffers it.

§ 3769. *Indemnification for Eviction.*—Art. 4114. He who suffers an eviction shall be indemnified by the co-heirs in proportion to their hereditary quotas.

§ 3770. *Part Lost, how Paid.*—Art. 4115. The portion which must be paid to him who shall lose his part by eviction shall not be that which his primitive part represents, but that which shall correspond to him by deducting from the whole of the inheritance the part lost.

§ 3771. *Insolvency.*—Art. 4116. If any of the co-heirs should be insolvent, the quota with which he ought to contribute shall be divided among the others, including him who lost his part by eviction.

§ 3772. *Payers for Insolvents.*—Art. 4117. Those who shall pay for the insolvent shall preserve their action against him when he shall better his fortune.

§ 3773. *Collectible Credits.*—Art. 4118. If a credit is adjudicated as collectible, the co-heirs shall respond for the subsequent insolvency of the hereditary debt; and they are only responsible for his solvency at the time of making the partition.

§ 3774. *Uncollectible.*—Art. 4119. For the uncollectible credits there is no responsibility.

§ 3775. *Attachments and Judgments.*—Art. 4120. The heir whose hereditary property shall be attached, or against whom shall be pronounced a judgment in the ordinary court on account of said property, has a right to ask that his co-heirs give bond for the responsibility which may follow said property; and that otherwise they be prohibited from selling the property which they received.

### Of the Rescission of Partitions.

§ 3776. *Rescission of Partition.*—Art. 4121. The partitions made extrajudicially can only be rescinded in the cases in which contracts in general can be.

§ 3777. *Rescission of Judicial Partitions.*—Art. 4122. The partitions made judicially can only be rescinded in the cases and manner which the code of procedure establishes.

§ 3778. *Preterition of Heirs.*—Art. 4123. A partition made with preterition of any of the heirs shall not be rescinded, unless that it is proved that there was fraud or bad faith on the part of the others interested; but these shall have the obligation of paying to the omitted heir (preterito) the part which shall belong to him.

§ 3779. *False Heir.*—Art. 4124. The partition made with a false heir is null so far as it shall have any relation with him, and as to his personality prejudicing the other interested parties.

§ 3780. *Not Rescindable.*—Art. 4125. The other points comprehended in the division of which the preceding articles speak are not rescindable except for another legal cause.

§ 3781. *Supplemental Division.*—Art. 4126. The partition being made, if any property should appear omitted in it, a supplementary division shall be made, in which the provisions contained in this title shall be observed.

# CHAPTER XXIV.

## PUBLIC REGISTER.

§ 3782. Public Register in Every Town.
§ 3783. Division of Office.
§ 3784. Mortgages.
§ 3785. Where Registered.
§ 3786. Various Properties.
§ 3787. Rightful Owner.
§ 3788. Who may be Registered.
§ 3789. Foreign Countries.
§ 3790. Third Parties.
§ 3791. Every Act to be Registered.
§ 3792. When not to be Registered.
§ 3793. Leases.
§ 3794. Wills.
§ 3795. Intestate Estates.
§ 3796. Death to be Noted.
§ 3797. Usufructs.
§ 3798. Marriage Settlements.
§ 3799. All to be Registered as in Article 3333.
§ 3800. Judgments.
§ 3801. Absent Persons.
§ 3802. Separation of Property.
§ 3803. Restitution.
§ 3804. Bankruptcy.
§ 3805. Title, Presentation of.
§ 3806. Defect in Title.
§ 3807. Registry must Contain What.
§ 3808. Date.
§ 3809. Fees.
§ 3810. Return of Title.
§ 3811. Time to Register.
§ 3812. Date of Registry, Effect of.
§ 3813. Judgments Noted.
§ 3814. Cancellation.
§ 3815. Total or Partial.
§ 3816. Total Cancellation, when.
§ 3817. Partial Cancellation, when.
§ 3818. Consent.
§ 3819. Conditions.
§ 3820. Cancellation as to Seller.
§ 3821. Judgments Reversed.

### General Provisions.

§ 3782. *Public Register.*—Art. 3324. In every town where there may be a tribunal of first instance an office denominated Public Register shall be established.

§ 3783. *Division of Office.*—Art. 3325. The office shall be composed of four sections: 1. A register of titles translative of the dominion of immovables or of real rights, diverse from the mortgages imposed upon them; 2. A register of mortgages; 3. A register of leases; 4. A register of judgments.[1]

§ 3784. *Mortgages.*—Art. 3326. The section of mortgages shall be governed by the provisions in chapter 4, title 8, of this book.[2]

§ 3785. *Where Registered.*—Art. 3327. The registry shall be made in the office to which the property in question belongs by its situation.

§ 3786. *Various Properties.*—Art. 3328. If the property should be situated in separate demarkations, the registry shall be made in all of them.

§ 3787. *Rightful Owner.*—Art. 3329. No inscription can be made if it does not appear that he who solicits it is the actual owner of the property, that he has a right to require the registry or proceeds with legal power from the proprietor.

§ 3788. *What may be Registered.*—Art. 3330. Titles which appear by public writing, and judgments and judicial decrees legally certified, can only be inscribed.

§ 3789. *Foreign Countries, Acts in.*—Art. 3331. Executed acts, contracts executed, and judgments pronounced in a foreign country shall only be inscribed when the following circumstances concur: 1. That if the acts or contracts should have been celebrated or the judgments pronounced in the District or in California, its inscription in the registry would have been necessary; 2. That they shall be properly legalized in conformity with what is provided in the code of procedure: 3. If they should be judgments, the execution of which might be ordered by the superior tribunal of the district or that of California.

§ 3790. *Third Parties.*—Art. 3332. The acts and contracts, which in conformity with the law must be registered, will not produce any effect against a third party if they should not be inscribed in the respective office.

### Of the Titles Subject to Registry.

§ 3791. *Every Act to be Registered.*—Art. 3333. All contracts and acts between the living which transmit or modify property,

[1] Article 3186 is a new article, and is as follows, in the code of 1884: "Art. 3186. In all the offices of public registry shall be kept, besides, an index of the documents to which article 2923 (3059) refers, with which shall be formed a special archive."

[2] Article 3326 is article 3187, and is amended by inserting "as well as all that relates to the registry thereof" after the word "mortgage."

the possession or the enjoyment of immovable property or real rights imposed thereon, must be registered.

§ 3792. *When not to be Registered.* — Art. 3334. When the property or rights do not exceed five hundred dollars the registry shall not be necessary.

§ 3793. *Leases.*—Art. 3335. Leases shall not be registered except when they shall be for more than six years, or when the rents shall have been paid for more than three years in advance.

§ 3794. *Wills.*—Art. 3336. Wills which transfer immovable property or real rights shall also be registered after the death of the testator.

§ 3795. *Intestate Estates.*—Art. 3337. In case of an intestate, the declaration which the judge shall make of those who may be legitimate heirs and titles of partition shall be registered.

§ 3796. *Death to be Noted.*—Art. 3338. In the registry of which the two preceding articles treat shall be noted the record of the death of the author of the inheritance.

§ 3797. *Usufructs.*—Art. 3339. Also shall be registered the titles in which are constituted a usufruct, use, habitation, service, concession of mines, quarries, bodies of mineral substances, or other similar ones.

§ 3798. *Marriage Settlements.*—Art. 3340. Shall also be registered marriage settlements and those which constitute dower, when in virtue thereof is established between the conjugal partners a community of real estate, or one of them acquires property of that kind by a dotal title, antenuptial donation, or any other.

§ 3799. *All to be Registered, as in Article* 3333.—Art. 3341. Also all transactions, reserves, conditions, novations, or any other act which may produce the effects designated in article 3333.

§ 3800. *Judgments.*—Art. 3342. Judgments which cause execution, including those of arbitros and arbitradores (two kinds of arbitration), shall be registered whenever they may produce the effects to which the preceding article refers.

§ 3801. *Absent Persons.*—Art. 3343. Shall also be registered the appointment of a representative of an absent person, and the judgments which shall declare the absence of a person or the presumption of death.

§ 3802. *Separation of Property.*—Art. 3344. Also shall be registered judgments in which shall be decreed the separation of property by necessary divorce, and those which shall approve said separation in the cases of voluntary divorce or by simple agreement.

§ 3803. *Restitution.*—Art. 3345. Also judgments in which shall be decreed restitution *in integrum* shall be registered.[1]

§ 3804. *Bankruptcy.*—Art. 3346. Likewise shall be registered judgments in which a bankruptcy shall be declared, or a cession of property shall be admitted, or a sequestration or an expropriation shall be ordered.[2]

Of the Manner of Making the Registry.

§ 3805. *Title, Presentation of.*—Art. 3347. The interested party shall present to the respective section the title in which may appear the act or contract, or the authentic copy of the judgment and the legal document which shall prove his representation, if he acts in the name of another.

§ 3806. *Defect in Titles.*—Art. 3348. If the recorder should not find the title or the representation legally proved, he will manifest it to the interested party and will require a judicial declaration.

§ 3807. *Registry must Contain What.*—Art. 3349. The registry must contain: 1. The names, ages, domiciles, and professions of the contracting parties. Moral persons (corporations) shall be designated by the official name which they bear, and companies by their firm name. 2. The date and nature of the act which shall be registered, the authority or notary who shall have authorized, and the day and hour in which the title shall be presented. 3. The kind and value of the property or rights which are transmitted or modified, expressing exactly the situation of the first, as well as all the circumstances relative to interest, burdens, rents, pensions, terms, and others which characterize the act.

§ 3808. *Date.*—Art. 3350. The register shall bear the date of the day on which the documents shall be presented in the office.

§ 3809. *Fees.*—Art. 3351. A special regulation shall establish the fees and obligations of the recorders, as well as the

[1] Article 3345 is suppressed in the code of 1884.

[2] Article 3346 is amended by suppressing all after the word "admitted," in the code of 1884.

The three following articles are new in the code of 1884:

"Art. 3207. Likewise shall be registered the judgments or decrees in which are ordered the fixing up of mortgage notices, an attachment, a sequestration, an intervention, or an expropriation."

"Art. 3212. In the index of which article 3186 speaks shall be contained the christian and family names of the contracting parties, the situation and boundaries of the immovable, the price and date of the sale, and the day on which the contract shall have been presented to the office."

"Art. 3218. The contracts to which article 2921 (3057) refer do not have effect against a third party except from the date of the presentation to the office."

formulas and other circumstances with which the registry shall be made.

§ 3810. *Return of Title.*—Art. 3352. The registry being made, the documents shall be returned to him who presented them, with a note of being recorded on such a date, and on such number and page of the register.

§ 3811. *Time to Register.*—Art. 3353. Contracts which shall be recorded within fifteen days from their date will produce their effect, with relation to third parties, from the date of their respective title.

§ 3812. *Date of Registry, Effect of.*—Art. 3354. Contracts which shall be recorded after the said term will only produce their effect, with relation to third parties, from the date of the registry.

§ 3813. *Judgments Noted.*—Art. 3355. If an act recorded shall be annulled or rescinded in virtue of a judgment, this shall be noted within thirty days, counted from the time it caused execution, on the margin of the respective register, otherwise it will only produce its effect with relation to third parties from the day on which it shall be noted.

### Of the Extinction of Inscriptions (or Registries).

§ 3814. *Cancellation.*—Art. 3356. Inscriptions are not extinguished as to third parties, except by cancellation or by the registry of the transmission of the dominion or real right inscribed to another person.

§ 3815. *Total or Partial.*—Art. 3357. The cancellation of the inscriptions may be total or partial.

§ 3816. *Total Cancellation, when.*—Art. 3358. The total cancellation may be asked for, and it may be ordered in case: 1. When the immovable, the object of the inscription, shall be completely extinguished; 2. When also the right inscribed shall be completely extinguished; 3. When the nullity of the title is declared in virtue of which the inscription has been made; 4. When the nullity of the inscription is declared for want of any of its essential requisites, in conformity with the provision in article 3349.[1]

§ 3817. *Partial Cancellation.*—Art. 3359. A partial cancellation may be asked for, and must be decreed in case: 1. When

[1] Article 3358 is article 3221, new code, and is amended by adding thereto the following: "5. When an immovable shall be judicially sold which supports the burden in the case prescribed in article 2928; 6. When, in treating of a mortgage notice or of an attachment, three years shall have transpired from the date of the inscription."

the immovable, the object of the inscription, shall be reduced; 2. When the right inscribed in favor of the owner of the estate burdened shall be reduced.

§ 3818. *Consent.*—Art. 3360. In order that the register may be canceled by the consent of the parties, it requires that they be legitimate, having the power to contract, and they shall make their will appear in an authentic manner.

§ 3819. *Conditions.*—Art. 3361. If, in order to cancel the register, any condition should be put, the fulfillment of this is also required.

§ 3820. *Cancellation as to Seller.*—Art. 3362. When property in favor of him who acquires it is registered, the relative registry to him who sells shall be canceled.

§ 3821. *Judgments Reversing Judgments.*—Art. 3363. When a judgment is registered which declares that the effects of another judgment already registered have ceased, the latter shall be canceled.

# APPENDIX I.

## FORMS FOR OBTAINING A TITLE BY DENOUNCEMENT.

[Stamp.]

To the Prefect of this Partido:

I, James Smith, a citizen of the United States, a native of the city of ........, state of ........, now a resident of ........, and by profession a ........, before your honor, in due form of law, make the following declaration:

That in conformity with article 8 of title 6 of the mining ordinance, I hereby make the location of a certain mine in the district of ........, designated by the name of ........, within your honor's jurisdiction, and which was formerly worked by its then possessor [Don ......], the same having been abandoned for more than .... years [or months, as the case may be]. I propose to work the same in accordance with the mining ordinance and laws, for gold, silver, or whatever may be found therein. Said mine is now designated by the name of "La Rosa" [or whatever the name may be].

Wherefore I ask your honor to accept this petition and grant my request.

Durango [or whatever place the petition may be in], [month and day], 1884. James Smith.

Durango, June 10, 1884.

This petition having been duly presented, the same was granted according to law.

Let the necessary proceedings be had in conformity with article 8, title 6, of the mining ordinances.

I, the prefect of this jurisdiction, thus order and sign the same in the presence of witnesses. Luis Mexia.

Attest: John Brown.
Henry Jones.

Notice of the same has been duly posted. I hereby certify.
Mexia.

This being the second Sunday, let notice be given for the second time. I hereby certify. Mexia.

This being the third Sunday, and it being necessary that notice should be given for the third and last time, let the same be known. I hereby certify. Mexia.

DURANGO, July 5, 1884.

No objection or protest of any kind having been made during the three Sundays in which said notices were made in conformity with the mining ordinances, against the proposed location of said mine by James Smith, let that gentleman be notified that within sixty days from date it will be required of him to have sunk on said mine a shaft of sufficient depth, and that after the same shall have been done, it will further be required of him to appear before the prefect and petition for due possession of the same.

I, the prefect, thus order, and subscribe this before witnesses. LUIS MEXIA.

Attest: JOHN BROWN.
HENRY JONES.

Mr. James Smith, the petitioner, having been duly notified of the above decree, declared that he heard and signed the same before me and the witnesses. I hereby certify.

JAMES SMITH.
MEXIA.

Attest: JOHN BROWN.
HENRY JONES.

I, James Smith, resident of this partido, personally appear before your honor, and in due form of law declare and make known to your honor that I have performed the labor required to be performed before taking formal possession of the mine known as the mine of [La Rosa], the same having been duly located by me, I hereby petition your honor to accompany me to said mine, and give me due possession of the same conformably to the mining ordinances, title 8, respectfully representing to your honor that in .... days hence the period fixed by law for the adjudication of possession will expire.

Wherefore may your honor be pleased to accede to my request, and to accept this petition. JAMES SMITH.

[Put here the name of the place of the mine and date], 1884.

DURANGO, August 1, 1884.

Possession is hereby decreed to the said petitioner of the said mine. I hereby appoint citizen Don Diego Bolaños to invest the petitioner with possession on the eighth day of this month.

I, the prefect of this partido, thus decree and subscribe the same before witnesses. LUIS MEXIA.

Attest: JOHN BROWN.
HENRY JONES.

La Rosa Mine, August 8, 1884.

Diego Bolañas being present as commissioner, appointed as aforesaid, to give possession of said mine to James Smith, having made his protest to speak the truth, promised faithfully and legally to discharge his duty in the premises, and without prejudice to the party interested.

Witness my hand as prefect.

Mexia.
Diego Bolaños.

Attest: John Brown.
Henry Jones.

La Rosa Mine, August 8, 1884.

I, the prefect of the partido of Durango, being present at the mouth of the mine known as La Rosa, in company with the commissioner heretofore appointed, Don Diego Bolaños, the aforesaid witnesses, and various other persons to witness the ceremony of investing said petitioner with possession of said mine, then and there, in a clear and intelligible voice, and while holding the hand of the said petitioner, Smith, did proclaim three times, to wit, as follows: "Gentlemen: In the name of the supreme government of the state of Durango [or whatever state the mine be in], and the supreme goverment of the Mexican republic, I am about to give to Mr. James Smith possession of the mine known as 'La Rosa.' Is there any person to oppose the same?" And all having answered favorably, I proceeded according to usage in such cases, to wit: Holding by hand the interested party, and walking along the claim, throwing stones, pulling grass, and going in and out of the mine, and such like acts of true possession. And thereupon the commissioner aforesaid proceeded to act in matters pertaining to his said commission, which having finished, he declared that he had examined the lode, and declared that the same was .... meters in width, with an inclination or dip of .... inches to the meter; that its ores were good, abundant, easily extracted, and of easy reduction [as the case may be], either by fire or amalgamation, and its cases solid; that there was a shaft and tunnel, or horizontal drift within [as the case may be]; that they were both worked according to the requirements of the mining ordinances; that there was no main shaft, but that one might be made when necessary; that the claim had been staked on its boundaries after the vein had been measured, thus: .... meters from the mouth of the mine, and from the same point .... meters below, and one hundred meters on each side of the vein.

And thus ended the proceeding, to which I certify.

LUIS MEXIA,
DIEGO BOLAÑOS.

Attest: JOHN BROWN,
HENRY JONES.

LA ROSA MINE, August 8, 1884.

All the proceedings having been completed, let the interested party be notified to appear before the prefect of Durango, to receive a certified copy of all the proceedings had and done in the premises, as an evidence of his right and title to the property.

Thus decreed by me, the prefect of the partido of Durango, and to which I certify. LUIS MEXIA.

Attest: JOHN BROWN,
HENRY JONES.

On this day, Mr. James Smith having been made acquainted with said order, declared that he would obey the same and obtain evidence of his title.

Answered and subscribed with me before witnesses.

MEXIA.
SMITH.

Attest: JOHN BROWN.
HENRY JONES.

I hereby certify that the foregoing is a full, true, and correct copy of the original record of proceedings in said case, the same having been transcribed this ninth day of August, 1884.

Certified by me before the witnesses.

LUIS MEXIA.

Attest: JOHN BROWN.
HENRY JONES.

Denouncements for a new mine must be changed to suit the facts.

# APPENDIX II.

## TIME OF ADOPTION OF THE MEXICAN CIVIL CODE OF THE FEDERAL GOVERNMENT BY THE SEVERAL STATES OF THE UNION.

| States. | Time when. |
|---|---|
| Aguascalientes | January 8, 1875. |
| Campeche | November 15, 1871. |
| Chiapas | November 18, 1871. |
| Chihuahua | March 1, 1883. |
| Coahuila | August 20, 1874. |
| Colima | June 24, 1878. |
| Durango | May 18, 1873. |
| Guanajuato | April 25, 1871. |
| Guerrero | June 27, 1872. |
| Hidalgo | September 23, 1871. |
| Jalisco | May 1, 1876. |
| Mexico | June 21, 1870. |
| Michoacan | August 9, 1871. |
| Morelos | July 30, 1871. |
| Nuevo Leon | January 5, 1875. |
| Oaxaca | December 17, 1878. |
| Puebla | May 17, 1871. |
| Querétaro | June 15, 1872. |
| San Luis Potosí | December 11, 1871. |
| Sinaloa | November 11, 1874. |
| Sonora | May 6, 1871. |
| Tobasco | June 15, 1874. |
| Tamaulipas | June 29, 1871. |
| Tlaxcala, once adopted and afterwards rejected; not in force. | |
| Vera Cruz | |
| Yucatan | August 18, 1871. |
| Zacatecas | December 4, 1872. |

# APPENDIX III.

## MINING CODE OF THE MEXICAN UNITED STATES.

NOTE.—The new mining code of Mexico, which is given in this appendix, was promulgated by the executive, under the authority of congress, to take effect January 1, 1885, after the body of "Hall's Laws of Mexico" went to press, hence it was impossible to include it in the earlier copies of the work.

Department of state, and office of public works, colonization, industry, and commerce of the Mexican republic. The president of the republic has been pleased to direct to me the decree which follows: Manuel Gonzalez, constitutional president of the Mexican United States, to all those to whom these presents may come: Know ye, that in exercise of the authorizations conceded to the executive by the law of the fifteenth day of December, 1883, I have thought proper to issue the following mining code of the Mexican United States:

### TITLE I.

#### OF MINES AND OF MINING PROPERTY.

Art. 1. The objects of this code are: 1. The mines and deposits (criaderos) of all inorganic substances which may be constituted in veins, in sheets or beds (mantos), or in masses of any form whatever, the composition of which may be distinct from the rocks of the earth, such as gold, silver, copper, iron, magnesia, lead, quicksilver, tin, antimony, zinc, sulphur, rock-salt (salgema), and other analogous substances, the enjoyment of which may require the work of miners; 2. Beds (placeres) of gold and of platina, with the metals which accompany them, and those of precious stones employed in jewelry; 3. The reduction-works (haciendas de beneficio) and sites on which to construct them, being understood under the first denomination all mining industrial establishments in which by any class of process may be separated any of the substances contained in the materials extracted from the mines or beds of which the foregoing subdivisions speak; 4. The waters extracted from the mines, and those which may be necessary for drink for the workmen and animals, for motor force, or for any other use in the mines and reduction-works (haciendas de beneficio).

Art. 2. The mines and beds of which subdivisions 1 and 2 of the foregoing article treat form an immovable distinct from the soil in which or under the superfice of which they may be found, although they may belong to one and the same owner.

Art. 3. The property of placer mines, of reduction-works (haciendas de beneficio), and of waters, to which article 1 refers, is acquired by virtue of discovery and denouncement, by the means of a concession made by the proper authority, in conformity with the rules and under the conditions which are hereafter fixed in the present code.

Art. 4. The law concedes to private individuals, in conformity with the foregoing article, the property in mines for an unlimited time, under the conditions of working and operating them according to the provisions of this code and of the regulations which may be dictated for their execution, in order to provide for the preservation of the mines and security of the workmen.

Art. 5. Every person capable of acquiring real estate in the Mexican republic may acquire the mines, placers, reduction-works, and waters comprehended in article 1.

Art. 6. Foreigners may acquire mining property on the terms and with the restrictions under which the laws of the republic consider them capable of acquiring, possessing, and transmitting common property; submitting themselves as Mexicans to the prescriptions of this law and to others which may be issued relative to the department of mining.

Art. 7. Mining property acquired in conformity with this code may be freely transferred, like any other real property, being subject to the relative prescriptions of the legislation in force.

Art. 8. Mining property shall not be forfeited except in the cases expressly determined in this code.

Art. 9. The title to the properties to which the four subdivisions of article 1 refer shall be an authentic copy (un testimonio) of the proceeding in the expediente of denouncement and of the act of possession which shall be given by the authorities or functionaries, and on the terms which are established in this code.

Art. 10. The following are of the exclusive property of the owner of the soil, who, therefore, can work and avail himself thereof, without the necessity of a denouncement or adjudication: 1. Beds of the divers varieties of coal (carbon de piedras); 2. Rocks of the earth and materials of the soil, such as calcareous (calizas) slate (pizarras), porphyry (porfidos), basalt, building-stone, earths, clays, sands, and other analogous substances; 3. The substances not specified in subdivision 2 of article 1, which are found in beds (en placeres), as iron, tin, and other minerals (de acarreo); 4. The salts which exist on the surface, the pure and salt waters, superficial or subterraneous, petroleum and gaseous springs, or thermal or medicinal waters. For the enjoyment of all these substances the owner of the land will be subject, nevertheless, in his works, to the provisions and regulations of police; and in the working of mineral coals and of other materials which require excavations to be made, to the provisions of this code relative to the preservation of the mines and the security of the workmen.

Art. 11. It is declared that the working of mines and placers, the establishment and the operating of reduction-works, and the enjoyment of waters, which in conformity with article 1 form the object of this law, are of public utility.

Art. 12. The mining grounds (fundos mineros) and the sites for reduction-works (haciendas de beneficio) may be denounced and acquired in any place in the republic, whether it be in vacant lands or public or private property, by previous indemnification, if the latter is in question as to the superfice occupied.

Art. 13. The possession and property which may be acquired in mines is understood only for what there may be in the interior thereof, and not of the superfice, which shall continue under the dominion of its proprietor, save the part which may be occupied by the miner, in conformity with the two prior articles.

Art. 14. The existence of a mine or deposit (criadero) being recognized, the lands, although they may be private property, shall be subject to occupation by the miner or beneficiator, to the extent necessary to open the shafts (boca minas), to construct edifices, habitations, stores, metallurgical offices, washing-places (lavaderos), dams, aqueducts, and roads, by the previous indemnification for the surface occupied, or of the service (servidumbre) which may be constituted on the land of another, according to the valuation by experts.

Art. 15. The superficial ground (fundo superficial) comprehended within the limits of the pertenencias of the mines or placers, as well as the immediate grounds, are subject to the service of passage of the workmen, necessary wagons and animals for the operating, and to the use of the waters which there may be, or which may pass through them, for drink for both the workmen and animals. Works to provide for the necessary waters for the movement of machinery may also be executed on said grounds, or for any other necessary use in the mines and reduction-works (haciendas de beneficio). The services (servidumbres) to which this article refers shall be established by the previous corresponding indemnification.

Art. 16. The open roads for one mine shall be used by the others which may be found in the same mining district; but in this case the costs of preservation shall be divided among the mines which use them, according to agreement, and in default of this, in proportion to the use which they may make of them.

Art. 17. The waters proceeding from the subterraneous works of the mines belong to the owners of the latter while they preserve their property, the rights of the proprietors of the lands through which said waters course being observed as established by the legislation in force.

## TITLE II.

### OF THE AUTHORITIES WHICH MUST INTERVENE AND TAKE JURISDICTION IN MINING AFFAIRS.

Art. 18. The branch of mining in governmental and economical affairs will belong to the department of public works, and the subordinate functionaries and authorities of the same, in conformity with this law; and in contentious affairs the trial of mining cases will belong to the respective judges and tribunals of each locality.

Art. 19. A body of engineers and miners is established, which shall be immediately subordinate to the department of public works, and shall be composed of three mining professors (peritos facultativos) and of three proprietors of mines, with the character of a consulting board and of improvement in mining (junta consultora y de formento de la mineria).

Art. 20. The body of engineers and miners of which the foregoing article speaks will take cognizance of all scientific, economiçal, or administrative questions which the department of public works may submit or propose to it, and move whatever may be proper relative to the improvement and advancement of the mining department.

Art. 21. In all mining districts in which it may be possible and deemed necessary to the department of public works, mining deputations shall be established, which must exercise all the governmental and economic functions assigned to them by this code.

Art. 22. The mining deputations shall be attached to the department of public works, and shall be immediately subject to it.

Art. 23. In the mining districts in which mining deputations can not be established, the local political authorities shall perform their functions, being dependent in the exercise thereof on the department of public works.

Art. 24. The organization, plant, and funds of the body of engineers and miners shall be the object of a regulation which the executive will issue.

Art. 25. The mining deputations shall in the same manner be regulated as to their formation by the election from the body of miners of each district; the number of its members, and the periodical renovation of the latter; the fees they may collect for the proceedings which they shall authorize and carry out; and the funds (dotacion) and obligations of their secretary.

Art. 26. In the mining districts in which his importance makes it possible and requires it, there shall be a mining professor (perito facultativo) associated with the respective deputation as assessor or adviser thereof, charged to perform all the work which the said deputation may commend to him, with the funds or the profits (obvencioñes) which the regulation and tariff (arancel) may assign to him.

Art. 27. The department of public works shall appoint the inspecting mining engineers which may be necessary, and they shall be obliged to visit the mines, to make reports, to make examinations or reconnoiters, and to perform the works which may be commended to them by the said department.

Art. 28. Under the direction of the department of public works, the mining deputations shall collect and remit all the *data* necessary and useful in the formation of mining statistics.

Art. 29. A special section of the department of public works will have in its charge all matters relating to the mining branch, in conformity with the provisions of this title.

## TITLE III.

### OF THE EXPLORATIONS FOR THE DISCOVERY OF MINES.

Art. 30. Every inhabitant of the republic, native or foreign, may undertake and freely execute on lands which are not private property works of exploration in order to discover mines and deposits of substances the object of the present law. The works of exploration may be made through the means of excavations, the depth or diameter of which shall not exceed five meters, or by drills (taladros) by boring (sonda) to any depth.

Art. 31. If the estate (finca) or land should be private property, and the owner, or his administrator or agent, should resist his carrying on the works of exploration for the discovery of mines to which the foregoing article refers, the works can not be made except with the express permission of the political authority of the place, with the limitations and requisites fixed in the following articles.

Art. 32. If the land on which one claims to make the exploration should not be inclosed nor cultivated, the said authority, by a previous audience with the owner of the land or his agent, shall grant authority to carry on the works of investigation on the terms fixed by article 30, provided that the explorer gives sufficient security, according to the judgment of the said authority, to answer for the damages he may cause to the proprietor of the land by such exploration.

Art. 33. If the exploration is to be made on lands inclosed or cultivated, the public authority, by a previous verbal hearing of the interested parties, a report relative to the propriety of the exploration and of the damages which it may cause, made by an expert appointed by the said authority, at the cost of the explorer, may deny the license or concede it, but the solicitor in this case shall give security on the same terms and with the object which is expressed at the end of the foregoing article.

Art. 34. The explorer must execute the security of which the two foregoing articles treat, for the sum which the political authority of the place may fix, in the term (improrogable, not to be extended) of ten days, which having passed, he forfeits his right.

Art. 35. After the execution of the respective security, the authority shall issue in writing the permit to which articles 32 and 33 of this title refer, expressing with clearness the site or sites where the explorations must be made, and the number of persons which may be employed in them; it being understood that it is conceded always with the following conditions: 1. That the time in which the investigation is to be made must not exceed one month, counted from the date of the permit; 2. That the investigation not being made by the means of the drill (sonda), the depth of the excavations or the diameter of the trial-pit (catas) must not exceed five meters.

Art. 36. If for justifiable causes the investigations can not be made in the time designated, the permit may be extended once, and for another month, by virtue of a decree by the authority.

Art. 37. During the time employed in carrying out the proceedings which are provided in the foregoing articles as necesasry for the authority to issue the permit of exploration, during the term conceded to make it, and a month after, neither the owner of the land nor any other person, except the explorer, can denounce mines or deposits (criaderos) of the material substances of the present law, in the place designated for the exploration, nor within a distance of 300 meters in any direction.

Art. 38. With the object of guaranteeing the right of which the foregoing article speaks, and the further object that on there being various denouncements the first discoverer shall have the preference, the authority which is to execute the permit for the exploration shall give notice to the proper mining deputation, or to the authority which acts in place thereof, of the petition presented, stating the place or places designated for the explorer to make his investigation.

Art. 39. The explorer must conclude his works of investigation within the term of one month, or within that of the extension should one be obtained. These terms having passed and one month more without the explorer having formalized his respective denouncement, in conformity with the provisions of this law, he will lose the exclusive right of so doing, as article 37 concedes it to him, and he shall not have a preference in respect to other denouncements.

Art. 40. Only with the consent of the proprietor can mining works of exploration be undertaken within an edifice or house of habitation, within their dependencies, as courts (patios), gardens, orchards, yards (corrals), etc., or within a distance of less than thirty meters from their exterior walls. No recourse can be admitted against the denial of the owner in the case of this article.

Art. 41. Neither can works of exploration be made for the discovery of mines in the streets or squares of towns, nor outside thereof, less than a distance of thirty meters from the exterior lines from the roads or canals, or any building, as a house, archway, aqueduct, dam, bridge, etc.

## TITLE IV.

### OF THE MODES OF ACQUIRING MINES, PLACERES, ABANDONED REDUCTION-WORKS (HACIENDAS DE BENEFICIO), OR SITES ON WHICH TO ESTABLISH THEM, AND WATERS THAT ARE USED IN MINES OR REDUCTION-WORKS AS A MOTOR POWER.

Art. 42. Property in mines, reduction-works, sites on which to establish the latter, and waters, to which this title refers, is acquired originally by adjudication and in virtue of a denouncement.

Art. 43. A denouncement may be made: 1. By title of discovery; 2. By title of abandonment; 3. By title of forfeiture or an extinction of the right of a prior owner in contravention of the present law, in the cases which it expressly determines.

Art. 44. A discovery may be: 1. Of a new mine; 2. Of a new deposit (criadero) in a known mining place (mineral); 3. Of a new mine in a known criadero and mineral.

Art. 45. The discoverer of a new mining place (mineral) shall have the right to a concession of three pertenencias following on the principal vein or deposit (criadero), and also to one more on the other veins or deposits (criaderos) of the same site or mining place (mineral) which may be discovered, and the possession of which shall be given separately. In the second case the discoverer has a right to two pertenencias contiguous, and to one pertenencia only in the third case.

Art. 46. The pertenencias shall have the extension and measurement which are determined in title 5 of this code, and in conformity with the provisions in article 106 of that title. There being various pertenencias in the same concession or adjudication, the measurement must be continuous, and each one in prolongation of the others.

Art. 47. The restorers of ancient mining places (minerales), decayed or abandoned, shall be considered as discoverers so far as regards what is established in article 45, and shall have the same rights as the latter; and those in which no work shall have been done for at least during one year shall be understood as such for the effects of this article.

Art. 48. If the discovery should be of placeres, horizontal ledges or beds (mantos ó capas), the discoverer shall have the right to three pertenencias, and those who afterwards denounce in the same deposit (criadero) shall only obtain one pertenencia, all in the form and under the measures which are detailed in title 5.

Art. 49. In any of the cases to which the preceding articles refer, if the denouncer, discoverer, or restorer should be a company constituted in the form and terms which in title 8 are established, it will only have the right to one concession of four pertenencias, with the measures which according to the nature of the deposit (criadero) are fixed in the respective articles of title 5.

Art. 50. A mine shall be considered as deserted and

abandoned, and may be adjudicated to him who may denounce it, when, in the term of a year preceding the day of the denouncement, or in a less period, any interior work (obra) comprehended in the pertenencias acquired by one sole concession has failed to be worked with six workmen during twenty-six (consecutive or interrupted) weeks. The failure of work anterior to the year which precedes that of the denouncement shall not be taken into consideration. The denouncement and adjudication of a mine as deserted and abandoned shall be subject to the proceedings provided in articles 61 to 67.

Art. 51. Only in the case of calamities or of disturbances of public order within twenty leagues around the place of the mines, and for the time which this inconvenience shall last, all the mines in the determined locality shall be considered in general protected, without the necessity of a special protection or declaration; but tranquillity being re-established, if within four months from the date which shall be fixed and published by the respective deputation or functionary which may act in its place work in said mines shall not be again established, they may be denounced by title of abandonment.

Art. 52. Those who for just and grave causes shall have had the necessity to suspend the works in their mines for more than twenty-six weeks can appear at the respective mining departments in solicitation of the necessary protection, stating and establishing the reasons for their petition.

Art. 53. The mining deputation, in view of the solicitation and report of an expert, or of other proofs, if it believes them necessary, can, without further recourse, deny the protection, or it will concede it for a term of six months, at the most.

Art. 54. If the miner should require a special protection for more than six months, he can solicit it through the deputation from the department of public works, which, with a report from the mining deputation and of an expert, or on examination of the proofs which may be presented to it, or which it may judge necessary, can, without further recourse, either deny the protection or concede it for a term which shall not exceed one year.

Art. 55. Pending the resolution relative to the protection solicited, the working of the mine in question must not be suspended, under the penalty of losing it by reason of abandonment, in conformity with the provisions of article 50.

Art. 56. The special protection conceded by the mining deputation, or by the department of public works, can not be extended, and whatever may be the causes alleged, in no case can a second protection be conceded to the same mine within the term of three years.

Art. 57. For the effect of declaring a mine deserted and abandoned in conformity with article 50, the miner can not be considered exempt from the obligation to work it, except during the term of the special protection, and the working must be re-established the day following that of the date on which the term shall have expired.

Art. 58. When a protection of any or various mines is solicited in order to undertake special works in other veins, and with which the former may be more conveniently worked, the mining deputation shall appoint an expert in whom they have confidence, in order that, by making the necessary surveys, he may report his opinion relative to the utility of the works and other points which may be deemed proper. The mining deputation, on examination of the decision of the expert, will deny the protection of that kind, or in the form solicited, or it will concede it for the time which the projected work may last; fixing the conditions which the said work must have or to which it must be subject.

Art. 59. The loss of property in a mine shall take place, and it may be adjudicated to him who may denounce it: 1. When for want of supports, fortifications, or by its bad condition, the lives of the workmen are found to be in danger, or when works are found to be ruined which are indispensable in order to continue the investigation and working the deposit (criadero), as shafts, pits, adits, general passages (canoñes generales), works of profit (labores de disfrute), etc. The ruin of ancient works useless for operation, and through which the workmen do not pass, is not a reason why the owner should lose his property; but the mining deputation can order its preservation if it judges it necessary so to do. 2. When the works (labores en trabajo) are badly ventilated, to such a degree that, by the scarcity of oxygen in the air, the health of the workmen is prejudiced or the combustion of the lights is difficult. 3. When the waters have failed to be removed which impede the prosecution of the working of the mine for twenty-six consecutive or interrupted weeks in the term of one year preceding the day of the denouncement, or within a less time. The suspension of the drainage prior to the year which precedes the date of the denouncement shall not be taken into consideration. In case a mine be denounced as abandoned for bad ventilation, or for suspension or want of drainage, the mining deputation, or the functionary who acts in its place, shall record the denouncement, and before three days shall cause the mine to be examined by an expert in whom he has confidence, and the expert shall be accompanied by the secretary and two witnesses, and for said examination the owner of the mine and denouncer shall be cited. If the denouncement should not be well founded, he shall reject it; and in a case to the contrary, he shall cite the owner of the mine and fix for him a term, which shall not exceed six months, in order that he may remedy the evil denounced which has been recognized to exist.

Art. 60. If within the term fixed in conformity with the foregoing article the infractions or faults shall not have been corrected, by doing what was ordered by the deputation, or if the drainage has not been established, the mine shall be immediately adjudicated to the denouncer, who shall, without further delay, be put in formal possession as established by the present law, provided the denouncer previously gives security, to the satisfaction of the mining deputation, for the cost of the drainage or the establishment of the works which it may be necessary to use, which he must commence to execute before a month from the date of the possession, and failing in which he shall lose his rights for not remedying the evil denounced before six months from said date.

Art. 61. The denouncement will be made in every case by the means of a writing, which shall be presented in duplicate to the mining deputation of the district, expressing therein by which title it is made of the three marked in article 43, and also the name of the denouncer and of his partners, if he should have any, the place of his birth, his profession or business, and residence, and the most distinguishable signs of the site, criadero, or mine denounced, or of which adjudication is asked, and it must conclude by asking that the interested party or parties shall hold as denouncers in some one of the three cases designated by article 43.

Art. 62. If the denouncement should be on account of abandonment or forfeiture, the writing shall contain the name of the last possessor, he being known, his domicile, the name of the mine, its situation and marks, as well as the names of the contiguous mines, and the names of the owners thereof, if they should be known.

Art. 63. The writing (escrito) being presented in duplicate, the hour and day of its presentation shall be immediately noted on both by the secretary of the deputation, and this note shall be entered in the book of registries which must be kept; and one of the duplicates shall be returned to the interested party for his safety.

Art. 64. The deputation shall pass upon said writing within twenty-four hours, and order the denouncement to be published on the three following Sundays by means of placards (carteles), put up in the customary places, and by the official periodical, if there should be one, in the capital of the district, or in the capital of the state, in order that, by reaching the notice of all, if any one should believe he had a right to oppose it, he may do so.

Art. 65. In the same decree in which the publications of the denouncement are ordered, the denouncer shall be admonished that within twenty-four hours from the date of the denouncement he must have works (una labor) opened on the site of the denouncement, in which the expert can examine the conditions of the deposit (criadero), as well as its course and inclination. These works (labor), when the deposit is a vein, shall be composed of a pit (pozo) and a level (cañon), worked on some of the sides (respaldas); each one of these excavations must have at least a section of one and a half meters on a side or diameter, and five meters of depth or length. If the deposit (criadero) should not be a vein, two excavations should be worked together (su masa) in distinct directions, each one at least of the dimensions indicated, but sufficient to give an idea of the nature and formation or position (yacimiento) of the deposit denounced. In case the owner of the soil claims, before giving possession of the mine, the value of the land, the surface of which the denouncer shall have the necessity to occupy in order to open the working (labor) of the examination (reconocimiento) to which this article refers, the mining deputation, or the authority which acts in place thereof, with a previous report of an expert in whom they have confidence, and a hearing of the interested parties, shall order the denouncer to satisfy the value of the surface which he requires to occupy, and the damages which may immediately follow, to the owner of the soil.

Art. 66. As soon as said works (labor) shall be open, and without waiting for the expiration of the four months from the date of the denouncement, provided the term of the publications shall have passed, a scientific expert shall be appointed, and in default thereof a practical one, in order that by previously examining in the prepared works the materials of which the vein or deposit is composed, their breadth, hardness, kind of minerals, with their course and inclination, or echado, he may measure and designate on the land the portion or portions (pertenencia ó pertenencias) which correspond, and mark the corners thereof, in order that the land-marks (mojoneras) may be constructed which shall serve as limits. The surveys or examinations being concluded, and the report and plan which the expert shall have made being attached to the expediente, and the contiguous mines having been also marked thereon, the adjudication shall be decreed in favor of the denouncer.

Art. 67. Within the term of the following ten days, and on the day designated for the act of possession, at the hour which shall have been fixed, one of the deputies of the district, accompanied by the secretary and the expert who made the survey, shall go to the site denounced, and shall give, in the name of the law, possession to the denouncer or denouncers of the mining ground measured and marked off. For this act and for that of the surveys the owners or agents of the contiguous mines shall always be cited, and all those who may be found within a distance of two hundred meters or less shall be considered as such in respect to the mine in question; and also the ancient possessor shall be cited if the mine in question be one denounced on the ground of abandonment, or of the infraction of the provisions of this code.

Art. 68. In the title (acta) of possession the person or persons who shall have taken possession shall be carefully made to appear, whether they shall be present or shall have appeared by an attorney in fact, for which a simple power (carta poder) with two witnesses without a notary shall be sufficient, which must be attached to the expediente, and in it must be designated the part which each interested party represents in the mine, in the terms of the parts in which it is considered by them to be virtually divided.

Art. 69. All this being concluded, the expediente shall be deposited in the archives. Each interested party who may ask for it shall be given a certified copy in form, at his cost, for the protection of his rights.

Art. 70. The proceedings established by the foregoing articles shall be observed in like manner in denouncements for discovery as in denouncements on account of abandonment.

Art. 71. In the denouncements on account of abandonment they shall not proceed, notwithstanding the publication, without citing previously the last possessor, when he may be known, and he shall be given a copy of the denouncement, and he shall be heard in a meeting to which the denouncer must also be cited. The deputation shall decide, in view of what the interested parties may set forth, if they appear at the meeting, and from the proofs and information which they may render, and which must be received within a term which shall not exceed ten days, whether the denouncement must be admitted or not. In the first case, the publications shall be made and the denouncement shall be substantiated in conformity with the foregoing articles; in the second, the mine shall continue in the possession of the former owner; in case of not agreeing, either of the parties may present their objections (oposicion) within the term of eight days.

Art. 72. Administrators, clerks, employés, and workmen of a mine are prohibited from denouncing other mines within the space of eight hundred meters around said mine, and can only do so for the owner of said mine by a power of attorney (carta poder) from him, or by a ratification of the latter during the terms established for proceeding with the denouncement and the taking of possession.

Art. 73. Every opposition to the denouncement is admissible which is founded on the ground that the opponent had previously denounced the mine in question, or any other legal cause or reason according to the provisions of this law, provided it shall be presented before the act of possession shall have terminated.

Art. 74. No opposition shall be admitted without the legal cause or reason on which it is founded be clearly and definitely expressed in the writing in which it is founded, nor beyond the term which is marked in the foregoing article.

Art. 75. In a case of controversy between two or more who may dispute about having discovered a mine, he who shall have first registered the denouncement shall be held as the discoverer.

Art. 76. When two or more denouncements occur in respect to the same site or deposit, or of contiguous sites or deposits, they shall proceed strictly in the order of dates, and in the same order must be given the survey of the pertenencias which correspond, and the possession to the denouncers.

Art. 77. If the opposition be presented during the term of the proclamations (pregones) or publications, the proceedings of the denouncement shall be suspended until the corresponding decision; but if it be presented after, the proceedings shall continue to the giving possession to the denouncer, and without prejudice of deciding on the opposition, should the same be substantiated in the proper time.

Art. 78. In every case of opposition, the deputation shall cite immediately the opponent and the denouncer, and try to conciliate them and to avoid the question; but if he does not succeed in doing so, he shall receive the proofs which they may present to him, and make or cause to be made the necessary examinations, within the term of twenty days; and afterwards, and within the following ten days, the deputation shall decide what it may deem just.

Art. 79. Of all that which relates to the opposition an expediente shall be formed, in which must be entered the proceedings, and therein must appear the proofs and the decision which shall have been given.

Art. 80. In case of opposition to the denouncement, and in case of any contention between the parties, if any one of them should not agree to the decision rendered by the mining deputation, he must so manifest it within eight days after it shall have been made known to him in writing or by appearance, which must be entered in the expediente, and this shall be remitted to the court of first instance which may be competent; and should there be various courts, to that which the opponent may elect.

Art. 81. The term of eight days which the foregoing articles determine having passed, there shall be no such recourse, and the decision shall be considered as consented to, and shall cause irrevocable effects; but if it is interposed within said term, the mining deputation shall admit it, and remit the expediente to the respective judge, in order that, the case (juicio) being opened and legally substantiated, the point or right controverted shall be definitely decided.

Art. 82. The same recourse may be interposed if the miner who thinks himself injured or prejudiced in his right should interpose it in the act of giving possession to the denouncer in the cases to which articles 50, 60, and 73 of this code refer.

Art. 83. In the mean time, no judicial sentence shall be rendered contrary to the resolution of the mining deputation; and notwithstanding the recourse of which the foregoing articles speak be interposed, the resolution of the deputation shall be executed without suspending the work of a mine, although it be in litigation.

Art. 84. Only in the cases of the lode or deposit denounced not existing, or not finding free ground in order to give the pertenencia or pertenencias which might have existed, shall a possession be suspended, and it shall never be done by reason of any opposition being made, or a right which may be alleged to the contrary; and it shall only be made to appear in the proceedings, reserving to the contradicter or opponent his right, in order that it may be alleged separately before competent judges and tribunals.

Art. 85. Until the question of a denouncement shall have been definitely settled, no other shall be admissible in respect to the same site, mine, or deposit, not even that it may be borne in mind and taken into consideration in case of the former being dismissed.

Art. 86. The foregoing prohibition comprehends the miner who denounced and his associates; and neither one nor the other shall present successive denouncements pending the proceedings and the resolution of the first.

Art. 87. The right acquired by a denouncer shall be forfeited if he shall not have opened the works (labor), or shall not have taken the possession within the terms or times designated by this code, or by the mining deputation, in conformity with articles 65 to 67.

Art. 88. Said terms may, for a justifiable cause, be extended by the deputation once; a second term being conceded to the denouncer, its duration shall not exceed two months.

Art. 89. The old sites of reduction-works (haciendas de beneficio), the new ones for the purpose of establishing them, and the haciendas abandoned, shall be denounceable, and shall be adjudicated to the denouncer in the same form established in respect to new or abandoned mines; and the same provisions shall be observed as in case of opposition or contradiction that shall be made to the denouncement.

Art. 90. A site or establishment for beneficiating metals shall be considered abandoned if it shall lack wholly the roofs, machinery (máquinas), tools (herramientas), and serviceable timbers, although the walls or construction materials subsist, and even without that circumstance a hacienda de beneficio may be adjudicated to whomsoever may denounce it, if during three years no work has been executed in it, and if the owner being required by the respective deputation shall not re-establish them within the term fixed, not exceeding six months.

Art. 91. As well in the case to which the foregoing article refers, as in that of the adjudication of a mine which may be denounced on account of abandonment, or forfeiture which may be found to have occurred by failure of working it according to the rules established, if the former possessor shall claim to have left in the mine or hacienda any exterior works and movables made at his cost, such as ore sheds (cubiertas de galeria), engines (máquinas), or other things of this class which may be used and which the denouncer may wish to preserve, the latter shall pay the owner according to the valuation thereof by experts, appointed one by each party; and a third, in case of disagreement, shall be appointed by the deputation.

Art. 92. The denouncements of surplus ground (de demasías) shall be subject entirely to the provisions in title 5, articles 111, 112, and 113.

Art. 93. If the denouncement of any running water or water-fall should occur, to be employed in the working of the mines or of the reduction-works (hacienda de beneficio), such as motive power or to wash metals, said denouncement shall be admitted and substantiated with the same proceedings as for mines, as well in the case in which the said water had been formerly used for said objects, if denounced as deserted or abandoned, as in the case where the water may have no known owner; but in no case shall such denouncement take place nor a forced occupation for a cause of public use, in favor of the miner, if the question is as to water which is the property of a private individual, and the owner is using it or requires it for his own use or for his possessions and industry. The property in running water or a water-fall may be lost, and may be adjudicated to him who shall denounce it, when it shall not have been used during twenty-six consecutive or interrupted weeks within the term of a year prior to the denouncement. The waters which shall have been utilized in the reduction-works (haciendas de beneficio) are not denounceable, except in case the said haciendas shall have been abandoned.

Art. 94. The refuse ores and rubbish heaps (desechaderos y terreros) of the abandoned mines are not denounceable, except by denouncing at the same time the mines from which they proceed. Neither are the slag-heaps (graseros) and slime (lameros) of the smelting-houses (fundiciones), and haciendas de beneficio which are abandoned, denounceable separately from the haciendas themselves.

Art. 95. In every case in which a miner, after having carried out the proceedings of possession, shall require the occupancy within or without his pertenencias, of any part of the surface of the land, whether in order to open the entrance of the mine (boca minas), to establish offices, roads, dams, aqueducts, or any other work, according to the right which articles 12 to

15 of title 1 concede to him, or in order to avail himself of the superficial part of the deposit in conformity with article 98 of title 5, he may do so, with the consent of the mining deputation, when the land shall be vacant (baldio), and if it should be public or private property, he shall pay previously the value of the soil which he may occupy, and that of the damages which immediately shall follow to the proprietor, without considering the value of the mineral, according to the valuation of experts, one of whom shall be appointed by each party, and a third, in case of disagreement, shall be appointed by mining deputation, without any one opposing with the title in fee the possession which shall be given to the denouncer, or the carrying on of the works and proceedings prior to it.

Art. 96. From the resolution dictated by the mining deputation, or by the functionaries who may act in place thereof, although there be no complaint nor opposition by any party, the interested parties may appeal to the department of public works (secretaria de fomento) and ask its revocation by presenting their established complaint within a month from the date on which they shall have been notified of the resolution in question.

## TITLE V.

### OF THE MEASURES WHICH THE PERTENENCIAS OF THE MINES OUGHT TO HAVE.

Art. 97. The pertenencia or unit of measure for mining concessions is a solid of indefinite depth, limited on the exterior by the projection on the surface of the earth of a square or of a horizontal right angle, and on the interior by four vertical planes which pass through their respective sides.

Art. 98. The dimensions of the square or right angle which must serve as an upper or superior base to the solid which constitutes the pertenencias are fixed in the following articles, the nature and position of the deposit being considered, under the conception that the miner may work and avail himself of all the mineral substances which exist in the interior of his pertenencia, and by a previous indemnification for the value of the soil, without considering that of the ore which may be the object of the working; and he may also use the part of the deposit which may be on the surface, and occupy that which may be necessary for his operations and works, in conformity with the provisions in articles 12 to 15, title 1.

Art. 99. The mining pertenencia, or the whole of the pertenencias which constitute one sole concession, is indivisible among the owners thereof in all cases of the transfer of the dominion of said property, whatever may be the title by which it is done.

Art. 100. In the concessions relative to veins or lodes, the upper surface (cara superior) of the pertenencia shall be a right angle, of which the parallel sides on the course of the vein shall have 200 meters level measure, and the length of the other two, perpendicular to the first, shall vary with the inclination of the vein, between 100 and 300 meters, in conformity with the bases which are detailed in the following article, with the object that the miner may enjoy 400 meters, approximately, on the vein in the direction of the inclination (echado).

Art. 101. When the vein shall be vertical (clavada), or when it shall have an inclination (echado) of more than 85°, the square (cuadra) shall be of 100 meters, which shall be measured from one to the other side of it, or they shall be divided between both, in conformity as the miner may wish it, whenever for that purpose no damage shall result to a third party. When the vein shall have less than 85° of inclination, the length of the sides of the square (cuadra) shall be measured in the direction (en el sentido) of the inclination (echado), and it shall be what appears in the following table:

| | | | |
|---|---|---|---|
| When the inclination is | 85° | to 75½°, | the square is 100 meters. |
| | 75½ | to 72½, | 120 meters. |
| | 72½ | to 69½, | 140 meters. |
| | 69½ | to 66½, | 160 meters. |
| | 66½ | to 63¼, | 180 meters. |
| | 63¼ | to 60, | 200 meters. |
| | 60 | to 56¾, | 220 meters. |
| | 56¾ | to 53¼, | 240 meters. |
| | 53¼ | to 49½, | 260 meters. |
| | 49½ | to 45½, | 280 meters. |
| | 45½ | to less, | 300 meters. |

Art. 102. The measure of the sides of the right angle of the pertenencia parallel to the course of the vein may be divided with both sides of the working of the survey (reconocimiento), to which article 65 of title 4 refers, according to the will of the miner, in ground free from other mining possession.

Art. 103. When, the vein having less than 85° of inclination, the miner shall solicit that some part of the square (cuadra) which belongs to him be measured to him in a direction (en sentido) contrary to the inclination, 25 meters may be conceded to him, provided that by it no damage shall result to a third party. Only in case that by the existence of another pertenencia on the inclination (echado) of the lode denounced the length of the square is not sufficient can more than 25 meters be measured contrary to the inclination.

Art. 104. In the concessions of placeres, of precious stones, of gold, and of platina, with the metals which accompany them, the upper face (cara superior) of the pertenencia shall be a square of twenty meters on a side, which shall be measured on a level, as the denouncer may indicate.

Art. 105. In the concessions relative to beds (mantos) or relative to irregular deposits (criaderos) not specified in the foregoing articles, the upper surface (cara superior) of the pertenencia shall be a square of 300 meters on a side, which shall be measured on a level, dividing them according to the will of the denouncer. If the deposit is of iron, the upper surface (cara superior) of the pertenencia shall be a square of 500 meters on a side.

Art. 106. The marking out (señalamiento) of the pertenencias shall be made with the following conditions: 1. That the working (labor) or excavations to which article 65 of title 6 refers must be comprehended within the limits of the pertenencia; 2. That whatever may be the unevenness (accidentes) of the ground, the horizontal projections of the sides of the right angle or of the square, in their respective cases, shall have the lengths designated in the preceding articles, but for no cause shall a fraction of a pertenencia be measured; 3. That the measures must be made on land which is not occupied by another mining possession, so that one pertenencia must not overlap that of a contiguous one; 4. That when one concession shall be composed of various pertenencias, they must be continuous and must be measured each one in prolongation of the others, so that each concession be limited by a square or by a right angle, although in order to comply with this condition it shall be necessary to reduce the number of pertenencias which ought to belong to the miner.

Art. 107. The experts shall mark the courses of their measurement according to the magnetic meridian; but they shall state the declination of the magnetic needle and assign it in their plans, when it shall be known in the place of their operations; and they shall fix, whenever it is possible, the position of the workings (labor) of the survey, that of one monument or that of some of the lines, noting their respective distances from other fixed objects.

Art. 108. The vertexes of the right angle or of the square of the concession shall be designated with monuments solidly constructed, which shall be distinguishable by their form or by some sign from those of contiguous concessions.

Art. 109. These monuments are immutable, and the miner shall preserve them in good condition, making the necessary repairs on them, and shall abstain from changing the places thereof.

Art. 110. If any miner shall observe that his vein has suffered a sensible change in its course or in its inclination, and shall wish to modify his pertenencias in order to place them in relation with the observed alterations, he shall solicit a new measurement from the mining deputation, which may be conceded to him by a previous survey and report of an expert, if there shall be no prejudice to a third party, and if this petition shall be presented before a year after the first possession shall have been given.

Art. 111. If between two or more immediate pertenencias shall exist a portion of free ground which shall not be sufficient in extent to contain a pertenencia, it shall constitute an overplus (demasia), which shall only be adjudicated to one of the adjoining miners, or be divided between the pertenencias separated by the overplus.

Art. 112. If the surplus or unappropriated ground (demasía) should be denounced by one of the miners on account of his having extended from his pertenencia and entered into the surplus with his interior works more than 100 meters in extension or depth, it shall be entirely adjudicated to him.

Art. 113. If the surplus (demasia) should be denounced before having been occupied in the interior by any working (labor), it shall be distributed between the adjoining pertenencias according to the agreement of their respective owners, and in default of this, in equal parts, each one paying the expenses of measurement and of possession in proportion to the part which he shall have received.

Art. 114. In case any miner shall have advanced so much in his subterraneous works that he shall have extended beyond the termini of his pertenencia, whether in length or in square measure (por el rumbo ó por la cuadra), he may prosecute his works provided he finds himself in free ground, and he may acquire it by a previous denouncement; but each concession shall not exceed its former size, and with the obligation of removing the land-marks to the new limits.

Art. 115. If the necessities of the working (laborio) of a mine, such as ventilation, drainage, etc., shall oblige the extending of the works into the pertenencias of another, this shall be permitted, provided that, in conformity with the opinion of an expert appointed by the mining deputation, the projected works shall be useful, and that by them no damage shall result to the contiguous miner. These works shall be executed in conformity with the orders of the deputation, in view of the report of the expert appointed by it, and at the exclusive expense of the miner interested in what may be done.

Art. 116. If on executing the works to which the foregoing article refers metal of any value shall be found, the miner who shall perform the work shall be obliged to give notice immediately to the deputation and to the owner of the pertenencia, and to divide with the latter thenceforth the metal or fruits and their costs in equal parts, provided that its enjoyment shall have cost anything. This shall be observed so long as the owner of the pertenencia is extending his communication with the works in metal (frutos), but after the communication shall have been made, the miner shall cease operations (hacer el disfrute) in the pertenencia of the other, and shall only prosecute the works proper for the working of his mine, in conformity with authorization which is granted to him in the foregoing article.

Art. 117. When a miner shall reach the limit of his pertenencia with any work which is giving fruits or metal he may continue it into the pertenencia of another, but he shall be obliged to give notice immediately to the mining deputation and the owner of the pertenencia, and to divide with him thenceforth the fruits and costs in equal parts, provided that the profits thereof shall have cost anything; all of which shall be observed so long as said owner is making the communication with the works not which may be in paying condition. If the miner should give the notice provided in this article and in the prior one, he shall pay the value of all the fruits or metal, without deduction of expenses, which he shall have extracted from the pertenencia of the other, and he shall be prohibited from continuing to avail himself of the part which might belong to him.

Art. 118. The communication once made to which the foregoing article refers, each miner shall keep within the limits of his pertenencia, and shall fix on the dividing line, whenever it may be necessary, an iron grate (reja), which shall impede the transit of the workmen, and which shall not prevent the free circulation of air.

## TITLE VI.

### OF THE MANNER OF WORKING MINES.

Art. 119. The mines must be worked in conformity with the rules of art and with subjection to the provisions of this title, and without prejudice also to the observance of the police regulations which may have relation to the works or workings undertaken in the mines.

Art. 120. In the working (laborio) of the mines the following conditions shall be fulfilled: 1. That by natural or artificial means the necessary ventilation shall be maintained; 2. That the interior roads shall be sufficiently ample, and that whenever the number of workmen shall exceed fifty there shall not be less than two roads which shall communicate with the exterior; 3. That the soft works (labores blandas) shall be fortified with timber, or masonry of stone and mortar, and in the proper places arches, bridges, pillars, and massive bulks (macizos) which may be necessary shall be constructed, in order to avoid any precipitation or downfall (derrumbe ó hundimiento); 4. The works of fortification which the security of the mine and that of the workmen may demand shall likewise be made, in case the natural pillars or massive bulks (macizos) of the deposit are not preserved which are ordinarily left to sustain the paying works (de disfrute); 5. That the works (labores) and the roads shall be kept clean, placing the rubbish (escombros) in the interior, or in the holes which arise from the working of the deposit, or on the surface of lands on which they will not obstruct the public roads, nor impede the course of the streams; 6. That when the operation of the mine requires the drainage of its works, this shall be continually maintained.

Art. 121. In order to insure the fulfillment of these conditions and those of the police regulations relative to the working of the mines, the authority shall exercise timely vigilance through the medium of the mining deputation, of the engineers of the mines, or of the agents which it may be considered proper to employ.

Art. 122. It is the duty of the mining deputations to visit or to order the mines comprehended within their respective districts to be examined whenever they shall deem it proper, or at least once in two years.

Art. 123. The mining deputation may make these visits in company with any expert, or order that an expert shall make them, accompanied by a notary, or with witnesses of assistance. In the report (acta) of the visits, the condition in which the mine shall be found shall be made to appear, and what shall be observed in relation to article 120 of this title. If any failures shall be noted, the mining deputation shall give timely orders in writing to the owner of the mine, in order that he may correct them within the reasonable term which it shall fix for him.

Art. 124. If the owner of the mine should not comply with the order of the deputation to remedy the failures which it shall have noted, he shall be fined according to the judgment of the deputation and according to the gravity of the failure, in the sum of from fifty to two hundred and fifty dollars for the first time. If the disobedience should be repeated, the deputation shall duplicate the fine, determining upon the partial or entire suspension of the works until the work it has ordered shall have been executed.

Art. 125. If, through the medium indicated, or by any complaint which shall be made, in which case the visit to the mine must in like manner be made, it should appear that the fault or faults are grave, to the extent that the prosecution of the work of the mine is thereby embarrassed, or that the lives and health of the workmen are put in danger, the mining deputation shall dictate the orders which it may judge opportune, and it may resolve, as a precautionary measure, the suspension of the works in the whole mine or in certain places, according to the cases. If the suspension decreed of the works should be total, and the miner should not correct the evil indicated within the term of six months, he shall lose the property in the mine, and it may be adjudicated to whomsoever shall denounce it on account of abandonment in conformity with the provisions in article 50.

Art. 126. If the parties interested in the mine should not agree to these orders, they shall be executed, notwithstanding, and the respective expediente shall be sent to the judicial authority for its decision in court. This authority, after hearing the interested party and receiving the proofs he may render, shall adjudge what is proper within a term which shall not exceed fifteen days, and from the judgment which it shall pronounce there shall be no recourse but that of responsibility.

Art. 127. In these cases the judgment shall be pronounced with citation of the functionary who ordered the suspension, and the proofs shall be received also with his citation; but if there should be a denouncer who shall ask for the adjudication of the mine, the judgment shall follow in the terms prescribed in articles 70, 71, and 78 to 83, of title 4.

Art. 128. The direction of the interior and exterior works of the mines, the beneficiating of the metals, and the establishment, construction, and preservation of the machineries, shall be necessarily commended to scientific or practical experts of recognized fitness.

Art. 129. The miner shall be responsible for the accidents which, on account of unskillfulness, may happen in the working (laborio) of a mine, or in the service of the engines, when he does not employ professional or practical experts in conformity with the foregoing article.

Art. 130. In the mines which may not be directed by professional mining experts, in places where such experts are, the mining deputations shall take care to intervene: 1. In the plans (trazos) of works of importance, such as adits (socavones), general shafts (tiros generales), galleries of communication, etc., with the obligation of visiting the works once every month or once in two months, as the progress of it may require, in order to avoid in time any error in the execution; 2. In the communications which shall be made with inundated works, or which may contain noxious gases; 3. In the execution of works (labores) near the surface which may compromise the security of the edifices or inhabitants.

Art. 131. The administrators of the mines shall make known to the respective mining deputations, and in case thereof to the political or judicial authority, the death of or any great injury to any workman which may happen in the interior of the mine, and any misfortune which may take place therein, such as falling of the earth (derrumbe), inundation, fire, etc.

Art. 132. In the affairs of mines, the people of which exceed two hundred workmen, there shall be a medicine-chest (botiquin), and they shall have at their service a surgeon, who shall make the first healings or cures (curaciones) of said workmen in cases of accidents happening during the work.

## TITLE VII.

### OF THE DRAINAGE OF MINES, VOLUNTARY ADITS (SOCAVONES AVENTUREROS), AND GENERAL GALLERIES OF INVESTIGATION.

Art. 133. The owners of mines, by means of shafts (tiros) or adits (socavones), and by employing the resources and means (arbitrios) of art which may be adequate, shall maintain drainage continually in said mines; so that if a miner limits himself to working the upper works (labores altas), without maintaining the drainage of his mine, it may be denounced in conformity with what is established in articles 59 and 60.

Art. 134. If the owner of any mine whose works are lower than those of his neighbors shall be burdened with costs of drainage on account ofs aid neighbors not maintaining the drainage, or not maintaining it to the extent necessary, and the water flows from the mines of said neighbors into his, he shall have the right of being indemnified by the owners of said mines, and they shall contribute for the cost of the drainage in proportion to the benefit they may receive.

Art. 135. The owners of the mines which shall be completely drained shall deliver, as indemnification to him who sustains the drainage, the tenth part of all the fruits which they shall take out below the level previously fixed by experts.

Art. 136. If the drainage should not be complete, but only should be made in part, the contribution mentioned shall be diminished more or less, according to the taxation of experts, appointed, one by each party, and a third one, in case of disagreement, by the mining deputation.

Art. 137. Mines which shall be newly opened in points where they may be beneficiated by means of the drainage already existing in other mines, shall be subject to the provisions in the preceding articles.

Art. 138. The provisions in the three foregoing articles shall only take place when the interested parties shall not agree in the matter; but there being an agreement, they must be subject to it.

Art. 139. If by means of an adit (socavon) the drainage, the investigation, or the working of various open mines of any kind of deposits should be facilitated, and all the mine-owners should offer to make it, or any of them, or an outside person alone or associated with various partners, although none of them be owner of the pertenencias which the adit must traverse, their claim and the denouncement which they may present shall be admitted by the contractor or contractors (empresario ó empresarios), with the following conditions: 1. That the work must be possible and useful, according to the judgment of an expert appointed by the mining deputation; 2. That with the petition of denouncement shall be accompanied a plan formed by an expert, in which shall be designated the survey of the road which the adit must follow, the pertenencias of the mines it must cross, and those which are within fifty meters on each side.

Art. 140. In the denouncements of these adits the proceedings established for the acquisition of new mines shall be observed, and the measurements of their pertenencias as in the portions of free ground shall be the following: 1. If the voluntary adit (socavon aventurero) has to be worked on the vein, the width of the square (cuadra) shall be that which corresponds to the greater or less inclination (echado) of the square, in conformity with what is established in article 101, and the length shall be the length of the projected adit; 2. If the adit must be made in its greater part outside of the vein or in another deposit (criadero), its pertenencia shall have a width of one hundred meters, divided in equal parts on both sides of the line or lines fixed by its survey, and a length the same as that of the adit. In the portions of ground on which possessed mines exist, the free surplus (demasías) may be ceded to the adventurer, and he may be permitted to cross the property of other pertenencias with his measurements.

Art. 141. The owner or the managing company (compania empresaria) of a voluntary adit (socavon aventurero) shall comply with the special provisions which the mining deputation, with the consent of an expert, shall fix for its execution on giving him the possession; and he or it shall subject himself or itself besides, in the execution and protection of the work, to the provisions of the foregoing titles. The workings of these adits (socavones) shall follow approximately the line or lines designated in the concession; but if it should suit the contractor (empresario) to vary the direction, he shall solicit the right, and it may be conceded to him without prejudice to third parties by the previous proceedings of a new denouncement.

Art. 142. The owner or contractor of a voluntary adit (socavon aventurero) shall enjoy the following concessions: 1. He may make it not only on free ground, but also within the pertenencias of mines occupied without prejudicing the security of said mines; 2. He may denounce, on projecting the adit (socavon) or when he is executing it, and may acquire five new or abandoned mines, each one of them with pertenencias of a company, provided they are less than one hundred and fifty meters from the line (trazo) of the adit (socavon); 3. If in the prosecution of the adit, veins or new deposits (criaderos) shall be found, the owner or contractors (empresarios) may, by a previous denouncement and the respective proceedings, and besides from what is conceded in the foregoing subdivision, acquire on each one of them (veins or deposits) three pertenencias if one alone works, and four if they work by a company, as well as the surplus (demasias) entirely if it should not contain a complete pertenencia; 4. The concessions to which the two foregoing subdivisions refer shall be considered annexed to the adit (socavon) and protected by the working in the latter; but the adit (socavon) being once terminated, each concession shall be worked separately.

Art. 143. When the adits shall have for their principal object the drainage of the mines, its owner or contractor (empresario) shall receive, in default of an agreement, the indemnification which is expressed in articles 135, 136, and 137 of this title, without prejudice to the other prerogatives, such as aventureros.

Art. 144. If the contractors (empresarios) of an adit with their works find profits (frutos) in the pertenencia of another, they are obliged to give immediate notice to the deputation and to the owner of that pertenencia, and to divide with him from that time the profits (frutos) and the costs in equal parts, provided that the enjoyment thereof shall cost anything; all of which shall be observed so long as the owner of the pertenencia is blasting or making the communication with the works (laborio); from the moment the communication is made, the contractors (empresarios) of the adit shall cease to profit by the fruits or metal found.

Art. 145. If the projector or contractors (empresarios) of the adit (socavon) should not give the timely notice which is provided in the foregoing article, they shall pay to the owner of the pertenencia, and by a valuation of experts, all the value of the metals (frutos) without deduction of expenses, which they shall estimate as having been extracted, and they shall be prohibited from availing themselves of the part which would belong to them.

Art. 146. If any mines use the adit for transport and extraction, they shall pay the projector what they shall have agreed to pay; and in default of an agreement, they shall deliver to him five per cent of the metals which they may transport through the adit.

Art. 147. Neither the owner of a voluntary adit (socavon aventurero), nor in general any miner, shall have a right to indemnification for the services of ventilation which he may do to other mines with his works of communication.

Art. 148. When in any mine shall be furnished one or more shafts (tiros) for the general drainage of various mines with competent machinery (máquinas) to force the water to the surface, upon a previous corresponding petition and the favorable report of two experts appointed by the mining deputation, they shall be considered as general shafts, and the levels or cross-cuts (cañones ó cruceras) which shall run from them as if they were voluntary adits (socavones aventureros), with the rights and obligations of the latter, which may be prosecuted into pertenencias of other persons.

Art. 149. Whenever, starting from a shaft or any subterraneous work, any gallery of investigation or other work of common utility for the working of various mines shall be projected, although it may not have drainage for its object, and shall have to be made in the pertenencia of another, the right to make it may be conceded, if, according to the judgment of the two experts appointed by the mining deputation, the work would be really useful.

Art. 150. The conditions in order to execute the works of which the foregoing article speaks shall be fixed for the voluntary adits (socavones aventureros). The distribution of their costs and of the ores or profits (frutos) shall be made according to agreement, and in default thereof, proportionally according to the judgment of experts, applying the provisions referring to voluntary adits (socavones aventureros) in like cases.

## TITLE VIII.

### OF MINING PARTNERSHIP.

Art. 151. Partnerships or companies which shall be formed for the working of mines and of reduction-works (haciendas de beneficio) shall be governed by the provisions of the civil code of the federal district, so far as they are not modified by the special provisions of this title.

Art. 152. Every mine, whether constituted of one, two, or more pertenencias, according to the title of its concession, is indivisible in the sense that it can not be made into fractions in order to be divided among distinct owners, and in the sense that the partners of a mining company shall not have the right to claim to work on their individual account any determined pertenencia, or works of the mine or mines which shall form the object of the company, unless the works shall be made in common, and the expenses and profits (frutos) shall be divided according to agreement, and in default thereof, proportionally according to the representation of each one.

Art. 153. Every company formed for the operating of mines, in conformity with what is determined in article 49, may acquire by denouncement four contiguous pertenencias on the same lode or deposit (criadero).

Art. 154. The mining partnership must be made to appear by a public writing (escritura publica), as an essential requisite for its validity.

Art. 155. The contract of partnership must absolutely contain the name and domicile of each one of the copartners, and the representation of each one of them on the part which he holds in the company, which, without such requisites, shall not be reputed as constituted.

Art. 156. In every partnership or mining company the mine shall be considered as divided into a certain number of shares, and each copartner shall have a right to one or many of these according to the agreement.

Art. 157. Any one of the copartners is free to alienate the part of his representation, without the others having the right of preference (tanto); and he shall give notice to the director or superintendent of the partnership of the person to whom he shall have sold, save in case the shares shall be represented by certificates transferable to the bearer.

Art. 158. The death of a copartner shall not dissolve the company, which shall continue with his heirs; and the latter may make use of the right established by the foregoing article.

Art. 159. It shall not be required in a partnership formed for the operating of mines that the capital shall be fixed and determined.

Art. 160. In mining partnerships the copartners are only responsible to the amount or value of their shares, deducting what on their account they may have already paid for the operating, if on forming the company a determined value had been fixed for them; in a contrary case they shall not respond for the obligations contracted for the partnership, except with the value of the mine or business comprising all that belongs to it.

Art. 161. Notwithstanding a mine is real estate and immovable, and being in this quality subject to all the provisions of the civil code of the federal district, relative to real estate, as to its alienation or transfer of dominion, mortgage, etc., the shares in a mining company or mining partnership shall be reputed movables for all legal effects.

Art. 162. The shares of which the foregoing article speaks, of mines or reduction-works (hacienda de beneficio), shall be represented by certificates transferable to the bearer, or to order, and transmissible by simple indorsement, without any right in the other shareholders of being preferred in the purchase thereof by paying the same (el tanto).

Art. 163. In default of stipulations contained in the company contract, the decision of the points which may be offered with relation to the workings, administration, etc., shall be what the copartners may determine by a majority of votes; but for every resolution which imports an alienation of the property in the mine the unanimity of votes shall be required.

Art. 164. In the deliberations of the partnership the owner or owners of one share shall have one vote, and he who may be the owner of more shall be considered in the voting according to the representation which shall correspond to the number of shares which he may have; but if one alone should be the owner of the half or more of the shares, his vote shall be valued one less than half.

Art. 165. In all cases in which by equality of votes there shall be a tie, they must appear at the mining deputation in order that it may decide, without any more proof than the knowledge of what occurred and was manifested at the meeting; and the deputations must solve the question, taking into account the equities between the copartners and the mining interests.

Art. 166. In order that the resolutions may be valid, the citation or convocation of all the shareholders must precede, expressing the object of the meeting or business which must be treated, with at least fifteen days' notice; and a meeting of the majority, or of one more than half of the shares, shall be required; but if for want of a meeting a new citation should have to be made, the meeting shall be formed with the number of shares which may be represented by those who may meet.

Art. 167. The citation of which the foregoing article speaks shall be personally made on the shareholders known who may reside or shall have a representative in the same place, and on the others by means of the official periodical of the district, if there should be one; and if there should be none, by means of the official periodical of the capital of the state.

Art. 168. The copartner who shall fail to contribute the part of the expenses that corresponds to him, and should not pay his quota within the term of two months, shall lose his shares, and these shall be declared forfeited, and shall be added proportionally to the others, on the terms and conditions which are expressed in the following articles.

Art. 169. In order to declare a share forfeited, a prior notice must be given by the contributing copartners, or by the director or administrator of the mine of the respective deputation, in order that a record of the date on which the owner of the share failed to contribute being made, the share may be declared forfeited by the said deputation if two months shall pass without the contribution having been made.

Art. 170. If it shall not appear that the shareholder shall have had a knowledge of the assessment made (exhibicion acordada) or asked, and of the payment which belongs to him to make, and that he has resisted or refused to make it, the two months of the term fixed in the foregoing article shall only run from the time at which he shall have been notified by the deputation of the obligation which he is under and of the sum of which he ought to contribute, which notice, if he should not be known or should be absent, shall be given by the periodicals, and within the term of fifteen days, as is provided for the citations for meetings in article 167.

Art. 171. In case of any shares having been declared forfeited or lost by the deputation, the owner thereof who shall not agree thereto may ask for the respective trial against the partnership that shall have asked for said declaration, and he may appear before the corresponding civil court, provided he shall do so within fifteen days, counted from the time he shall have been notified of said resolution, and not afterwards.

Art. 172. The copartner whose shares have been declared forfeited, save an agreement to the contrary, shall only preserve the right of reimbursement for what he shall have paid. This reimbursement shall be made with fifty per cent of the profits of the mine after all the expenses made by the present copartners before and after the forfeiture shall have been paid.

Art. 173. The copartners are under no obligation, save an agreement to the contrary, to beneficiate in common the ores (frutos), or contribute to purchase or establish reduction-works (haciendas de beneficio). The division of the profits (frutos) extracted among the copartners, proportionally according to their representations, shall not be made until each one shall have paid his part of the expenses of the mine.

Art. 174. The foregoing rules and provisions shall only be applicable in default of a stipulation, since, if in an agreement made or in their respective by-laws (estatutos) others shall be adopted, those shall be applicable; but those contained in articles 152, 154, 155, 156, 158, and 161, of this title, are not renounceable, nor can they be altered or modified by private individuals.

## TITLE IX.

### OF THE CONTRACT OF SUPPLIES (AVIO), AND OTHERS RELATIVE TO MINES.

Art. 175. The contract for supplies (avio) may be made by the supplier (aviador) acquiring a part in the mine, or as a simple loan (prestamo ó refaccion), and in both cases the stipulations of the contract shall be observed, and in default thereof, the following rules; and those contained in articles 181, 183, and 186 can not be modified nor renounced.

Art. 176. When the contract of supplies (avio) is agreed upon, the supplier (aviador) acquiring a part of the mine, this and his administration shall be preserved while the contract is maintained; and the profits in the first place shall be destined to pay the debt of said contract, and afterwards they shall be divided between the owner and the supplier (aviador), in proportion to the representations which each one shall have of them. The supplier or suppliers (aviádor) may terminate the contract (avio) whenever they may wish, losing in doing so that part of the mine which they had conditionally acquired, which shall revert to the original owner or owners; the supplier (aviador) preserving the right to the payment of what he may have spent, until he shall have lost the property in the mine.

Art. 177. If the capital of the supplies (caudal del avio) should be exhausted, or a part thereof not being covered by the remaining effects, the miner shall not be responsible for the same with his property, except only with the profits of the mine, fifty per cent of which shall be destined, after covering the last supplies (avio), to paying the former suppliers (aviadores) one after the other, commencing with the last or most recent, provided that the qualifications of restitution (refaccion) shall concur. The debts, burdens, or mortgages which a mine may have shall be extinguished in case its property is lost on account of abandonment or by the non-observance of the precepts of this code, and they shall not be demandable when the mine is in possession of a new owner.

Art. 178. The contract of supplies (avio) being made in the character of a loan, whether bearing interest or not, or with the condition of receiving in payment the silver (las platas) or ores (frutos) with some profit, shall only be reimbursed with the products of the mine, and shall not have any other guaranty than the said mine, unless in the contract there shall have been constituted or expressly stipulated mortgages on distinct property or other securities.

3*

Art. 179. With the exception of days' works due, the credit of the supplier (aviador), of whom the foregoing article speaks, shall be preferred to any other credit which may not proceed from supplies (avio), said credit having the character of restitution (refaccion), and among divers suppliers (aviadores) the preference shall belong to the last, or to the one posterior to the former ones.

Art. 180. If the said mine and its machinery, stock on hand (existencias), and other values which form a part of the business should be attached or sold, what is provided in the foregoing articles relative to the preference shall be observed in favor of the suppliers (aviadores) among themselves, with their credits, and in respect to other creditors.

Art. 181. Every contract of supplies (avio) must appear by a public writing (escritura publica), without which requisite it shall have no validity, nor shall it produce any legal effect.

Art. 182. If the contract of supplies (avio) should be made for a definite time, or should the supplier (aviador) compromise himself to facilitate the miner with a fixed capital or sum, he shall lose the right to collect what he may have furnished if he suspends or withdraws the supplies (avios) before fulfilling his compromise, without prejudice to the right which the miner shall have to demand of him the fulfillment and to solicit a new supplier (aviador).

Art. 183. The miner to whom the supplier (aviador) shall not furnish in time the workmen's pay (raya) may take and sell, to make the payments, notwithstanding an agreement to the contrary, the effects or useful goods (utiles) on which the same can be most easily realized; and the loss suffered thereby shall be on account of the supplier (aviador).

Art. 184. Every supplier (aviador) may put in an inspector (interventor) if he himself could not administer, and the miner or owner may in his turn put in one with the supplier, if the latter should have the administration according to the terms of the contract.

Art. 185. The inspectors of which the foregoing article treats shall not interfere with the administration, and they shall limit themselves to watching and reviewing the operations, books, and accounts; and they must inform the supplier (aviador) or owner whom they represent of what may interest them to know, and in grave or urgent cases, and when the question is of preventing any abuse or damage, they must inform the respective mining deputation.

Art. 186. In the sales and contracts respecting mines or the shares thereof, there shall be in no case any recourse for a rescission for a cause of damage (lesion),[1] nor restitution *in integrum*.

Art. 187. The salary, daily pay, or pay by a share of the profits (á partido), or other system which may be adopted for the working of the mining business, is a matter of private contract between the owners thereof and the employés or workmen, and the contracts relative thereto shall be governed by the provisions of the common law.

## TITLE X.

### OF THE PROCEEDINGS IN MINING CASES.

Art. 188. In economical and administrative affairs, the proceedings to which the deputations must be subject in mining cases are those which have been determined in titles 4 and 6 of this code.

Art. 189. The causes (juicios) in the matter of mines shall be tried and definitely decided in the federal district, in the territory of Lower California, or in each state, by the judges and tribunals which may there be competent, and in conformity with laws of procedure thereof; but always observing the rules assigned in the following articles.

Art. 190. The trial shall be summary, provided that by its nature it ought not to have a special or shorter form, according to the law of procedure of the state where the mine is, or of the federal district or territory in case thereof.

Art. 191. The working of a mine or reduction-works shall not be suspended on account of litigation, sequestration, or execution; a party can only intervene.

Art. 192. The machinery, tools, utensils, and necessary provisions or stock on hand in the mine or hacienda, can not be attached or sequestered separately from the business for a mining debt; and only for the payment of the accounts (rayas) of the workmen can be taken and sold of said objects those which may be sufficient and necessary to pay said accounts.

Art. 193. In every case of sequestration or execution the preservation of the works shall be considered in preference and with the products of the mine or hacienda.

Art. 194. In cases of bankruptcy (con curso), or testamentary cases, or of intestacy, if in the estate there be any mine or

---

[1] This is understood to mean that if the mine after a sale should become of much greater value, that the sale on that account can not be rescinded or restored to the seller.

reduction-works, the preservation of the works shall be considered by the judge, or by the representative of the bankruptcy or of the testamentary case (testamentaria), and if the products of said business shall not be sufficient therefor, and all the interested parties shall not present themselves to contribute, any one of them may pay the expenses, in which case he shall have the rights of the supplier in order to reimburse himself for the amount he may have furnished and invested therein, and also for what may be due him as a creditor, if anything; and in default of any of the interested parties so doing, an extraneous supplier (aviador) shall be solicited.

Art. 195. The executing creditor shall have the same right expressed in the final part of the foregoing article, if the products be not sufficient to preserve the works; and the possessor or person in execution not providing therefor, the creditor himself may offer to do it.

## TITLE XI.

### OF THE IMPOSTS ON MINING.

Art. 196. During the term of fifty years, counted from the date of this law, mines of coal, in all their variety, of iron and of quicksilver, as well as the products thereof, shall be excepted from all direct taxation.

Art. 197. The circulation in the interior of the republic of gold and silver, in bullion or in coin, that of the other metals, and that of all of the products of the mines shall be free from all impost.

Art. 198. Quicksilver shall continue to be excepted from importation duties and from all direct taxation.

Art. 199. Besides the duties of coinage and of exportation established, or which may be established, the mines not excepted in article 196, and their products, shall not bear more than one sole direct impost, which shall be fixed upon the value of the metal or of the substance worked, without deduction of costs, and which shall never exceed two per cent of that value.

Art. 200. The direct impost of which the foregoing article treats shall be for the state in which the mine is situated, or for the federation when it is in the federal district, or in the territory of Lower California, and therefore the amount of that impost, within the limit marked, the respective legislatures of the states shall annually fix, and the congress of the Union, in its turn, shall attend to the necessities of its exchequer and to the protection which it may accord to mining.

Art. 201. The reduction-works or metallurgical offices of any class shall only pay to the state where they are, or to the federation if they should be situated in the federal district or in the territory of Lower California, the same taxes which in the respective demarkation shall be fixed for other industrial establments, without any difference.

Art. 202. The federation shall receive, accordingly as it is established, twenty-five per cent of the taxes which, in conformity with the foregoing articles, belong to the states.

## TITLE XII.

### GENERAL PROVISIONS.

Art. 203. It is the duty of the mining deputations, besides what is specially determined in this law, to watch over the exact observance and fulfillment of their orders in the mines and reduction-works of their respective districts, under the dependence and direction of the department of public works (secretaria de fomento). In grave or urgent cases, which do not give time to consult said department, the deputations may decree, under their responsibility, the measures or orders which they may estimate necessary and opportune for the preservation and regularity of the works and working of the mines, and the local authorities must give them their aid in the execution thereof, if necessary.

Art. 204. The considerations which by the laws are due to the authorities and public functionaries must be preserved by the individuals who form the mining deputations, and in case of an accusation against any of them by reason of their charge, the tribunal which may be competent to try causes of the judges of first instance shall only be competent to try them.

Art. 205. The mining deputies and the employés of the deputations shall be responsible for the crimes and abuses which they shall commit in the exercise of their functions, in conformity with the provisions of the penal code of the federal district.

Art. 206. For light faults which they may incur, and in cases of complaint for unduly delaying the dispatch of business without justifiable cause, the individuals who form the mining deputations may be suspended and fined by a resolution of the department of public works.

Art. 207. The deputations shall receive the fees which the tariff formed by the department of public works shall designate, for the proceedings which they may execute or in which they may intervene.

Art. 208. The fees of which the foregoing article speaks, and those which said tariff shall designate for the experts, shall be paid by the denouncer or moving party; but in case the denouncement shall have been made of a mine badly worked, and the denouncer not having taken possession, in order that the owner or possessor of the mine may remedy the faults within the term which shall be fixed for him, the costs of the denouncement shall be satisfied by the said owner or possessor.

Art. 209. Every proprietor or supplier (aviador) must have in the district in which the mine is situated of which he is owner, or which he supplies, if he is absent from the district, an agent or attorney in fact duly accredited, with whom the authorities may communicate on all business which may arise. In default of said agent or attorney in fact, the authorities may communicate and transact business, without the necessity of citing the owner, with the administrator or person charged with the business, if he is at the mine, and in default of him, with any of the clerks or dependents (dependientes). In default of all of these persons, judgment by default shall follow in conformity with the respective law of procedure.

Art. 210. The executive shall designate, in the terms of article 21 of the constitution, the penalties which those shall incur who infringe the provisions of the regulations which he may issue for the application of this code, and he shall empower, in their turn, the mining deputation or the functionaries who act in place thereof to impose the said penalties.

Art. 211. The owners of mines or of reduction-works, or the the administrators thereof, shall be obliged to furnish the statistical *data* and information (noticias) which shall be asked of them by the deputations, or functionaries who may act in place thereof, according to the instructions which the department of fomento or general direction of statistics shall dictate; and said persons, in case of not complying therewith, shall be subject to the penalties established in the regulations of statistics.

### Transitory Provisions.

Art. 212. Every mining property legally acquired before the date on which this law shall commence to govern shall remain subsisting, although they may be of deposits or substances not comprehended therein, or the pertenencias of which may have an extension different from that now established.

Art. 213. If the properties acquired prior to the date on which the present law shall commence to govern, by way of denouncement, are of deposits or substances which, in conformity with article 10, belong to the owner of the soil, the proprietors to whom said properties shall have been adjudicated as mines shall continue to possess them as until now, and for once they shall enjoy a special protection for two years, counting from the date on which this code shall commence to govern, in order that within that term they may be put in operation; and in case that after said term shall have expired the owners shall abandon them or lose their rights by forfeiture, said mines shall be considered thereafter as the property of the owner of the soil. The denouncements presented before this code commences to be in force shall be decided in conformity with the laws in force at the date on which they shall have been presented; but in the proceedings the provisions of the present code shall be observed.

Art. 214. The mines which until the issuing of this code may be in operation or legally protected (amparadas) shall preserve the measures which they may have, although their pertenencias may be different from those which now are established, and they may be ratified if the interested parties should solicit it.

Art. 215. In any case, in order to continue preserving rights acquired with priority, it is a necessary condition that the possessor shall comply in the future with the provisions of this code, under the penalties which it establishes.

Art. 216. The salt mines (salinas) which on the coasts of the republic, or in other points of the national territory, the federation may possess, shall be operated in conformity with the regulations which the department of public works shall form respecting the leases or other contracts, which shall have been made relative to them, until their termination. As to those which may have been alienated by the national government, the present possessors shall continue enjoying them on the terms of their respective contracts, and the owners of the soil on which such salt mines (salinas) shall be found shall respect the rights acquired.

Art. 217. The states, the imposts of which on mines and their products, as well as on the reduction-works or metallurgical establishments of any class, shall not be regulated according to the provisions of title 11 of this code, shall issue the necessary laws in order that said imposts may be in accord with the provisions of that title from the first of July, 1885.

### Final Provision.

Art. 218. This code shall commence to govern in all the republic the first day of January, 1885, and thenceforth the mining ordinances of May 22, 1783, shall be repealed, as well as the other laws and provisions of the colonial epoch of the federation or of the states relative to the branch of mining, even in the part in which they should not be contrary thereto.

Wherefore, I order it to be printed, published, circulated, and that due compliance be given it. Given in the palace of the executive power of the Union, in Mexico, on the twenty-second day of November, one thousand eight hundred and eighty-four. Manuel Gonzales. To the citizen Manuel Fernandez, assistant secretary, charged with the office of the department of public works. And I communicate it to you for your understanding and consequent ends. Liberty and the constitution. Mexico, November 22, 1884. M. Fernandez, assistant secretary.

# REGULATIONS

## FOR THE ORGANIZATION OF MINING DEPUTATIONS, AND TARIFF FOR THE COLLECTION OF FEES AND SALARIES.

### CHAPTER I.

#### OF MINERS.

Art. 1. All those who, knowing how to read and write, shall be registered in the book of registry to which article 6 refers, by having some of the following requisites, shall be considered as miners in each locality for the purpose of being able to vote at the elections of mining deputies: 1. Those who for the term of one year prior to the date of the registry were owners or suppliers (aviadores), wholly or in part, of one or various mines or reduction-works; 2. The engineers of mines and the beneficiators of ores, after residing one year in the locality; 3. Those who, being already registered in some other mining deputation, shall acquire property in that locality, although they have not possessed it a year.

Art. 2. Those comprehended in subdivision 1 of the foregoing article may be registered as miners of the locality by expressly asking for it themselves; for which effect they shall present in writing the respective petitions to the mining deputation having jurisdiction, with the documents which shall prove their property, in order that the deputation may determine what corresponds thereto.

Art. 3. The petitions for registry to which the foregoing article refers may be made through the means of an attorney in fact, and a power of attorney (carta poder) legalized before two known witnesses shall also be sufficient therefor.

Art. 4. Those comprehended in subdivision 2 of article 1 shall present with petitions the documents which prove in a legal manner their residence in the locality for the time which said function requires.

Art. 5. Those comprehended in subdivision 3 of said article 1 shall annex a certificate from the respective deputation in which they shall have been registered, with the proof of their property in that locality.

Art. 6. In view of the petitions of which the preceding articles treat, and of the resolutions which may be made thereon, if they should be favorable, a book shall be formed which shall be entitled, "Of the registry of miners of the mining deputations of [such a part]."

## CHAPTER II.

### OF THE MINING DEPUTATIONS.

Art. 7. The mining deputations shall exercise the economical and administrative powers which in the mining code are conceded to them, and shall be under obligation of furnishing informations (noticias) and of rendering reports which the political or judicial authorities and the department of public works shall ask of them.

Art. 8. The mining deputations shall exercise their functions under the immediate dependency and direction of the department of public works.

Art. 9. For the present there shall be mining deputations in the places which article 56 determines. In the future, when any miners or mining deputations shall solicit, or when new mining places (minerales) shall be discovered, the department of public works may establish new mining deputations, designating their respective jurisdictional limits; but in order that this may take effect, it is indispensably requisite that there shall be in the principal town of the locality in question at least fifteen persons capable of performing the duties of mining deputies, which shall be proved by a certificate from the first local political authority.

Art. 10. The limits for the jurisdiction of the mining deputations shall be regulated, provided it be possible, by those of the political divisions of the state, federal district, or territory in which they are.

Art. 11. The mining deputations shall be renewed by halves every year, and shall be composed of two proprietary deputies and four substitutes, elected directly by the miners registered in each locality.

Art. 12. The mining deputies and their substitutes shall not have a fixed salary, but shall enjoy the fees which are fixed in article 47. The duration of these offices shall be two years, and they may be re-elective.

Art. 13. In order that the ordinary election may be had, there shall be issued by the acting deputations the corresponding proclamations (convocatorias) before the fifteenth day of November of each year, stating therein the day, hour, and place in which the election shall take place. The omission of what is here provided shall be punished by the department of public works with a fine of from ten to fifty dollars, which shall be imposed on the deputies who shall not comply with this provision. When the establishment of a new mining deputation is in question, the order of the department of public works relative thereto shall designate the date on which the president of the ayuntamiento, or municipal corporation, must issue the proclamation for the election, and the day on which it must take place. The municipal president having once received the order from the department of public works establishing a new deputation, he shall issue the proclamation, and from that date until three days before the election he shall have open a provisional register for the registry of miners, in order that the persons may be registered therein who, in order to fulfill the requisites which article 1 expresses, shall have a right to take part in the election. The decisions of the municipal president admitting or rejecting petitions for registry are not reviewable; but the department of public works, on petition of an aggrieved person, shall punish with a fine of from ten to fifty dollars the wrongs which, relative to this matter, the municipal president may commit.

Art. 14. The regular election, in the localities where mining deputations are established, shall take place on the first day of December of every year, although it may be a holiday. The election shall be presided over by the deputy of the unexpired term, and the ballot counters (escrutadores) shall be two of the parties present, who shall be chosen by a majority of voters. One deputy and two substitutes shall be elected every year, for the renewal, in part, of the deputation. Where there is no mining deputation, the first election for all the members of one shall be made under the presidency of the municipal president of the place in which the deputation shall act, and, after the expiration of one year their functions shall cease unless they shall be re-elected.

Art. 15. To be eligible as a mining deputy proper, or substitute, one is required to be a miner registered in the books of that deputation, a Mexican citizen in the exercise of his rights, and a resident of the place in which the deputation performs its functions.

Art. 16. All the miners who shall have been registered in the book to which article 6 refers, at least three days prior to the day of election, have a right to appear at said elections in person, or by an attorney in fact, who shall be a miner.

Art. 17. In order that there be an election, it is necessary that at least fifteen registered miners shall appear in person or by proxy. If for want of number the election can not be had, it shall be called again with an interval of ten days, at the most, until a sufficient number is present.

Art. 18. Every miner shall have for himself one vote, and he may represent four more by having special authority therefor, either by a formal power, or by a carta poder[1] legalized before two known witnesses; so that in no case the representation by one person shall exceed five votes. If it should happen that any one of the voters present should have a greater number of proxies, the total representation thereby shall only be computed as five votes.

Art. 19. The election of each officer shall take place separately and by secret ballot, by the means of election tickets. If on the first ballot no one should obtain an absolute majority, the election shall be repeated between the two who shall have had the highest number of votes. In case of a tie, the election shall be repeated, and if there should be a tie again between two persons, chance shall designate the person who shall be elected. The corresponding declaration of those who have been elected having been made by him who presided over the board, the respective return shall be drawn up, corrected, and approved, and it shall be signed by the individuals of the board.

Art. 20. If, before or during the election, one of the miners in the minority shall present or allege a protest of nullity, the same shall be annexed to or included in the return.

Art. 21. Authorized copies of said election return and of the protests, if there shall have been any, shall be remitted by the citizens who formed the board to the department of public works, and the election shall be communicated to the persons elected in order that they may take possession of their respective offices on the first day of the following January.

Art. 22. In case the election should be disapproved by the department of public works, the miners shall be again called together, in order that the election may be repeated, within a new term which shall not exceed ten days; but such disapproval shall not invalidate the acts of the deputy or deputies who shall have taken possession of their offices.

Art. 23. The office of mining deputy, proper or substitute, can not be renounced except for a cause justified before the same deputation. He having performed the duties of said office during the two prior years is a cause for an excuse.

---

[1] Not made before a notary.

Art. 24. When, on having the regular election, the deputation should be incomplete through an impediment or absolute default of any one member or substitute having occurred during the year, besides these deputies who legally ought to take the place of those who shall have completed their time, those who ought to fill the vacancy or vacancies which there may be shall be elected by the same electoral board. The person or persons so elected shall hold their office for the time which the person or persons whose place they have to fill shall be required to complete their unexpired period of two years.

Art. 25. In order that there may be no delays in the denouncements and in the other economical affairs, and of the simple proceedings which may occur, the two deputies proper shall act by turns in the office for the period of three months each.

Art. 26. The grave affairs or affairs of importance which shall be presented, such as the decrees of adjudication, the protections (amparas) and declaration of desertion, or of forfeiture, shall be dispatched by the two deputies jointly, for which they shall meet once a week, and shall hold special meetings whenever it may be necessary.

Art. 27. When the opinions of both deputies shall disagree on any business, they shall call one of the substitutes in the order of their election, so that by the three studying the points in question they may adopt a resolution which the majority may approve, and the three who intervene shall sign the resolution with the explanations which they may think proper.

Art. 28. The deputies shall consult with an attorney at law (asesor letrado) chosen by themselves upon the doubts which occur to them, as to whether the questions before them are within their jurisdiction, and relative to the procedure which they ought to follow, but without its being obligatory upon the deputies to adopt the opinion of the asesor.

Art. 29. For the dispatch of business before the mining deputations, each one shall have a secretary.

Art. 30. This secretary shall have a salary of six hundred dollars annually, and he shall be appointed by the department of public works, on the proposal of the mining deputations.

Art. 31. In order to be a secretary of a mining deputation one must be a Mexican citizen in the exercise of his rights, and shall have the practice and knowledge which are required for the dispatch of the business, according to the judgment of the deputation.

Art. 32. Without prejudice to the regular and extraordinary meetings which the mining deputations may have, the secretary shall have his office open to the public during four hours a day, in order to receive therein the denouncements and other documents of the miners.

Art. 33. The deputies, secretaries, and experts may be excused from any special matter, provided that for a cause wholly conformable to the laws in force for the administration of justice in the respective locality it may be done; but the point shall be determined by the deputation formed by the other deputy proper, and the substitute to whom it shall belong to act, exclusively for the case only, of the person in question.

Art. 34. When the first deputy shall be in default, either temporarily or absolutely, the second shall be substituted in his stead; and in the place of the second, the substitutes shall be called in the order of their election.

Art. 35. Through the default or impediment of said members, those who shall have been deputies proper or substitutes during the previous year or years shall be substituted in their stead.

Art. 36. The substitutions of which the two foregoing articles speak shall continue, in case of the defaults being permanent, until a new election shall be had according to article 24.

Art. 37. When the secretary shall be absent for less than a month, or in any special case, the deputations shall act with two assisting witnesses; but if his default, through sickness, license, or absence, exceed more than a month, a secretary *pro tem.* may be appointed, with the approval of the department of public works, who shall act until the return of the secretary proper.

Art. 38. The members of the mining deputations, during the period for which they shall have been elected, may be excused from any municipal office.

Art. 39. In every deputation a book shall be kept, which shall be entitled "Experts of the mining deputation of [such a place]," which shall contain the petitions of the interested parties which have been granted by the respective deputation, and of the extract or copy of their vouchers, the originals of which shall be returned after a comparison has been made.

Art. 40. All mining engineers, metallurgists or assayers, bridge and road builders, mechanics, surveyors, and hydrometic experts, may be registered at their own request as scientific experts to exercise their professions, but they shall be considered only as practical men in branches not included under their proper title.

Art. 41. In conformity with the provisions of article 26 of the mining code, the deputations shall appoint from among those registered one titled expert, with whom they shall consult upon such official business as may present itself.

Art. 42. In matters of dispute, mining deputations shall appoint, with preference, as experts in their respective branches, those who have been registered with titles as such. Only in default of such experts shall the mining deputations appoint according to their judgment the most intelligent practical men of the locality in their place.

Art. 43. Mining deputations, besides the books for the registration of miners and experts, of which mention has been made, shall keep the following: Of elections; of the registry of denouncements; of the possession of mines and of reduction-works; of maintenance of possession (amparas); of visits to mines; of the withdrawal of expedientes remitted to the courts; and a general inventory of the archives thereof.

Art. 44. When the mining deputations shall give any decision by which any one of the interested parties may feel himself aggrieved, he may, without prejudice to the provisions of articles 80 and 96 of the mining code, present his substantiated complaint to the secretary of public works, who shall immediately ask for the corresponding report of the deputies in question, and shall remit to them for that purpose the original complaint and proofs (justificantes), or a copy thereof.

Art. 45. The complaints to which the foregoing article alludes can only be made and considered within a month from the notification of the decision in question. That term having passed, or when the respective proofs are not annexed, the complaints shall be immediately dismissed.

Art. 46. The secretary of public works, considering the accusation, and the report and proofs (justificantes) shall decide according to the case: 1. If the offense be light and proved, he shall impose administratively on the guilty party a fine not exceeding one hundred dollars; 2. If the offenses should be grave, the fine shall be from one hundred to five hundred dollars; and if it should be a crime, the expediente (proceedings) shall be remitted to the respective tribunal or court, and the accused shall be committed thereto, who, after trial and conviction, shall have the penalty of the law applied to him.

## CHAPTER III.

### OF THE FEES WHICH MUST BE PAID IN MINING CASES.

Art. 47. Mining deputies shall have no right to receive fees except in the following cases: 1. For every resolution which they shall dictate for the admission of denouncements, for registering any document, protection of possession (concesion de amparo), adjudication, etc., they shall receive one dollar; 2. For attendance at meetings, two dollars an hour or a fraction of an hour in which they have been engaged; 3. For the possession which they shall give of a mine, whatever may be the number of its pertenencias, for the possession of a surplus ground (demasia) or a reduction-works, five dollars; 4. For a personal examination of the interiors, whether it is a question of one or various pertenencias, surplus grounds (demasias), or reduction-works, five dollars; 5. For the exterior inspections, visits, or examinations, five dollars for each pertenencia, when the depth shall not exceed one hundred meters, and five more for each one hundred meters or fraction thereof which shall increase the depth. If the examination shall extend to another or other pertenencias, they shall also receive the half of what is fixed in this subdivision for each one; 6. For each league traveled to carry out the proceedings mentioned, at the rate of one dollar in going and the same for returning.

Art. 48. The secretaries of the mining deputations shall receive: 1. For certifying to any resolution (acuerdo), registry, or certificate of the mining deputies, one dollar; 2. For making copies of the leases which the expedientes and other documents may contain which they may have to extract, or with which to make a report, at the rate of five cents each one; 3. For drafting and writing the decrees, resolutions, acts (titles), examination, appearances, notifications, citations, entries, official notes, notices, extracts, etc., at the rate of twenty-five cents for each ten lines or fraction thereof, besides the fees designated in subdivision 1; 4. For the writing, comparing, and certifying to copies (testimonios[1]), certificates, and other literal copies, at the rate of one dollar for every hundred lines or fraction thereof, and one half when they shall be simple copies; 5. For attendance at meetings, at the rate of one dollar for every hour or fraction thereof in which they shall have been engaged; 6. For attendance on giving possessions and personal examinations, and for exterior examinations, five dollars for each act,

[1] Second copies—the first, given by a notary, is called the original.

whether it be of a surplus ground (demasia), or of one or more pertenencias, or of a reduction-works; 7. For the searching of expedientes or any other documents of the archives, at the rate of one dollar for every year that it shall be registered; 8. For the notifications or citations which shall be made in going to the houses of the interested parties, fifty cents, besides what is expressed in subdivision 3; 9. For the inspections (veedurias), interior visits, or examinations, and for the leagues which they shall travel, the same as that assigned to the deputies; 10. For a copy of a plan, five dollars.

Art. 49. When in default of the secretary the deputies shall act with assisting witnesses, they shall receive the fees designated for the secretary, which shall be paid to the witnesses.

Art. 50. The titled mining experts shall receive, save a contract to the contrary: 1. For the survey of a lode or deposit (criadero) which they shall make of a new or old mine in order to designate its pertenencias, and the report and respective plans, five dollars for each concession, whatever may be the number of pertenencias; and they shall receive besides, for the measurement which they shall make for the designation of the boundary lines, at the rate of five cents for every meter they may measure; 2. For the rectifications which they shall make in order to explain the respective boundary lines of each mine, or in order to mark the forms (figuras) and periphery of the surplus grounds (demasias), five dollars for the report and respective plans, and five cents besides for every meter which they shall measure; 3. For the inspections, interior visits, or personal examinations, being simple examinations without measurements, and for the corresponding report, ten dollars for each pertenencia, when the depth does not exceed one hundred meters, and another ten for every one hundred meters or fraction thereof which shall increase the depth; if the examination should extend to another or other pertenencias, they shall receive besides the half of what is designated in this subdivision for each one of them; 4. For the interior measurements which they shall make, at the rate of fifteen cents for every meter of the hypothenuse; 5. For the construction of plans, which shall not be of those already expressed in subdivisions 1 and 2, in which they shall have to calculate and construct a horizontal and vertical projection, whether the measurement be exterior or interior, fifteen cents for each meter; but if these should be very few, or the plan should refer to a simple work, they shall collect therefor ten dollars as the minimum; 6. For each copy which they shall draw of the plans already constructed, the fourth part of what the plan may be worth, with the conception that the minimum value of the copy shall be five dollars; 7. For the written reports which they shall give relative to the business of this branch, and which are not comprehended in subdivisions 1, 2, and 3, at the rate of one dollar for every twenty-five lines; 8. For attendance at meetings, two dollars an hour or fraction thereof, in which they shall be engaged; 9. For the formation of estimates or valuations, besides the fees which are fixed, they shall receive: on the amount of these when they do not reach one thousand dollars, ten dollars; when the amount does not reach ten thousand dollars, besides what is expressed in the foregoing paragraph, for the excess above the value of one thousand dollars, five dollars per thousand; when the amount of the estimates and values exceed ten thousand dollars, besides what is expressed in the two preceding subdivisions, they shall receive two dollars per thousand for the excess above ten thousand dollars; 10. If the expert is interrupted in the execution of his works, he shall be paid ten dollars for every day the interruption shall last; 11. The works made for the measurement of water, levelings, and analogous operations, ten dollars for every half-day or less, of the time employed for its execution, besides what is fixed for the measurements, reports, etc.; 12. For the leagues which they shall travel in or to comply with the commissions which they may be charged with, at the rate of one dollar for every one in going and the same in returning.

Art. 51. The titled beneficiating experts shall receive, save an agreement to the contrary: 1. For the work which they shall perform in the reduction-works, ten dollars per day; 2. For the other work which they may do, what is designated for mining experts in the preceding article.

Art. 52. The assayers of ores shall receive, save an agreement to the contrary: 1. For a dry assay, to determine one sole substance, two dollars; 2. For an assay of silver mixed with gold, three dollars; 3. For a moist assay, five dollars; 4. For an analysis, fifty dollars.

Art. 53. Practical experts in case thereof shall receive the same fees which are designated for scientific ones in the preceding articles.

Art. 54. Cases not provided for in this tariff, in default of agreement, shall be paid for by the valuation of experts.

Art. 55. The fees designated for deputies, secretaries, and experts shall be the same, whether they are to be paid by private individuals or by companies.

TRANSITORY PROVISIONS.

Art. 56. For the present, and until the *data* relative to the necessities of all the mining districts of the republic are obtained, mining deputations shall be established in the following localities: Tasco, Zacualpan, Tlalpujahua, Angangueo, Pachuca, Zimapan, Cadereita, Guanajuato, Catorce, Zacatecas, Durango, Chihuahua, Batopilas, La Paz, Culiacan, Hermosillo, Alamos, and Oaxaca. The said deputationes being once installed, each one shall report within fifteen days to the department of public works relative to the jurisdictional limits which it may estimate proper for the public interest should be assigned it, and until said department shall decide, said deputations shall exercise their functions within the political districts of their residence (ubicacion).

Art. 57. The municipal authorities of the towns which are cited in the foregoing article shall issue a proclamation before the fifteenth day of January next, in order that at the place and at the hour which they designate all the persons may meet who, in conformity with article 1 of this regulation may be miners of the respective localities, in order to elect, the first of February next, the first mining deputation, the persons who are considered as having a right to vote being registered before the twenty-eighth day of said January.

Art. 58. The persons elected on the first of February next shall immediately take possession of their offices, protesting[1] before the municipal authority which shall have presided over the election that they will faithfully comply with duties of their offices.

Art. 59. The mining deputations being once constituted, they shall appoint temporarily a secretary, and shall propose to the department of public works the person who is to fill the place.

Art. 60. The mining deputations elected on the first of February next shall receive from the authority or authorities which shall have been acting up to that date in mining affairs all the expediente relative thereto, and shall make an inventory thereof and execute the corresponding receipt.

Art. 61. Of the mining deputies proper and substitutes who

[1] Under the constitution no oaths are administered.

are to be elected the first of February next, the first deputy proper and the first and second substitutes shall continue in office until the first of January, 1886, and the second deputy proper and the third and fourth substitutes shall perform their functions until the first day of January, 1887, in order to be substituted for those who, in conformity with article 14, shall be elected respectively on the first of December of 1885 and 1886, provided they shall not be re-elected.

Wherefore, I order it to be printed, published, circulated, and that due compliance be given it. Given in the palace of the executive power of the Union, in Mexico, the twenty-eighth of November, one thousand eight hundred and eighty-four. Manuel Gonzales. To the citizen Manuel Fernandez, assistant secretary, charged with the office of the department of public works. And I communicate it to you for your understanding and consequent ends. Liberty and the constitution. Mexico, twenty-eighth of November, 1884. M. Fernandez, assistant secretary.

# INDEX.

www.ingramcontent.com/pod-product-compliance
Lightning Source LLC
LaVergne TN
LVHW062241200926
848484LV00006B/1586
*9781584779957*